Graphic.

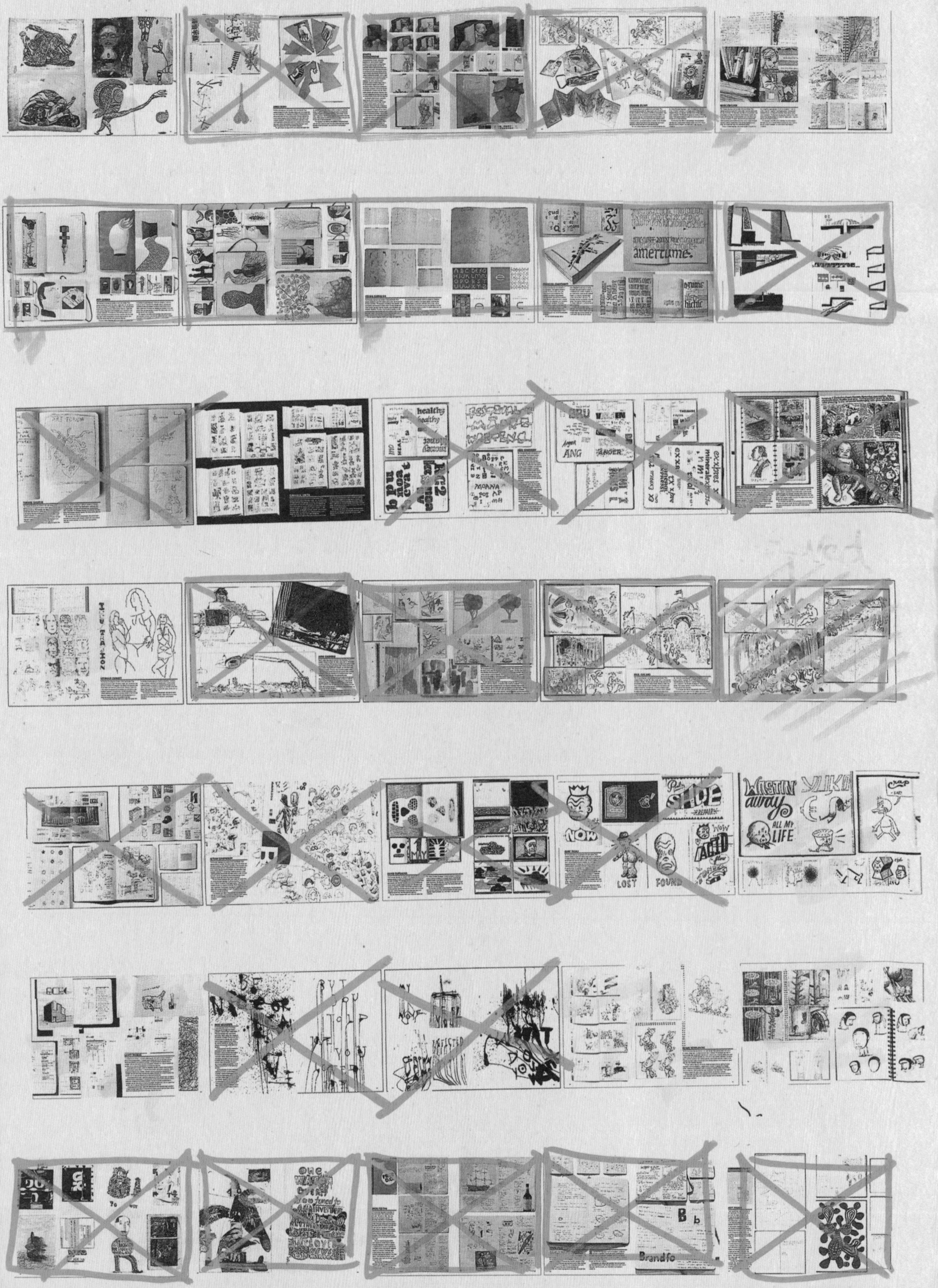

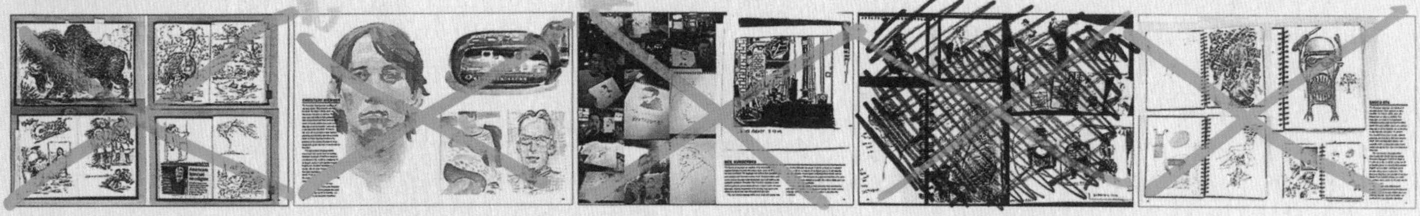

Graphic.

Thames & Hudson

Inside the Sketchbooks of the World's Great Graphic Designers

Steven Heller & Lita Talarico

With 922 illustrations, 654 in color

Contents.

Sketch-book Appeal.

Steven Heller
& Lita Talarico

What is it about sketchbooks that makes them so appealing to touch and smell? Why are illustrators, designers, and others hypnotically drawn to them in their pristine, fallow state? Is it the size, shape, color? Or perhaps the heft, or lack thereof. Is it the brand? In recent years, Moleskine has made filling sketchbooks as popular a pastime as sports and as common a practice as thinking. Perhaps the blank pages are what beckon most of all? The invitation to fill those pages with one's own scribbling is an irresistible force.

The sketchbook is a portal into a world where anything can happen: another dimension beyond that of space and time, a veritable twilight zone, where innermost thoughts, ideas, and feelings can be expressed freely. The sight of those blank pages is enough to set hearts and minds racing in some, yet can trigger uncontrollable seizures in others. A sketchbook is a *tabula rasa* and, therefore, a creative double-edged sword. Those empty sheets say freedom, but they can also be chains that enslave. While the sketchbook is the least judgmental and most forgiving of any communications medium, for the creatively insecure it may be just too free – too rasa.

Some designers use sketchbooks as repositories for random ideas, both grand and minor; others throw everything of value into them. For the latter, sketchbooks are major works, at least inadvertently (like Leonardo's famous books, which feature his extraordinarily prescient inventions). In this case the book is not an indulgence but a sanctified reliquary of precious artifacts. These sacred books are, however, no more nor less significant than those containing simple, unpretentious notations.

A sketchbook cannot be measured by the same standards as a finished work. Nonetheless, some are more ambitious than others – although, granted, ambition is a relative distinction. There are those who are driven by concept (say, the concept of one landscape rendered for each day of the year, or a single word placed neatly on each page every hour). Yet most books are more ad hoc. The discipline imposed is simply to maintain the book in the first place. Some are ambitious by virtue of their brevity and economy, while others are ambitious because they are filled with layer upon layer of remarkable material. But ambition is not the only yardstick for judging a sketchbook. Sometimes the most obsessive is the least compelling, just as a cluttered attic is less impressive than a well-ordered library (or, at the very least, a well-organized second-hand bookstore). There must be a balance between the everything-including-the-kitchen-sink and the excessively studied sketchbook; usually this is the book where not every page is pristine, but neither is it unappealingly chaotic.

Of course, this might suggest that there is a right or wrong way to work a sketchbook; yet nothing is further from the truth. A sketchbook is, first and foremost, a means, not an end. It is the result of the natural urge of artists and designers to make marks on paper, to explore, analyze, and refine ideas and notions.

There are sketching classes in art schools, but despite the fad in scrapbooks and "scrapbooking," there is no such thing as a sketchbook class. How can a teacher impose a method of making a sketchbook? It is like imposing a protocol for pure creativity. A sketchbook is a physical manifestation of unfettered thought. What is imagined is converted into a graphic idea and recorded. Governments, religions, and political parties may have attempted to control minds, but the sketchbook should never be subject to such influence. By virtue of being unfiltered, it should be free from stricture.

So how were the sketchbooks selected for this book? If freedom is the watchword, what was the standard for inclusion? The answer is simple: each was judged on its own merit and context. First, the artists and designers were invited to submit what they wanted to see published. Surprisingly, some of the most prolific do not keep and never kept sketchbooks. Some keep only small notebooks with notations so spare that they are not visually interesting. As this is a visual book, visuality was the primary determinant. But not all visuals are created equal. Some books are indeed elaborate, filled with color or fragments of cultural material; others are decidedly economical, with fewer inclusions, but are no less interesting to look at (and to read).

The object is to survey how illustrators and designers see themselves, informally, through the lens of their sketchbooks, and this was accomplished by recruiting a range of known and lesser-known keepers of the book. The selection of which pages to present was more intuitive, and was based almost entirely on the graphic impact of each piece. It might be argued that one page of a sketchbook is as good as the next, but that is simply not the case. Some days are better than others, in the same way that some works have greater impact. Although a sketchbook may not be a continuous narrative, it is still an entity; excerpting pages is not necessarily the most effective means of showing it. However, given the constraints of this format, it will have to do.

What overall impression will this book produce? In other words, why is a book about sketchbooks meaningful or useful? As an anthology, it may be compared with a collection of short stories or poems. Each page or assortment of pages tells one or more tales about the maker. Some are probably more revealing than others – some may be more profound. But in the final analysis the sketchbooks provide insight into individuals who, as illustrators and designers, are usually known only by their formal commercial endeavors and not by their purely expressive ideas. That is sketchbook appeal.

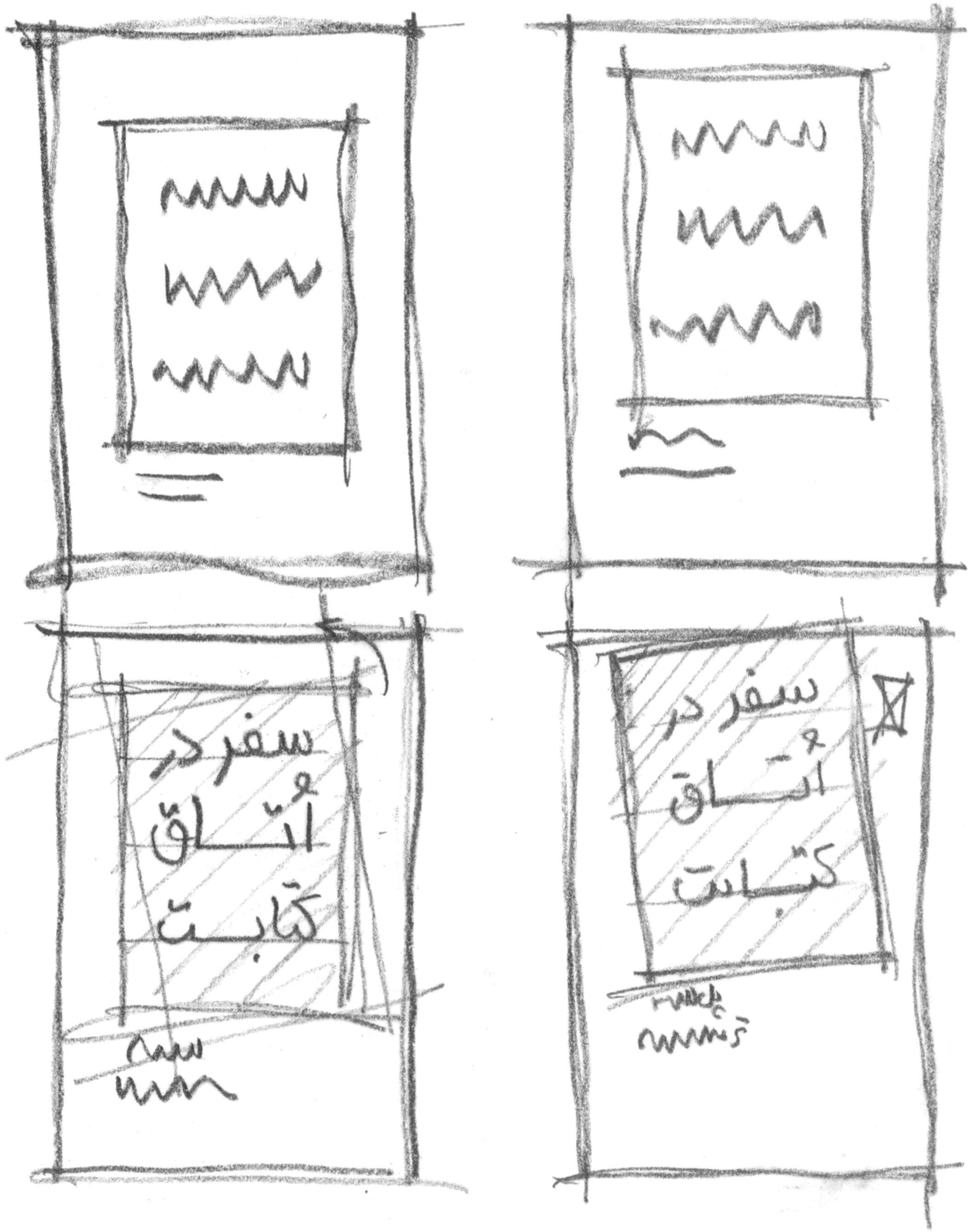

MAJID ABBASI

Majid Abbasi, Tehran-based creative director of Did Graphics, admits that many of his sketches are digital, not drawn: "Normally I do my designs using graphic software on my computer, and sometimes I file these scribbles in folders labeled 'Practices' for different projects." These roughs, he adds, "remind me of the process I have undergone to attain results." Since most are done on the computer, the sketches are similar to the finished works, "except for the details," he notes.

Sometimes the method and the design are influenced by an occasion or a special work. For instance, in designing the cover of Paul Auster's novel *Travels in the Scriptorium* (in 2008; shown here), "I was inspired by a romantic message." Abbasi keeps "a load of sketches" in small notebooks, as well as single sheets of A4 paper and "several folders on my computer." The pieces here are recent, but the books themselves span nearly fifteen years – "though all are few and far between."

سفر در اُتاق کتابت

پُل اوستر

ترجمه‌ی احسان نوروزی

سفر در اُتاق کتابت

سفر در اُتاق کتابت

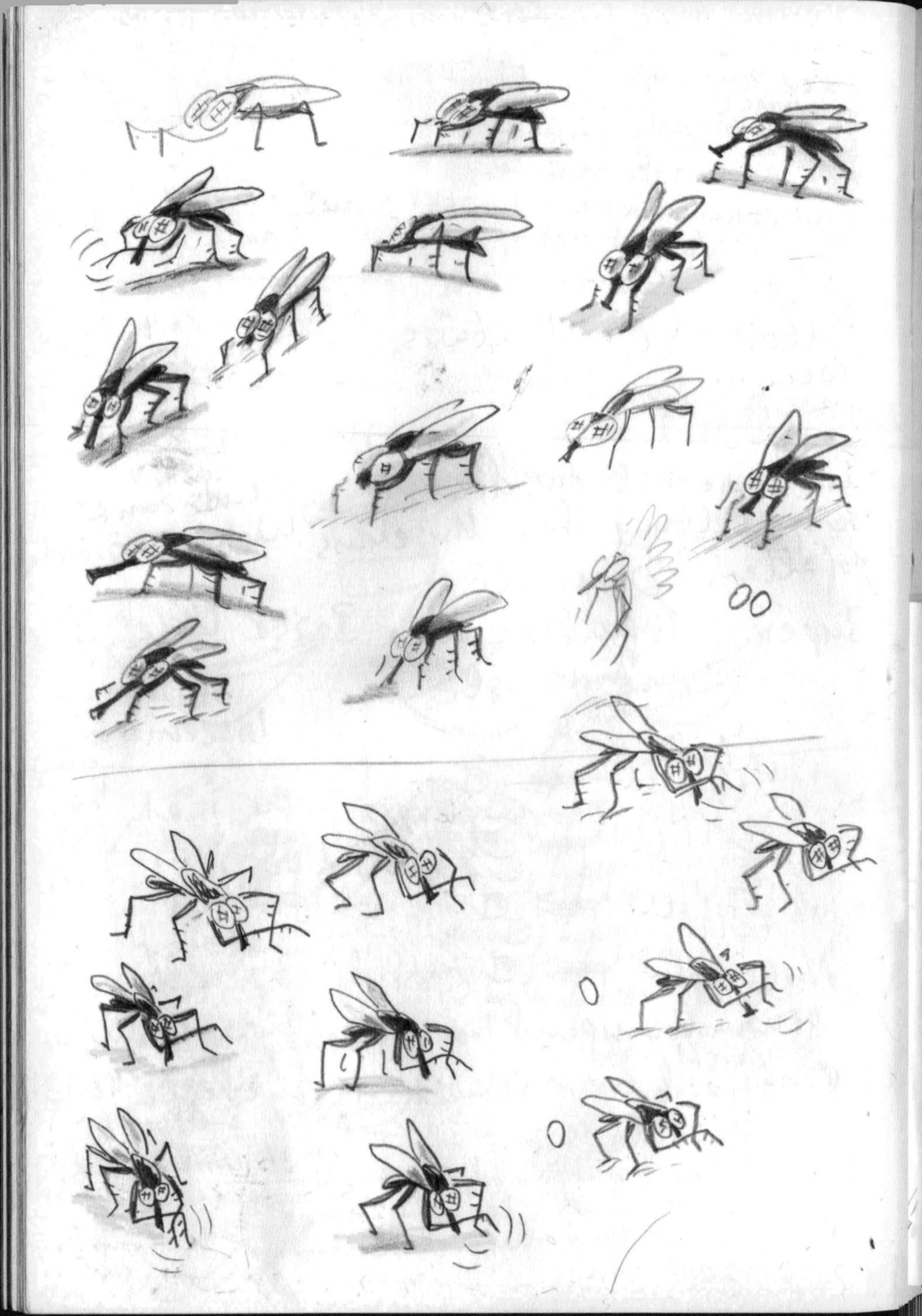

CHRISTOPH ABBREDERIS

For the past twenty-five years, Christoph Abbrederis, an Austrian illustrator and designer who spent many years living in Spain, has kept sketchbooks to help him "develop creative ideas while I'm resting after lunch." Now, that is a fine way to pass the siesta. "I make sketches about things that come to my mind while in the satisfied haze. I call these books 'siesta books'."

There is a critical distinction, however, between these sketches and his professional work because "in these 'siesta books' I allow my mind to associate freely, and I find that the ideas flow easier than when I am working on a project for a client." Visualizing Abbrederis lounging and sketching after a fine meal is almost as satisfying as seeing the sketchbooks themselves.

"Sometimes those sketches contain a special wit or catch a certain situation in a way I can never, ever reproduce," he confides. And although there might be thematic recurrences, Abbrederis feels that these are "less important than the ideas that emerge."

In addition to his "siesta sketchbook," from which images created in 2008–9 are shown here, Abbrederis has "a 'while I watch television book,' a 'travel sketchbook,' a book for stories and comics and a little booklet I take with me wherever I go to make notes." For professional work he keeps the sketches and binds them, depending on the project, into different booklets.

30.1
Der Hut brennt an allen Ecken
Vermeer

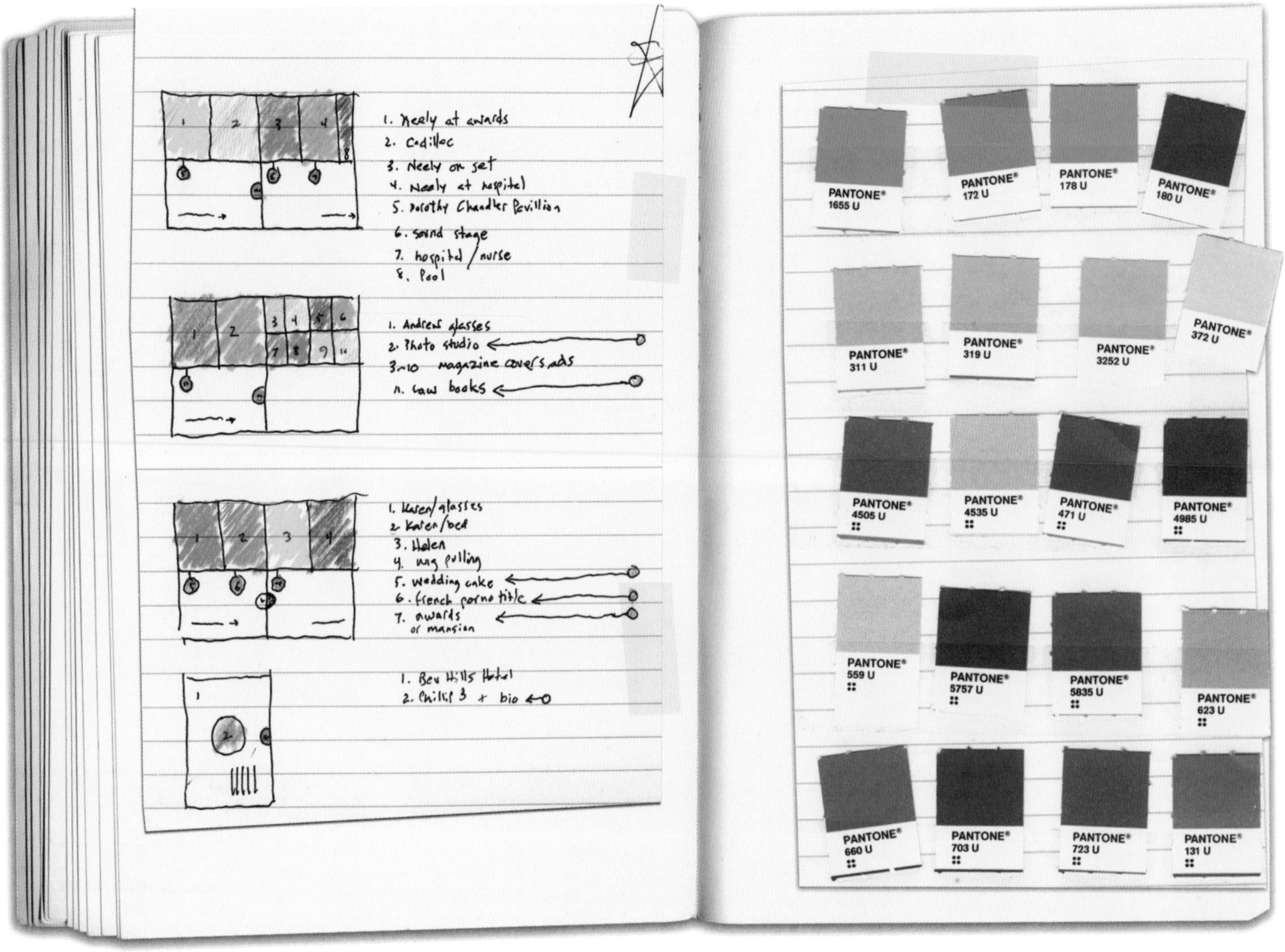

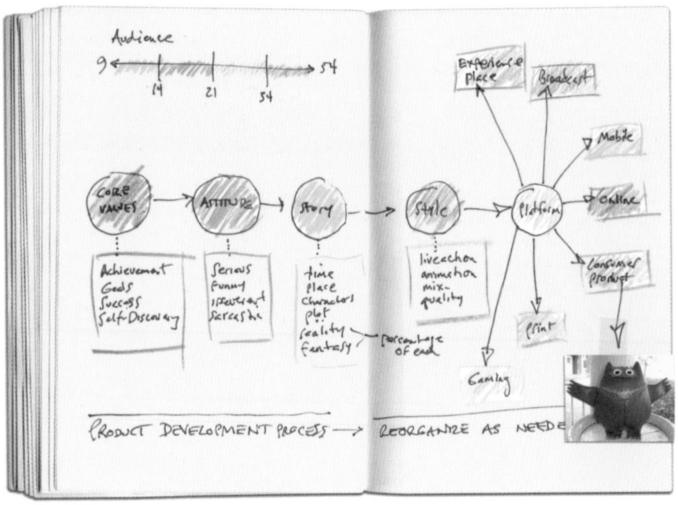

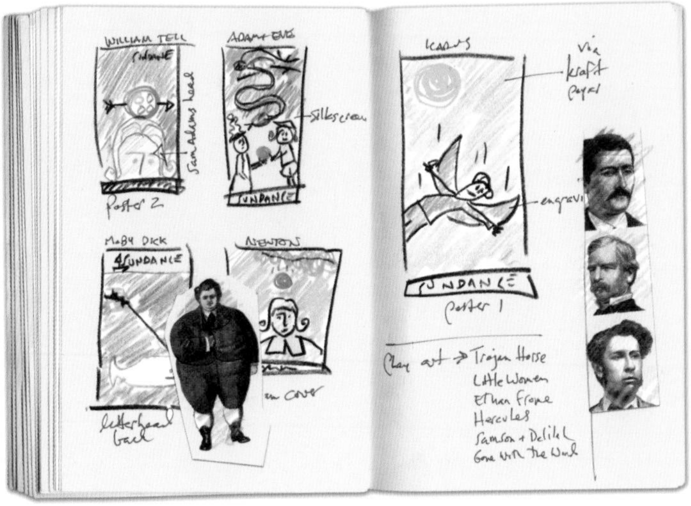

SEAN ADAMS

Sean Adams, co-founder of AdamsMorioka in Beverly Hills, California, has kept a sketchbook since his first day at CalArts in 1982. The purpose is "to help my quickly fading memory," Adams admits. "I'll have what seems to be a good idea and write it down, or come across an object and tape it into the book. I'll find a wonderful color palette in a strange place, such as Mary Blair's for the movie *How to Succeed in Business Without Really Trying*, and simply shoot the screen, print out the images and attach matching Pantone® colors. I also use them in meetings. I'm terrible at taking notes about important issues like deliverables, but good at doing strange charts that diagram the client's business."

Keeping the sketchbooks is a discipline for Adams: "When I look at them as a whole, the common theme of the notebooks is popular culture combined with a Surrealist process. Sounds fancy, but there is often no premeditation of the objects or images selected. For example, the spread with a product narrative diagram was created for a global entertainment brand. I cannot remember what prompted me to attach a Nauga Monster to the page. But the final identity for the client did incorporate some of the attitude that George Lois used for the Naugahyde Nauga Monster advertisements. There is no rational association beyond family connection and memory."

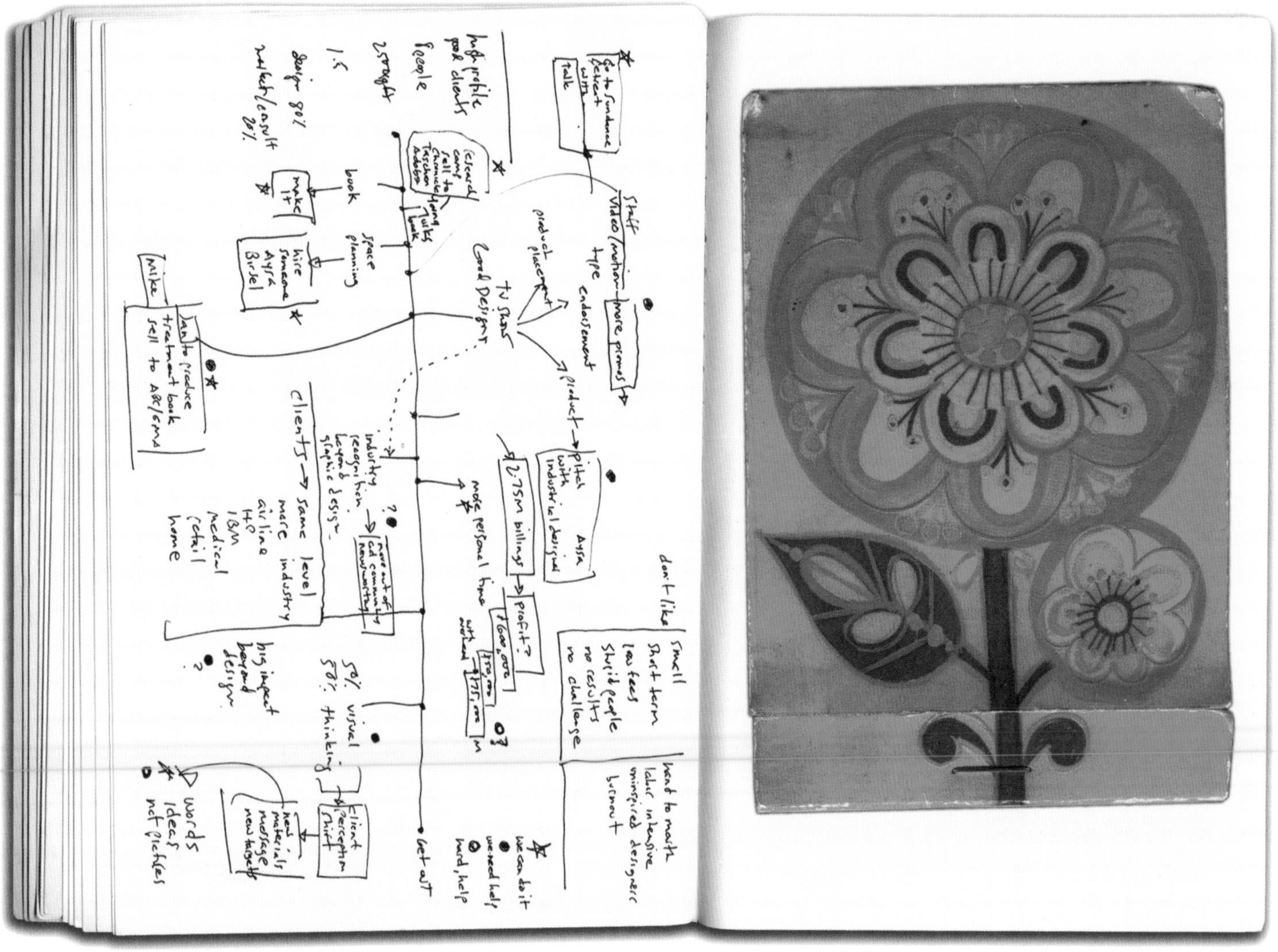

CALIENTE NEV.
STEVENSON
STEVENSON
28240
Essays
CASE STUDIES

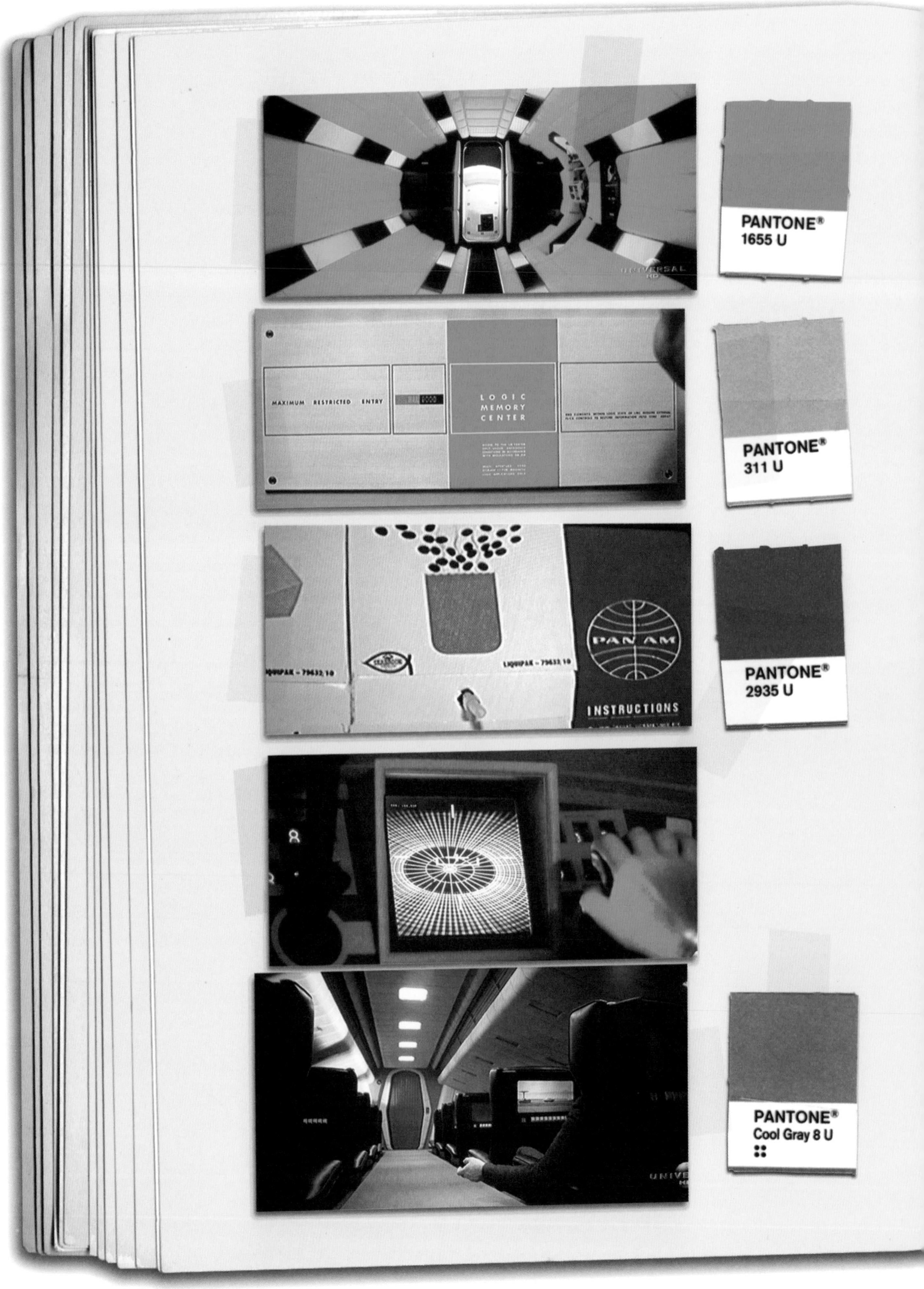
PANTONE®
1655 U
MAXIMUM RESTRICTED ENTRY
LOGIC
MEMORY
CENTER
PANTONE®
311 U
PAN AM
INSTRUCTIONS
PANTONE®
2935 U
PANTONE®
Cool Gray 8 U

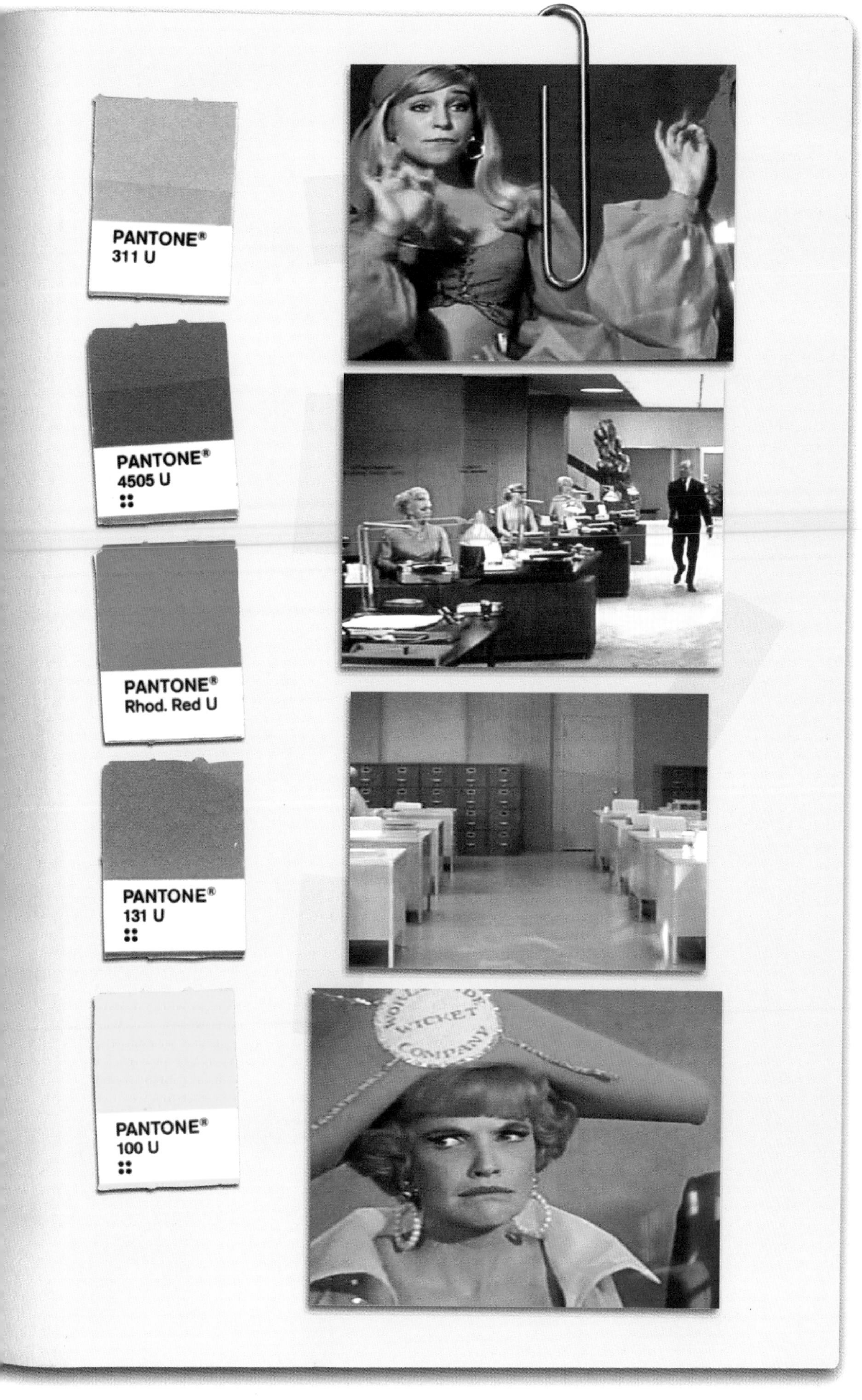
PANTONE®
311 U
PANTONE®
4505 U
PANTONE®
Rhod. Red U
PANTONE®
131 U
PANTONE®
100 U
WICKET
COMPANY

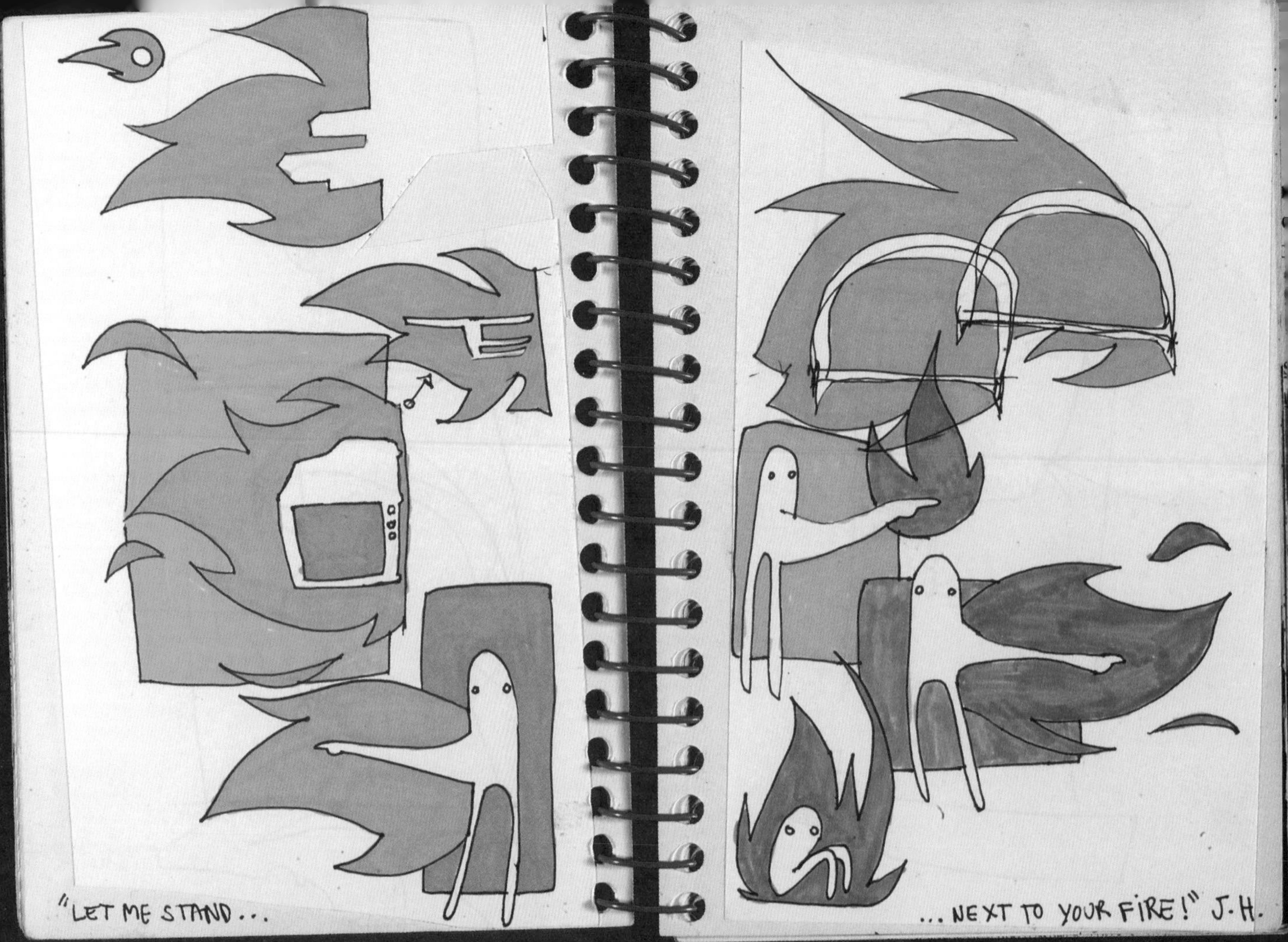
"LET ME STAND...
... NEXT TO YOUR FIRE!" J.H.

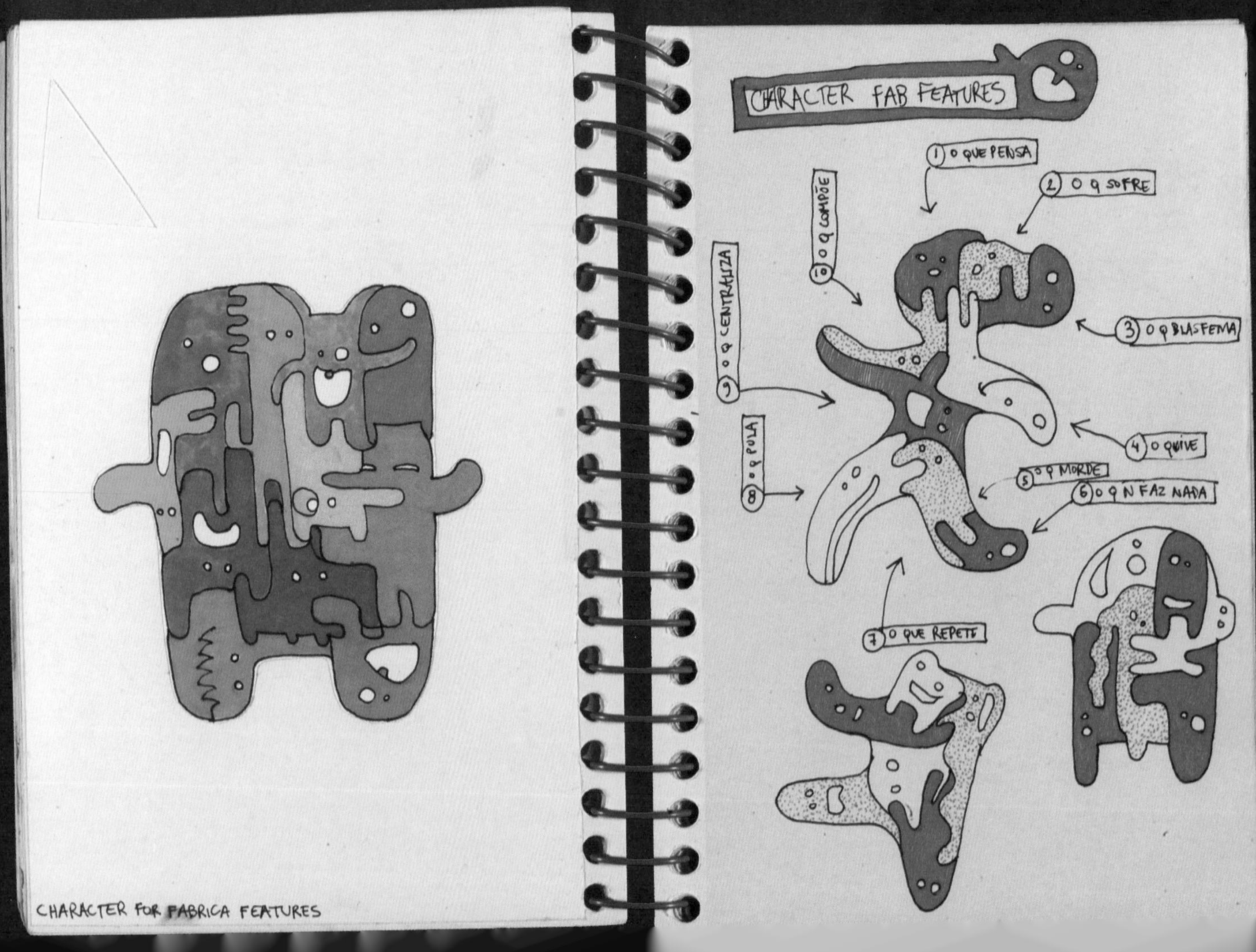
CHARACTER FOR FABRICA FEATURES
CHARACTER FAB FEATURES
1 O QUE PENSA
2 O Q SOFRE
3 O Q BLASFEMA
4 O QUIVE
5 O Q MORDE
6 O Q N FAZ NADA
7 O QUE REPETE
8 O Q PULA
9 O Q CENTRALIZA
10 O Q COMPÕE

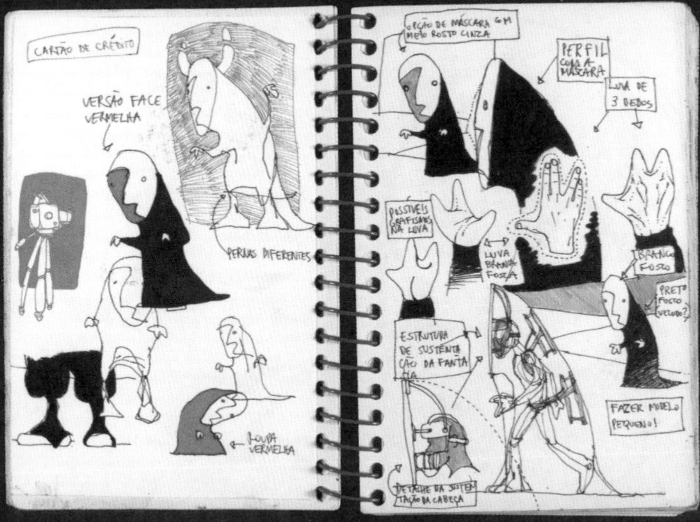

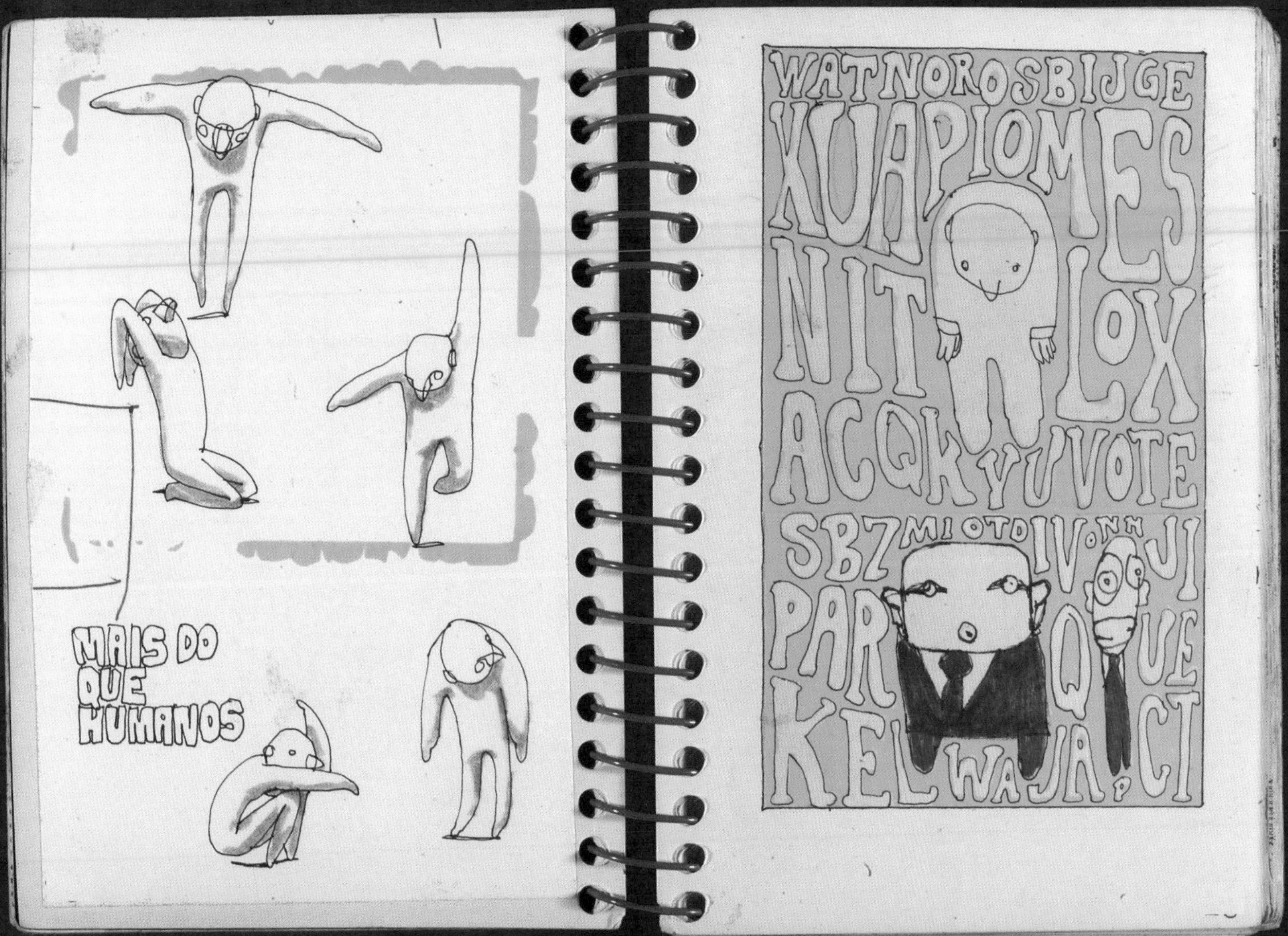

CONRADO ALMADA

Brazilian designer Conrado Almada started filling sketchbooks eight years ago and usually takes around three months or so to complete each one. He does this so he won't lose his ideas. "Before my sketchbooks I used to draw and write everywhere and because of that I lost so many drawings and forgot good ideas," Almada reveals.

With sketchbooks, Almada has "the complete freedom of creation and no fear to experiment with different things. In a professional job you often have to change the idea you really trust to get the work same time the creative director, the agency owner and the client!" The sketchbook is his contemplative space.

Almada never uses a pencil in his sketchbooks; everything is drawn directly in pen. The fact that he cannot erase and redraw something gives him "more freedom and confidence in what I'm doing. There's no undo button; what is done is done." He also uses his books as a record of his past. "When I look back at my old sketchbooks I can clearly see the psychological and emotional aspects of my life at those times. All

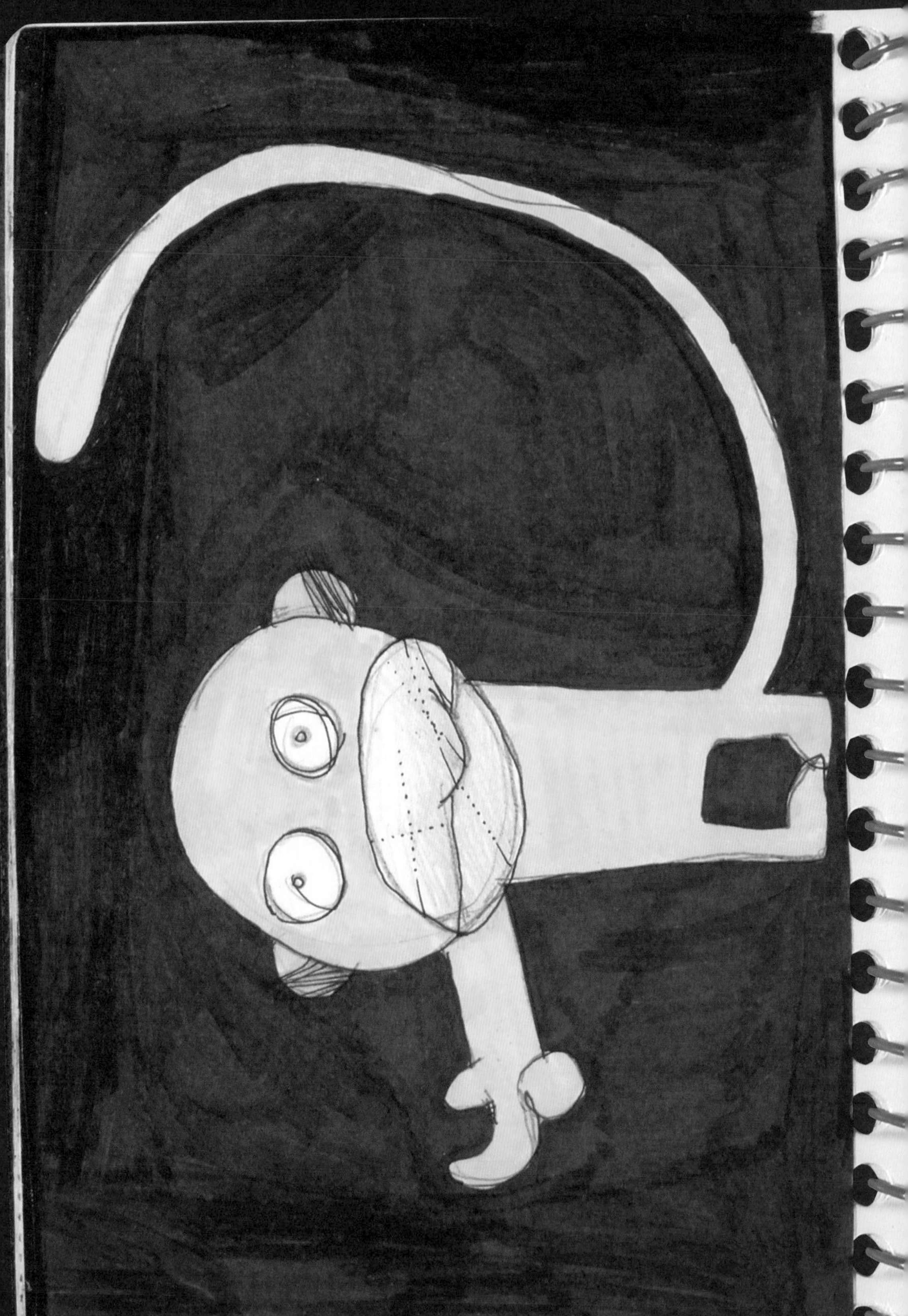

CANTORA NUM PALCO COM CORTINAS VERMELHAS EM BAIXO DE UM FOCO DE LUZ
DEPOIS DE UNS 30 SEG VOA O PRIMEIRO OVO ...
PÚBLICO COMEÇA A ARREMESSAR OVOS, TOMATES, ETC...
QUANTO MAIS ELA RECEBE OS OVOS E TOMATES MAIS ELA CANTA
COMPLETAMENTE SUJA!!!
NO FIM UM ALÇAPÃO SE ABRE E ELA CAI
UM BALDE DE LAVAGEM VAI BEM TB!

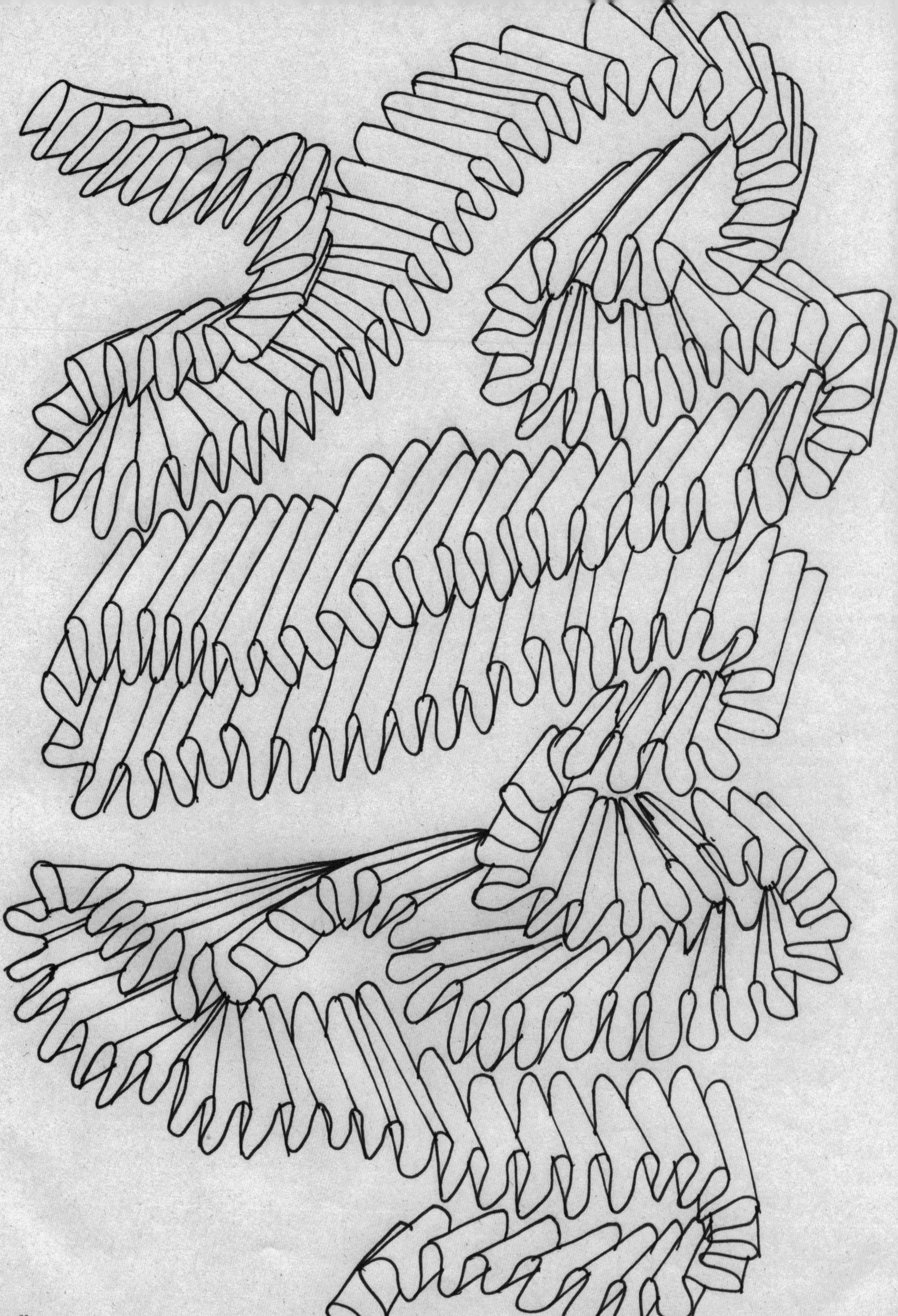

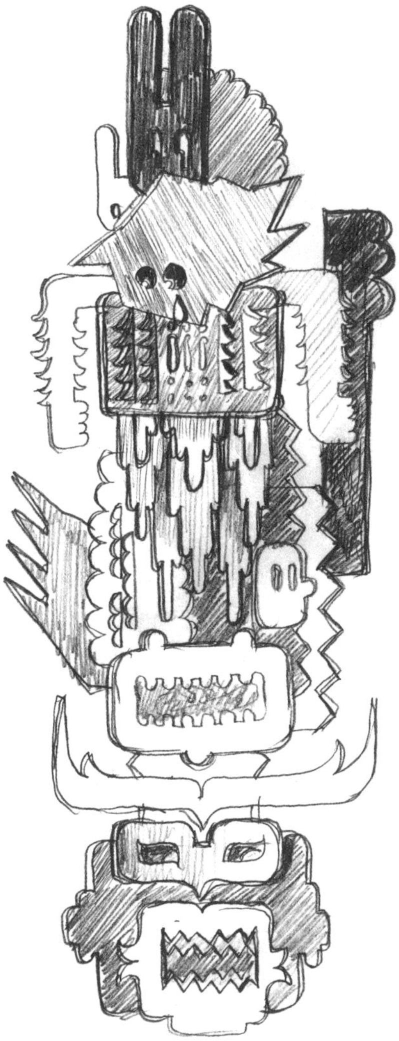

ANTOINE + MANUEL

Parisian designers Antoine + Manuel have always used sketchbooks, "since we met at school," says Antoine. "Manuel had many, but unfortunately most were left behind in Parisian basements. That's when I decided to use them too."

Their books are for putting down the ideas that pass through their heads. "Often we would regret that we had not recorded them. We also use the books as a basis for our commercial illustrations. For example, for the past two seasons at La Comédie de Clermont-Ferrand, the printed program has been the same dimension as my sketchbook, in which I worked directly to the same scale. The illustrations in those sketchbooks are, for the most part, the final versions."

Often their sketches have the charm of originals. The content is also much freer and lighter. However, "The majority of these images remain in the books. It is very unusual for them to be part of the final work."

"Manuel's work is always about objects, furniture and cards," says Antoine, "and my work is about color and gesture in general."

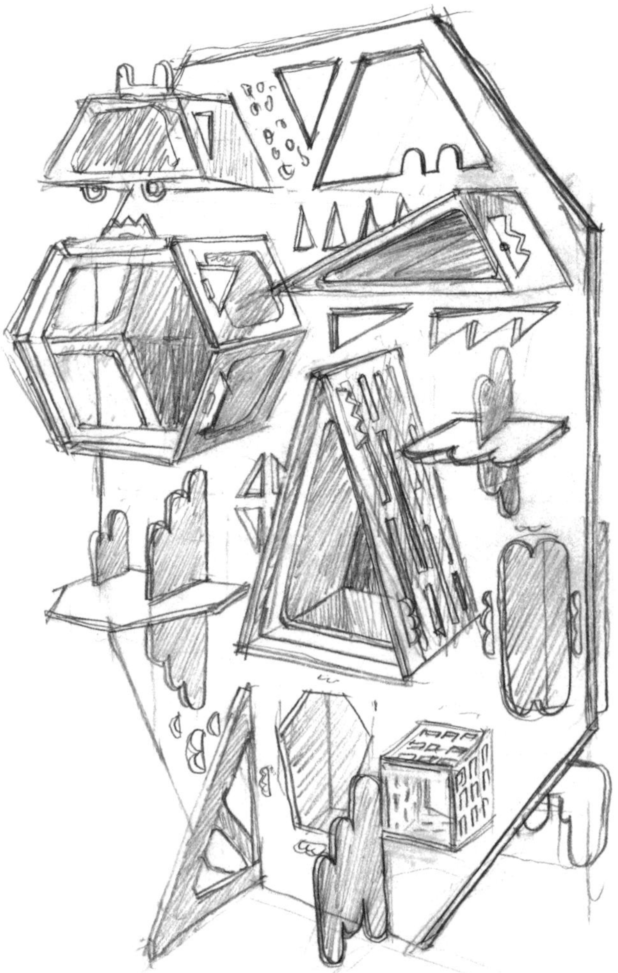

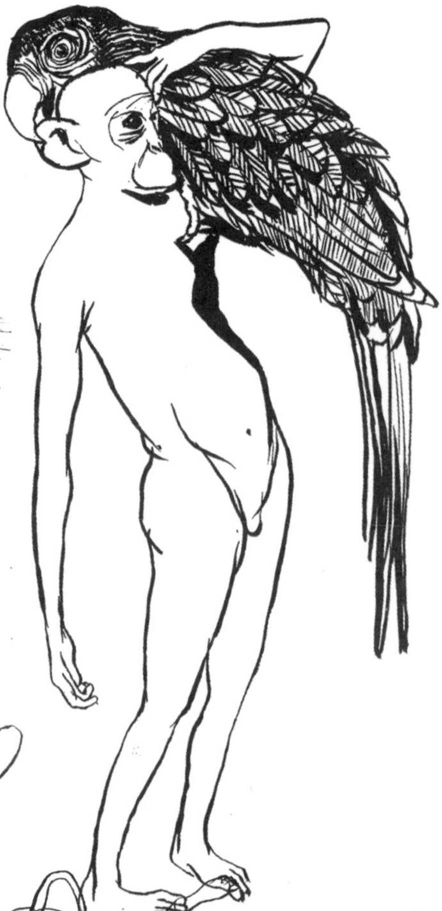

MARSHALL ARISMAN

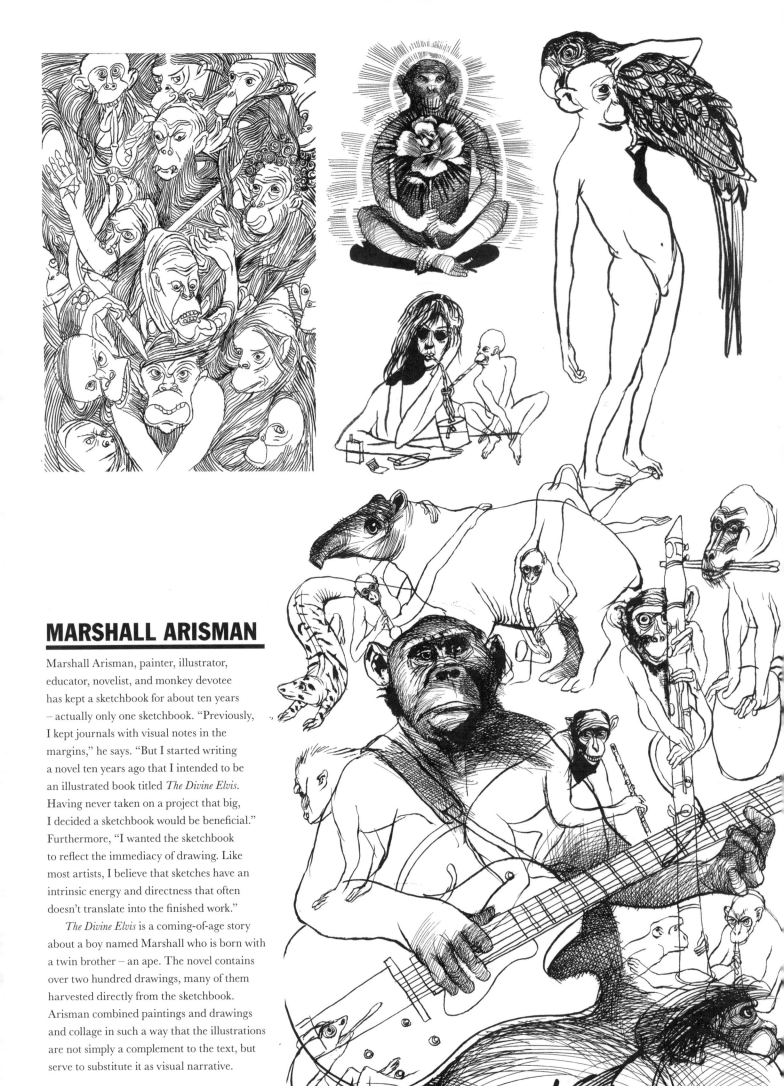

Marshall Arisman, painter, illustrator, educator, novelist, and monkey devotee has kept a sketchbook for about ten years – actually only one sketchbook. "Previously, I kept journals with visual notes in the margins," he says. "But I started writing a novel ten years ago that I intended to be an illustrated book titled *The Divine Elvis*. Having never taken on a project that big, I decided a sketchbook would be beneficial." Furthermore, "I wanted the sketchbook to reflect the immediacy of drawing. Like most artists, I believe that sketches have an intrinsic energy and directness that often doesn't translate into the finished work."

The Divine Elvis is a coming-of-age story about a boy named Marshall who is born with a twin brother – an ape. The novel contains over two hundred drawings, many of them harvested directly from the sketchbook. Arisman combined paintings and drawings and collage in such a way that the illustrations are not simply a complement to the text, but serve to substitute it as visual narrative.

Marshall Arisman
SKETCH BOOK
THE JAZZ MONKS
Blue Devil Jazz Lounge
Blue Devil Lounge
Buffalo N.Y
202 River Street
BIRD
565-345
ALL STAR QUINTETTE
SALT PEANUTS
(CLARKE-GILLESPIE)
DIZZY GILLESPIE
AND
CHARLIE PARKER SYDNEY CATLETT
AL HAIG-CURLY RUSSELL
1003 A

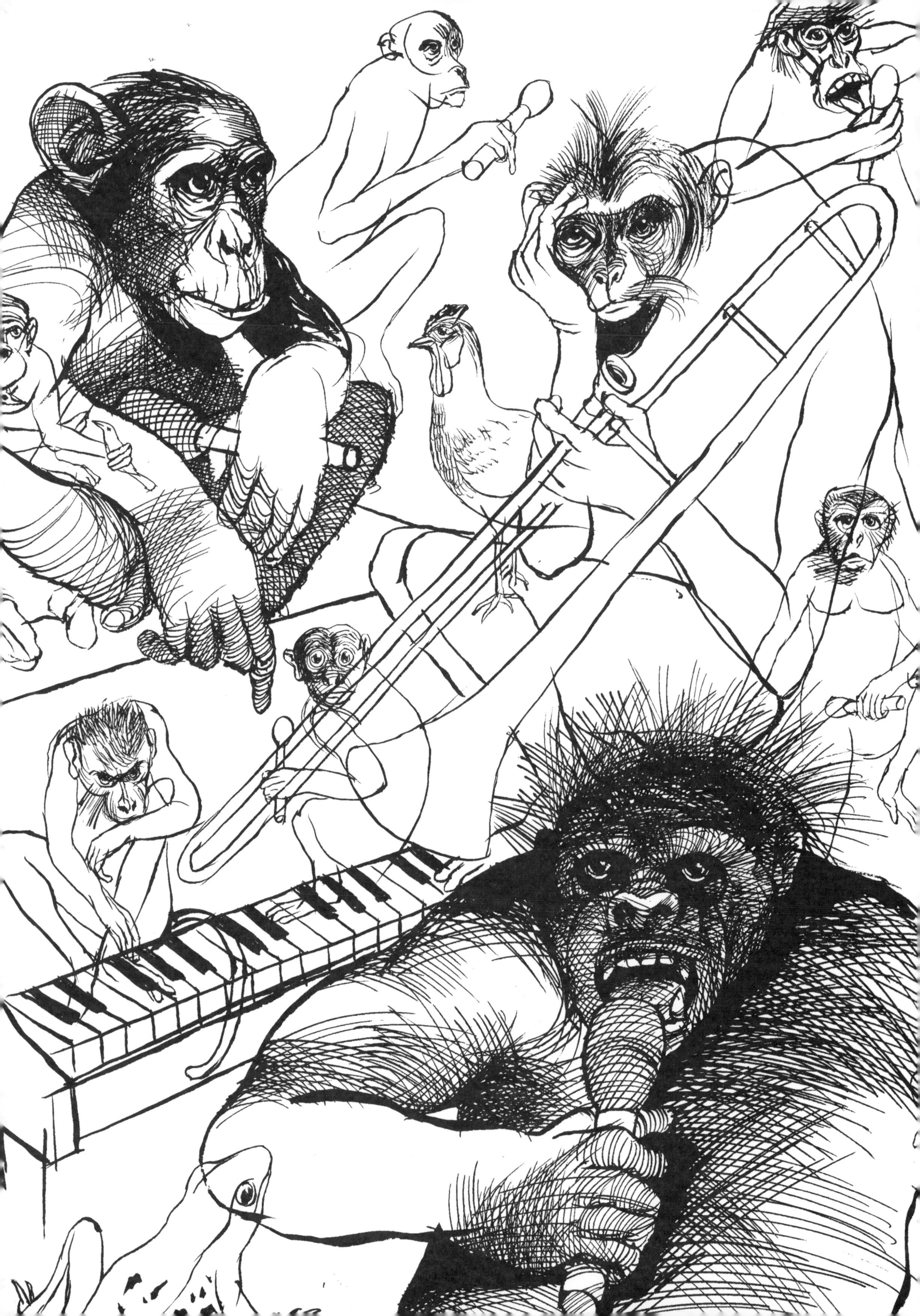

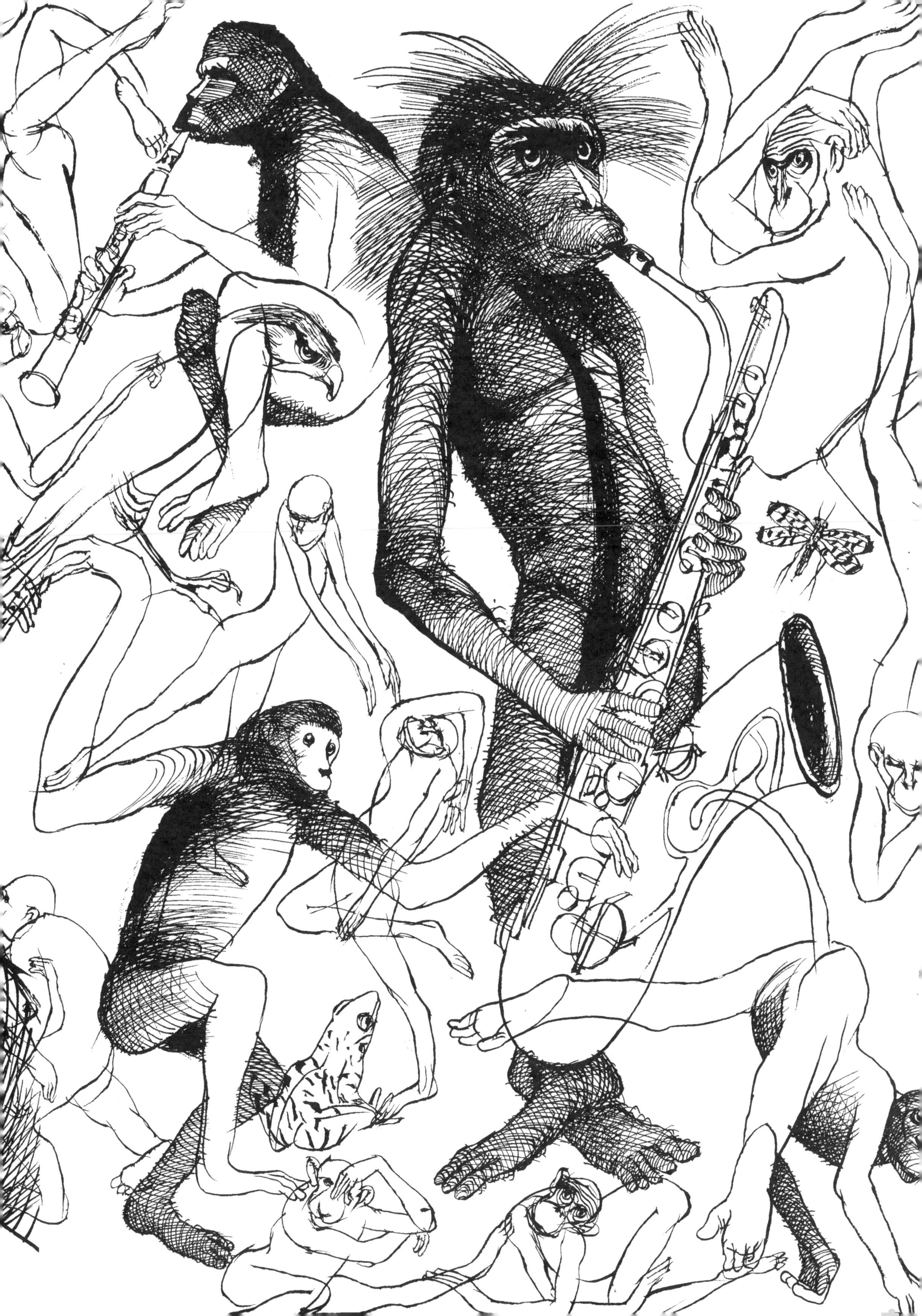

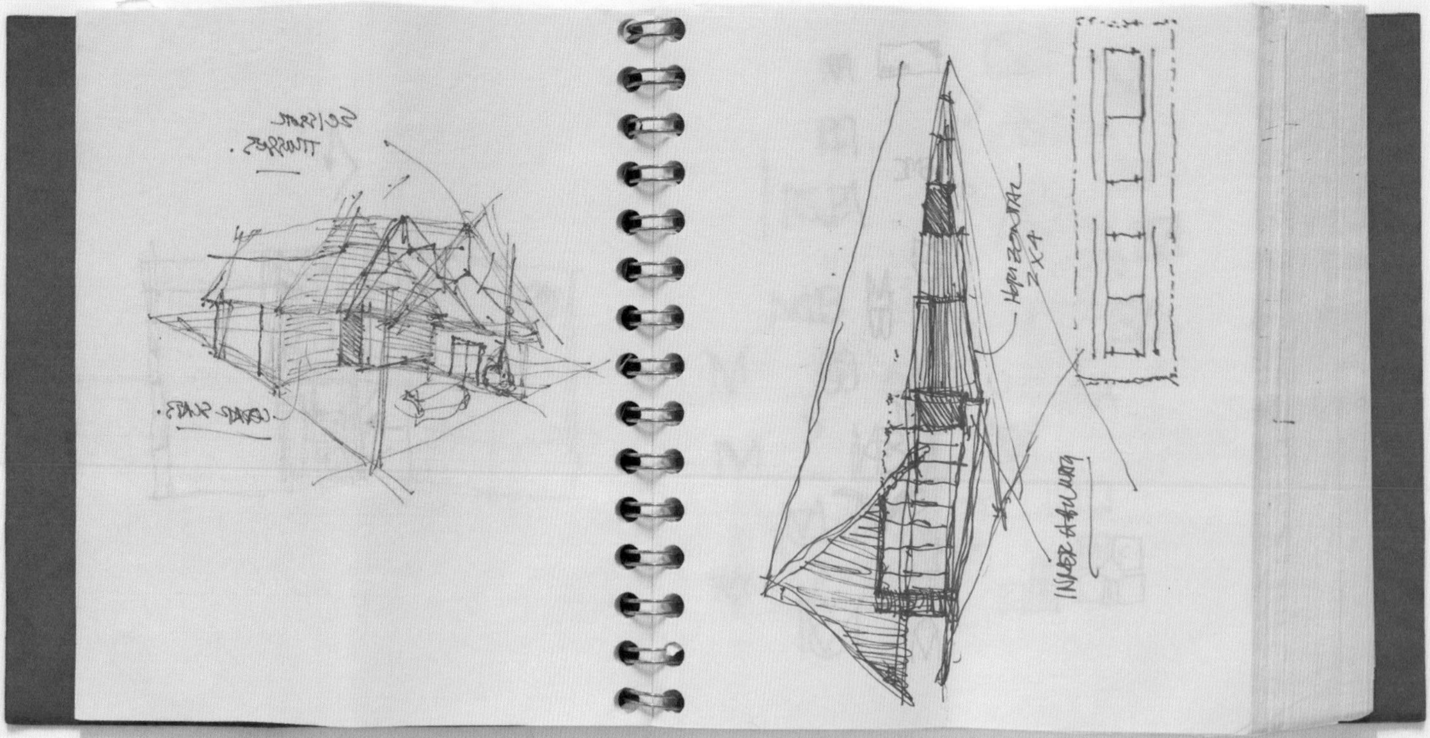
HORIZONTAL
2X4

MIXED
MATRIX
IN MENU BOARDS

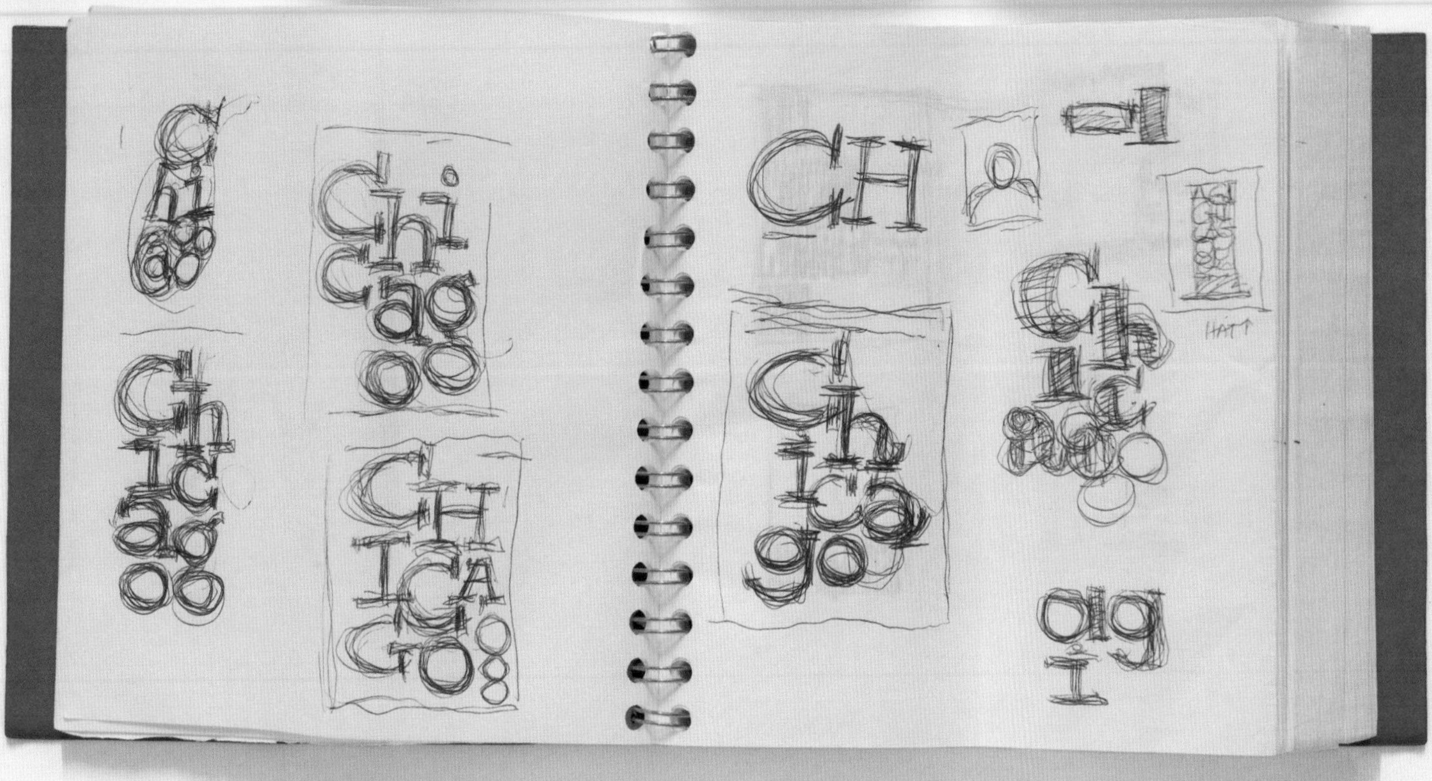

DANA ARNETT

Dana Arnett, founder of VSA Partners in Chicago, recalls that "as a kid, my mother would buy me those infamous Academy sketchbooks – I'd fill them up as fast as I could get my hands on them." His books "capture my thinking before it vaporizes. When I taught beginning design classes at university, I began by writing these words on the blackboard: 'Record, remember, relish, and relive.' It was my way of expressing the importance of owning and using a sketchbook."

He continues, "My first boss trained me to enlarge my sketches to scale as a part of the production phase. This helped me to understand how effectively a conceptual idea could translate to a finished product." Arnett estimates that 70 per cent of his sketches are architectural. "Judging by the content in my sketchbooks, I'm a frustrated architect at heart. I'm constantly consumed by the urge to draw buildings, decorative façades, elevations, and home improvement projects."

He treats these books as diaries that are not intended to be shared. He refers to "the inherent sincerity of the sketches themselves," and says they remind him of why he got into this profession in the first place: "To conceive things by hand that are emotional and real."

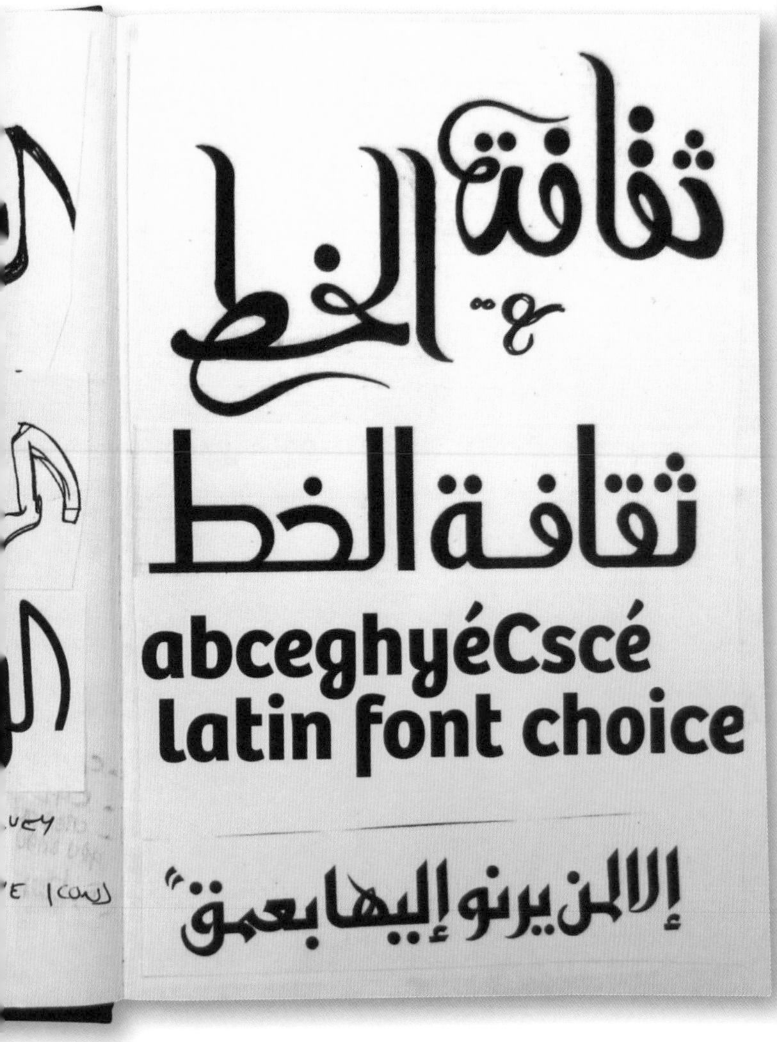

TAREK ATRISSI

Tarek Atrissi, a Lebanese-born, Amsterdam-based designer, says a sketchbook has many purposes. "It is a tool, where you collect all your scribbles, notes, and ideas," he says, adding that "it reminds you to work 'manually' and avoid falling into the trap of working digitally all the time. On the other hand, it is documentation for the process of any project. Scanning spreads from the sketchbook helps the client to understand how much work was behind any suggested design, even a simple one."

Typography takes up a lot of Atrissi's sketch space. "Typography doesn't look good accidentally," he says. "Good type always results from a lot of sketching, trials, and visual exploration. This process is what you see in my sketchbook. Logo design is also prominent because it is a discipline that requires considerable sketching."

Atrissi keeps specialized books, at least one for each large project. He also dedicates one to Arabic calligraphy. "I document nice examples of calligraphy or lettering I find in projects, in historical material, vernacular design pieces, or even on the streets and in old sign shops." And in another he stores photos of street graphics and posters that he takes when traveling across the Arab world.

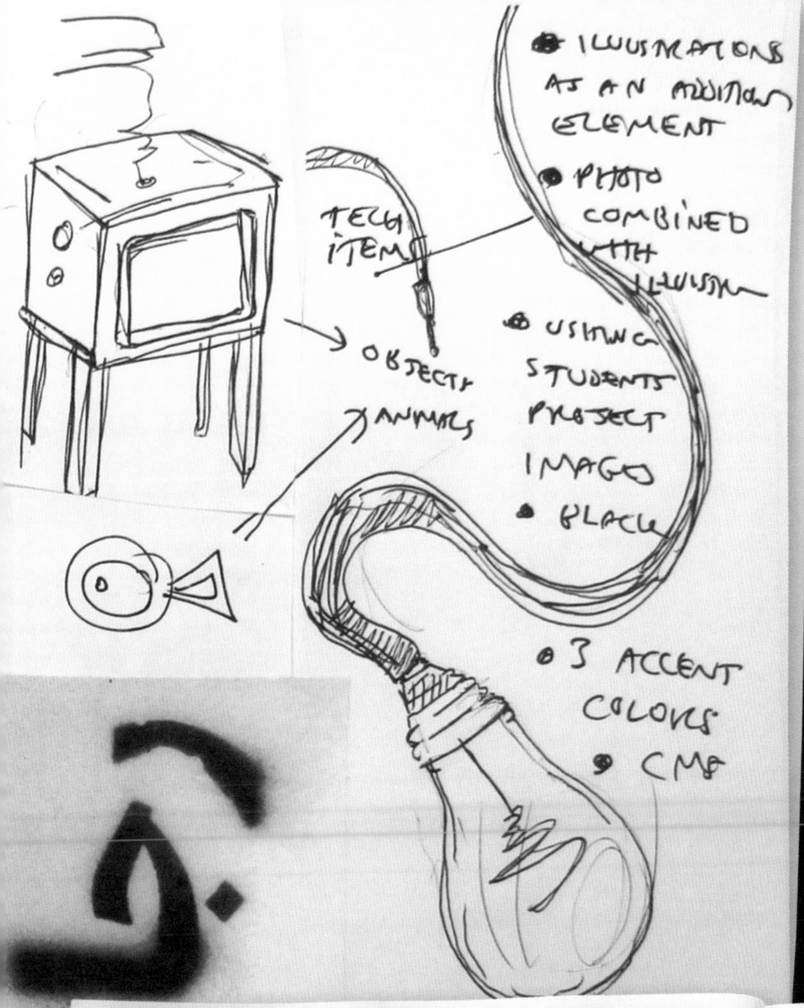
ILLUSTRATIONS AS AN ADDITION ELEMENT
PHOTO COMBINED WITH ILLUSTRATION
USING STUDENTS PROJECT IMAGES
BLACK
3 ACCENT COLOURS
TECH ITEM
OBJECTS
ANIMALS

HORSE VS GAZELLE DETAILS.

شادي
الخط
ARABIC GRAPHICS
THE WORK OF TAREK ATRISSI
ARABIC GRAPHICS
THE WORK OF TAREK ATRISSI
ARABIC GRAPHICS
ARABIC GRAPHICS
THE WORK OF TAREK ATRISSI
ARABIC GRAPHICS
THE WORK OF TAREK ATRISSI
ARABIC GRAPHICS
THE WORK OF TAREK ATRISSI
ARABIC GRAPHICS
THE WORK OF TAREK ATRISSI
ARABIC GRAPHICS
THE WORK OF TAREK ATRISSI
ARABIC GRAPHICS
THE WORK OF TAREK ATRISSI

MARIAN BANTJES

Canadian letterer and script-meister Marian Bantjes has been obsessively ("but not meticulously") keeping all her sketches on whatever scraps of paper they are produced on since mid-2003. Her rationale for keeping all this material, Bantjes explains, is that "I have this fantasy that one day I will be famous and my sketch piles will serve as a treasure trove for some student or group of students after I am dead. They will go through the piles and assemble them into mini-piles for each project, and they will exclaim over my fumbled beginnings and wrong turns. Then they will layer up the tracing-paper sketches and see how the form changed from one to the next. They will read the little scribbles on the edges of the pages and wonder: Whose phone number? What meaning? They'll make connections from one project to the next, and excitedly discover things that never made it to print. They will closely examine the eraser marks, looking for the changes in a single sketch. They will find pieces of patterns and link them back to the final piece: a shard of the *Wallpaper** cover, a detail of the Pop!Tech poster. Endless hours of scholarly fun, no? Hubris, I know."

The examples from 2003–8 shown here are kept chaotically. "I love them, but I disrespect them by tossing them into a drawer in handfuls, and later stuffing them into envelopes or shopping bags." Bantjes has thousands of sketches piled one on top of the other: just waiting until her piles are worth more than the paper they are written on.

A Death on Terminal Island By Ben Ehrenreich
Sandra Tsing Loh Is One Angry Mother By Ariel Swartley
My Synagogue's Struggle to Survive By Ed Leibowitz
Los Angeles
Marian Bantjes

ELIZABETH KNOWI
A Treas
of
QUOTATIONS
for all
OCCASIONS

WOMEN
DESIGN

From: kofi_mills@walla.com
Date: August 7 2007 5:05:24 AM PDT (CA)
Subject:
My Dear can we work together
My Dear,
With my humble fidelity and enthusiastic mind I greet you.
Dear this is a
golden opportunity
that am bringing to you which will change your life in a positive way.
I need your keen interest towards this
I will like us to be one and work together as one body,
and
this deal has to be between you and I
you have to promise me that!
Because my life will be in danger, if
any other person gets to find out.
I know as a mature person who known business and life,
you will do that for me.

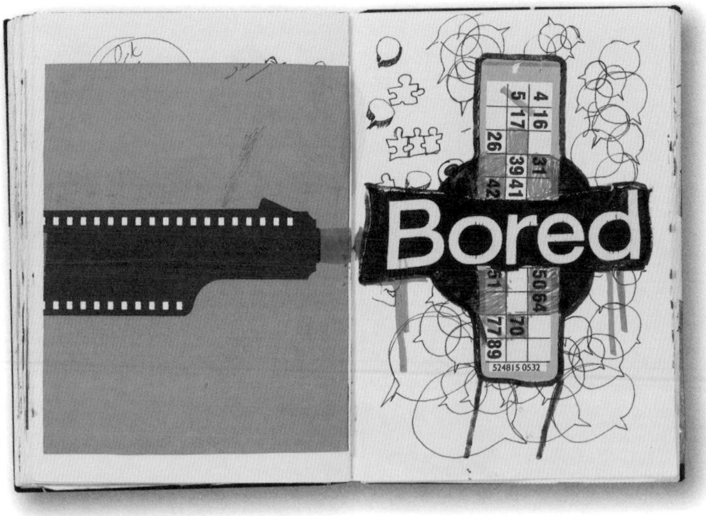

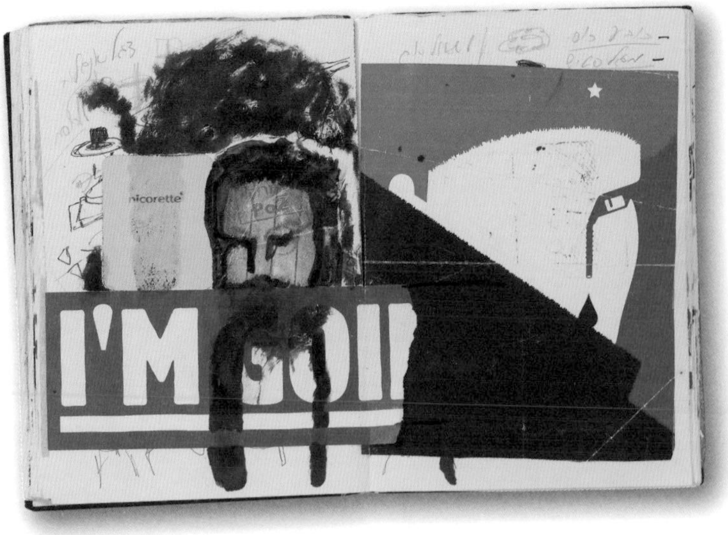

NOMA BAR

Israeli-born, London-based caricaturist Noma Bar has an exceptional ability to use objects related to his subject's life as features comprising the face or body. The result is both abstract and recognizable, but always clear and clean. Not so with his sixty-plus sketchbooks; the loose, expressionist images are a respite from the rigors of detail.

"What is the common thing between the two? Both are telling a story," Bar explains. "The story in my finished work is structured and designed to communicate with the viewer, while the sketchbooks reflect moments and are designed to communicate with one viewer: me."

Bar notes that "they are a diary of moments and events, rather than backstage drawings towards the finished work. For example, when I'm looking again at some images they take me back to my late father's hospital bed in Haifa, opposite the sea. He was unconscious and the only thing that I could do for hours was sit next to him and pull some bits of toilet paper, tissue, and medical packaging that surrounded his bed and revive them in my sketchbook. By using those I have captured some moments in a way that is stronger than any photo, realistic drawing, or written text." These images span the years 2000–9.

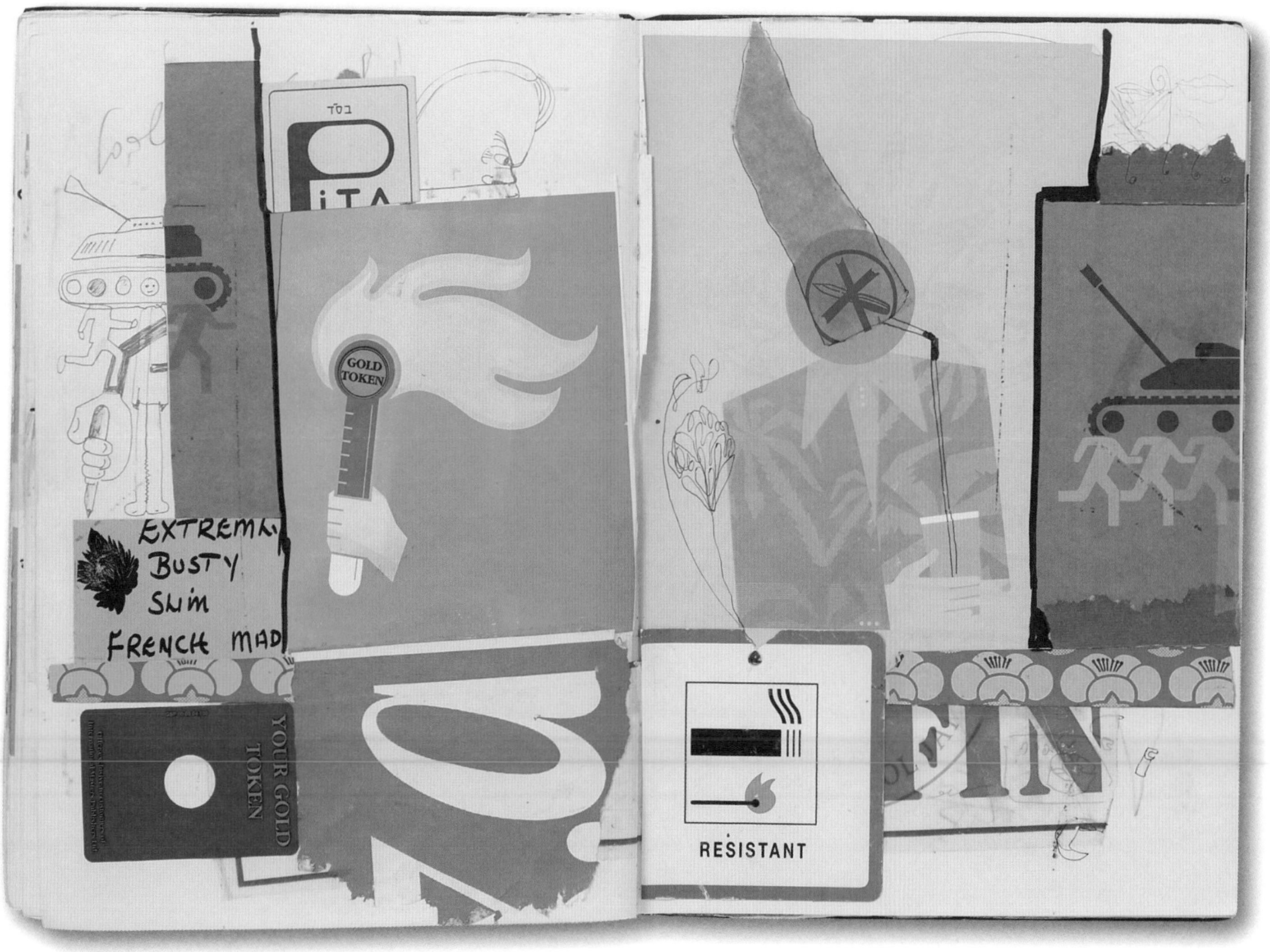
GOLD TOKEN
EXTREMLY BUSTY SLIM FRENCH MAD
YOUR GOLD TOKEN
RESISTANT

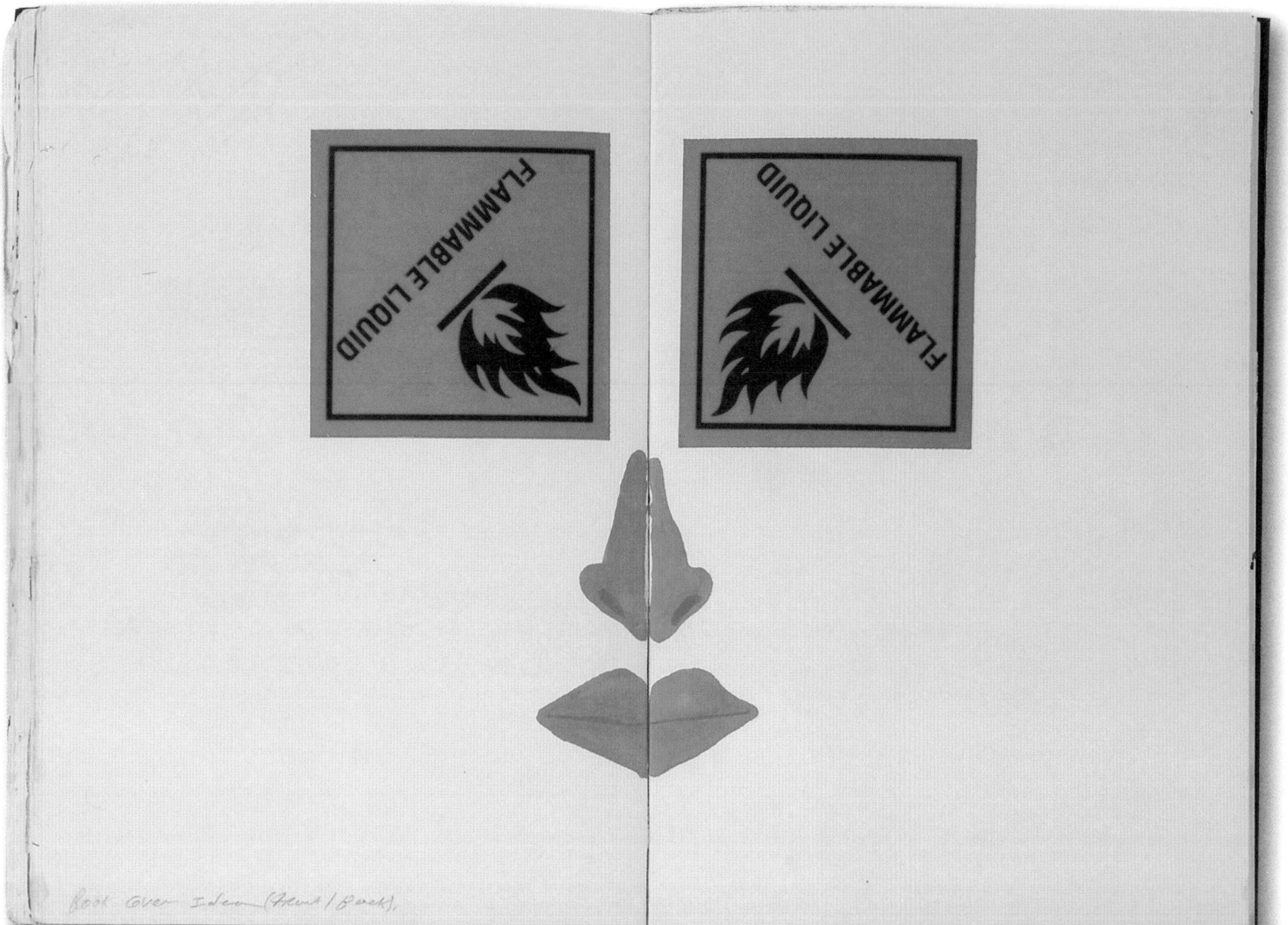
FLAMMABLE LIQUID
FLAMMABLE LIQUID
Book Cover Ideas (Front / Back).

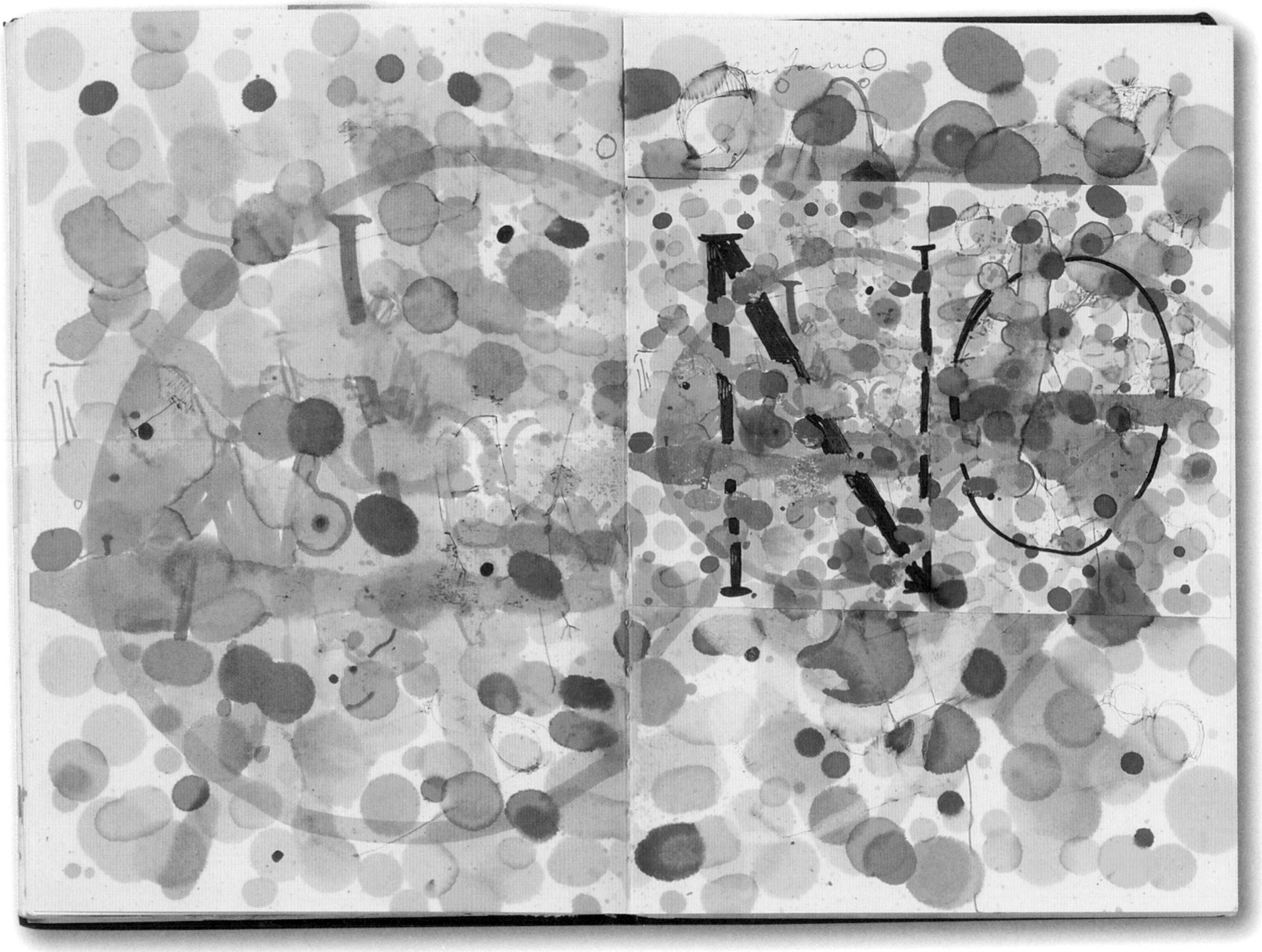
NO

CK.801-1101/G
Chartwell
come
done
drunk
driven
eaten
fallen
felt
found
flown
got
given
gone
had
held
kept
known
learnt
made
met
paid
put
read
said
chose
chosen
bought
brought
been
drove
ate
fell
flew
gave
went
eat
fall
feel
find
fly
get
give
go
have
hold
keep
know
learn
make
meet
pay
read
say
see
speak
take
teach
tell
think
wear
write
wrote
cost
bring
buy
was/were

Free
Me

559519
UniChem
ABSORBENT COTTON GAUZE
S/WAY
Store Description
1st Del
S/WAY
GUZZI
CALL

FRAGI

FRAGILE
Quality Cigarette
READY BY
REPAIRS
PRICE
THIS TICKET MUST BE GIVEN UP FOR REPAIRS
8750
KUNMING CIGARETTE FACTORY
YUNNAN
HAND
WITH
presente
DON'T
we are always here to help.
HELLO
MY NAME IS
NU-GEL
WASTE PAPER
MEDICAL
SOVENIER BOOK OF DESIGN TERMINOLOGY
TOY MOEDL
FIELD WITH
AVARIETY OF
FANCY FOOL COLORED PICTURES & SCENES
STUFF TO LOOK AT
and
LIQUID CENTER
JAN-7
HAND FINISH
TUFFTAPE
ATTA
PETER PINNER
020 8863 1528
e-mail: peter@peterpinnerents.com

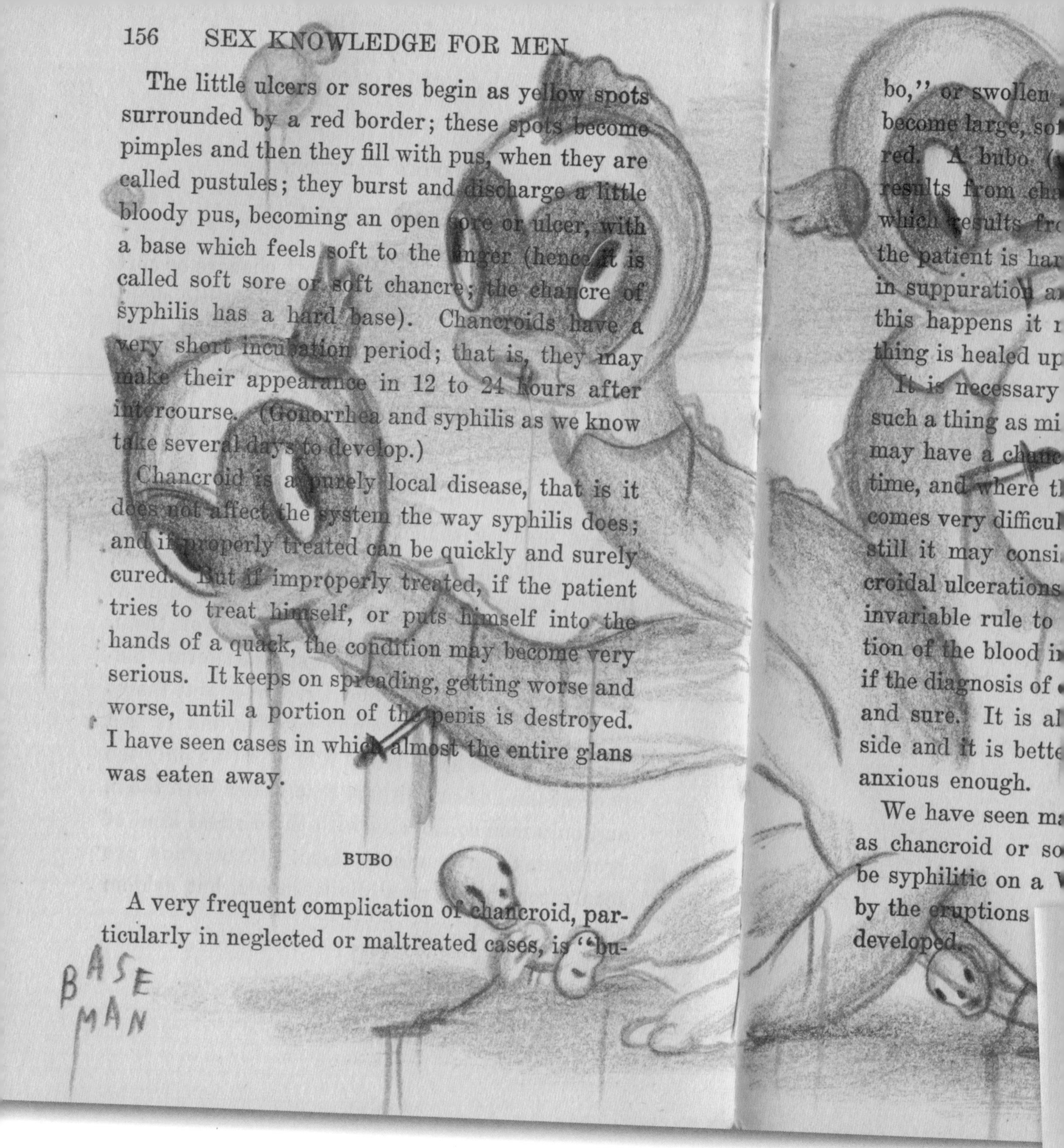

156 SEX KNOWLEDGE FOR MEN
The little ulcers or sores begin as yellow spots surrounded by a red border; these spots become pimples and then they fill with pus, when they are called pustules; they burst and discharge a little bloody pus, becoming an open sore or ulcer, with a base which feels soft to the finger (hence it is called soft sore or soft chancre; the chancre of syphilis has a hard base). Chancroids have a very short incubation period; that is, they may make their appearance in 12 to 24 hours after intercourse. (Gonorrhea and syphilis as we know take several days to develop.)
Chancroid is a purely local disease, that is it does not affect the system the way syphilis does; and if properly treated can be quickly and surely cured. But if improperly treated, if the patient tries to treat himself, or puts himself into the hands of a quack, the condition may become very serious. It keeps on spreading, getting worse and worse, until a portion of the penis is destroyed. I have seen cases in which almost the entire glans was eaten away.
BUBO
A very frequent complication of chancroid, particularly in neglected or maltreated cases, is "bu-
BASEMAN

GARY BASEMAN

Los Angeles-based illustrator, animator, comics artist, and toymaker Gary Baseman carries a sketchbook every day. He also carries an old published book to draw in, starting with a Chinese prayer book he was given in Taiwan, then an old book on Communism found in Berlin, and now he retains a book titled *Sex Knowledge for Men*.

"Sketching allows my subconscious to escape onto the paper. I will always surprise myself. When I was an illustrator, I used to sketch out ideas. As a painter, I allow my id to roam free and try to find simple truths about the human condition. And they have a recurring theme," he says. "All of them contain a dragon character I call Ooga, which means 'cake' in Hebrew. Ooga was the protector of my parents but the imprisoner of me, who kept me from my own personal destiny and growth. I acknowledge now that I need to become my own liberator. I need to forge my own path of 'good,' even if my 'good' is imperfect and bittersweet, mixed with the pure and the impure, right and wrong, vulnerability and strength, selflessness and selfishness, creating both achievement and failure. My parents were successful in nurturing a soulful son who loves life and people, and who does not take things for granted; who, as an adult, loves to pinch cheeks, to hold others, to feed and be fed, and who still loves cake."

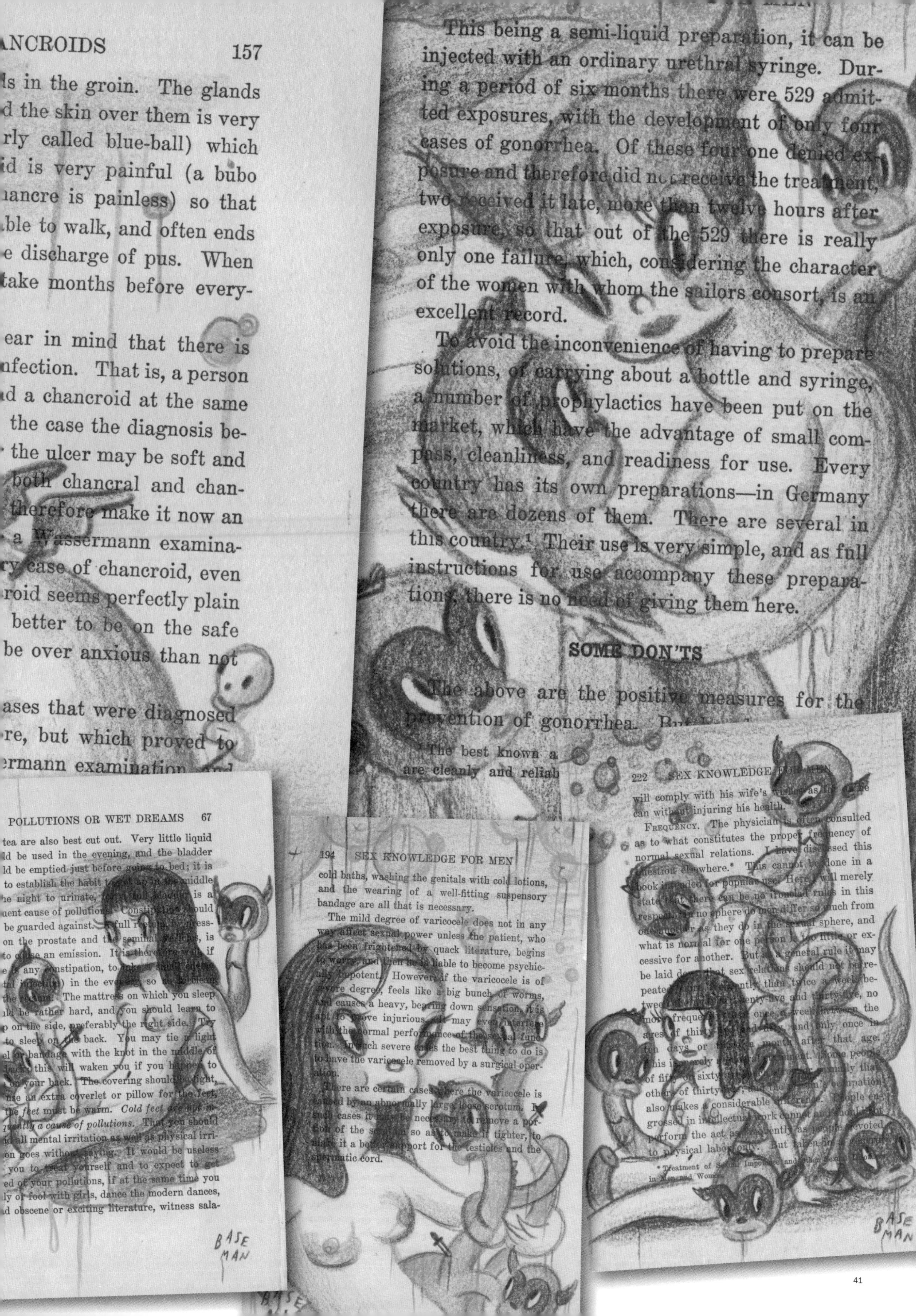
ANCROIDS 157
ls in the groin. The glands
d the skin over them is very
rly called blue-ball) which
id is very painful (a bubo
hancre is painless) so that
ble to walk, and often ends
e discharge of pus. When
take months before every-
ear in mind that there is
nfection. That is, a person
d a chancroid at the same
the case the diagnosis be-
the ulcer may be soft and
both chancral and chan-
therefore make it now an
a Wassermann examina-
ry case of chancroid, even
roid seems perfectly plain
better to be on the safe
be over anxious than not
ases that were diagnosed
re, but which proved to
ermann examination
This being a semi-liquid preparation, it can be injected with an ordinary urethral syringe. During a period of six months there were 529 admitted exposures, with the development of only four cases of gonorrhea. Of these four one denied exposure and therefore did not receive the treatment, two received it late, more than twelve hours after exposure, so that out of the 529 there is really only one failure, which, considering the character of the women with whom the sailors consort, is an excellent record.
To avoid the inconvenience of having to prepare solutions, of carrying about a bottle and syringe, a number of prophylactics have been put on the market, which have the advantage of small compass, cleanliness, and readiness for use. Every country has its own preparations—in Germany there are dozens of them. There are several in this country.[1] Their use is very simple, and as full instructions for use accompany these preparations, there is no need of giving them here.
SOME DON'TS
The above are the positive measures for the prevention of gonorrhea.
[1] The best known a
are cleanly and reliab
POLLUTIONS OR WET DREAMS 67
tea are also best cut out. Very little liquid
ld be used in the evening, and the bladder
ld be emptied just before going to bed; it is
to establish the habit
he night to urinate,
uent cause of pollutions. Constipation should
be guarded against. A full rectum, by press-
on the prostate and the seminal vesicles, is
to cause an emission.
the rectum. The mattress on which you sleep
ld be rather hard, and you should learn to
p on the side, preferably the right side. Try
to sleep on the back. You may tie a light
el or bandage with the knot in the middle of
back; this will waken you if you happen to
on your back. The covering should be light,
use an extra coverlet or pillow for the feet,
the feet must be warm. *Cold feet are not in-*
quently a cause of pollutions. That you should
all mental irritation as well as physical irri-
on goes without saying. It would be useless
you to treat yourself and to expect to get
ed of your pollutions, if at the same time you
ly or fool with girls, dance the modern dances,
d obscene or exciting literature, witness sala-
BASE MAN
194 SEX KNOWLEDGE FOR MEN
cold baths, washing the genitals with cold lotions, and the wearing of a well-fitting suspensory bandage are all that is necessary.
The mild degree of varicocele does not in any way affect sexual power unless the patient, who has been frightened by quack literature, begins to worry, and then he is liable to become psychically impotent. However, if the varicocele is of severe degree, feels like a big bunch of worms, and causes a heavy, bearing down sensation, it is apt to prove injurious. It may even interfere with the normal performance of the sexual function. In such severe cases the best thing to do is to have the varicocele removed by a surgical operation.
There are certain cases where the varicocele is caused by an abnormally large, loose scrotum. In such cases it may be necessary to remove a portion of the scrotum so as to make it tighter, to make it a better support for the testicles and the spermatic cord.
222 SEX KNOWLEDGE FOR MEN
will comply with his wife's wishes
can without injuring his health.
FREQUENCY. The physician is often consulted as to what constitutes the proper frequency of normal sexual relations.
what is normal for one person is too little or excessive for another.
to physical labor only.
BASE MAN

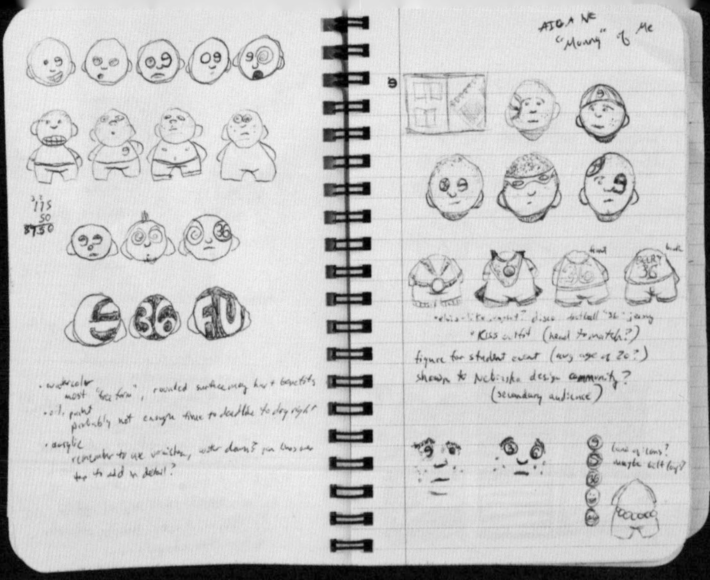

DONOVAN BEERY

Donovan Beery, co-founder of the design firm 36Point, has tried over the years to have what he calls an actual sketchbook, but "I always forget to carry it around," he declares. So, technically speaking, his sketchbooks are simply notebooks, "which I happen to sketch in between meeting notes."

Beery uses his books to come up with as much of the finished idea as possible before moving to the final medium. "I love working on the computer," he notes, "but I easily fall into the trap of doing what the program I am using does easiest. Working these things out in pen first forces me to try other solutions. It's also the fastest way to brainstorm for me."

His sketches "are terrible, and normally unfinished. I only sketch projects for my own reference, so quit each one as soon as I see the design I need in it, and move to the next." He adds, "I get as much or more from the notes I write down as from the images drawn."

For Beery, the books are "based on whatever project I am working on. I have only been good at keeping the notebook I am currently using. I probably need to do a better job at finding an archiving method. I started making my own notebooks two years ago, so I have a pile of blank ones to use. They are small enough that I actually carry them around sometimes."

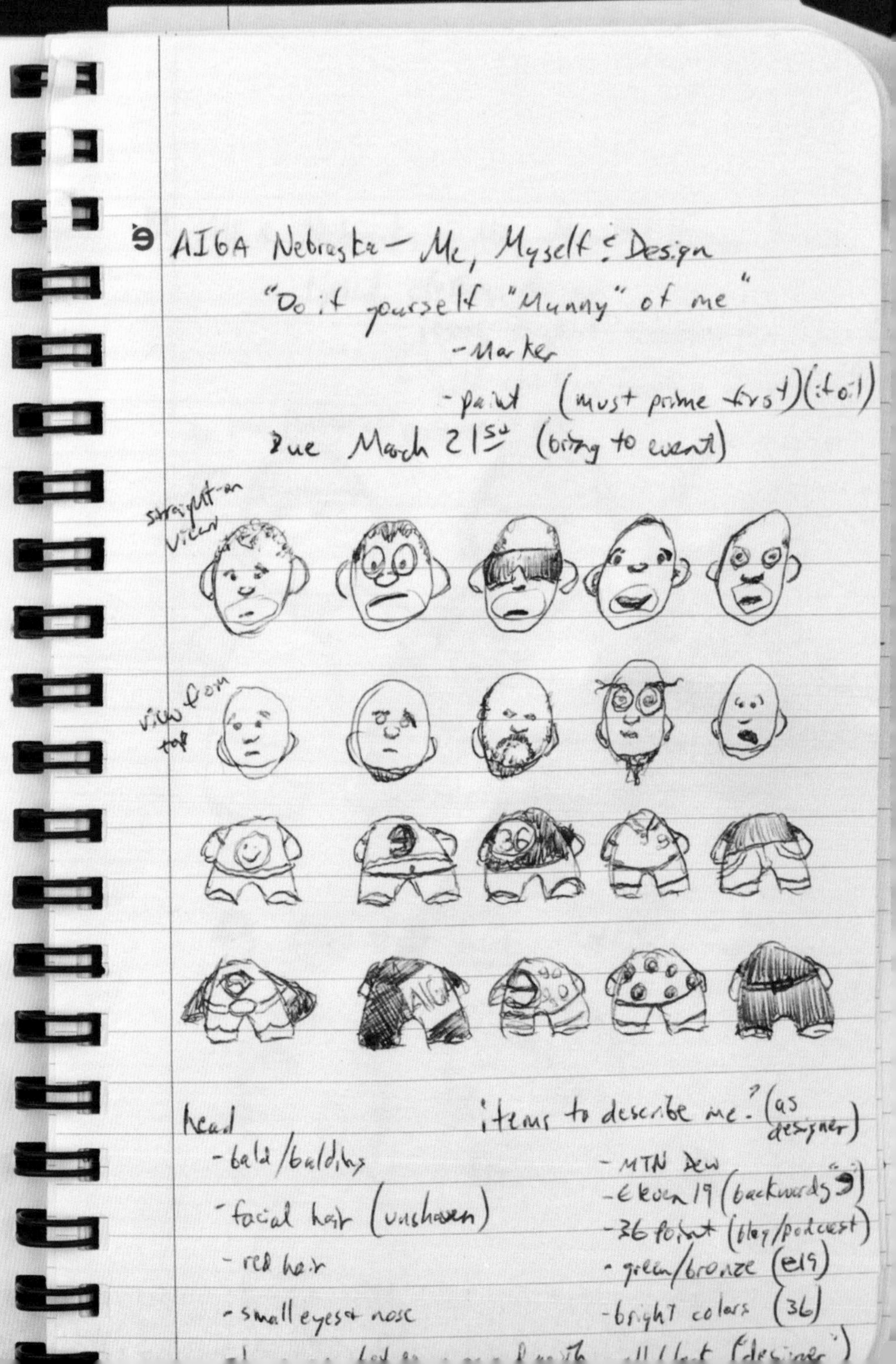

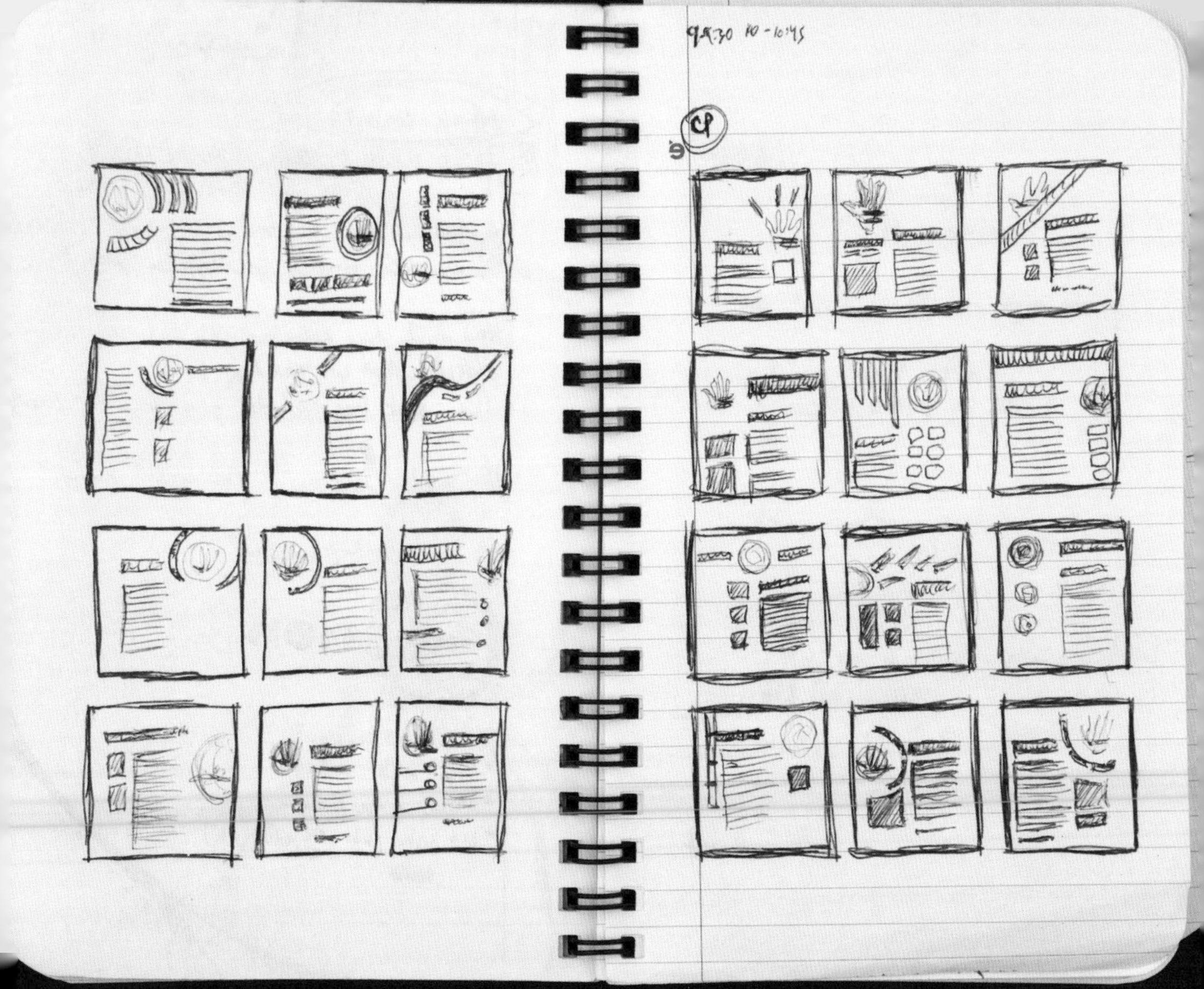

9:30 10-10:45

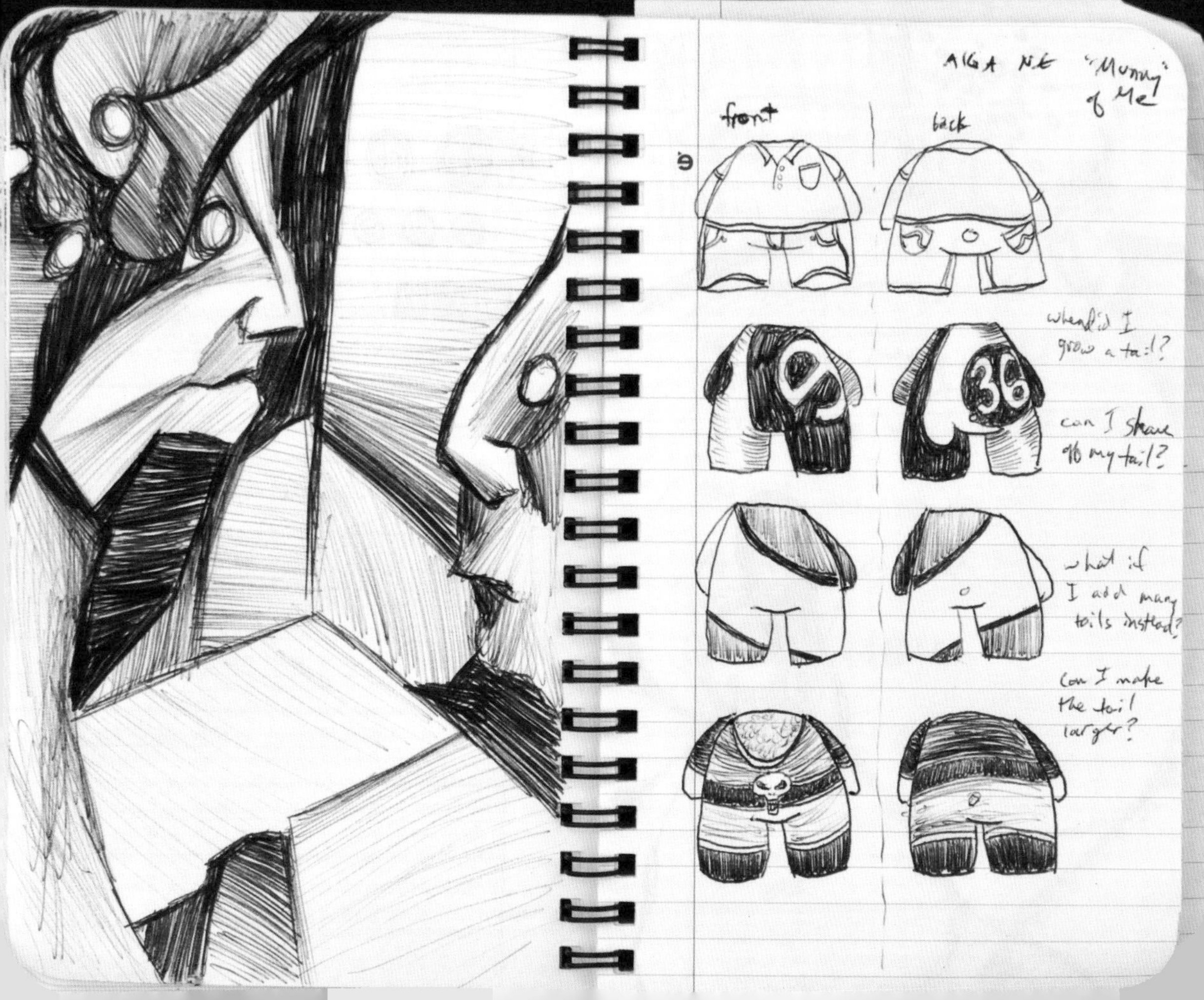

AIGA NE "Mummy" of Me!
front
back
when did I grow a tail?
can I shave off my tail?
what if I add many tails instead?
can I make the tail larger?

POLICY WOMANUAL
Farmers Rock
Pig People
WE ARE WHAT WE EAT!
VT
May
BUZZZZ
FF MTG. 4/6/09
WITH PENNY CANDY
MAPLE SUGAR
MAY BASKETS
JAMS THEY SAY "MADE IN ME" BUT HOW MUCH OF THE INGREDIENT ARE?
THESE BERRIES ARE ACTUALLY MADE IN
HOW TO HANDLE?
EX.
EAT
IDEA
PECHA KUCHA NAME TAGS AS T-SHIRTS?
AXE MAN

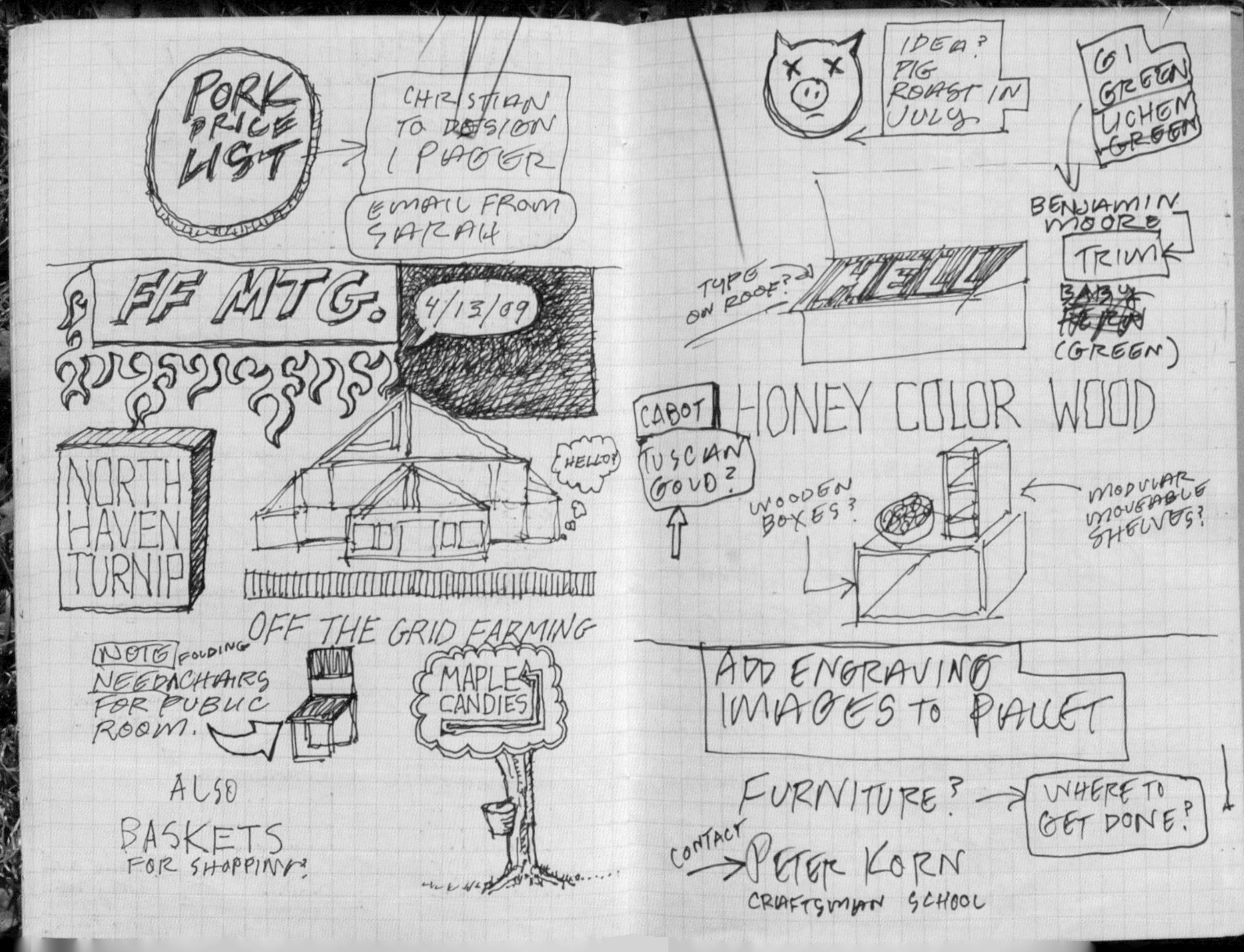
PORK PRICE LIST
CHRISTIAN TO DESIGN 1 PAGER
EMAIL FROM SARAH
FF MTG.
4/13/09
NORTH HAVEN TURNIP
HELLO!
OFF THE GRID FARMING
NOTE FOLDING NEED CHAIRS FOR PUBLIC ROOM.
MAPLE CANDIES
ALSO BASKETS FOR SHOPPING!
IDEA? PIG ROAST IN JULY
GI GREEN
LICHEN GREEN
BENJAMIN MOORE
TRIM
BABY FERN (GREEN)
TYPE ON ROOF?
CABOT
HONEY COLOR WOOD
TUSCAN GOLD?
WOODEN BOXES?
MODULAR MOVEABLE SHELVES?
ADD ENGRAVING IMAGES TO PALLET
FURNITURE?
WHERE TO GET DONE?
CONTACT PETER KORN
CRAFTSMAN SCHOOL

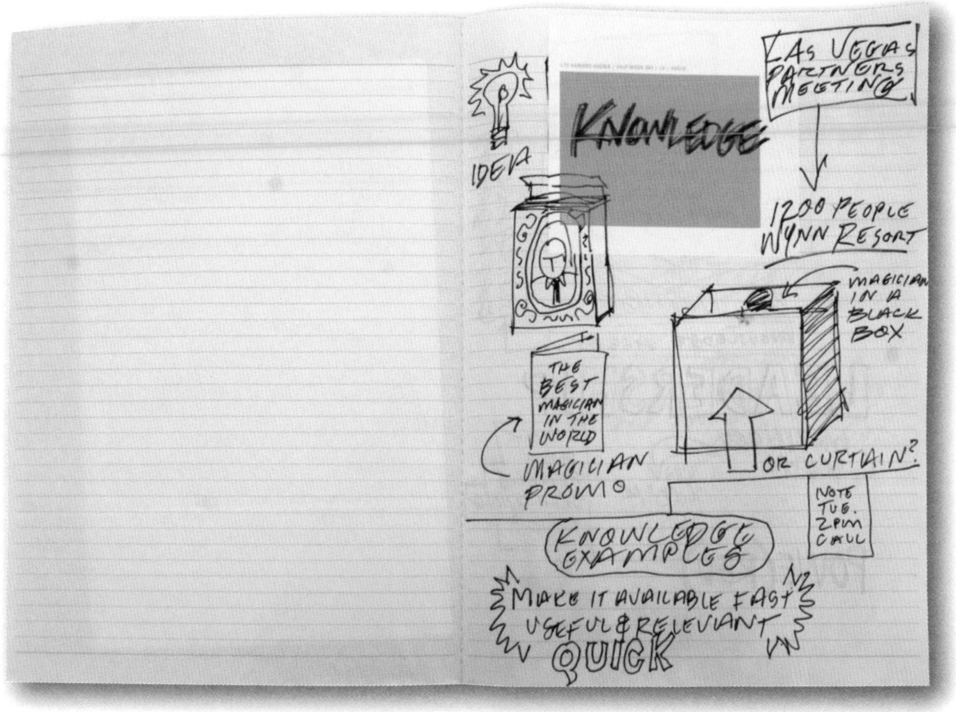

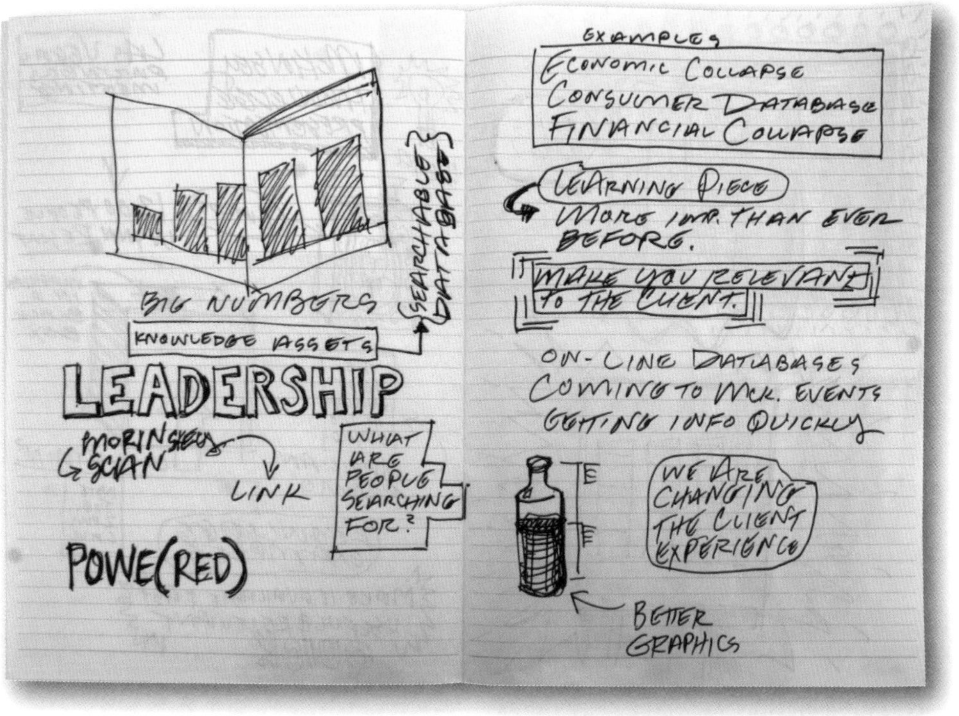

JOHN BIELENBERG

The peripatetic San Francisco-based designer John Bielenberg, who founded Project M, a "designer as citizen" advocacy group, is a longtime sketchbooker, "ever since I started working professionally at a crummy little advertising agency in Palo Alto in 1980," he notes.

They are mostly for writing down notes in meetings. "Although I rarely look at them again, the process of taking notes and doodling helps me remember stuff from the meetings." The sketches are mostly about documentation and ideas. "I heard Milton Glaser [see page 156] describe this as the 'fuzzy zone.' They rarely translate into execution," he says.

Bielenberg does admit to fostering a certain graphic style in the books. "I like to draw dimensional boxes around text. Maybe it helps me keep thoughts distinct and separate from other thoughts."

And, despite his protestations, "I've saved maybe fifty. I never refer back to them so I don't know why I keep them. Maybe it's the idea that I might someday need them. Who knows...?" The books shown here are from late 2009.

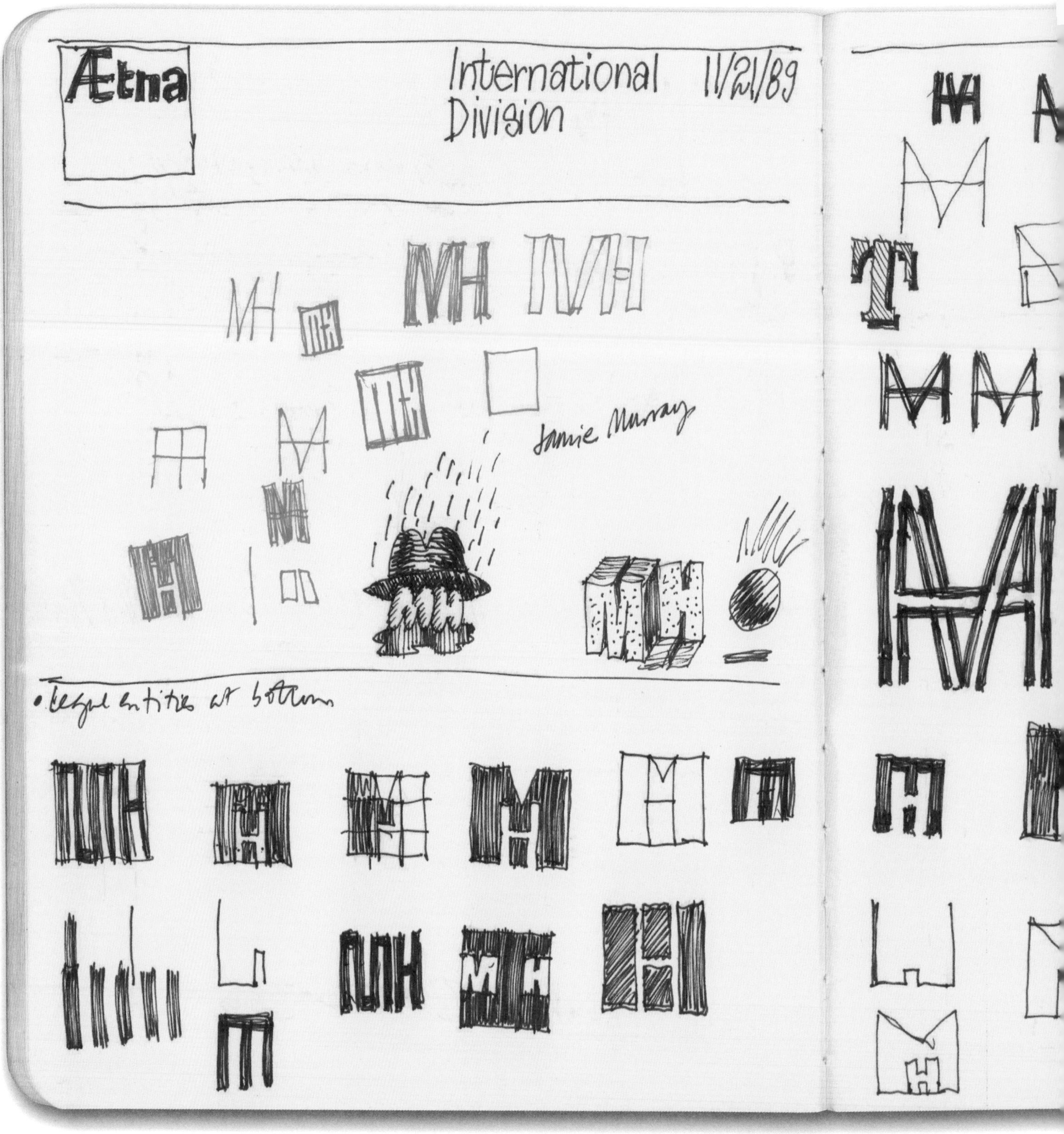

MICHAEL BIERUT

New York-based Pentagram partner Michael Bierut wrote on the website *DesignObserver*: "I tend to be obsessive-compulsive, and I am very picky about notebooks. No fancy Moleskines for me, just standard-issue office supply composition books." And so it has been since he started in 1982 – he has now reached number eighty-seven. The drawings are very rough, sometimes unintelligible. They are a kind of shorthand to get to the next stage.

"I hate gridded paper (but not as much as lined). There have been times when it's been difficult to get unlined composition books, which are oddly unpopular. Once I found a supplier who would only sell them in bulk and I bought a whole boxful. I thought these would last the rest of my life, but I gave a lot away, which I regret. Now they're gone."

"They function like a security blanket for me," he further confides. "I can't go into a meeting unless I have my book in my hand. Because I carry one everywhere, I tend to misplace them. Losing one makes me frantic. Everyone who works with me gets used to me asking, 'Have you seen my notebook anywhere?', which I assume gets irritating after a while: sorry. Once I left one on the roof of a cab on the Upper West Side. I ended up walking ten blocks, retracing the taxi's route, until I found it on Broadway at 63rd Street, intact except for some tire marks."

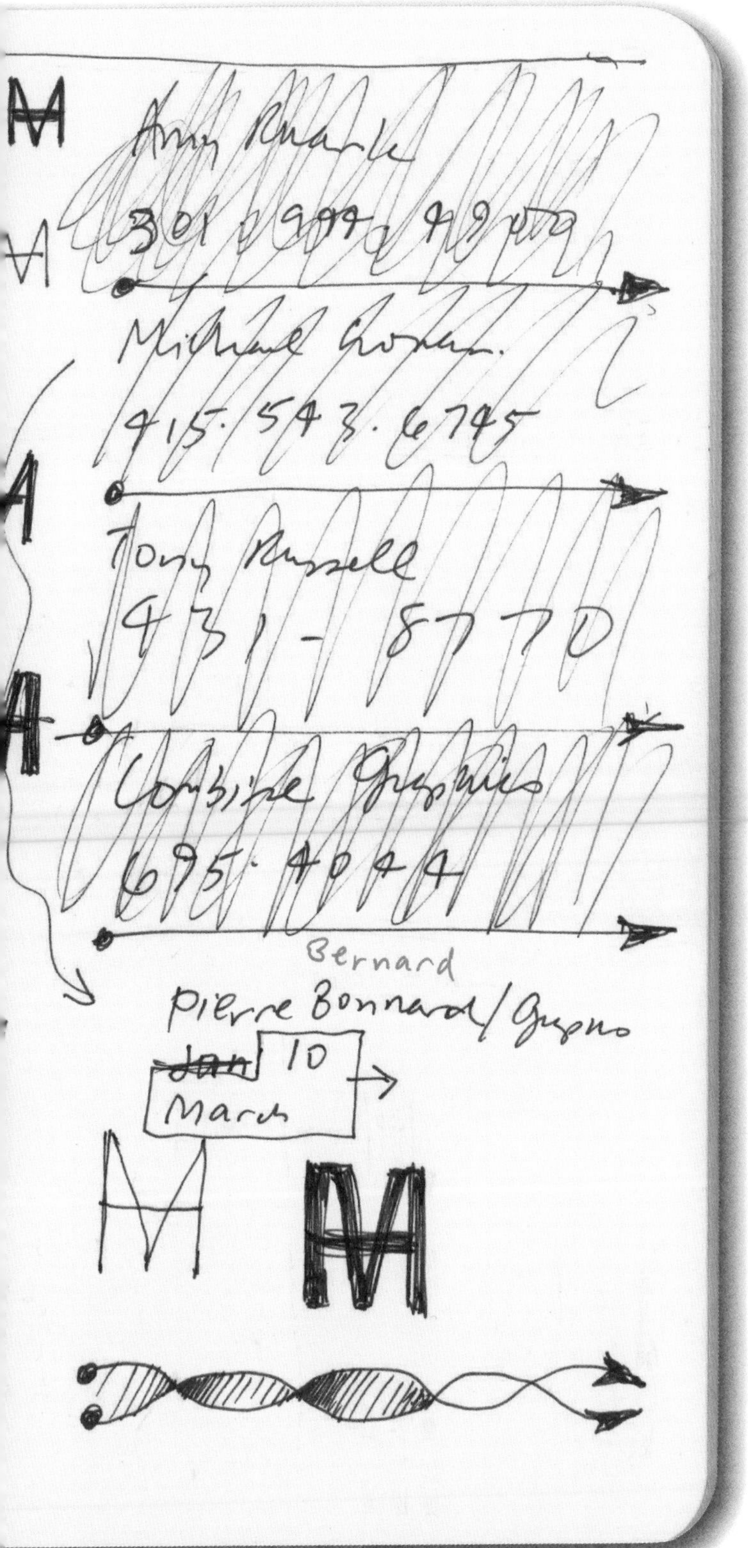
415.543.6745
Tony Russell
431-8770
695.4044
Bernard
10
March

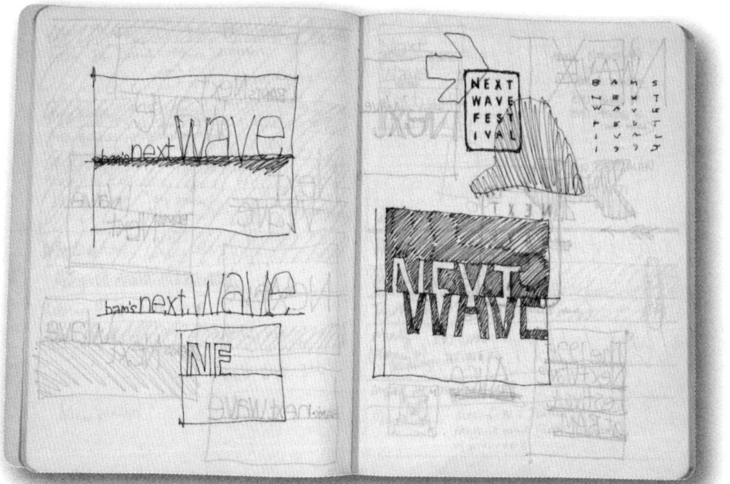
bam's next wave
NEXT WAVE FEST IVAL
NEXT WAVE
NE

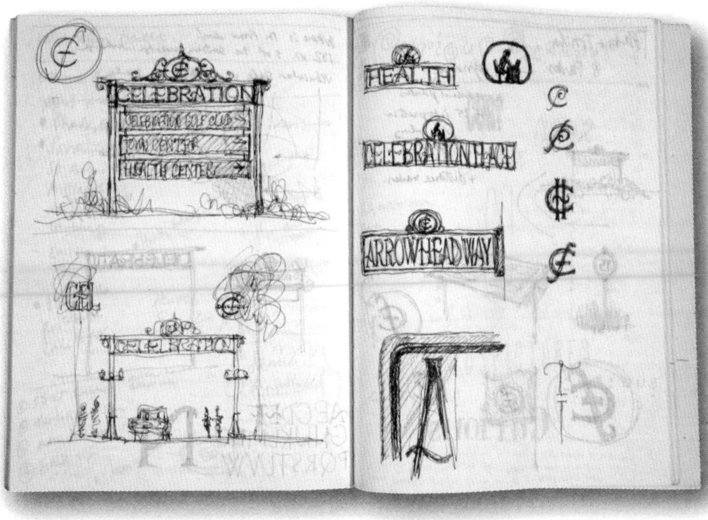
CELEBRATION
CELEBRATION GOLF CLUB
TOWN CENTER
HEALTH CENTER
HEALTH
CELEBRATION PLACE
ARROWHEAD WAY

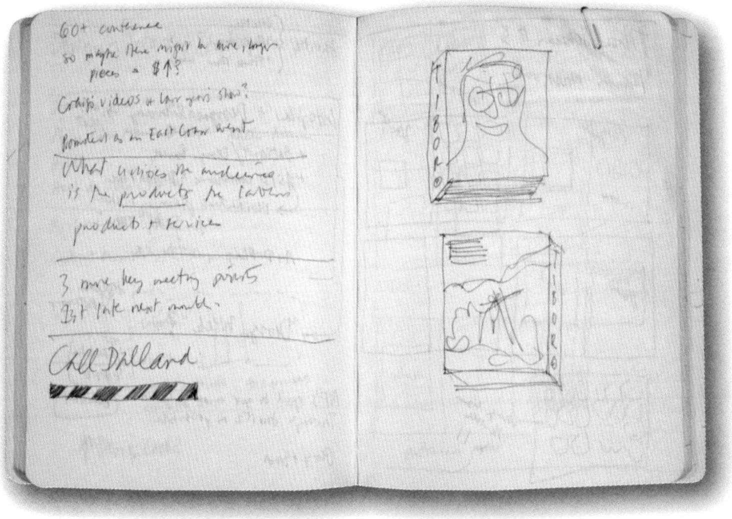
TIBOR

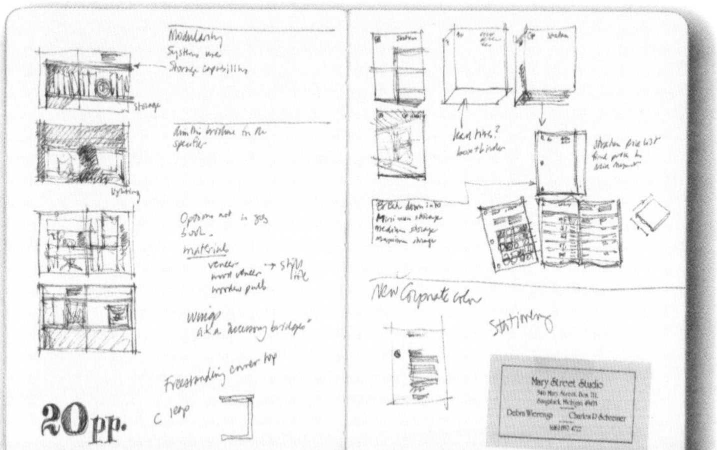
20pp.
Mary Street Studio
Debra Wierenga
Charles P. Schermer

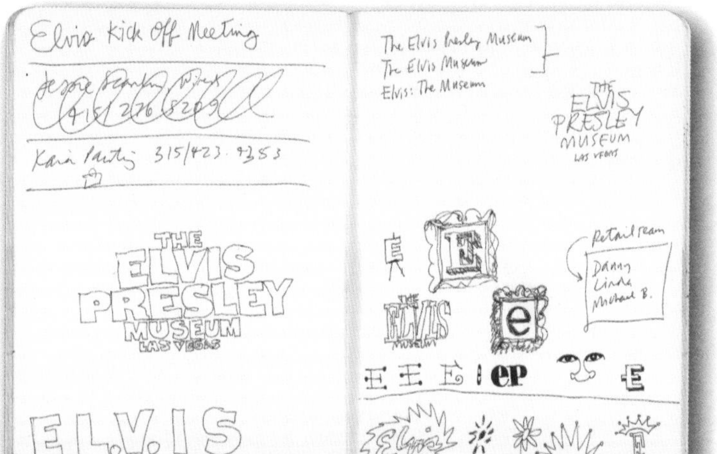
Elvis Kick Off Meeting
The Elvis Presley Museum
The Elvis Museum
Elvis: The Museum
THE ELVIS PRESLEY MUSEUM LAS VEGAS
Retail team
E.L.V.I.S

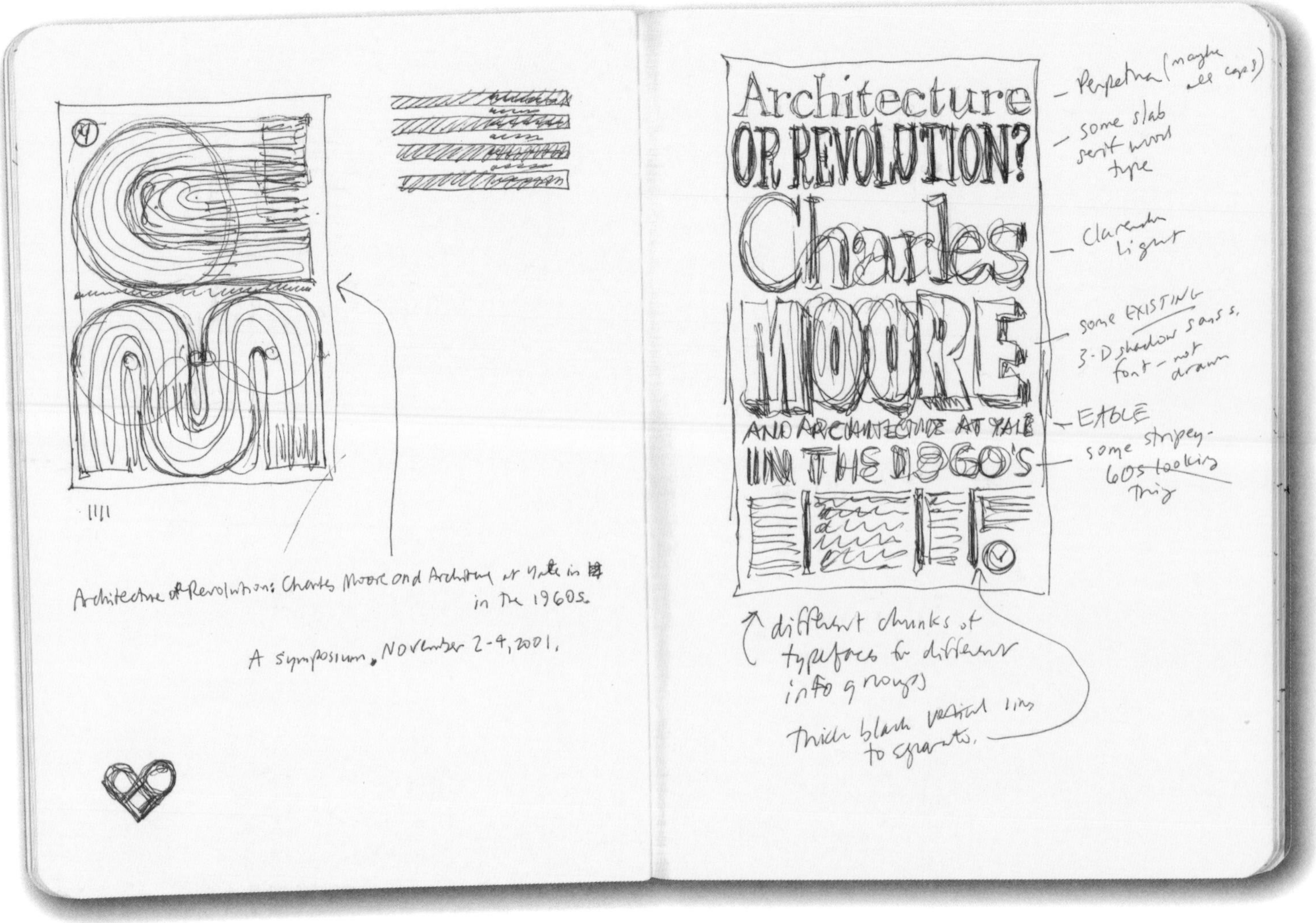
Architecture
OR REVOLUTION?
Charles
MOORE
AND ARCHITECTURE AT YALE
IN THE 1960'S
Perpetua (maybe all caps)
some slab serif wood type
Clarendon Light
some EXISTING 3-D shadow sans s. font - not drawn
EAGLE
some stripey-60s looking thing
different chunks of typefaces for different info groups
Thick black vertical lines to separate.
Architecture or Revolution: Charles Moore and Architecture at Yale in the 1960s.
A symposium, November 2-4, 2001.

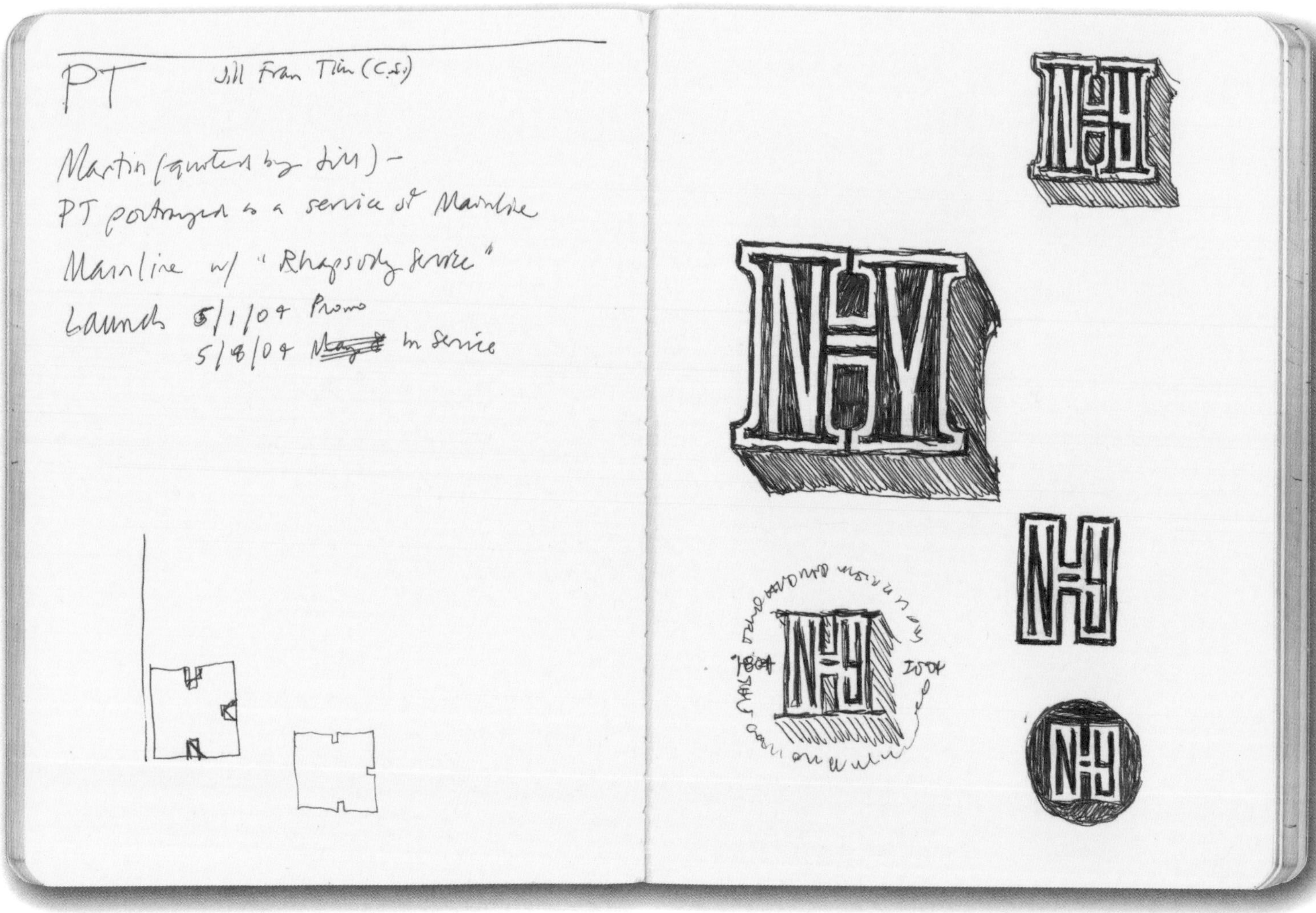
PT
Jill Fran Tim (C.S.)
Martin (quoted by Jill) -
PT portrayed as a service of Mainline
Mainline w/ "Rhapsody service"
Launch 5/1/04 Promo
5/8/04 in service
N-Y
1804
1904

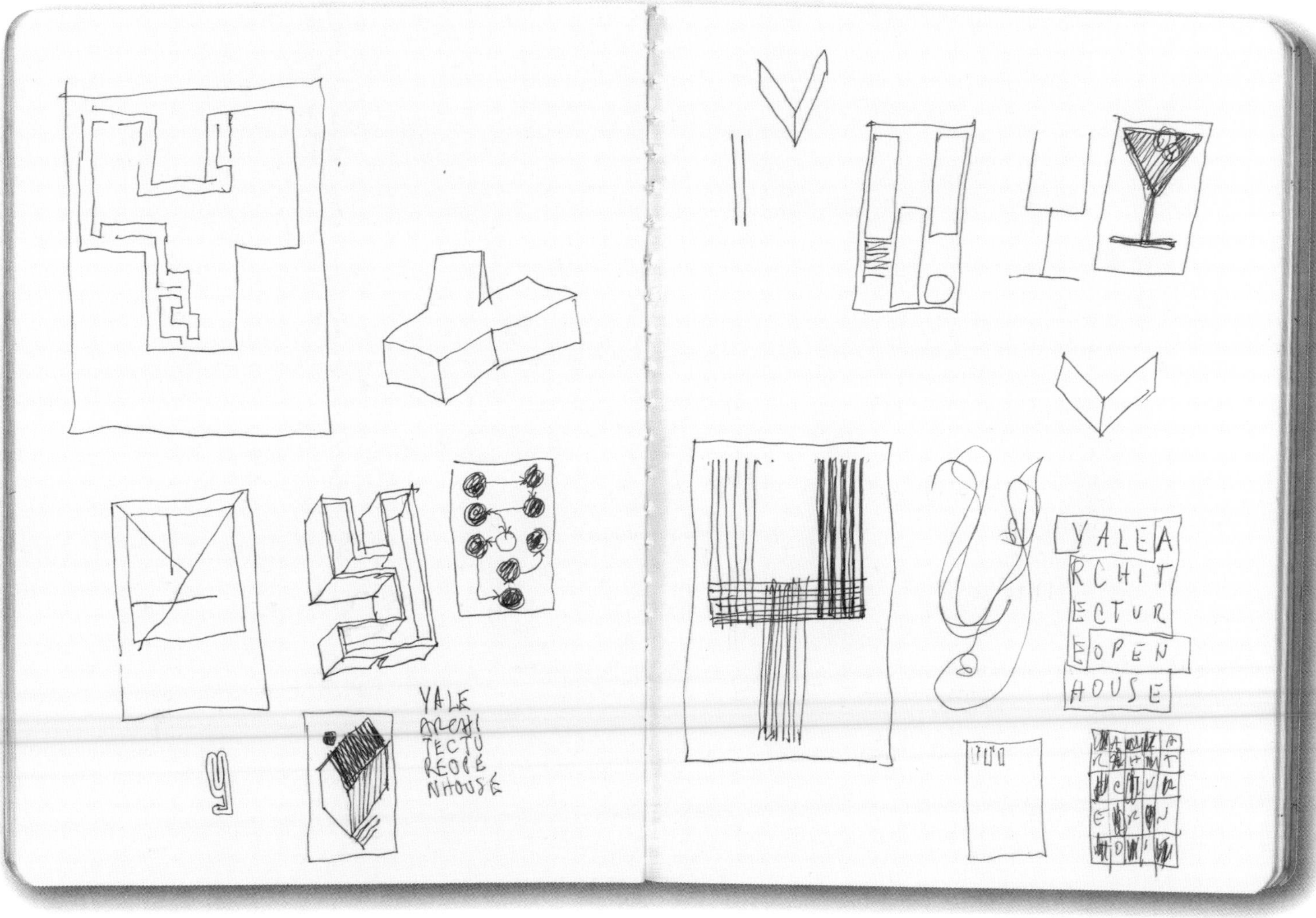
YALE
ARCHI
TECTU
REOPE
NHOUSE
YALEA
RCHIT
ECTUR
EOPEN
HOUSE

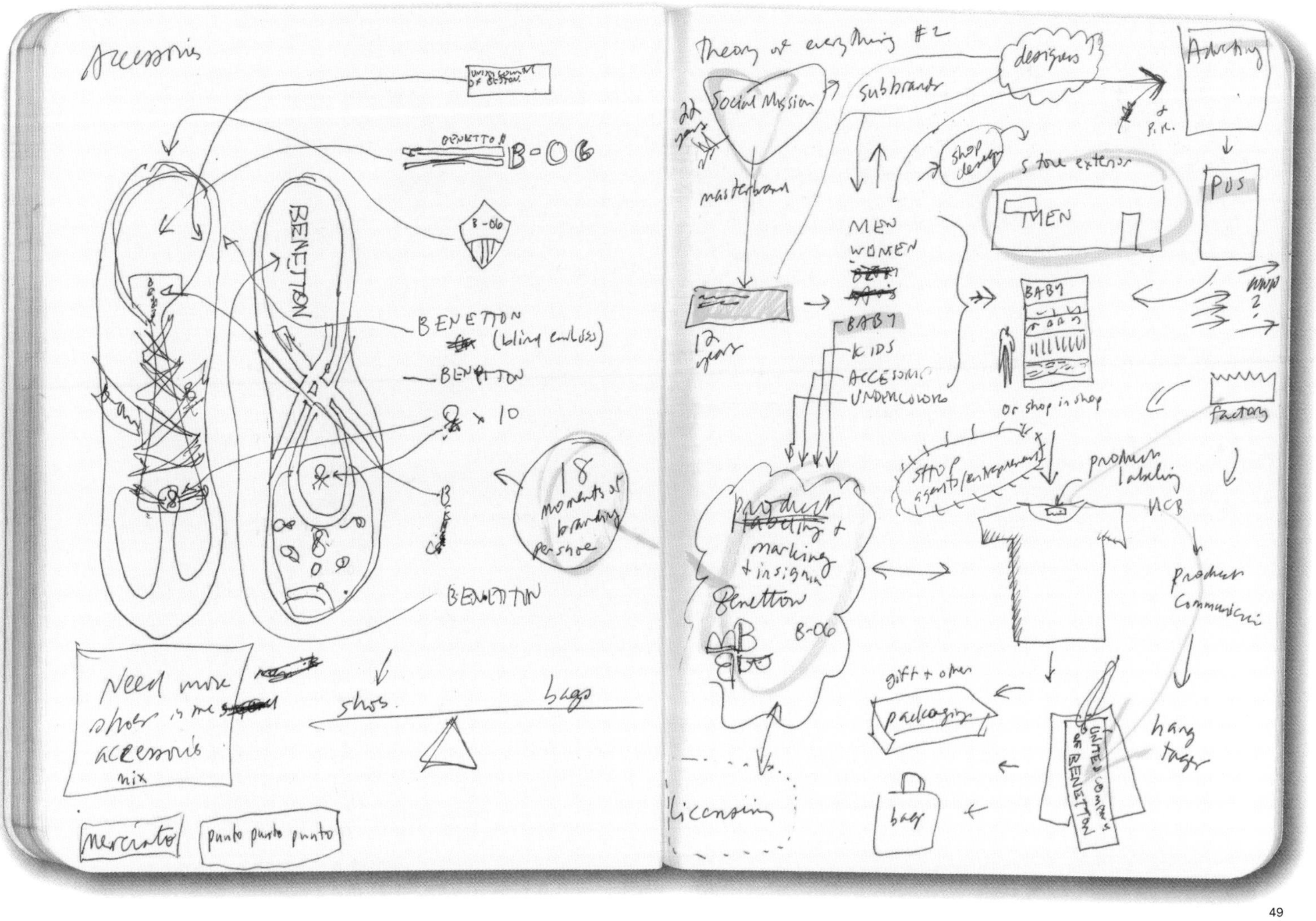
B-06
BENETTON
BENETTON
(blind emboss)
x 10
18
moments of
branding
per shoe
BENETTON
Need more
shoes in the
accessories
mix
shoes
bags
punto punto punto
Theory of everything #2
Social Mission
designers
subbrands
masterbrand
shop design
store exterior
MEN
WOMEN
BABY
KIDS
UNDERCOLORS
or shop in shop
factory
product
labeling
product
marking
+ insignia
Benetton
B-06
gift + other
packaging
hang
tags
UNITED COLORS
OF BENETTON
bags
licensing

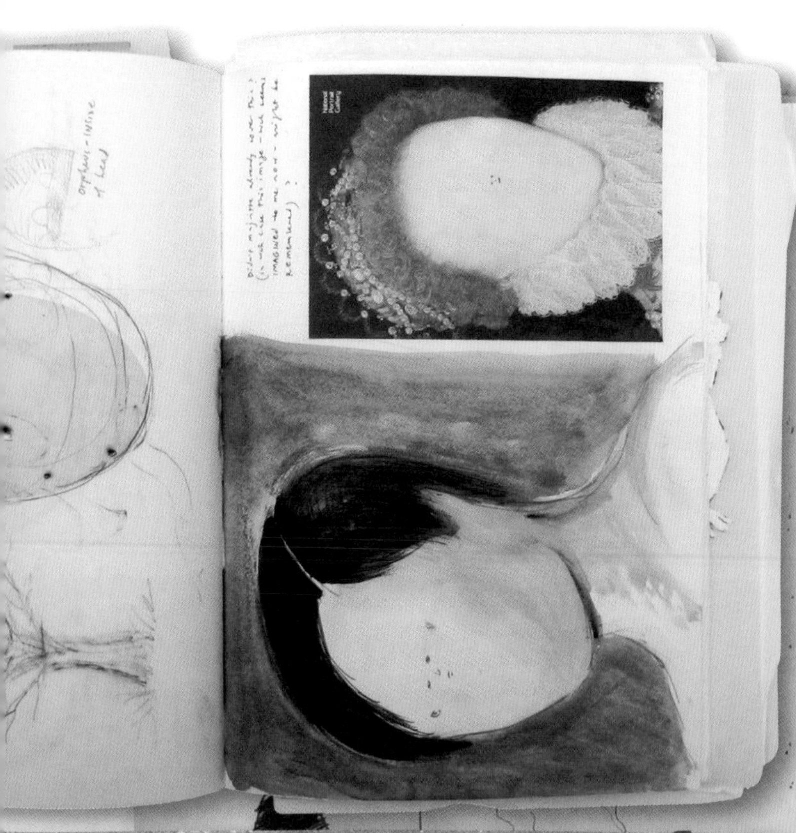

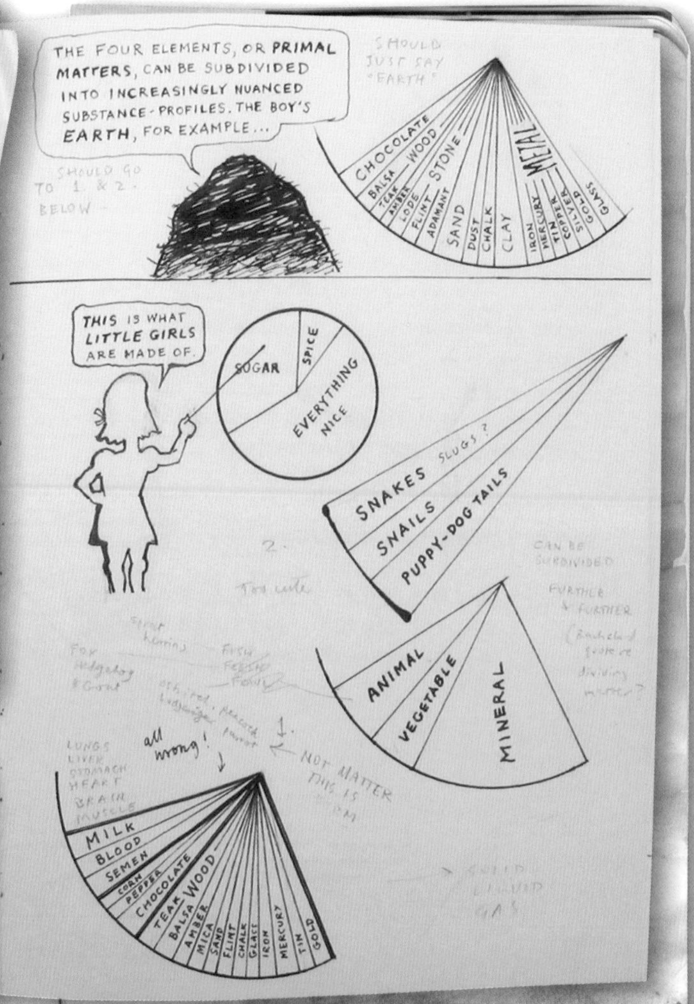

PETER BLEGVAD

Peter Blegvad, American-born, London-based cartoonist, children's book illustrator, and satiric author is an avid sketchbook maven. "I have disintegrating sketchbooks in the archive dating back to 1964, when I was thirteen," he proudly proclaims.

For Blegvad, the sketchbook is "a place where it's safe to goof off, to fail, to exercise what Keats called 'negative capability' and be an amateur again. And because it's a record of one's development on various levels, it's a kind of mirror, too; a reminder, sometimes encouraging and sometimes an admonition."

Sketchbooks record process more than product. "Finished work is cooked," he continues, "sometimes overcooked, while work in a sketchbook is usually raw, freer, more honest." By honest he also means there is "chaos" in some of them. "An accurate portrayal of the inchoate splatterfest that passes for 'thought' between my ears," he declares. "There's the ongoing struggle to draw – either by overcoming, circumventing, or cultivating my flaws as a draftsman."

He estimates having around forty books. The earliest shown here dates from 1987 when he was developing his *Leviathan* comic strip. "I had no idea how to draw cartoons. I suspected big noses might be part of the formula," he says.

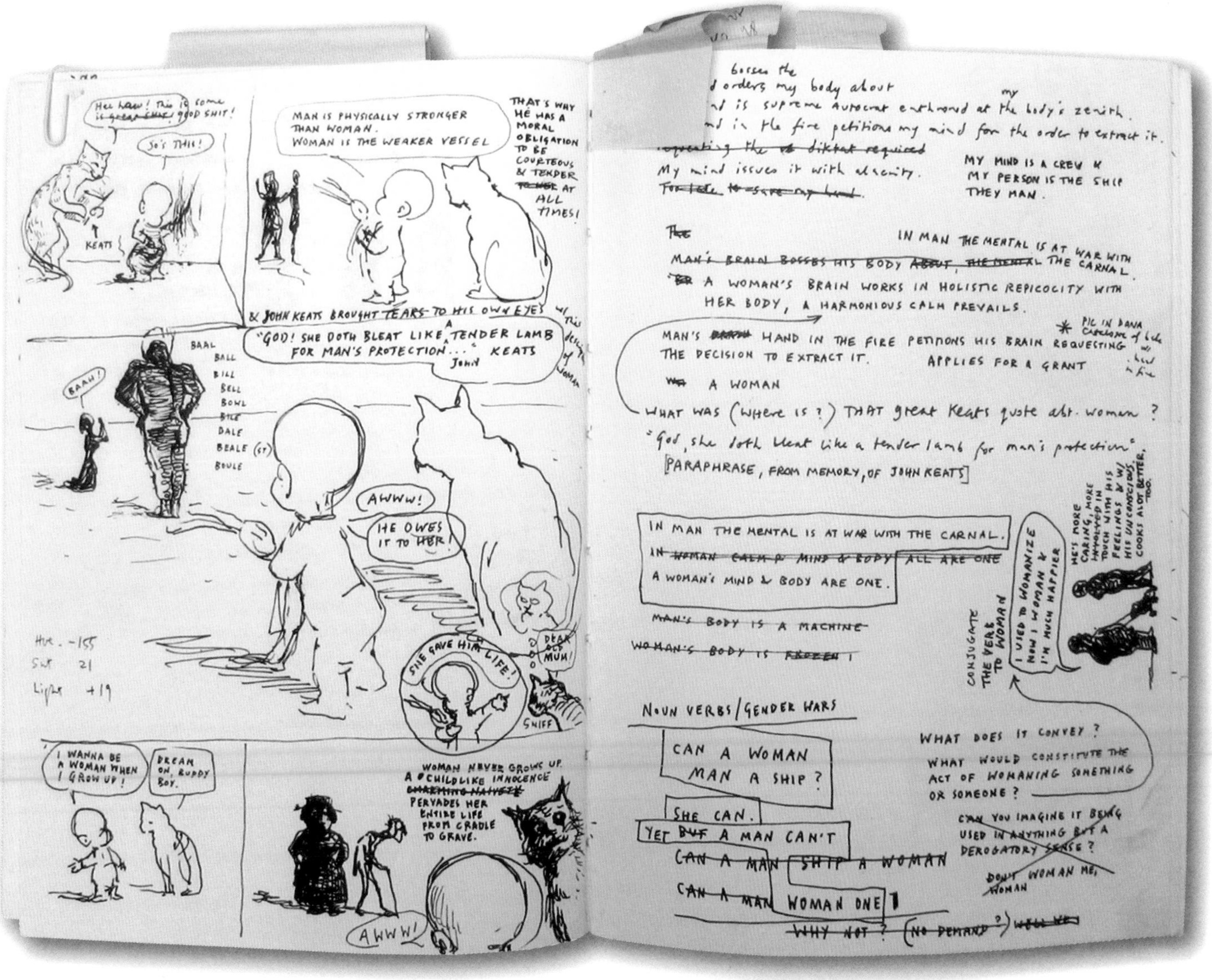
Hee haw! This is some good shit!
So's THIS!
KEATS
MAN IS PHYSICALLY STRONGER THAN WOMAN. WOMAN IS THE WEAKER VESSEL
THAT'S WHY HE HAS A MORAL OBLIGATION TO BE COURTEOUS & TENDER AT ALL TIMES!
& JOHN KEATS BROUGHT TEARS TO HIS OWN EYES
"GOD! SHE DOTH BLEAT LIKE A TENDER LAMB FOR MAN'S PROTECTION..." JOHN KEATS
BAAL BALL BILL BELL BOWL BILE DALE BEALE BOULE
BAAH!
AWWW!
HE OWES IT TO HER!
SHE GAVE HIM LIFE!
DEAR OLD MUM!
SNIFF
I WANNA BE A WOMAN WHEN I GROW UP!
DREAM ON, BUDDY BOY.
WOMAN NEVER GROWS UP. A CHILDLIKE INNOCENCE PERVADES HER ENTIRE LIFE FROM CRADLE TO GRAVE.
AWWW!
bosses the
orders my body about
is supreme autocrat enthroned at the body's zenith.
is the fire petitions my mind for the order to extract it.
My mind issues it with alacrity.
MY MIND IS A CREW MY PERSON IS THE SHIP THEY MAN.
IN MAN THE MENTAL IS AT WAR WITH THE CARNAL.
MAN'S BRAIN BOSSES HIS BODY
A WOMAN'S BRAIN WORKS IN HOLISTIC REPICOCITY WITH HER BODY, A HARMONIOUS CALM PREVAILS.
MAN'S HAND IN THE FIRE PETITIONS HIS BRAIN REQUESTING THE DECISION TO EXTRACT IT. APPLIES FOR A GRANT
A WOMAN
WHAT WAS (WHERE IS?) THAT great Keats quote abt. woman?
"God, she doth bleat like a tender lamb for man's protection"
[PARAPHRASE, FROM MEMORY, OF JOHN KEATS]
IN MAN THE MENTAL IS AT WAR WITH THE CARNAL.
ALL ARE ONE
A WOMAN'S MIND & BODY ARE ONE.
MAN'S BODY IS A MACHINE
WOMAN'S BODY IS FROZEN
CONJUGATE THE VERB TO WOMAN
I USED TO WOMANIZE NOW I WOMAN & I'M MUCH HAPPIER
HE'S MORE CARING, MORE INVOLVED IN TOUCH WITH HIS FEELINGS & W/ HIS UNCONSCIOUS. COOKS ALOT BETTER, TOO.
NOUN VERBS/GENDER WARS
CAN A WOMAN MAN A SHIP?
SHE CAN.
YET A MAN CAN'T
CAN A MAN SHIP A WOMAN
CAN A MAN WOMAN ONE?
WHY NOT? (NO DEMAND?)
WHAT DOES IT CONVEY?
WHAT WOULD CONSTITUTE THE ACT OF WOMANING SOMETHING OR SOMEONE?
CAN YOU IMAGINE IT BEING USED IN ANYTHING BUT A DEROGATORY SENSE?
DON'T WOMAN ME, WOMAN

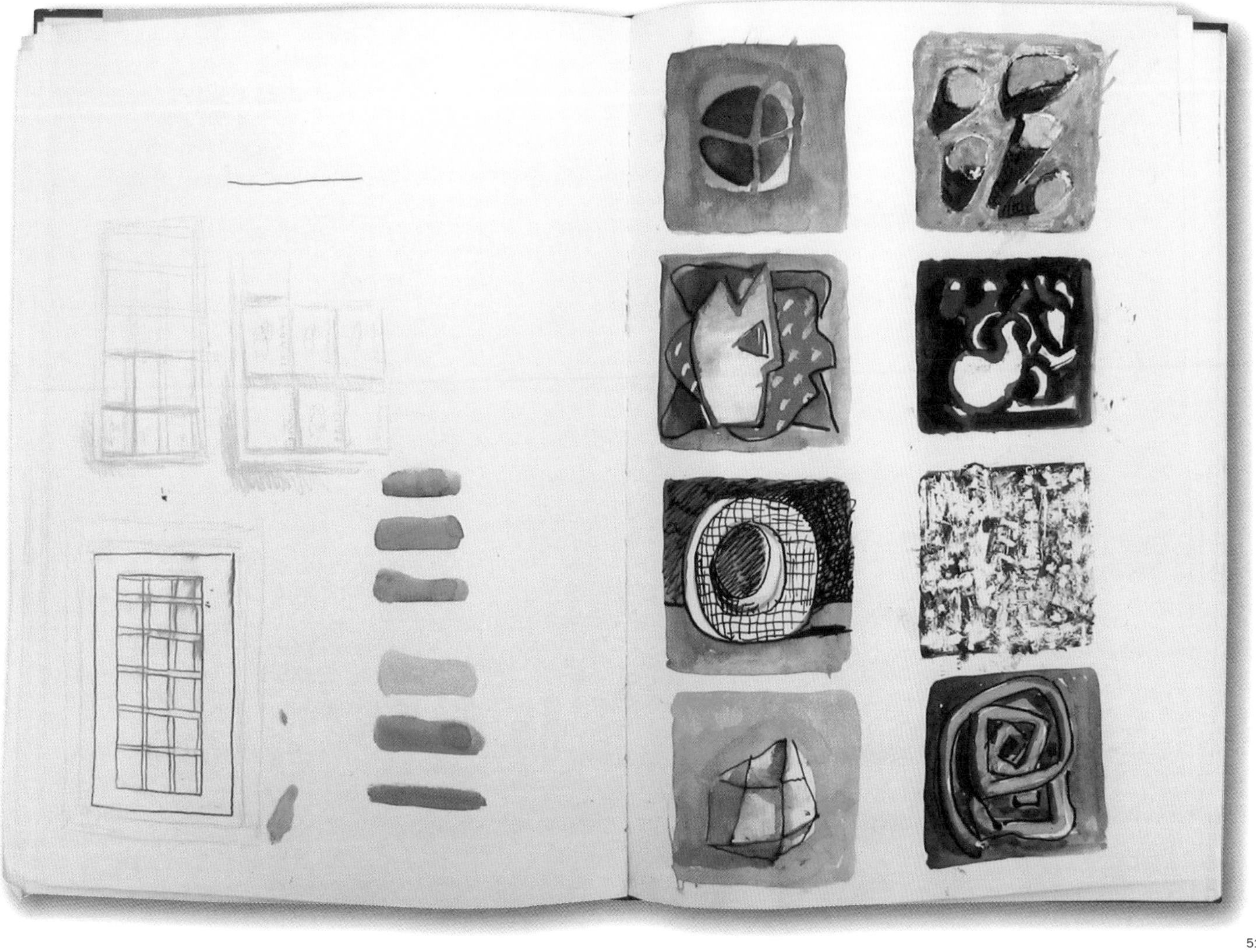

FLOWER

IMAGINED

OBSERVED

REMEMBERED

ROSE

IMAGINED

OBSERVED

REMEMBERED

seventeenth-century German poet Angelus Silesius: "The rose has no why, it flowers because it flowers".

Mallarmé

Stein

NERVAL – on how one "spoils" the places one loves in imagination by going to see them – "... it is Egypt that I most regret having hunted from my imagination, to let it find sad lodgings in my memory! You still believe in the magic ibis, the purpled lotus, & the yellow Nile ... Alas, the ibis is nothing but (see ★ → over

In these unsettled (overcrowded) times

it's only worth attempting if it seems impossible

(a way to draw the eidolon's of memory & imagination, fr instance)

SIGNS *for* THINGS

except for EYE, all OBSERVED & copied from works by other artists . . .

a series of these? - If this is a group of Imagined (by other "artists") Things, Observed by me - couldn't you have a bunch of things Observed by other
Remembered by me - etc.?

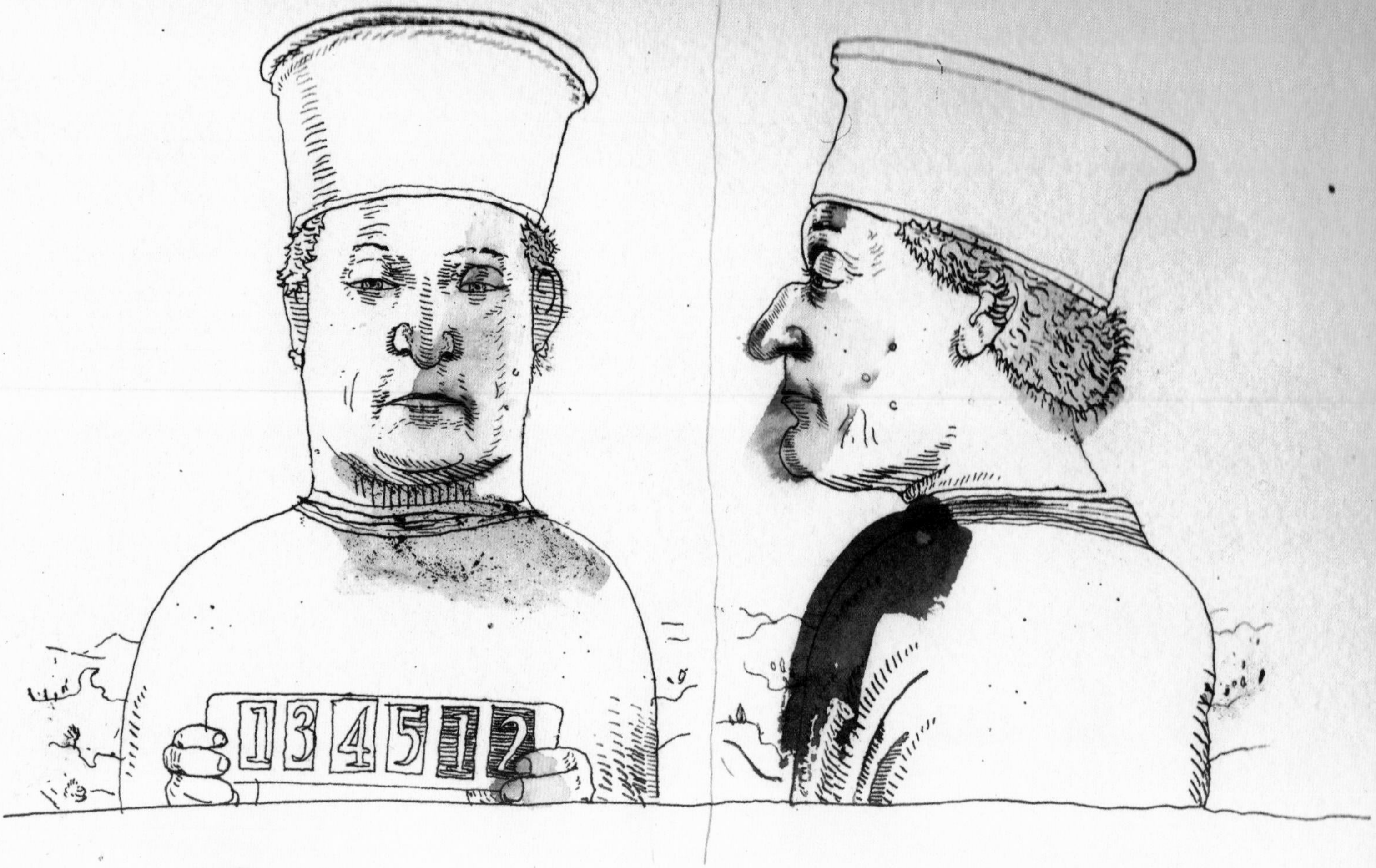

BARRY BLITT

Connecticut-based illustrator and caricaturist Barry Blitt, best known for his satiric "fist bump" cover of *The New Yorker* that showed President and Mrs Obama in all the stereotypes affixed to them, has kept sketchbooks since he was a kid. That is over thirty years, with "some gaps during my difficult adolescence," he adds.

He keeps the books "partly to remember stuff that occurs to me, to record ideas, partly to work on concepts for assignments, and also to isolate myself, to keep myself from having to interact and converse with those in the room. And for fun." The sketches are distinct from his finished work in that "some of these drawings have a little life left in them," he drily states. "I try not to self-edit too much. You're seeing the least messy pages – the vast majority of them are impossible to read or make sense of. They are all attempts at being funny, but other than that, if there is some theme, I think I'd rather not know about it."

Although they are not chronological, there are a lot of them. "I start one, don't finish it, start another two, go back to the first one," says Blitt. "Some books have incoherent scribbling from years apart, from one page to the next."

MY PET GOATEE

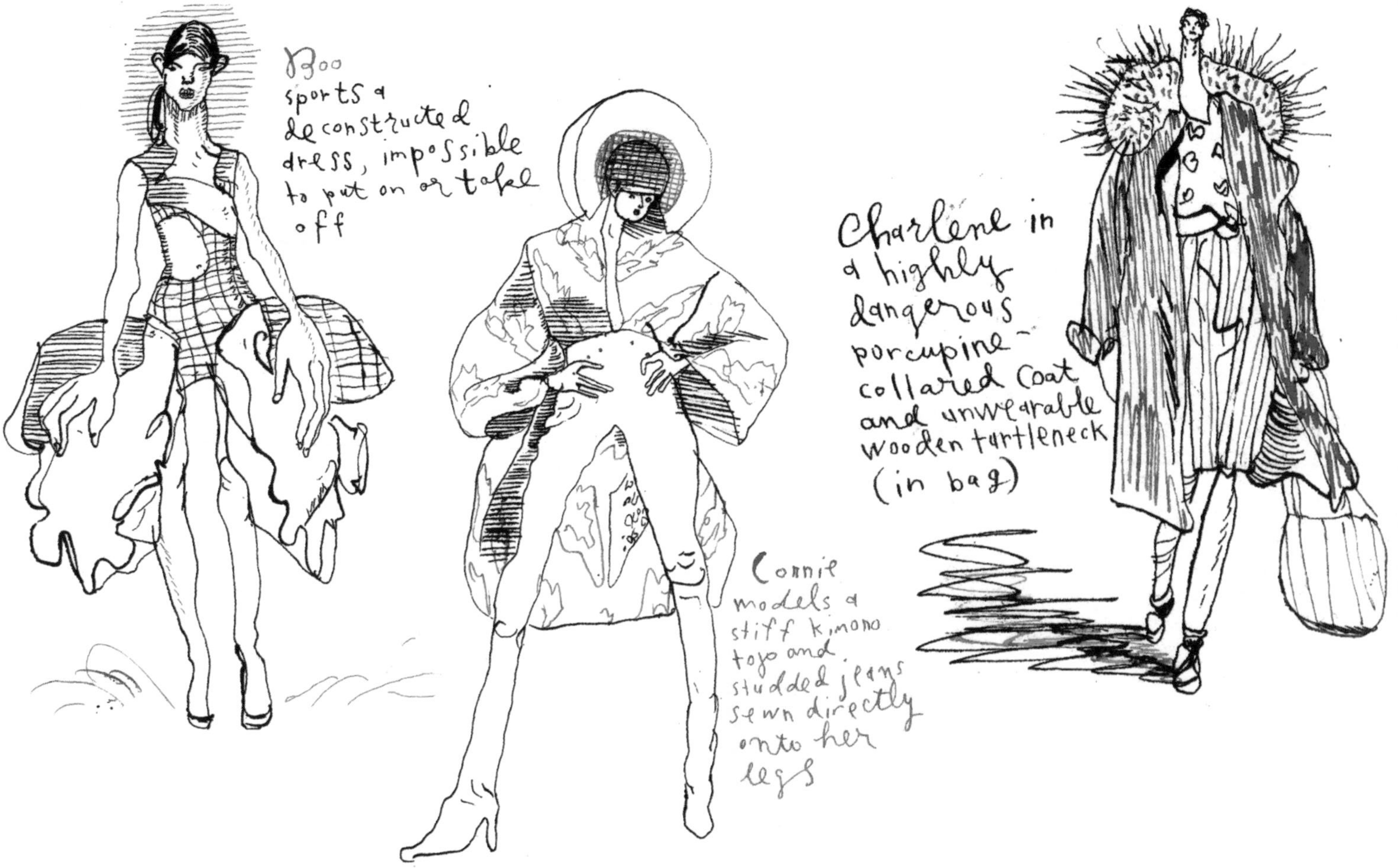
Boo sports a deconstructed dress, impossible to put on or take off
Connie models a stiff kimono toyo and studded jeans sewn directly onto her legs
Charlene in a highly dangerous porcupine-collared coat and unwearable wooden turtleneck (in bag)

To Peacock
Forever Yours
Mrs Simpson

Was Babe Ruth a Jew?
a surprising new documentary says no.
YANKEES
YANK

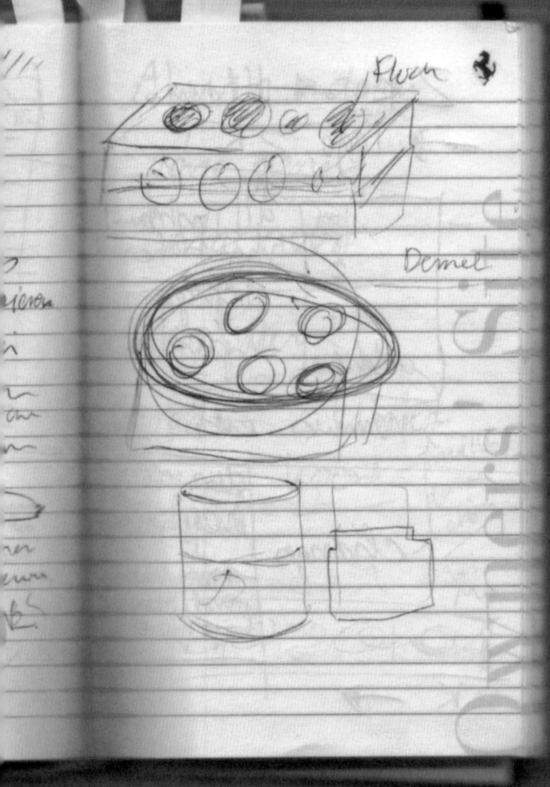

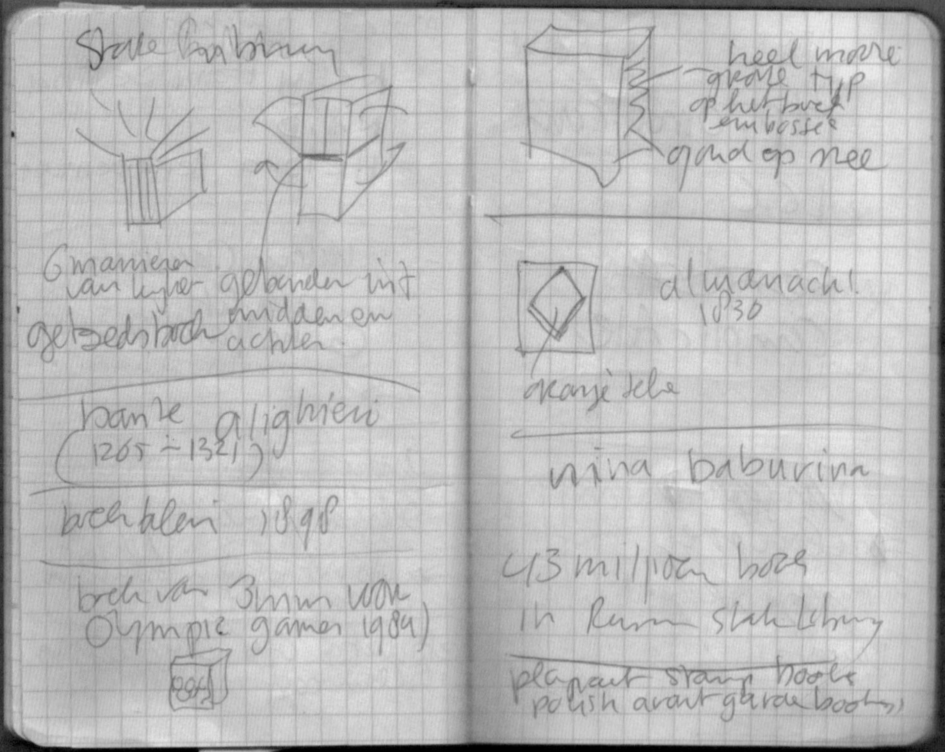
almanach!
1930
nina baburina
polish avant garde books

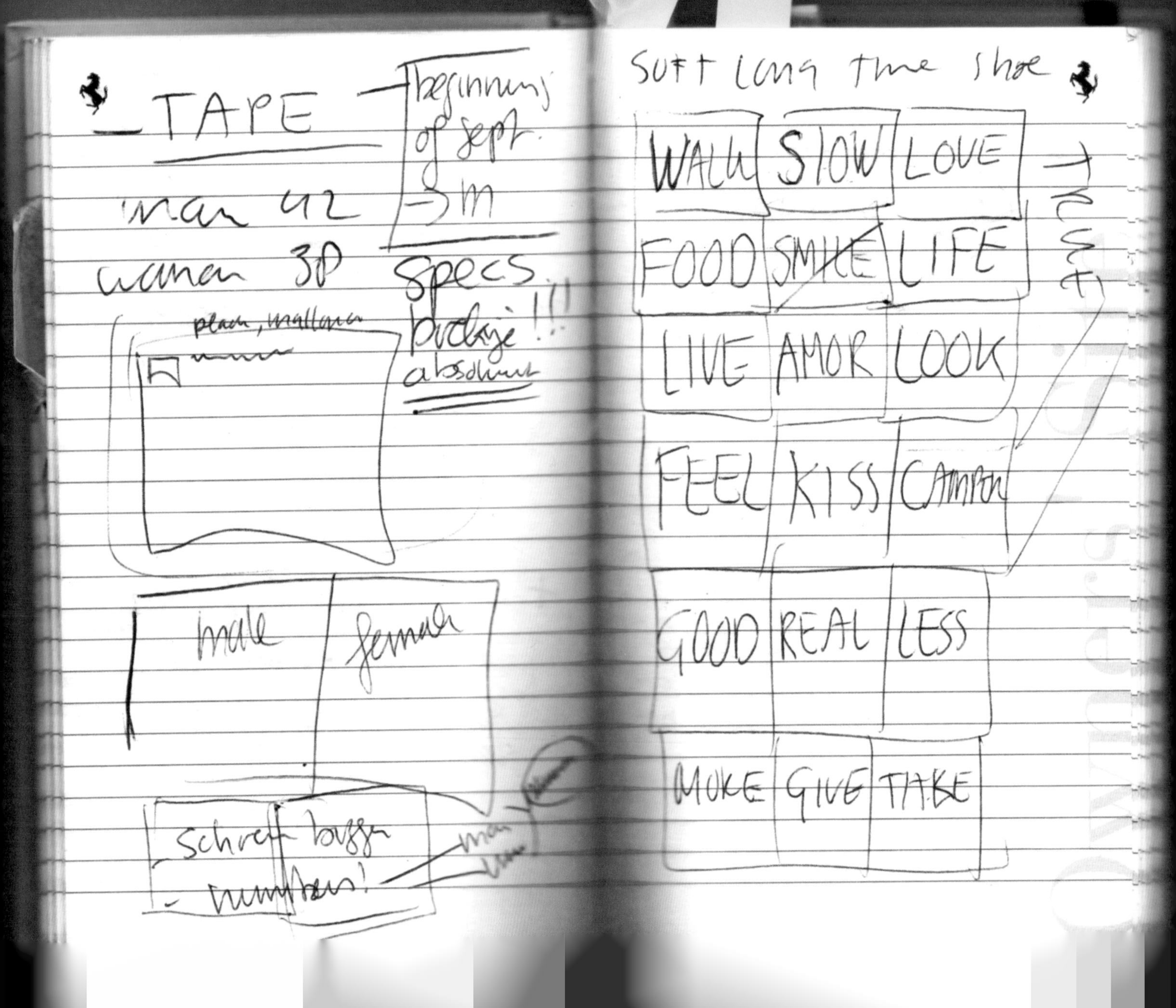
TAPE
beginning of sept.
specs
male
SOFT LONG TIME SHOE
WALK SLOW LOVE
FOOD SMILE LIFE
LIVE AMOR LOOK
FEEL KISS CAMPER
GOOD REAL LESS
MAKE GIVE TAKE

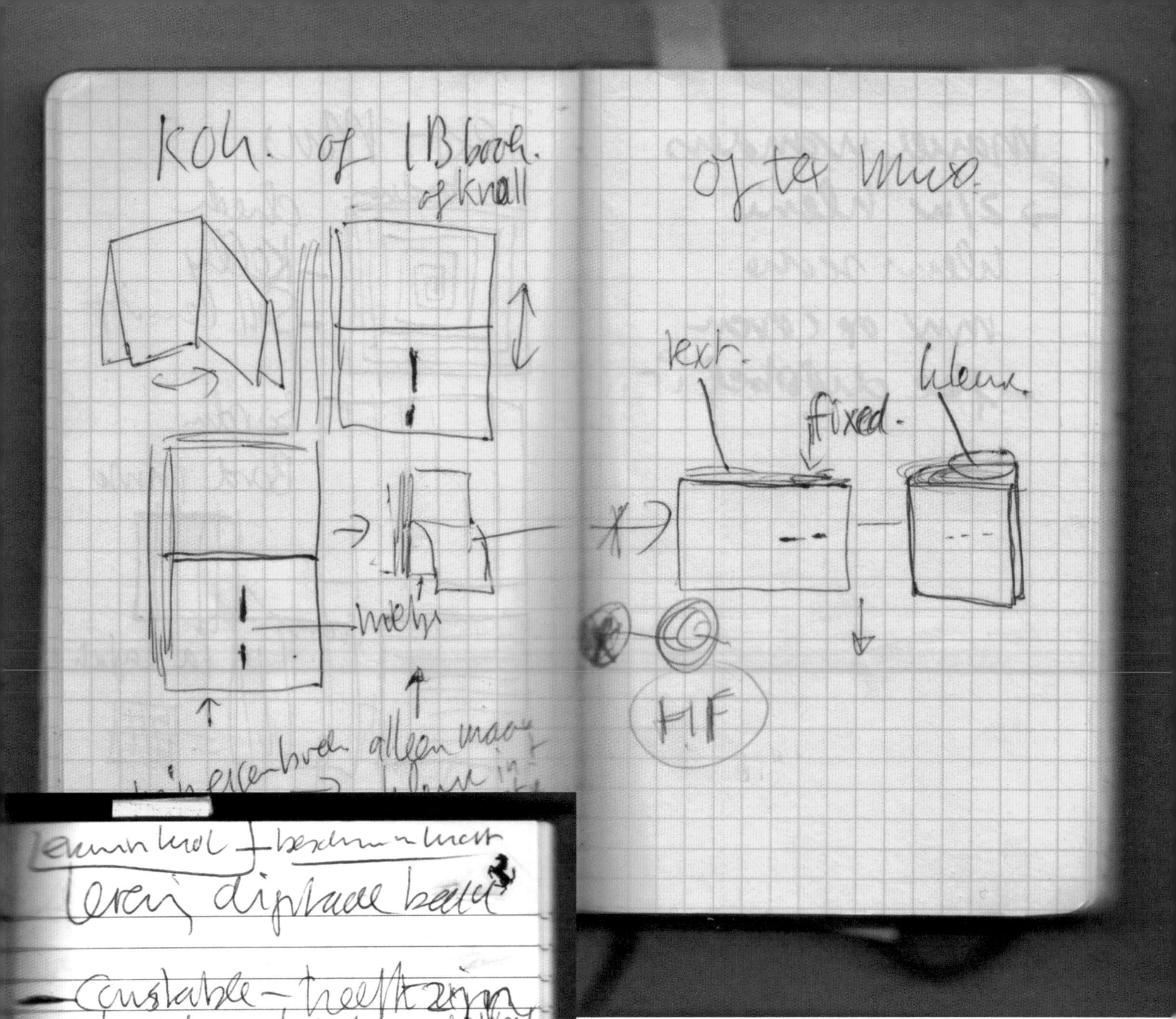

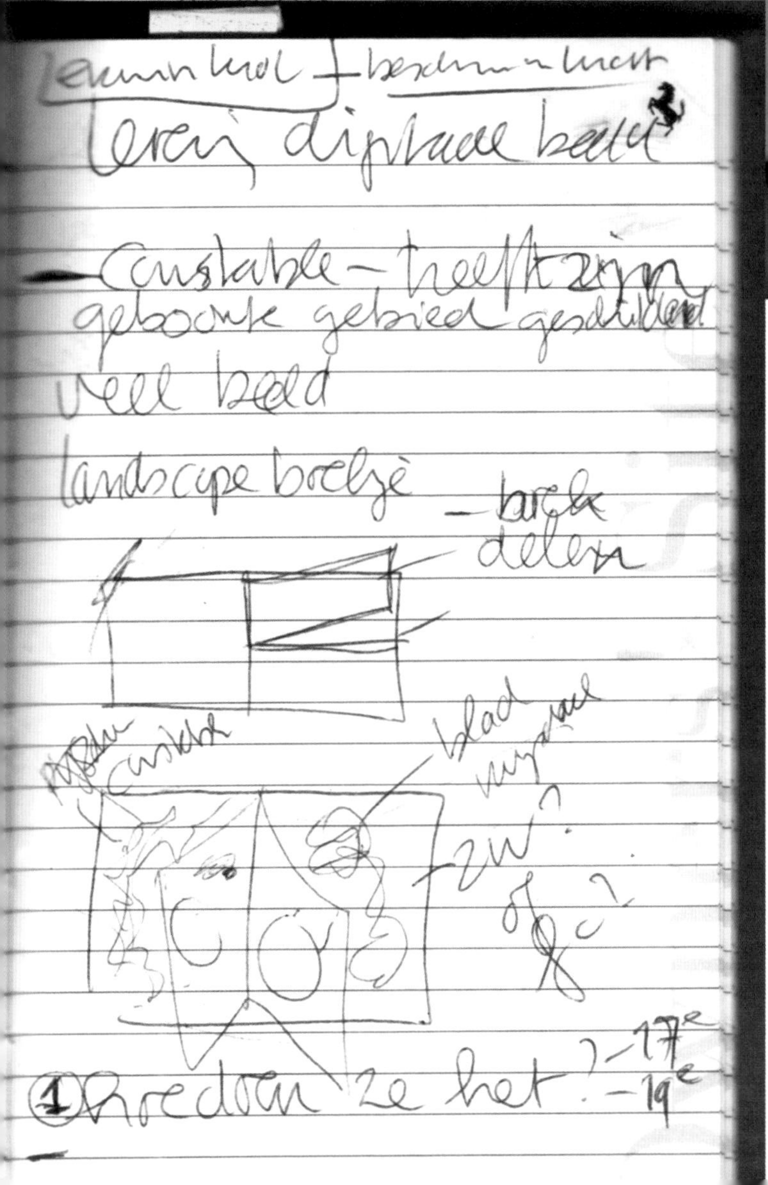

IRMA BOOM

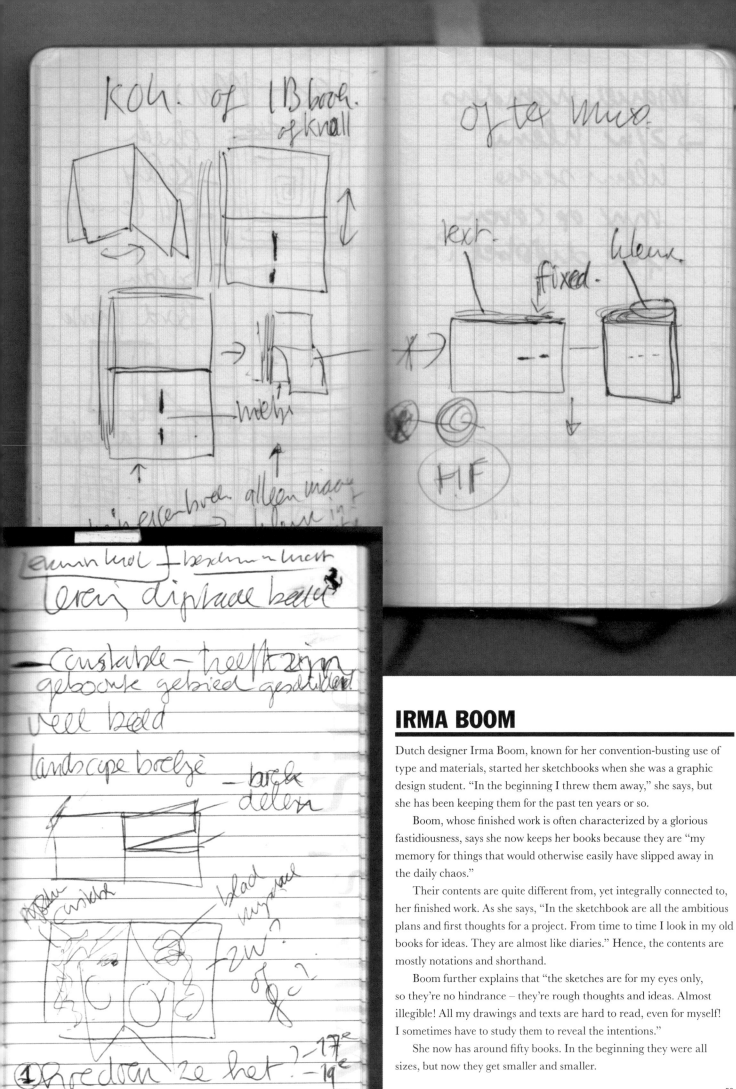

Dutch designer Irma Boom, known for her convention-busting use of type and materials, started her sketchbooks when she was a graphic design student. “In the beginning I threw them away,” she says, but she has been keeping them for the past ten years or so.

Boom, whose finished work is often characterized by a glorious fastidiousness, says she now keeps her books because they are “my memory for things that would otherwise easily have slipped away in the daily chaos.”

Their contents are quite different from, yet integrally connected to, her finished work. As she says, “In the sketchbook are all the ambitious plans and first thoughts for a project. From time to time I look in my old books for ideas. They are almost like diaries.” Hence, the contents are mostly notations and shorthand.

Boom further explains that “the sketches are for my eyes only, so they’re no hindrance – they’re rough thoughts and ideas. Almost illegible! All my drawings and texts are hard to read, even for myself! I sometimes have to study them to reveal the intentions.”

She now has around fifty books. In the beginning they were all sizes, but now they get smaller and smaller.

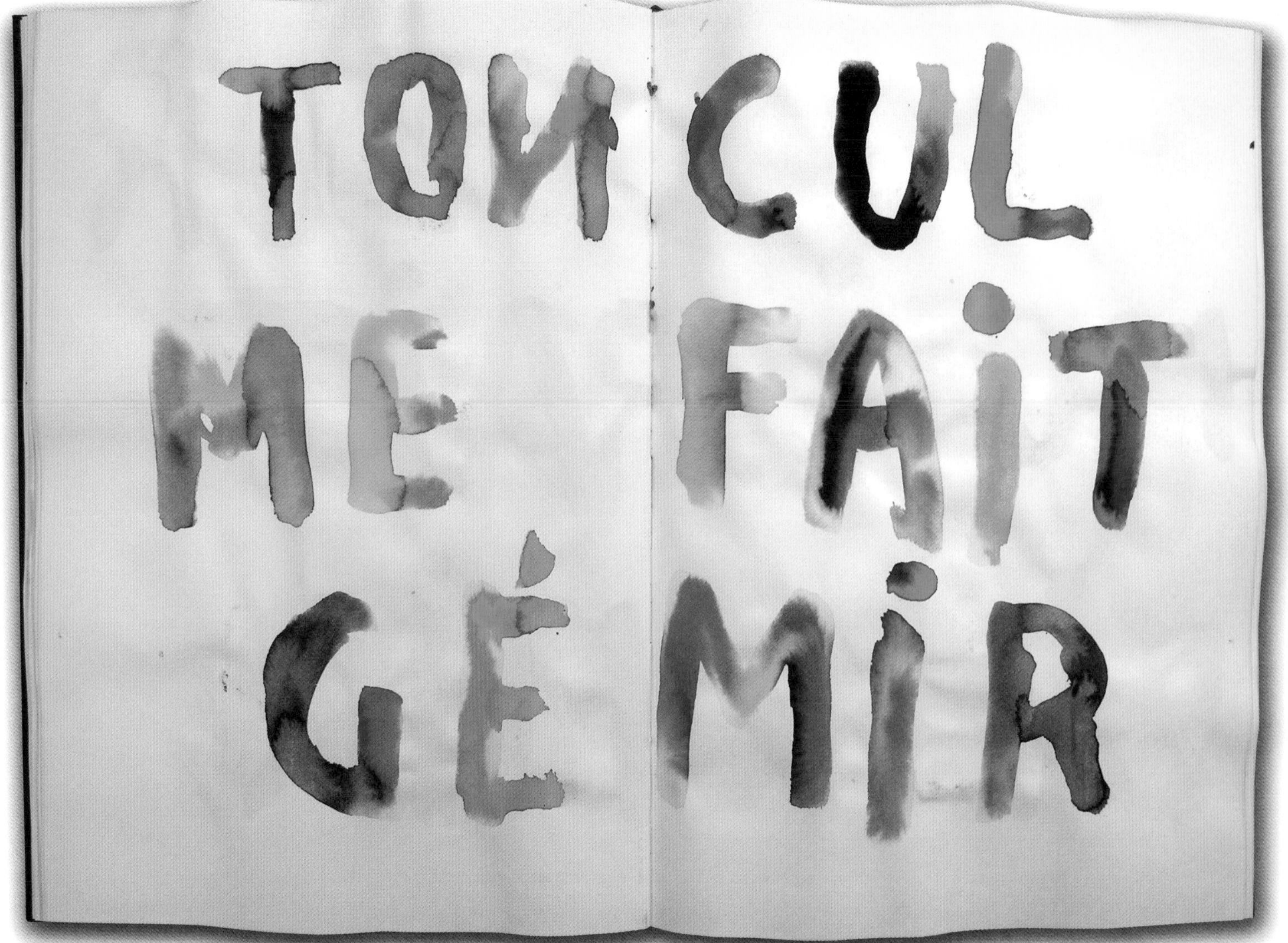

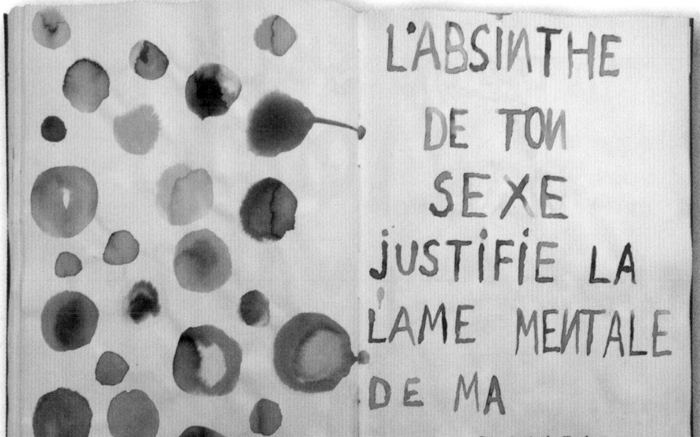

BRUNO BRESSOLIN

Bruno Bressolin, a Paris-based painter, photographer, and illustrator whose commercial work is mostly for upscale advertising campaigns, is a decade-old sketchbooker. "Almost every day I jot down whatever comes through my mind: ideas, projects, unpublishable thoughts – politically correct or not – drawings, paintings, newspaper clips, stickers. It's a memory place, a work in progress," he says.

He uses sketchbooks to experiment with solutions to problems, whether or not he intends to turn them into paintings or illustrations. What's more, "I flip through my sketches every day," he says. "I mix some of the concepts or ideas I find there, change colors or messages. They are a data bank of concepts and ideas. Sometimes my teenage twin daughters, Clémence and Prudence, draw into them as well."

Bressolin insists: "I do not edit my thoughts. I do not censor myself. The themes are news, sex, politics, and philosophy. My sketchbooks are my shrink. All the material is somewhat psychoanalytical." They are an inexpensive shrink at that.

Within his thirty or more sketchbooks of various sizes, some quite large, "I draw over everything, from accounting books to books written in Braille for the blind. I draw on newsprint, Bible paper, tracing paper, thick vellum, whatever appeals to me at that moment."

TU VAS FAIRE
TON DEUIL
DE MA VIE

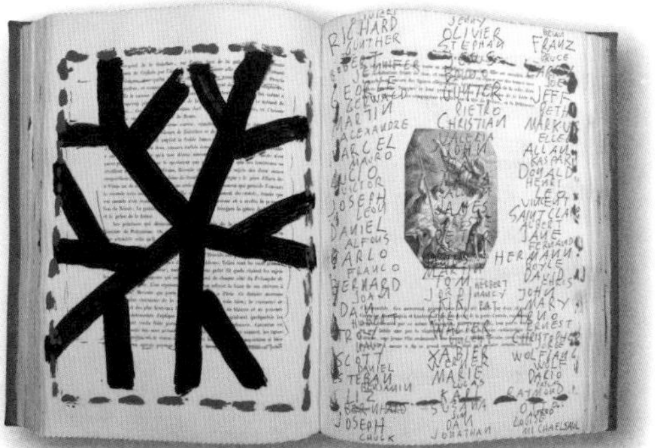

LES GEANTS
DE
SILENCE

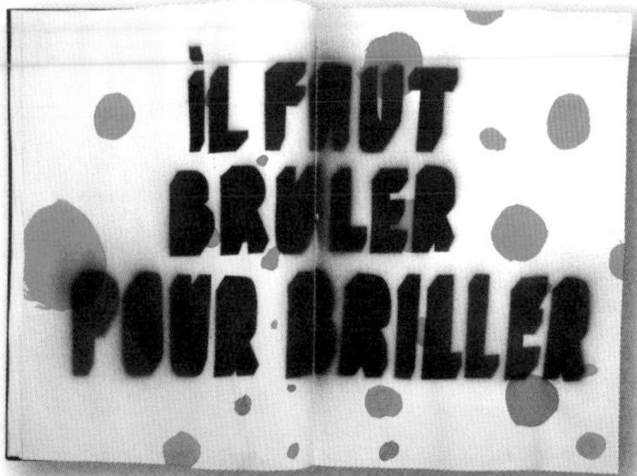
IL FAUT
BRULER
POUR BRILLER

oui
au Darwinisme
Social

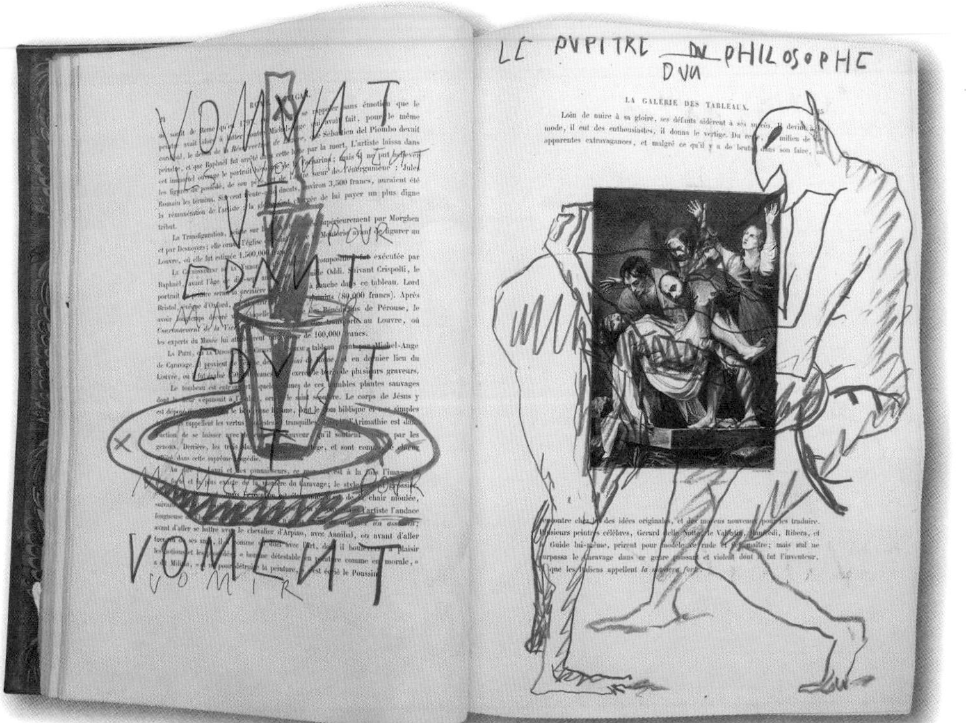
LE PUPITRE DU PHILOSOPHE
LA GALERIE DES TABLEAUX.

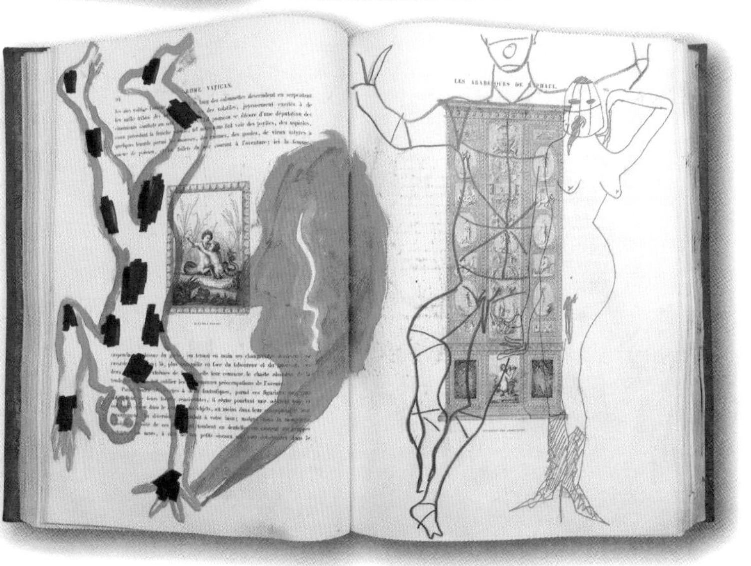

STEFAN BUCHER

German-born, California-based Stefan Bucher started keeping a sketchbook at Art Center, Pasadena, where the teacher insisted on a 14 × 10 in. (35 × 25 cm) format. He recalls that it was "a Big Book for Big Ideas! And I hated that thing. There isn't a single drawing in it. My drawings have always been small and the vast expanse of white wasn't so much daunting as annoying."

After college, Bucher started to use his preferred size: 6 × 4 in. (15 × 10 cm). Each book takes a long time to fill because "I have such bad discipline about sketching and taking notes." For Bucher, "Keeping the sketchbooks is like going to the gym – it's sort of a chore, but I'm always happy when I've filled a page. Every now and again there's a sequence of drawings that I hated because they were somehow not as nice or as accurate as I wanted them to be. But with the passage of time I can see those pages as pleasing marks, which has given me some confidence. I'm creating a little time capsule for myself. Hopefully I'll learn something." The one thing Bucher really uses his book for is logo design: "Logos come out better when they're the result of many scribbled pages. A good logo simply has to work as a tiny scribble."

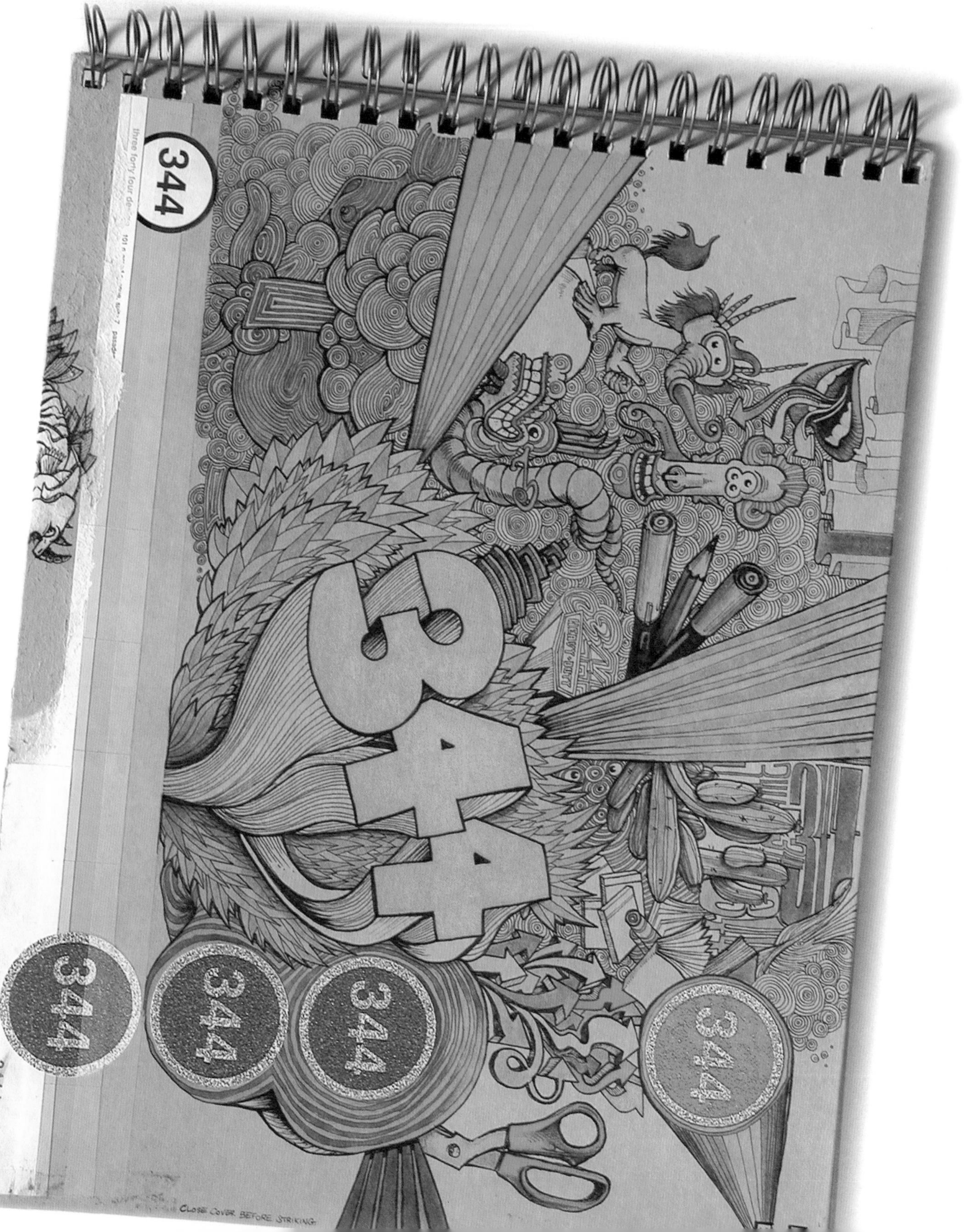

NUTS 4 NUTS
WHEN I TELL MY CIVILIAN FRIENDS ABOUT MY WORK AND ABOUT HOW LONG STUFF TAKES AND HOW MUCH EFFORT + BULLSHIT IS INVOLVED + HOW MANY LONG NIGHTS AT THE DESK ALONE, THEY OFTEN ASK: "WOW! SO YOU'RE GONNA MAKE A LOT OF MONEY OFF THIS, HUH?"... CIVILIANS DON'T GET IT!
THEY ALSO THINK THAT IT'S VOLUNTARY. "OH. SO WHEN DID YOU DECIDE TO BE AN ARTIST?" "HM. I'M NOT SURE. WHEN DID YOU DECIDE TO START BREATHING?"
GREED CONTROL©
BE HONEST ABOUT YOUR DESIRES!
QUALITY OF WORK
GREED
AS GREED INCREASES AND MONEY BECOMES YOUR MOTIVATION THE QUALITY OF WORK INEVITABLY DECREASES.
BECAUSE YOU'VE GOT TO BEND YOURSELF EVERY WHICH WAY TO GET AT THAT CHECK AND YOU BECOME WHAT BILL HICKS CALLS "JUST ANOTHER WHORE AT THE CAPITALIST GANG BANG." THE STUFF MAY STILL LOOK NICE,
BUT THE SPIRIT WILL BE ALL GONE. ONE MORE HACK, COMING RIGHT UP!
DON'T GET ME WRONG: I LIKES TO GET PAID, TOO, ESPECIALLY SINCE MONEY IS THE NEW RESPECT, BUT IF THAT IS WHAT DRIVES YOU ...MAKING $$$
GET THE HELL OUT OF MY BUSINESS! GET A REALTOR'S LICENSE OR SOMETHING.

YOUR WINSOME SMILE WILL BE YOUR SURE PROTECTION
23 27 37 43 48 51
PULL
KILL BILL SOUNDTRACK
KILL BILL SOUNDTRACK VOL 1
STEFAN G. BUCHER
344 DESIGN, LLC
626.796.5148
stefan@344design.com
Please RETURN THIS SKETCHBOOK for good karma + a cash reward.
THANK YOU!
"I feel strongly that Oliver Wendell Holmes was right. Not to share in the activity and passion of your time is to count as not having lived.

WHAT ARE WE ALL ABOUT?

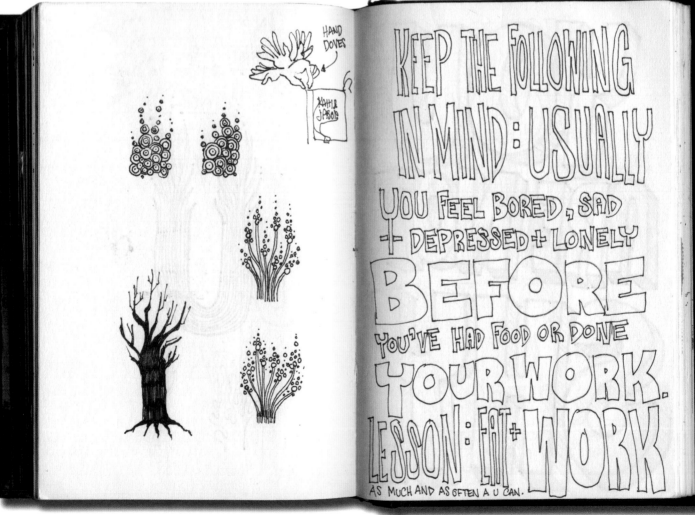

HAND DOVES
KEEP THE FOLLOWING
IN MIND: USUALLY
YOU FEEL BORED, SAD
+ DEPRESSED + LONELY
BEFORE
YOU'VE HAD FOOD OR DONE
YOUR WORK.
LESSON: EAT + WORK
AS MUCH AND AS OFTEN A U CAN.

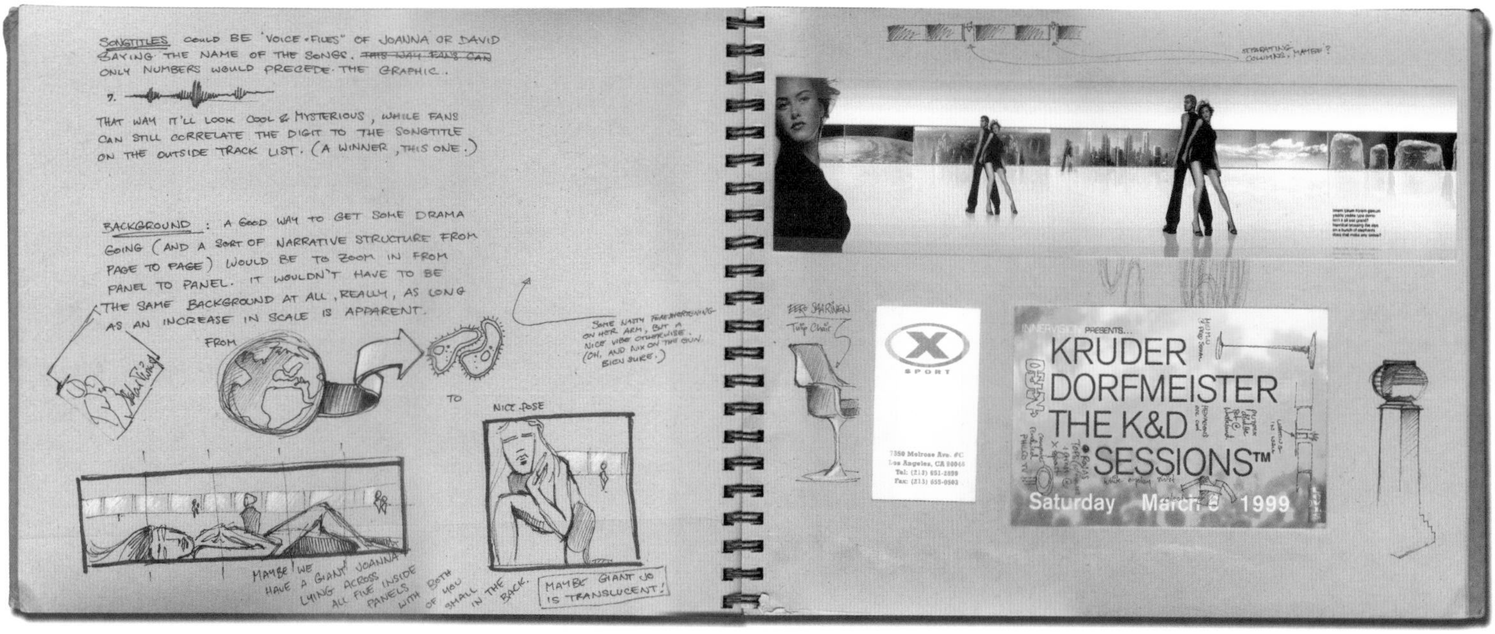
SONGTITLES COULD BE 'VOICE-FILES' OF JOANNA OR DAVID SAYING THE NAME OF THE SONGS. ONLY NUMBERS WOULD PRECEDE THE GRAPHIC.
THAT WAY IT'LL LOOK COOL & MYSTERIOUS, WHILE FANS CAN STILL CORRELATE THE DIGIT TO THE SONGTITLE ON THE OUTSIDE TRACK LIST. (A WINNER, THIS ONE.)
BACKGROUND: A GOOD WAY TO GET SOME DRAMA GOING (AND A SORT OF NARRATIVE STRUCTURE FROM PAGE TO PAGE) WOULD BE TO ZOOM IN FROM PANEL TO PANEL. IT WOULDN'T HAVE TO BE THE SAME BACKGROUND AT ALL, REALLY, AS LONG AS AN INCREASE IN SCALE IS APPARENT.
FROM
TO
NICE POSE
MAYBE WE HAVE A GIANT JOANNA LYING ACROSS ALL FIVE INSIDE PANELS WITH BOTH OF YOU SMALL IN THE BACK.
MAYBE GIANT JO IS TRANSLUCENT!
KRUDER DORFMEISTER THE K&D SESSIONS™
Saturday March 6 1999
X SPORT

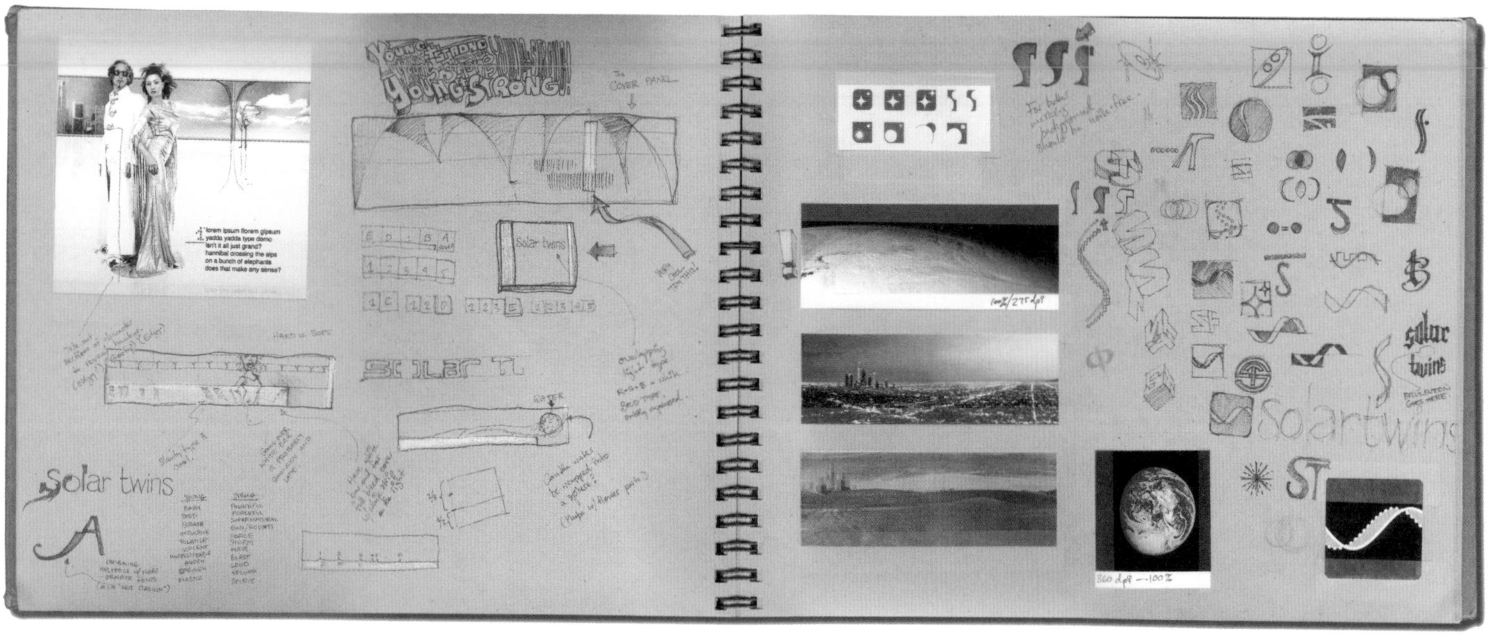
lorem ipsum florem gipeum yadda yadda type demo isn't it all just grand? hannibal crossing the alps on a bunch of elephants does that make any sense?
YOUNG & STRONG!
solar twins
Solar twins

TO INAUGURATE NEW WORLDS, ASTRAL TV WILL SOMETIMES PLAY MUSICAL EVENTS. AND IF YOU'RE LUCKY, JOANNA WILL WOW THE CROWD WITH COOL SILVER PANTS + TWO ADDITIONAL ARMS.
OF COURSE, TWO ADDT'L ARMS WON'T DO MUCH FOR DAVID, WHO MAY JUST GO FOR THE GUSTO AND SHOW UP WITH SOME CLONE PROXYS TO HANDLE SECONDARY KEYBOARDS.
OF COURSE, ALL FUTURE KEYBOARDS CARRY THEIR OWN ANTIGRAV UNITS.

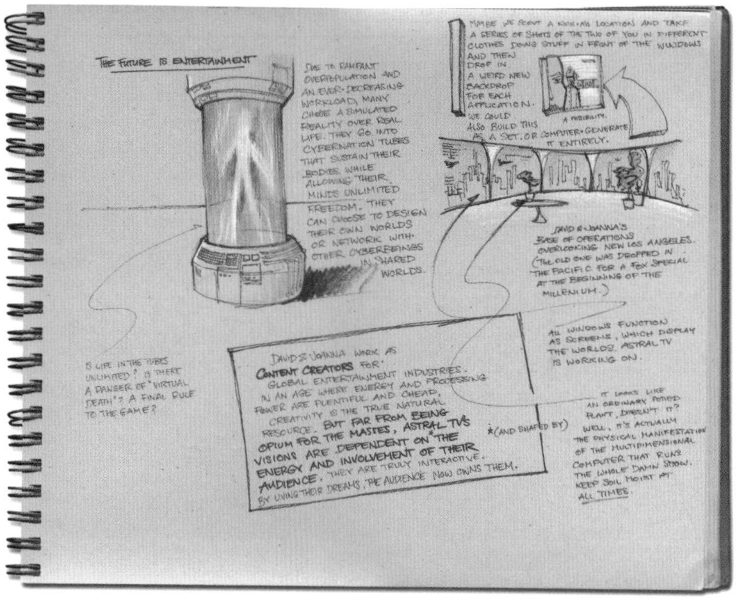
THE FUTURE IS ENTERTAINMENT
DUE TO RAMPANT OVERPOPULATION AND AN EVER-INCREASING WORKLOAD, MANY CHOSE A SIMULATED REALITY OVER REAL LIFE. THEY GO INTO CYBERNATION TUBES THAT SUSTAIN THEIR BODIES WHILE ALLOWING THEIR MINDS UNLIMITED FREEDOM. THEY CAN CHOOSE TO DESIGN THEIR OWN WORLDS OR NETWORK WITH OTHER CYBERBEINGS IN SHARED WORLDS.
DAVID & JOANNA'S BASE OF OPERATIONS OVERLOOKING NEW LOS ANGELES.
AS WINDOWS FUNCTION AS SCREENS, WHICH DISPLAY THE WORLDS ASTRAL TV IS WORKING ON.
DAVID & JOANNA WORK AS CONTENT CREATORS FOR GLOBAL ENTERTAINMENT INDUSTRIES. IN AN AGE WHERE ENERGY AND PROCESSING POWER ARE PLENTIFUL AND CHEAP, CREATIVITY IS THE TRUE NATURAL RESOURCE. BUT FAR FROM BEING OPIUM FOR THE MASSES, ASTRAL TV'S VISIONS ARE DEPENDENT ON THE ENERGY AND INVOLVEMENT OF THEIR AUDIENCE. THEY ARE TRULY INTERACTIVE. BY LIVING THEIR DREAMS, THE AUDIENCE NOW OWNS THEM.
IS LIFE IN THE TUBES UNLIMITED? IS THERE A DANGER OF 'VIRTUAL DEATH'? A FINAL RULE TO THE GAME?

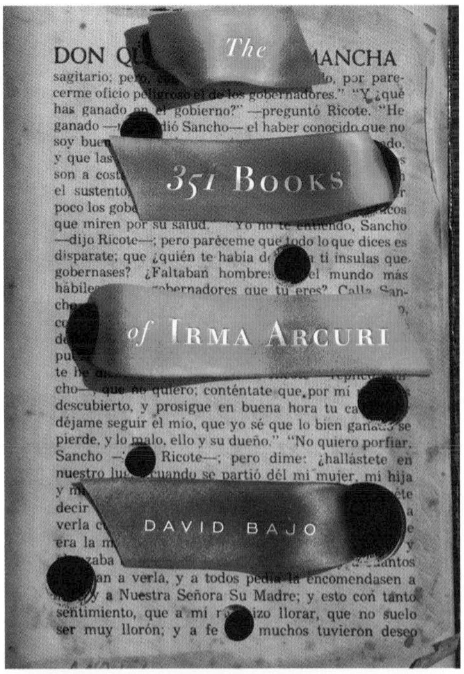

PAUL BUCKLEY

Paul Buckley, art director for New York's Penguin Books, does not use a sketchbook, but retains most of his sketches, often in a book. "I use whatever scrap of paper is around," he says. "Usually that means a Post-it on my home or work desk, or one of those 5 × 3 in. [12.5 × 7.5 cm] spiral notepads, which I keep in my back pocket and by my bed."

Buckley's sketching habits are fairly pedestrian, but nonetheless revealing in terms of process, as the images here attest. "My design sketches are never precious, and always utilitarian. The goal is only to jot the visual thought down and move on. As many of my ideas come on during sleep, I probably just want to go back to bed. So they ain't pretty."

He insists that "there is nothing unusual about my sketches, other than their poor quality, despite the fact that I used to make my living as an illustrator." In fact, the School of Visual Arts in New York gave him an illustration scholarship solely based on his drawing portfolio.

"I can draw when I truly want to or need to, but it's never been easy for me," he explains. "My father, like many comic artists, drew effortlessly. Tattoo artists seem to have the same sort of ease and speed as well – it's a beautiful thing to witness someone who can draw and make it look easy."

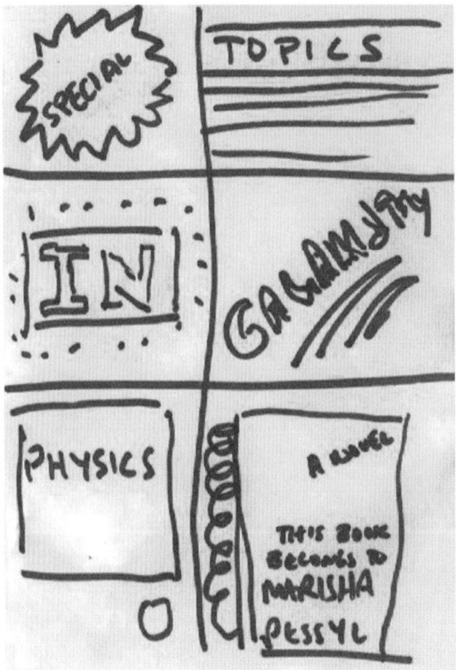

BIG CLOUD
SMOKE IN THE DISTANCE
CIVIL WAR ERA CAPITOL BLDG
ROAD LEADING UP TO CAPITOL

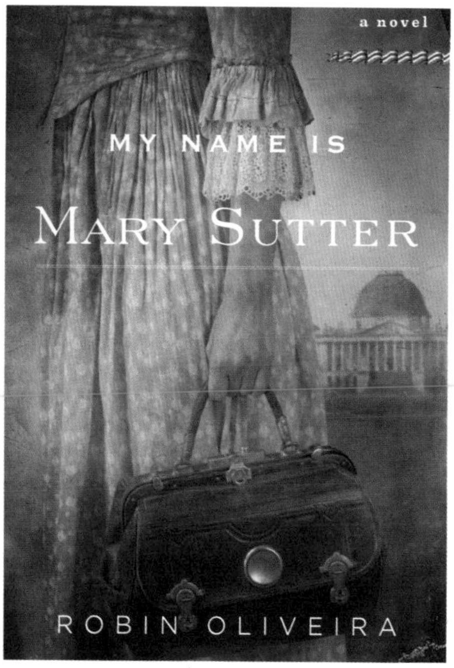
a novel
MY NAME IS
MARY SUTTER
ROBIN OLIVEIRA

7·12·07

PHILIP BURKE

Buffalo, New York-born caricaturist Philip Burke is known for the expressively painted facial distortions that he has often drawn from life. His work, produced at a monumental scale, integrates the abstract essence of modern art with the critical commentary of the cartoon. His sketchbooks are less monumental – more human scale.

Burke's sketchbooks have always been for preliminary work – "that is, preliminary to finals in ink, charcoal, colored pencil, watercolor, or oil. I also occasionally do some personal work in my sketchbooks, such as drawings of family or friends." What distinguishes these sketches of politicians and celebrities from his final works is primarily the medium, a 4B pencil. His finishes are almost all paintings.

He adds, "In my sketches I work from very straight to very wild – straight drawings to learn the subject's physiognomy, and wild drawings to push the distortion and see how far I can go without losing the character of my subject."

"I have far too many sketchbooks to count – the number of sketchbook pages on my database is somewhere around 10,000," he casually notes.

MIKEY BURTON

Philadelphia-based Mikey Burton has kept a sketchbook for about one year. "I wish I could say longer," he says, "because I've been designing and illustrating for a while. I'm good at starting sketchbooks, but horrible at finishing them. I think this is the first one I've ever completed. This was a big accomplishment for me. I felt as much pride in the sketchbook as I did the final project."

The book excerpted here was for Burton's MFA thesis project. "It was a great exercise and I learned so much from the physical act of drawing. I don't like to have blank spots in my sketchbook, so force myself to fill the page. Often the process of trying to come up with one extra sketch will result in my best idea."

Burton says, "I do the majority of my work on the computer, so before I start pushing pixels around I like to get out all my ideas on paper. Good ideas should communicate in a simple form. Usually, if it doesn't work as a sketch, it's not going to work in the long run."

He adds that "one technique I utilize (mainly because I can't draw realistically) is a blending/transfer pen. I take photocopies and transfer them right into my sketchbook, then sketch over the transfer. The transfer process also produces a lot of interesting textures that I often use in the final piece."

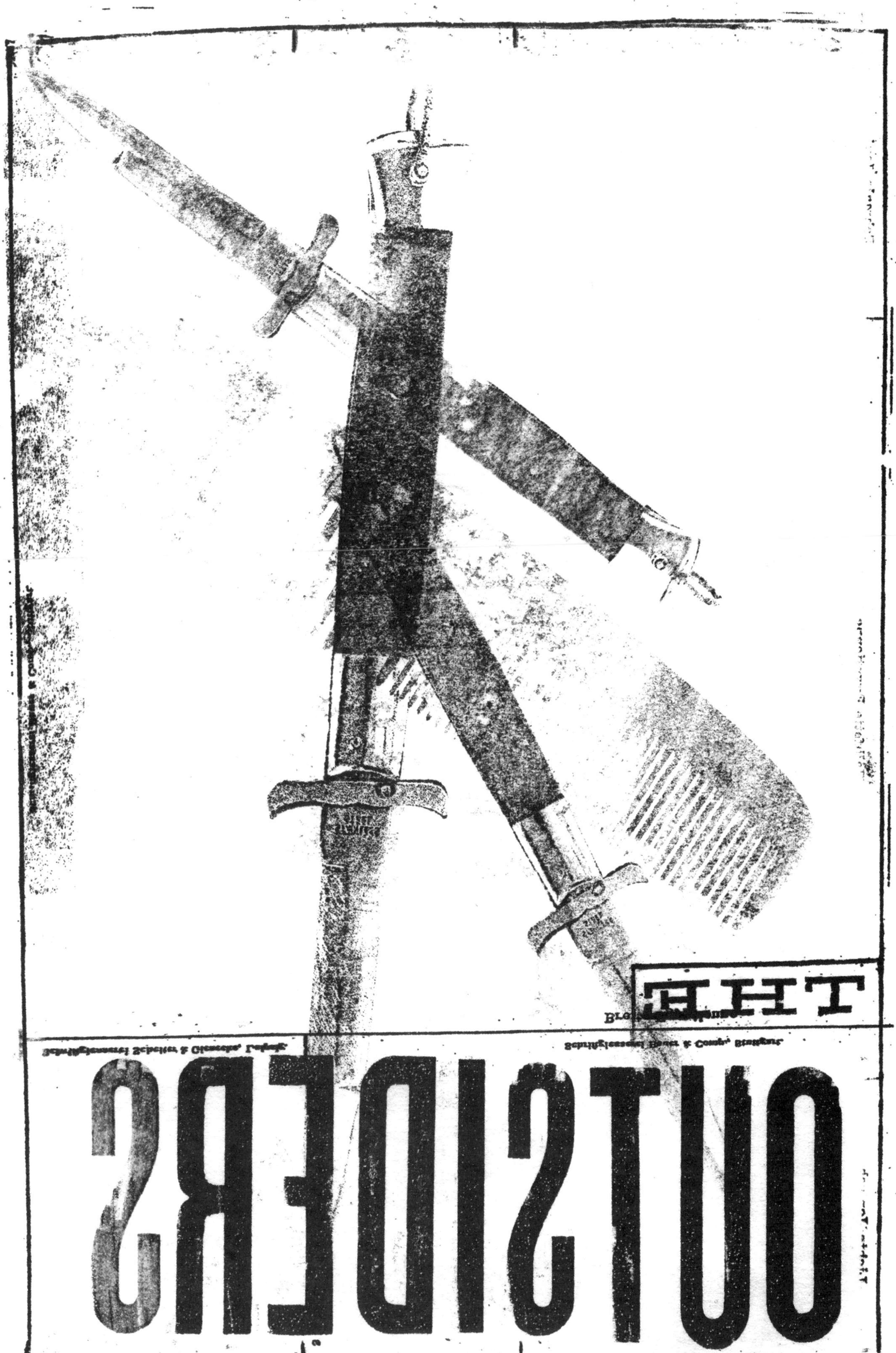
THE
OUTSIDERS

ANIMAL
FARM

ANIMAL
FARM

to Kill
a Mocking-
bird
HARPER
LEE

To Kill a Mock-ingbird

To Kill a Mocking-bird
HARPER LEE

451
The Great Gatsby
The Great Gatsby
The Great Gatsby
The Great Gatsby

CHRIS CAPUOZZO

Chris Capuozzo, illustrator, web designer, former partner of Funny Garbage in New York, and longtime graffiti tagger, has kept a sketchbook since 1980. "I keep a few going at the same time. A sketchbook must have a certain personality for me to be able to start working in it. I've kept a pocket-size book since 2004 to chronicle life going on around me. These have been very satisfying."

His first few sketchbooks in the early 1980s were graffiti books or "blackbooks." These blackbooks were passed around to other graffiti writers to work in, and served as great networking tools. "Street Island (where I lived), graffiti writers would travel from far away neighborhoods to see my blackbooks."

He has well over 100 books that have focused on various themes, including daily chronicles, illustrated stories, certain image-making techniques, and collections of printed ephemera. "In the early 1980s my own and Peter Girardi's [see page 152] sketchbooks became the basis for the Funny Garbage look. They were a crossroads of fine art, children's art, comics, typography, illustration, and collage. We were both plugged into pop culture on a lot of levels and this was reflected

KEN CARBONE

Ken Carbone, the co-principal of New York-based Carbone Smolan Agency, has used sketchbooks since the 1970s. "However," he says, "in 1990 a museum curator showed me a rare Paul Gauguin sketchbook. It was a remarkable work of art and I felt like I was peering into the soul of this great artist. Its raw beauty and breadth of personal expression left me awestruck. This was the epiphany that inspired me to keep a sketchbook journal as part of my daily life." He does not often use his sketchbooks for client projects. "It is the total aggregate of images, writings, and memories that filters down into my projects. These books are a creative database that I draw upon during the design process."

Carbone takes the sketchbook ethos to a high level of precision. For instance, "I have covers custom made of white goat skin, which I paint with leather dye when I start a new book. It's like a christening. These sketchbooks contain nearly 5,000 pages of 'beginnings.' I really don't consider any single page a finished work but more as fuel to explore a particular idea further. I'm not precious about how the pages are composed. The act of capturing an idea or recording the source of inspiration is more important than how it is entered into the book. I rubber stamp the date in the corner of the page when I make an entry."

FALLINGWATER

JAN. 2 4 2005
BUSH, AT 2ND INAUGURAL,
SAYS SPREAD OF LIBERTY IS THE
'CALLING OF OUR TIME'

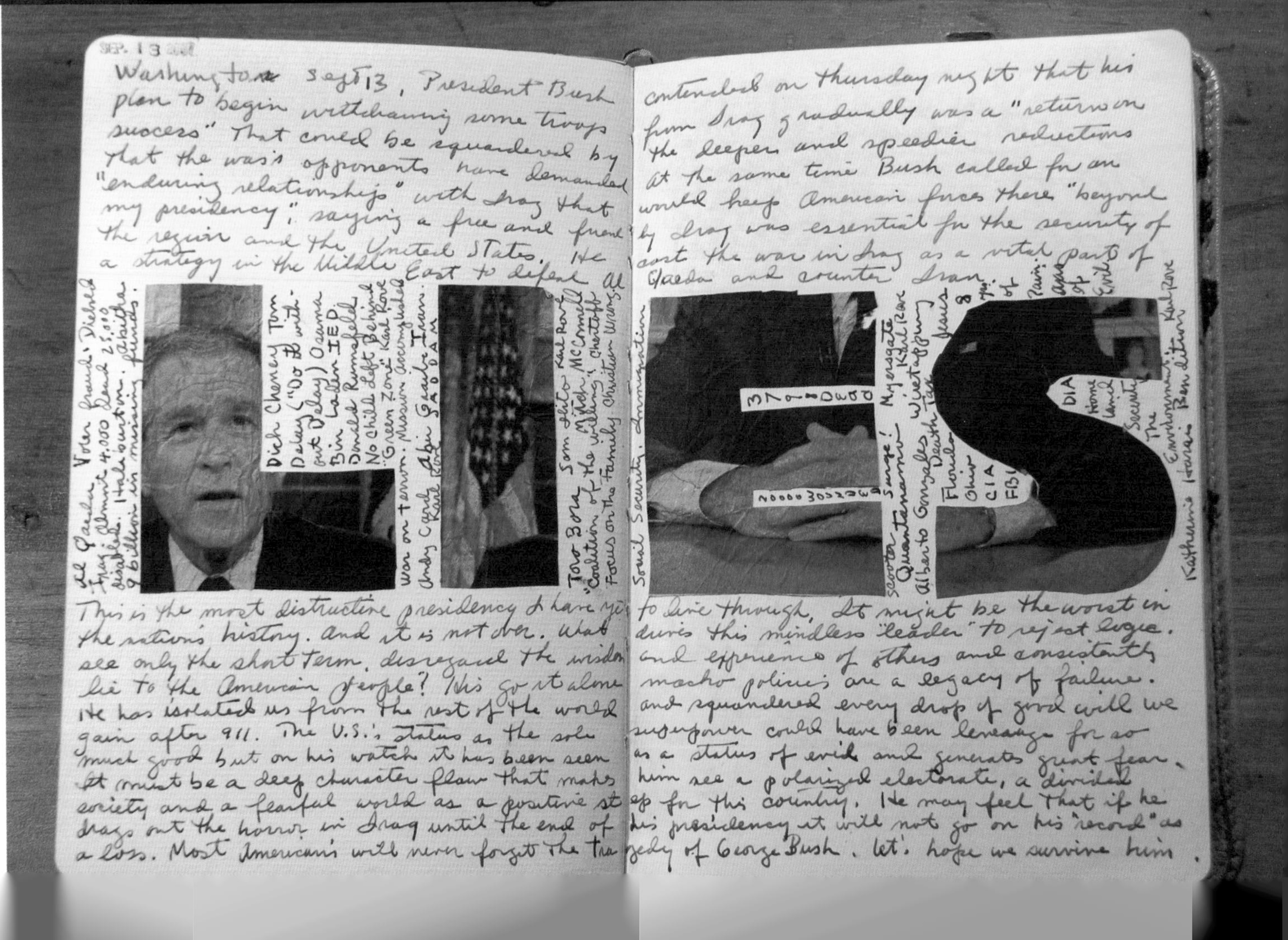
Washington sept 13, President Bush
plan to begin withdrawing some troops
success" That could be squandered by
that the war's opponents have demanded
"enduring relationship" with Iraq that
my presidency", saying a free and friend
the region and the United States. He
a strategy in the Middle East to defeat Al
contended on thursday night that his
from Iraq gradually was a "return on
the deeper and speedier reductions
At the same time Bush called for an
would keep American forces there "beyond
by Iraq was essential for the security of
cast the war in Iraq as a vital part of
Qaeda and counter Iran.
This is the most distructive presidency I have yet
the nation's history. And it is not over. What
see only the short term, disregard the wisdom
lie to the American people? His go it alone
He has isolated us from the rest of the world
gain after 911. The U.S.'s status as the sole
much good but on his watch it has been seen
It must be a deep character flaw that makes
society and a fearful world as a positive st
drags out the horror in Iraq until the end of
a loss. Most Americans will never forget the tra
to live through. It might be the worst in
during this mindless "leader" to reject logic.
and experience of others and consistently
macho policies are a legacy of failure.
and squandered every drop of good will we
superpower could have been leverage for so
as a status of evil and generates great fear.
him see a polarized electorate, a divided
ep for this country. He may feel that if he
his presidency it will not go on his "record" as
gedy of George Bush. Let's hope we survive him.

MAY 12 2006
PARIS
MAY 13 2006
AIR FRANCE
Hôtel de la Bretonnerie
BON VOYAGE
Brasserie FLO
7 Cour des Petite Ecuries
01 47 70 13 59
Perch with Pasta
22, rue Sainte Croix
de la Bretonnerie
75004 Paris
Tél. 01 48 87 77 63
Fax 01 42 77 26 78
E mail : hotel@bretonnerie.com
My biennial trip part business part pleasure all Paris!

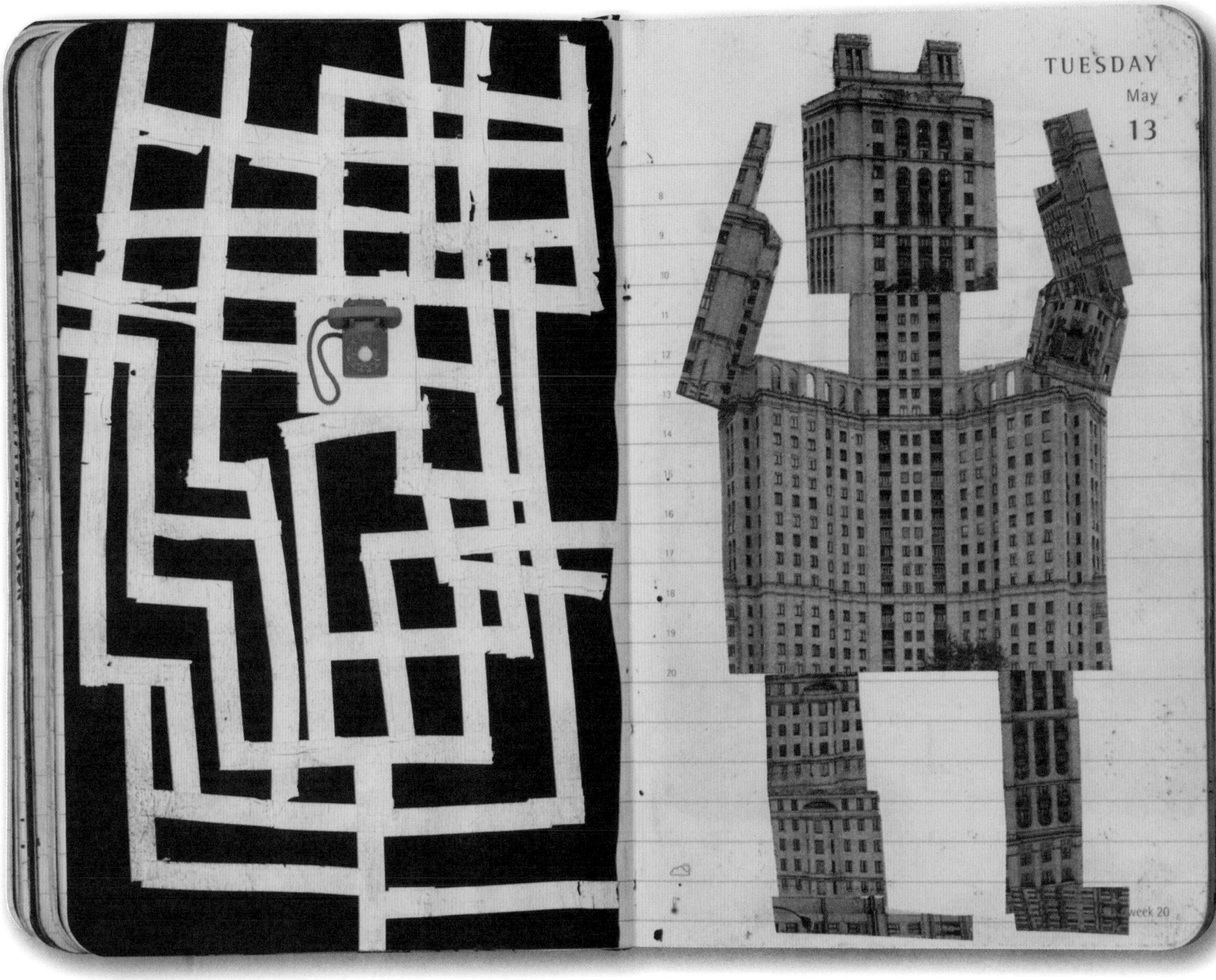
TUESDAY
May
13
8
9
10
11
12
13
14
15
16
17
18
19
20
week 20

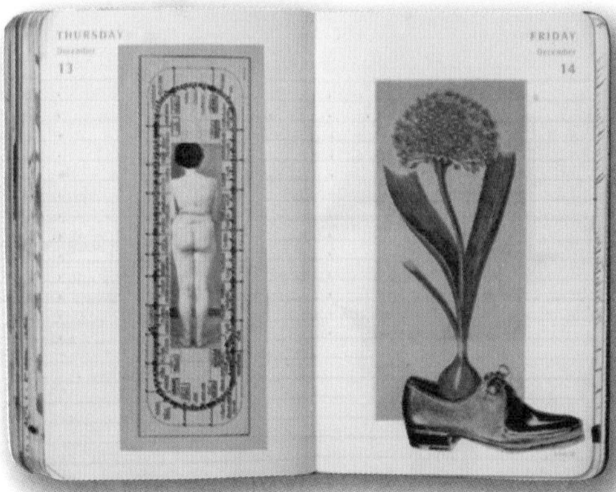
THURSDAY
13
FRIDAY
14

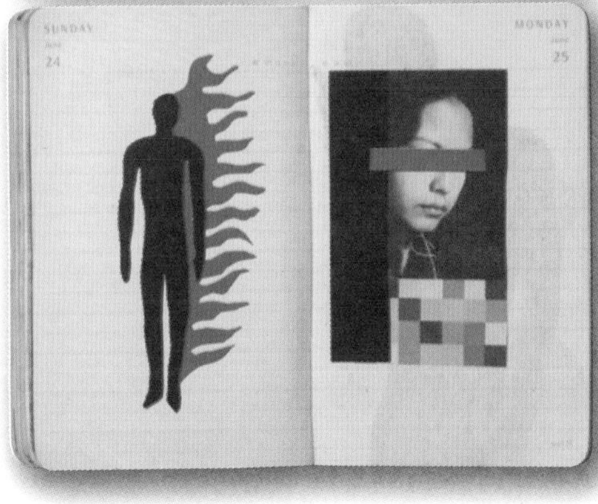
SUNDAY
24
MONDAY
25

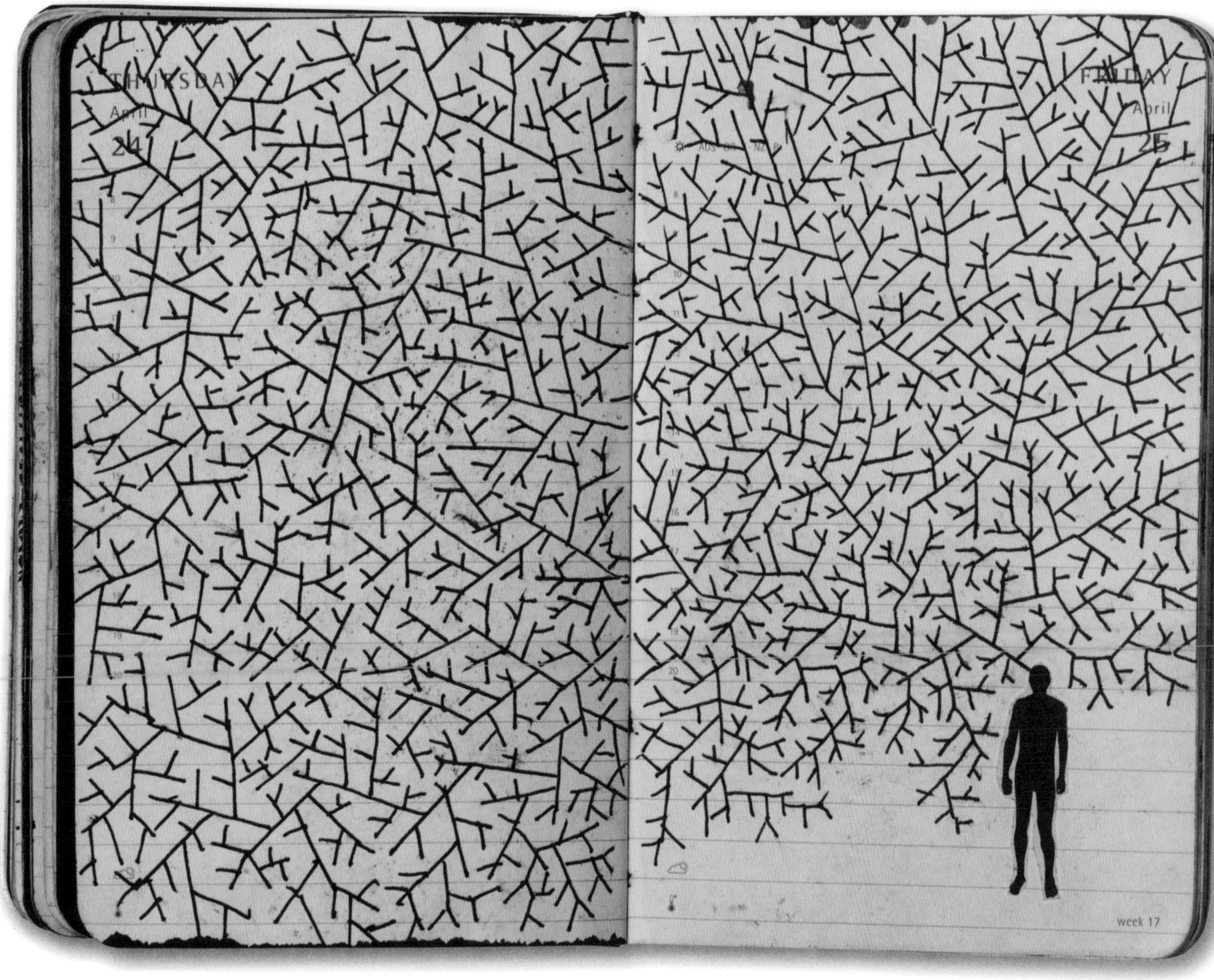

PEP CARRIÓ

Pep Carrió, a Spanish graphic designer with a painter's touch, says he began to work in these diaries in 2007 as a project to create an image every day. Carrió notes that the book "is a portable laboratory, where I can work with different ideas and found images."

As a graphic designer, Carrió is used to working on long-term projects, with enough time to reflect. But the diary is a different space, "with more freedom to experiment and with no fear of failure." Hence, he allows himself greater licence. Since he is doing one image per day, the end result must be finished every day. But this can be done anywhere: "At work, on the bus, at home, in a hotel, without a fixed idea or style. Anything goes."

He adds, "I try not to have any special subject, using a different technique or style every day. When the diary is finished, after a whole year of different images, you can see that there are many subjects."

Carrió says he is always working with a notebook near him. "Now it is an essential companion. I have notebooks with collages, with drawings done during telephone calls, or during travels." If nothing else, his drawing skills have improved at an incredible speed.

FRIDAY
October
12
13

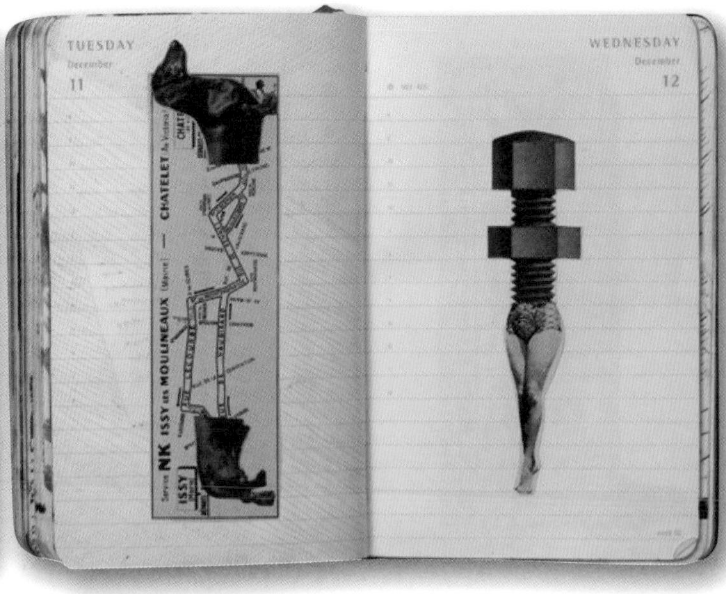
TUESDAY
December
11
ISSY les MOULINEAUX
CHATELET
WEDNESDAY
December
12

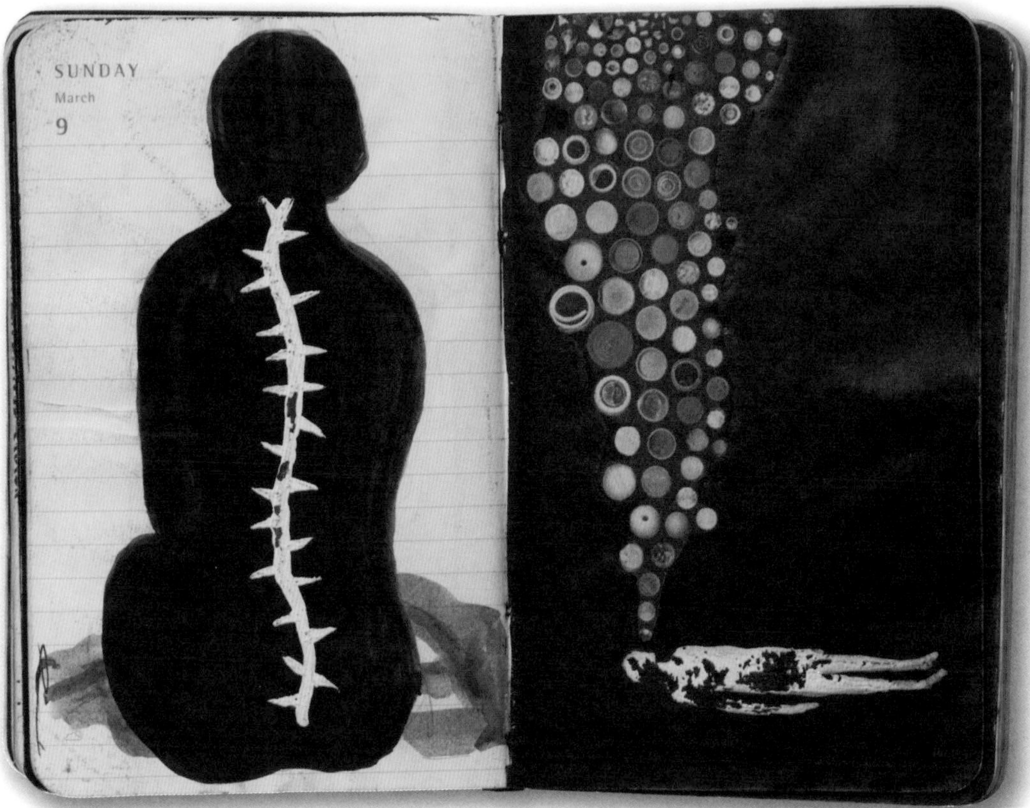
SUNDAY
March
9

FRIDAY
February
16

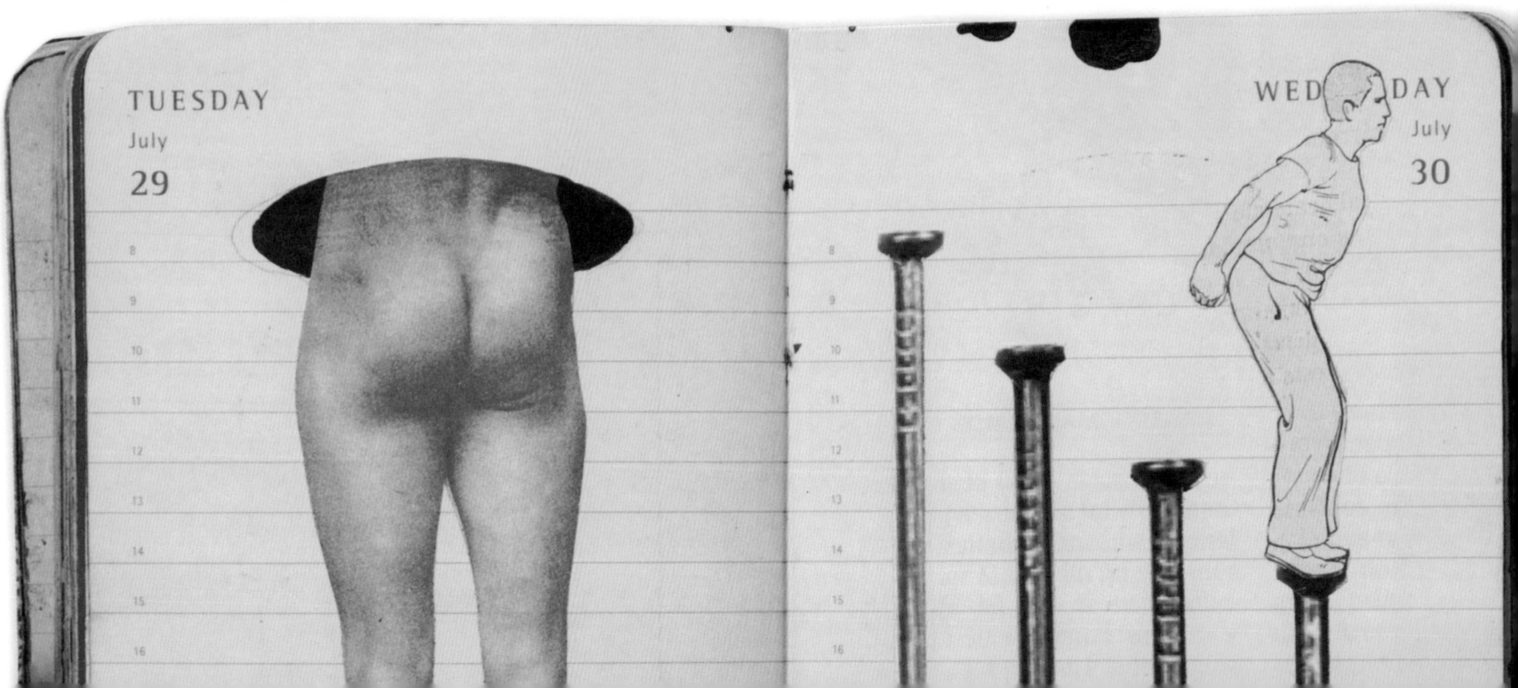
TUESDAY
July
29
WED
DAY
July
30

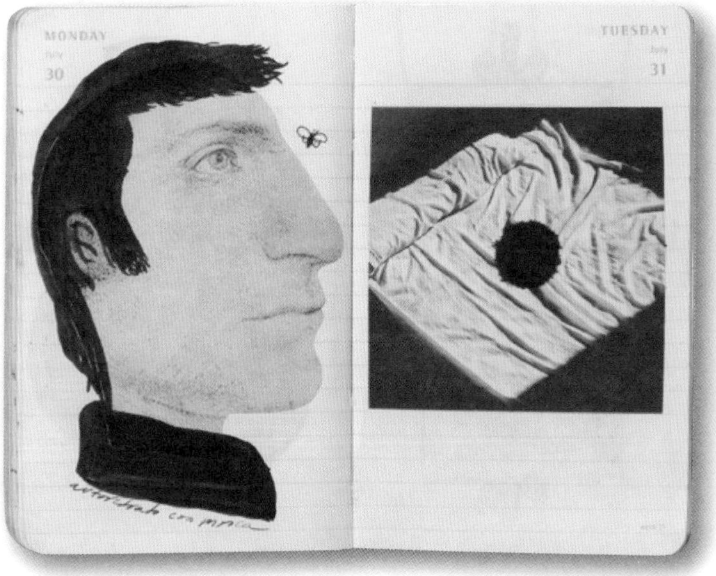
MONDAY
30
TUESDAY
31

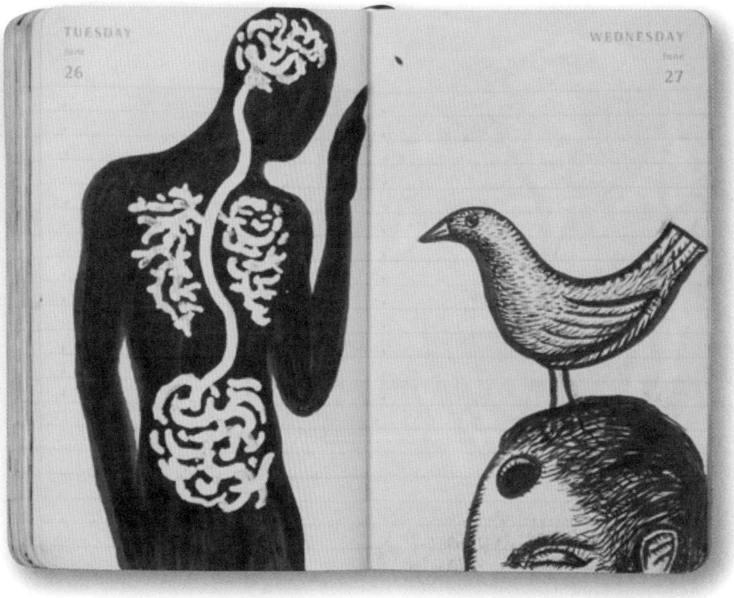
TUESDAY
26
WEDNESDAY
27

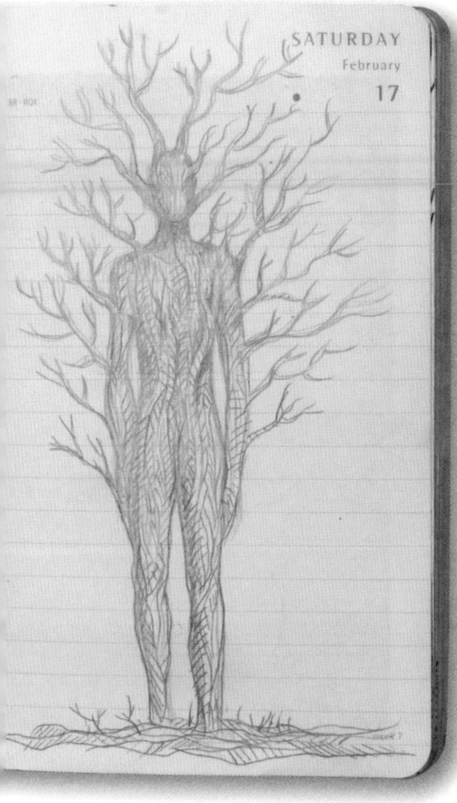
SATURDAY
February
17

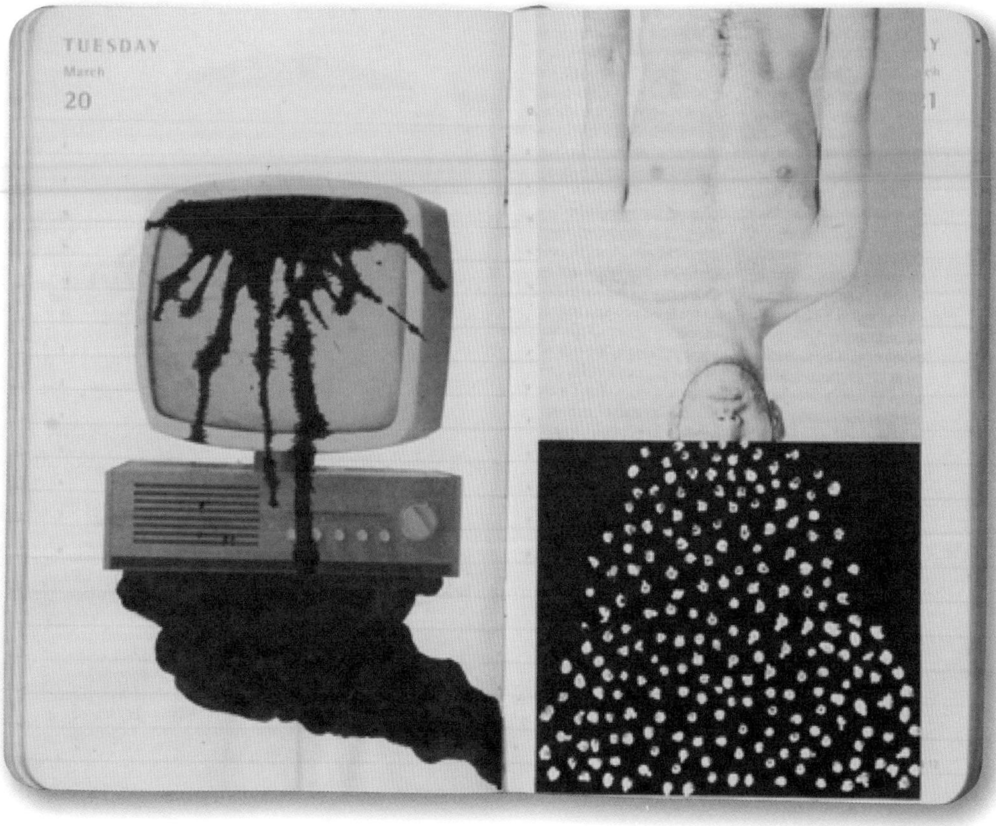
TUESDAY
March
20

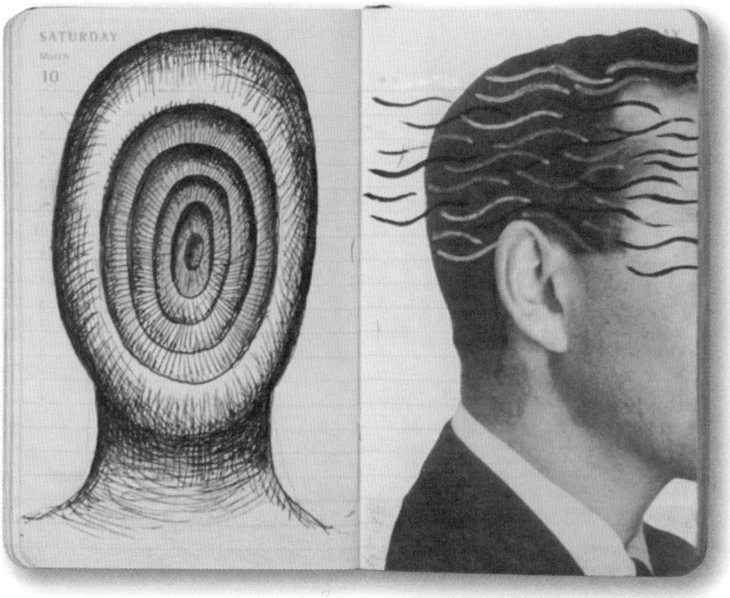
SATURDAY
March
10

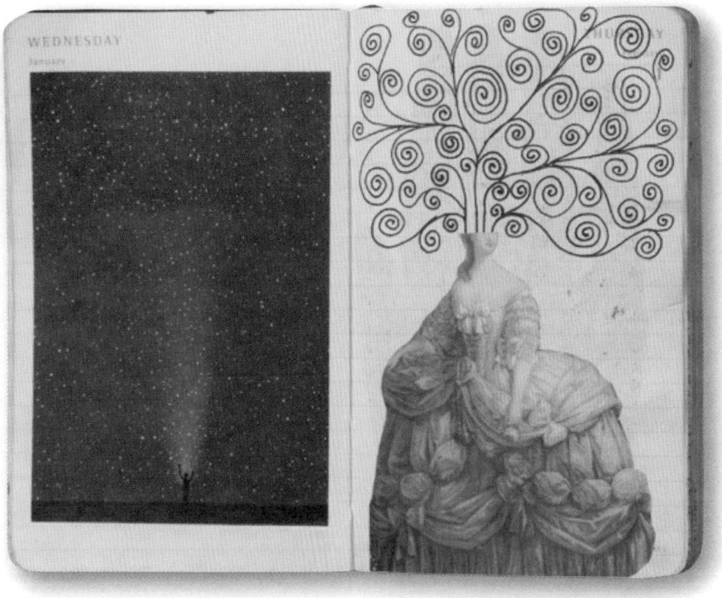
WEDNESDAY

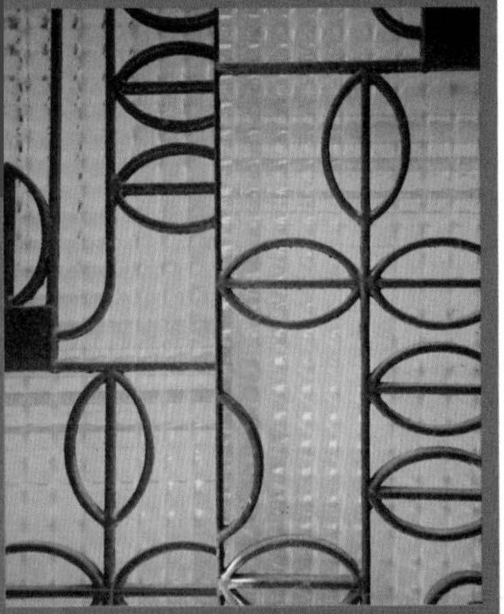

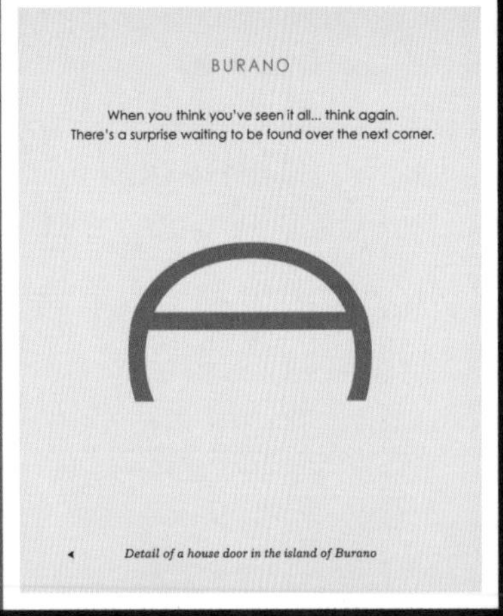

BURANO
When you think you've seen it all... think again.
There's a surprise waiting to be found over the next corner.
Detail of a house door in the island of Burano

Is it easy to paddle on a gondola?

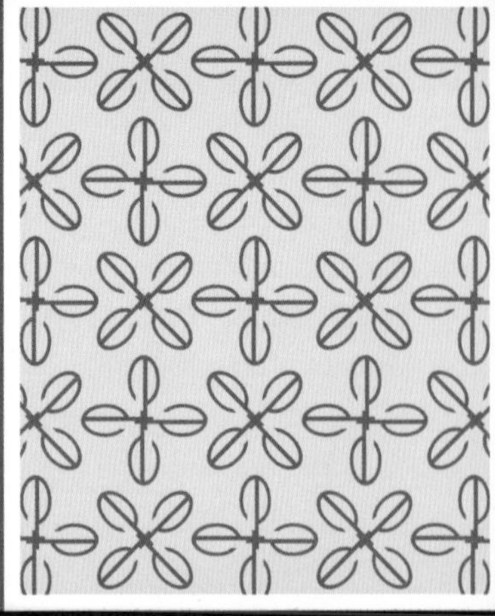

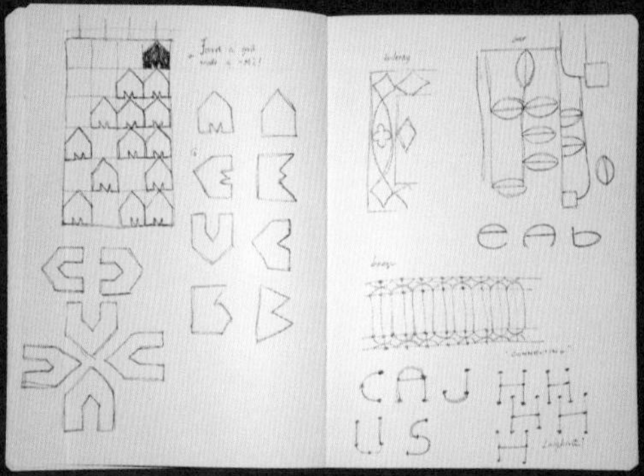

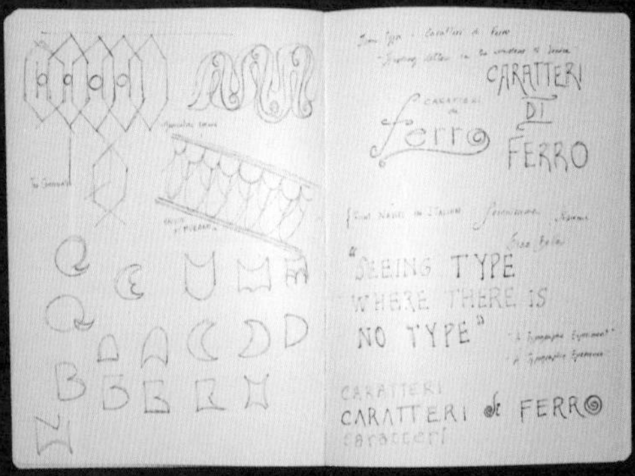

CARATTERI DI FERRO
"SEEING TYPE WHERE THERE IS NO TYPE"
CARATTERI di FERRO

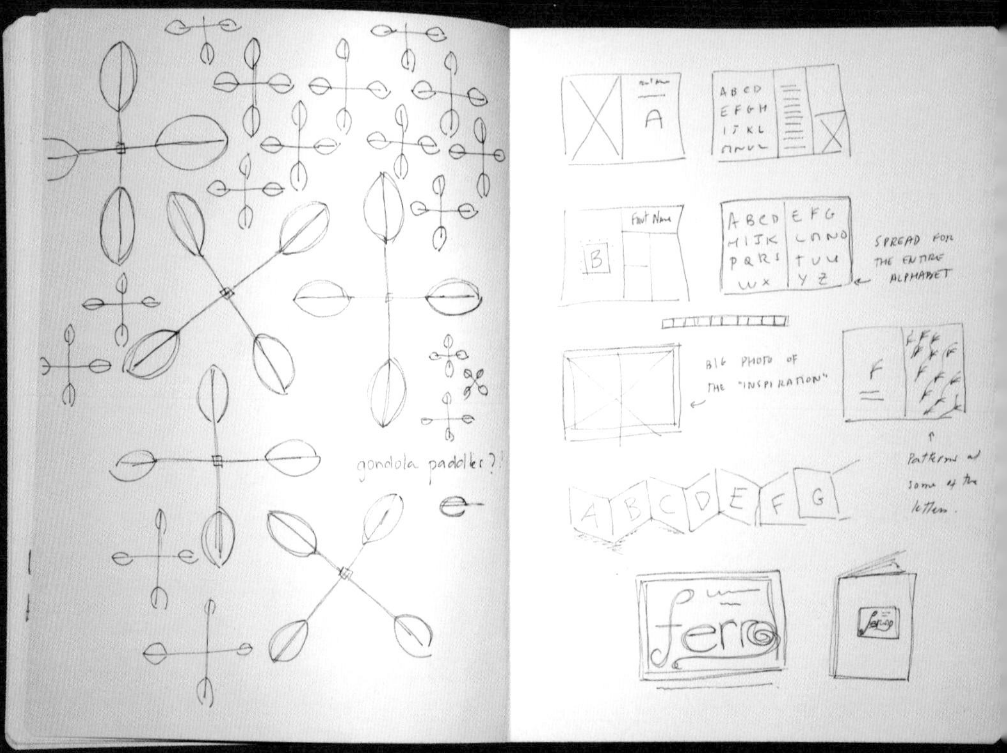

gondola paddles?
SPREAD FOR THE ENTIRE ALPHABET
BIG PHOTO OF THE "INSPIRATION"
A B C D E F G
ferro

IRON TYPE

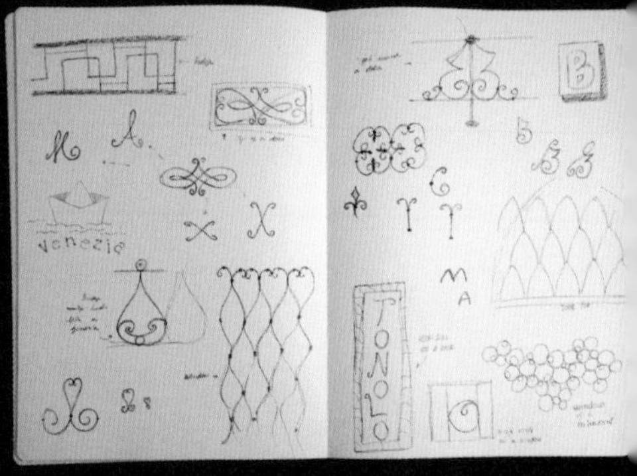

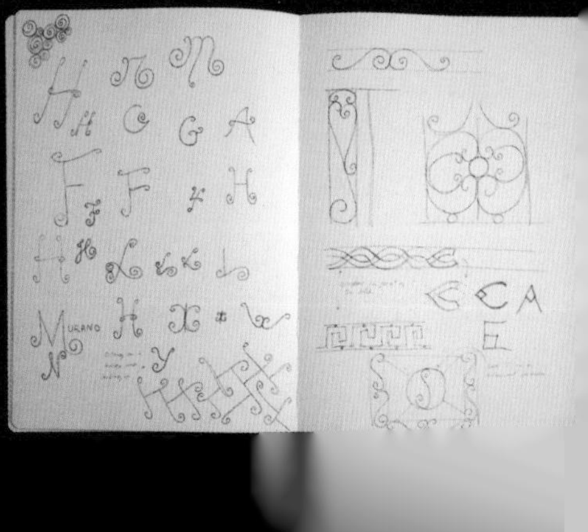

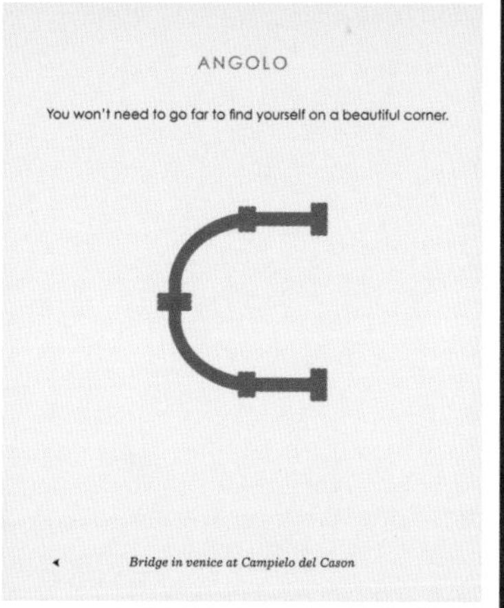

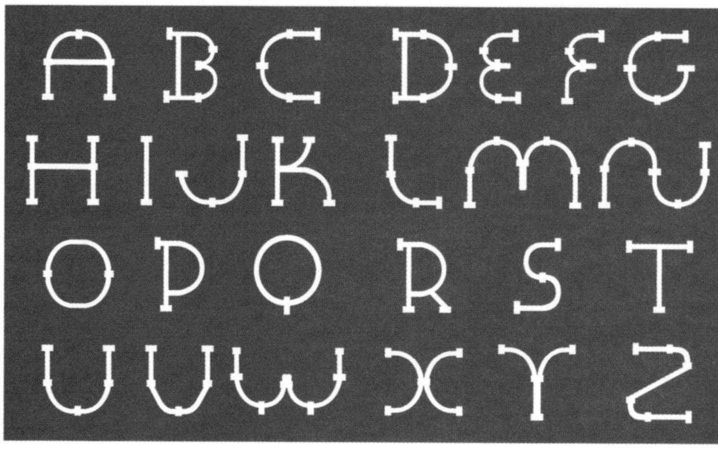

CELINA CARVALHO

For São Paulo-based Celina Carvalho, the purpose of the sketchbook "is to get started," she says. "It is much harder to begin designing if I sit at the computer with a blank 'page' in front of me. With the sketchbook, I can simply scribble with no concerns. I can draw whatever comes to mind, even if it has nothing to do with what I need to achieve in the end. And this leads me to the beginning of my ideas."

Carvalho hardly ever uses colors in her sketchbooks, while her finished work is usually very colorful. "I find it more practical to use around to make my sketches. In the sketchbook I draw what my inspirations are and write what comes to my mind (which are two things that won't appear in the final work). When I draw in one medium, what I see and what I think connect faster than if I was to have a photograph (of my 'inspiration') next to a blank page on the computer screen."

The images shown here were created during the last week of May 2009, in Venice, and were the basis for a guidebook devoted to the iron railings Carvalho found throughout the city. She ultimately used the

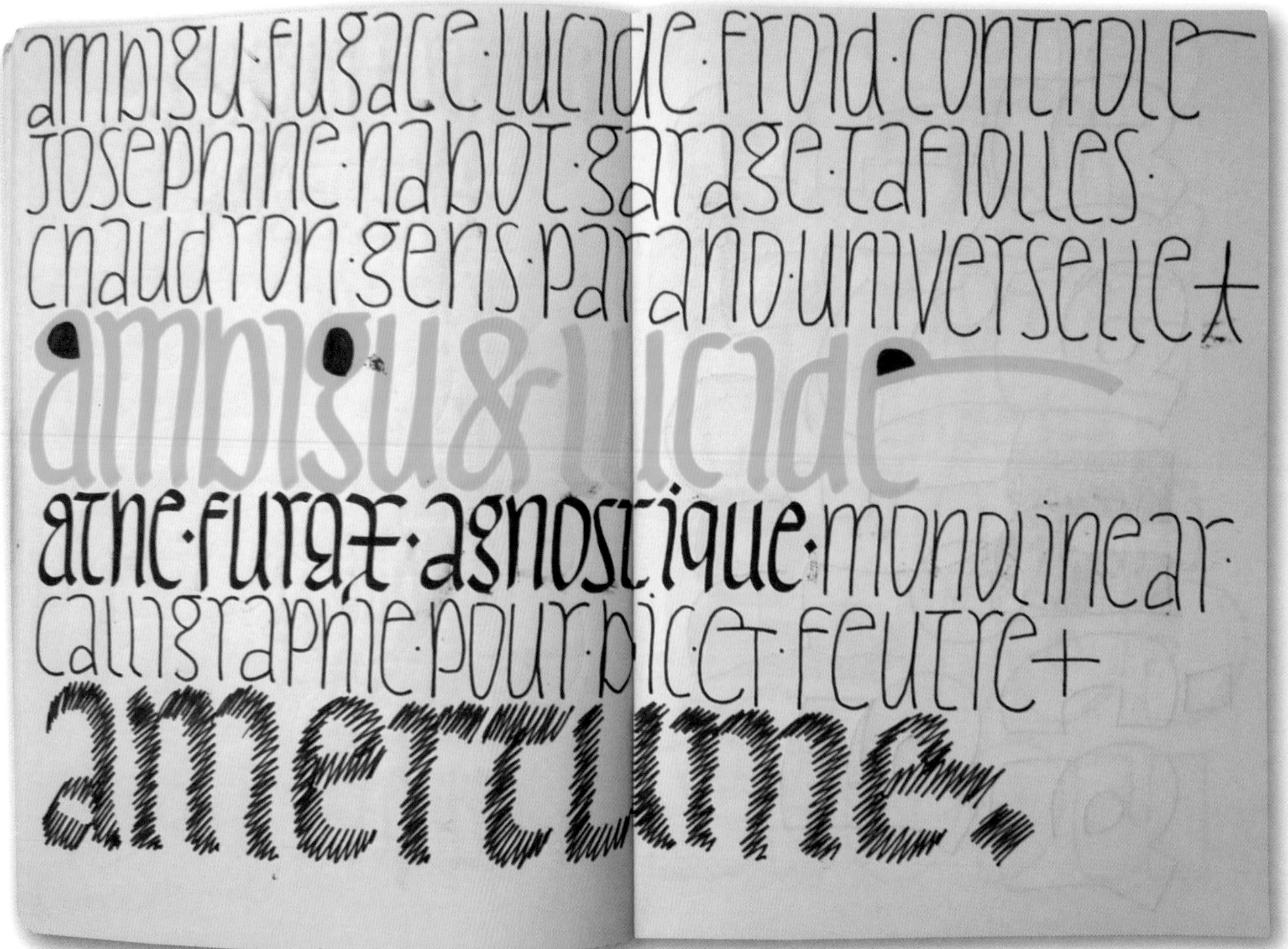
ambigu · fugace · lucide · froid · contrôle
Josephine · nabot · garage · tafiolles ·
chaudron · gens · parano · universelle +
ambigu & lucide
atne · furax · agnostique · monolinear ·
calligraphie · pour bic et feutre +
amertume.

you · can't · bring

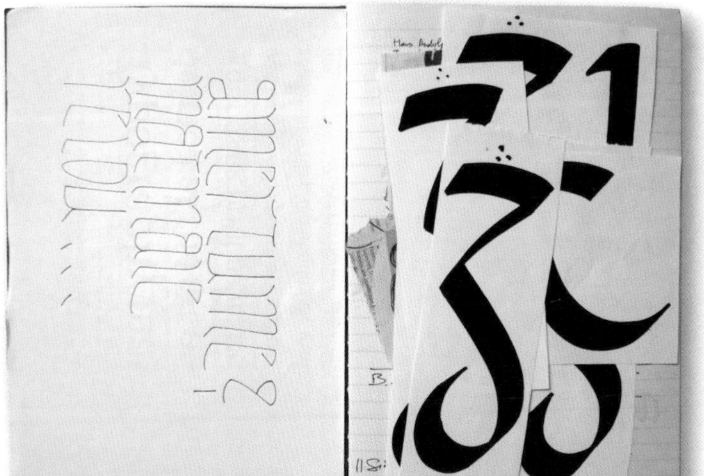

FRANÇOIS CHASTANET

François Chastanet, a Paris-based typographer, photographer, architect, teacher, and street art historian, used to sketch on sheets of A4 paper, but destroyed them all. However, since the age of twenty-five, "I have kept some of my drawings, although I still throw away a lot."

For Chastanet, it is about "progressing in drawing, both figurative and abstract, noting and remembering places and shapes; structuring and making syntheses with diagrams and patterns is more efficient for me than a continuous and linear way of thinking. My finished works are much calmer; the empty space plays its full role of tension. I am a perfectionist in shapes, and often minimalist."

The examples shown here are mainly from 1999–2000. This sketchbook represents the complete process of "my diploma work as an architect about subway stations, architectural space, and signage systems. At that time I was using the small portable Japanese brush-pen from Pentel with black ink. It permitted me to make very thin and thick lines with the same tool, which is highly practical when outside. At the same time, the drawing rendering is almost 'too nice' – too aesthetic in a way – and intentionally making a nice drawing is a trap. I learned to be wary of this pen, and now use the classic Pilot V5, which is the best ballpoint ever, producing a flowing and nervous monolinear thin line."

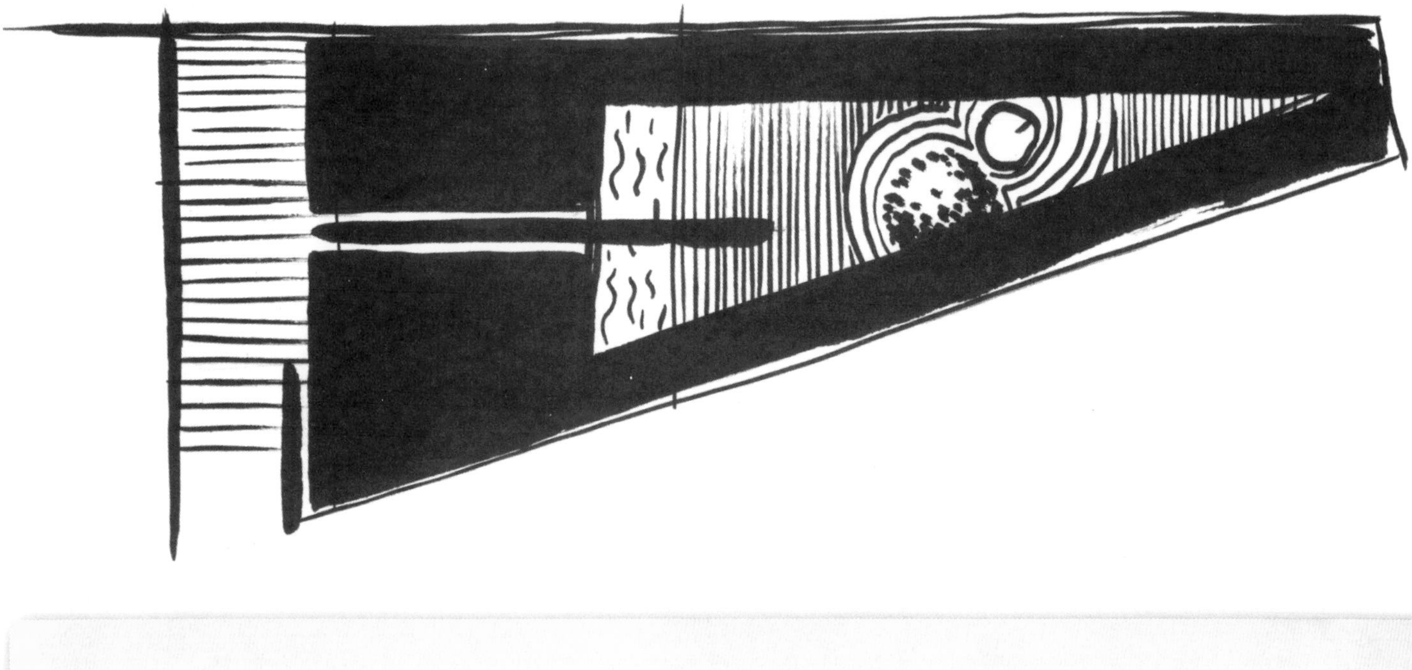

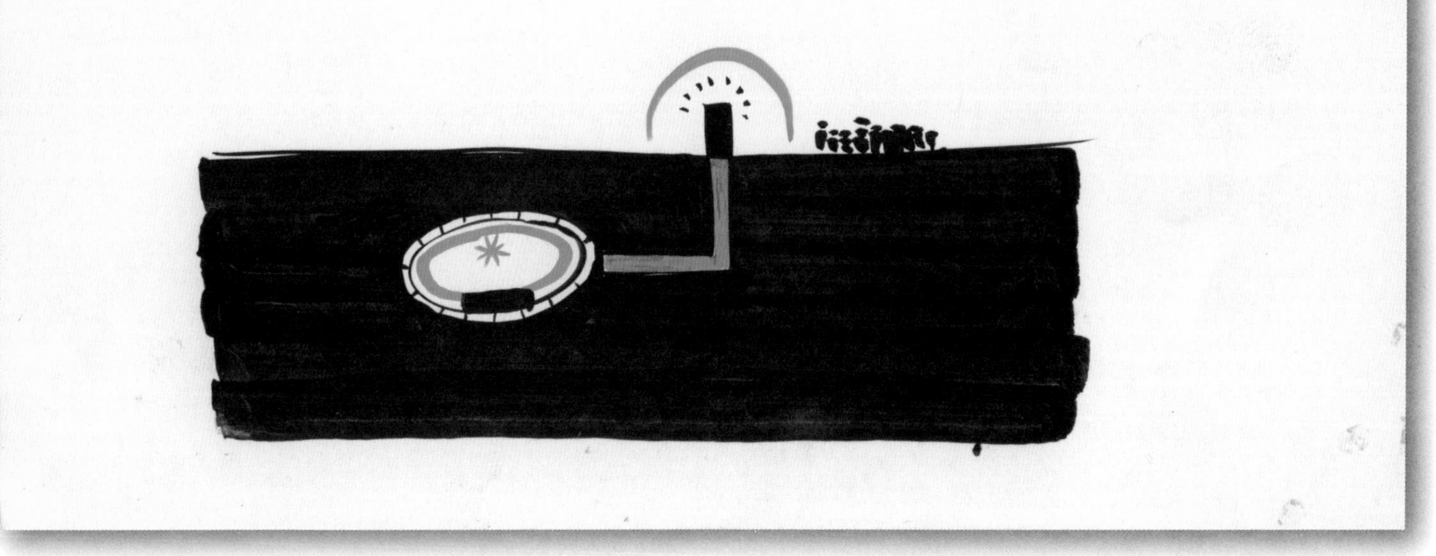

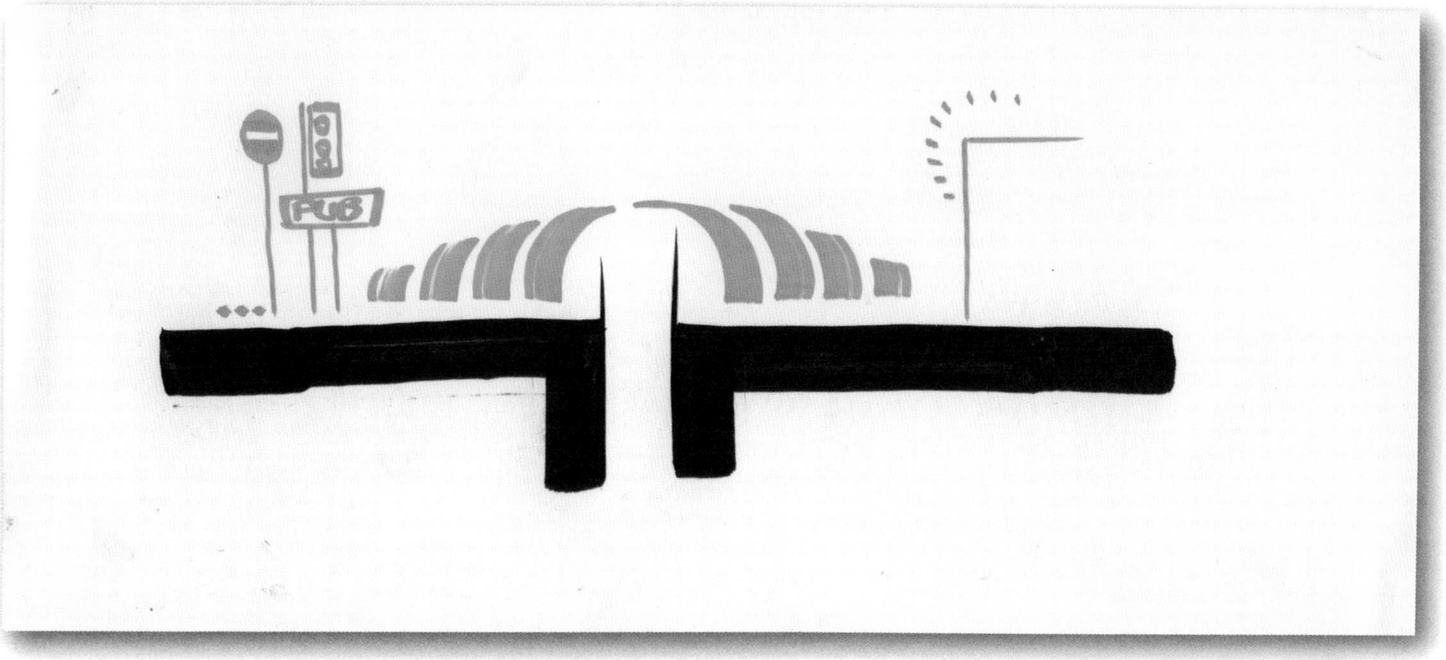
PUB

problématique PUB/CINETIQUE...
Flip

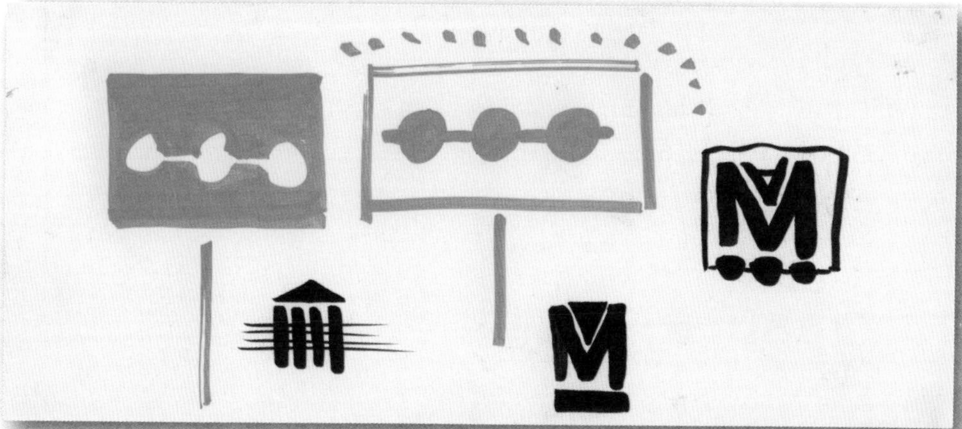

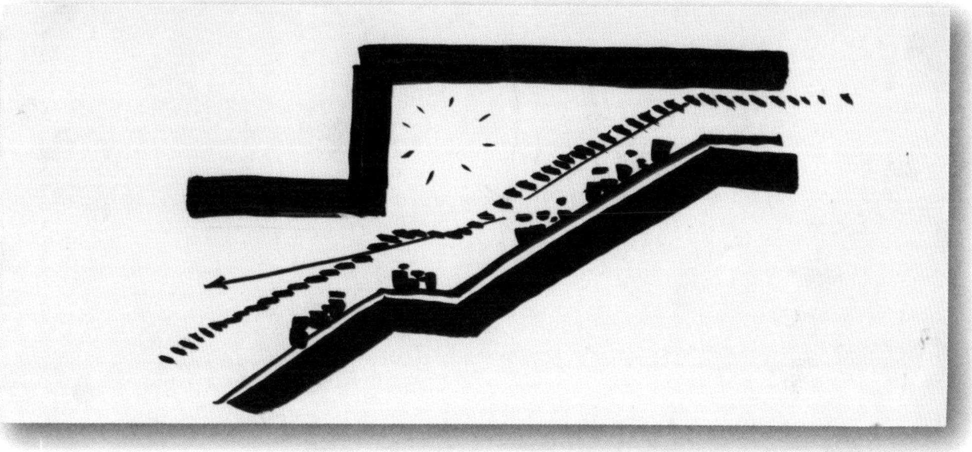

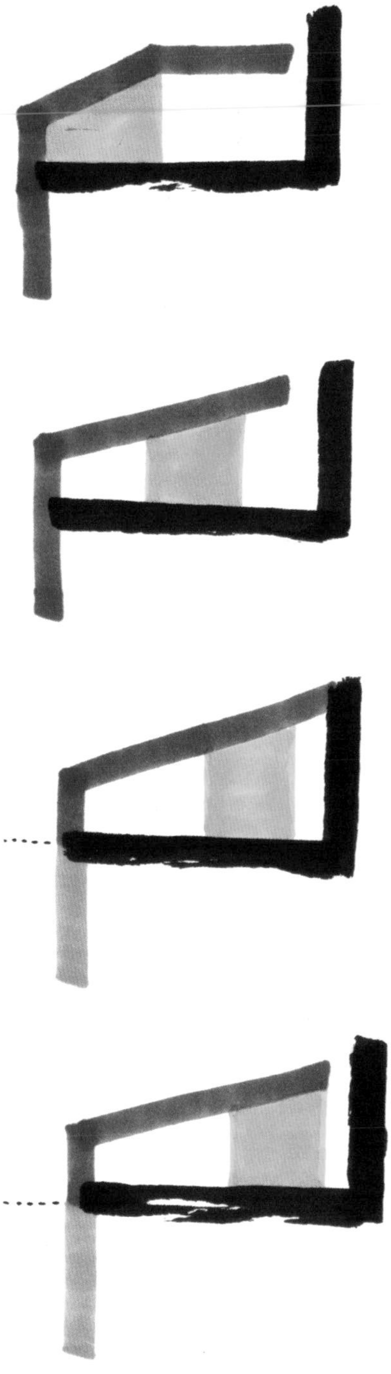

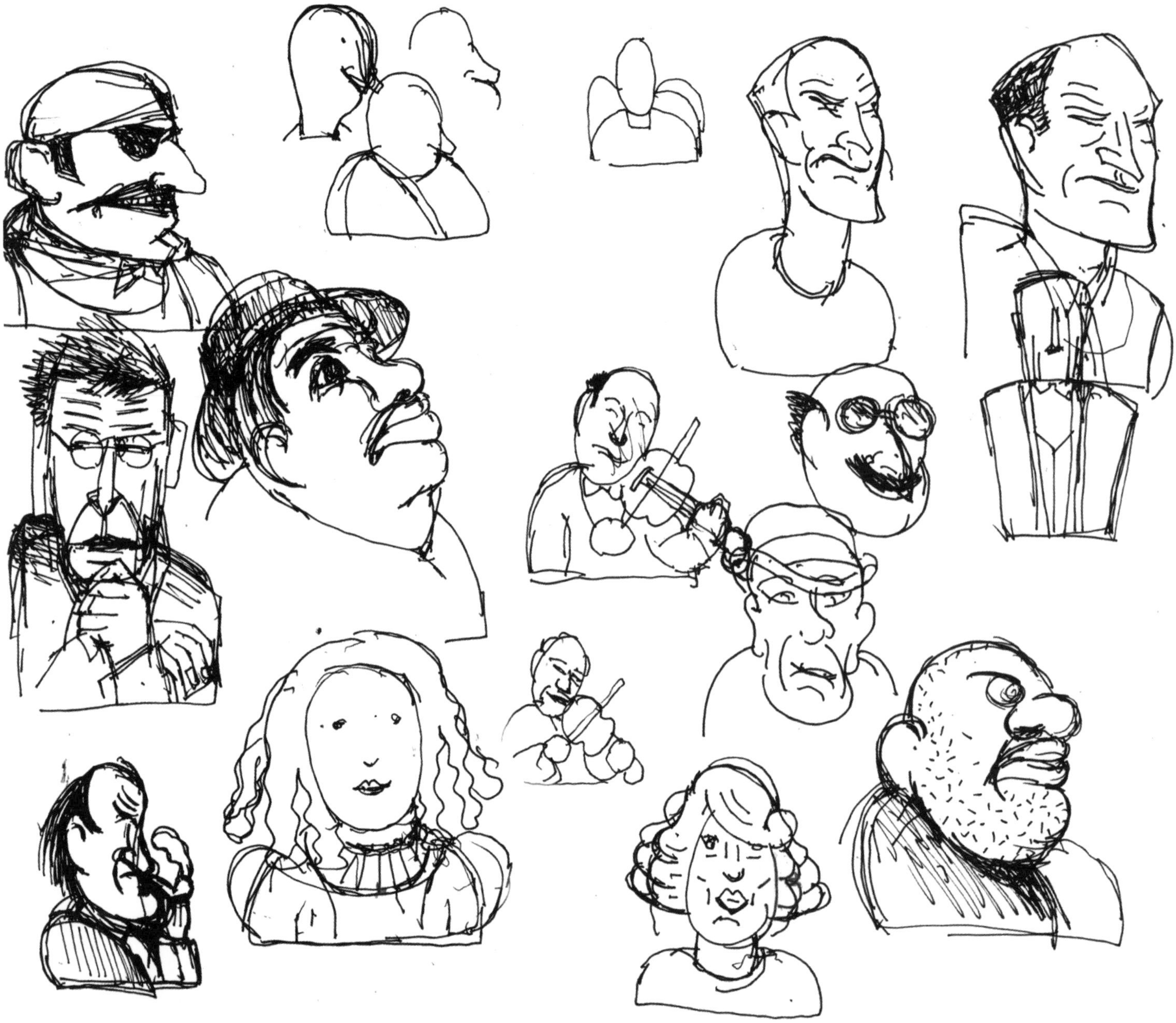

SEYMOUR CHWAST

Seymour Chwast, the co-founder with Milton Glaser (see page 156) of the legendary Push Pin Studios in New York in 1954, who is still actively illustrating, designing, and producing children's books, usually lets his art speak for itself. However, making art is not only his voice – for Chwast, it is tantamount to breathing. He is constantly making images, whether on canvas, in metal, on paper, or with the computer, and everywhere else too. He puts a blank book in his suitcase every time he travels, whether for business or pleasure, and the odds are that it will be filled by the time he returns home.

Since Chwast has probably never touched a camera, he keeps notebooks so that he can "sketch friends and colleagues in restaurants, sometimes to avoid boredom, but often to break the ice and stir conversation; also to sketch interesting buildings and typography." He has also sketched ideas that have come to him in restaurants in foreign places when he is with his wife, designer Paula Scher.

The images here from 2007 are mostly ideas for books. Rather than drawing for its own sake, his goal is to make as many published works as possible. He loves to make visual puns, of which these are but a few.

ILLUSTRATION

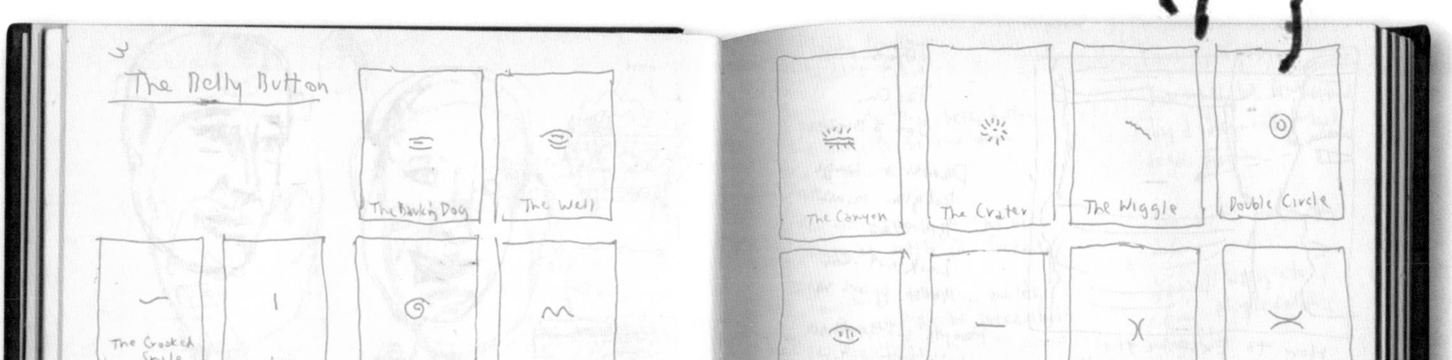

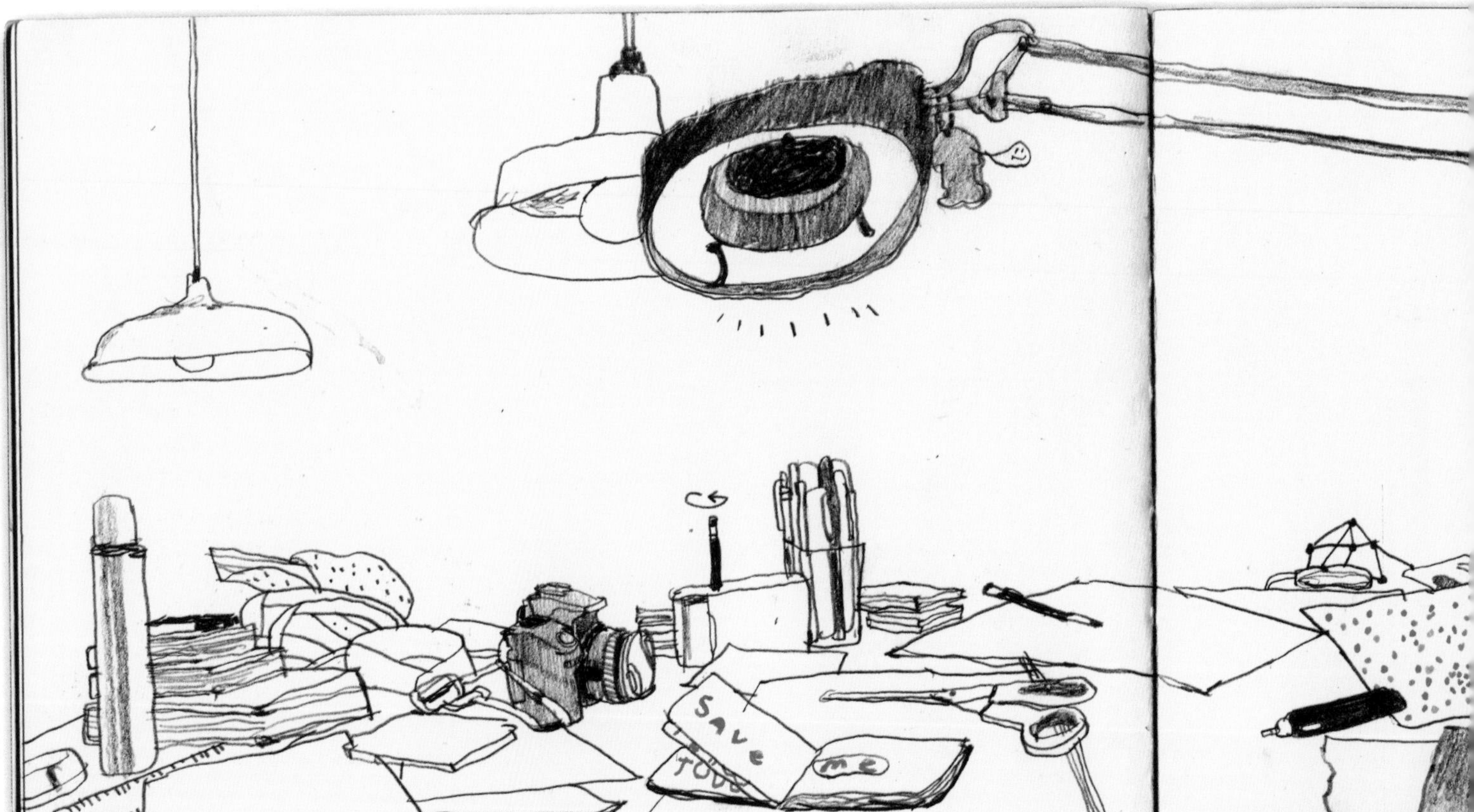
Save
me

JOSH COCHRAN

Josh Cochran, a conceptual illustrator with expressionistic flair, uses sketchbooks functionally: to try out new ideas, work out compositions, doodle, rant, and draw from life. "Often the marks I make in my sketchbook are much more raw and off-the-cuff than anything I do with my finished work. There is a certain amount of spontaneity that I really love, which is hard to replicate anywhere else," he confides.

On a personal note, he adds, "Most of these were done around December 2009, right before my dad passed away, and I think they capture this particularly intense moment of my life." Indeed, there is a solemn mood here that is not found in his more exuberant illustrations.

Cochran admits that there is "not too much of a theme. I like to be pretty free-flowing when I start a new page. Whatever mood I'm in, I'll put it down. Usually I am working out ideas for assignments or whatever I'm obsessed with at that moment."

He works in four different sketchbooks at a time. "I try to have one with me at all times but sometimes I'll forget it in the studio or leave one at home, so they can be a bit scattered."

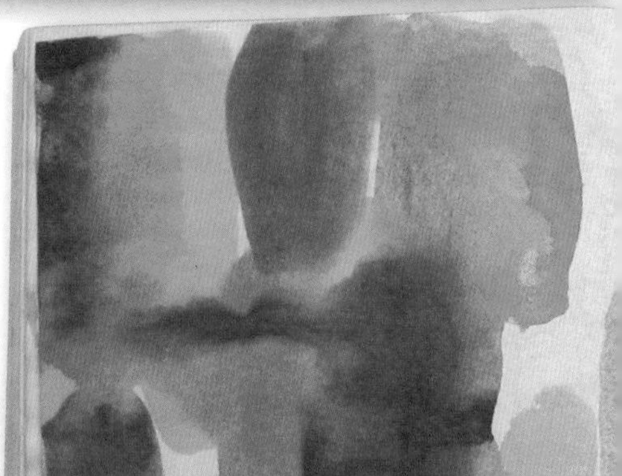

PAUL COX *FRANCE*

French illustrator Paul Cox has kept sketchbooks since childhood. “I prefer to draw in books rather than on loose pages. It was the pleasure of making books that appealed to me.”

His books are, first and foremost, “what Le Corbusier called the ‘daily record’ (*la continuité quotidienne*),” he says. “It is a way of not losing the thread of my life.” And he tries to devote at least one hour a day to drawing in them. “Whatever ideas pass through my head are set down. This is where I keep memories, research of forms and colors, things I see throughout the day, and also observational drawings and portraits. It is a very free type of experience, without any direct connection to projects – I have dossiers for client work. There is not much writing in them, as I have special books for my notes. I never went to art school so my books are like my schooling.”

Cox notes “the freedom, as if I was singing in the shower. But this is an attitude I try to keep in my work in general. There is an absence of inhibition as well as the feeling that I have to do it well. And I hope this carries over to my professional life.”

Sea Baptism – Easter Sunday –
Negril

Verandah

Mark & Jo

PAUL COX *UK*

London-based illustrator Paul Cox's oldest extant sketchbook dates from 1972, when he was fifteen. His books are mainly visual diaries recording responses to various environments: figures and architecture, gestures and atmosphere. "Drawing in a sketchbook immediately connects me with a new location while I am away from the comfort of my studio," he notes.

He also uses a sketchbook "to warm up my drawing fluency before I start working on my larger drawings. It sharpens my responses and speeds up my hand–eye coordination." Cox finds sketchbook work a useful tool in developing images that balance figures, interiors, and architecture from observation. Much of his work is location drawing. "This always presents challenges, particularly working in busy urban environments on a large scale. A smaller book enables me to be more private," he says. "I often draw figures when they are unaware of my intent. However, a couple I was drawing once on a bus missed their stop so that I could finish my work. They waited to see the drawing and then for the bus to turn around to return them to where they wanted to get off. I have since developed more subtle ways of not being noticed!"

MICHAEL PATRICK CRONAN

Michael Patrick Cronan, a San Franciscan graphic and clothing designer, started using sketchbooks while traveling on a hiatus from school. "I kept a book because I couldn't afford a camera and film," he says. When later he could afford a camera, he photographed everything. But, he adds, "after a while I began to realize that I wasn't actually seeing things, so I went back to a sketchbook. I am sure I was annoying when I was photographing everything, and probably more interesting when I was making sketches." These days, he uses both. "The camera is for documenting and the sketchbook is for taking the time to draw something to understand it visually."

Most quick notes in his sketchbooks refer to much more than the sum of the words and scribbles. They represent a series of thoughts, feelings and pictures in shorthand. "Everything is easily recalled, even when I look at them years later. The only theme is the wildly different kinds of design challenges that come my way, one after another."

Within Cronan's fifty sketchbooks, "Very little editing takes place. The ratio of signal to noise is low. Some signal, good ideas, and a great deal of noise. No idea is scribbled out but potentially good ideas get circled. Finished work is just that: finished, where the signal to noise ratio is hopefully very high."

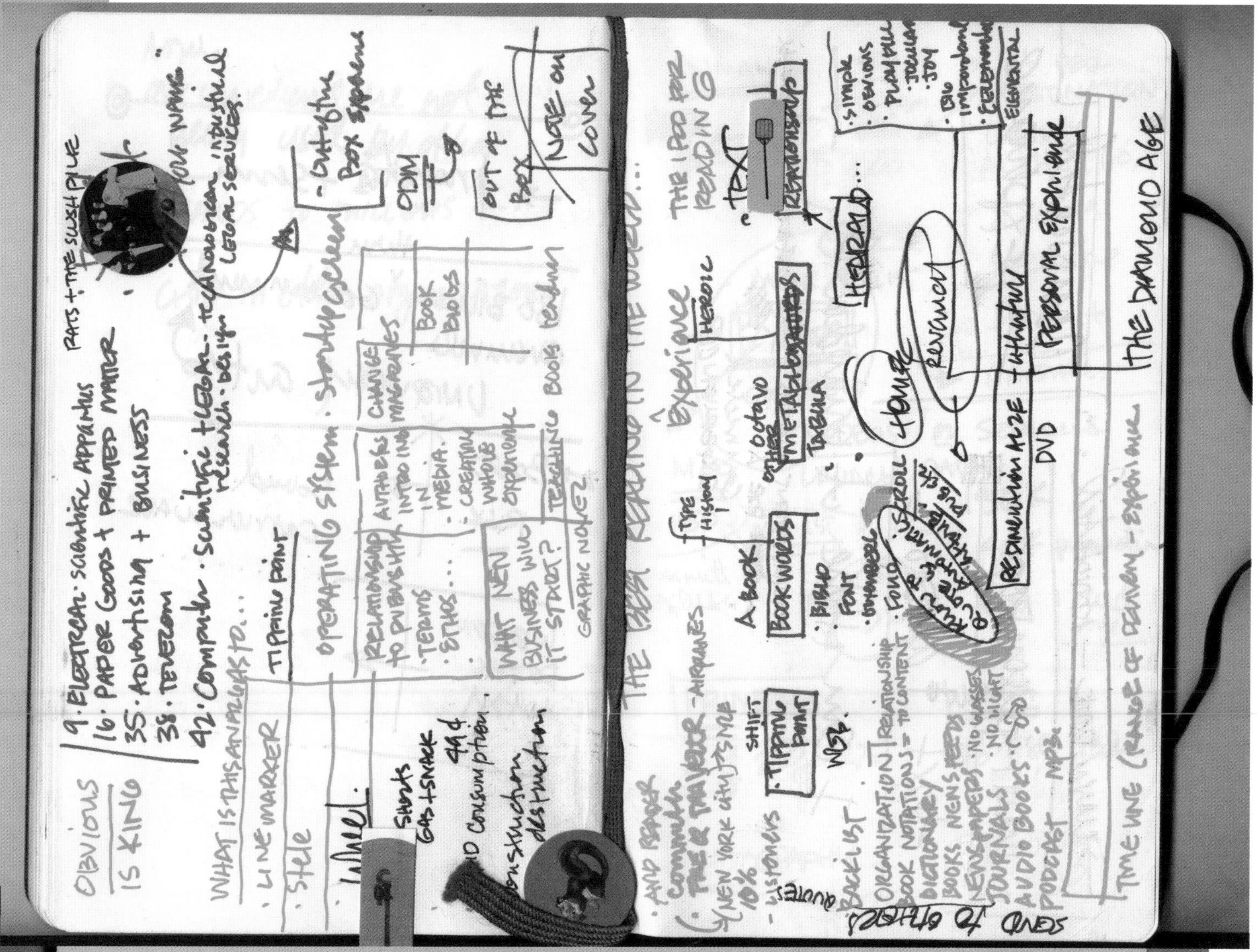

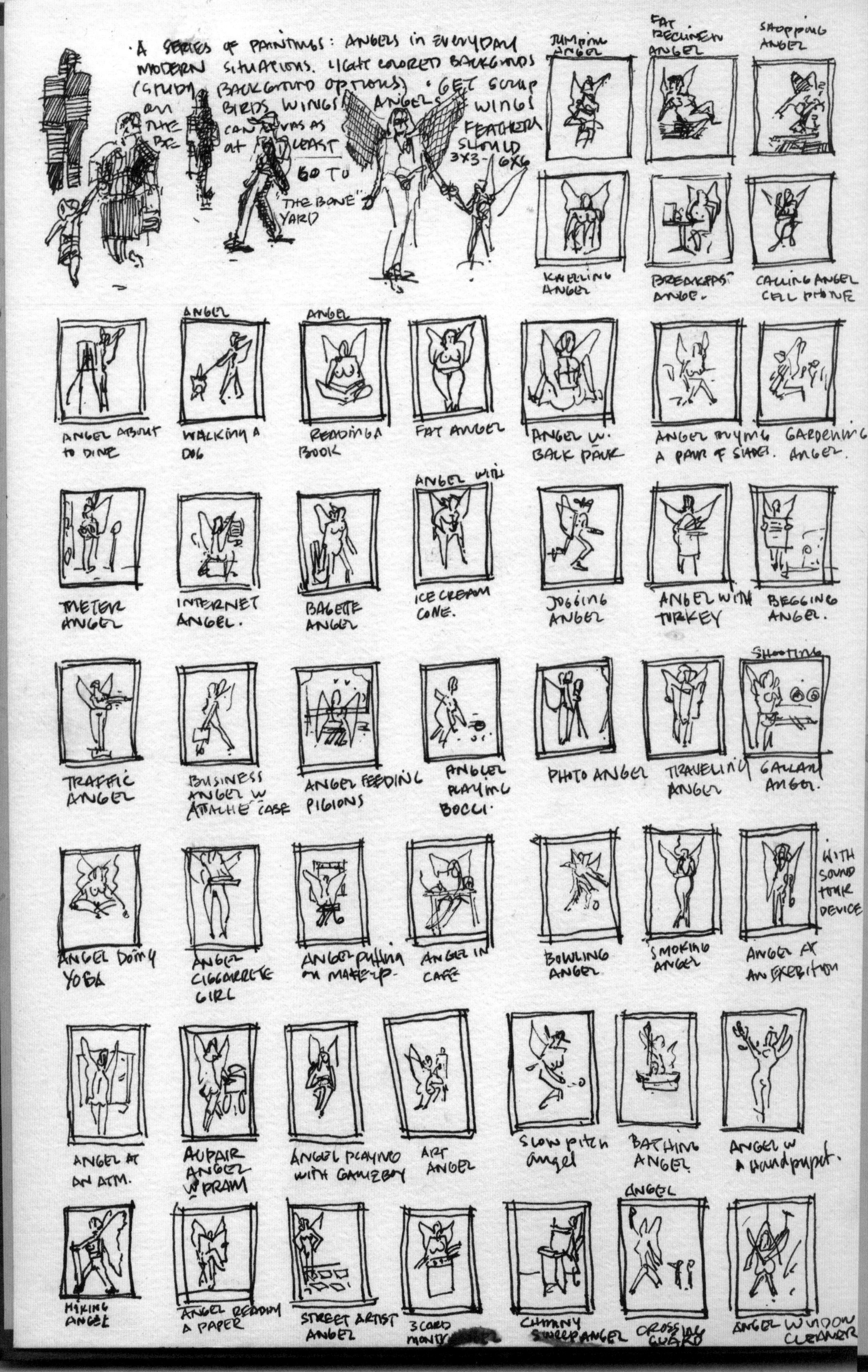

A SERIES OF PAINTINGS: ANGELS IN EVERYDAY MODERN SITUATIONS. LIGHT COLORED BACKGROUNDS (STUDY BACKGROUND OPTIONS). GET SCRAP ON THE BIRDS WINGS ANGELS WINGS FEATHERS
BE CANVAS AS AT LEAST SHOULD 3X3 - 6X6
GO TO "THE BONE" YARD
JUMPING ANGEL
FAT RECLINEN ANGEL
SHOPPING ANGEL
KNEELING ANGEL
BREAKFAST ANGEL.
CALLING ANGEL CELL PHONE
ANGEL ABOUT TO DINE
ANGEL WALKING A DOG
ANGEL READING A BOOK
FAT ANGEL
ANGEL W. BACK PACK
ANGEL BUYING A PAIR OF SHOES.
GARDENING ANGEL.
THEATER ANGEL
INTERNET ANGEL.
BAGETTE ANGEL
ANGEL WITH ICE CREAM CONE.
JOGGING ANGEL
ANGEL WITH TURKEY
BEGGING ANGEL.
TRAFFIC ANGEL
BUSINESS ANGEL W ATTACHE CASE
ANGEL FEEDING PIGIONS
ANGEL PLAYING BOCCI.
PHOTO ANGEL
TRAVELING ANGEL
SHOOTING GALLARY ANGEL.
ANGEL DOING YOGA
ANGEL CIGGARRETE GIRL
ANGEL PUTTING ON MAKE-UP.
ANGEL IN CAFE
BOWLING ANGEL
SMOKING ANGEL
ANGEL AT AN EXEBITION WITH SOUND TOUR DEVICE
ANGEL AT AN ATM.
AUPAIR ANGEL W PRAM
ANGEL PLAYING WITH GAMEBOY
ART ANGEL
Slow pitch angel
BATHING ANGEL
ANGEL W A handpuppet.
HIKING ANGEL
ANGEL READIN A PAPER
STREET ARTIST ANGEL
3 CARD MONT
CHIMNY SWEEP ANGEL
ANGEL CROSSING GUARD
ANGEL WINDOW CLEANER

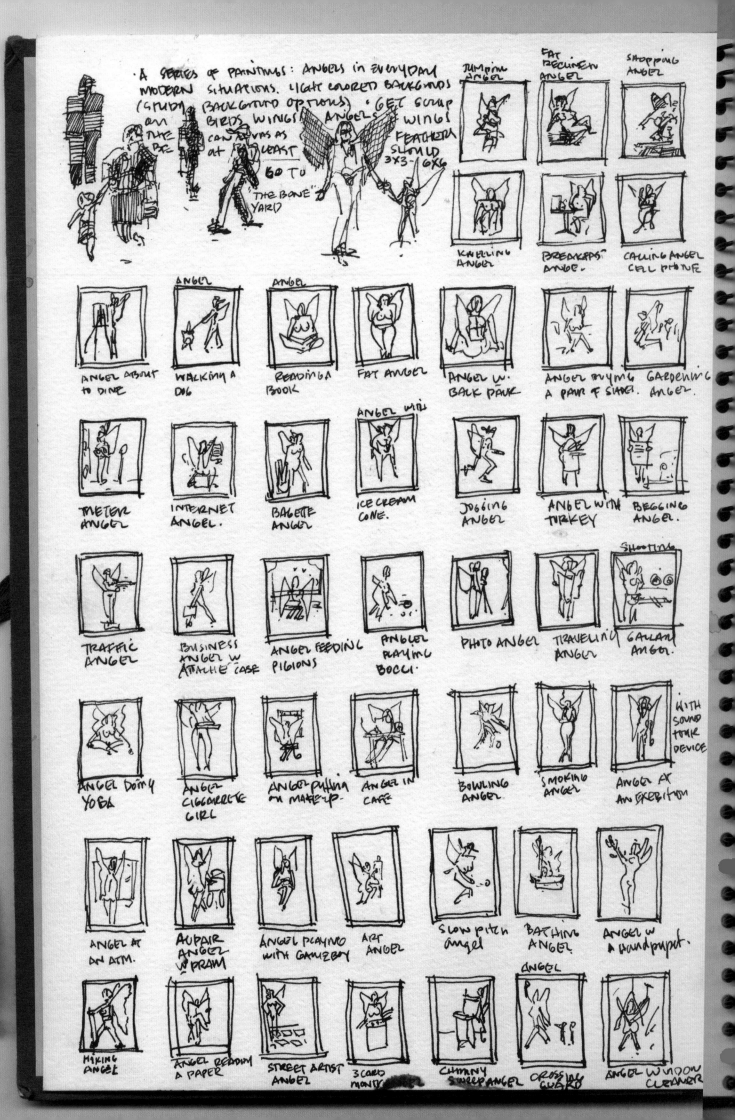

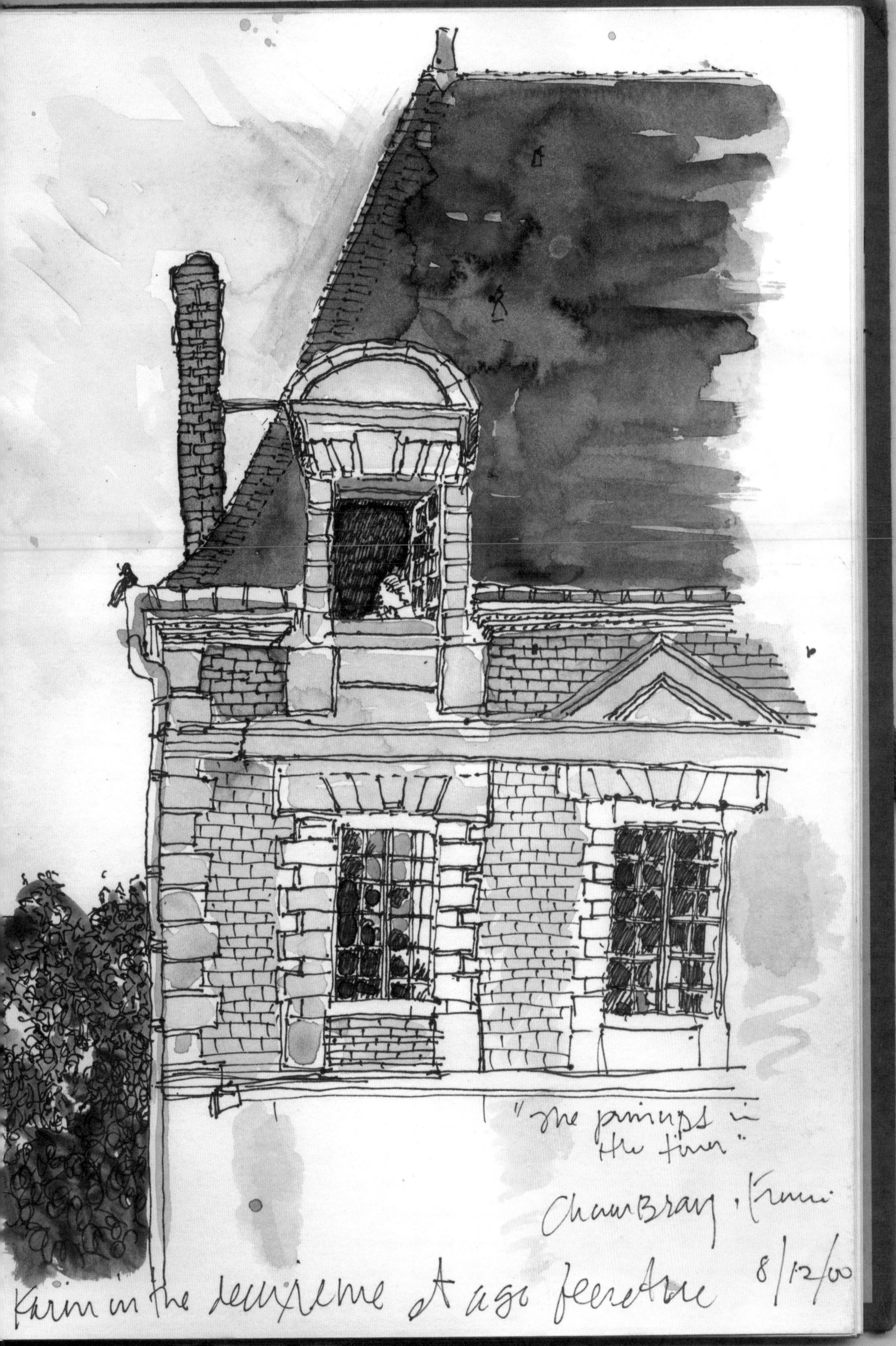
"the princess in the tower"
Chambray, France
8/12/00

EUROTRASH,
CASH TO BURN,
SMELLS LIKE
CHEAP COLOGNE
AND SPERM.

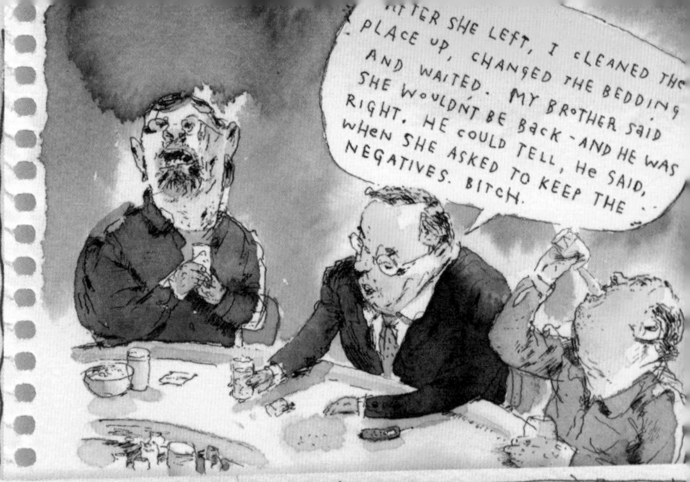
AFTER SHE LEFT, I CLEANED THE PLACE UP, CHANGED THE BEDDING AND WAITED. MY BROTHER SAID SHE WOULDN'T BE BACK - AND HE WAS RIGHT. HE COULD TELL, HE SAID, WHEN SHE ASKED TO KEEP THE NEGATIVES. BITCH.

HAVE YOU SEEN THE REMOTE?

JOHN CUNEO

John Cuneo, a humorous artist and stand-up comedian, has kept sketchbooks for a couple of decades. "I work in them for a number of reasons, but not having 'purpose' is probably one of the most appealing," he chuckles. "I'm almost always disappointed with my finished work, and getting back into a sketchbook helps me reconnect with the fundamental pleasure of making a line on paper, which is where the whole thing gets started for many of us."

Like an athlete, Cuneo uses his books to get limber before a job. "My stuff is usually just done to relax, or practice, or loosen up," he says. "I really admire the folks who have a more disciplined approach." He cites fellow comic illustrator Barry Blitt (see page 54) as an example. "I should probably doodle less and emulate his approach more."

Cuneo enjoys working in his books. "Some older books are a deliberate effort to 'draw myself' out of some stylistic influences and bad habits. One is mostly filled with caricatures of writers, while another has a bunch of interiors – I was trying to figure out how to put figures inside a room convincingly. There are lots with nothing but sexual stuff, and other, more recent ones, with random little characters, animals, and drawings from photos all crammed onto pages along with bad poetry, assignment notes, and doomed ideas for children's books."

69 Speare Rd
Woodstock, NY 12498-1119

BREATH INTO IT..
GIDDY UP.
FREUD
WEATHERAUTHORITY
CRAFTADVISORY
FIXTHIS
I'M REALLY FEELING A CONNECTION HERE.
HOW'S THE WIFE?

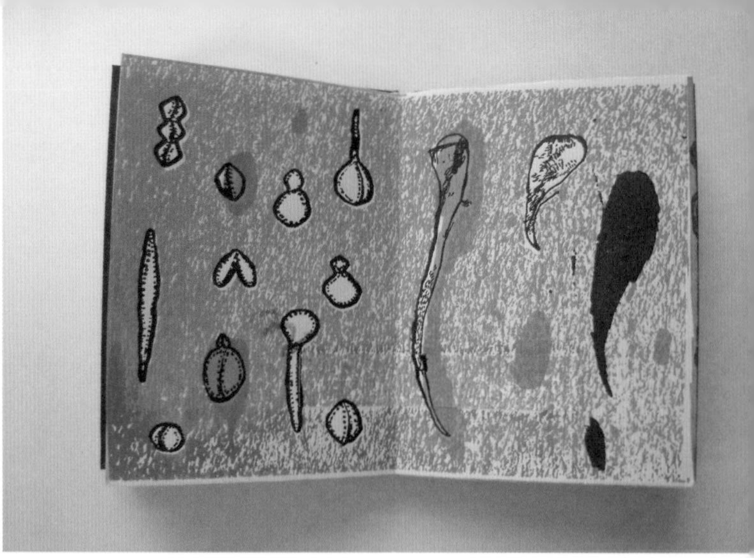

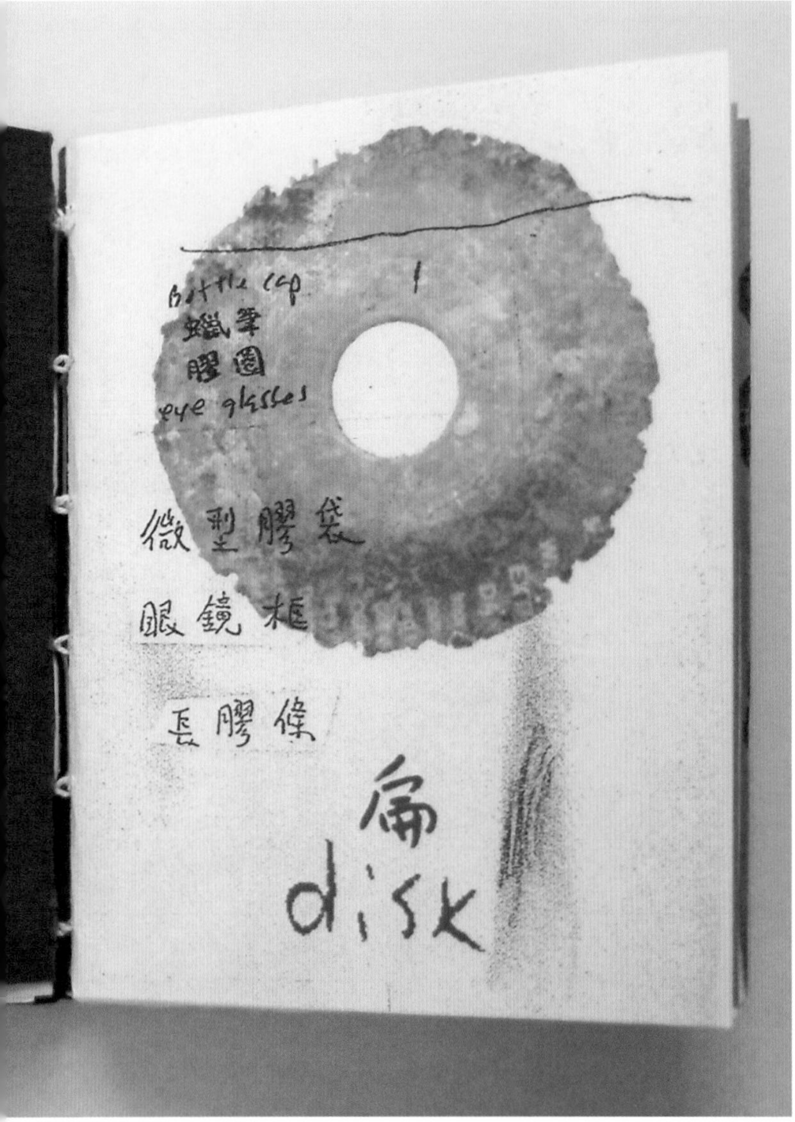

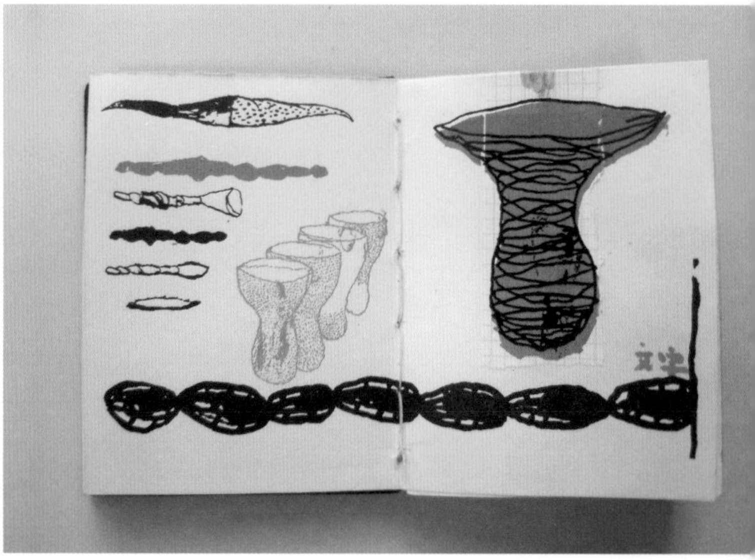

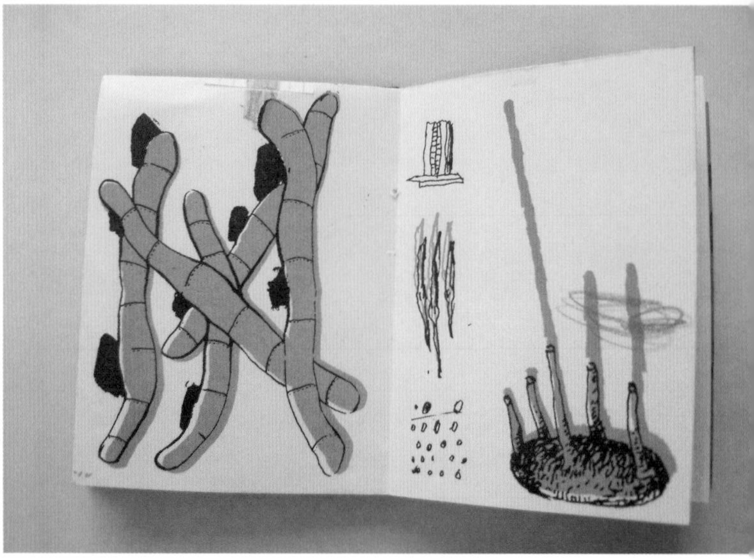

HENRIK DRESCHER

Henrik Drescher, who alternately lives in Denmark, China, Canada, and the United States, has been keeping sketchbooks since he was seventeen years old. He thinks of them as his "file cabinet of ideas." Since Drescher's work is so loose and ad hoc, there is no real distinction from his finished pieces. It is more of a symbiotic relationship where each part, according to Drescher, "spills into" the other. "The sketchbook pages become part of the finished pictures. The finished pictures get funneled into the sketchbooks."

Drescher does not feel that the images are unusual; what he does find remarkable is "that they get made in spite of, and because of, my peripatetic life." He has so many sketchbooks that he has stopped counting.

"The inherent themes in my sketchbooks are categorization and pseudo-science," he says. The books are also windows onto what Drescher will do next as an artist and author. In a way, they predict his authorial future.

FORGOTTEN BOMB
infidels
Salon
PICTURE MECHANIC
PLAYBOY
THAT'LL TEACH YOU TO QUESTION CREATIONISM
HOLY BIBLE
26 SEP 2001
MERCHANDISE AND SERVICES
OFFE
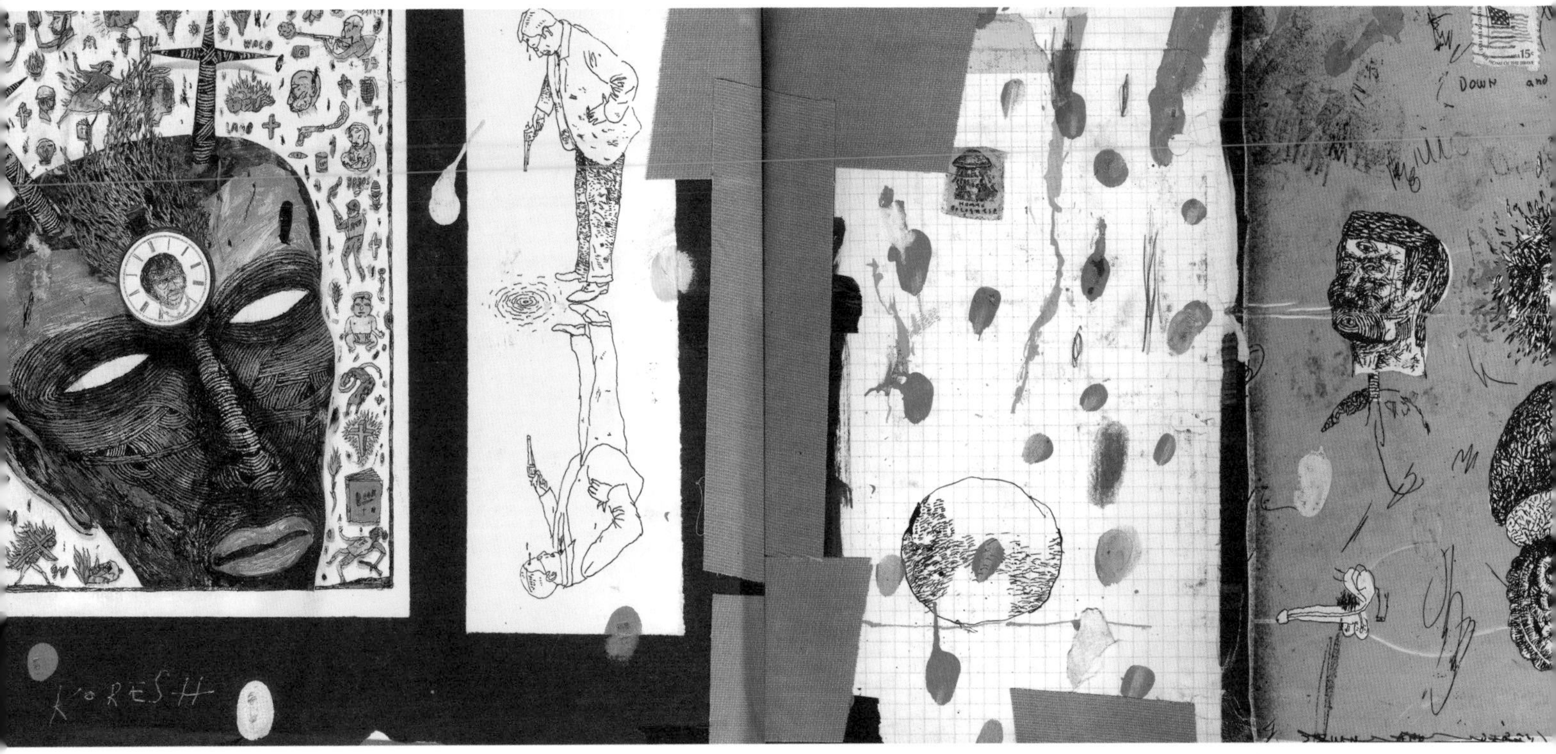
KORESH
DOWN and
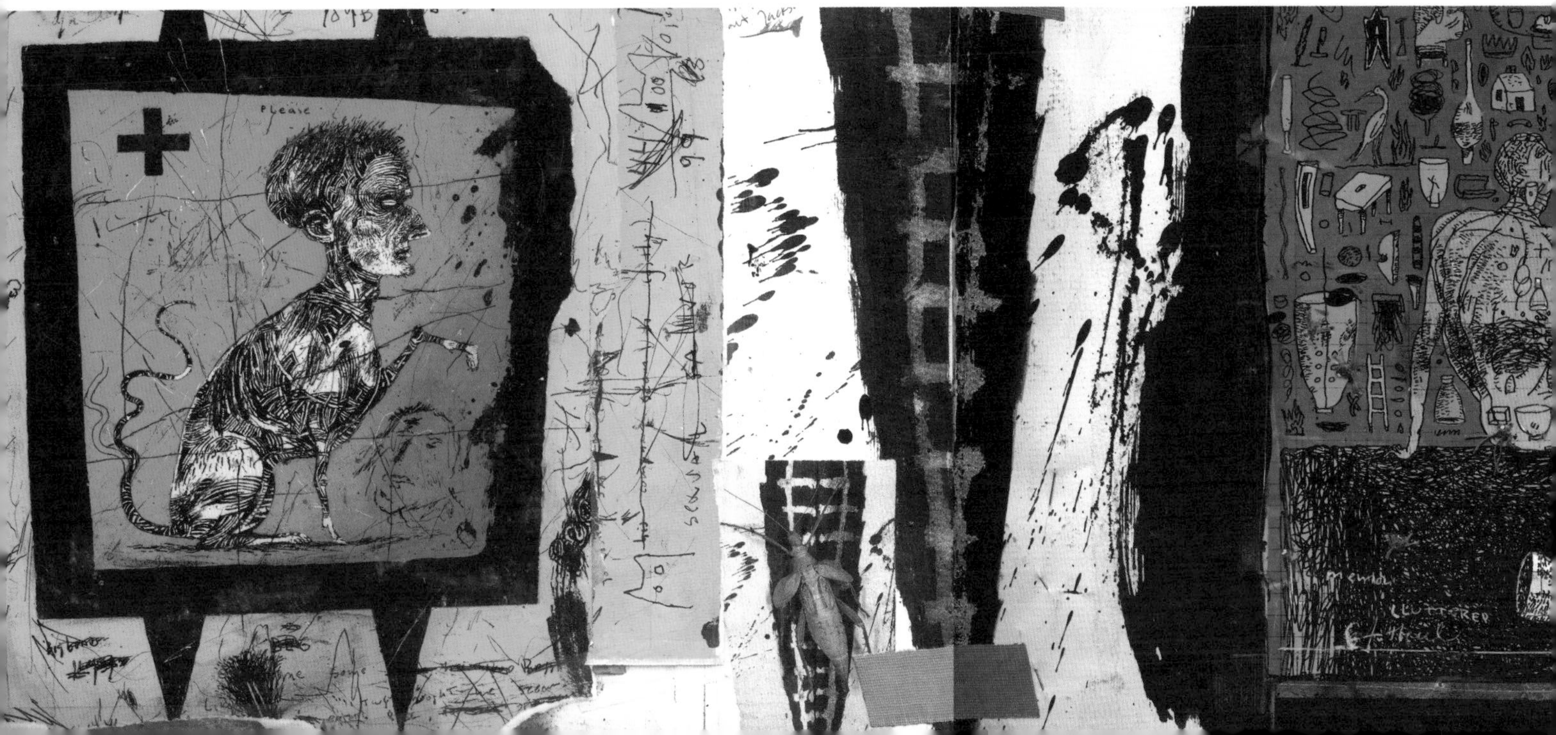
Please

WEDNESDAY
im achild of that which im a child of

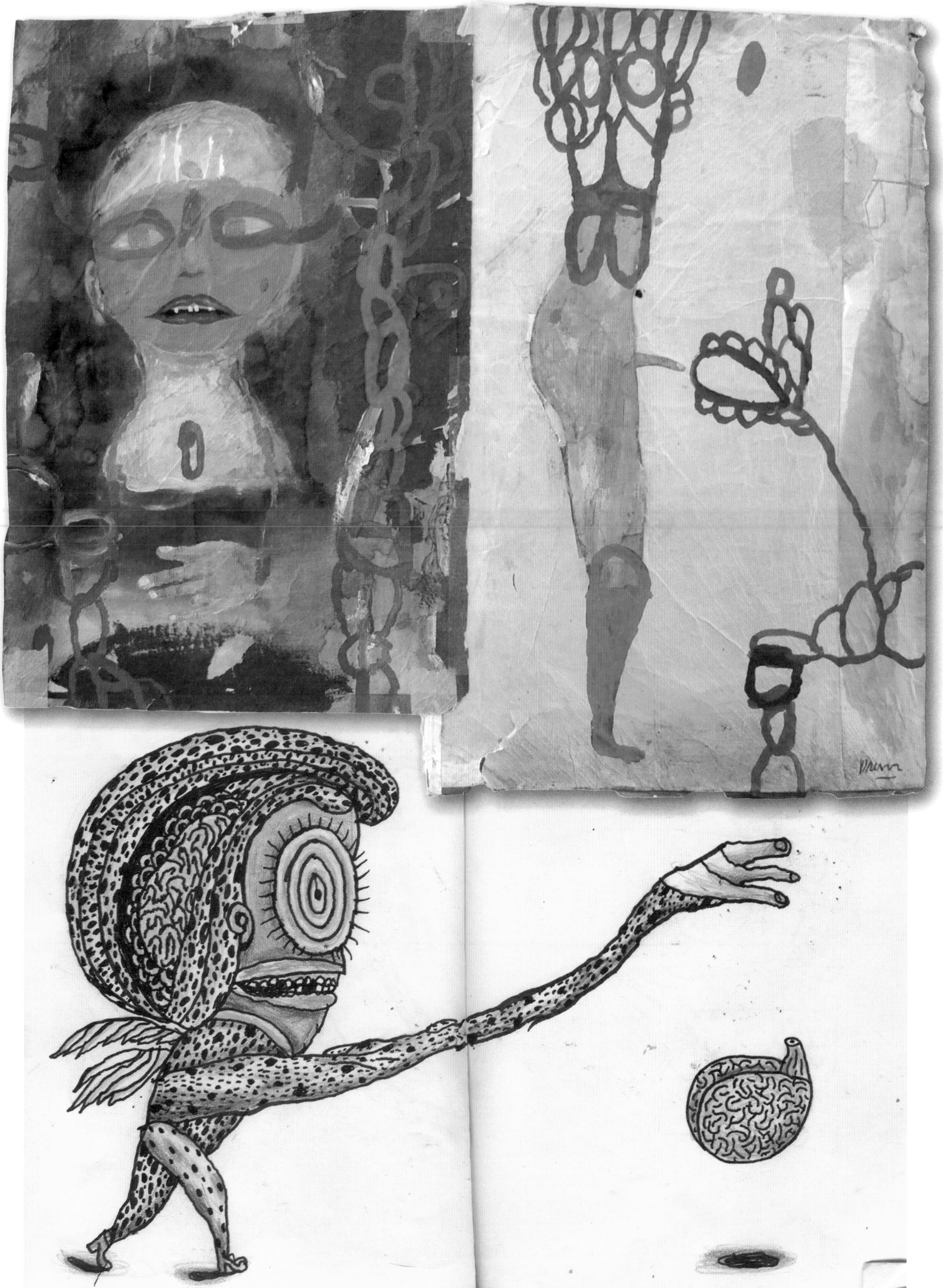

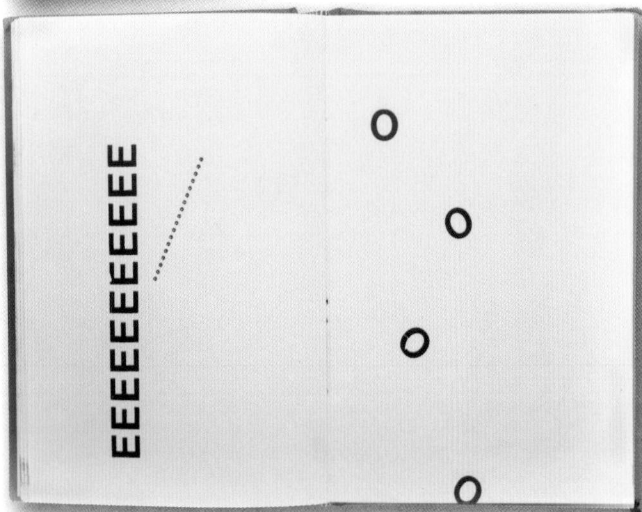

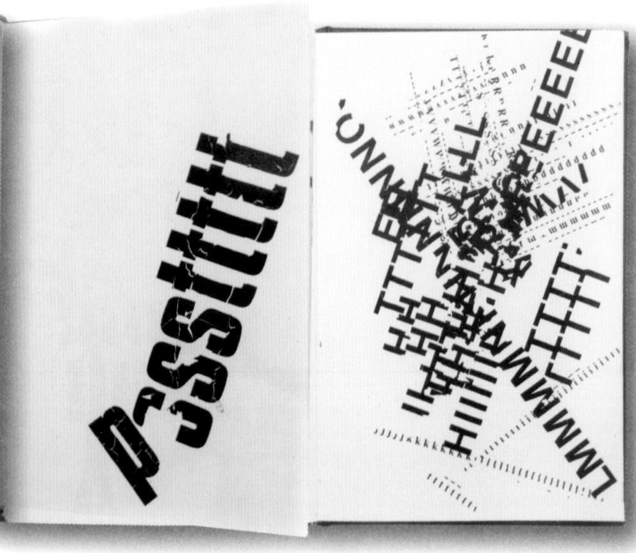

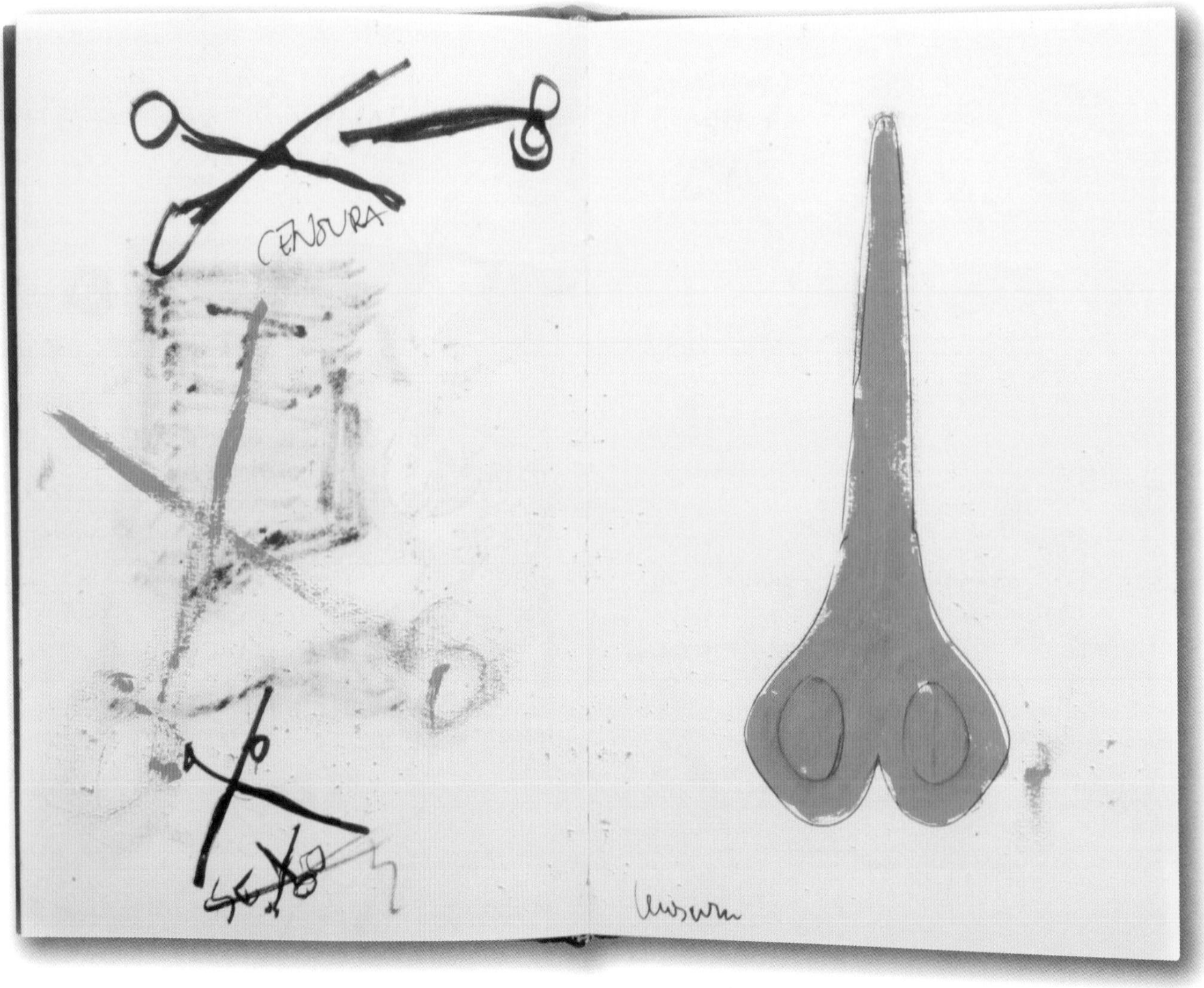
CENSURA

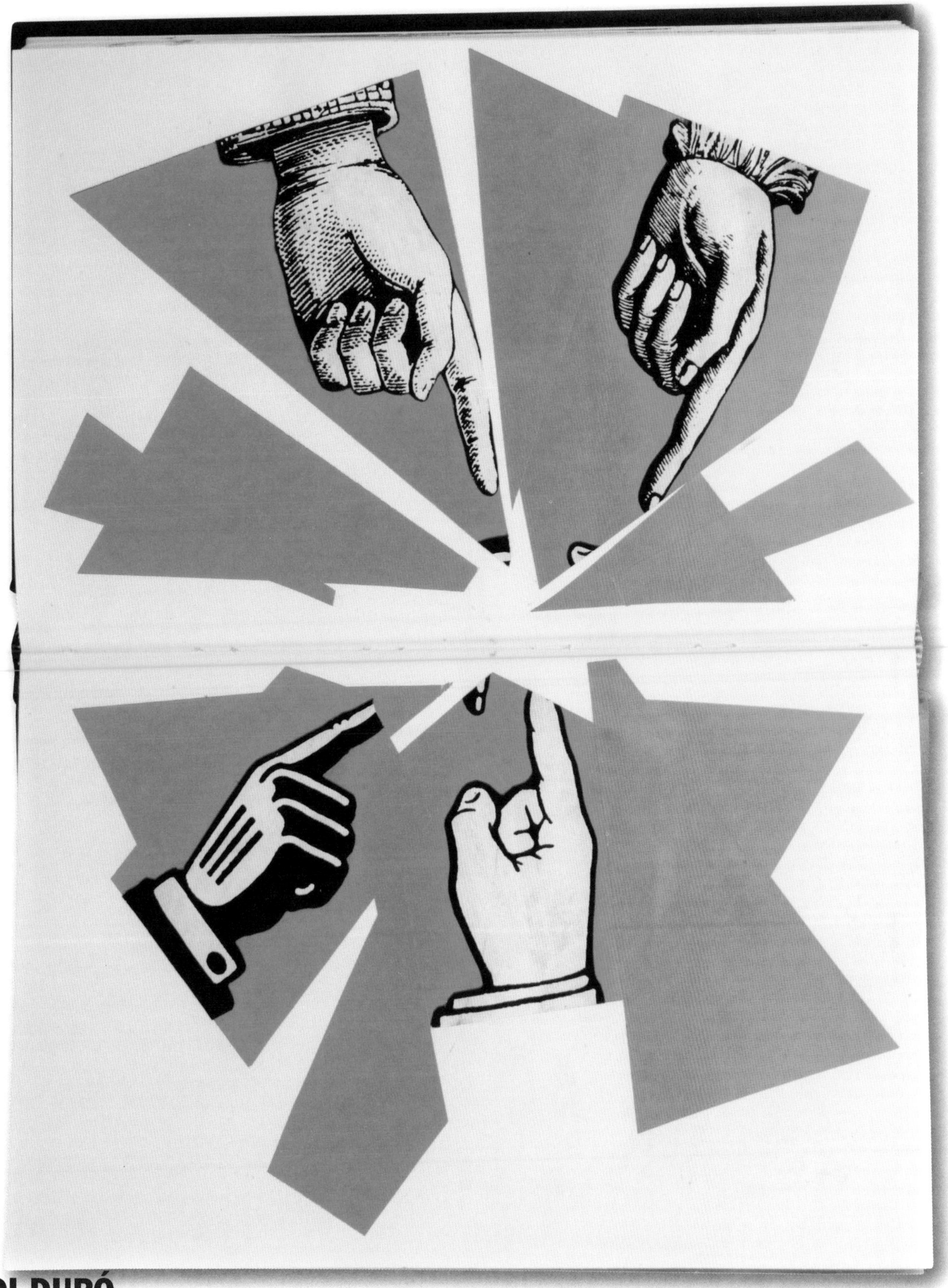

JORDI DURÓ

Barcelona-based designer Jordi Duró is a maven of Spanish design history and ephemera. He likes to collect artifacts of all kinds and incorporate them into his work. Mostly, they are thrown into boxes, but sketchbooking has become a convenient means of storing and sorting. "I have gone back to keeping a scrapbook," he reports, "but this time the books are made out of loose cardboard squares, which are easier to layer. The last books were hard to close with so much stuff pasted inside them."

One cannot have books that are hard to close, after all. What's more, Duró likes to "keep track of ideas, to experiment with different media and, oddly enough, keep track of the concerts I attended." He is a music maven, too.

These books are from the mid-1980s to the late 1990s. "I was living in the United States, so there are a lot of cut-outs of found type that was very exotic to me," says Duró, who adds that his books are a "constant experiment with composition and typography."

In his twenty-one books, Duró says he was surprised to see a few pieces directly related to Spanish news of the time. "I suppose a lot of them were the reaction to very personal emotions ... so spontaneity would probably be the main theme of my books."

STASYS EIDRIGEVICIUS

Stasys Eidrigevicius, Lithuanian-born Polish designer, painter, and illustrator, whose work is filled with Surrealist quirks and tics, is a perpetual image-maker. Since he is constantly drawing, the sketchbook is a source of solace as well as nourishment. "I have made sketches from the beginning of my creation," he says, "from 1968 in Kaunas, to finishing Art School in Vilnius, through to the present." The sheer number of books – estimated at over 300 – in his collection would probably make most artists seem like slackers.

The books are at once laboratories and storehouses. They are used "to find ideas for my work," he says, "and fix what, for me, is important in real life. They are also there for me to make notes of my poetry."

The books represent Eidrigevicius at his "most free, independent, and personal. Any time, anywhere," he poetically adds. "They are like my mini studio in an airplane, train, or hotel. They are my theater and cinema."

The images in these books, which date from the 1970s to the present, derive from his travels throughout Europe. But the theme that recurs is also the most common element of his art: men in face masks, hiding, waiting, emoting.

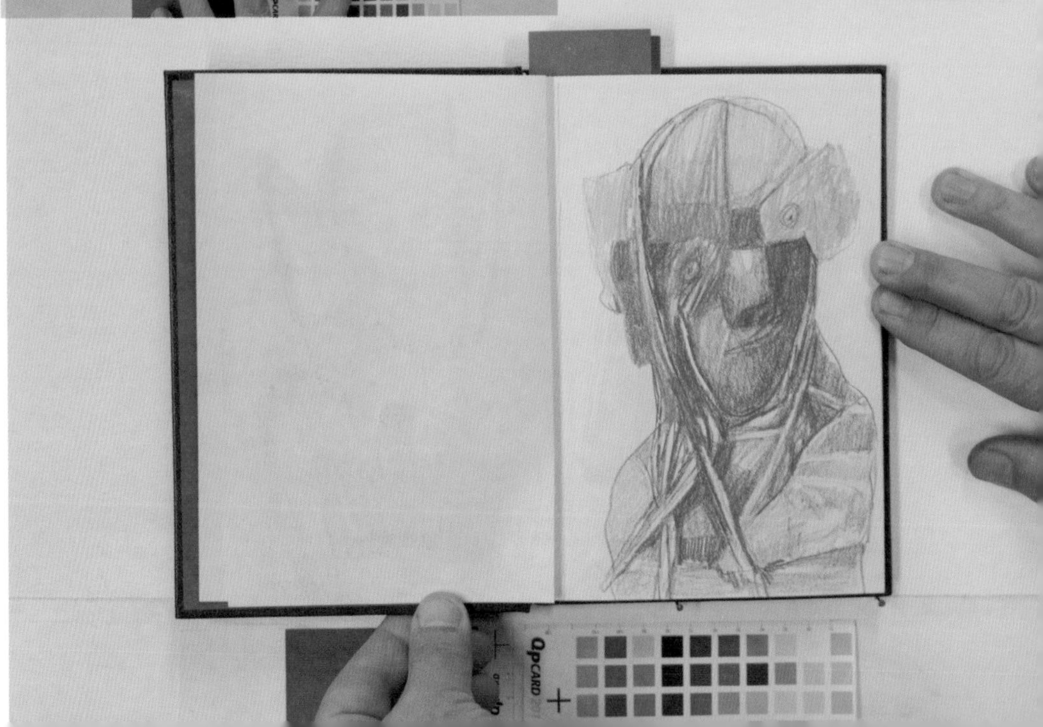

Japan
England
QPCARD

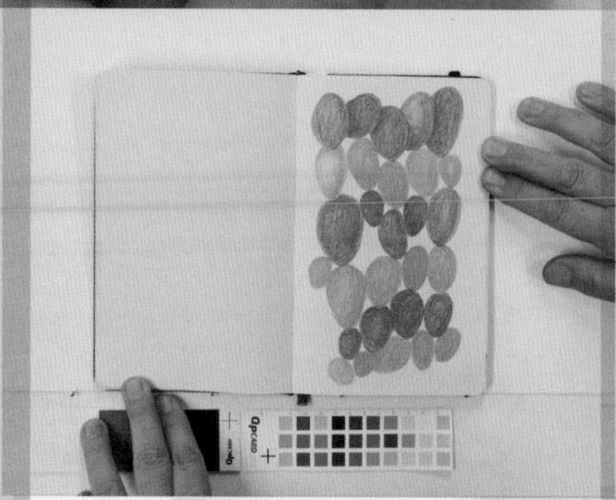

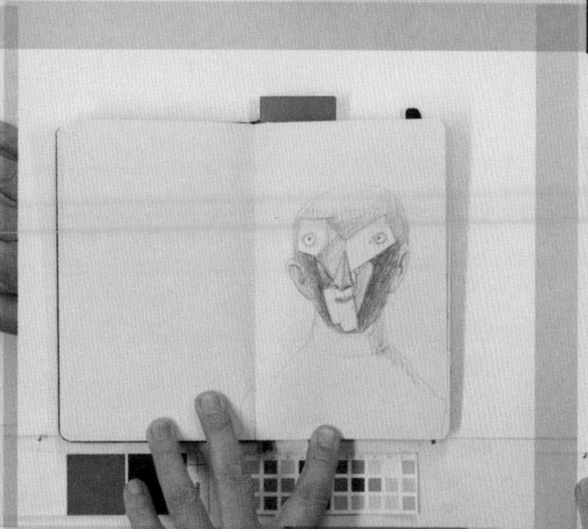

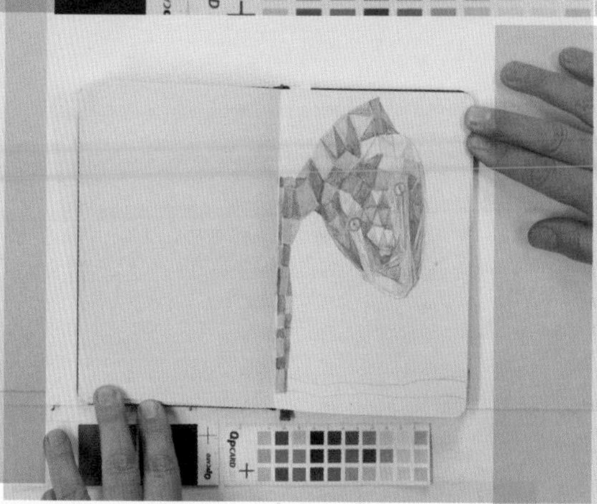

QPCARD

GRAHAM ELLIOTT

Graham Elliott, British-born, Brooklyn-based music video designer and producer, is a fiend when it comes to keeping sketchbooks. He started when he was ten, as if he knew that someday he would need all the imagery that was floating around in his head.

Yes, he uses them, as he says, "to collect creative bursts, to be used later in projects," but also "to have a creative outlet when working more corporate projects, especially commercials. A lot of ideas don't make it into the final piece so the sketchbooks act as a reservoir." Reservoir to be sure, yet there is something crazily carnivalesque about them, too. he "feels detached from the work, as if someone else did it, and this is exhilarating." Also, he notes that as the democratization of the moving image marches forward, "I look back at my sketchbooks and realize I can make many of these ideas exist, by myself, with no tech geeks or expensive edit facilities. When many of these books were created over ten years ago, After Effects, Final Cut Pro and digital cameras were no available."

In the 100-plus books that Elliott has made, including those shown here from 2003–9, the inherent theme for him is a "playfulness that is

MARC ENGLISH

Texas-based designer Marc English began his journals in 1968, when "we drove from Boston to Mexico and I recorded the exact minute I first crossed into Texas, hardly knowing I would live here as an adult." But he adds that it is only a sometime thing. "While we may do a sketch or two around the studio, much of the work springs from my head and is then art directed by myself. The rare times when I break out my sketchbook, much of it involves words, not images.

The importance of the journals, says English, is that "I like to think my varied experiences allow for an experiential design, which lets my recollections focus in a certain way. For instance, packaging for Italian pasta for Whole Foods springs from observation, not theory; from being in small-town America as well as small-town Italy. I think it all adds up, and I suppose my photo archives complement my mostly written journals."

Included in these excerpts is a project for an educational group called Alliance Abroad Group (AAG), for which English used an illustration from his journal (not intended for the project) as well as actual covers from his books. Other pages from English's journals over the past few years "are more observations of myself and the situation or circumstances of where I am or going or have been, along with the ephemera I find along the way."

Royaume du Maroc
Ministère des Affaires Culturelles
المملكة المغربية
وزارة الشؤون الثقافية
الصندوق الوطني للعمل الثقافي
Fonds National pour l'Action Culturelle
10 DH
Série A
Droits d'entrée aux Musées, Sites et Monuments Historiques
واجبات رسوم الدخول إلى المتاحف والمواقع والمباني التاريخية
Dahir n° 1-82-332 du 15 Rabia 1er 1403 (31-12-82) Art. 33
N° 5559050
SALON
السهول والمنخفضات
الهضاب والحمادات
الكتل المرتفعة
العروق
النيجر
2286 m
MUSICIANS WITH HUGE MOROCCAN CASTANETS, ABOUT
DRUMS, & A BENDIR, MADE GREAT MUSIC.
IN HEADPHONES WHO WANTED TO SHOW ME
& SQUATTED DOWN AGAINST A WALL TO
WOMAN SITTING ON A CANAR SMA

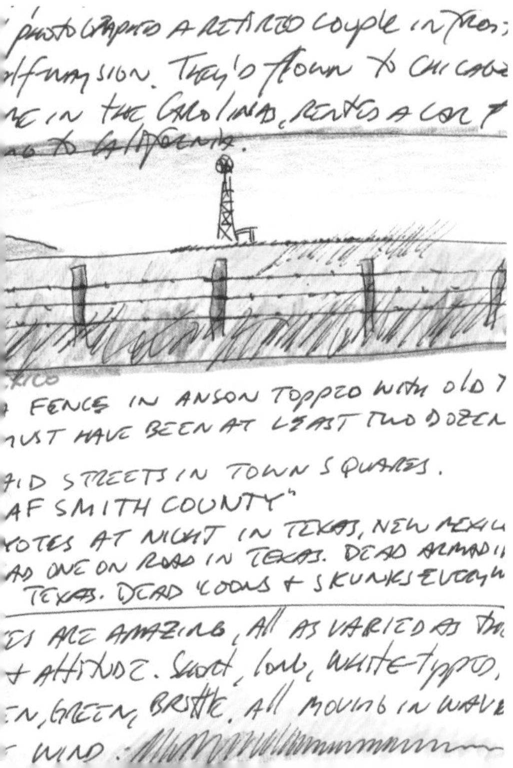

PHOTOGRAPHED A RETIRED COUPLE IN TAOS;
THEY'D FLOWN TO CHICAGO
IN THE CAROLINAS, RENTED A CAR
TO CALIFORNIA.
FENCE IN ANSON TOPPED WITH OLD
MUST HAVE BEEN AT LEAST TWO DOZEN
STREETS IN TOWN SQUARES.
OF SMITH COUNTY"
COYOTES AT NIGHT IN TEXAS, NEW MEXICO
ONE ON ROAD IN TEXAS. DEAD ARMADILLO
TEXAS. DEAD COONS & SKUNKS EVERYWH
ARE AMAZING, ALL AS VARIED AS THE
ATTITUDE. SHORT, LONG, WHITE-TOPPED,
GREEN, BRITTLE. ALL MOVING IN WAVE
WIND

EL SO
RESTAURANTE
TELFS.:950 611 100 - 950 380 216
04118 - SAN JOSÉ - NIJAR (ALMERÍA)
ARA MOL
GARRUC
644 484

ODED EZER

Oded Ezer, an Israeli designer and typographer, has kept a sketchbook since starting his graphic design studies at the Bezalel Academy in Jerusalem. Given all the typographic experimentation that Ezer undertakes, it is inconceivable that he would not be well endowed with sketchbooks.

"I treat it as an extension of my brain," he notes, "as a storage space for unfinished or half-baked ideas. It is also some kind of visual diary. The difference between my ten or so sketchbooks and my finished work is like the difference between an inner conversation with myself and a talk to an audience."

The work is not entirely typographic, but in each image there is a fundamental form that plays a role in his graphic design. The theme in these excerpts from 2003–9 for Ezer is more philosophical than concrete. It is, he says, the "search for the essence of each idea, feel, or shape." But along the way there are messages born of time and place that are waiting to emerge.

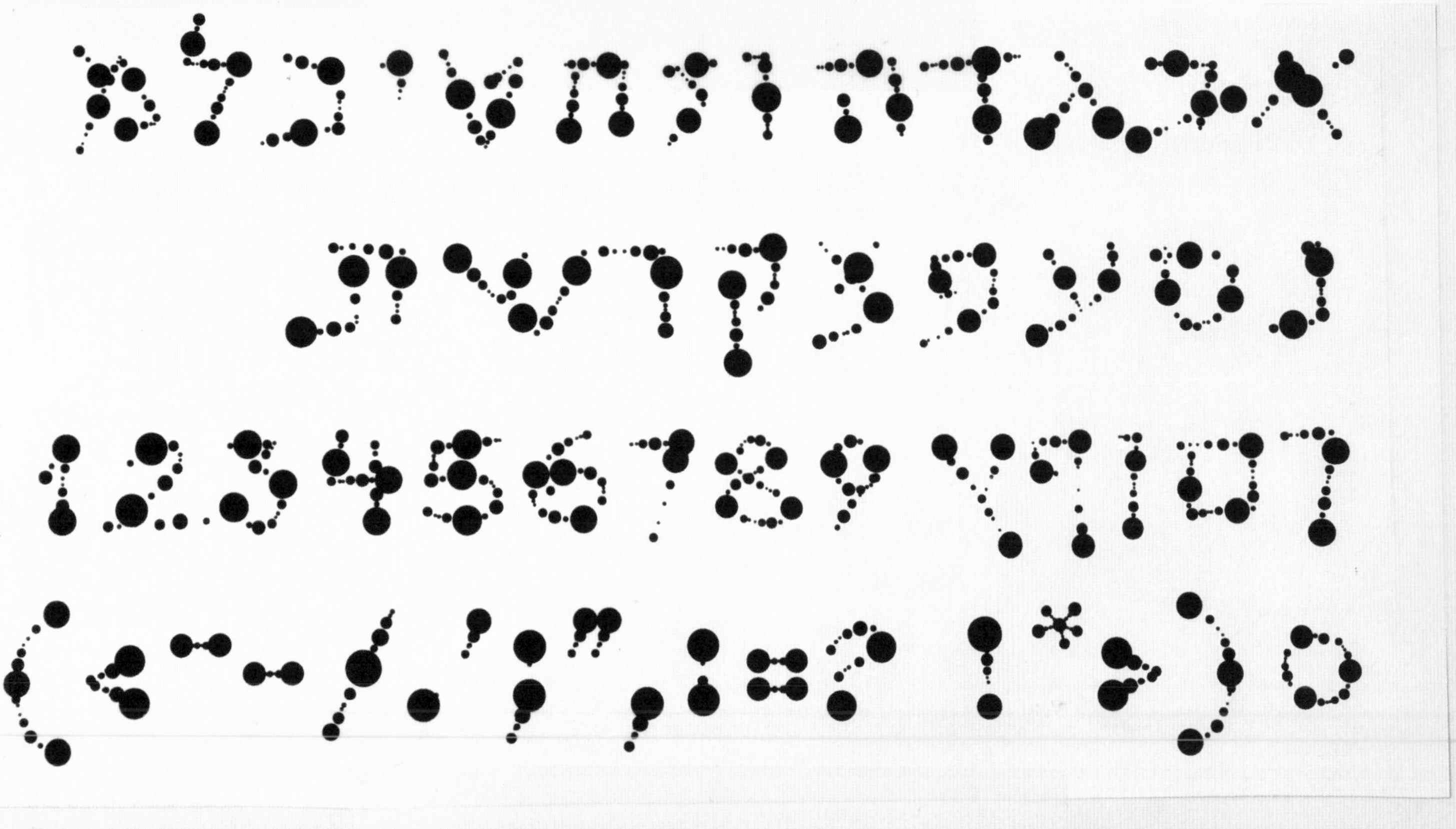
123456789

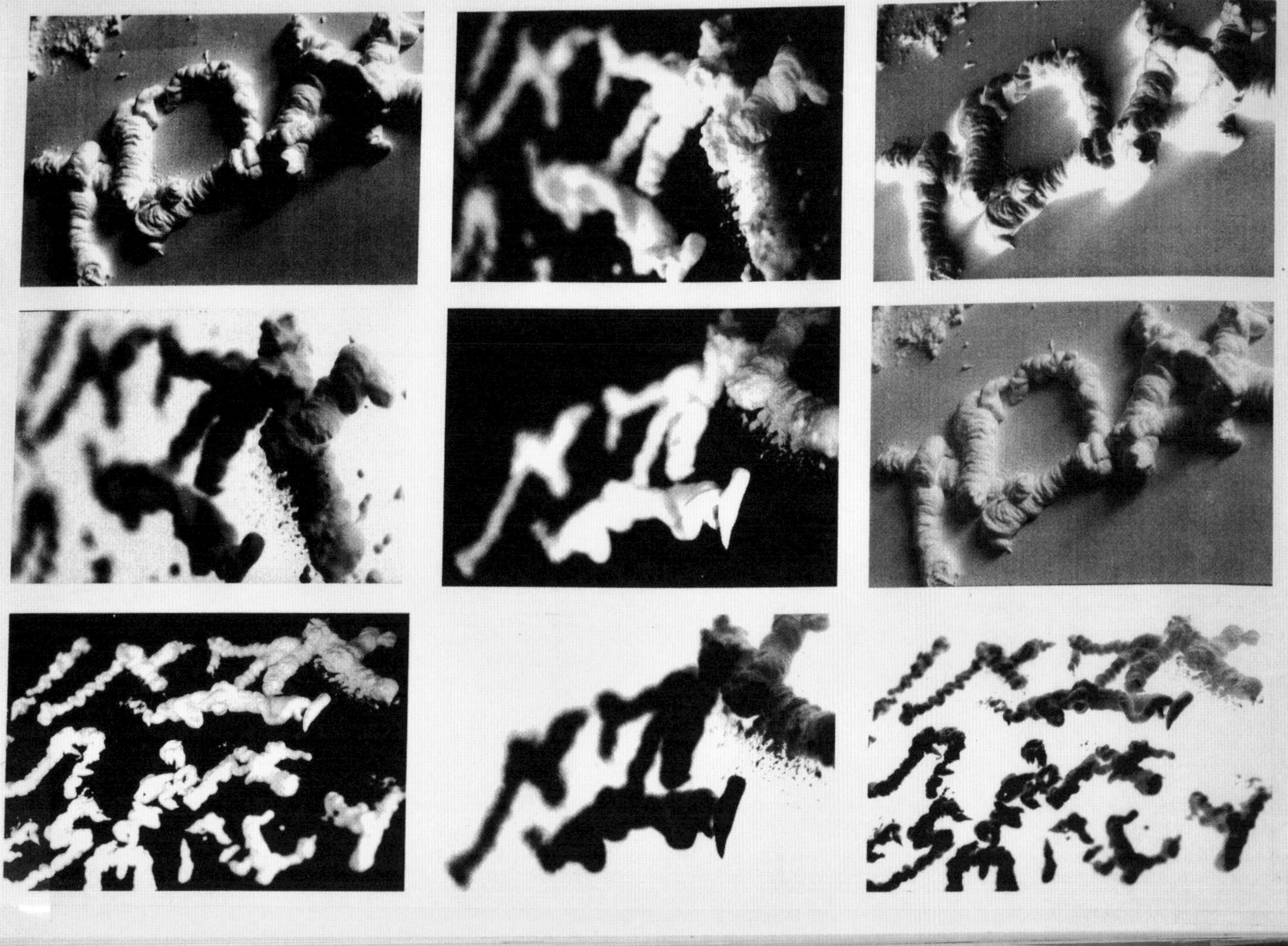

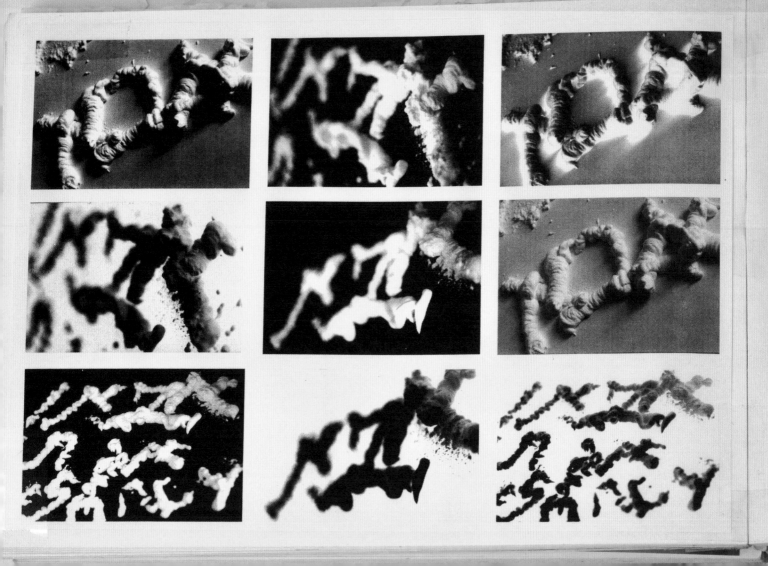

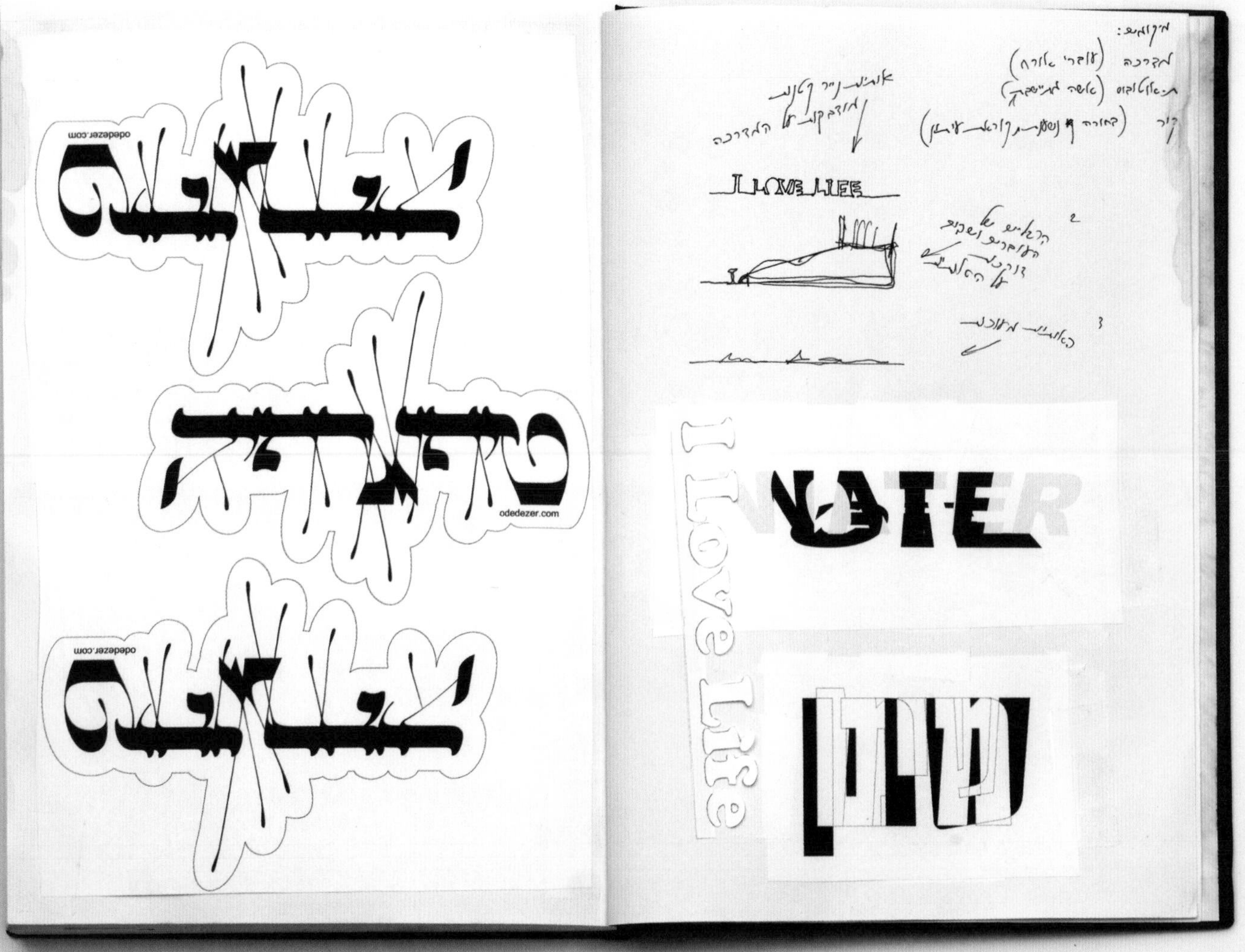
odedezer.com
I Love Life

27

abcdefghijklmnopqrstuvwxyz
0123456789 (!?*&%$"[/~)
0123456789
Aa
Impact
Hebrew version designed by Oded Ezer 2000
MCA
ARCHITECTURE

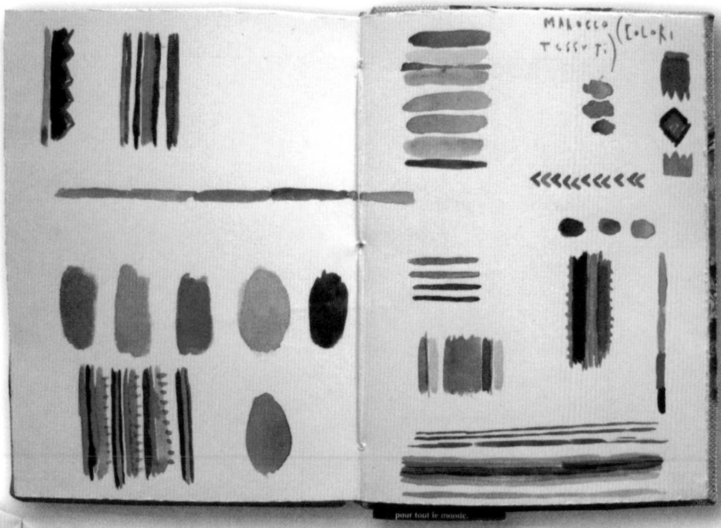

SARA FANELLI

Italian-born, London-based children's book author and illustrator Sara Fanelli's first sketchbooks were a record of her travels when she was in her teens. She began keeping books at twenty years old, which is when she started developing visual languages at college.

Now, Fanelli explains, "I have several sketchbooks all at once. One is to keep ideas, some are for visual research (different paper for different media), and then usually a new one when traveling." However, often "the subject is completely unrelated to commissioned briefs. And occasionally some of these images are finished artworks." But equally important is that the images are personal, "not only from the visual, formal point of view, but also when the subject matter relates to a journey. They can afford the freedom of not having to be too explicit."

Currently Fanelli has about six sketchbooks, of different sizes and papers, but adds: "I have not counted all the sketchbooks I've ever had – there must be dozens." The images shown here cover different periods from 2000–9.

a-fanning →
THERE WAS A
YOUNG person
of JANINA
whose uncle WAS ALWAYS
A-FANNING
HER;
WHEN he fanned
OFF
her HEAD,
she smiled
sweetly
AND SAID,
"YOU
PROPITIOUS
OLD
person
of
JANINA"

I don't want to TEACH
I WANT to SMOKE

Madame
PACE

THE frumious
BANDERSNATCH
!
B.

AN → OLD man REMEMBERS his CHILDHOOD sweetshop
SUGAR Bombs
bubblesludge
TOOTH-twisters
SHERBET SHOCKS
glueballs
5-DAY FIZZERS
1 2 3 4 5
TREACLE demons
whopper ROCKS
green SMILES
WOLF mints
oozy-woozies
1.
2.
chompsticks
GOBBLEDROPS
jelly GIANTS
SLOW slurps
LIQUORICE BRICKS

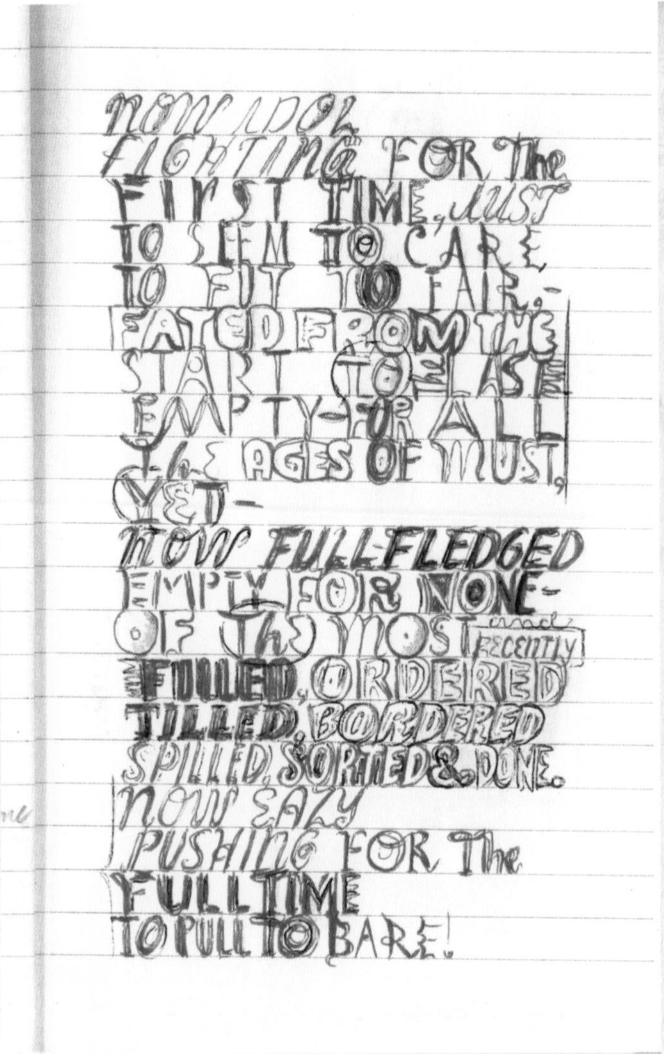
NOW IDOL
FIGHTING FOR THE
FIRST TIME, JUST
TO SEEM TO CARE
TO FIT TO FAIR,-
FATED FROM THE
START TO ELASE
EMPTY-FOR ALL
THE AGES OF MUST,
YET-
NOW FULLFLEDGED
EMPTY FOR NONE-
OF THE MOST and RECENTLY
FILLED, ORDERED
TILLED, BORDERED
SPILLED, SORTED & DONE.
NOW EAZY
PUSHING FOR THE
FULLTIME
TO PULL TO BARE!

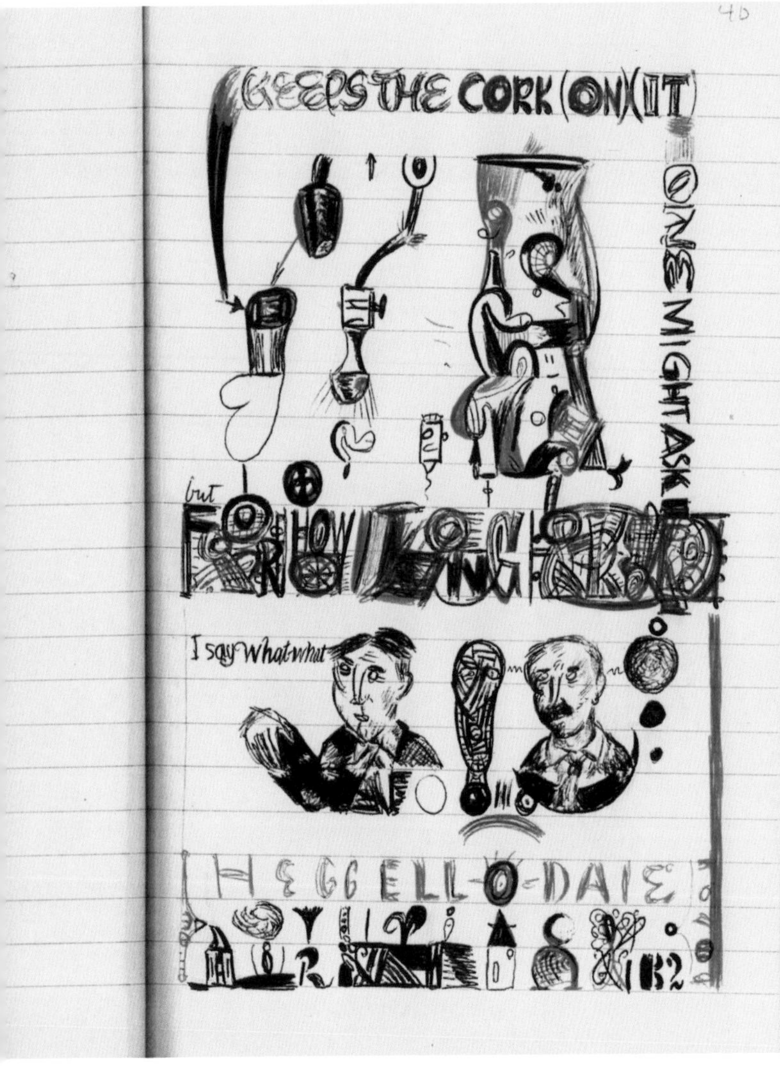
40
KEEPS THE CORK (ON)(IT)
ONE MIGHT ASK
but
I say What-what

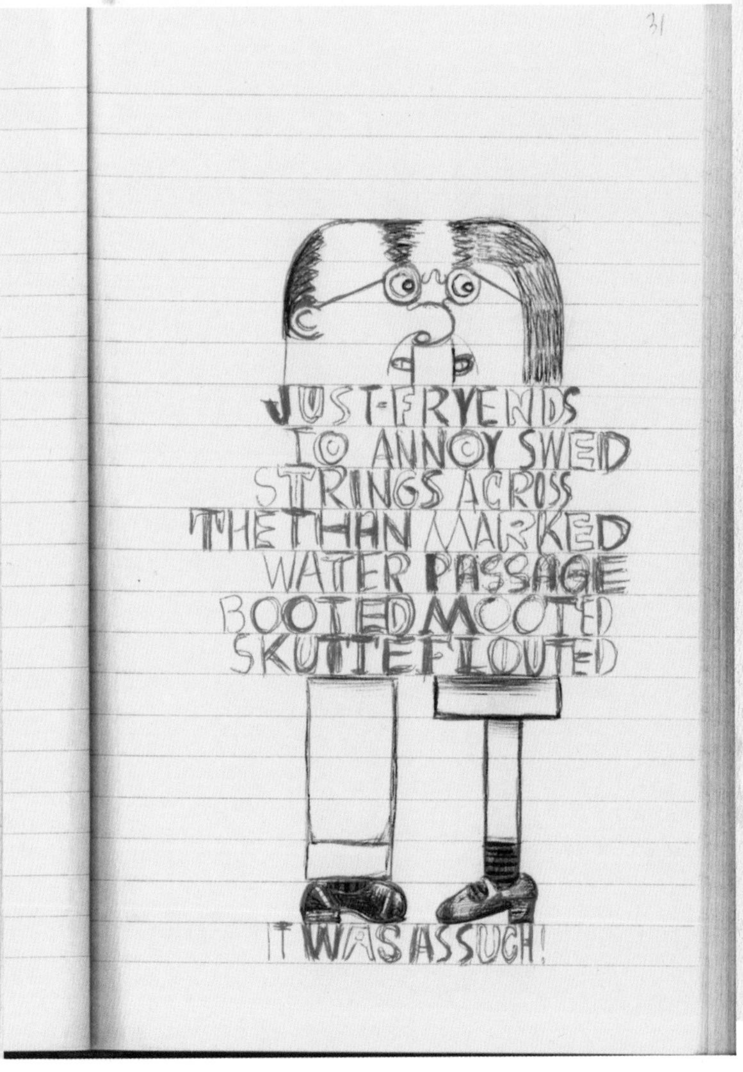
31
JUST-FRYENDS
TO ANNOY SWED
STRINGS ACROSS
THE THAN MARKED
WATER PASSAGE
BOOTED MOOTED
SKUTTEFLOUTED
IT WAS AS SUCH!

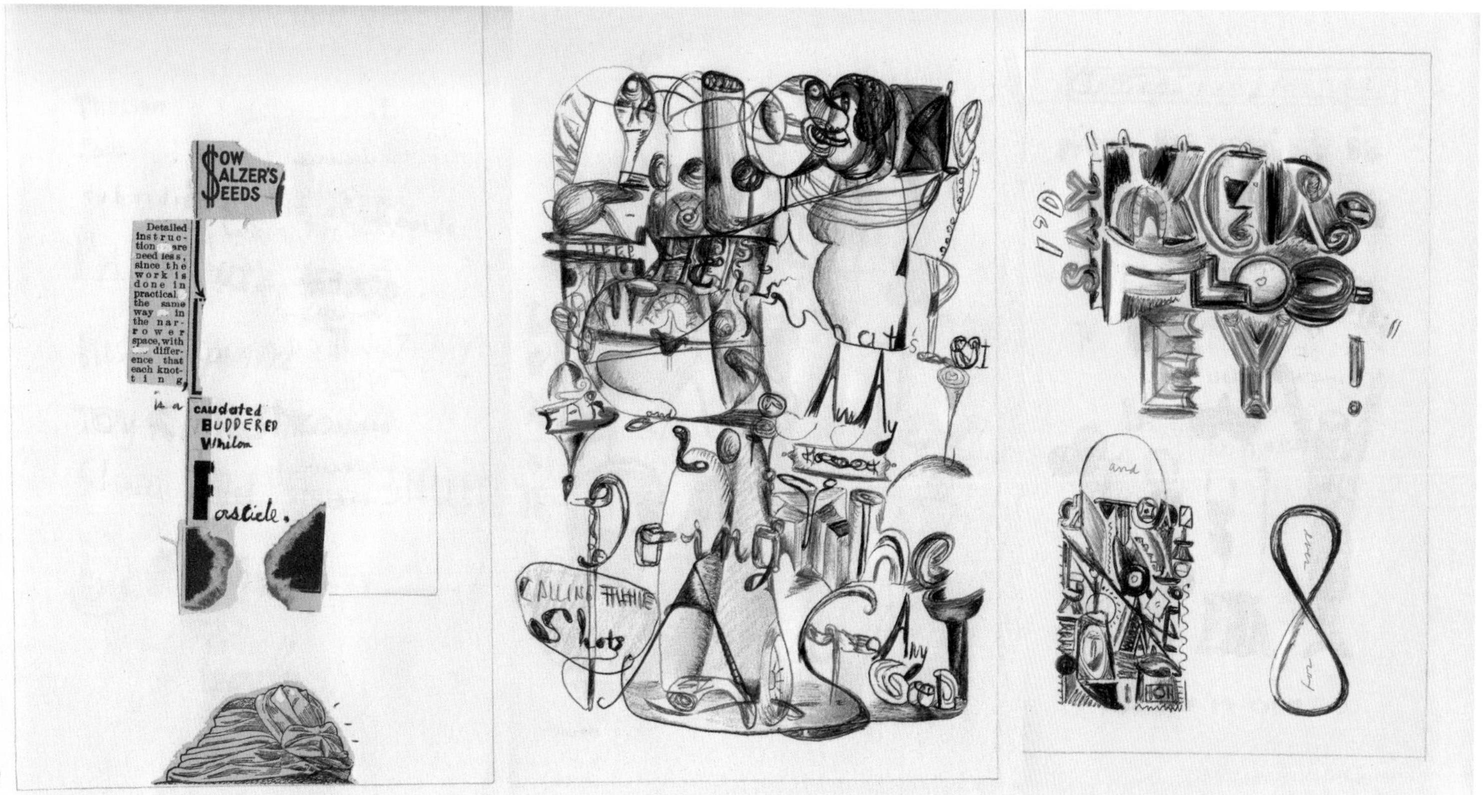

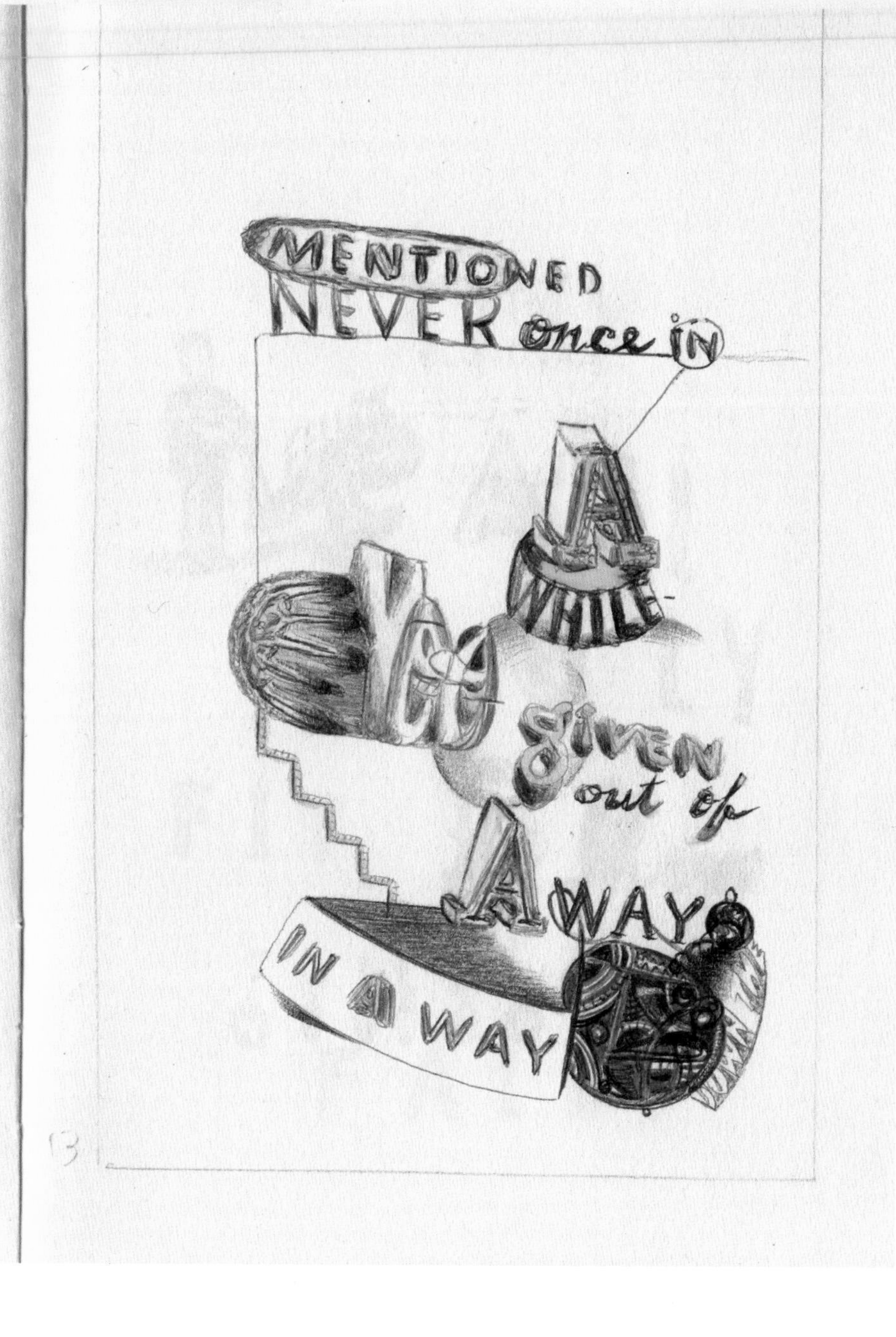

ED FELLA

Ed Fella, the former Detroit "commercial artist," turned Cranbrook student, turned guru for a generation of deconstructivist designers, has kept a sketchbook since 1976, "which is over thirty years; no wonder I have so many," he notes with a sly grin.

"During my career as a commercial artist I would always be drawing, sketching, or collaging on bits and pieces of paper around me (as an aside to my assignments)," he adds. "Originally I used books just to keep all the stuff together and have one place for doing it in a continuous form, which in time became an end in itself."

Fella's pages contain separate and discrete images; the books are not sequential, nor do they have a connecting narrative or any reason for being other than a kind of play, "which for me is making something out of my commercial art vernacular crossed with 'avant-garde' art styles and practices (which I learned about in high school in the mid 1950s – mainly Surrealism!)," he continues. "They are not true 'sketch' books, in that they contain finished drawings – but with, I hope, the quality of sketches: no revisions, no working up to a preconceived idea, more like a form of 'automatic' writing."

Fella has 115 or so books, "which makes for about 10,000 pages!"

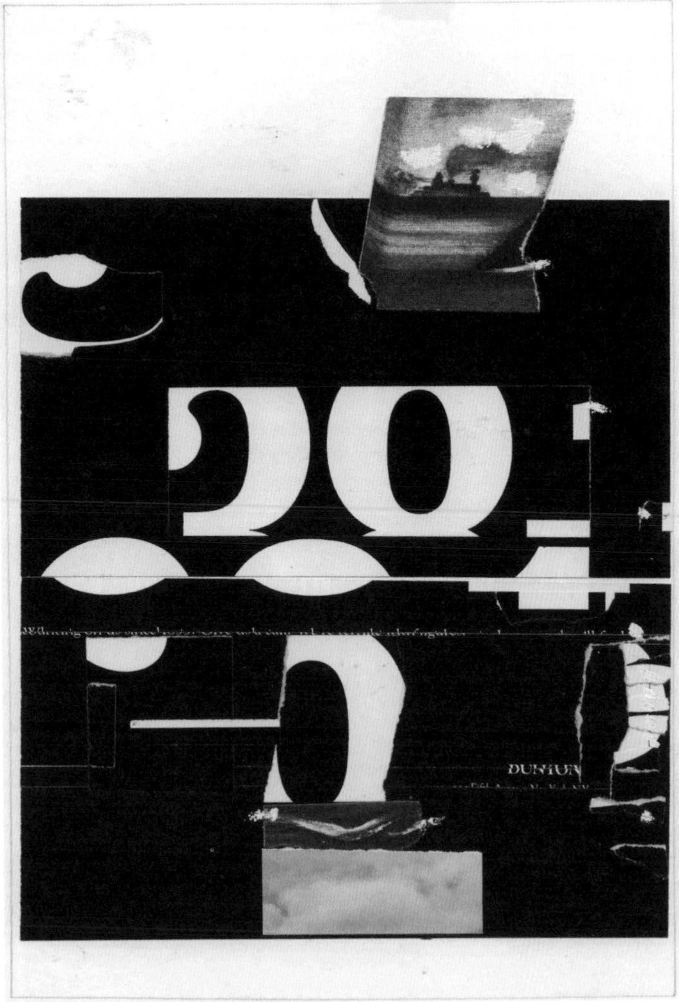

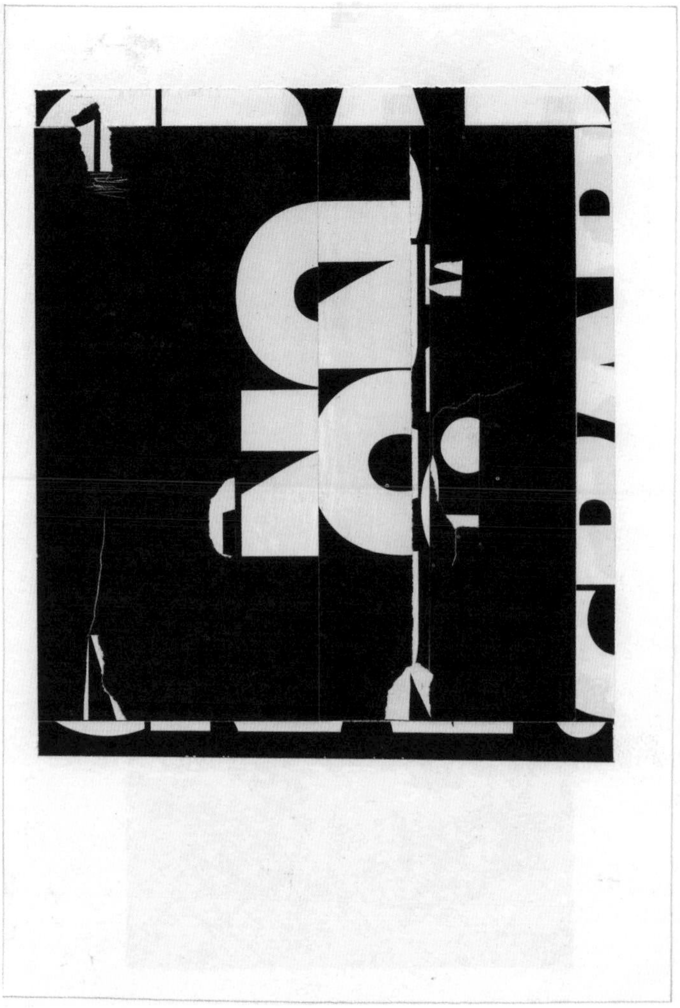

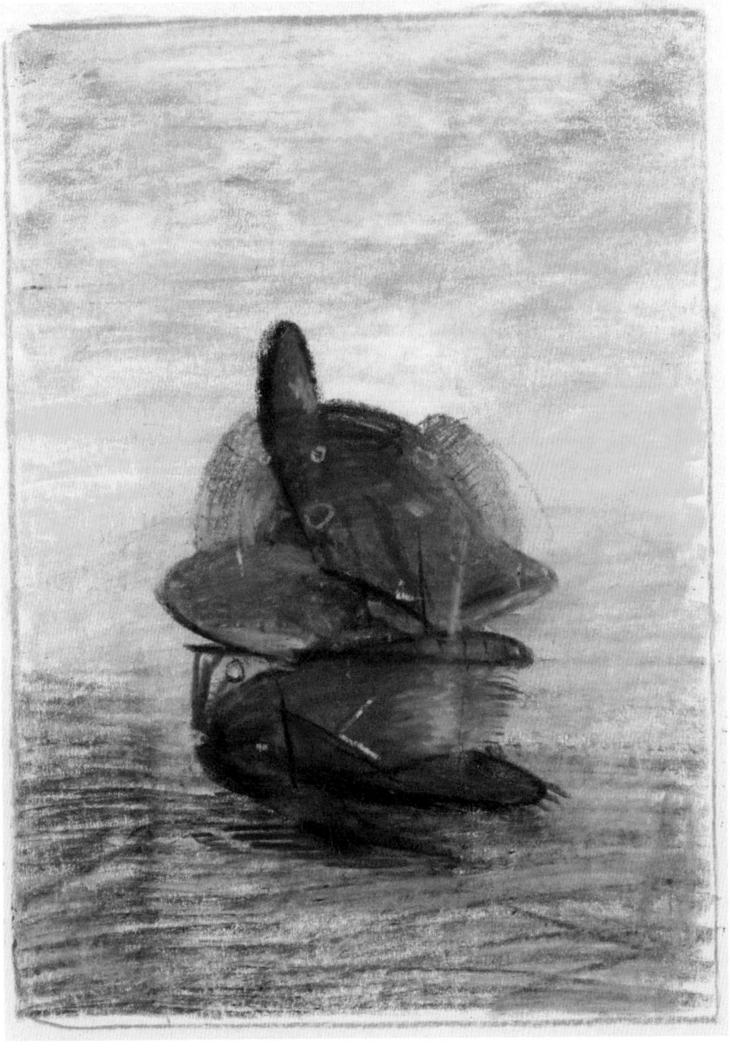

collage w/old stuff

TO
WIT

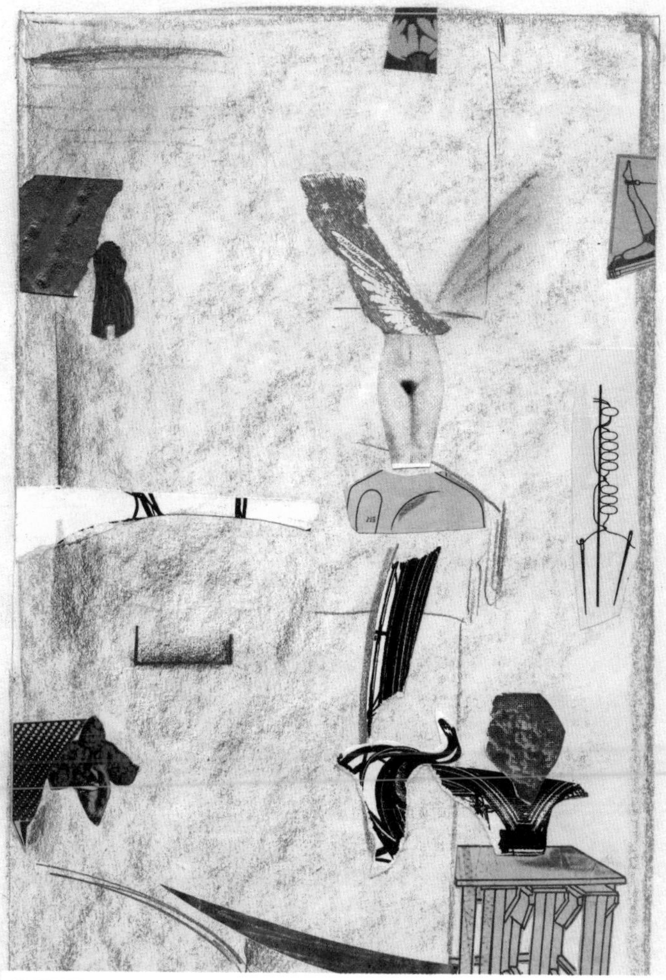

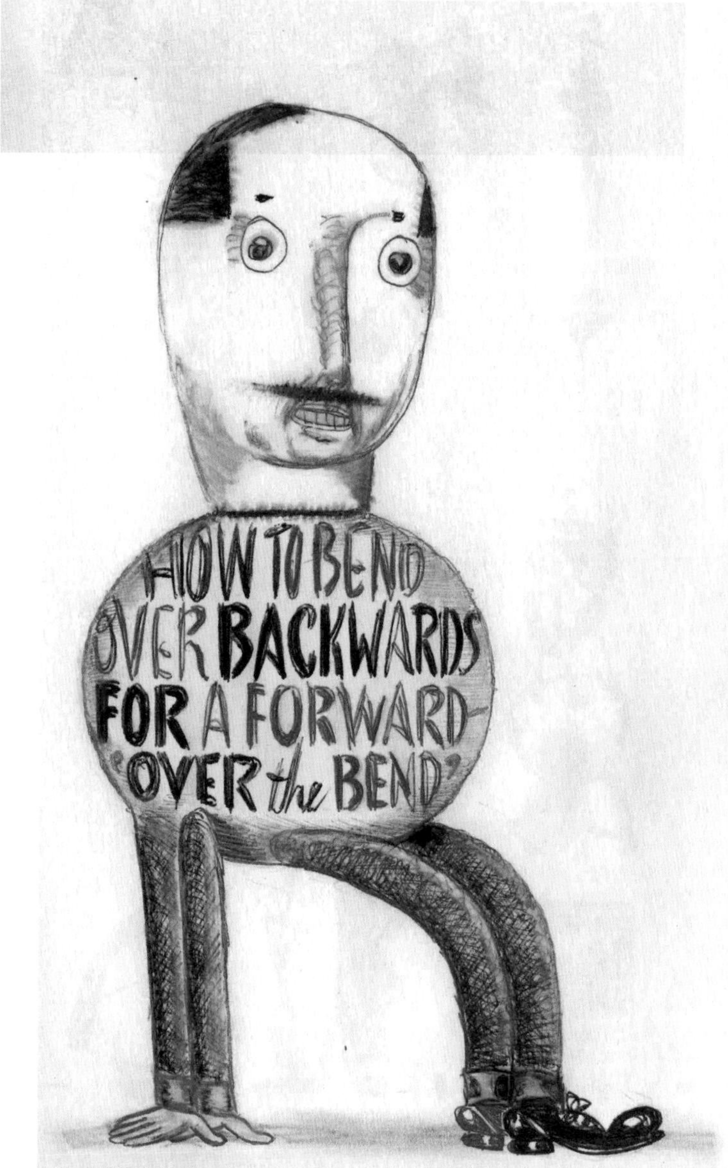
HOW TO BEND
OVER BACKWARDS
FOR A FORWARD
OVER the BEND

one
a
time
WATCH
AN
OVERSEE
of
you tuned to
AN
INVESTIGATE
YET
A
DEAD END
as
to
it
ANOTHER
to
FOLLOW
HERE
&
THERE
after
IMPROVED
AND ALL
UP TO
the
task
NEWLY
minted
and
NOW
AGAIN
page

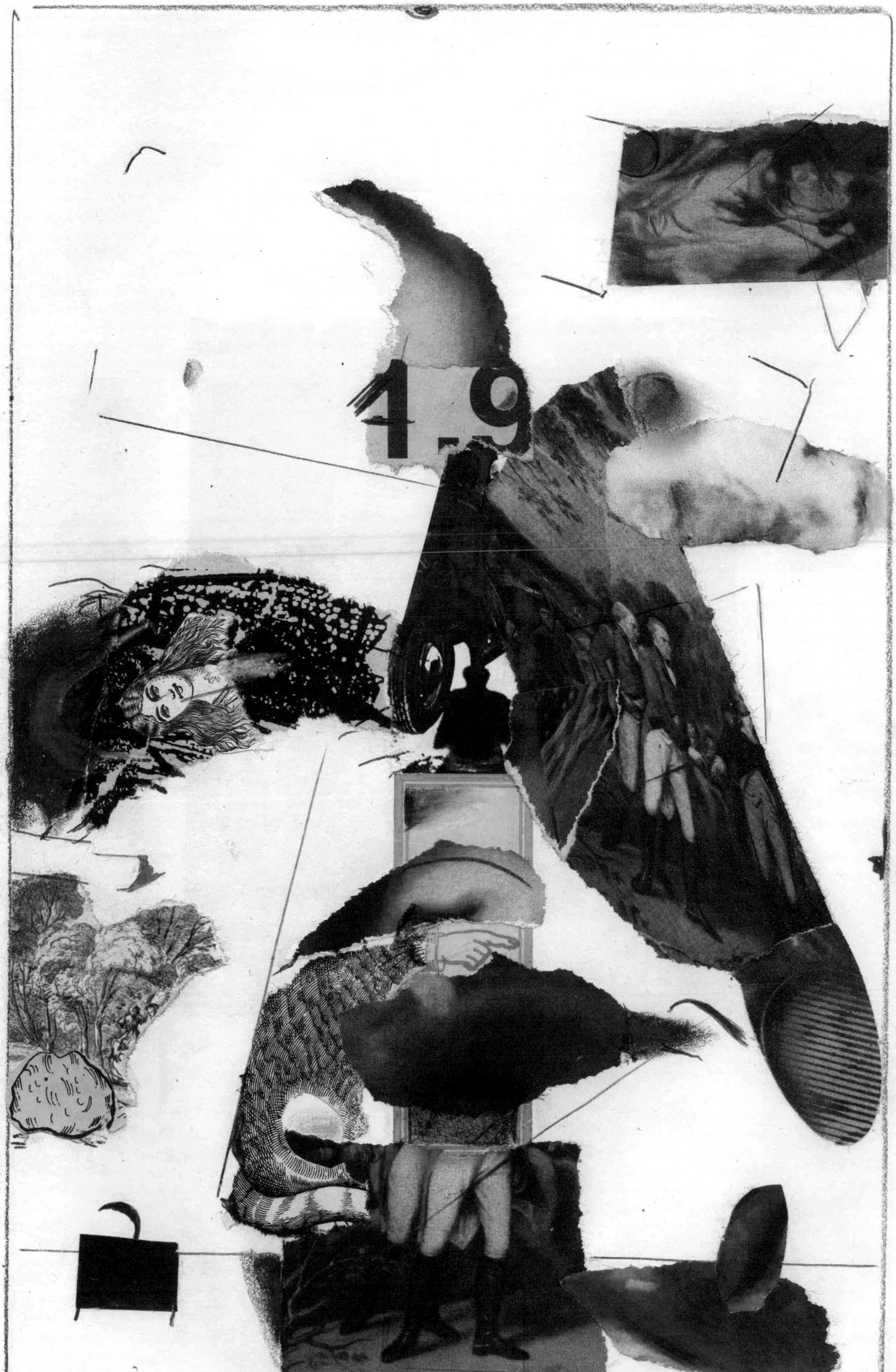
4.9

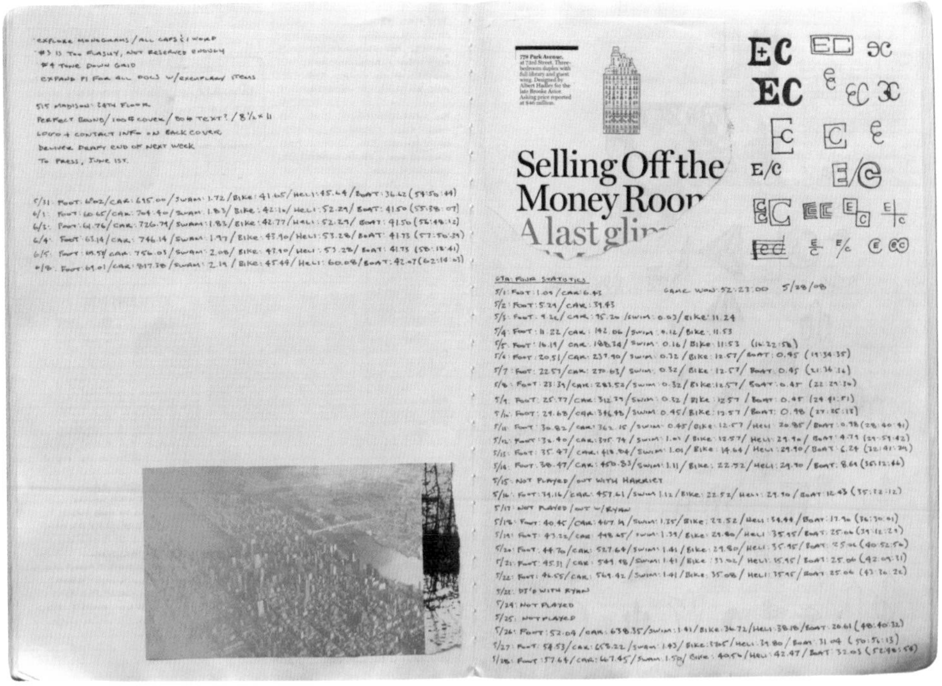

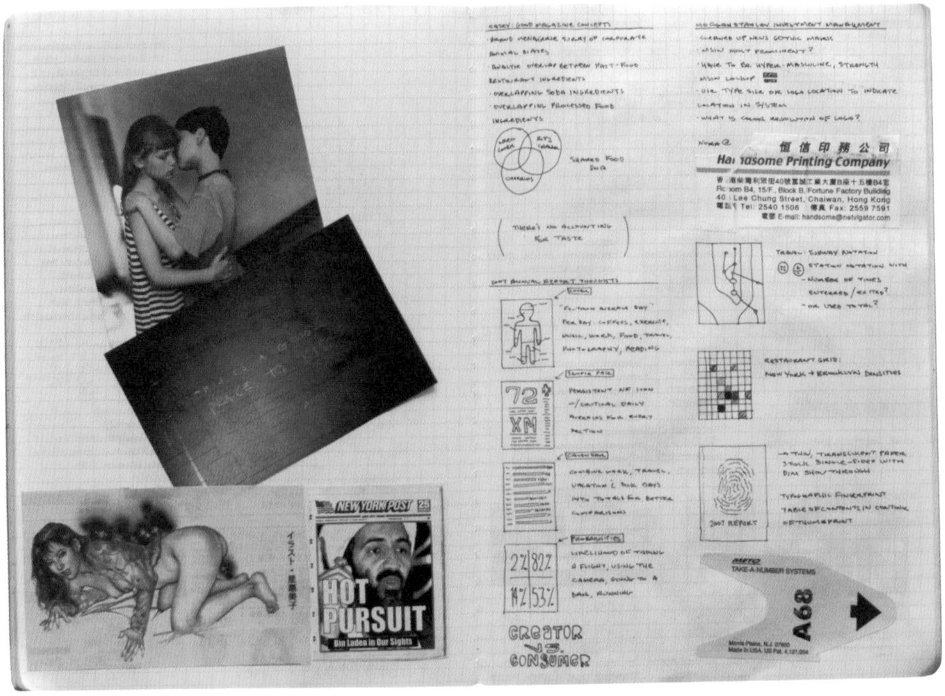

NICHOLAS FELTON

Nicholas Felton of Feltron in New York began as a generalist, doing work in advertising, identity, and editorial and web design. He enjoyed working on projects in several different media simultaneously. "The influence of personal projects like my 'Annual Report' series has been the most surprising twist in my career. While I lost sleep and sweated every detail of notable professional projects that were largely overlooked, the smaller projects I made for myself have had a profound effect on my career," he says.

The sketchbooks that he maintains reflect the detailed work he does professionally, only a tad looser. They are models of graphic erudition. Much of what he puts in them is what might be called "faux information." It looks real but has a wry edge.

He quotes Lord Kelvin (1883): "I often say that when you can measure what you are speaking about, and express it in numbers, you know something about it; but when you cannot measure it, when you cannot express it in numbers, your knowledge is of a meager and unsatisfactory kind; it may be the beginning of knowledge, but you have scarcely in your thoughts advanced to the state of Science, whatever the matter may be."

"I find that pseudo-information is even more amusing when considered under this mantle," says Felton.

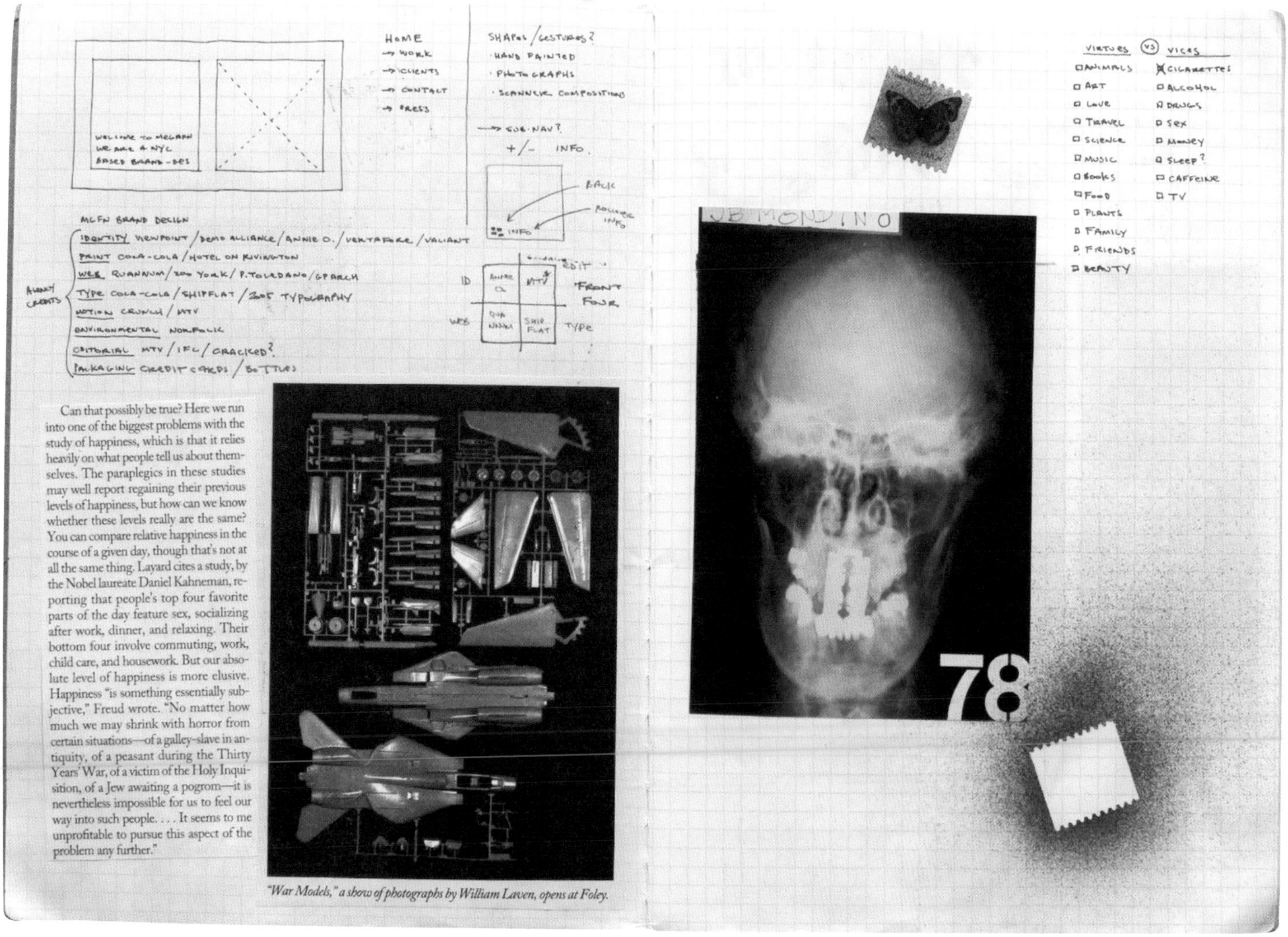
HOME
→ WORK
→ CLIENTS
→ CONTACT
→ PRESS
SHAPES / GESTURES?
· HAND PAINTED
· PHOTOGRAPHS
· SCANNER COMPOSITIONS
→ SUB-NAV?
+/– INFO
BACK
INFO
MCFN BRAND DESIGN
IDENTITY
PRINT
WEB
TYPE
MOTION
ENVIRONMENTAL
EDITORIAL
PACKAGING
EDIT
TYPE
VIRTUES VS VICES
ANIMALS
ART
LOVE
TRAVEL
SCIENCE
MUSIC
BOOKS
FOOD
PLANTS
FAMILY
FRIENDS
BEAUTY
CIGARETTES
ALCOHOL
DRUGS
SEX
MONEY
SLEEP?
CAFFEINE
TV
JB MONDINO
78
Can that possibly be true? Here we run into one of the biggest problems with the study of happiness, which is that it relies heavily on what people tell us about themselves. The paraplegics in these studies may well report regaining their previous levels of happiness, but how can we know whether these levels really are the same? You can compare relative happiness in the course of a given day, though that's not at all the same thing. Layard cites a study, by the Nobel laureate Daniel Kahneman, reporting that people's top four favorite parts of the day feature sex, socializing after work, dinner, and relaxing. Their bottom four involve commuting, work, child care, and housework. But our absolute level of happiness is more elusive. Happiness "is something essentially subjective," Freud wrote. "No matter how much we may shrink with horror from certain situations—of a galley-slave in antiquity, of a peasant during the Thirty Years' War, of a victim of the Holy Inquisition, of a Jew awaiting a pogrom—it is nevertheless impossible for us to feel our way into such people. . . . It seems to me unprofitable to pursue this aspect of the problem any further."
"War Models," a show of photographs by William Laven, opens at Foley.
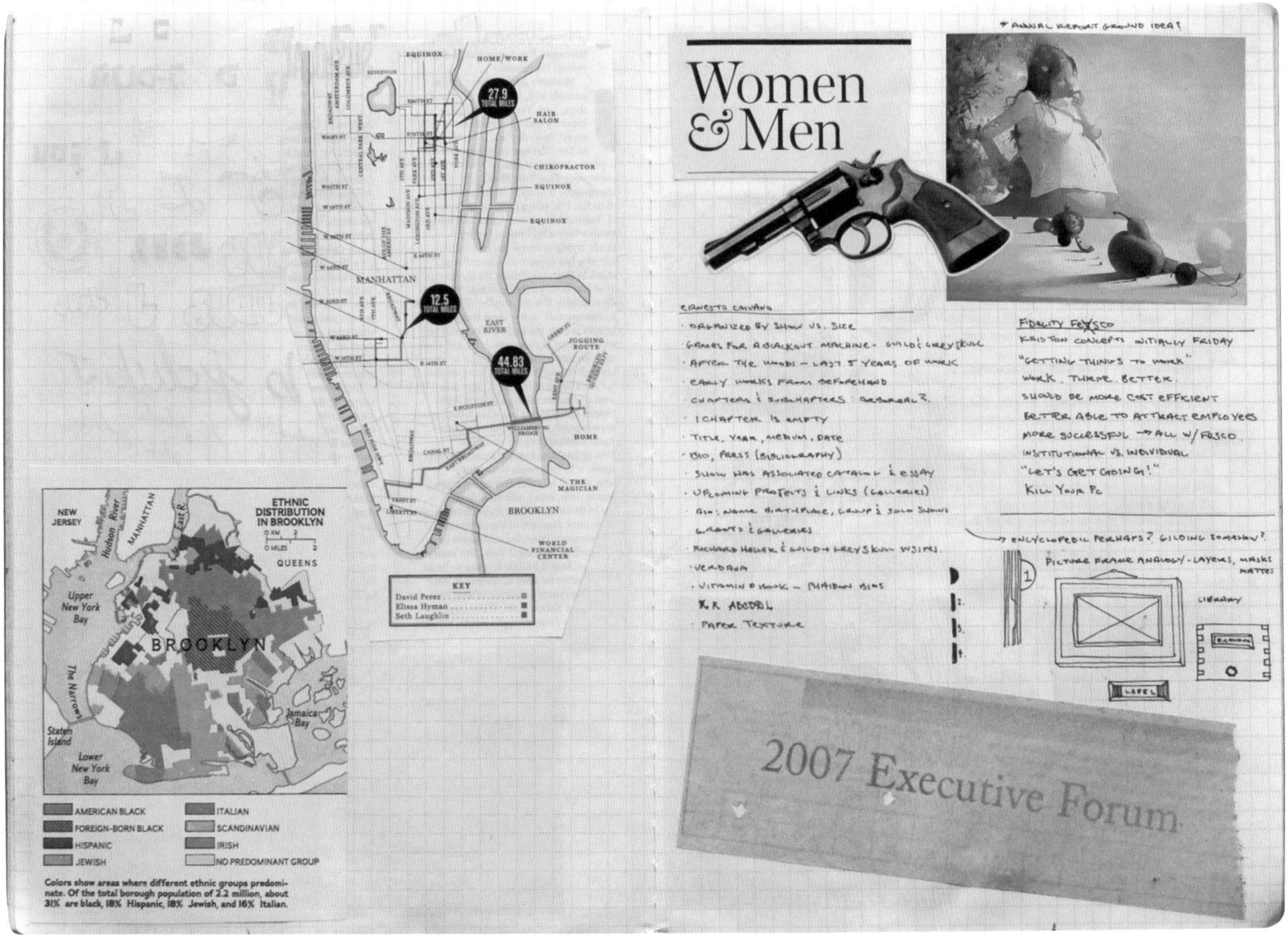
EQUINOX
HOME/WORK
27.9 TOTAL MILES
HAIR SALON
CHIROPRACTOR
EQUINOX
MANHATTAN
12.5 TOTAL MILES
EAST RIVER
44.83 TOTAL MILES
JOGGING ROUTE
HOME
THE MAGICIAN
BROOKLYN
WORLD FINANCIAL CENTER
KEY
David Perez
Elissa Hyman
Seth Laughlin
ETHNIC DISTRIBUTION IN BROOKLYN
NEW JERSEY
MANHATTAN
QUEENS
Upper New York Bay
BROOKLYN
The Narrows
Staten Island
Lower New York Bay
Jamaica Bay
AMERICAN BLACK
FOREIGN-BORN BLACK
HISPANIC
JEWISH
ITALIAN
SCANDINAVIAN
IRISH
NO PREDOMINANT GROUP
Colors show areas where different ethnic groups predominate. Of the total borough population of 2.2 million, about 31% are black, 18% Hispanic, 18% Jewish, and 16% Italian.
Women & Men
VERDANA
PAPER TEXTURE
KILL YOUR PC
2007 Executive Forum

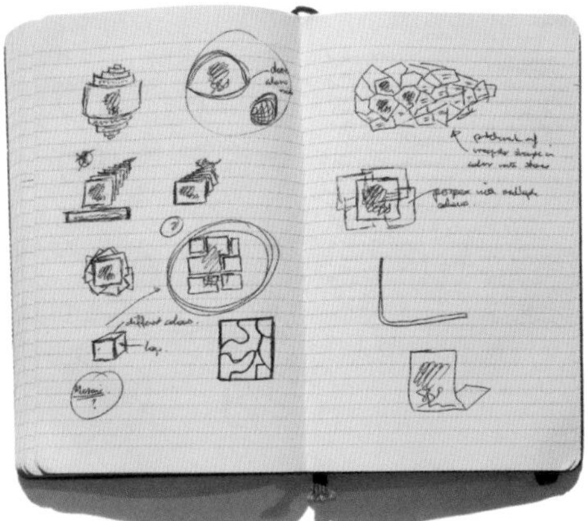

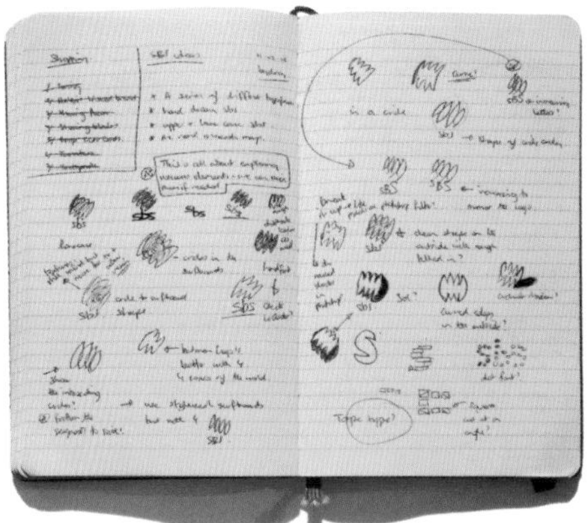

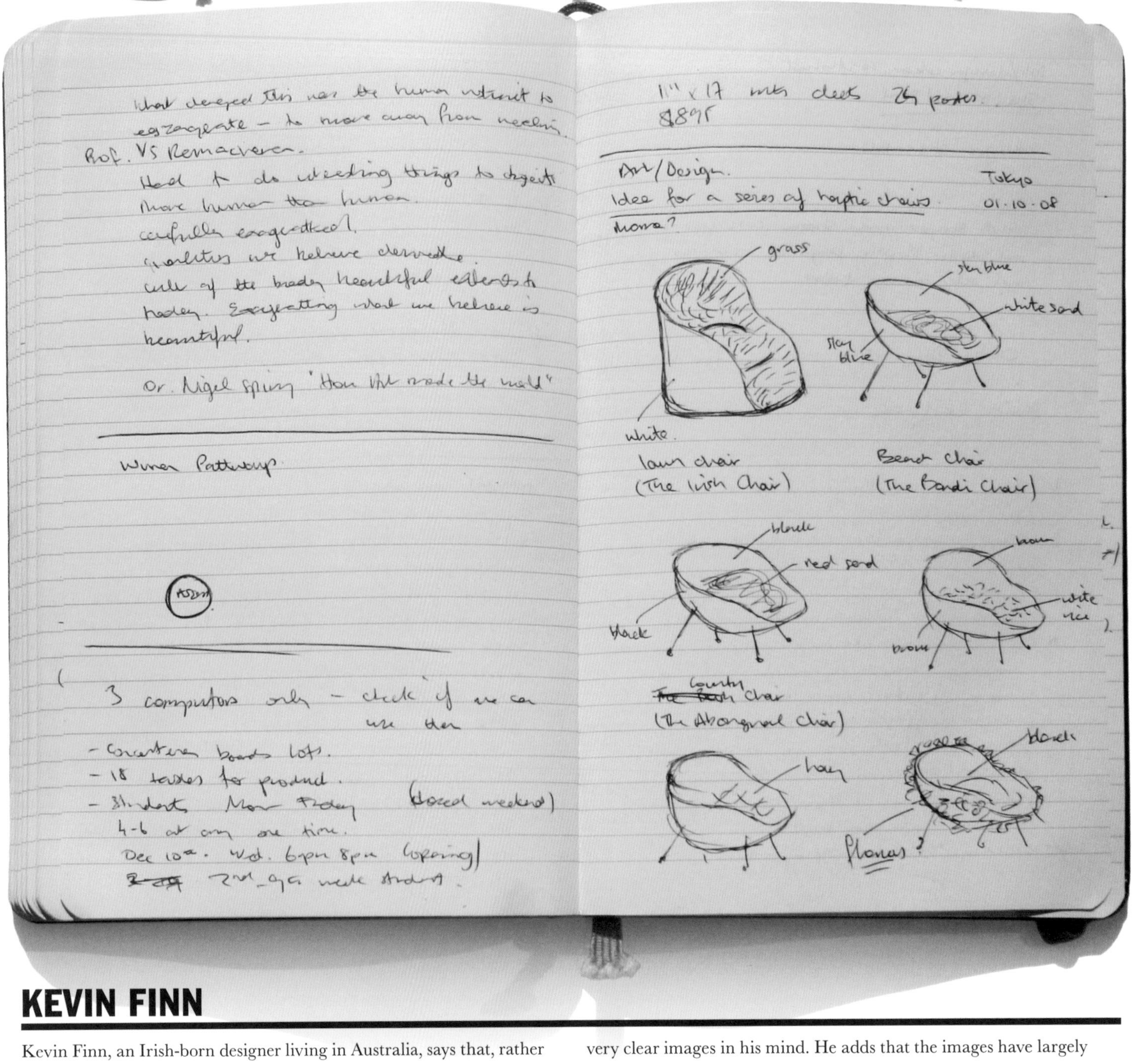

KEVIN FINN

Kevin Finn, an Irish-born designer living in Australia, says that, rather than keeping sketchbooks, "I've kept notebooks for a number of years. However, I started a regular book in mid-2005 to keep track of ideas. Some ideas are directly related to projects that I am working on. Some are random thoughts that occur to me."

The other purpose for working in a notebook is to keep things simple. "My book centralizes my thoughts, be they notes from meetings, ideas, visuals for projects, or even, on occasion, a shopping list," he says. Finn's notebook jottings are a type of shorthand, which jogs very clear images in his mind. He adds that the images have largely been driven by (or rationalized with) words. "That may not seem particularly unusual to some people but, as a visual communicator, it was a surprising discovery for me. In many respects this has become a theme for how I work through my ideas, doodles, and sketches," he says.

"I used to have two books – one smaller, pocket-sized notebook and one A5. However, I now prefer to keep one notebook at a time so I can keep track of everything." The images shown here span the years 2006–7.

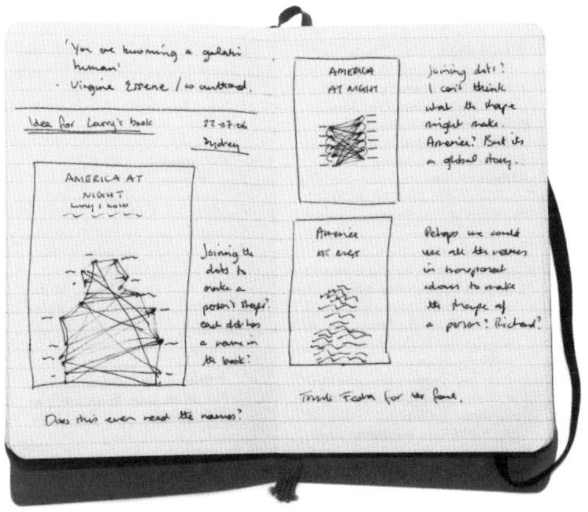
AMERICA AT NIGHT
Does this even need the names?

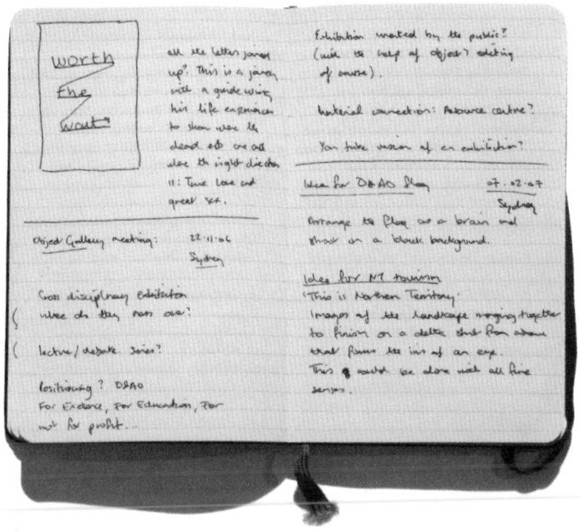
worth the wait

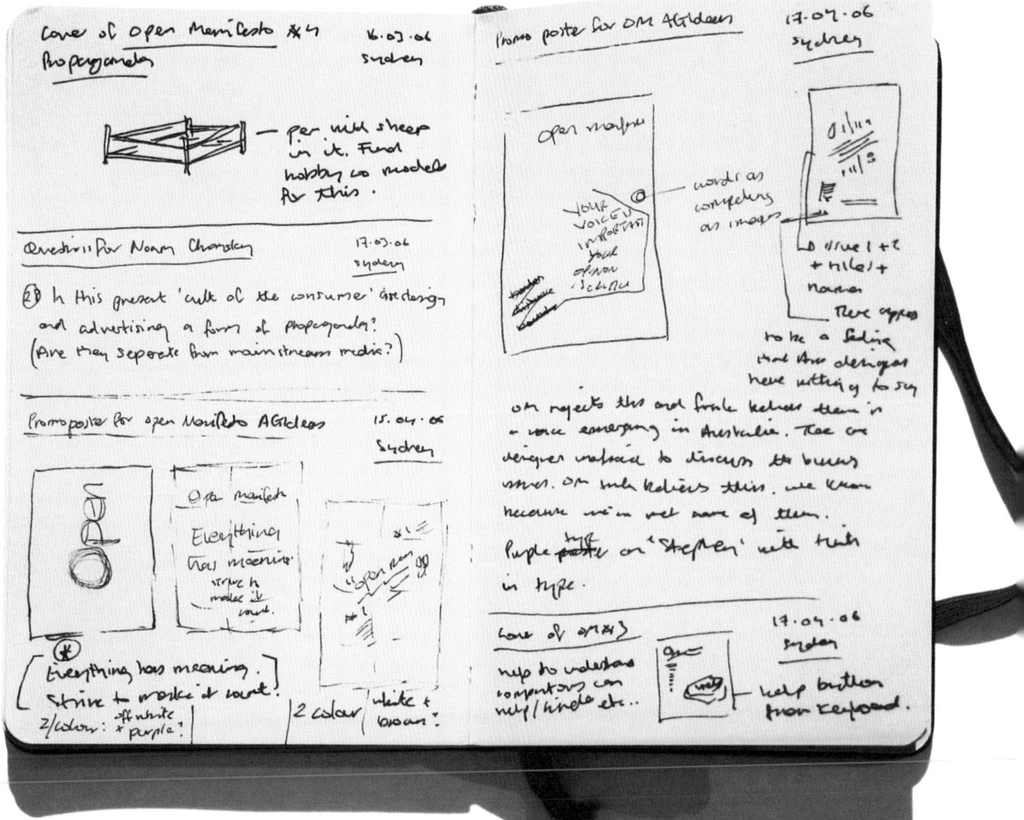
Cover of Open Manifesto #4 Propaganda
Sydney
Questions for Noam Chomsky
17.03.06
Sydney
Is this present 'cult of the consumer' are design and advertising a form of propaganda?
(Are they separate from mainstream media?)
Promo poster for Open Manifesto AGIdeas
15.04.06
Sydney
Everything has meaning.
Strive to make it count.
2 colour
Promo poster for OM AGIdeas
17.04.06
Sydney
words as computers as images
Purple type on 'Stephen' with text in type.
Help button from keyboard.

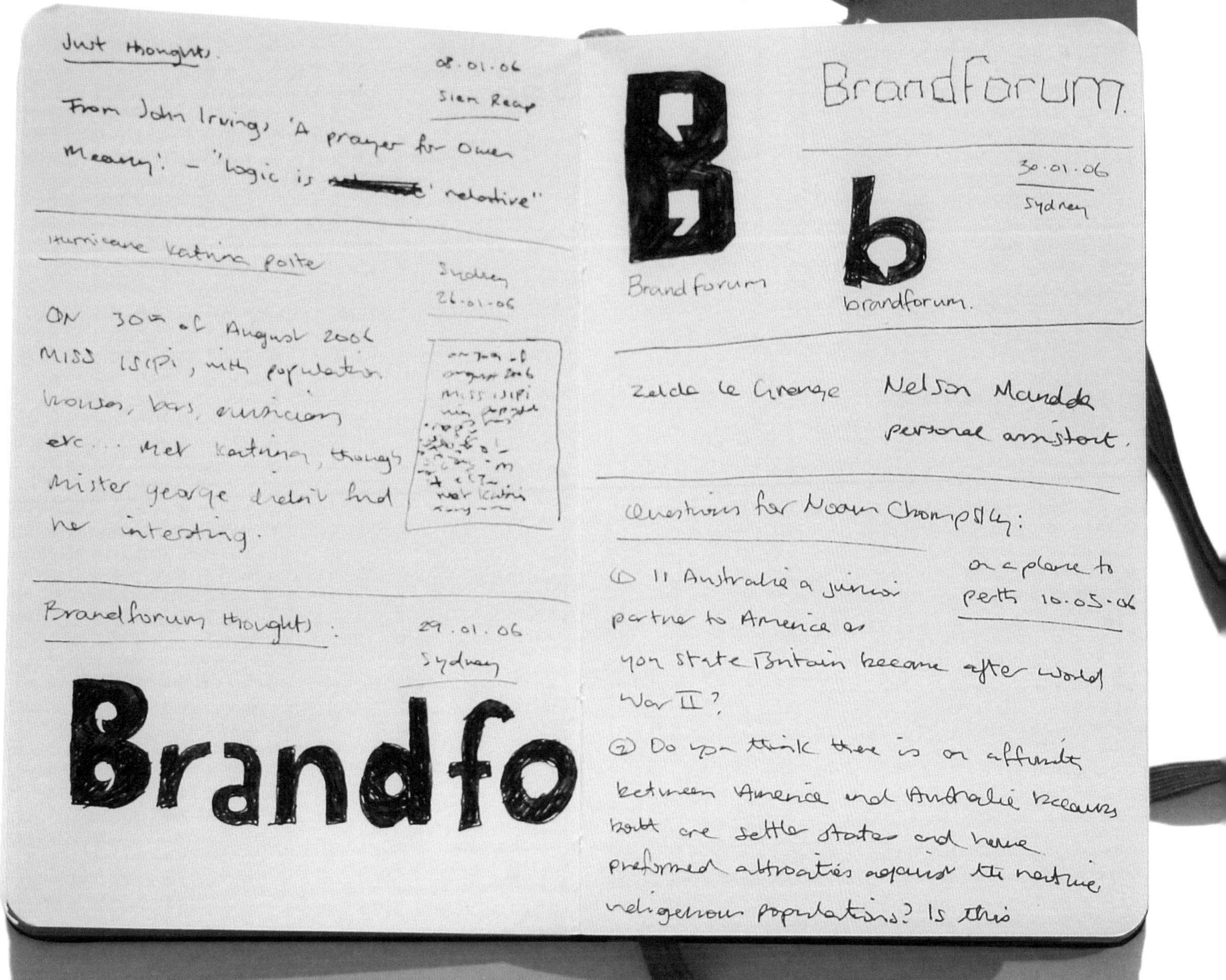
Just thoughts.
08.01.06
Siem Reap
From John Irving's 'A prayer for Owen Meany': – "logic is relative"
Hurricane Katrina poster
Sydney
26.01.06
ON 30th of August 2006
MISS ISIPi, with population houses, bars, musicians etc... Met Katrina, though Mister George didn't find her interesting.
Brandforum thoughts:
29.01.06
Sydney
Brandfo
Brandforum
Brandforum.
30.01.06
Sydney
brandforum.
Zelda le Grange
Nelson Mandela personal assistant.
Questions for Noam Chomsky:
on a plane to Perth 10.05.06
① Is Australia a junior partner to America as
② Do you think there is an affinity between America and Australia because both are settler states and have

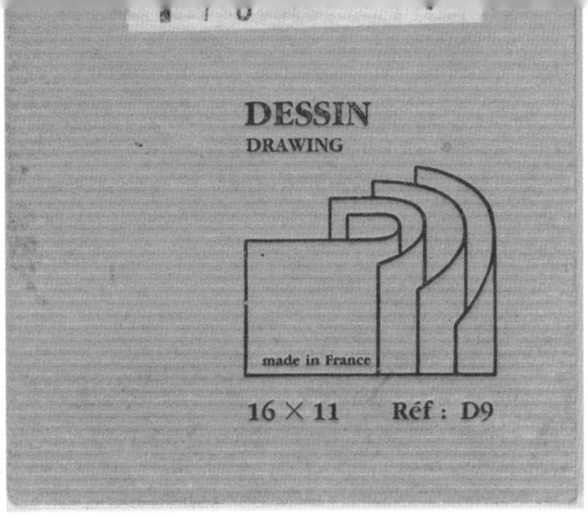

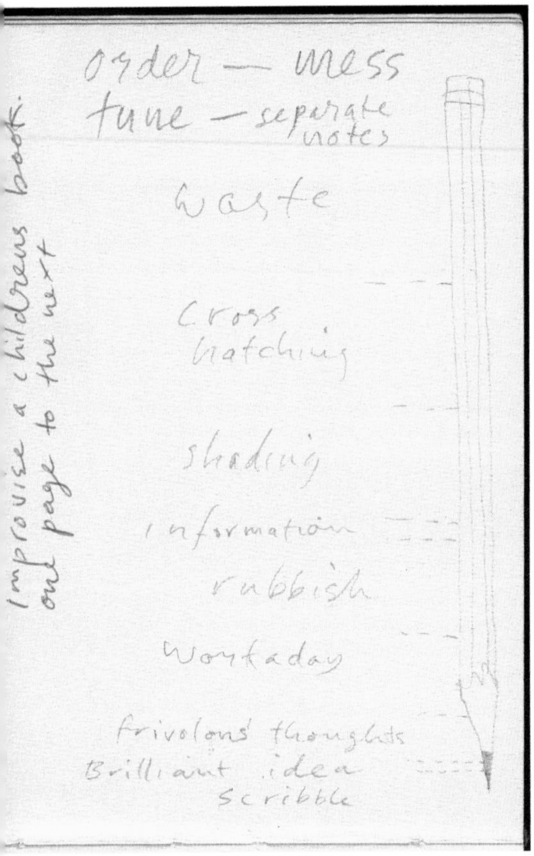

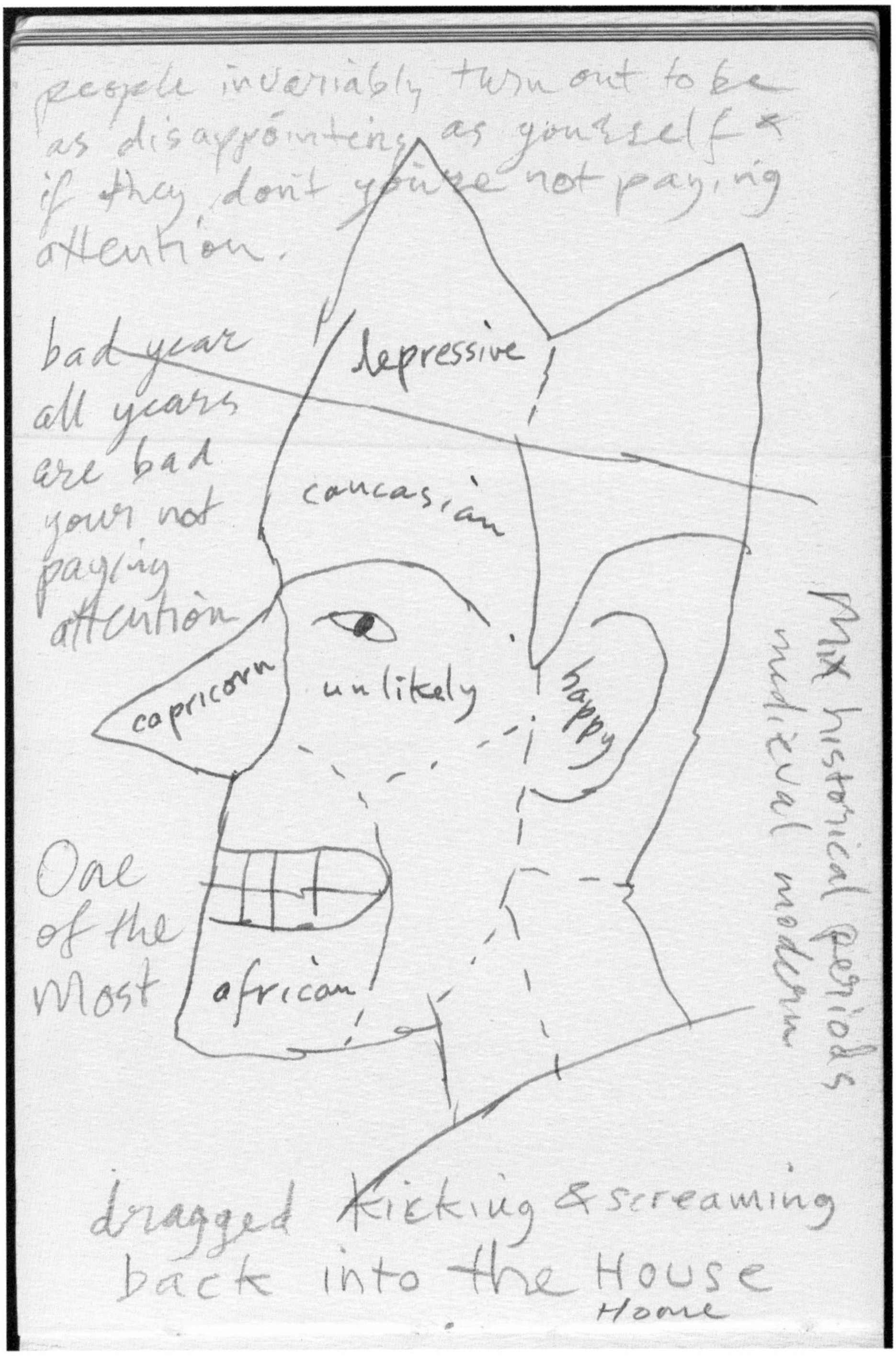

JEFFREY FISHER

Jeffrey Fisher, a British-born illustrator who lives in the South of France, is known for his raw, comedic, linear wit, and a very distinct hand-lettering style. In fact, his style has influenced a generation of illustrators working during the 2000s who use words as a colorful complement to pictures.

Although he says he is not a compulsive sketchbooker (a claim that is hard to fathom, given his style and method), he nonetheless has kept them for almost twenty years. "I have always had a sketchbook. I don't carry one with me but have a number scattered here and there." There is no lofty philosophical rationale – no higher artistic purpose. For Fisher, his books function "purely as a memory aid. More and more they become notes to myself rather than drawings. I practically never sketch things." And yet, at the risk of contradiction, he believes that the sketchbooks are much funnier, more relaxed, and less self-conscious than his finished work.

There are no themes to the five or so books that he has. For Fisher, "It is about randomness, although I can have one book going for fifteen to twenty years."

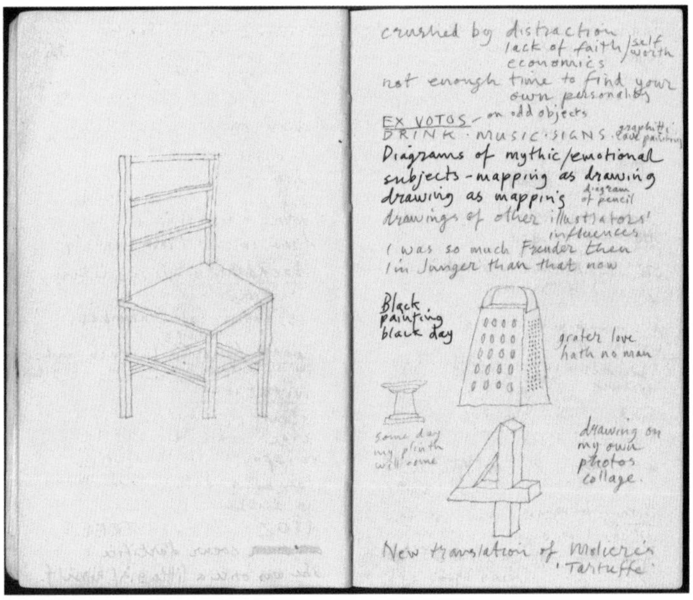

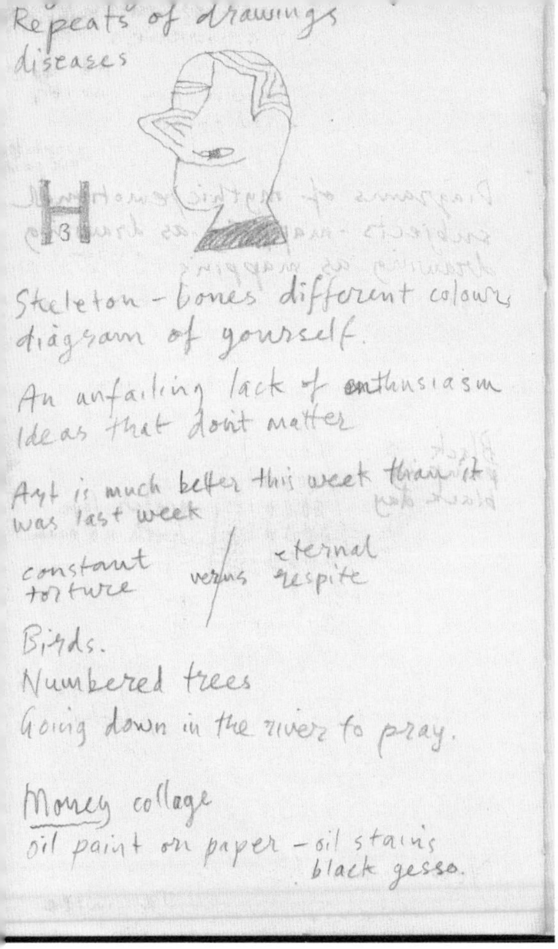
Repeats of drawings
diseases
Skeleton - bones different colours
diagram of yourself.
An unfailing lack of enthusiasm
Ideas that don't matter
Art is much better this week than it was last week
constant torture versus eternal respite
Birds.
Numbered trees
Going down in the river to pray.
Money collage
oil paint on paper - oil stains
black gesso.

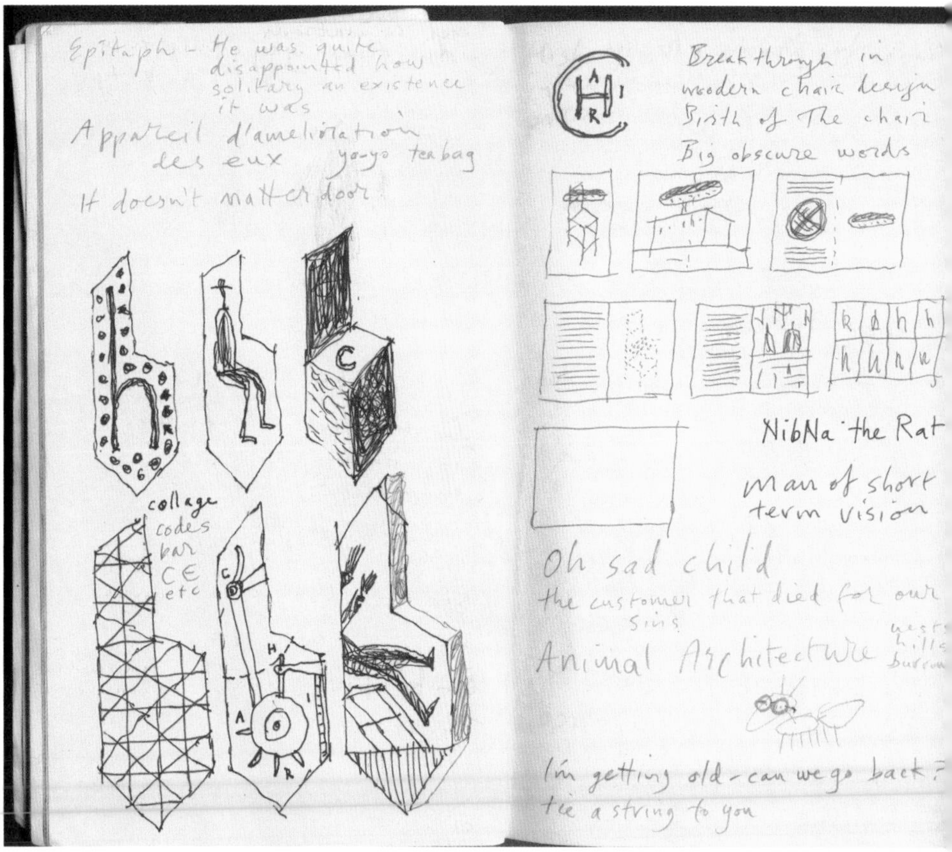
Epitaph - He was quite disappointed how solitary an existence it was
Appareil d'amelioration des eux
yo-yo teabag
It doesn't matter door
collage
codes
bar
CE
etc
Breakthrough in wooden chair design
Birth of The chair
Big obscure words
NibNa the Rat
Man of short term vision
Oh sad child
the customer that died for our sins
Animal Architecture
I'm getting old - can we go back?
tie a string to you

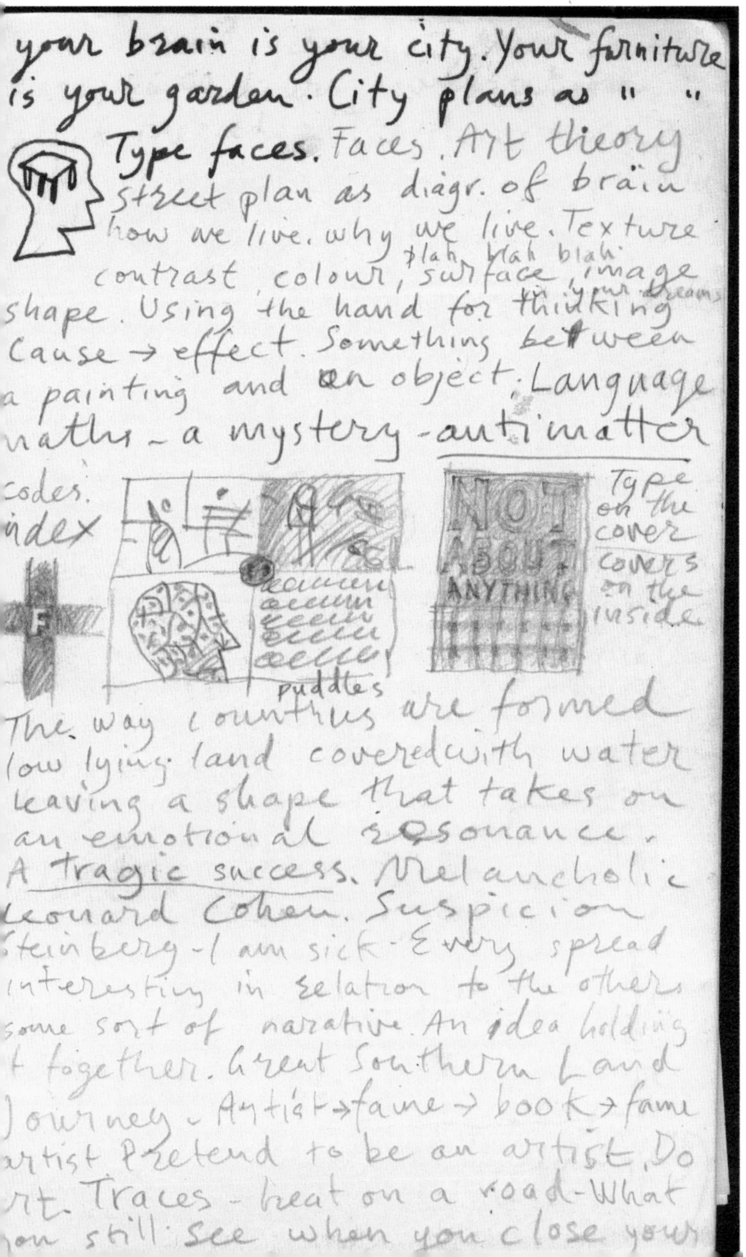
your brain is your city. Your furniture is your garden. City plans as " "
Type faces. Faces. Art theory
street plan as diagr. of brain
how we live. why we live. Texture
contrast colour, surface, image
blah blah blah
shape. Using the hand for thinking
in your dreams
Cause → effect. Something between a painting and an object. Language
maths - a mystery - antimatter
codes.
index
NOT ABOUT ANYTHING
Type on the cover
covers on the inside.
puddles
The way countries are formed
low lying land covered with water leaving a shape that takes on an emotional resonance.
A tragic success. Melancholic
Leonard Cohen. Suspicion
Steinberg - I am sick - Every spread interesting in relation to the others
some sort of narative. An idea holding it together. Great Southern Land
Journey. Artist → fame → book → fame
artist Pretend to be an artist. Do art. Traces - heat on a road - What you still see when you close your

STEG
MAN

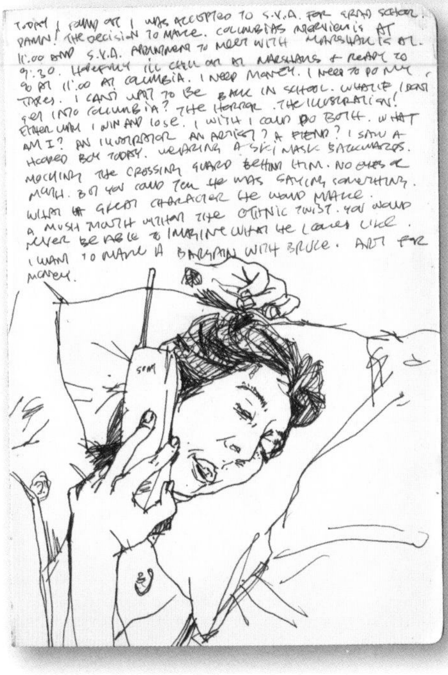

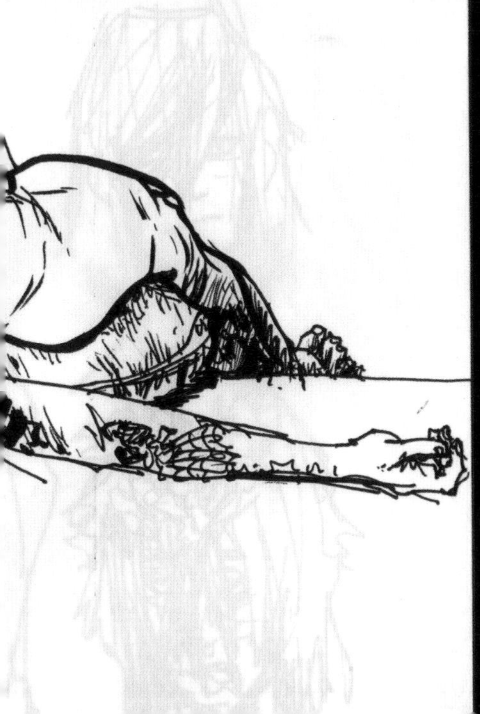

NATHAN FOX

Nathan Fox, a New York-based illustrator and comic artist, has been keeping a book off and on for years, though he never finishes one. "I'd love to say I draw in them every day," he laments, "but there seems to be less and less time to keep one."

Fox keeps them for "random thoughts, character design ideas, location drawing, and really bad freelance sketches and concept stuff. There's no real 'finish' approach. Even my sketches for illustration work are off-the-cuff, moment kind of drawings."

Fox adds: "I don't really go back and look at them, aside from notes I make for larger images. I used to do sketches that were used for the finished work but they always felt contrived or forced. Like re-doing an image over again. Over the years I've found that I would rather just start again from scratch. But once you get a sketch approved you can't really do that. In keeping sketches loose and almost elaborate-stick-figure-simple, I can retain the freedom to flesh them out. So all the creation and the details are in the moment and focused on the finished image, and not on the sketch with a repeat for the larger piece."

Fox does have a few smaller sketchbooks that he keeps entirely to himself. The longest-running one is about "heads."

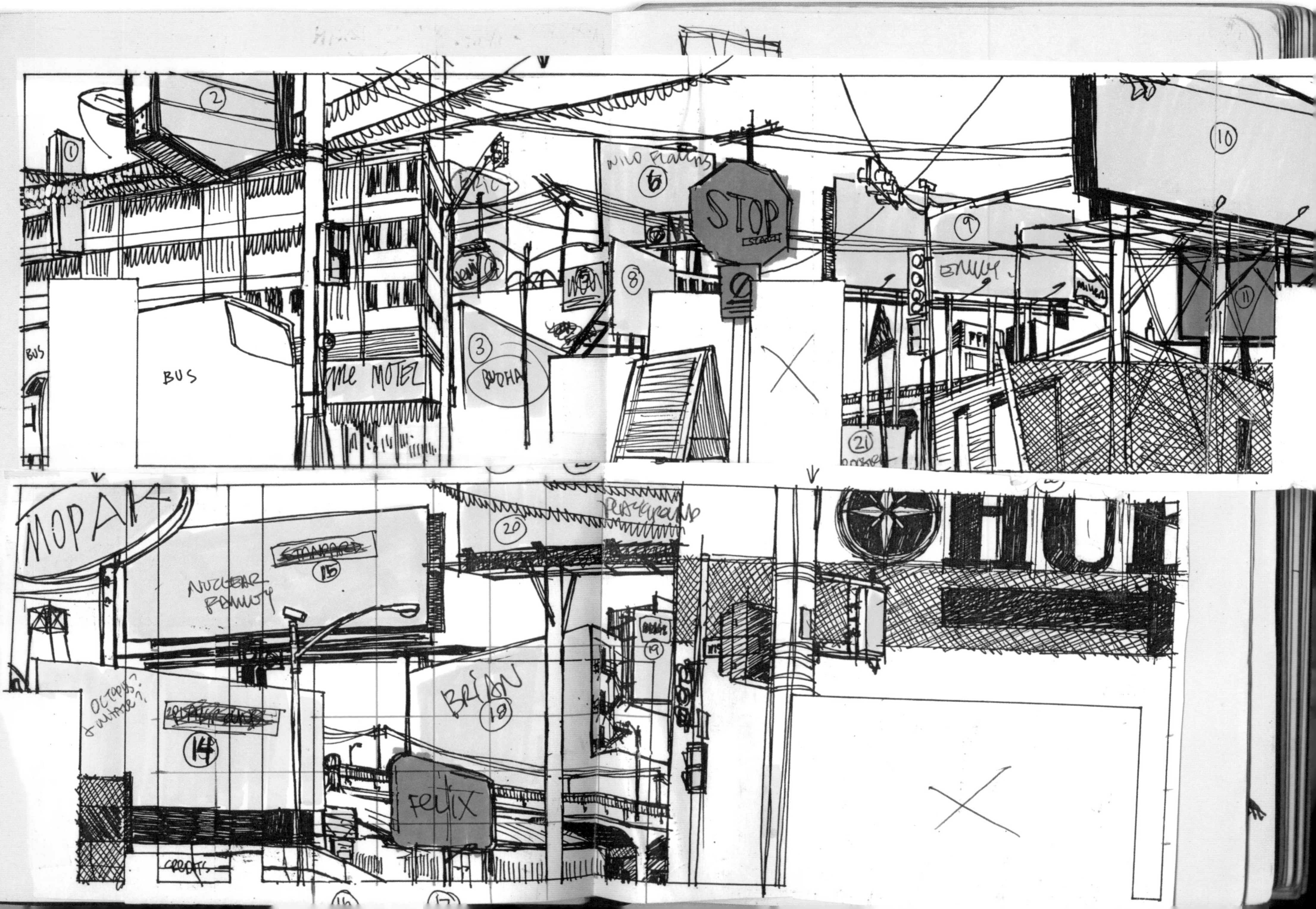
BUS
MOTEL
STOP
WILD FLOWERS
MOPAR
NUCLEAR FAMILY
BRIAN
FELIX
CREDITS
OCTOPUS? & VINTAGE?

8/9/02

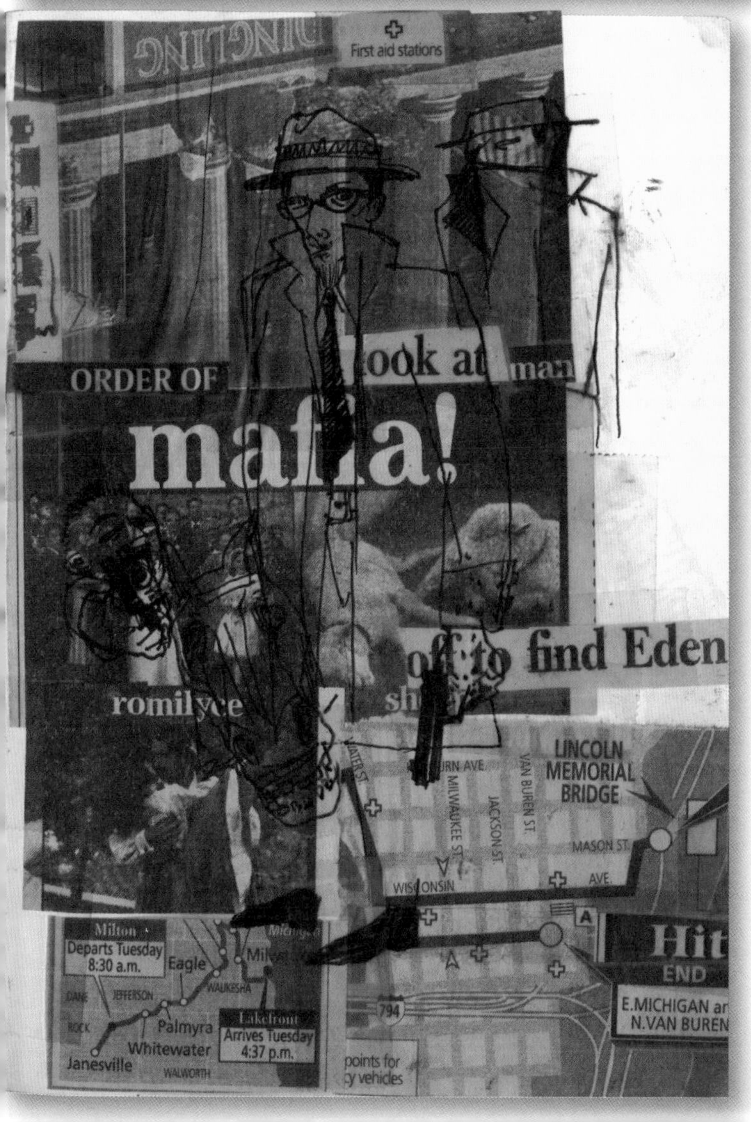
First aid stations
ORDER OF
look at
man
mafia!
off to find Eden
romilyce
LINCOLN
MEMORIAL
BRIDGE
MILWAUKEE ST
VAN BUREN ST
JACKSON ST
MASON ST
WISCONSIN
AVE
Milton
Departs Tuesday
8:30 a.m.
Eagle
Palmyra
Whitewater
Janesville
Lakefront
Arrives Tuesday
4:37 p.m.
Hit
END
E.MICHIGAN an
N.VAN BUREN
points for
cy vehicles

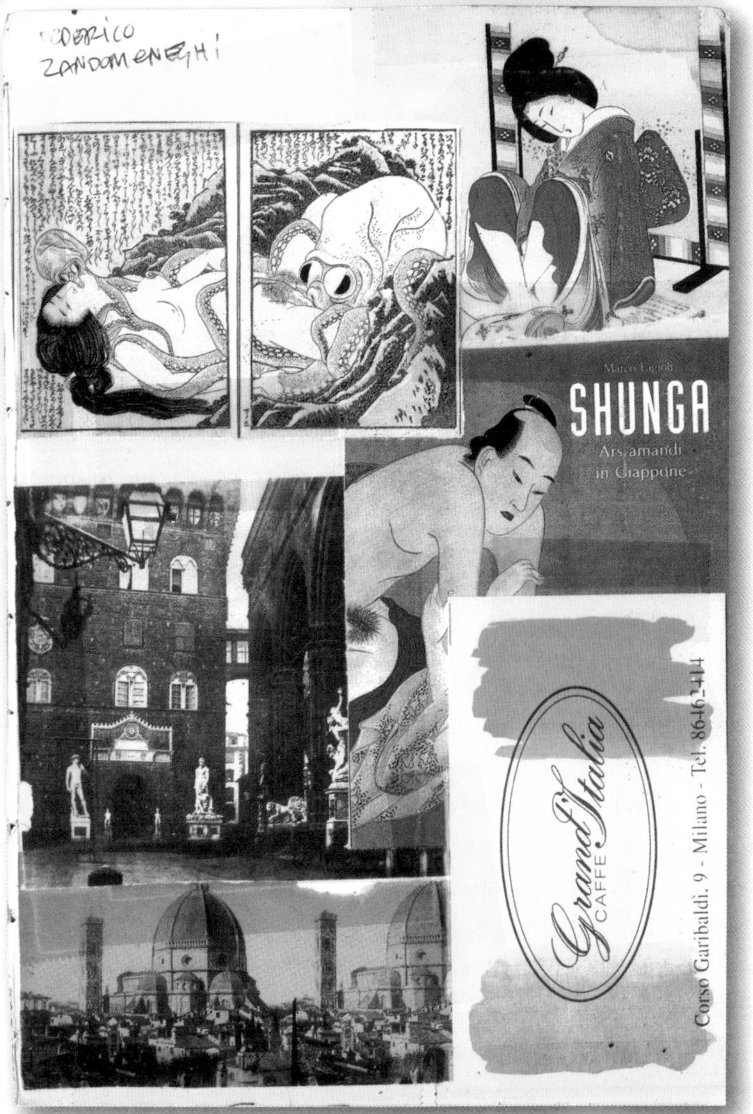
ZANDOMENEGHI
Marco Fagioli
SHUNGA
Ars amandi
in Giappone
Grand Italia
CAFFE
Corso Garibaldi, 9 - Milano - Tel. 86462414

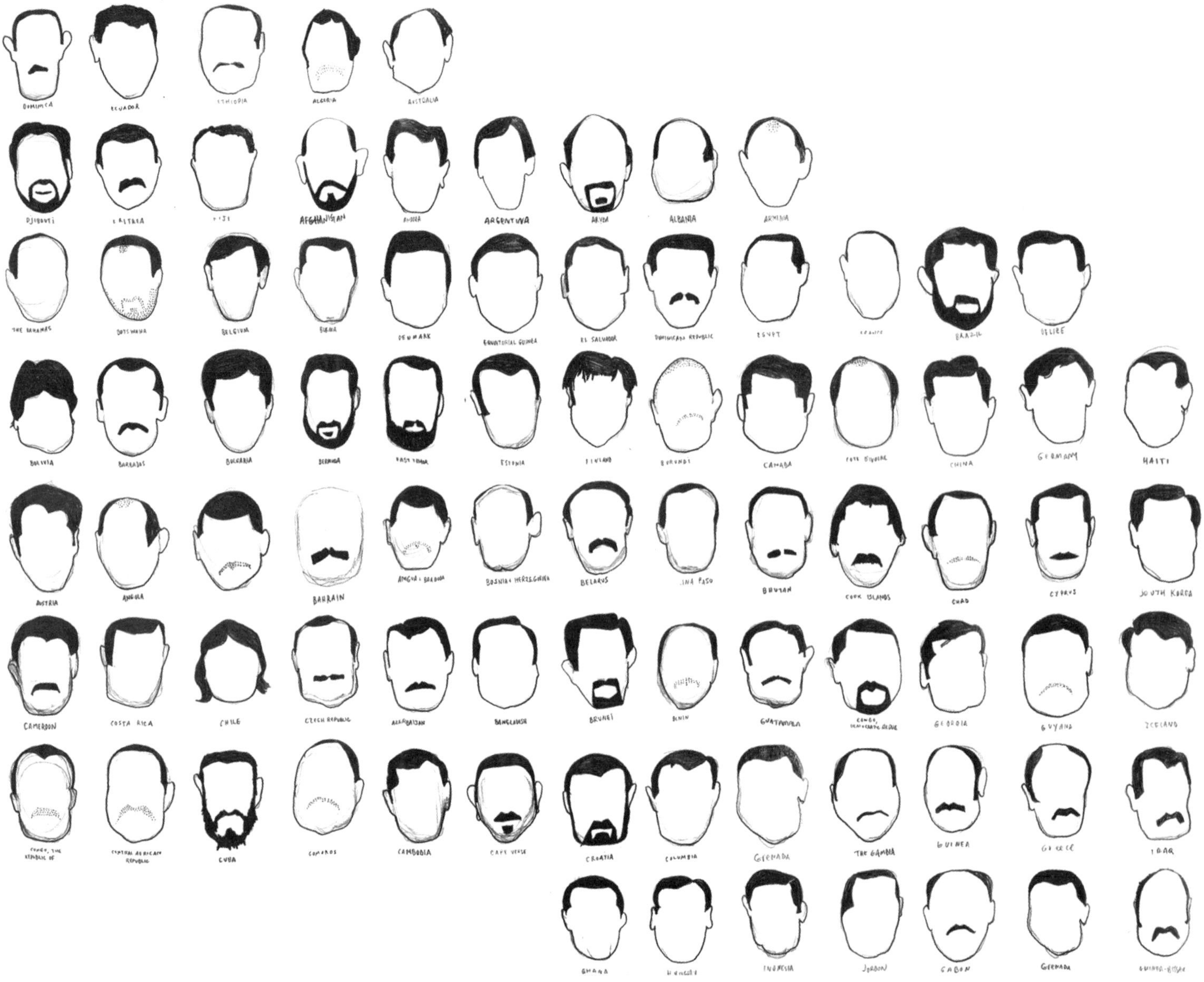

AMY FRANCESCHINI

Amy Franceschini, of multimedia design firm Futurefarmers in San Francisco, has kept a sketchbook since she could write. Her father bought her a sketchbook and a set of pens each Christmas. As soon as she would open the package her father would start practicing his lettering with her. "I think the gift was more for him than me," she notes. She now has over 100 in all different sizes and shapes, many of which she makes herself on an industrial sewing machine.

Franceschini's sketchbooks go everywhere with her "as notebooks or process logs. They are my brain. I use them to daydream during meetings, to take notes while I read, to log the many ideas I have that I never have time to do, but maybe someday...."

For Franceschini, the sketchbooks offer freedom from constraints. "My sketchbook does not think of an audience or form. For a finished work I think about how the idea must take form and what that form will mean in different contexts. When I look at my book it feels much fresher than most of my finished work."

The sketchbooks show she is fixated on drawing "cute" characters. "I enjoy drawing them, and they are definitely a reflection of my mood." The images shown here range from 2004–9.

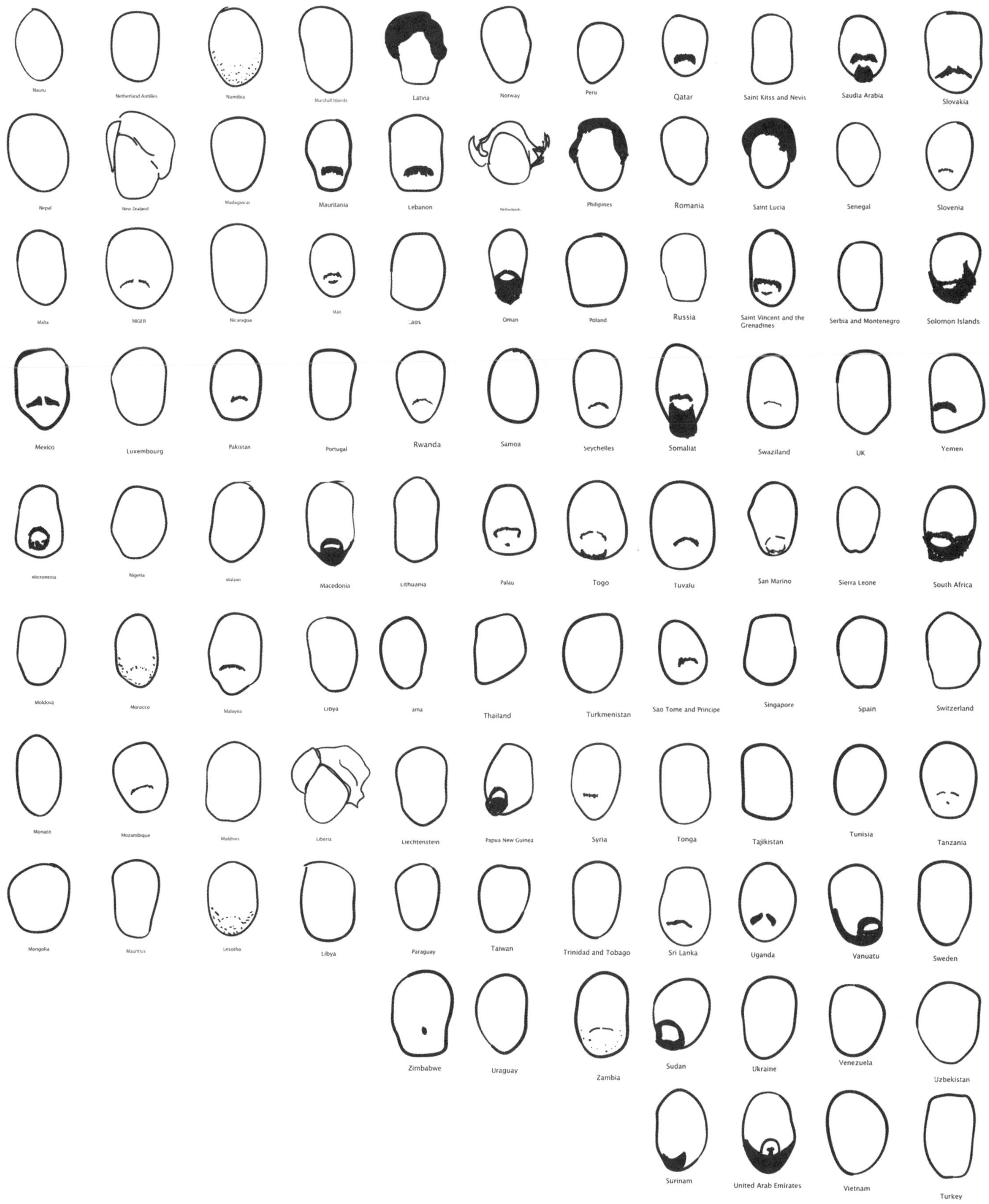
Nauru
Netherland Antilles
Namibia
Marshall Islands
Latvia
Norway
Peru
Qatar
Saint Kitss and Nevis
Saudia Arabia
Slovakia
Nepal
New Zealand
Madagascar
Mauritania
Lebanon
Netherlands
Philipines
Romania
Saint Lucia
Senegal
Slovenia
Malta
NIGER
Nicaragua
Mali
.aos
Oman
Poland
Russia
Saint Vincent and the Grenadines
Serbia and Montenegro
Solomon Islands
Mexico
Luxembourg
Pakistan
Portugal
Rwanda
Samoa
Seychelles
Somaliat
Swaziland
UK
Yemen
Micronesia
Nigeria
Malawi
Macedonia
Lithuania
Palau
Togo
Tuvalu
San Marino
Sierra Leone
South Africa
Moldova
Morocco
Malaysia
Libya
ama
Thailand
Turkmenistan
Sao Tome and Principe
Singapore
Spain
Switzerland
Monaco
Mozambique
Maldives
Liberia
Liechtenstein
Papua New Guinea
Syria
Tonga
Tajikistan
Tunisia
Tanzania
Mongolia
Mauritius
Lesotho
Libya
Paraguay
Taiwan
Trinidad and Tobago
Sri Lanka
Uganda
Vanuatu
Sweden
Zimbabwe
Uraguay
Zambia
Sudan
Ukraine
Venezuela
Uzbekistan
Surinam
United Arab Emirates
Vietnam
Turkey

SOCIAL FABRIC:

small gestures, art's angelic program, a set of tasks carried out beside or beneath the "real" ecoomic system, so as to patiently RE-STITCH THE RELATIONAL FABRIC.
pg. 36.

WEARING THE SHOES OF OTHERS.

SOCIAL CONTRACTS:

CREATE A FASHION VIDEO BY CAPTURING STILL OR SHORT SNIPS OF MOVIES, T.V. NOW IF YOU HAD TO CAPTURE FASHION OF TODAY.

⇒ IMOVIE DEMO
- CHECK OUT VIDEO CAMERA'S
TEAM PEOPLE UP →
VIDEO MAKERS – W/ PAINTERS
PAINTERS W/ PHOTOGRAPHERS.

SHOES
HATS
PANTS
CASUAL
COUTURE

YOU HAVE... THE RIGHT TO KNOW!

"The spotted plane trees, the square plot of earth at the foot of each."
pg 165
The Waiting
Borges

166
"each day is a translucent network of minimal surprises."

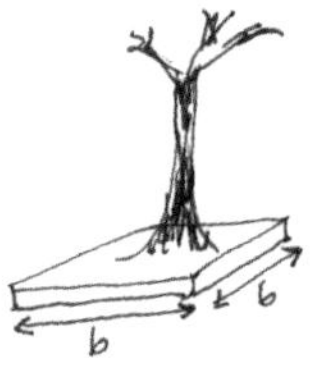

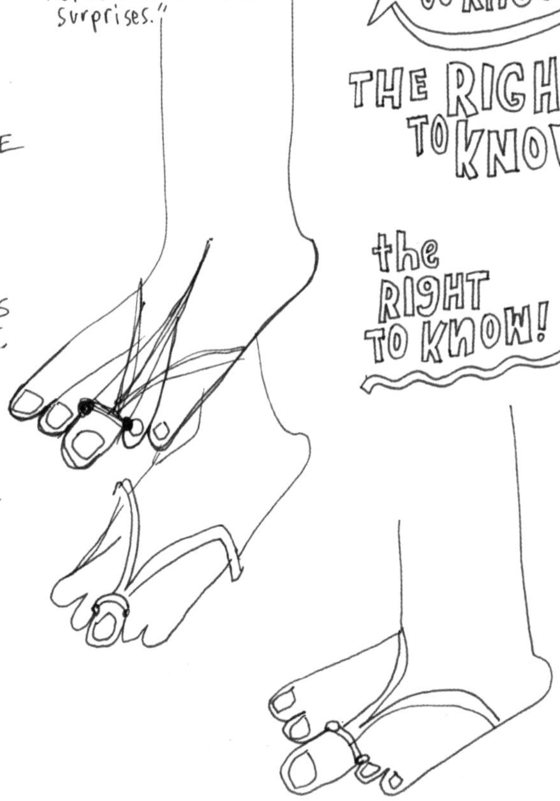

the right to know!

THE RIGHT TO KNOW

the RIGHT TO KNOW!

ORDER	DREAMS
SYSTEMATC	7513462
REALITY	ARBITRARY
1234567	NON-LINEAR.

redirected by notes of someone else found in a second hand book.

FREE SOIL: FERTILE TERRAINE

FACILITATING COMBINATIONS OF FERTILE EXISTENCE.

~~WORKING TOWARDS~~ A SUSTAINABLE FERTILITY.

ART, ACTION, + DISCOURSE TOWARDS SUSTAINABLE FERTILITY.

~~SUSTAINING~~ CULTIVATING FERTILE ART, ACTION, + DISCOURSE

KEEP IT FRESH!

USER-FRIENDLY
HANDS ON
AMATEUR.

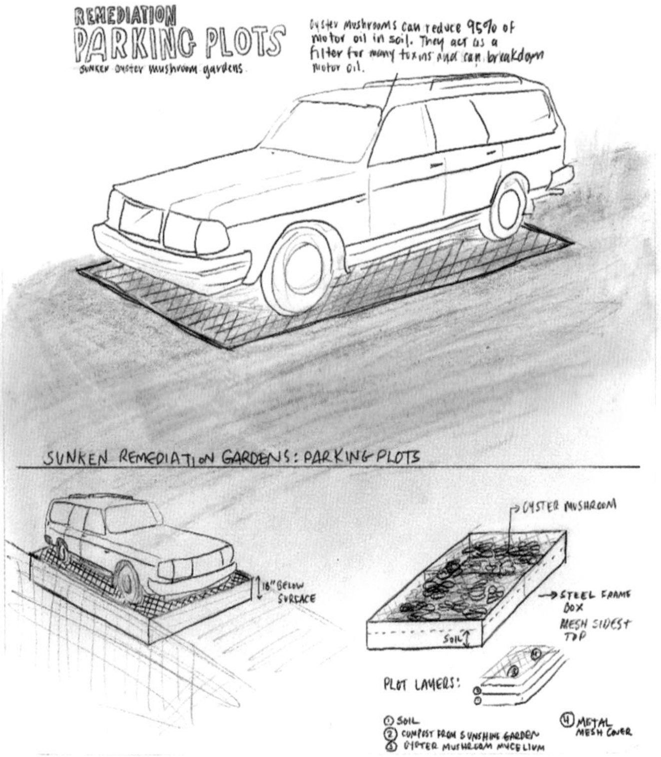

remediation beds

mycoremediation is a form of bioremediation, the process of using microbes to return an environment (usually soil) contaminated by pollutants to a less contaminated state.

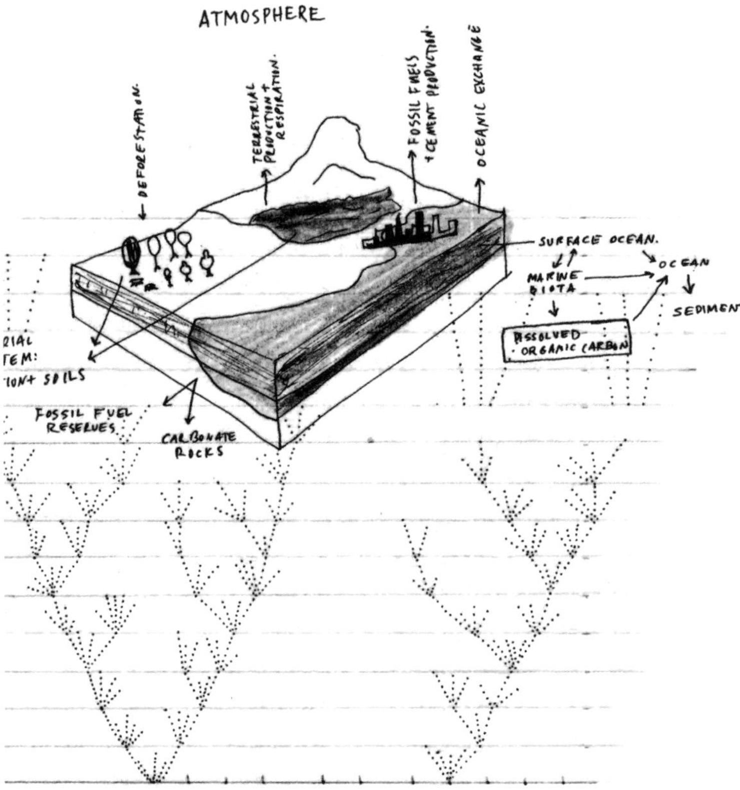

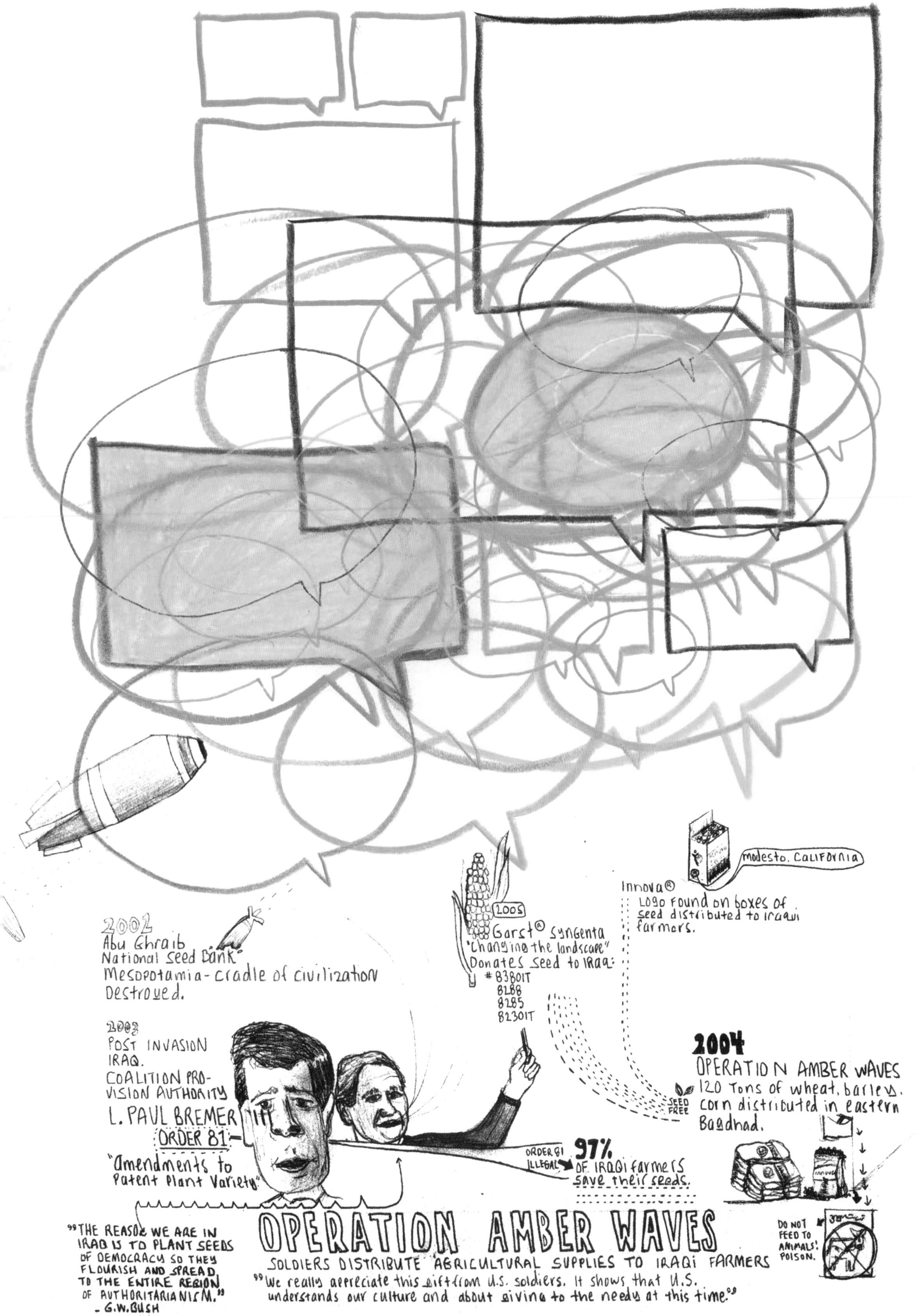

2002
Abu Ghraib
National Seed Bank
Mesopotamia- cradle of civilization
Destroyed.
2005
Garst® syngenta
"changing the landscape"
Donates seed to Iraq:
B3801T
8288
8285
B2301T
modesto, California
Innova®
Logo found on boxes of seed distributed to iraqi farmers.
2003
POST INVASION IRAQ.
COALITION PROVISION AUTHORITY
L. PAUL BREMER
ORDER 81
"amendments to Patent Plant Variety"
ORDER 81 ILLEGAL
97% OF IRAQI farmers save their seeds.
SEED FREE
2004
OPERATION AMBER WAVES
120 Tons of wheat, barley, corn distributed in eastern Bagdhad.
DO NOT FEED TO ANIMALS! POISON.
"THE REASON WE ARE IN IRAQ IS TO PLANT SEEDS OF DEMOCRACY SO THEY FLOURISH AND SPREAD TO THE ENTIRE REGION OF AUTHORITARIANISM." - G.W.BUSH
OPERATION AMBER WAVES
SOLDIERS DISTRIBUTE AGRICULTURAL SUPPLIES TO IRAQI FARMERS
"We really appreciate this gift from U.S. soldiers. It shows that U.S. understands our culture and about giving to the needy at this time."

CRAIG FRAZIER

Craig Frazier, an illustrator and designer from Mill Valley, California, writes a lot of text in his sketchbooks, including "speeches, essays, and to-do lists." In addition, he records ideas for websites, book projects, businesses, and a lot of things that never come to be. "I suppose I am practicing drawing, though I think it is really practicing seeing and thinking," he says, as though pondering the real rationale.

Frazier is known for posting a new drawing on the internet every Monday morning, but that is not what the books are for. "I use my sketchbook to record idea blips before they escape. At times I can work in it very deliberately and purposefully, at others with great randomness and spontaneity. There is a certain sense of 'staying on your game' that comes from keeping a sketchbook."

For Frazier, these images from 2007–8 "are unfinished work, usually very poor drawings. I am much more concerned with documenting an idea. The privacy of a sketchbook creates a completely different response in me than work that I know will be seen and judged in the public eye. There is no theme, as only I can decipher what the sketches are really about. I suppose there is a repeated effort to mine for wit."

34

67

79

76

54

55

78

50

8

9

35

14

96

97

24

6

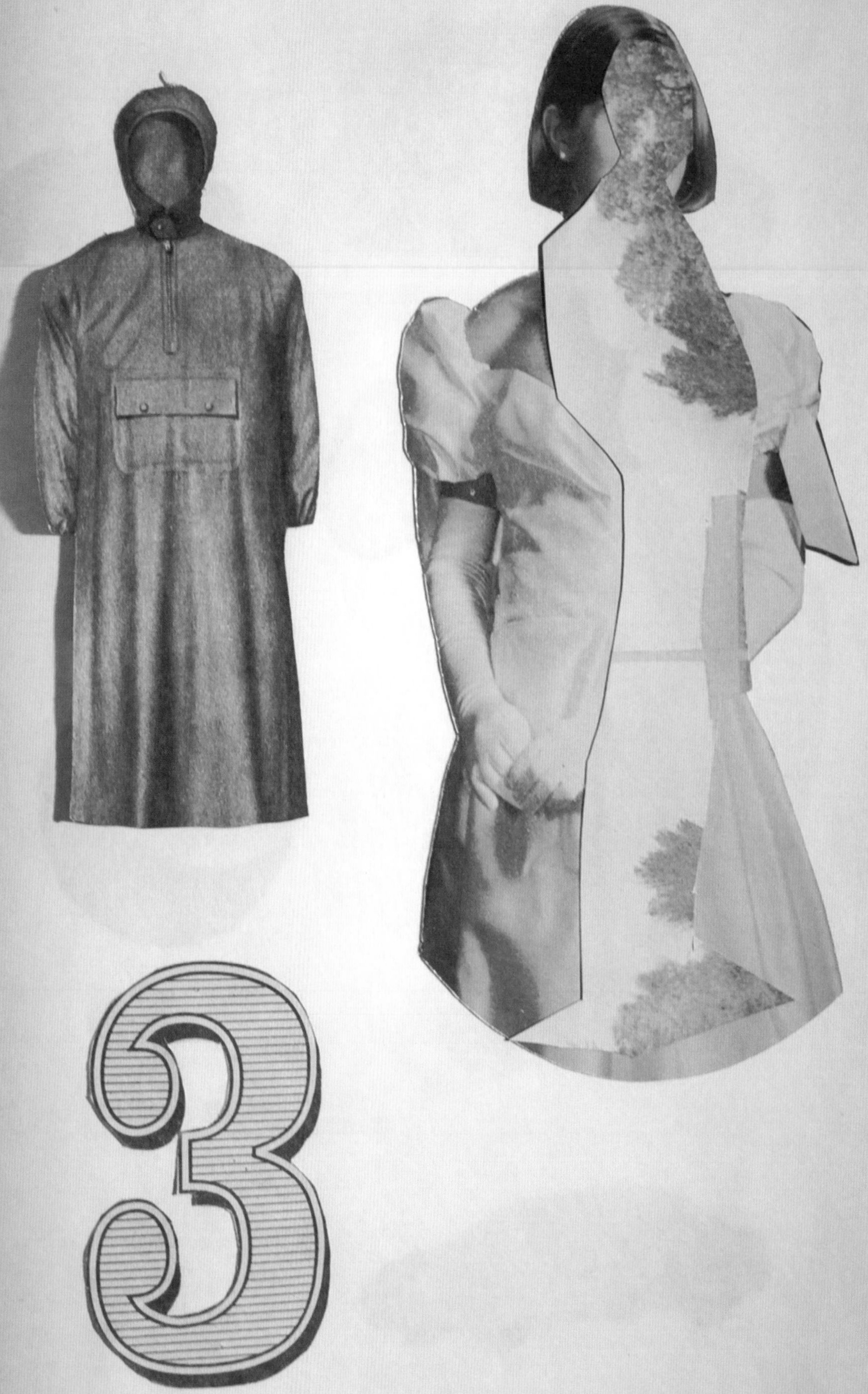
3

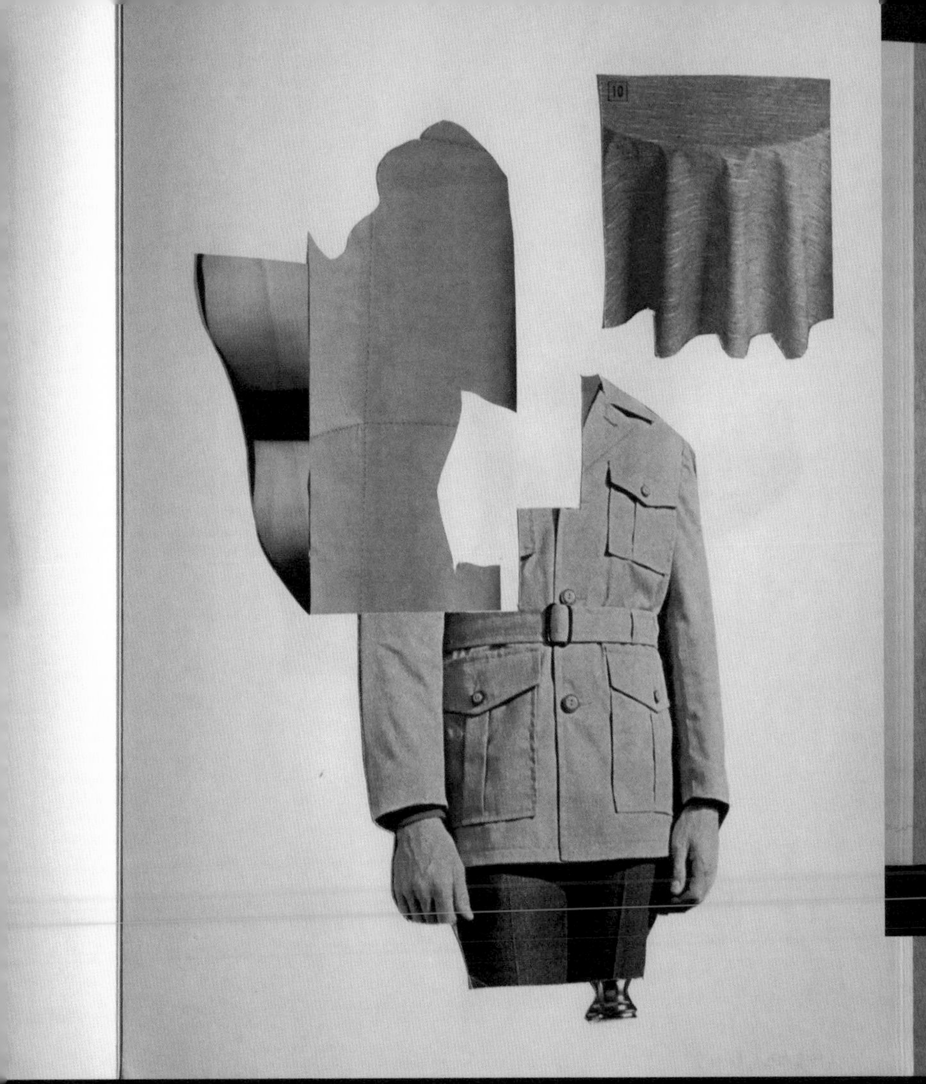

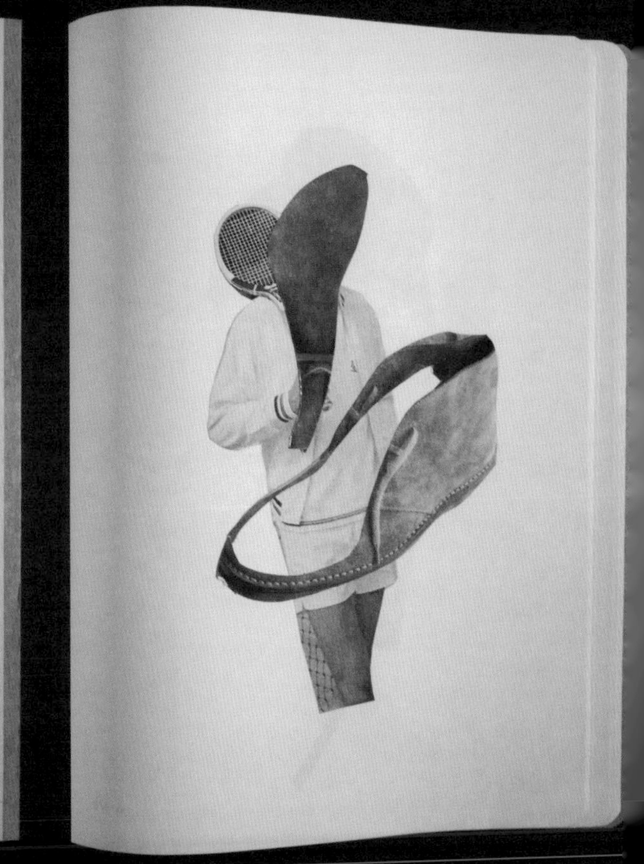

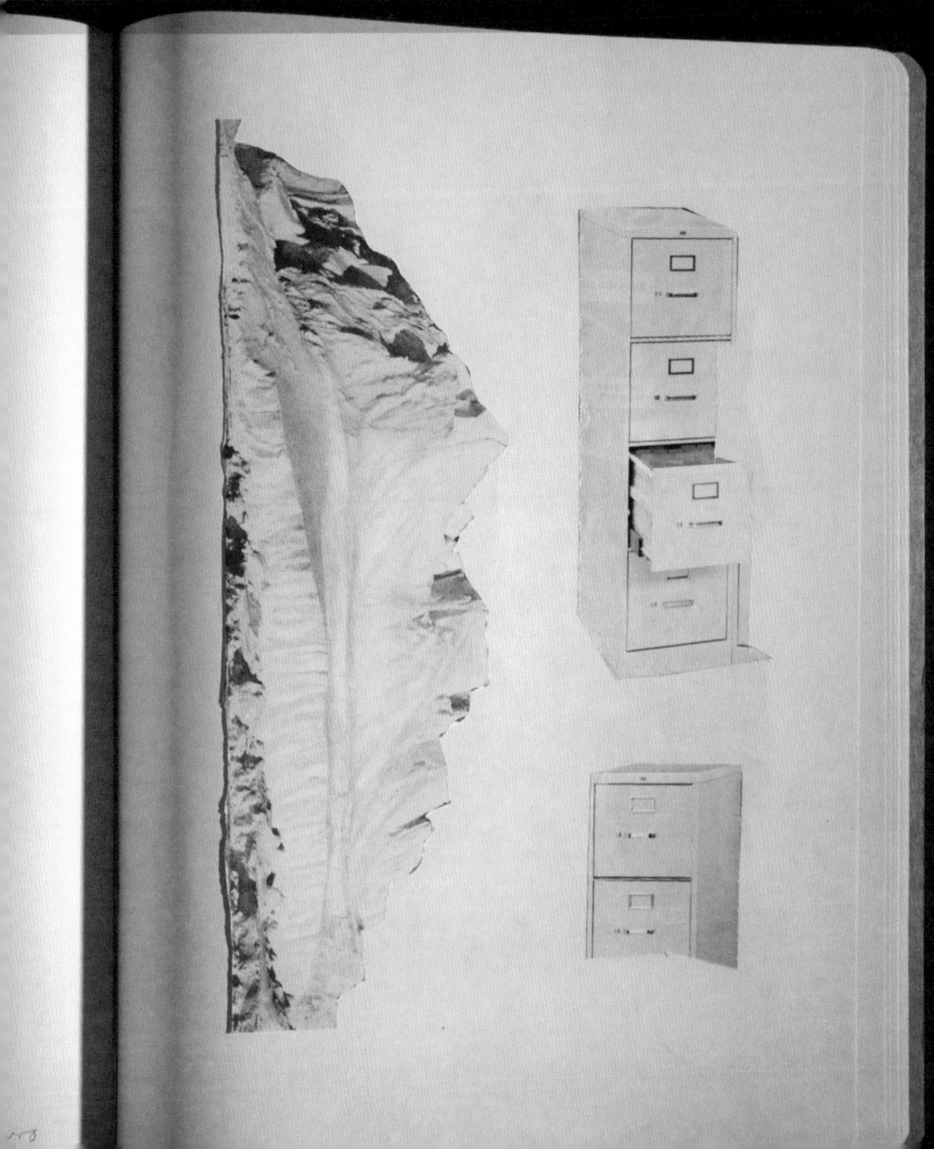

JOHN GALL

John Gall, longtime art director of Vintage Books, is a packrat who has used some kind of sketchbook his entire student and professional life. "I use them as an escape from the day job – a place to get away from 'design think' and problem-solving," Gall wistfully explains. "I can use my hands, cut things up, paste them down, free associate, make wrong decisions, that kind of thing."

Gall's book covers are as airtight as possible. But of late, he says, "I have been trying to get a little looser with the concept – adding more ambiguity." That's where the sketchbooks play a role.

"Even though there is a free associative element to these images, I do present myself with rules when approaching a page, mostly to do with things I tend not to like about collage in general. It will be something like: 'no funny heads made out of appliances,' 'no surreal-looking narrative,' 'no foreground and background,' and 'no type(!).' Of course, I break these rules as often as I follow them. I also try not to work with anything of any inherent beauty or value. I prefer recycling the dregs of our visual culture."

These books from 2001–9 are best characterized as "labored spontaneity," says Gall, revealing his penchant for paradoxical thinking.

PETER GIRARDI

Los Angeles-based animation producer and designer Peter Girardi started his design career as a graffiti artist in the New York City train yards. So subway trains were his original sketchbook. But he has had one since age thirteen. "My sketchbook contains everything from ideas to finished drawings, sketches, reference images to notes," he says. But, he abruptly adds, "It's not a journal. I don't like 'journals'."

Of course, it's all semantic. Girardi says, "I get too precious with the sketchbooks. Most of these are finished works. Sometimes I'll take pieces and make them into larger paintings, or some of the lettering I might use in projects."

These intense lettering sketches from 2002–8 are influenced by his graffiti days, but transcend them. "The more I draw these lettering pieces, the more they turn into strange pieces of poetry," he says. "That's not something I've ever thought of or wanted, but I can't avoid the by-product."

Girardi is not sure how many sketchbooks he retains but thinks there are a lot of them. "In the last ten years I've only used black composition notebooks (they are less precious and therefore less pressure than fancy bound 'artist' sketchbooks), and I have at least twenty-five of those, from which these examples are taken."

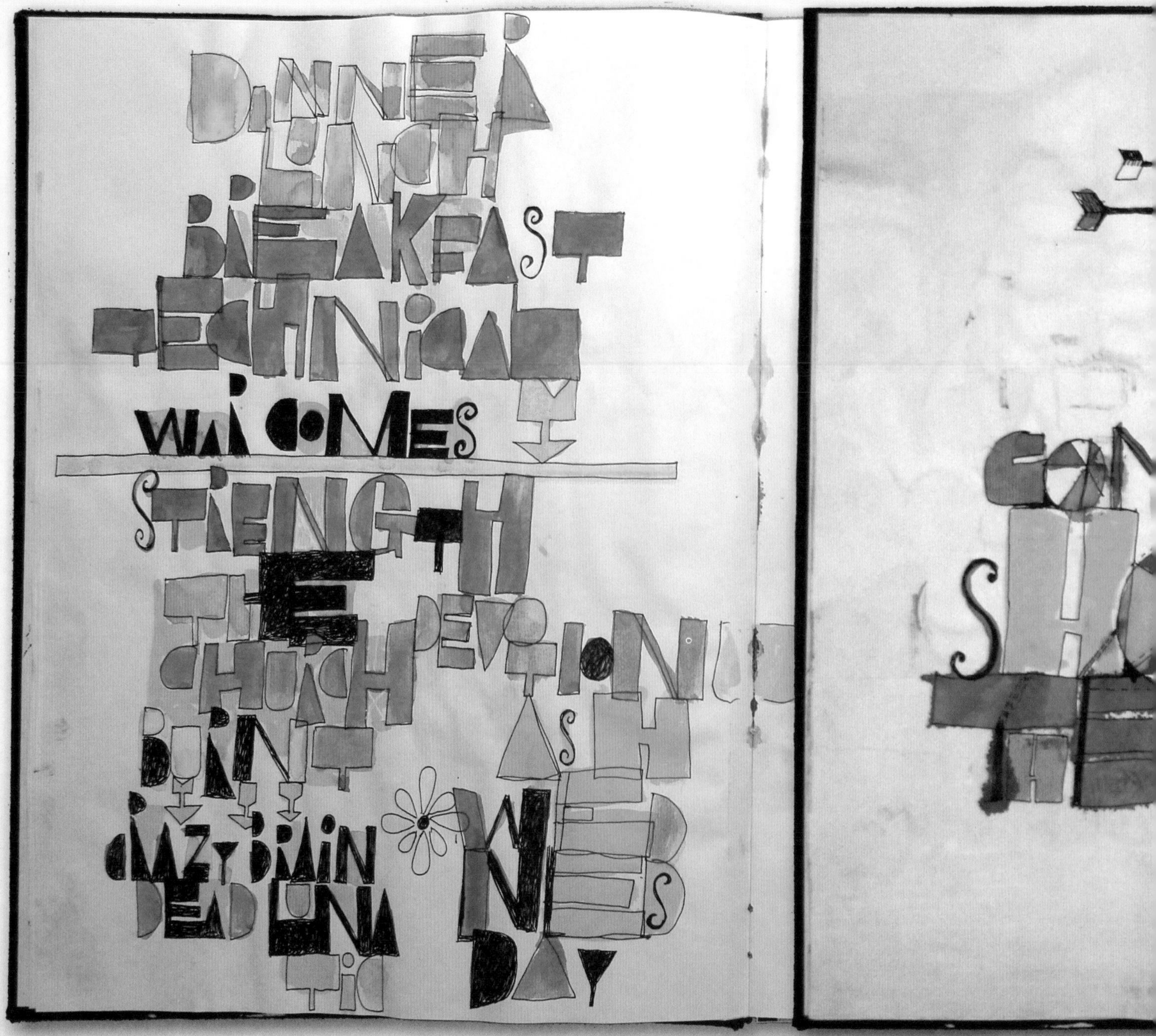
COMES
WEDNESDAY

MOCKING
WOOD AND WATER
FLESH
BONE
SHUT
GEN-POP
SPOFFORTH
MED:GATE

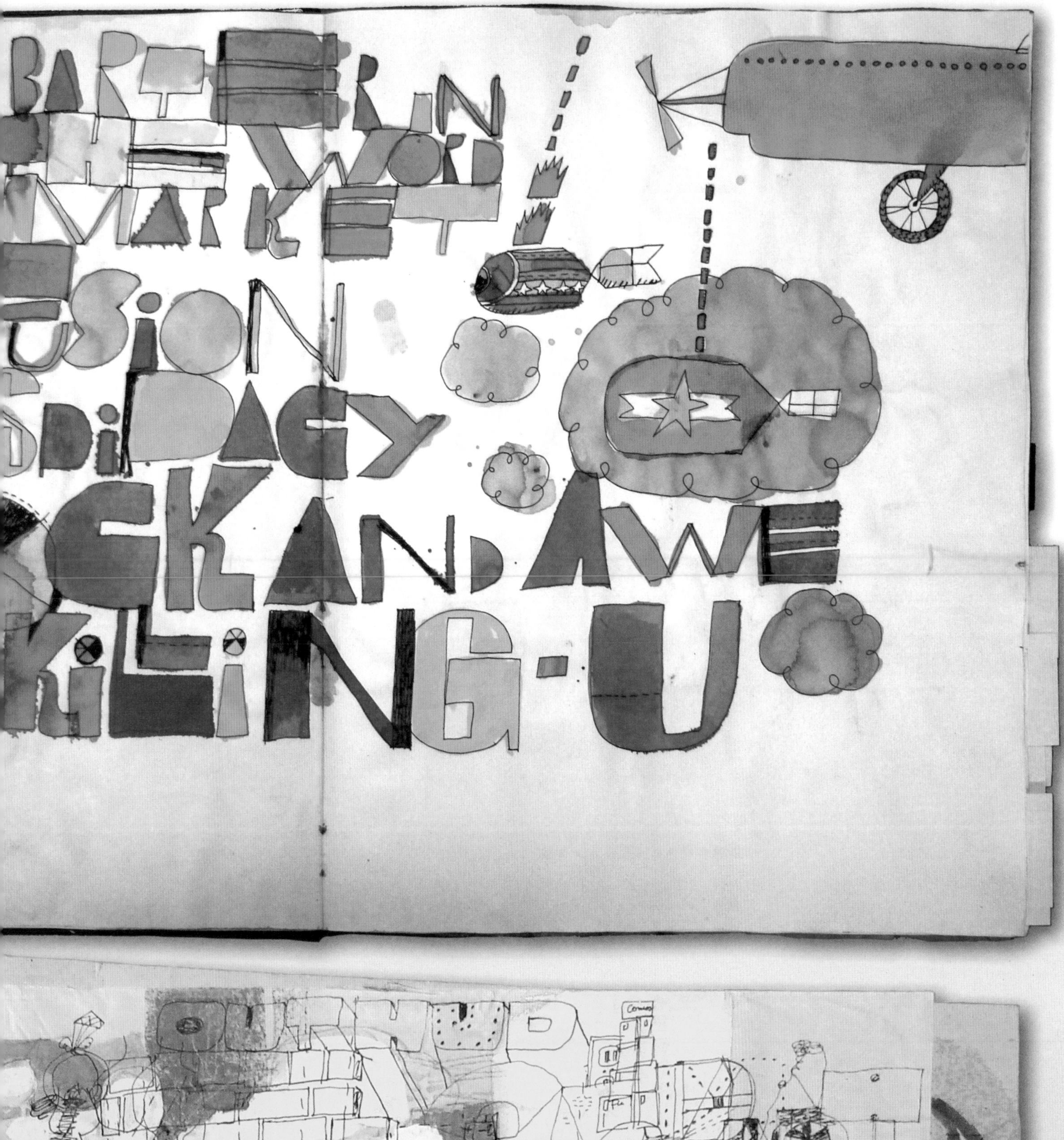
AND AWE
KILING-U

ASK
MORE
RELAX
SHOW
THEN
FIX
ALL
THE
BOT
DROWNED

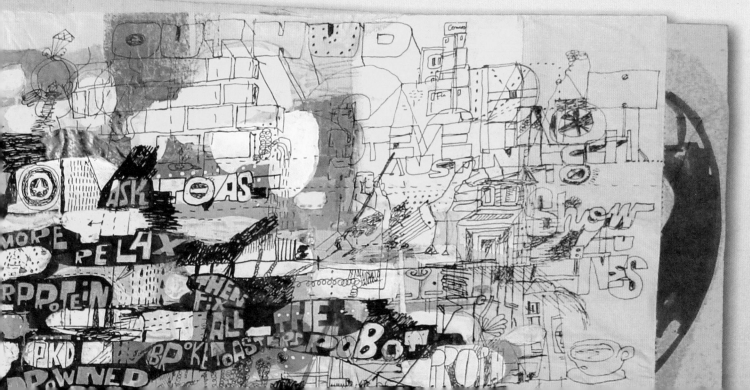

MILTON GLASER

With Seymour Chwast (see page 92), Milton Glaser co-founded Push Pin Studios in New York in 1954. He is currently the principal of Milton Glaser Inc., and designs posters, packages, publications, environments, and more. He is an icon of American design.

Glaser has kept a sketchbook since he was at the High School of Music & Art in New York. Given his historic output, it would be wonderful actually to see some of these earliest objects, now lost. Nonetheless, enough of Glaser's work is documented to give a fairly accurate picture of his creative evolution. The reason why he still keeps sketchbooks is pretty logical: "To remind me of what I've forgotten," he says. What is distinct about these sketchbooks is that "they are more tentative, less professional," than Glaser's finished work, and are "made for my own viewing," although the finish brought to these sketches is not all that dissimilar from some of his posters and illustrations.

Asked if there is any kind of thematic strand, he simply notes "how particular it is to recognize any themes from a few thin lines." Many of the images here are from past travels, especially in Italy. Glaser admits he takes great pleasure from these lines. And the sixty or so books he retains are full of pleasurable encounters.

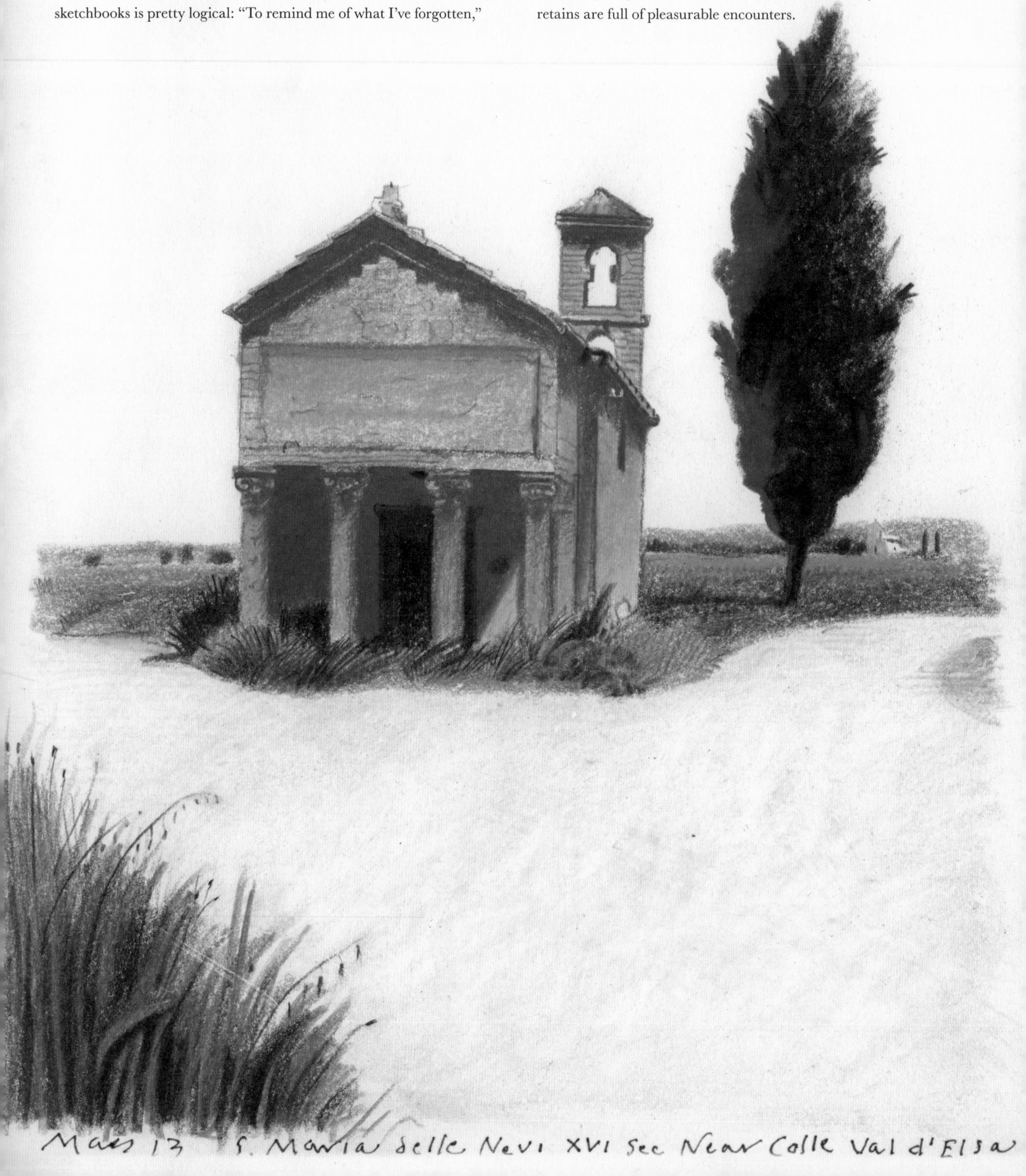
Mar 13 S. Maria delle Nevi XVI Sec Near Colle Val d'Elsa

Thursday April 6 San Giovanni Valdarno

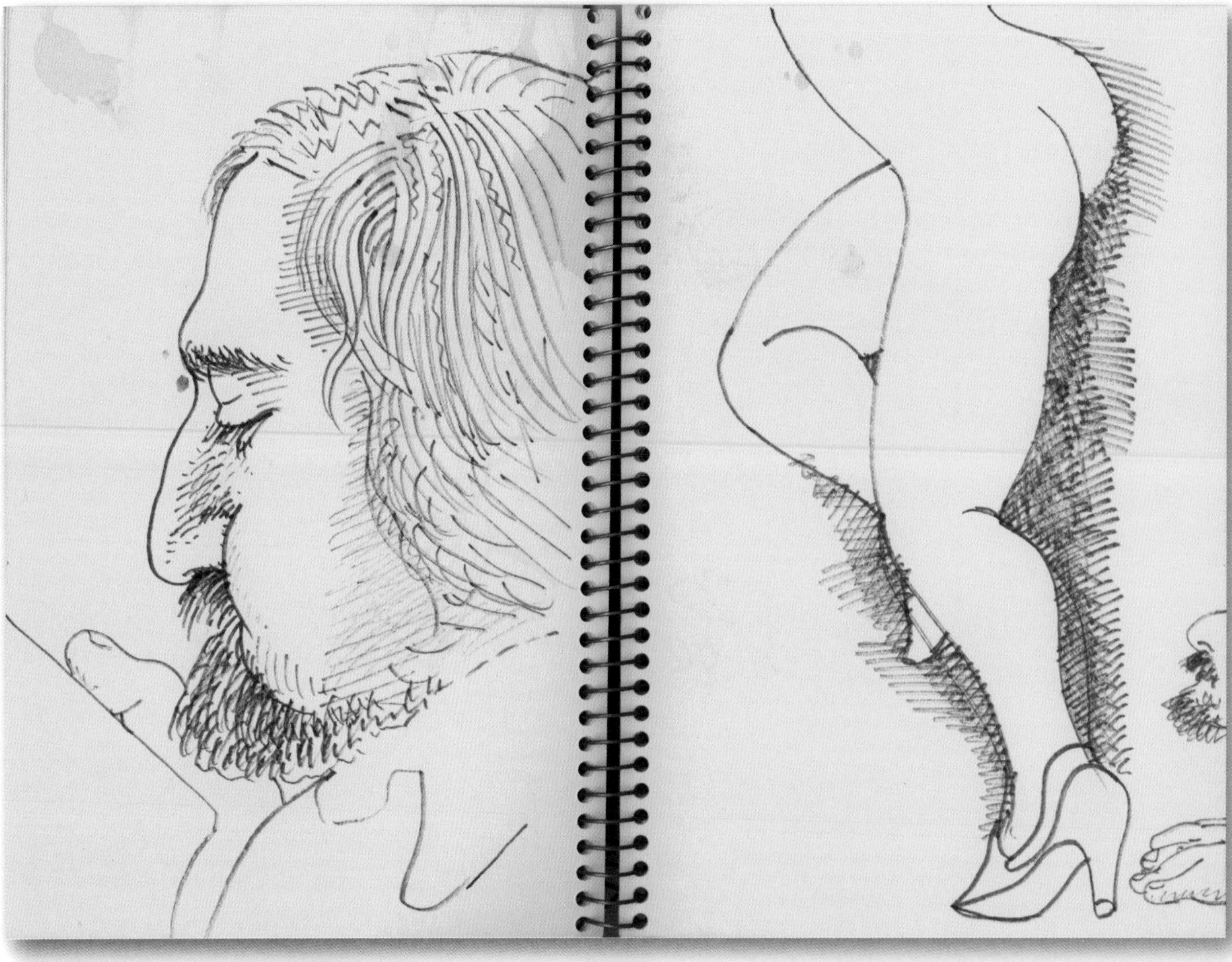

Friday Morning
Milton Glaser

Grilled filets of Beef grilled on one side only aflavored with olive oil and Rosemary
Verdura alla Bracia
Tomato
Radicchio
Finnocchio
Eggplant
mushroom
1989
Sfurfantino
BIANCO DEI COLLI DELLA TOSCANA CENTRALE
VINO DA TAVOLA
Duck medalions of porcini a sauce made of asparagus
← NICE LOCAL HOUSE WINE
Then panna cotta and a beautiful arrangement of fresh cut fruit
we began with a green risotto
SAT. MAY 13 L'ANTICA TRATTORIA - COLLE D'ALELSA

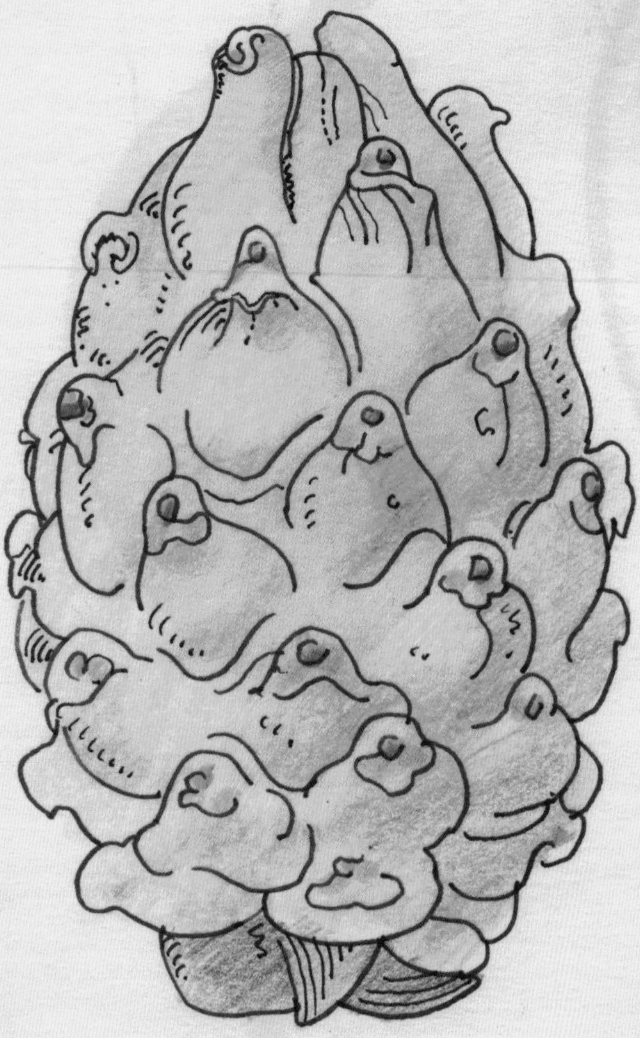

Pitahaya
a kind of cactus
many black seeds
that are said to be
laxative when chewed

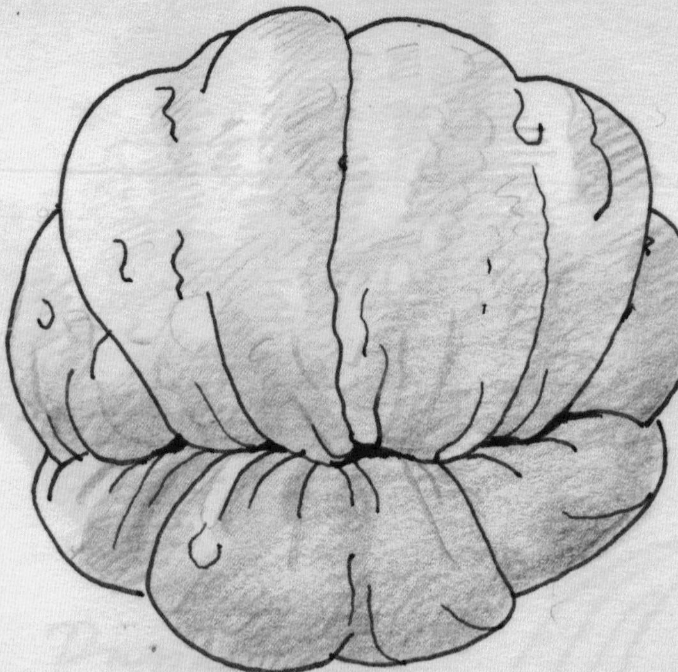

ciorayota
least expensive vegetable
white potato like

Zapote
yellow flesh
sweet, large pit
not unlike mango

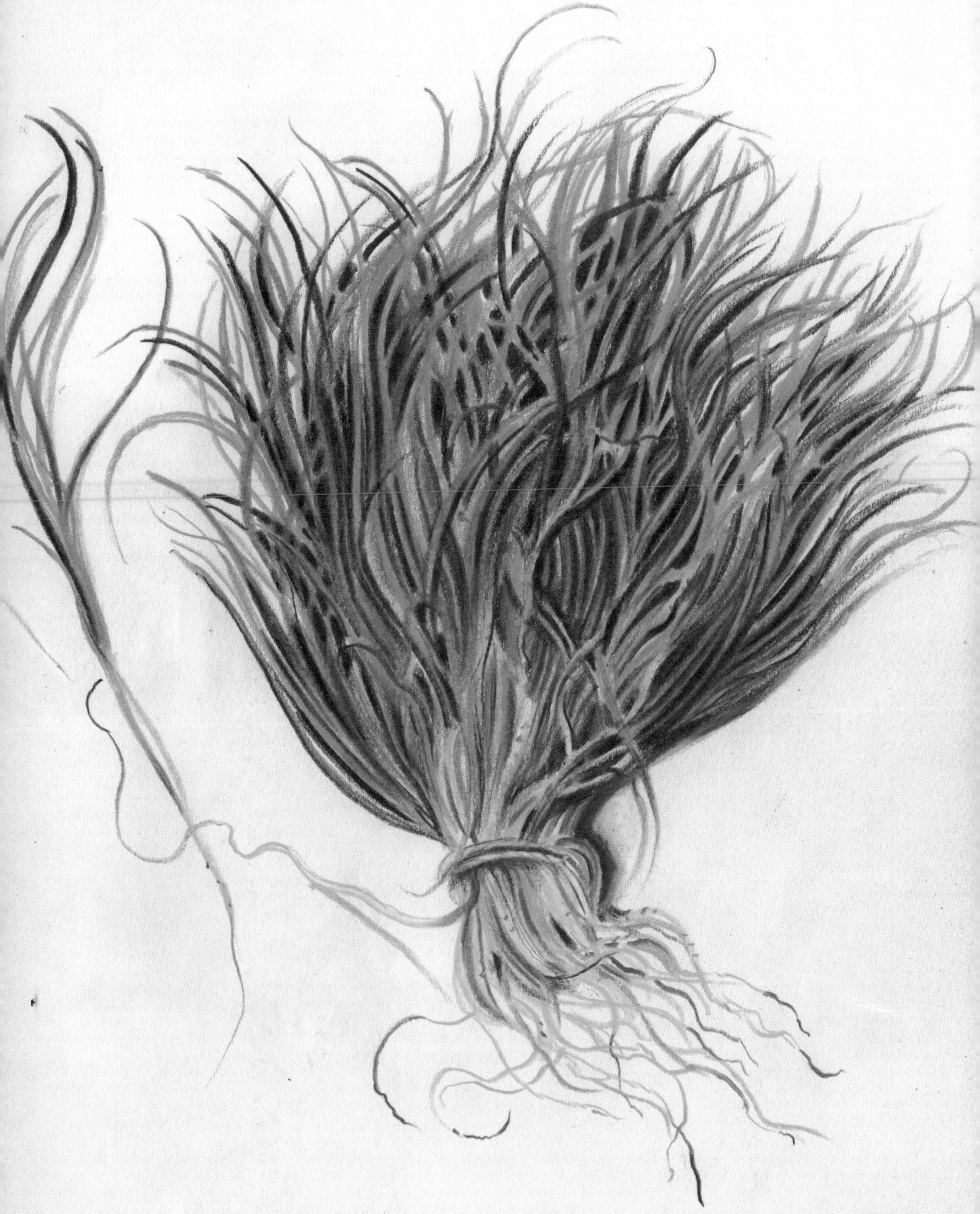

Monday April 10 – Agretti can be eaten cooked or raw

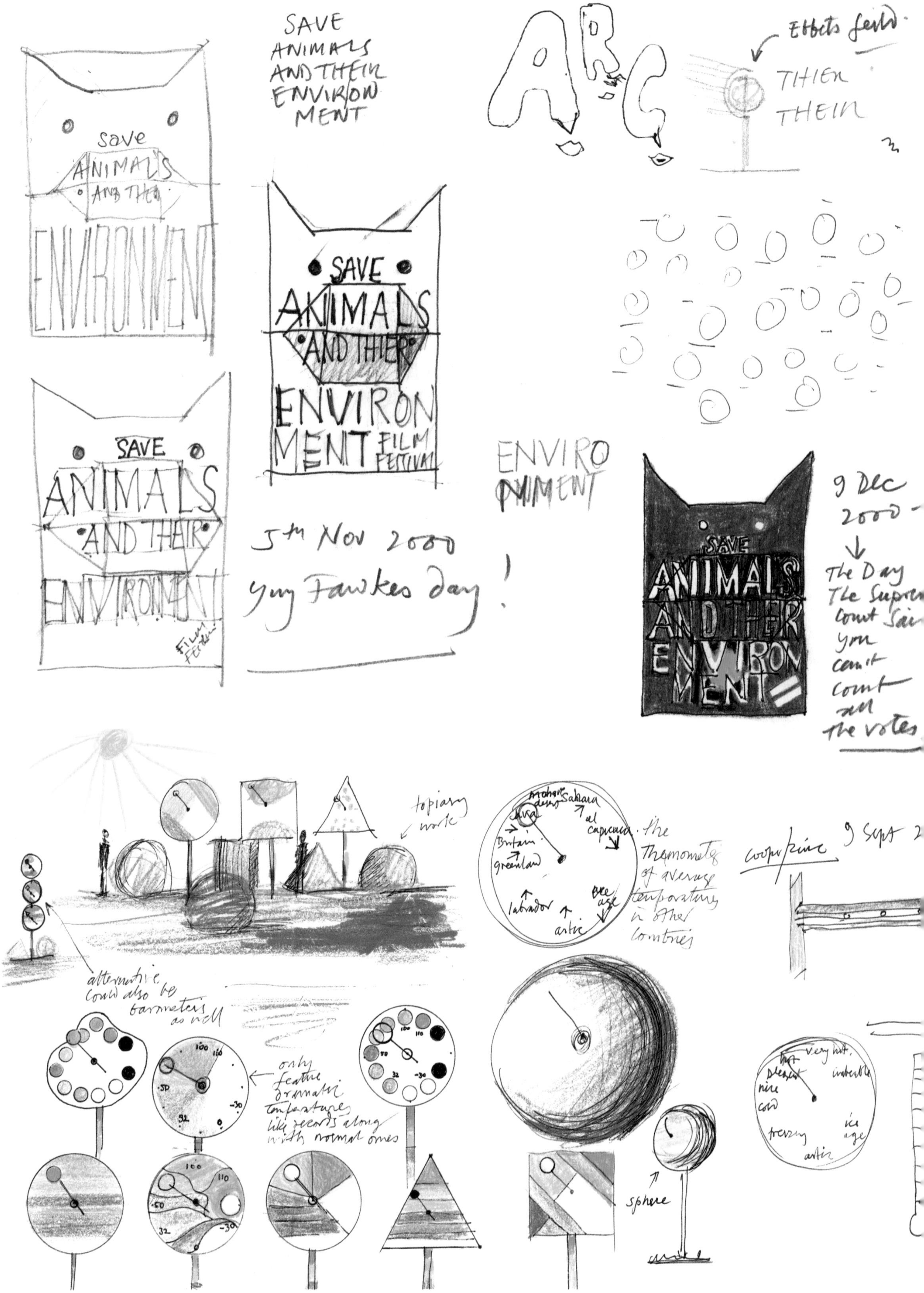
SAVE ANIMALS AND THEIR ENVIRONMENT
ENVIRONMENT
SAVE ANIMALS AND THIER ENVIRONMENT FILM FESTIVAL
SAVE ANIMALS AND THEIR ENVIRONMENT
FILM FESTIVAL
ARC
THIER
THEIR
ENVIRO NMENT
5th Nov 2000
Guy Fawkes day!
SAVE ANIMALS AND THER ENVIRONMENT
9 Dec 2000
The Day
topiary work
alternative could also be barometers as well
only feature dramatic temperatures like records along with normal ones
sphere

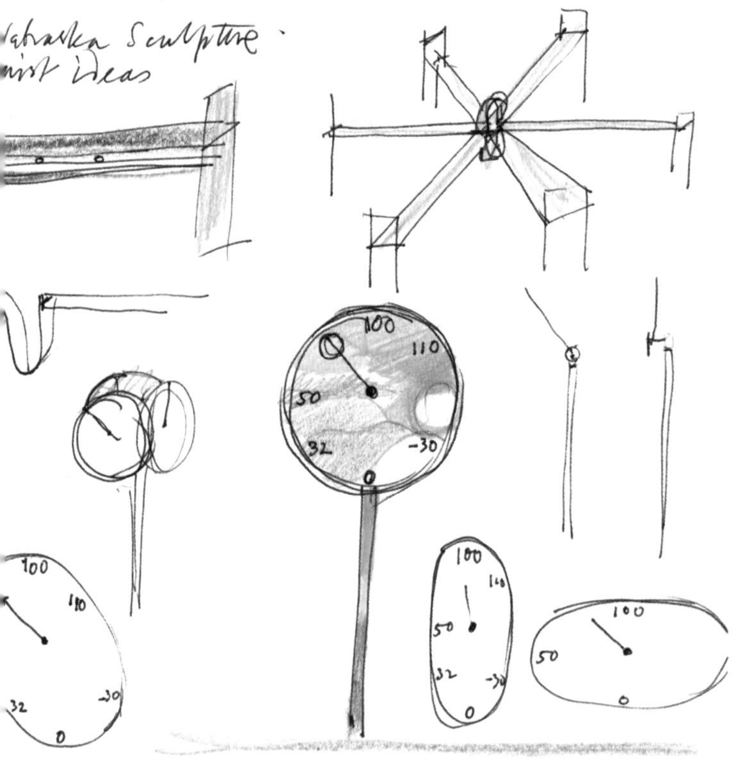

KEITH GODARD

London-born, New York-based multimedia designer Keith Godard's first sketchbook dates back to 1958. He says, "I started at the London College of Printing and continued drawing in the Royal Army Medical Corps and on my travels to Europe," some of which is shown here.

For Godard, who was one of the first to teach graphic design history as a discipline, the sketchbooks are intended "to improve my visual memory, as I believe one draws what one knows probably more than what one sees. I was gifted as a small kid in remembering things I had seen, specifically memories of London at the end of the war and in the beginning of peace in 1946–47. The later sketchbooks are more for developing ideas for graphic designs and exhibition design as well as visual notes for public art projects and competitions."

The contents of Godard's crusty sketchbooks are "spontaneous thoughts, made with heart and hand, which are often lost in the development and mechanical production process for printing or fabrication." He notes that the most important aspect of his six sketchbooks is "the written notes about the concepts. Also, although the technology of producing design work has changed over the last fifty years, the keeping and making of sketchbook drawings that have the nucleus of an idea of a project have remained the same."

Continent Tables for UNICEF February 2006

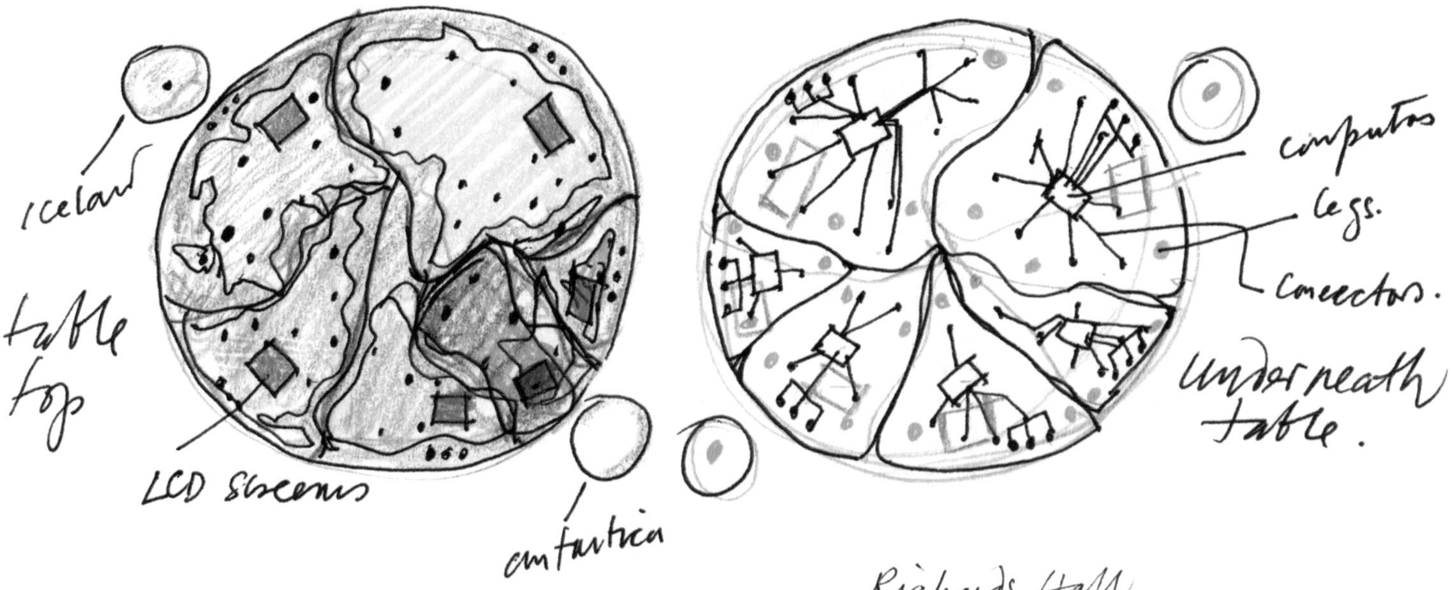

Richards Hall Sculptures.

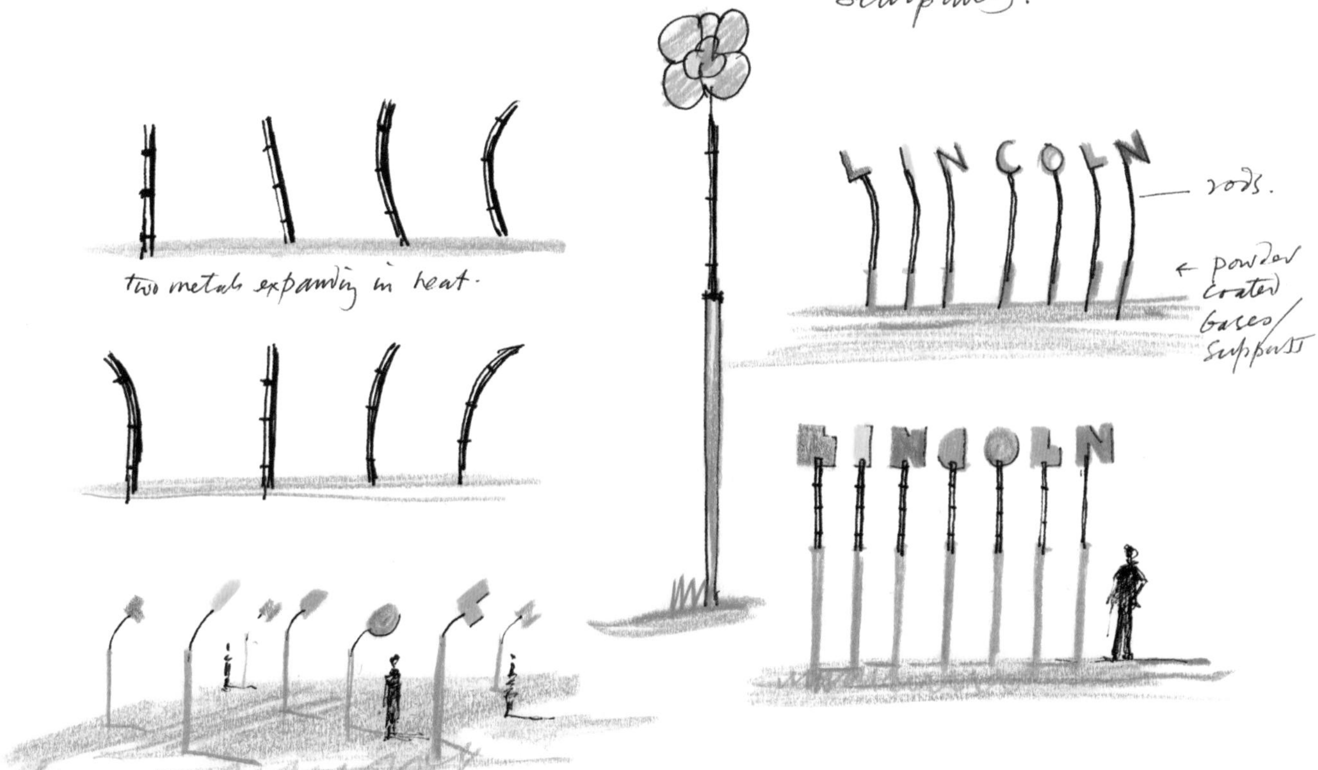

Ways of Seeing
BBC T.V series
John Berger
Pelican Original
ISBN 0140216316

TILLY
LOSCH

I want to live!
Planet Earth
allegro = lively
allegretto = not
moderato = moderate

CAROLYN GOWDY

London-based illustrator Carolyn Gowdy has been sketching for as long as she can remember. "When inspired, I just make a scribble or a sketch, usually accompanied by words. As a child I drew a new picture every day on a fresh brown paper lunch bag before taking it to school."

For Gowdy, the sketches and scrapbooks, which are too numerous to count, "help me remember and especially to explore the ideas I have. I love to document interesting people, places, events, and things about the world that I encounter or read about."

The distinction is that "there is often a very fine line between a sketch and a finished piece. It helps me to approach almost everything as a sketch. My process usually begins with a scribble from the imagination and proceeds until I feel I've arrived at something that breathes and is convincing." The ongoing theme Gowdy has worked with since 1994 is "Life is an Adventure ... Life is a Gift." Another is "Theatre of Women," which began around 1979.

"Dressing Up," the early sketch shown here, Gowdy "just threw in for fun. It is from the early 1960s." The others were made over the years 2004–6.

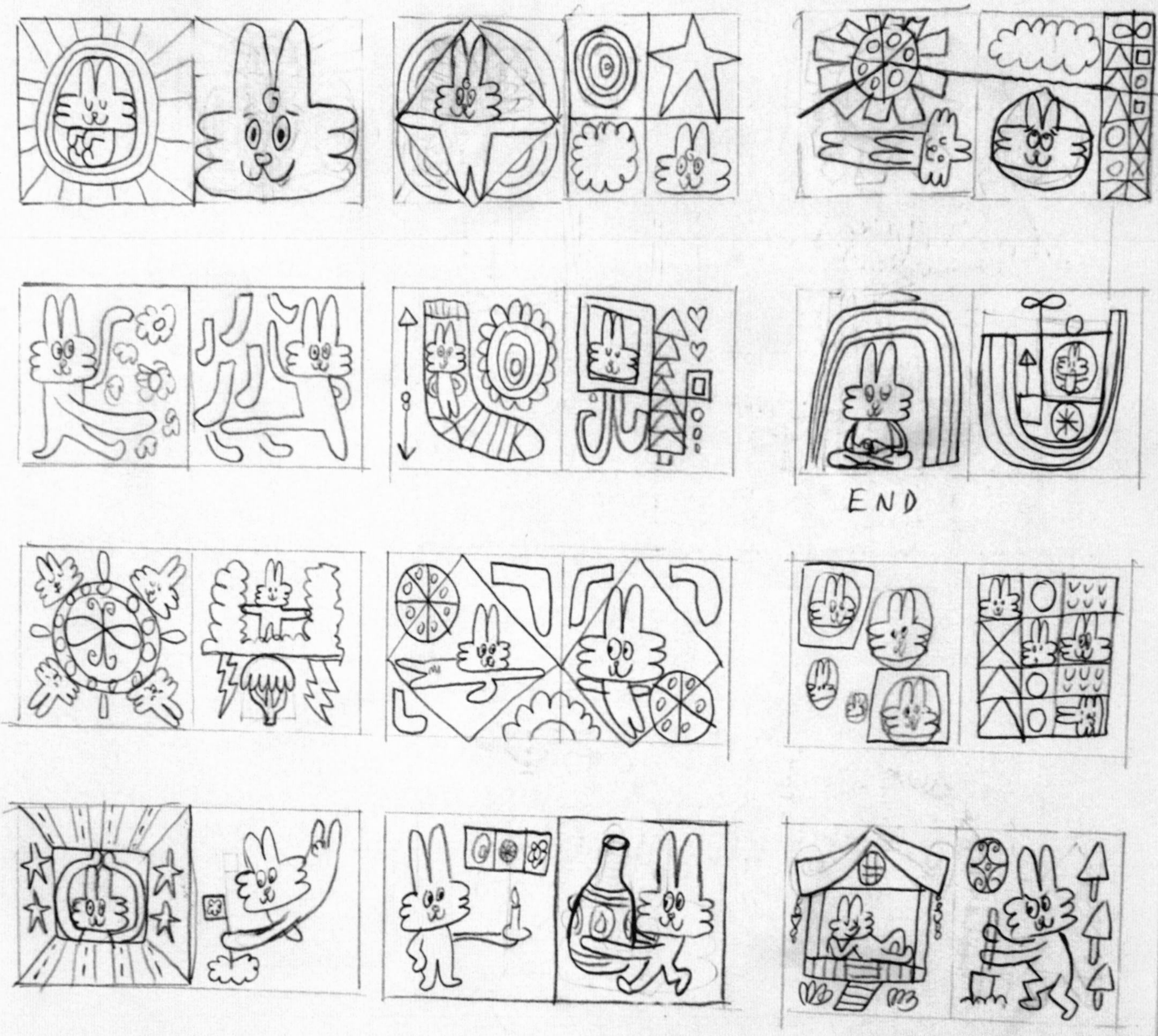

RODNEY ALAN GREENBLAT

Rodney Alan Greenblat, New York artist, illustrator, and pioneer digital game creator, started formally keeping sketchbooks when he began at the School of Visual Arts in 1978, and has kept them in a remarkably orderly fashion ever since.

His books are what he philosophically terms "the fundamental and intimate dominion of infinite time and space. I use them to daydream, test notions, relax, and explore the infinite workings of the vast mind. I illustrate goofy poems, record my profound realizations, feature quotes from books, and emphasize important notes to myself. Sometimes I simply entertain myself with the wonder of drawing."

Within the books, Greenblat notes, "often unresolved propositions reoccur at different intervals. It's interesting to notice my pencil digging back into an idea buried a week, a month, or even a year previous. There are explorations of nuts-and-bolts commercial projects like character design, then snapping back to the sublime mystery of sculpture and painting. I think my sculptural studies are interesting as I wrestle with very specific and often practical engineering issues." The excerpts here are from books 47 to 51 (out of 52, all numbered), from May 2006 to July 2008.

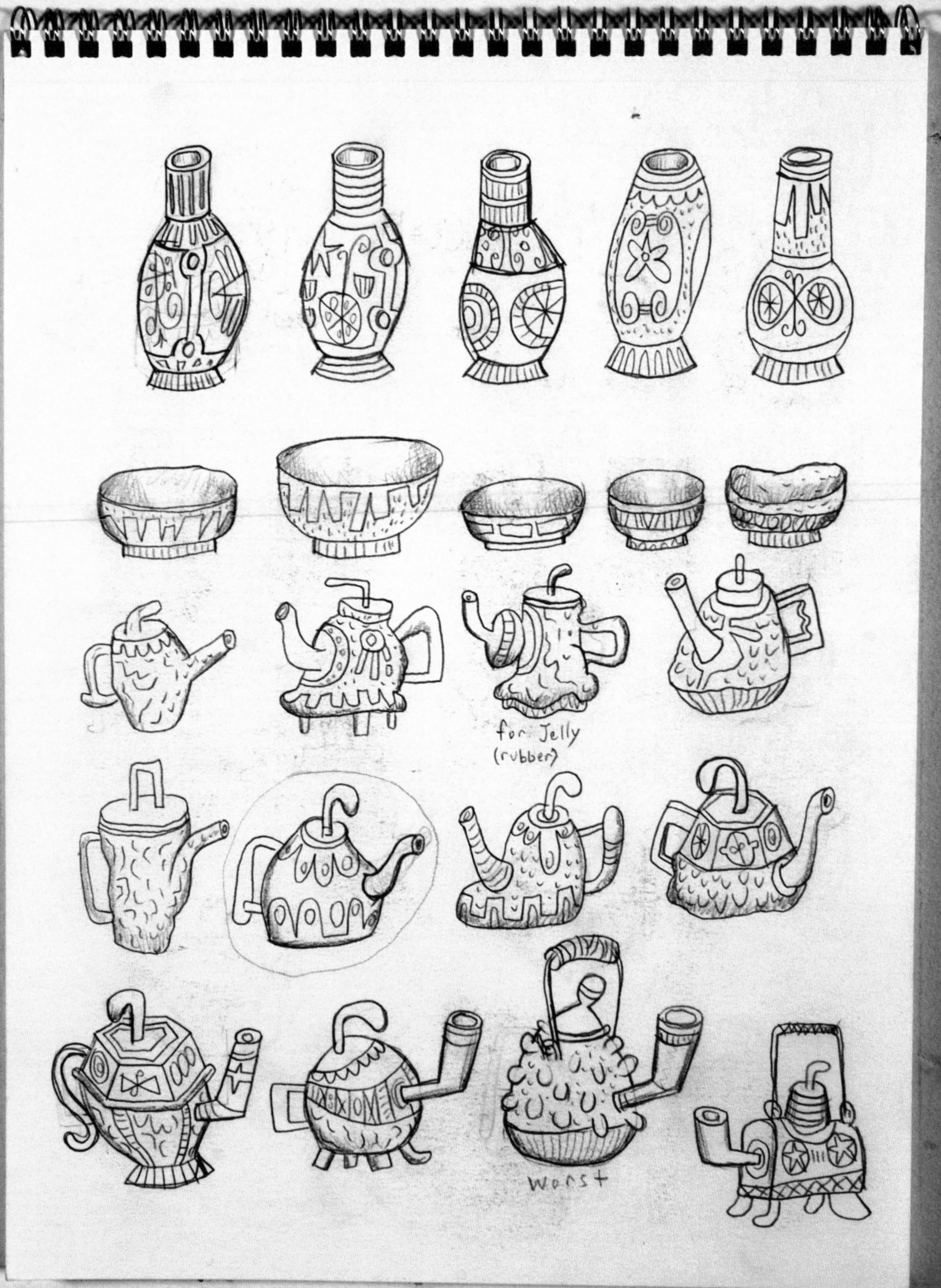
for Jelly
(rubber)
worst

Kumajitomokai
NOT Pleasurable or un-Pleasurable
NOT That Good NOT That Bad
not comfortable or uncomfortable
JUST as it is...
recognizable and un-recognizable
without yin or yang
No Substance Ahhh!
beginningless and Endless.......
appears and then disappears
not Comfortable
not un-comfortable
Treasury of The True Dharma eye
not Pleasurable or Unpleasurable

Fudo?

ALL TIME + SPACE INCLUDED INSIDE INFINITELY
electric Guitar Solo
NOW
Past Future
(look into it)
Temple Bell
don't try to accomplish anything

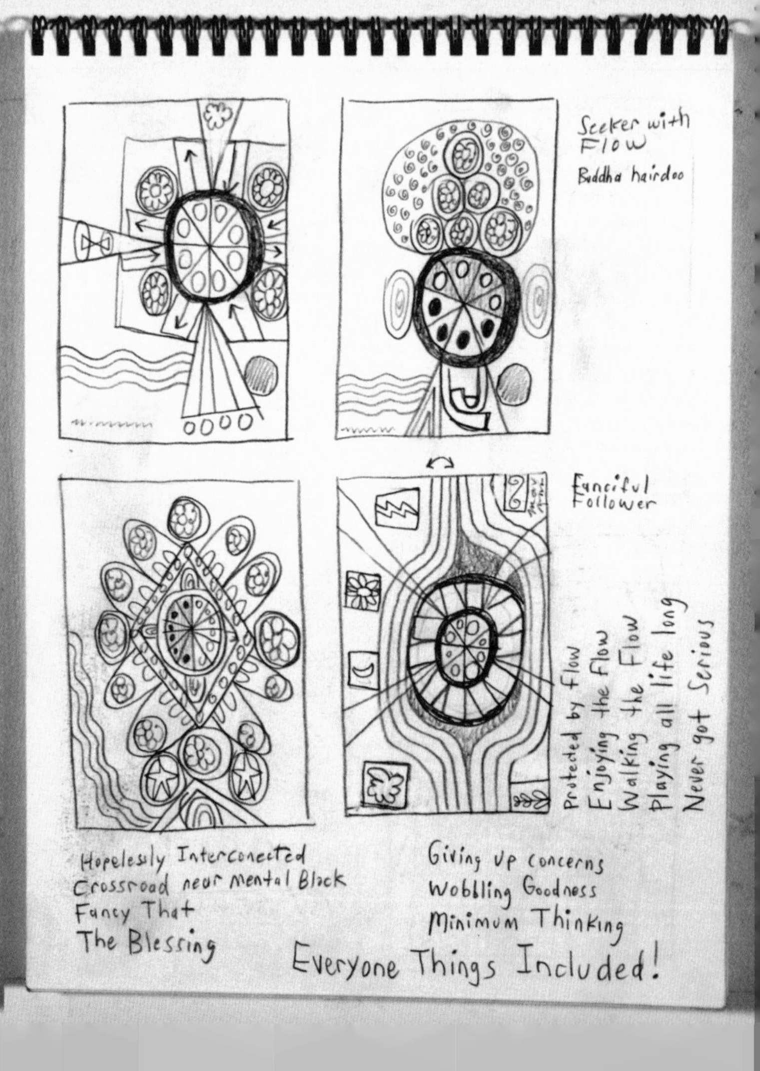
Seeker with Flow
Buddha hairdoo
Fanciful Follower
Protected by flow
Enjoying the Flow
Walking the Flow
Playing all life long
Never got Serious
Hopelessly Interconected
Crossroad near Mental Block
Fancy That
The Blessing
Giving up concerns
Wobbling Goodness
Minimum Thinking
Everyone Things Included!

3/21/08

3/22/08

FOOD SNOBS

the rarified tastes of gourmets & gourmands of note

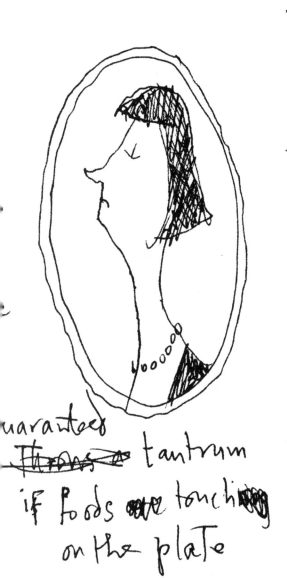

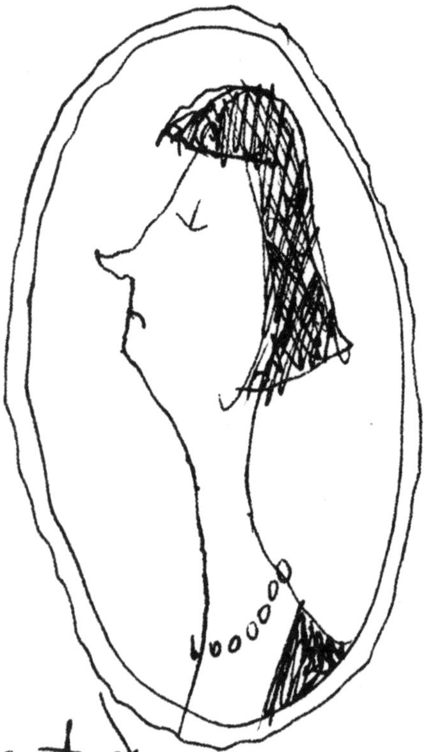

uaranteed ~~Throws a~~ tantrum if foods ~~are~~ touching on the plate

Only white food - bread, mashed po rice, pasta. Color icky!

FRIENDS

Chevy II

Chris

Alex ~~&~~ von Pamplemousse

M

Merrit

Ma

Mar

Mar

Mic

must have the crusts cut of his peanut-butter-and-jelly sandwiches

STEVEN GUARNACCIA

When Steven Guarnaccia, illustrator, art director, children's author, and textile designer, went out looking for his first job thirty years ago, his portfolio was his sketchbook. As loose as it was, it earned him an editorial spot assignment from *The New York Times*. He didn't realize most illustrators had formal presentations. But he had kept sketchbooks since high school, and this was the best way to show off his talents.

He explains: "I couldn't draw directly in them at the time, out of self-consciousness. Instead, I used them more like scrapbooks to paste my doodles and jottings in." These days, Guarnaccia says, "my sketchbook is where I think visually and, increasingly, verbally. It's also a constant and comforting companion. When I'm alone, bored, on the subway, drawing in my sketchbook is my activity of choice. It allows me to carry on a conversation with myself. I never draw from life in them." Better than an iPhone any time.

"Sketchbooks are often X-rays of my current obsessions," he says about the book here (from 2008) with heavily "tattooed" people doing leaps and flips. He now has hundreds of them. "I finish one about every month and a half," he explains. "I work in one at a time."

AND then
HE says,
SO IT
BEGINS,
needles & pins

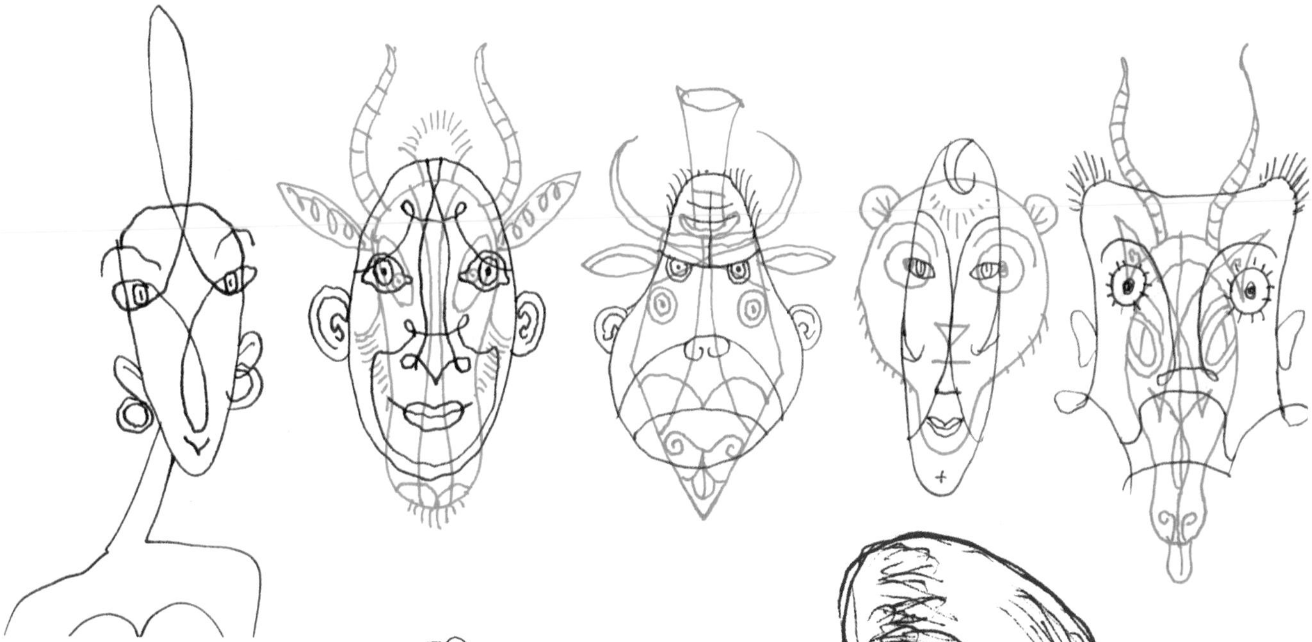

JONNY HANNAH

Jonny Hannah, a Southampton-based illustrator known for his hand-drawn adaptations of Victorian typography and witty children's book illustrations, is one of those inveterate sketchbook keepers, and has been "ever since the first year on my degree course at Liverpool."

Since Hannah is a master of the hand-wrought, ad hoc rendering, the fundamental difference between the books and his finished work is their relaxed quality. "There are no time constraints; I still work quick, but in a different way. They're just random scribbles, but they sometimes appear as finished artwork, or end up as a part of it."

Many of Hannah's sketches are from New York, some from Coney Island, "my favorite place." He likes to draw places and things he couldn't possibly find anywhere else. "After one particular visit, I had an exhibition called 'Hot Dogs & Rocket Fuel,' and I referred back to some of those pages a lot," he says. "And as Coney Island is being redeveloped, it was my last chance to draw some of those things."

Hannah usually has a couple of books going at any time. These images from 2006 (a field trip with Kingston University students) are "my good, going away sketchbook. But I always have another that's for notes and ideas, and sometimes shopping lists.

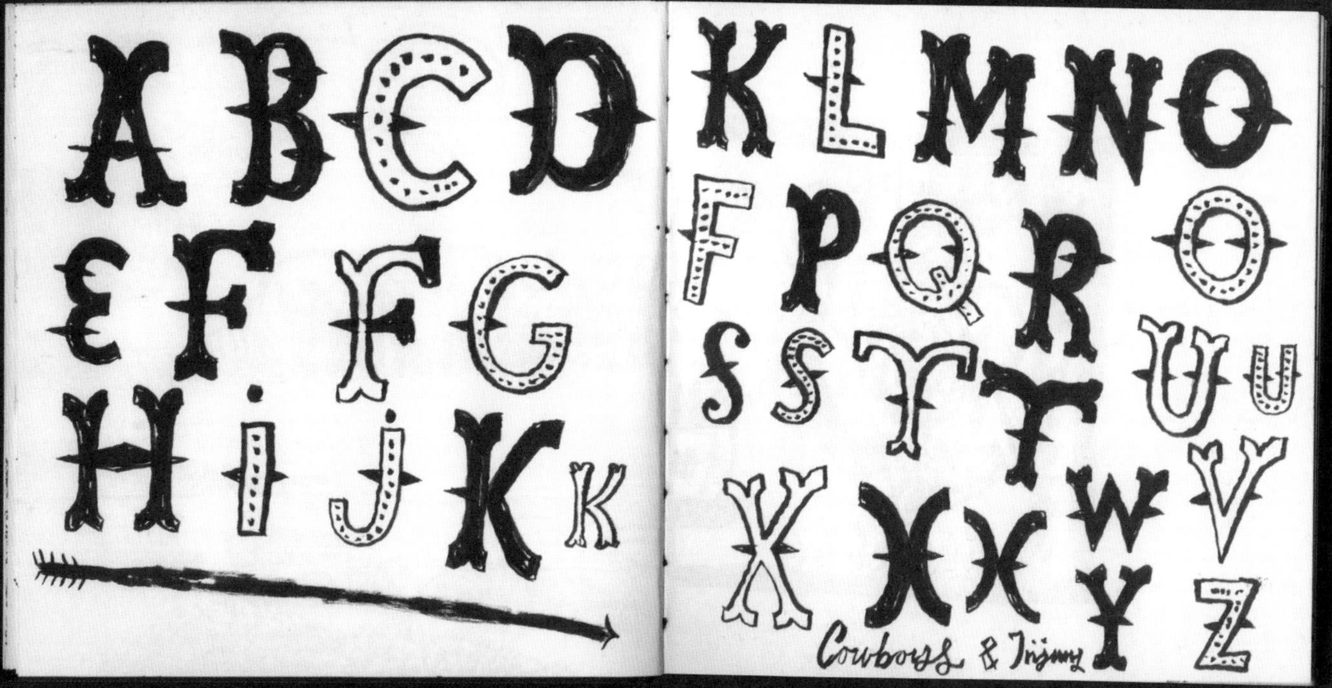
Cowboys & Injuns

all Beef
HOT CORN
FRUIT PUNCH

THE WHiZ
MAN NEVE
R FiT HiM
LiKE THE
WHiZ KiD
DID
BASTARD
WHIZZ
MAN

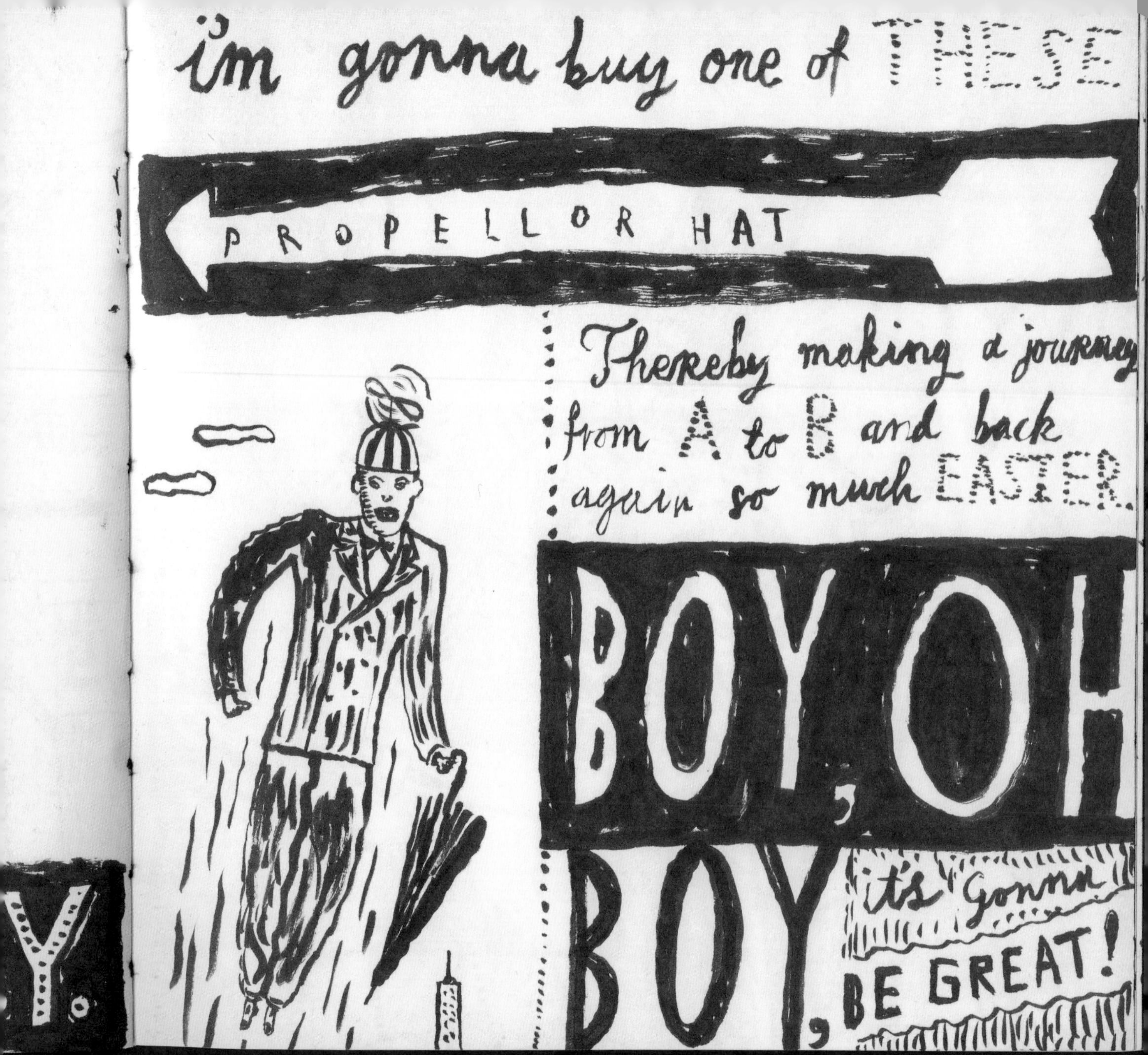
i'm gonna buy one of THESE
PROPELLOR HAT
Thereby making a journey from A to B and back again so much EASIER.
BOY, OH BOY,
it's Gonna BE GREAT!

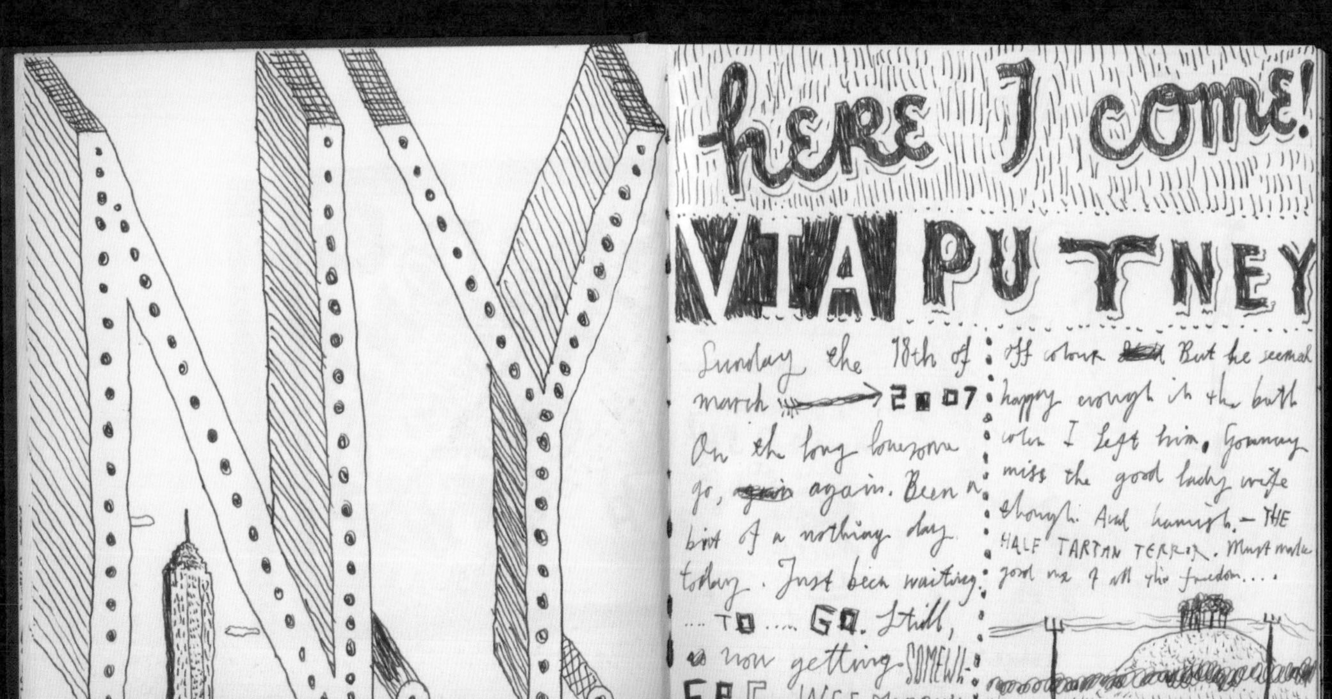
NY
here I come!
VIA PUTNEY
Sunday the 18th of march 2007
On the long lonesome go, again. Been a bit of a nothing day today. Just been waiting ... TO .... GO. Still, now getting SOMEWHERE.
Off colour But he seemed happy enough in the bath when I left him. Gonna miss the good lady wife though. And hamish. – THE HALF TARTAN TERROR. Must make good use of all the freedom....

S

E

IS FOR

ELEMENTARY

H

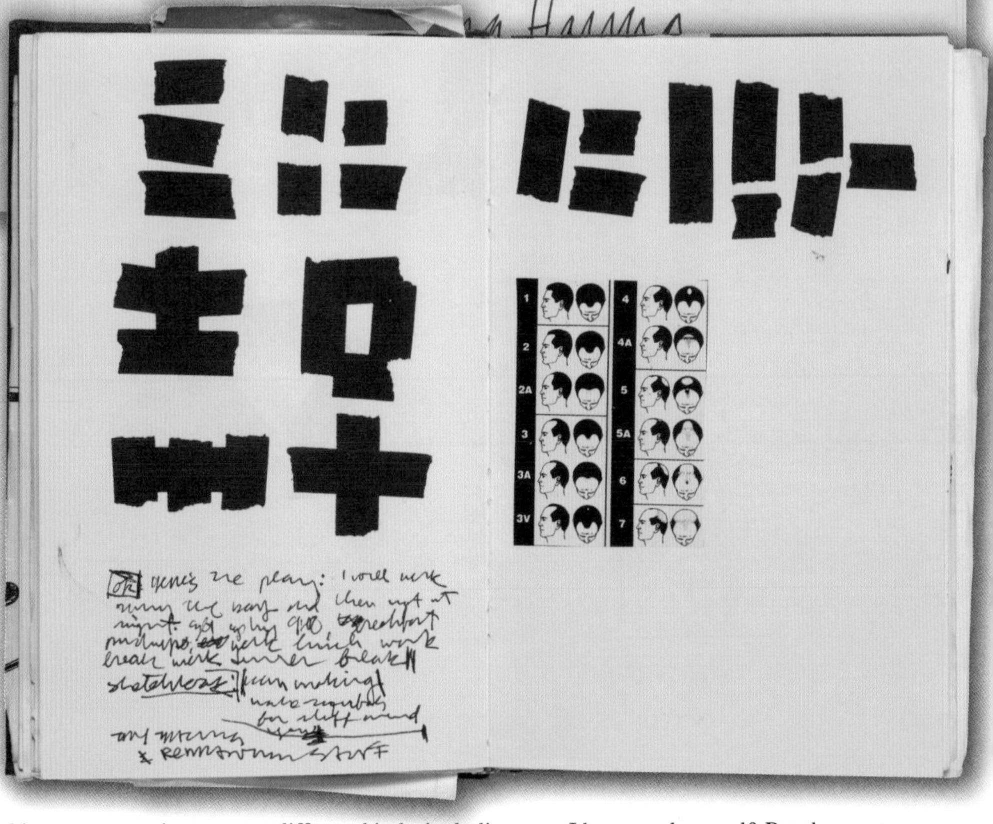

CYRUS HIGHSMITH

Type designer Cyrus Highsmith, senior designer at Font Bureau in Boston, develops new type series. Yet he draws a calligraphic script for a wedding invitation as comfortably as an industrial-strength sans serif. Despite his reliance on the trusty computer, he considers himself above all a draftsman. He combines an energetic illustrative approach with enthusiasm for innovation and has developed a large library of original designs.

Aside from the functional reasons for keeping sketchbooks, he offers this admission: "It's very simple – I enjoy it!"

What he looks for in a sketchbook is "blank white pages," he remarks. "Then it should be easy to carry. I have used several different kinds, including ones I have made myself. But the most important thing is blank white pages." Highsmith sees his sketchbook as a journal. "It's where I do a lot of thinking. Ideas start in a sketchbook but I prefer to do work for specific projects on loose paper. That way I can spread them out and see all the pages at once."

In his sixty-seven books, one recurring theme is chairs: "I never get tired of drawing chairs."

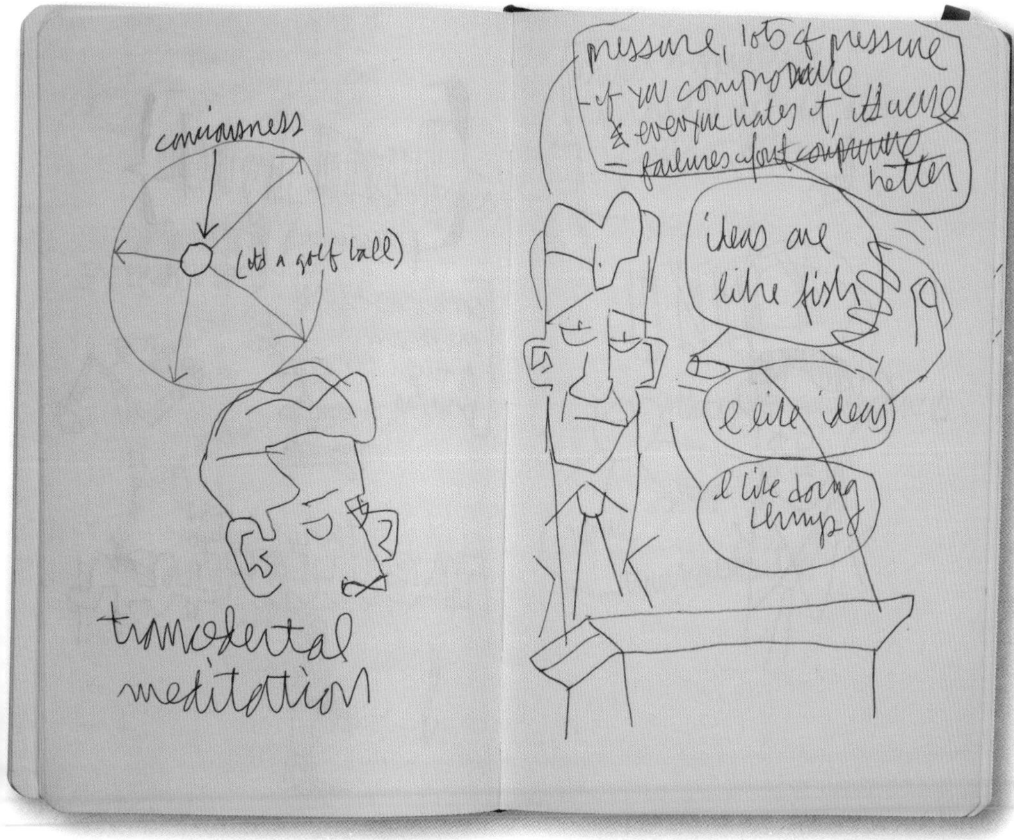
conciousness
(its a golf ball)
meditation
pressure, lots of pressure
ideas are like fish
I like ideas
I like doing things

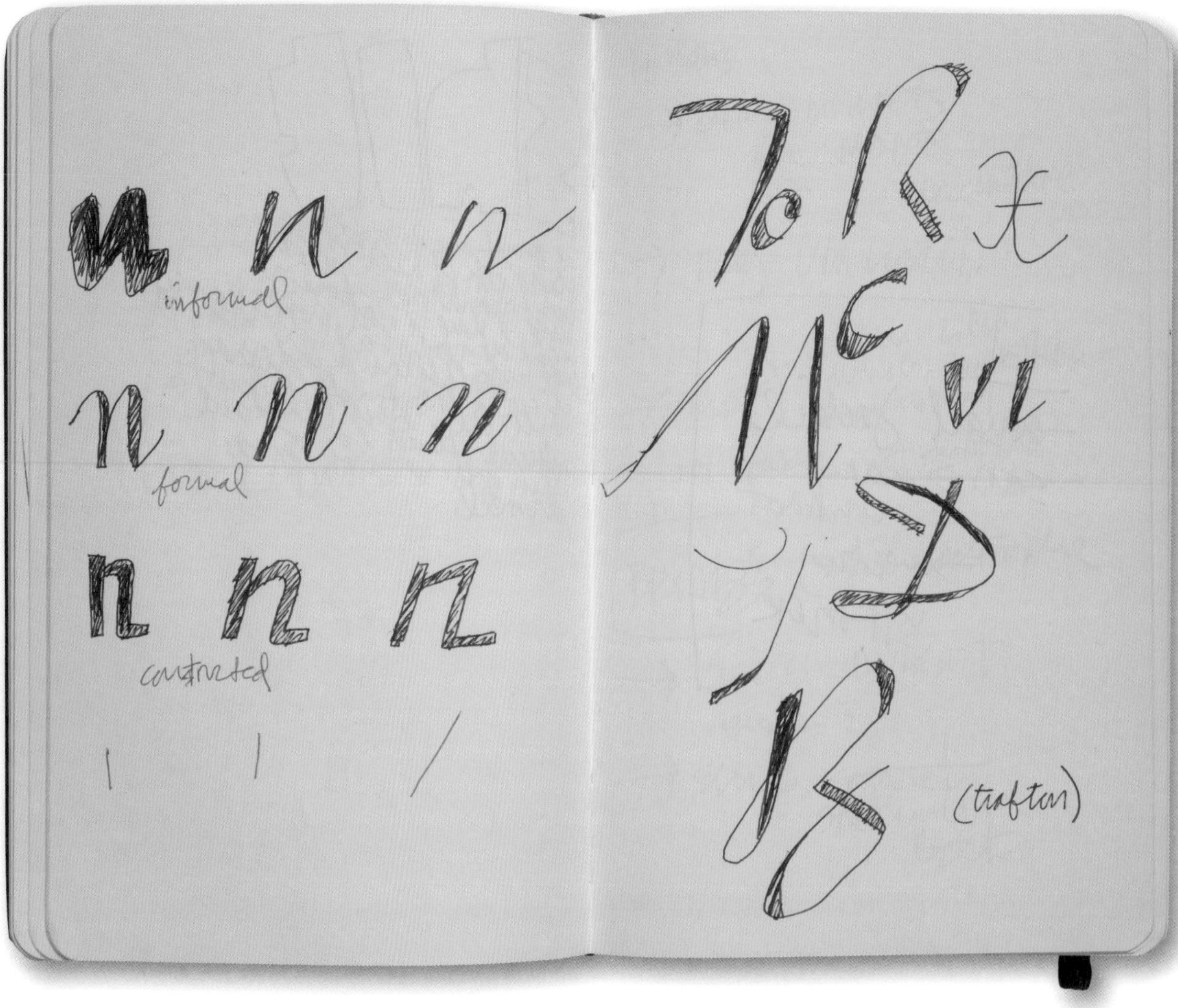
informal
formal

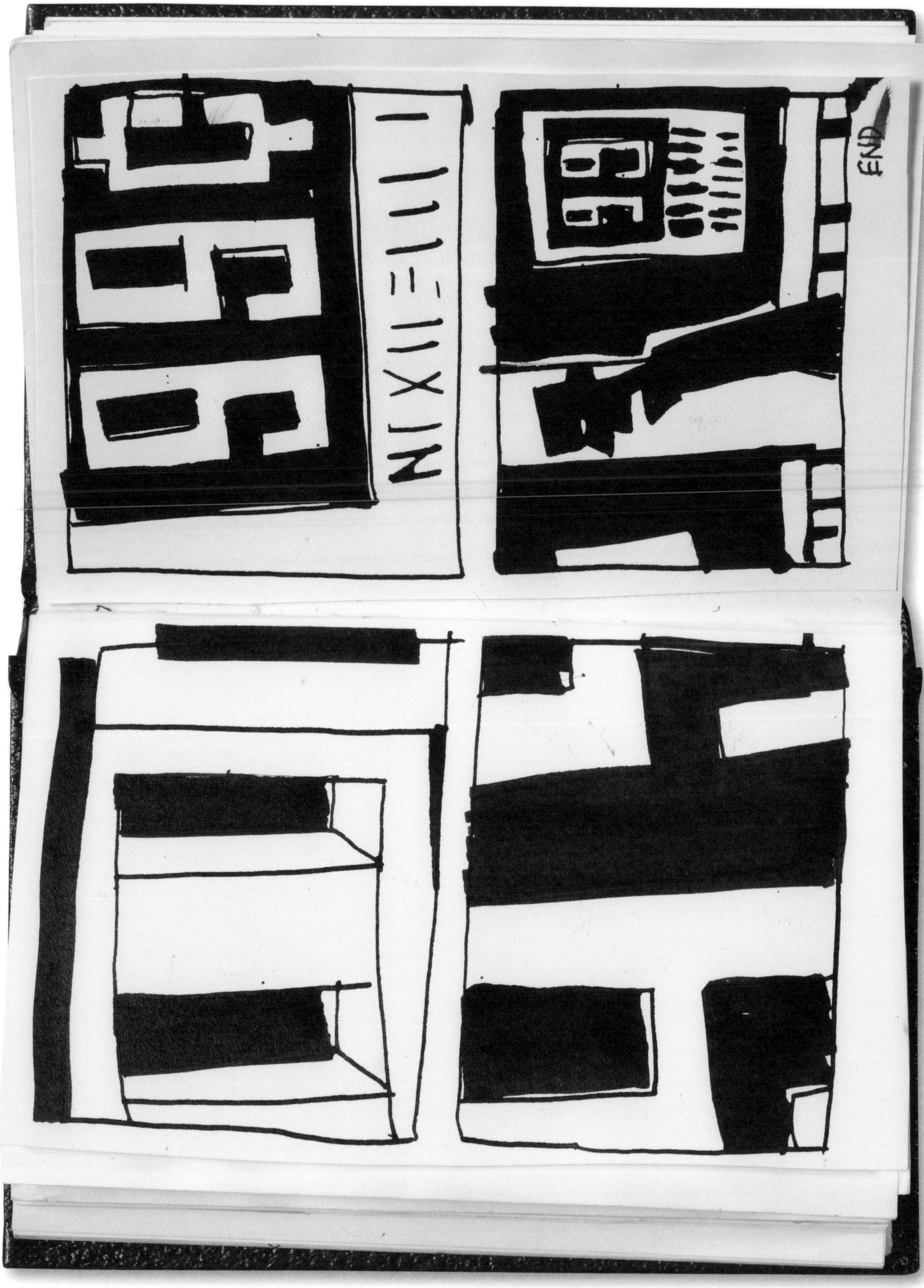
END

BRAD HOLLAND

New York illustrator Brad Holland "started to buy those cheap sketchbooks they sell in art stores when I was a kid." He also drew on typing paper – or on order forms from a grocery wholesaler where his uncle worked.

He took his books on trips "to Japan, Brazil, Turkey, Germany, Russia, the Nordic countries. Each drawing had a particular experience behind it that was different from a story behind a photograph. It changed the way I saw sketching."

The sketches here are from a project called "Hair America." "The kids are real, though they might not recognize themselves. These were all done within a day or two, some years ago." He made up names for all of the haircuts – except one. "When I was a kid in Ohio, there was a barbershop where all the jocks hung out. The barber, Pete Zimmerman, only had one haircut on the menu. It was an army buzz cut with a Woody Woodpecker kind of topknot. He called it the Pineapple. Since all the jocks got their hair cut there, the school was full of Pineapples. When I drew one of these kids in Washington Square, he looked like he had a Pete Zimmerman Pineapple. That's when I decided to give the other haircuts names too."

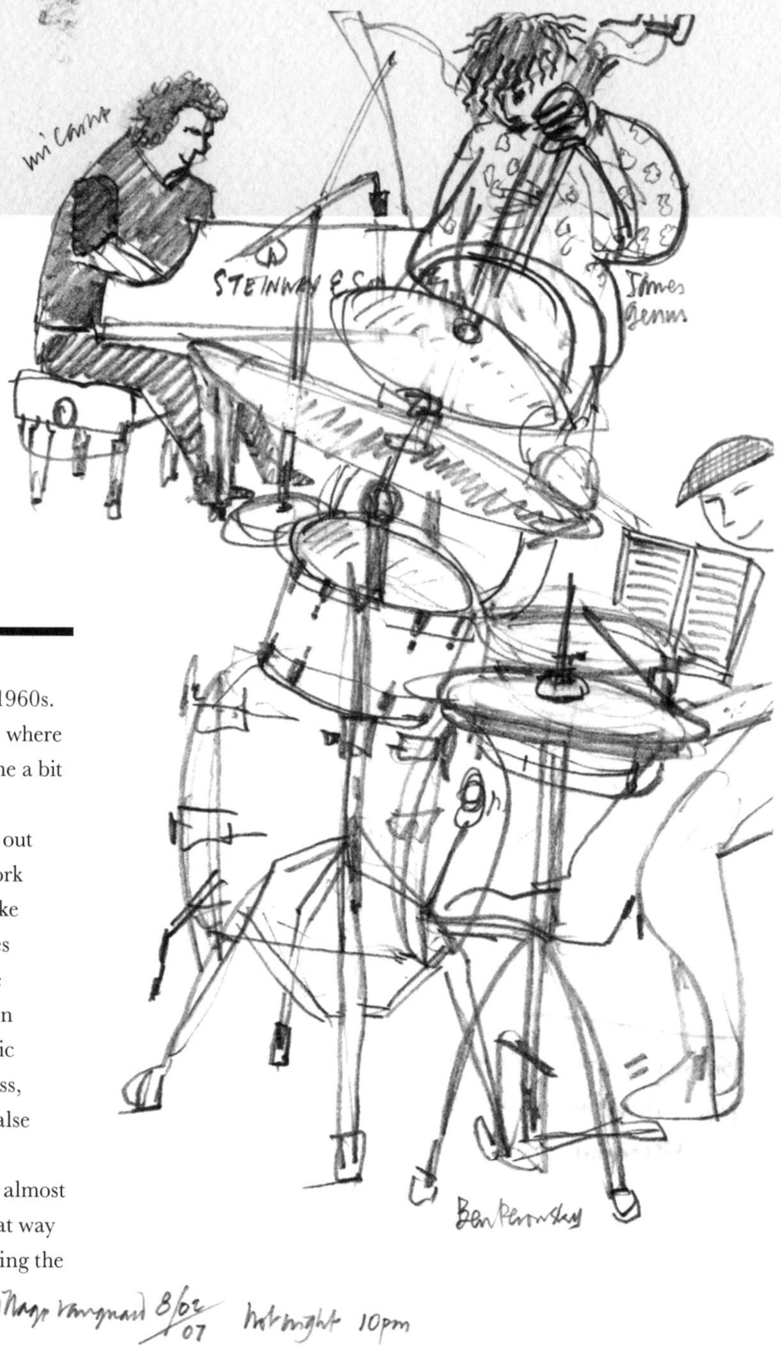

NIGEL HOLMES

Nigel Holmes, who helped revolutionize the iconic information graphics of the 1970s, first kept sketchbooks in art school in the 1960s. He started again in earnest when he left *Time* magazine in 1994, where he was the information graphics director. "Since then, it's become a bit obsessive!" he says.

Of course, Holmes uses his books "to record thoughts; to try out different iterations; to practice drawing; to make mistakes; to work out details; to create a visual diary; and to collect images that take my fancy: from magazines, newspapers, tickets, etc. Lots of pages are not sketches at all, but words that will eventually become the text of diagrams and charts." He takes liberties with the precision that typifies his published work. He also allows his impressionistic side to be revealed. The sketches are, as he says, "about roughness, spontaneity, relaxation, a mix of styles, lots of crossing out and false starts, and all hand-done as opposed to computer-generated."

The sketchbook has certain parameters, though. "When I'm almost at a solution, I won't finish that thought in the sketchbook. In that way there is still something to discover and to excite me while I'm doing the finished piece."

Ventana Pool
7/31/97

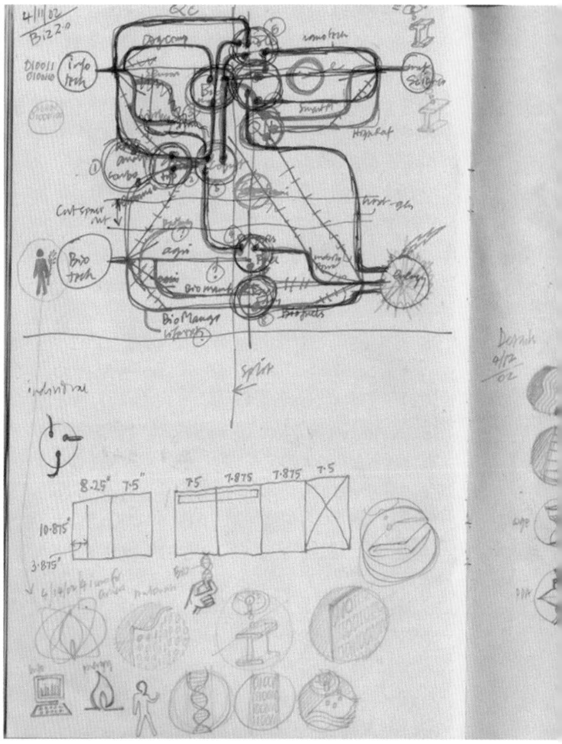

View Inn, Elk, California July 25th/03

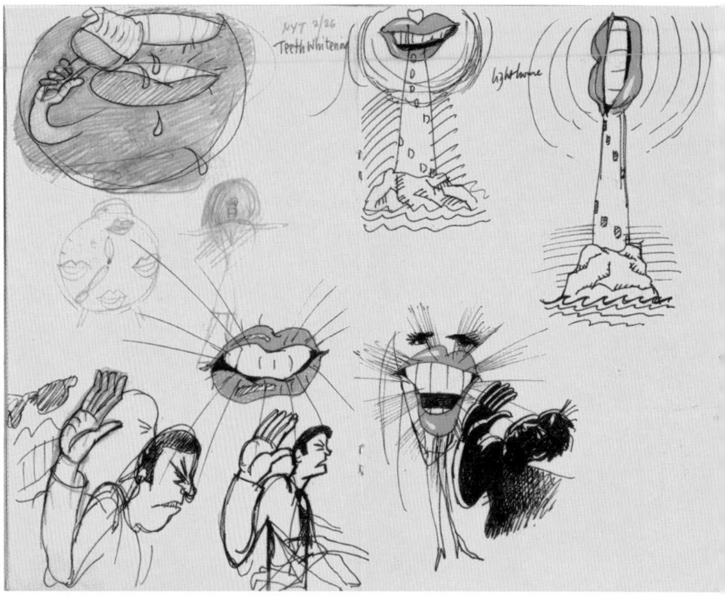
NYT 2/26

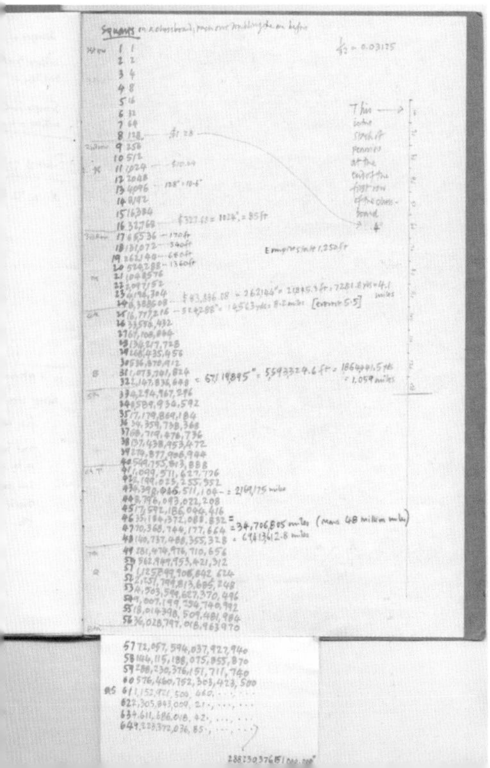

NEPENTHE
TUESDAY
7/00

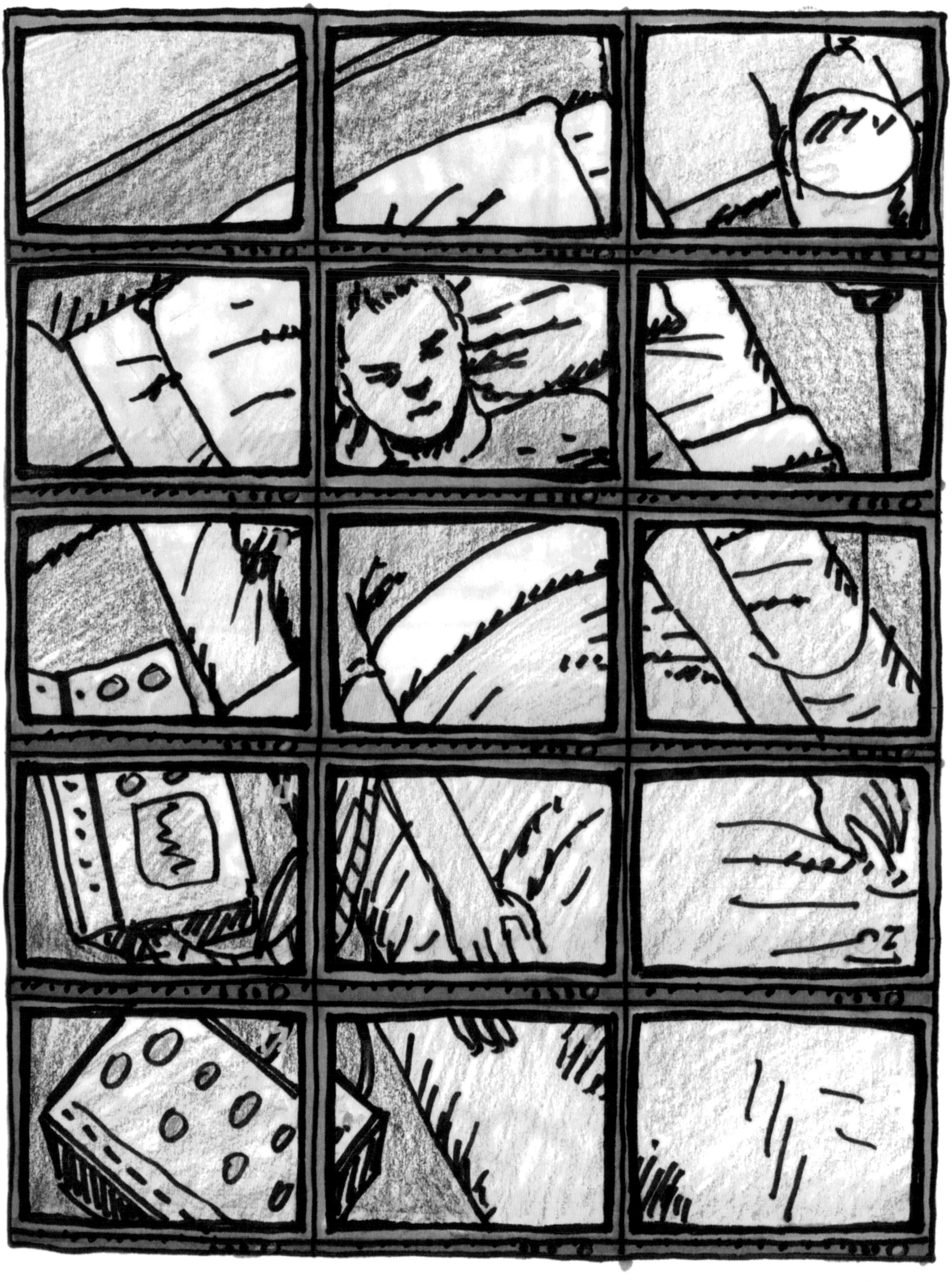

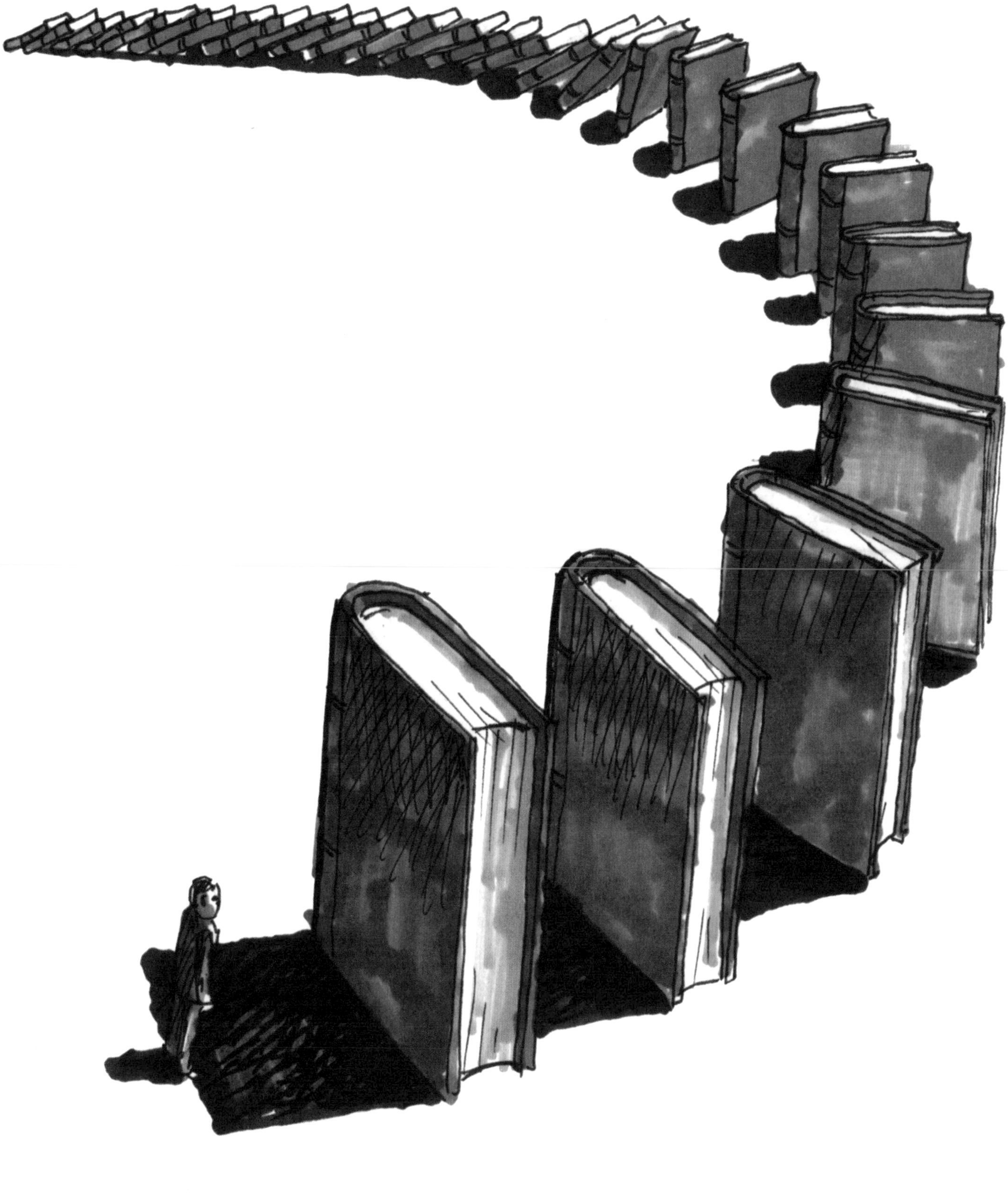

MIRKO ILIĆ

Bosnian-born, New York-based designer and illustrator Mirko Ilić's first sketchbooks were his composition books in elementary school. Then later, "in the United States, I used sketchbooks for the first time – mostly for illustration jobs, sitting in the *New York Times* waiting room, where we would do sketches on the spot to show them to art directors."

But then they invented the fax machine and "we started faxing sketches," he recalls. When they invented the computer, "we started scanning them to e-mail them. In that process sketchbooks became obsolete, because the pages needed to be loose. I'm now back to keeping sketchbooks just for myself, for visual reminders."

"Idea-wise," notes Ilić, "the sketchbook contains 'virgin' work – untainted and untouched by art directors, editors, board members, vice presidents or CEOs. Technique-wise, finished works are usually better, but not always." The book shown here is uniquely for illustrations – he has a separate one for design work. Usually the first few pages contain neat drawings. "Then as I progress the sketches get looser and smaller, until the pages become empty. And then I go out and buy another one."

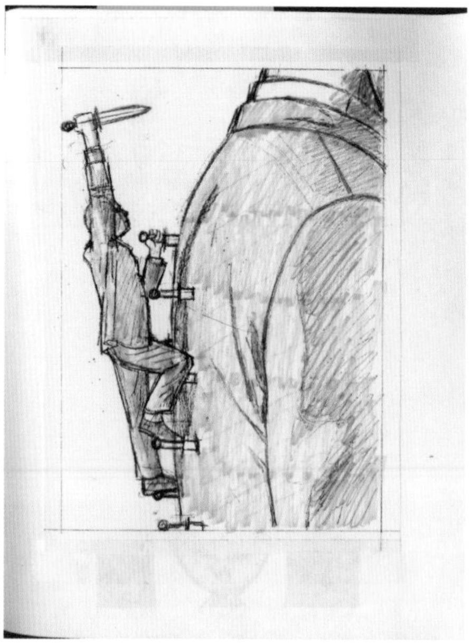

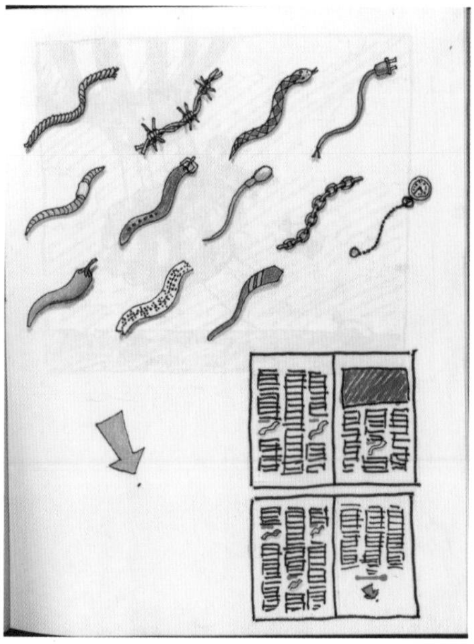

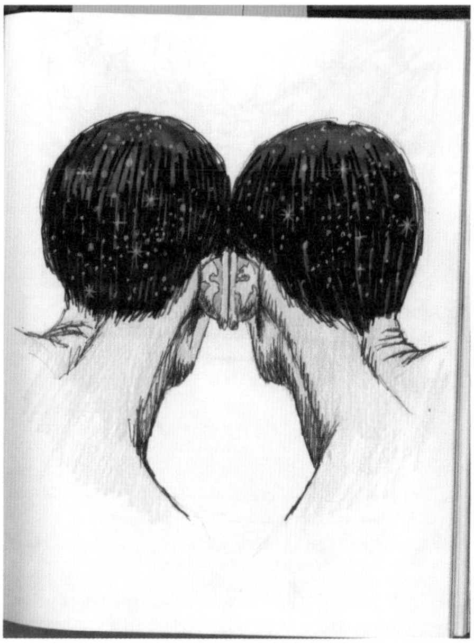

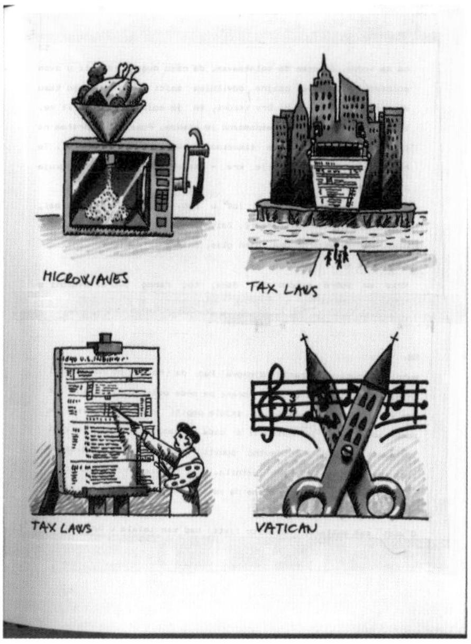

MICROWAVES
TAX LAWS
TAX LAWS
VATICAN

MICROWAVE

BULLDOZING

ARCHITECTURE

VATICAN

ARTIST

VATICAN

- PDF Istituto
- Respondre ... Alumni
93 352 30 11
LOW BLUE
TIRED GREY
CEREBRAL GREEN
PERMANENT WHITE
RUSTY PINK
PICTORIAL BLACK
EXIGENT ORANGE
IDENTICAL BLUE
EMPTY WHITE
USED BROWN
Experimenta
Maria
10 F
08010
mitjà.
display
- Helena
- Ramona
- Event
- Freelance
- Dentista
934046135
Summa Sports:
93459 1914

ENRIC JARDÍ

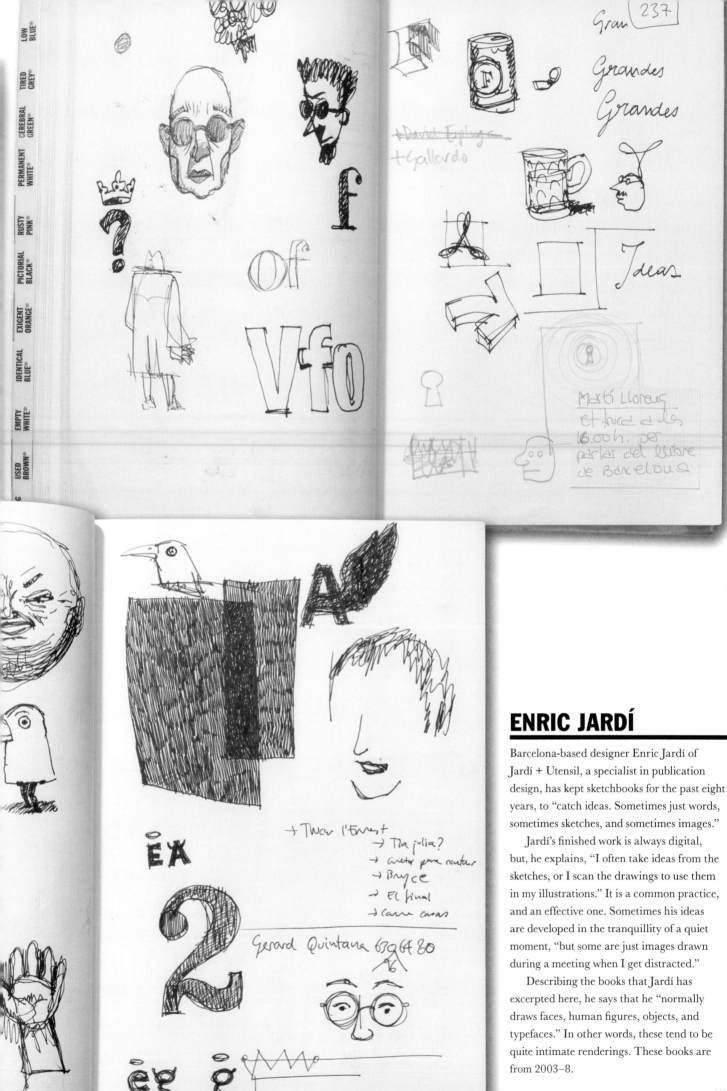

Barcelona-based designer Enric Jardí of Jardí + Utensil, a specialist in publication design, has kept sketchbooks for the past eight years, to "catch ideas. Sometimes just words, sometimes sketches, and sometimes images."

Jardí's finished work is always digital, but, he explains, "I often take ideas from the sketches, or I scan the drawings to use them in my illustrations." It is a common practice, and an effective one. Sometimes his ideas are developed in the tranquillity of a quiet moment, "but some are just images drawn during a meeting when I get distracted."

Describing the books that Jardí has excerpted here, he says that he "normally draws faces, human figures, objects, and typefaces." In other words, these tend to be quite intimate renderings. These books are from 2003–8.

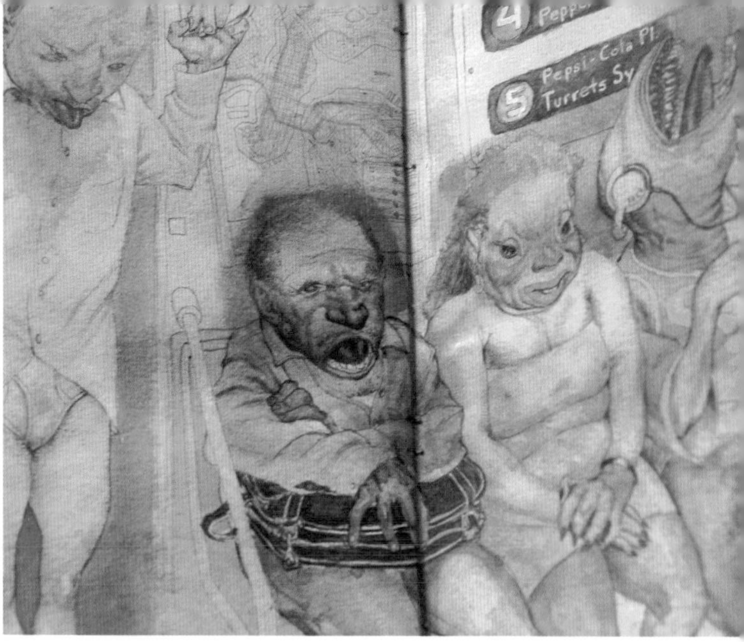

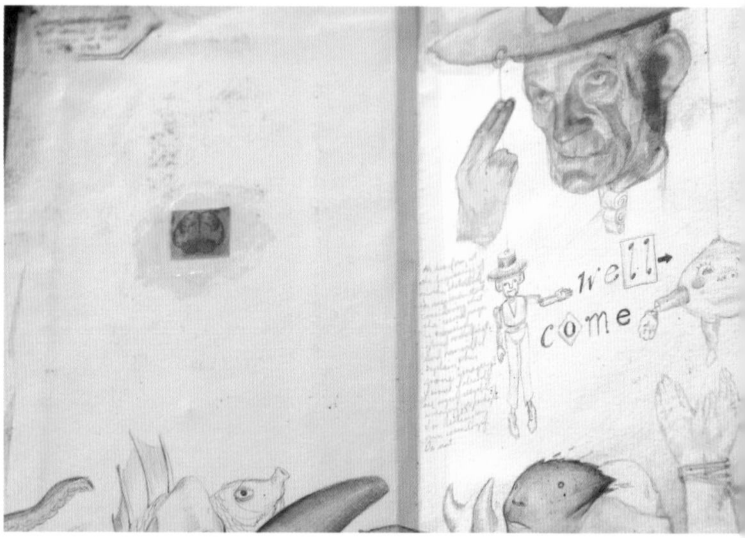

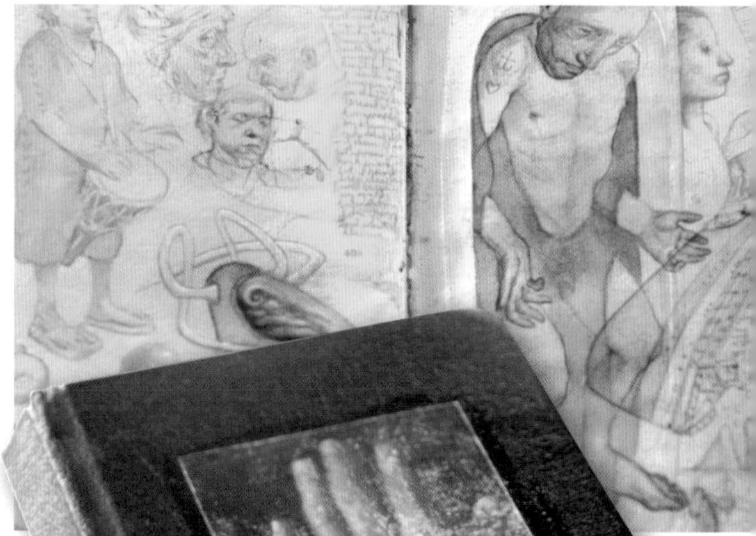

JAMES JEAN

James Jean, known for his Neo-Pre-Raphaelite paintings, layered fantasy comics, and ethereal metaphysical characters, has kept a sketchbook since 1997, when he started art school. Now they have become "a record of my life, as I pass the time in airports or cafés."

Jean insists that his sketchbooks "are created spontaneously, without any kind of planning. Most of my finished work of late is based on a completely imagined world, while the sketchbooks are grounded in observation and drawing from life."

He now has about fifteen sketchbooks. What he likes best about them is that "there is an overlapping of images, describing multiple timelines and perspectives."

Jean acknowledges that there is a difference between his sketchbooks now and the earliest books he did in art school, as those "were about an exploration of ideas, imagination, and honing technique," whereas "these days, it's about channeling intuition, and letting chance and accidents happen on the page." The colorful sketchbook images shown here are from 2001 and the line drawings date from 2007–8.

210

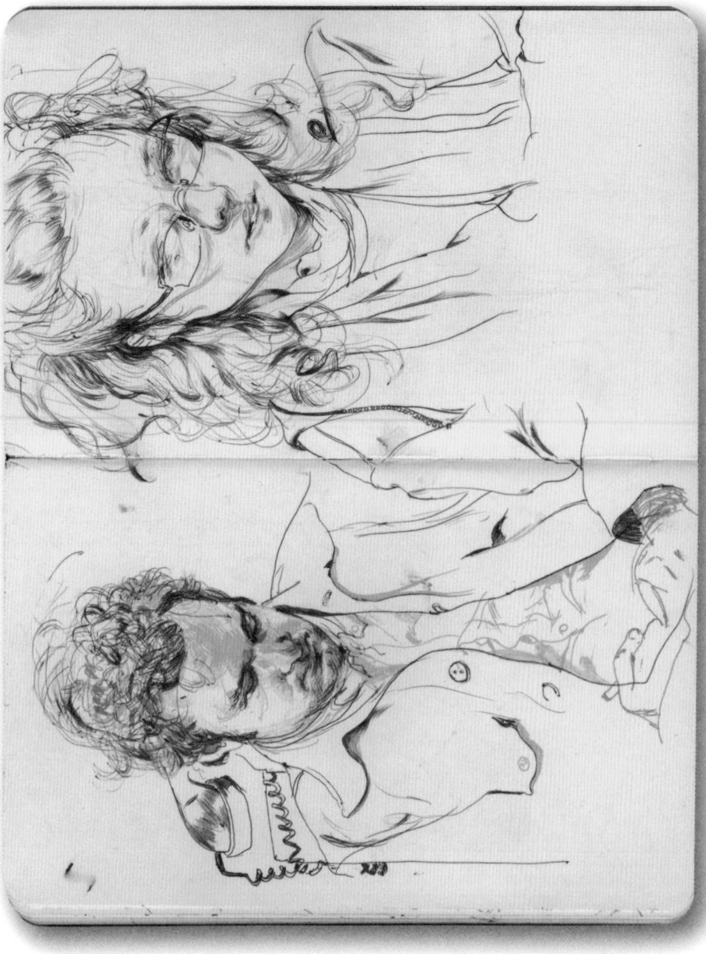

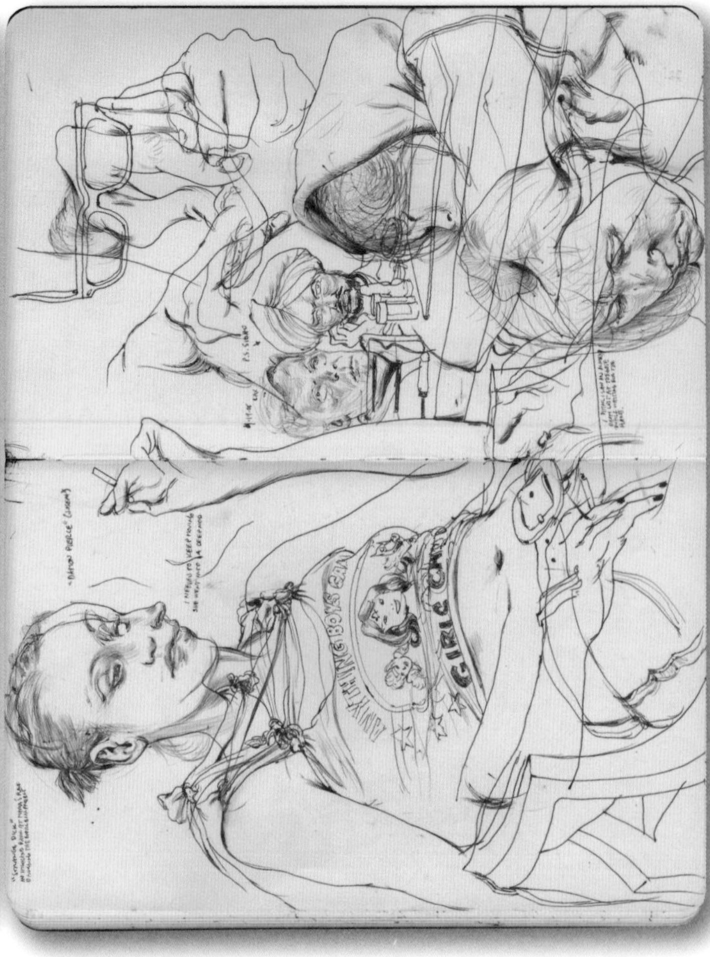

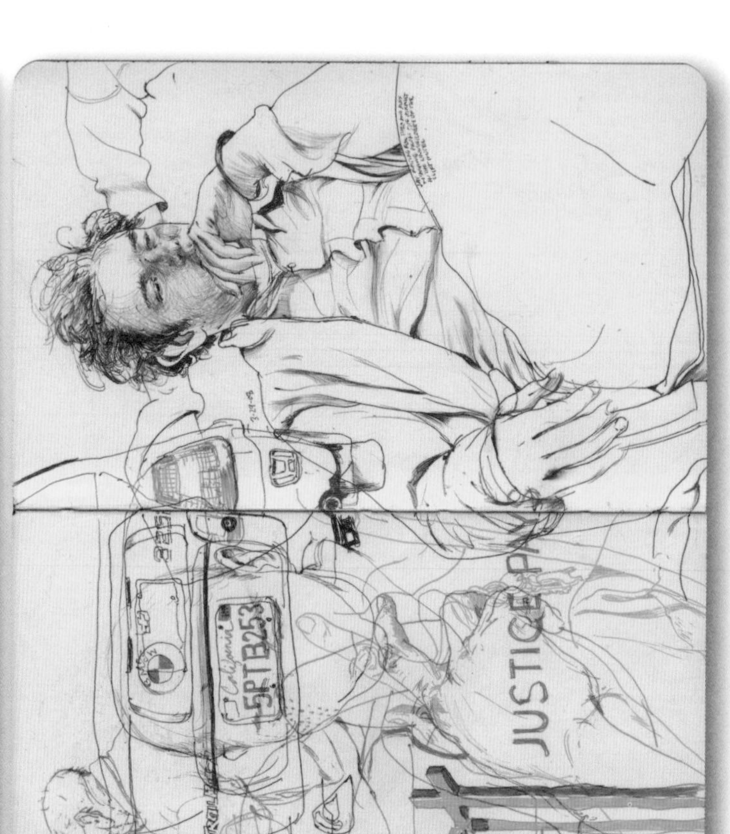
JUSTICE

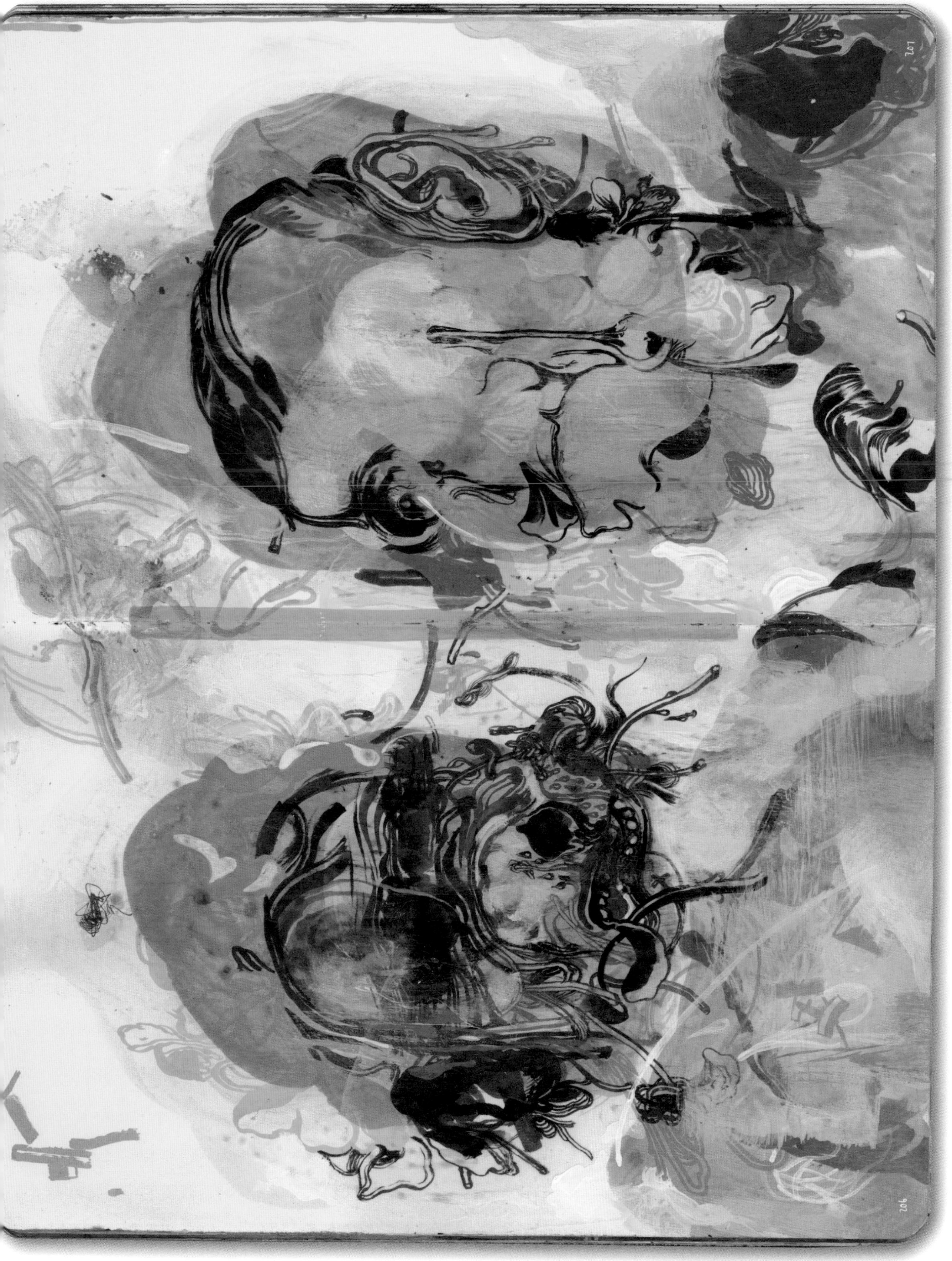

BEYOND
liquid fruit
GROUNDING GRAPEFRUIT
Skwish
ORANGE AWARENESS
totally Minute

16 fl. oz. (1 PT) 473 ml
fruitopia
POPS UP
seal is broken

100% PURE
EARTH JUICE
naturals
from minute maid
FRUIT PUNCH
DIRT → FRUIT → MOUTH
All white indicated in cyan
tropical 1
tropical 2
tropical 3
tropical 4
16 fluid ounces of fruit
Naturals
ALMIGHTY APPLE
totally natural. totally Minute Maid.
TROPICAL CONSIDERATION

NO PRESERVATIVES
real fruit beverage
fruitopia
TROPICAL HAZE

fruitopia
STRAWBERRY PASSION AWARENESS
totally natural.
sale sample only
real fruit beverage
LEMONADE LOVE

GAINING MORE AND MORE
ATTENTION AND SUCCESS,
KEITH BEGAN TO EXPAND
HIS CREATIVE
HORIZONS
BY PAINTING
MAJOR ON-SITE
MURALS
ALL
OVER
THE

16 fluid ounces of fruit
fruitopia
LEMONADE LOVE
totally natural. totally Minute Maid.

real fruit beverage
fruitopia
LEMONADE LOVE & HOPE

JEFF JOHNSON

Jeff Johnson, co-founder of Spunk Design Machine in Minneapolis and New York, says that he is "a bit of a freak when it comes to my sketchbooks. I have one shelf in our production room dedicated to the ongoing pile. I am imagining that when I die, I will have two things to leave behind. The first will be some sort of data storage device, about the size of a deck of cards, that holds a few dozen terabytes of my life's work. The other will be my pile of sketchbooks." Not a bad legacy.

So, it should come as no surprise that he uses the sketchbook as a means of addressing ideas, large and small, from thinkers and slackers, that have resonance with his own goals and aspirations. The books further include such personal expressions and professional iterations as "an embarrassing self-portrait from 1989, and an equally embarrassing Nietzsche quote."

Also shown here are "shots from my Fruitopia project in 1993. At the time I was also working on a monster project for the Keith Haring estate, and you can see here how immersion in Haring art affected the illustration and design that I authored for all of the Fruitopia brand work. I did all the design and illustration for Fruitopia for two years."

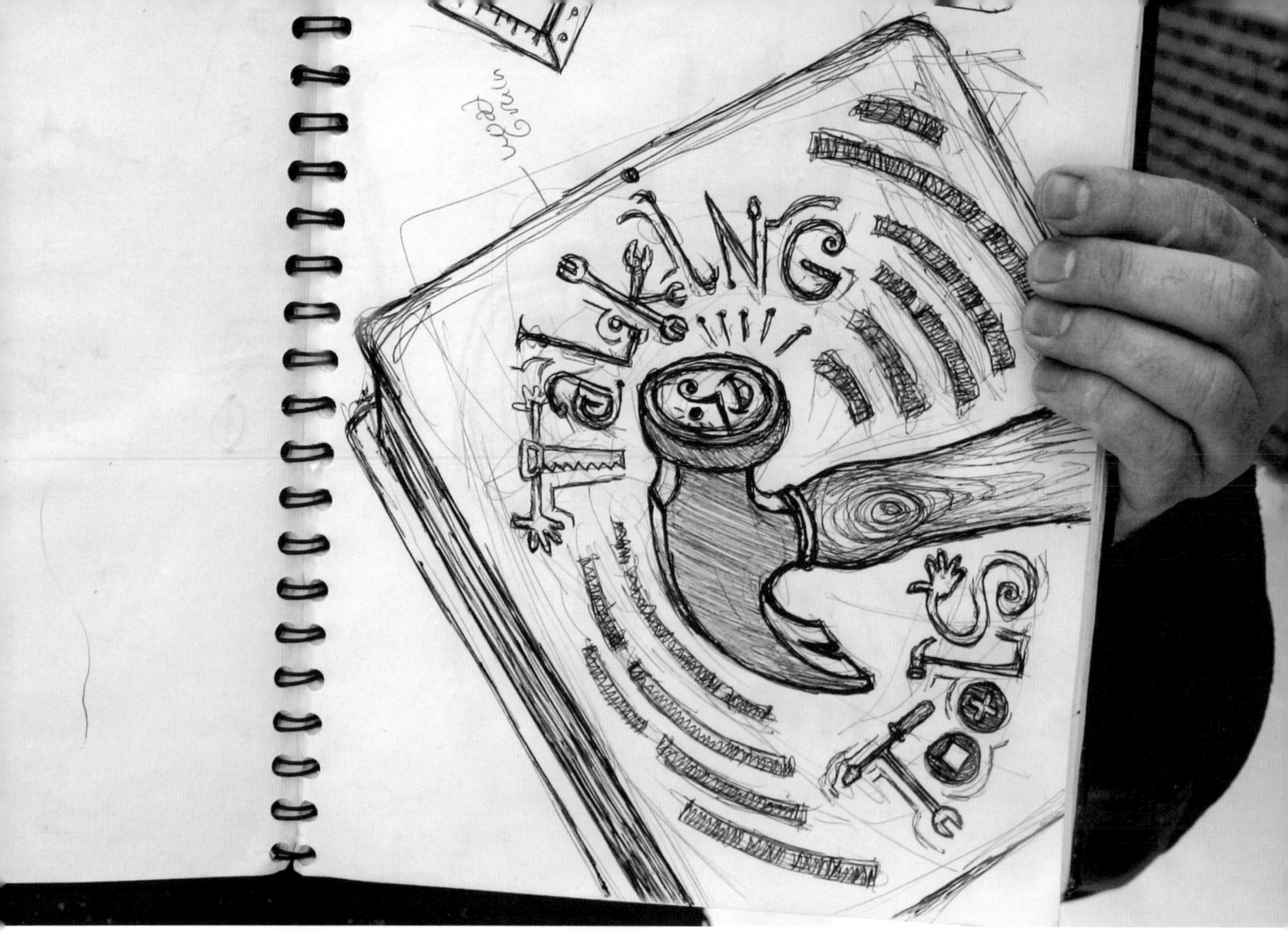
TaLkiNG
TooLS

ROLE play
ROLE play
act up
- TOOL Crib
- Mixer
- Bumper Crop

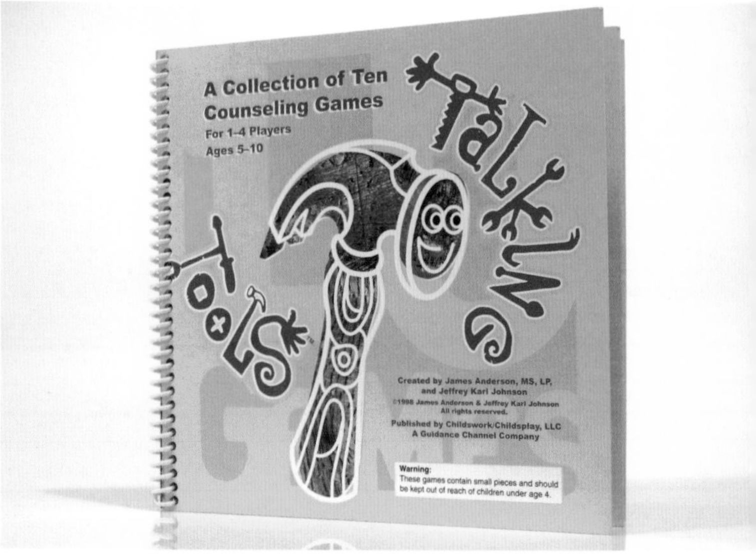
A Collection of Ten Counseling Games
For 1–4 Players
Ages 5–10
TaLkiNG TooLS
Created by James Anderson, MS, LP, and Jeffrey Karl Johnson
©1998 James Anderson & Jeffrey Karl Johnson
All rights reserved.
Published by Childswork/Childsplay, LLC
A Guidance Channel Company
Warning:
These games contain small pieces and should be kept out of reach of children under age 4.

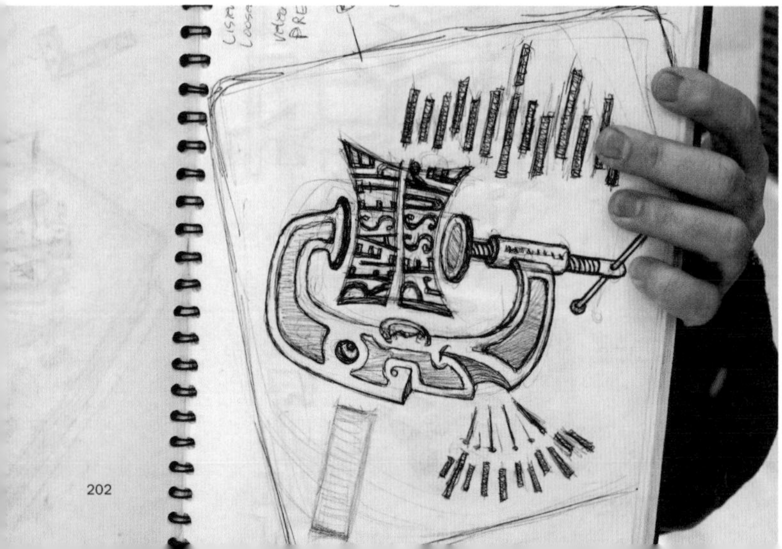
RELEASE THE PRESSURE

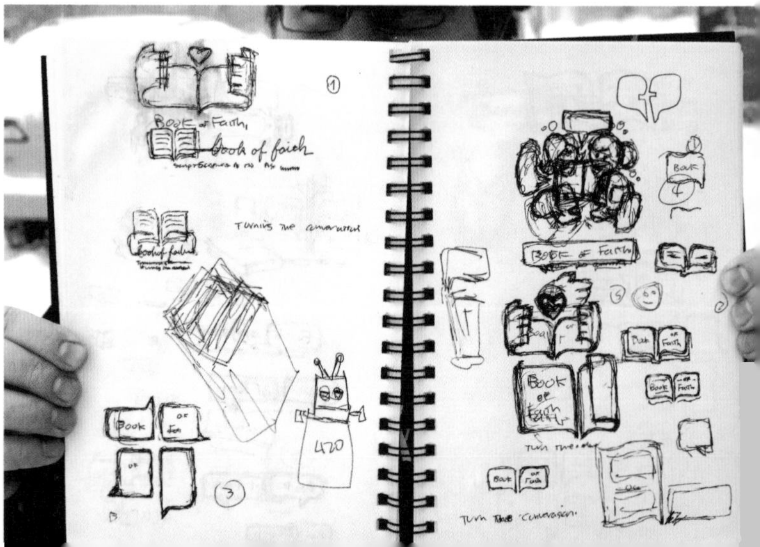
Book of Faith
Book of Faith

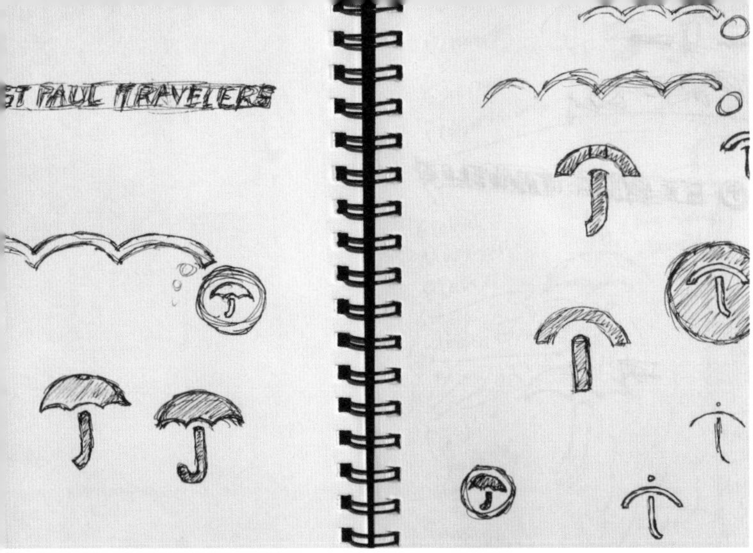
ST PAUL TRAVELERS

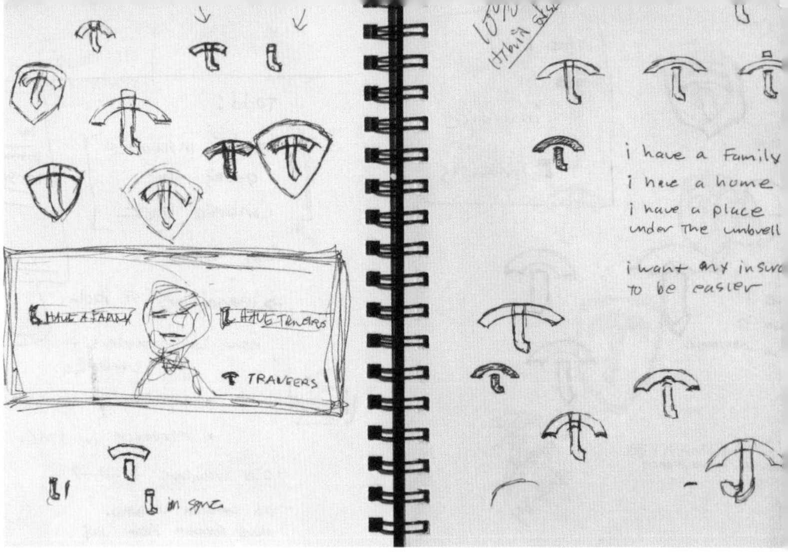
I HAVE A FAMILY
I HAVE TRAVELERS
TRAVELERS
in sync
i have a Family
i have a home
i have a place
under the umbrell
i want my insura
to be easier

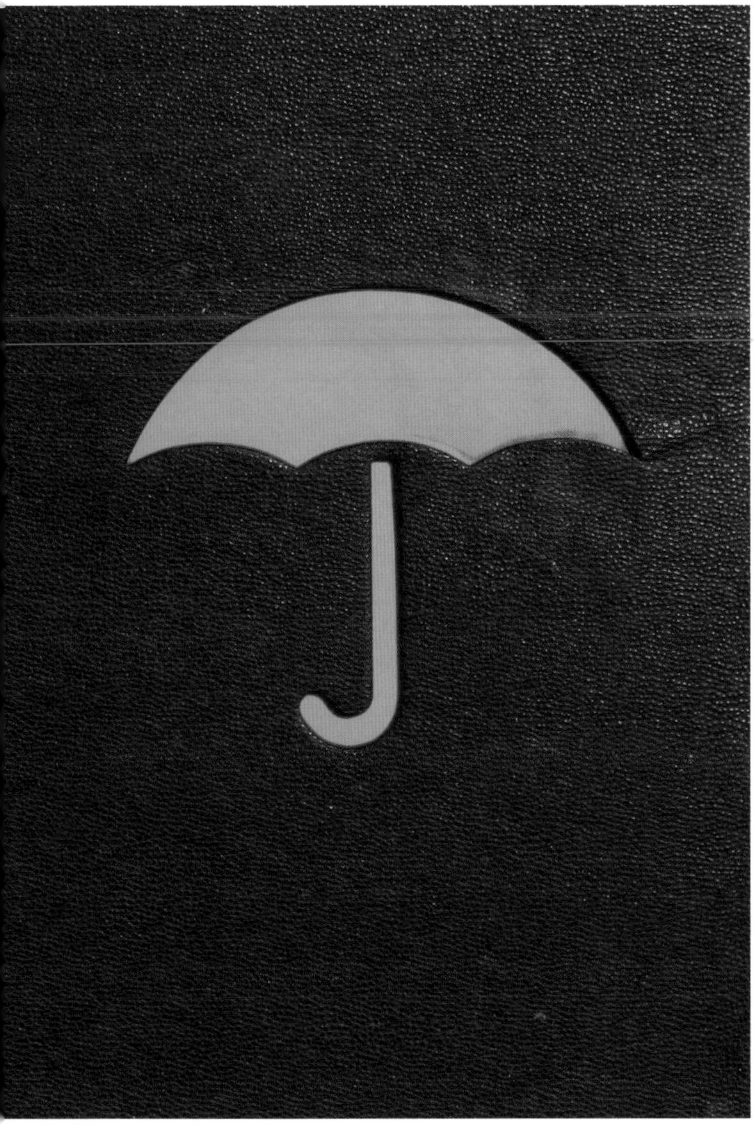

umbrella
ad photos?
TRAVELERS
TRAVELERS INSURANCE
ST. PAUL TRAVE

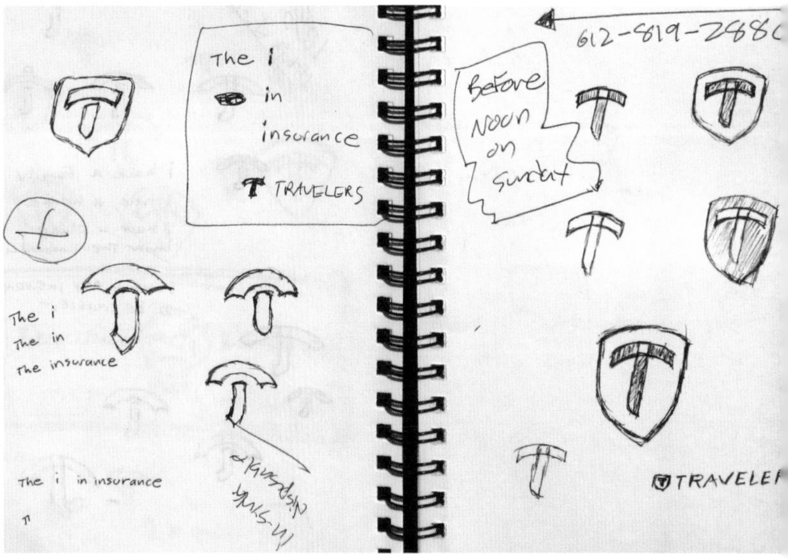
The i
in
insurance
TRAVELERS
The i
The in
The insurance
The i in insurance
612-819-2486
Before
Noon
on
Sunday
TRAVELE

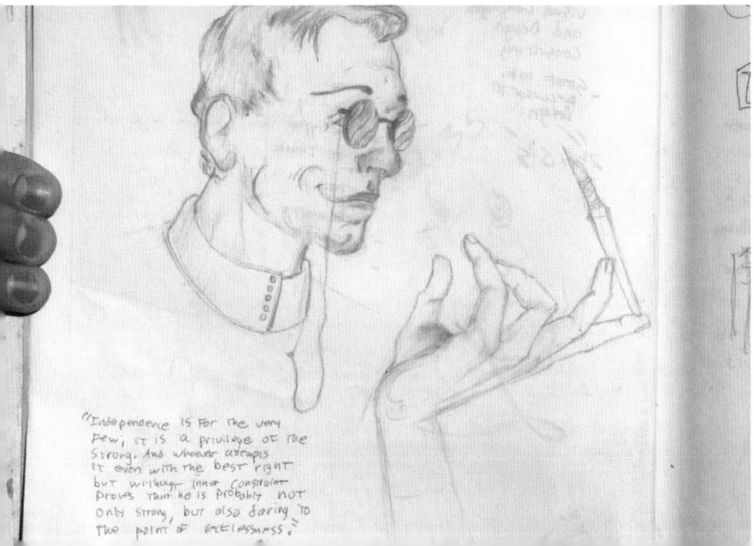
"Independence is for the very
few, it is a privilege of the
strong. And whoever attempts
it even with the best right
but without inner constraint
proves that he is probably not
only strong, but also daring to
the point of recklessness."

1989
2009

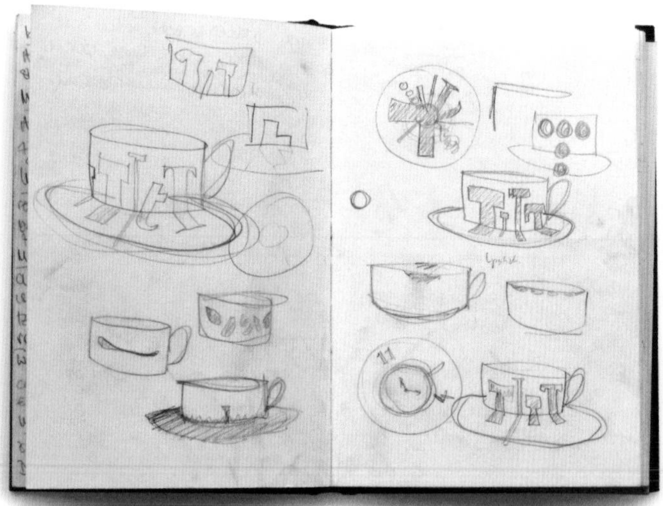

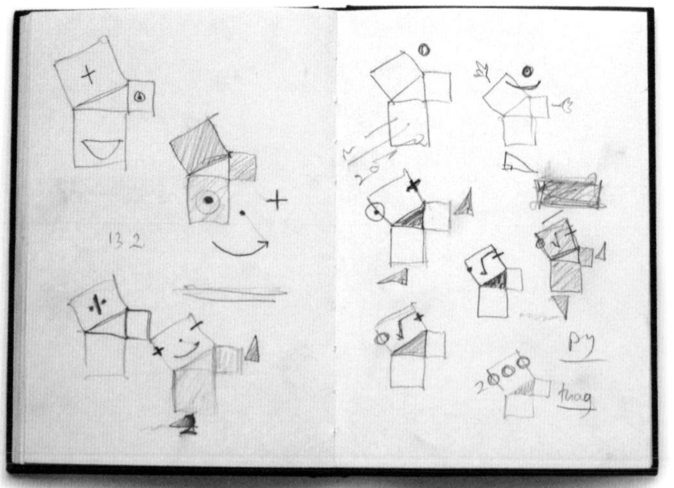

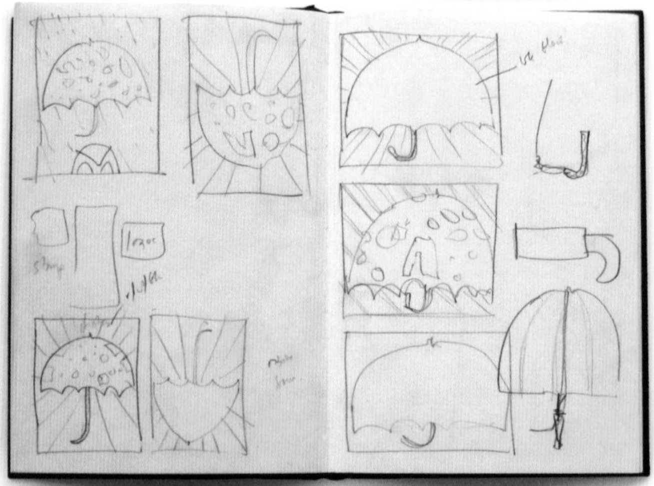

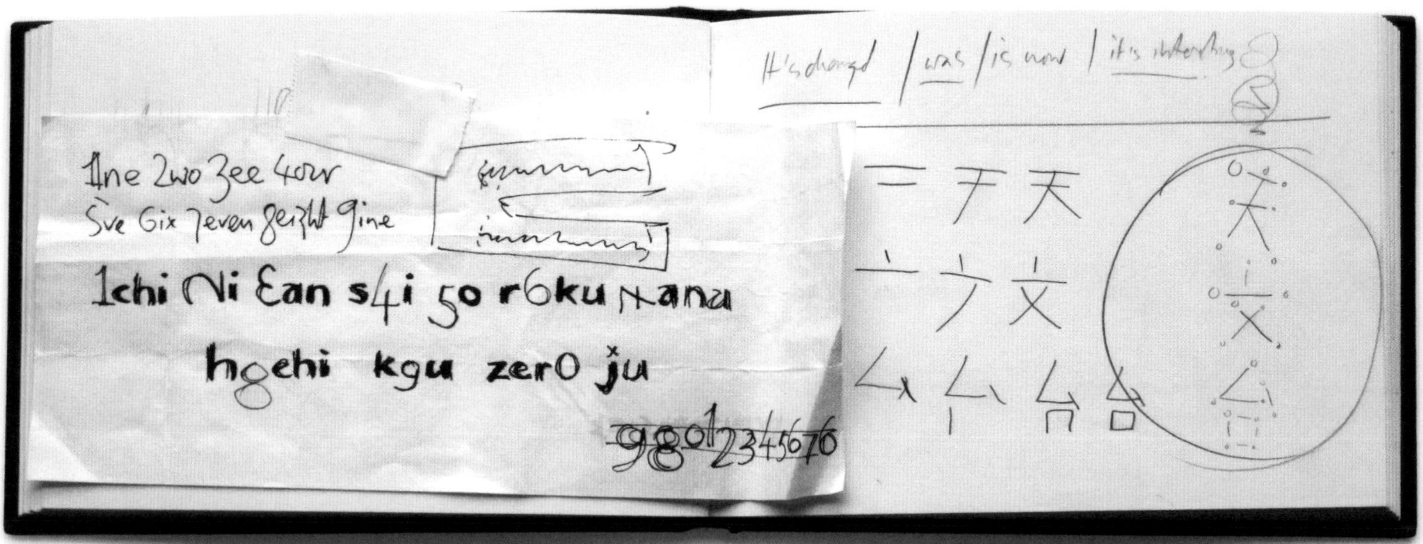

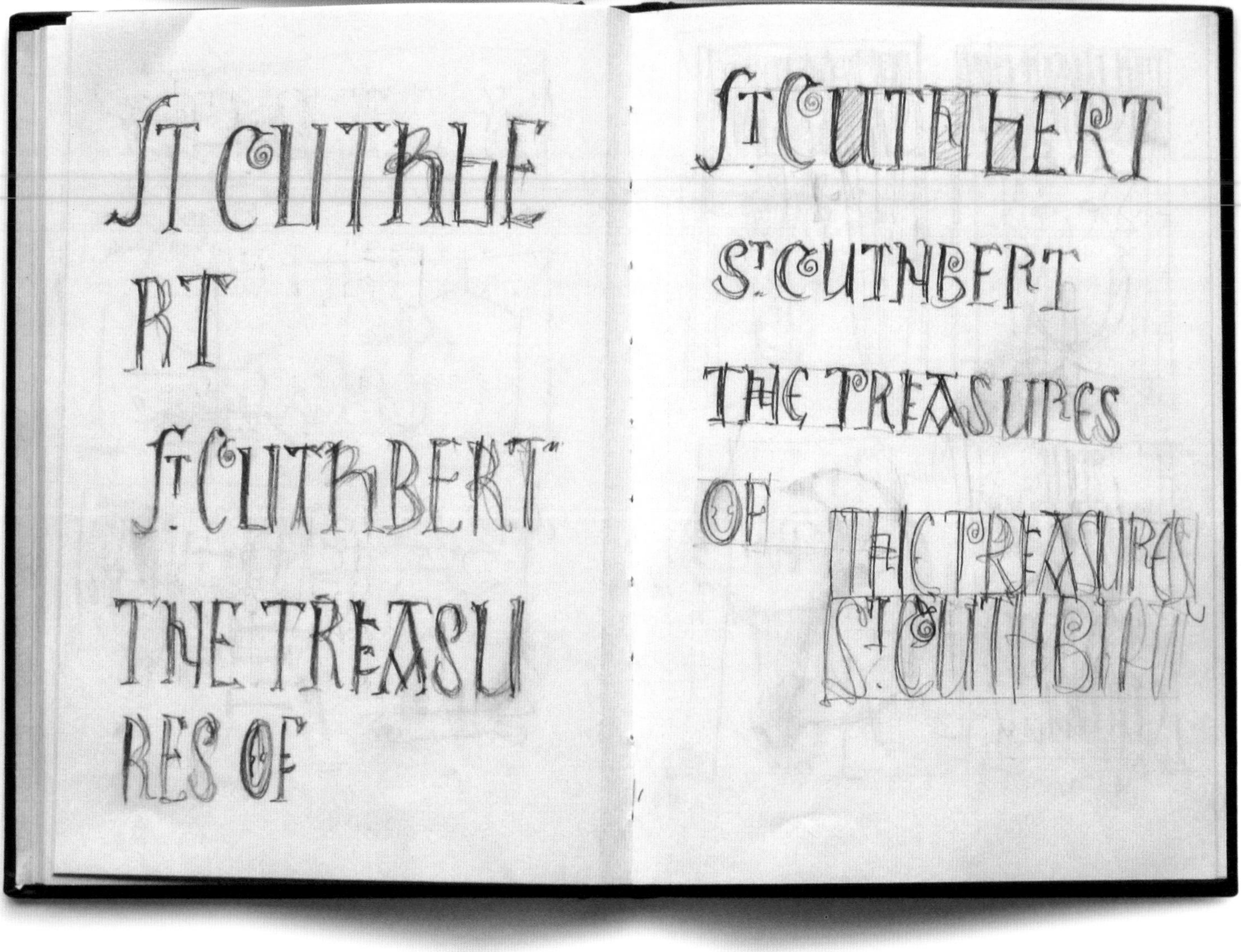

MICHAEL JOHNSON

During his decade "working for other people," Michael Johnson, principal of johnson banks in London, was always drawing in large typo pads, accumulating piles of crumply paper by his desk. "Then it began to dawn that having a record of what I was thinking, what someone said in a meeting, and maybe the odd half-decent idea would be a whole lot smarter. I've been filling four or five a year ever since."

The books are "a very linear, analogue form of memory. Sometimes the notes, scribbles, and sketches are almost indecipherable, but with luck I can look back at the marks and work out what I was thinking about." The main theme is the endless drawing and redrawing of logos. "Sometimes I'll virtually fill a whole book with the same few letters as I search for the most memorable juxtaposition of characters."

The weirdest thing about collecting books is going back and noticing ideas he has been trying for decades, "or, just occasionally, the roots of a really big idea, but drawn years earlier, almost unconsciously. The last time I went through them I found a sketch for some stamps using multiple parts to make faces. Nice idea. But the sketch was made in 1996, five years before I got the brief to do exactly that. Spooky."

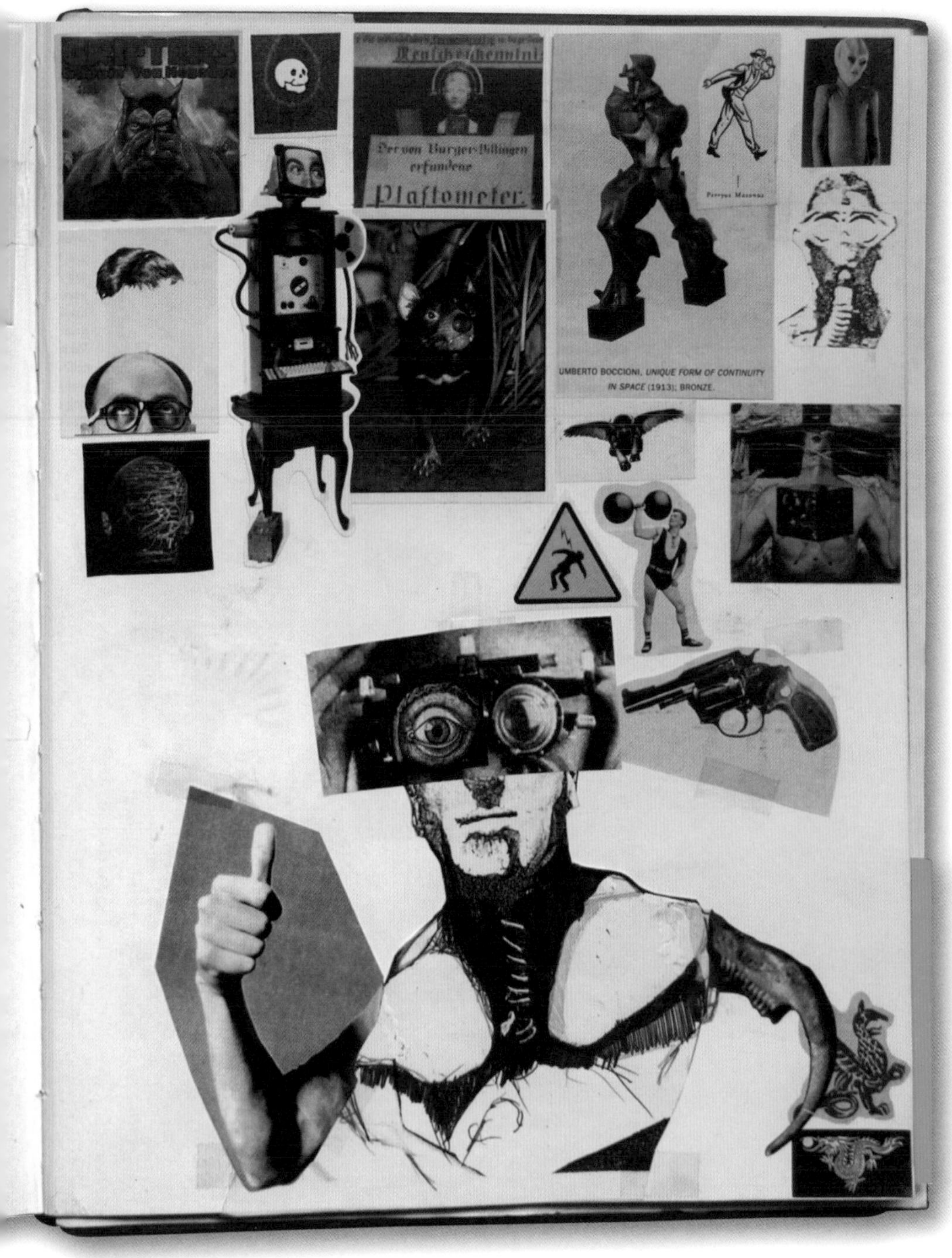

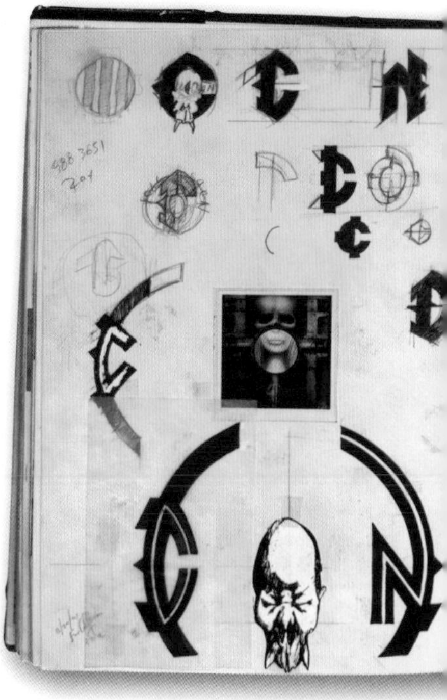

VIKTOR KOEN

Greek-born, Israeli-educated, and New York-based Viktor Koen says he has kept sketchbooks since his first year at Bezalel Academy of Arts and Design in Jerusalem. "We had a course where a minimum of seven sketches had to be turned in with every assignment. The school produces its own extra-thick paper books that I still use now. They were sort of a status symbol and we would sketch for hours at Tel Aviv coffee shops by the beach. Sketching almost became a way of life."

Since his finished work is digital and photography-based, "my sketches are very different from my finishes," he says. "I mostly sketch ideas and compositions that later are refined on screen. It's almost the only work I do traditionally, and this is very dear to me."

There are no thematic threads in his books, "since my sketches just resolve different assignments on a conceptual level (as well as compositional and proportional aspects), and most of the time have nothing to do with aesthetics or personal style."

These books span 1986–2009. Koen is only up to number six, "due to the small size of my images and my pathological organizational nature, where no inch goes unused."

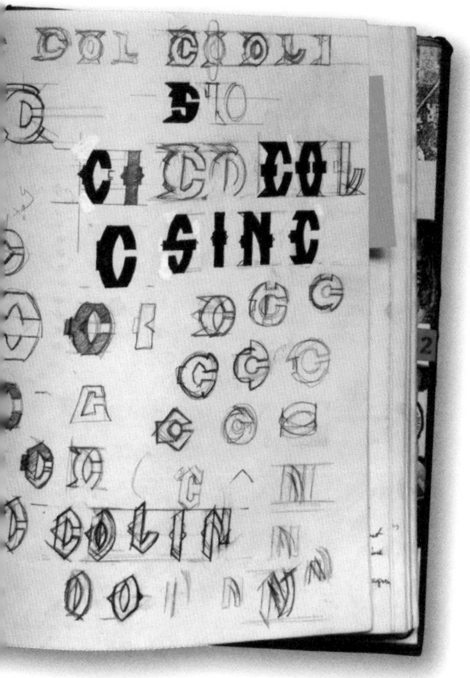

COLLISION
MAXIMUM RESPECT

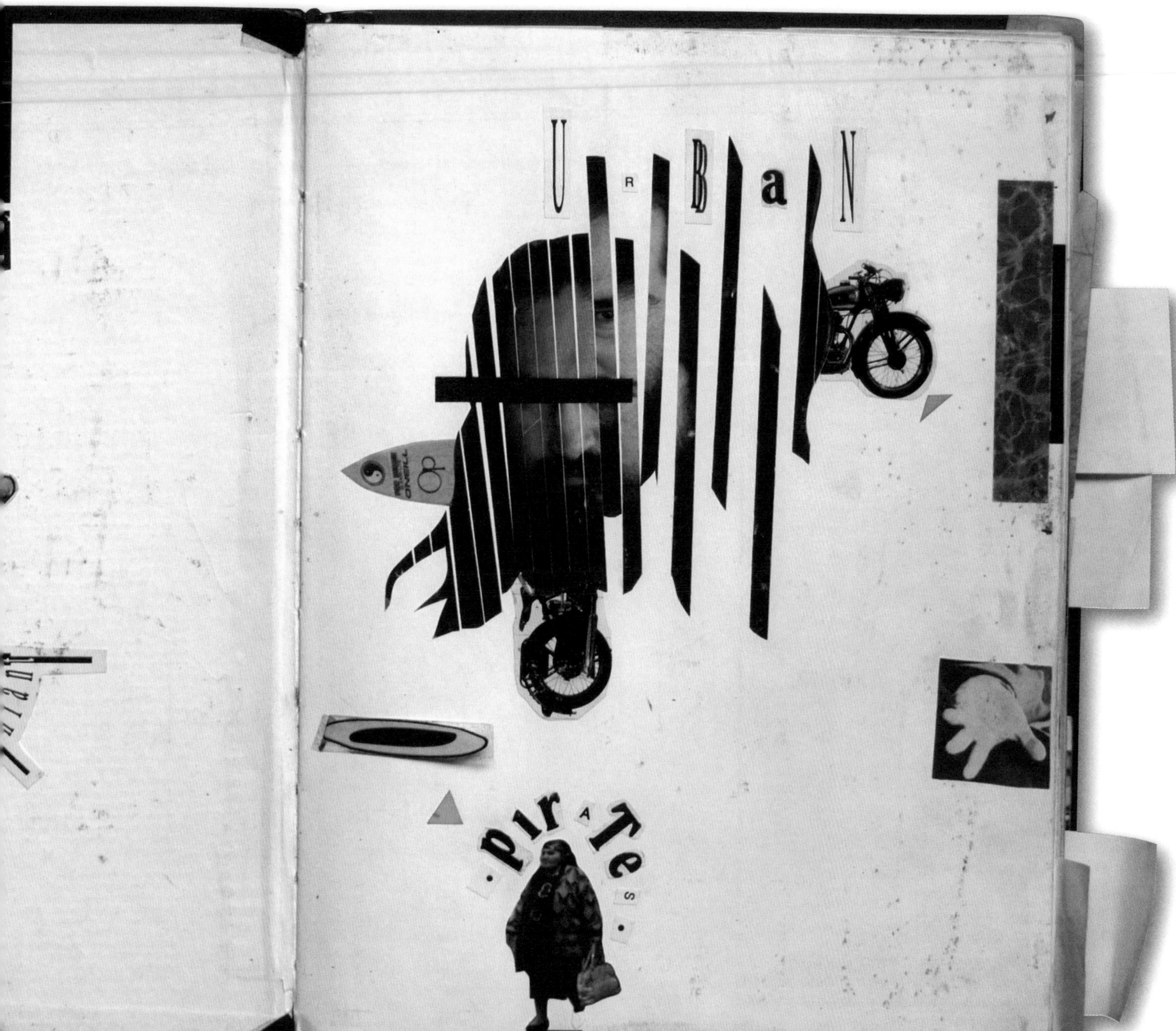
URBaN
pIrATeS

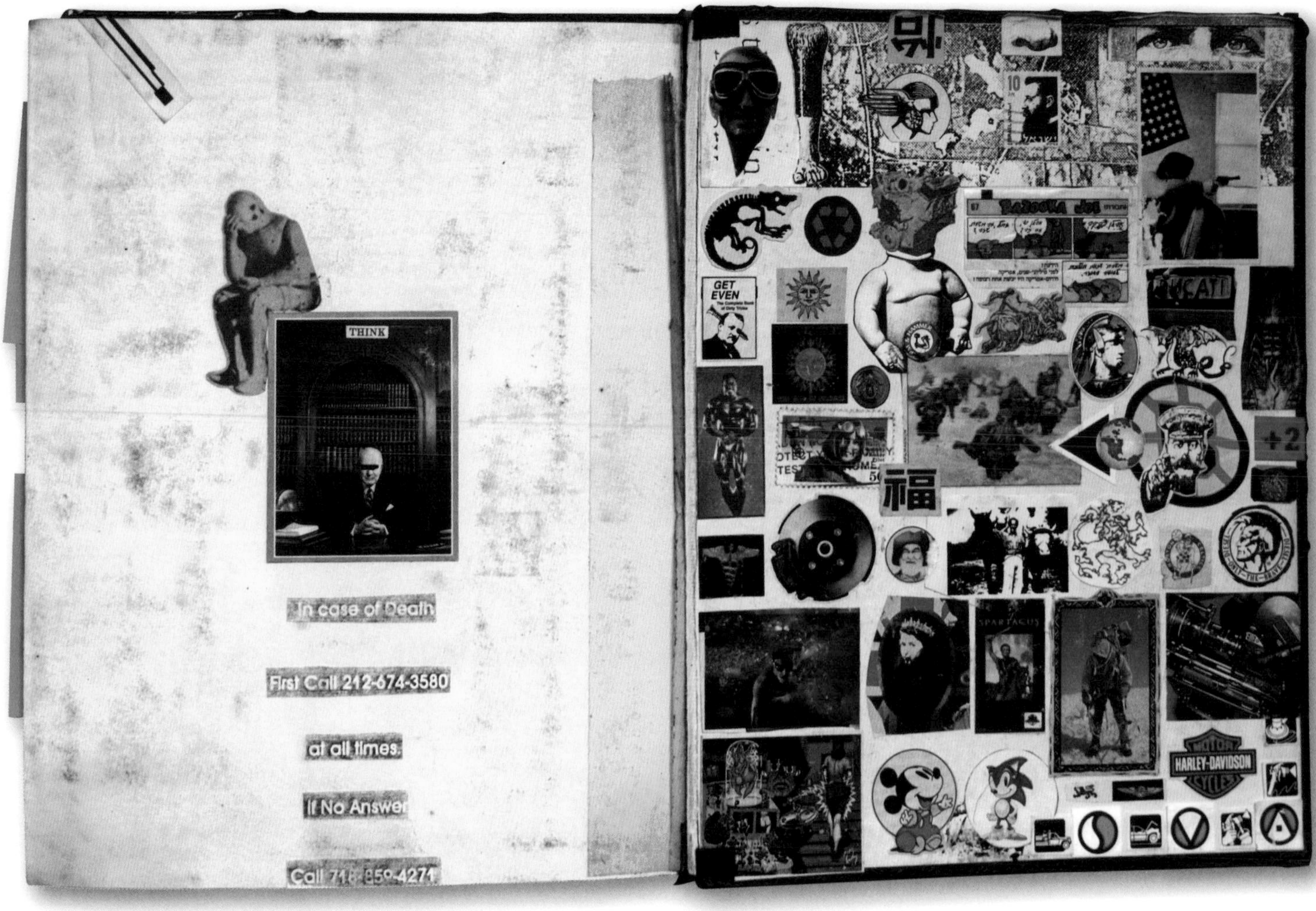
THINK
In case of Death
First Call 212-674-3580
at all times.
If No Answer
GET EVEN
SPARTACUS
HARLEY-DAVIDSON

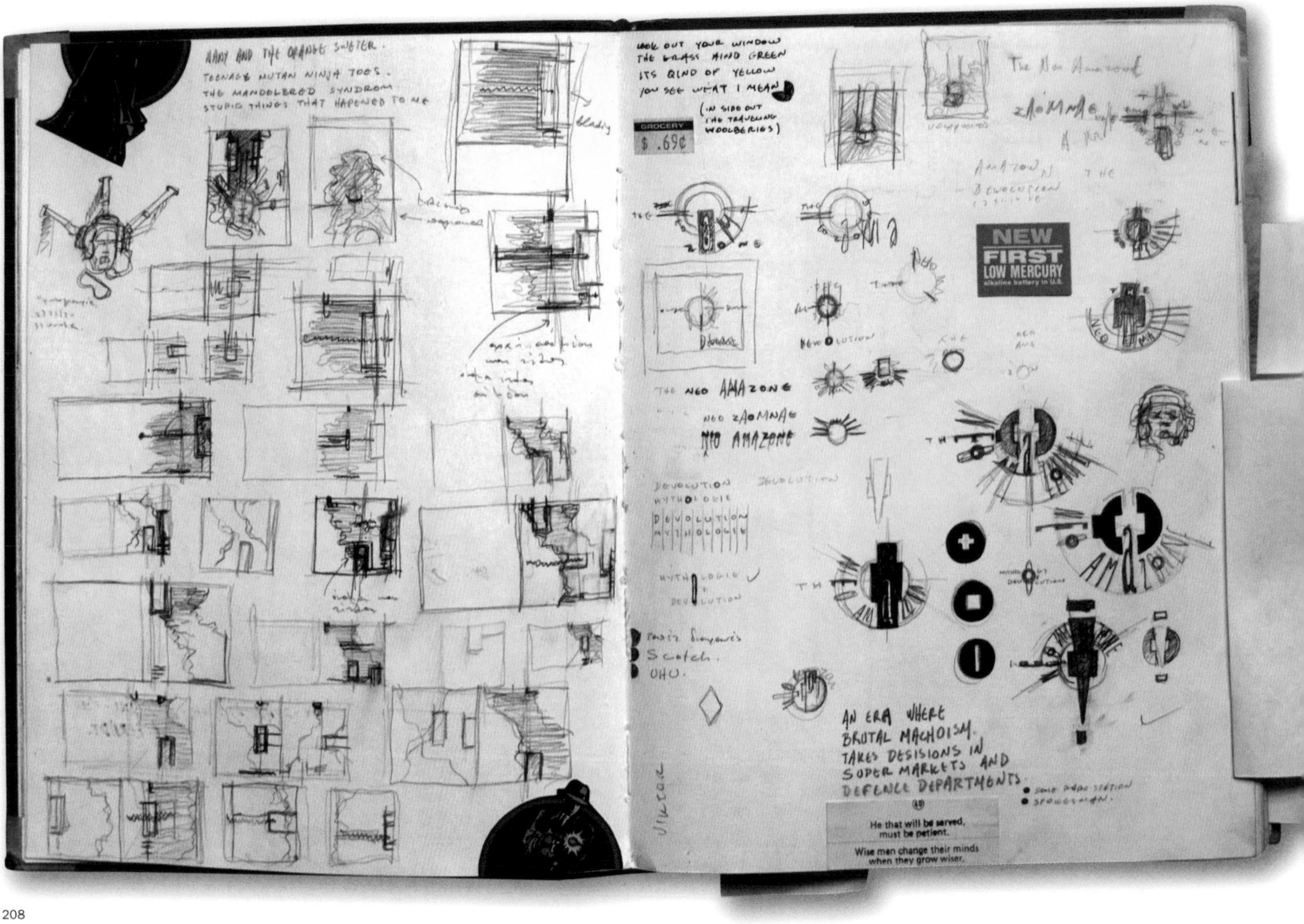
TEENAGE MUTAN NINJA TOES.
THE MANDELBROD SYNDROM
STUPID THINGS THAT HAPENED TO ME
LOOK OUT YOUR WINDOW
THE GRASS MIND GREEN
ITS KIND OF YELLOW
YOU SEE WHAT I MEAN
GROCERY
$ .69¢
NEW
FIRST
LOW MERCURY
alkaline battery in U.S.
THE NEO AMAZONE
DEVOLUTION
MYTHOLOGIE
AN ERA WHERE
BRUTAL MACHOISM
TAKES DESISIONS IN
SUPER MARKETS AND
DEFENCE DEPARTMENTS.
He that will be served,
must be patient.
Wise men change their minds
when they grow wiser.

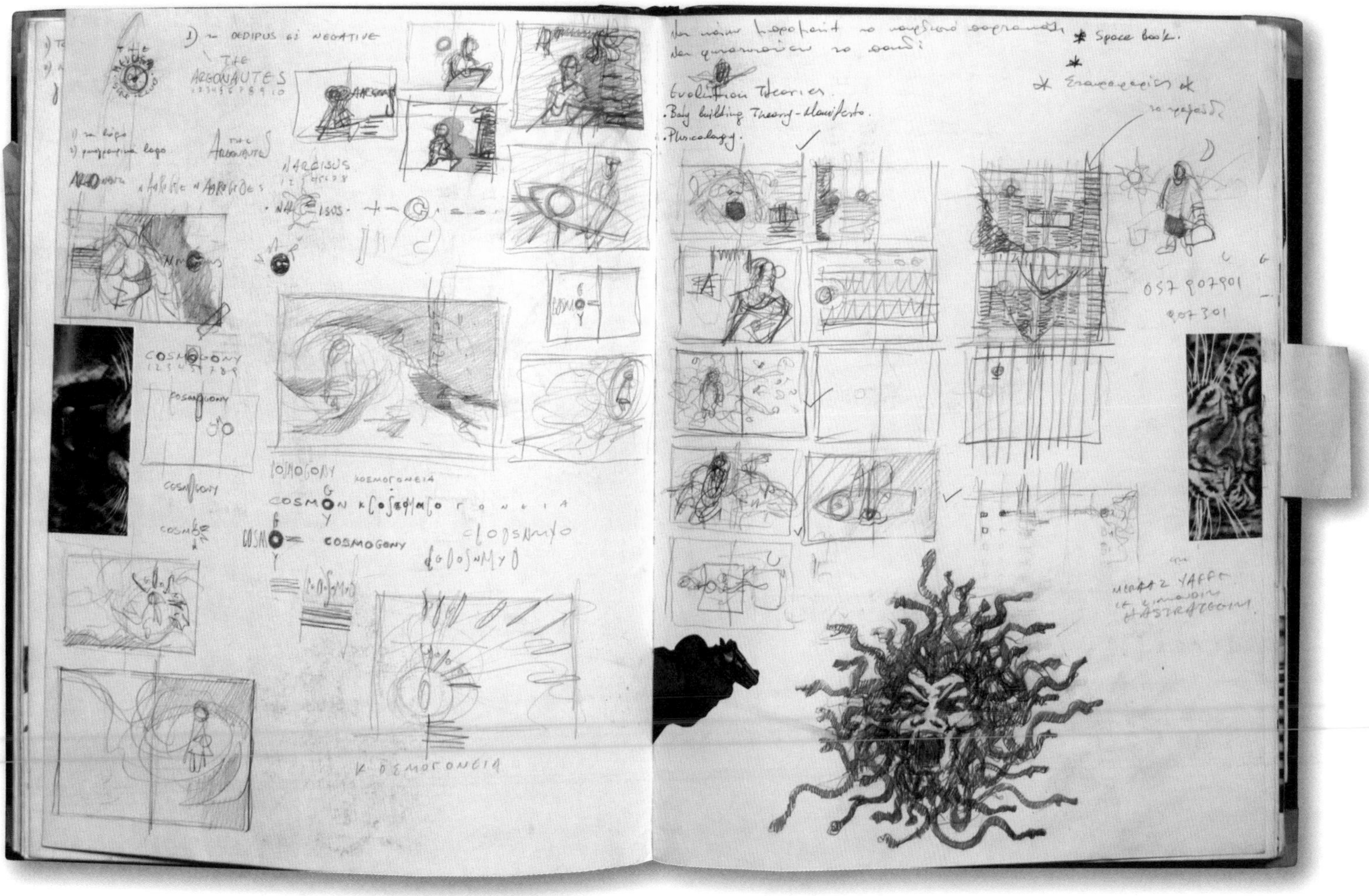
OEDIPUS AS NEGATIVE
THE ARGONAUTES
NARCISUS
COSMOGONY
COSMOGONY
KOSMOGONIA
Evolution Theories.
Physcology.
Space book.

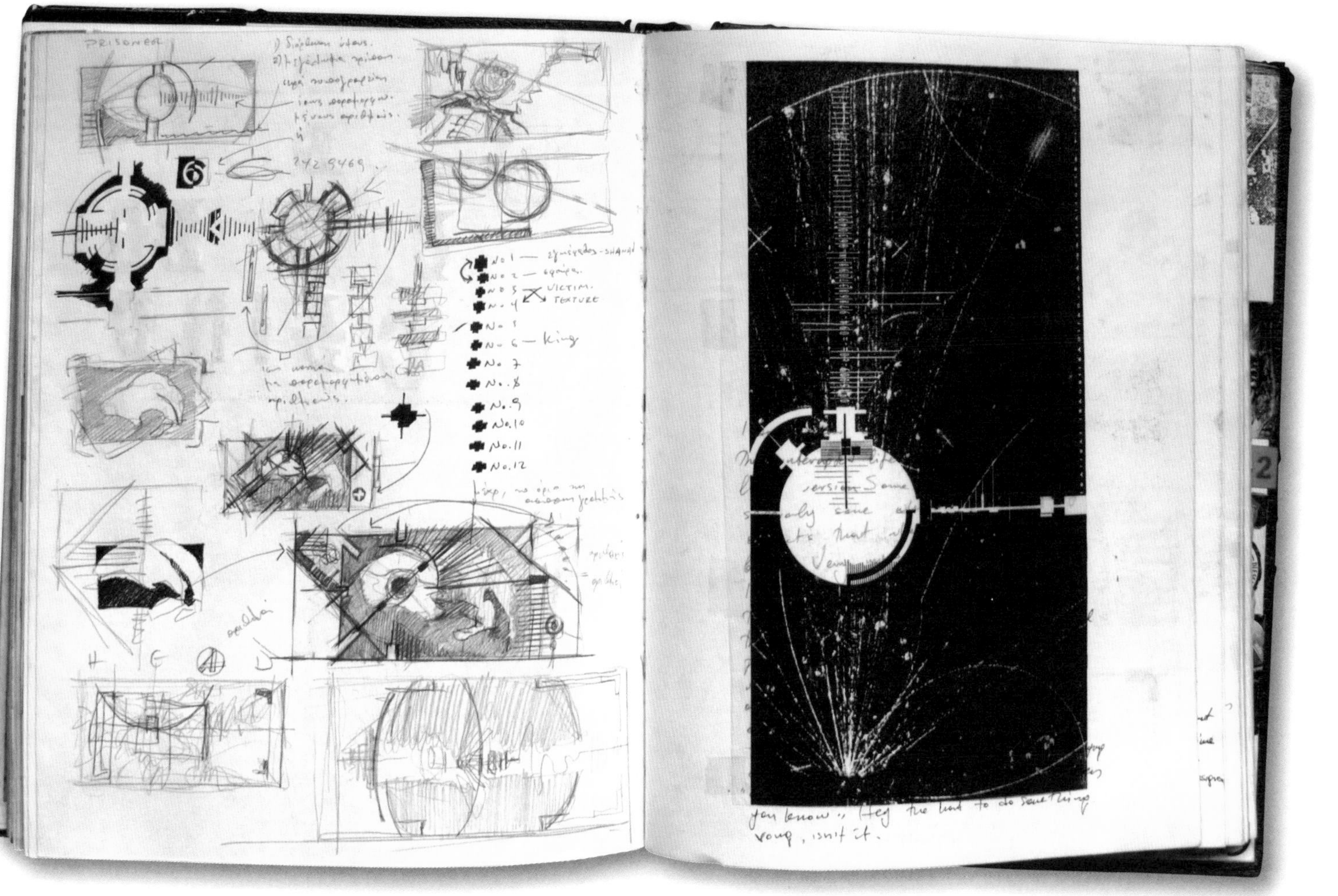
PRISONER
No.1
No.2
No.3
No.4
VICTIM.
TEXTURE
No.5
No.6 — king
No.7
No.8
No.9
No.10
No.11
No.12

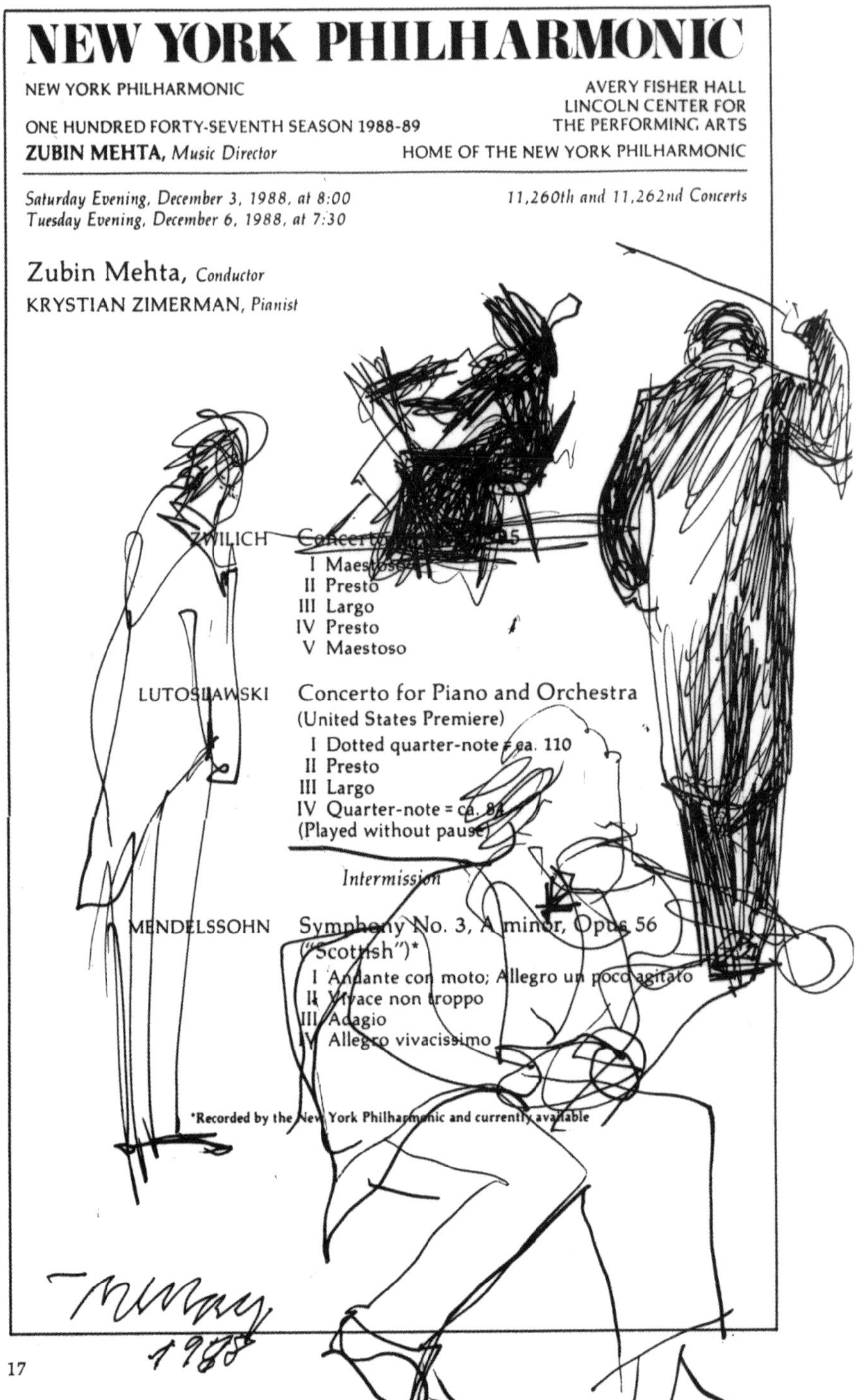

BILL LACY

Bill Lacy, an architect and designer based in San Antonio, Texas, has drawn from the moment he could hold a pencil. Lacy's sketch journals, half writing, half drawing, began in earnest when he won the LeBrun Traveling Fellowship, which required six months of travel in Europe and Mexico and a report illustrated with sketches. That was the first of some sixty to seventy black bound journals produced over the years.

His passion for drawings was represented in a book, *100 Contemporary Architects: Drawings and Sketches* (Abrams), which dealt with hand-drawn conceptual sketches at that point when an idea is still free from the constraints of client demands, timetables, and budget: what Frank Gehry calls the tentativeness, the messiness, the "in progress stage."

Although a licensed architect, for Lacy it has taken considerable unlearning in order not to make precise depictions in the tightly prescribed language of geometry. The sketches he aspires to do are gestural, those that capture the essence of the subject, with neither one line too many, nor one too few.

"Drawing is a strange business. After a certain point courage is more important than talent," he adds. For Lacy, "A drawing, properly viewed, has its own story to tell apart from what it depicts."

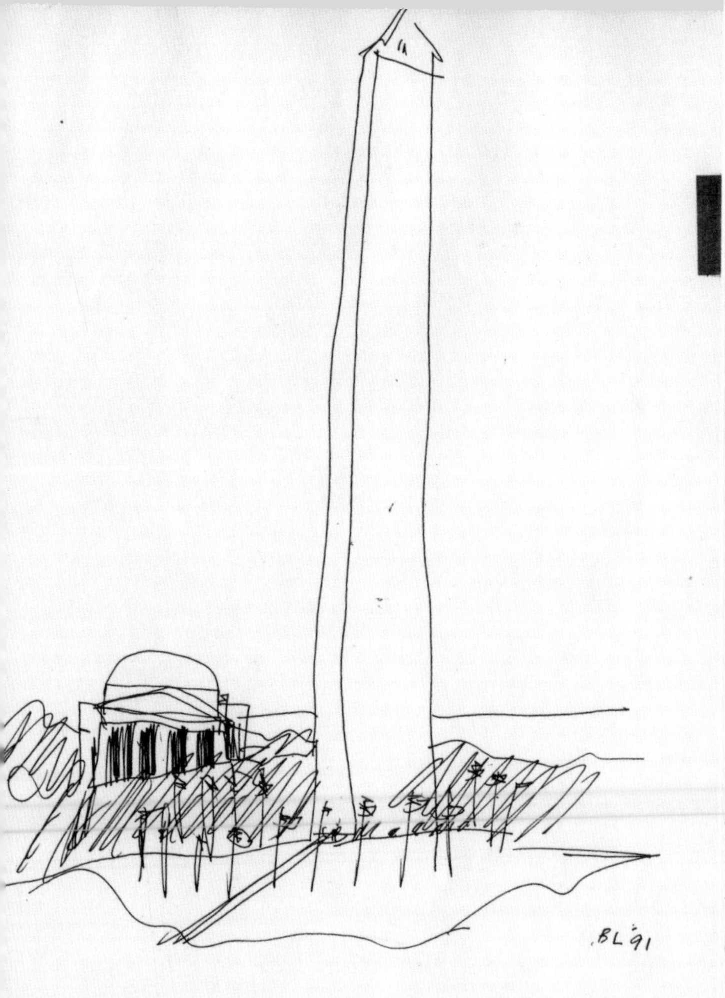
BL'91

BL
Watergate Looking South
Potamac view.
9-24 96
pencil
original
w/ LITA

DC
BL
Watergate

San Sebastian

Aspen IDCA
Design Tent '87
VOL. 15

EVELAND BL
2001

BL
CAMPO BEACH
WESTPORT.
AUG '96

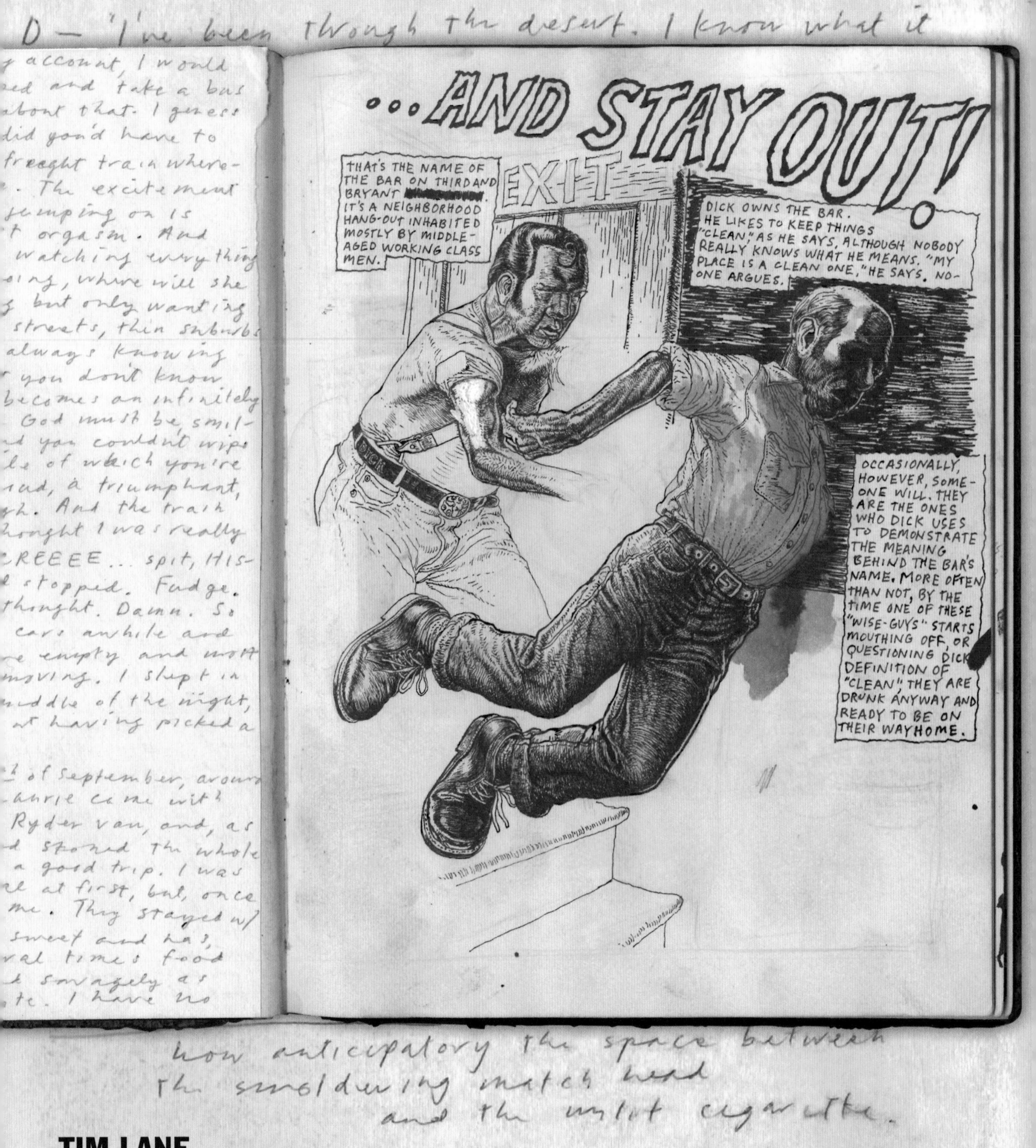

TIM LANE

For Tim Lane, a New York-based illustrator and comic artist, sketchbooks are a repository of ideas and experiences: "I keep different sketchbooks for different reasons." One is more like a journal, in which he documents interesting life experiences, story ideas, character sketches, weird dreams, and weird conversations. Another is a pocket-size Moleskine that he keeps with him at all times "to record things whenever I go out," which is then transferred, if it is important or memorable, to an 8½ × 11 in. (22.5 × 28 cm) hardbound sketchbook.

"I get very self-conscious 'sketchbooking' in public," he says, "so the Moleskines, which attract less attention, are perfect for me. I also keep a separate book for commercial illustration work. But lately I've been trying to connect those two worlds together a little more."

Lane notes that his books are "pretty battered. They look like they've been through the washing machine. I spent a good part of the 1990s – when I was in my twenties – traveling around and working odd jobs, so my sketchbook was an essential part of my life. That travel was critical to my artistic development, and I often return to those books in search of inspiration. But they're in really bad shape." Unfortunately, quite a few of Lane's books have been left in telephone booths at train stations and airports. The ones here range from the mid-1990s to 2009.

ARLIN — 1-9-95: "My dream is to find a rich woman with one foot on a banana peel and one foot in the grave."

LION OF THE VALLEY: ST LOUIS HISTORY HIGHLIGHTS
p. 166 – WHARF FIRE & RIOTS W/ IRISH THAT ENDED W/ HOWITZER CANNON
p. 169 – GERMANS & NATIVISTS RIOT @ THE POLLS
ST. LOUIS BLACKIE
30 YEARS OLD
FEBRUARY, 1933
Shane Co. USERNAME: TIMLIZ
PASSWORD: SAGE / PASSWORD QUEST: DOG
ANSWER: SAGE
NAME OF WISHLIST
TIMLIZ
Took what I could get. The train
now – rolls right out of the NE
w(return to earlier excerpt)
WOMAN AT THE PIANO
SCENE FROM "PHANTOM OF THE OPERA"
THE MOON –
… the moon here in St Louis always startles me.
"Sometimes the moon is you.
In any case, the moon."
THE TEXT MUST STILL REMAIN INFORMATIVE, UNIQUE TO ST LOUIS, DESCRIPTIVE & NOT SOO "OUT THERE" OR POETIC OR ARTSY. SHOULD REMAIN JOURNALISTIC — BUT AM THINKING ALSO NECESSARY TO BROADEN RIGIDITY OF FORMAT IN ORDER TO MAKE NEW REAL-ESTATE DOWNSIZE BE POIGNANT OR ENGAGING OR… SOMETHING! MUST STILL HAVE A VOICE – BUT DON'T TRY POETRY, TIM, WHATEVER YOU DO, DON'T WRITE FUCKING POETRY. IT'D BE BAD AND YOU'D EVEN LOSE YOUR LAST READER (IN OTHER WORDS) YOURSELF.
WHAT'S THE NOVEL OBJECT?
No-one will know how much I feel about things:

No one will know much about anybody's feelings, except maybe their own. It's not hard to understand why it is so important for one to
[redacted] himself
picks up speed,
hopping a train)
to unde
towards
SO THE GIRL – DOBB'S DAUGHTER – IS A BIT OF A GROUPIE. SHE'S INTO THE JAZZ SCENE AND GETS OFF ON KNOWING THE MUSICIANS. SHE CLINGS TO THE KID, ALTHOUGH HE DOESN'T REALLY NOTICE HER. SHE ENDS UP TRAVELING WITH THE KID ON HIS WAY SOUTH BY A FLUKE. SHE BRINGS MONEY AND HEROINE. STONED ON HEROINE ONE NIGHT, IN A MOMENT OF PARANOID HYSTERIA, SHE CALLS DADDY AND DIVULGES THEIR WHERE-ABOUTS. WITHIN A SHORT PERIOD OF TIME THE KID IS ASSAULTED BY A MOB OF GOONS HIRED BY DOBBS. THE POLICE COME, FIND LAURA'S DRUGS IN THE KIDS POSSESSION, AND ASSUME THEY ARE HIS.
BY THIS TIME, THE KID HAS ALREADY CONFRONTED THE DETECTIVE DOBBS HIRED & LAURA REMAINED OBLIVIOUS.
KISSES FOLDED PAPER TO CREATE THE IMAGE OF LIPS.
OLD FRIENDS
RUSS & CHARLIE
AND HE'D FALLEN ASLEEP WITH HIS DICK IN HIS HAND...
YOU DON'T KNOW WHAT YOUR TALKIN' ABOUT.
...WATCHIN' T.V. ON THE COUCH.
AH, YOU SHUT UP, YOU PAWN!
IN THE HABIT OF TALKING TO THE BARTENDER
MAY 17, MONDAY, 1996: I'm living now in El Cerrito, Ca. and have been since January. I'm now interested in creating a depth to my characters that is more expansive than others seen in graphic story-telling. Practice is necessary for this task. I plan to write a series of short stories whose sole intention is to develop a story line depending mainly on the relationships between characters and the dialogue which results from that relationships. The two characters below and to the left are two of these: Russell and Pip.
Not much is new at the El Cerrito place. Chris is unemployed and Emily is yelling at him for various reasons on a regular basis. She has refused to keep her new computer here because she believes it will either get stolen or Chris will spill
beer on it. All of her arguments are, of course, absurd. She's apparently "rented" a small room out at her friend's house in West Oakland as her "office." Kevin, being the wise man that he is, remains as quiet as a mouse, complaining about nothing and therefore receiving no complaints. I'm going home to Minnesota for two weeks in June, taking an Amtrak train over the Rocky Mountains and through Montana, etc. – a trip which I'm desperately looking forward to. I've been so stuck here for the last few months that a chance to move – just to be going anywhere, will be a remedy.
INFLUENCES!: When I lived in Amsterdam, I was impressed by the way friends would create compilation cassette tapes for each other. This was back in 1991, before the CD revolution. The compilation tapes would often have original cover designs, all manner of imagery, most often collages and pictures taken from various sources carbon copied, and folded into cassette covers. I'd never seen this sort of thing before, and it excited me. However, at the time, I had no immediate use for that kind of imagery – but it stayed in the back of
and his aesth
cassettes. I'd
NOTES ON [redacted]
RUDOLF ARNHEIM:
UNIDENTIFIABLE
INSISTENCE OF
AN ARTISTIC
DISAPPOINTME
CONTRARY TO
TEACHERS: Maybe we find character traits in our best teachers that we either need to recognize in ourselves or want to believe exist in the society around us. What one person (student) sees in a teacher another may not – it could be debatable that the trait is even there, whether it's not
COULD THIS BE A YAH ILLUSTRATION? IF SO, WHAT WOULD THE STORY BE? THE STORY'LL HAVE TO FIND THE ILLUSTRATION, OR VISA-VERSA.

EY'RE ~~G~~ GONNA BOO-GA-LOO DOWN BROADWAY." OUTSIDE St Peter & Paul Parish the line of men stood, woebegone, shivering in the cold, waiting for the
rs to open for dinner at 5PM. A few of them spoke to each other —
fact one seemed to be speaking or even possibly preaching to
ryone else — while they waited. One guy, a ~~nice~~ friendly loo
dude, wandered around the parking lot, a constant smile on
s face, chatting with new arrivals from time to time. He wore
sheepskinned cap; the ear flaps were pulled up and tied at
top of his head. All of the men waiting in line acted very
siness-like — there was a kind of vacancy about them that
own them in every way — their expressions, their posture, everythi

THE ENTIRE SONG CHOREOGRAPHED, BROKEN INTO FRAGMENTS. SEGMENT

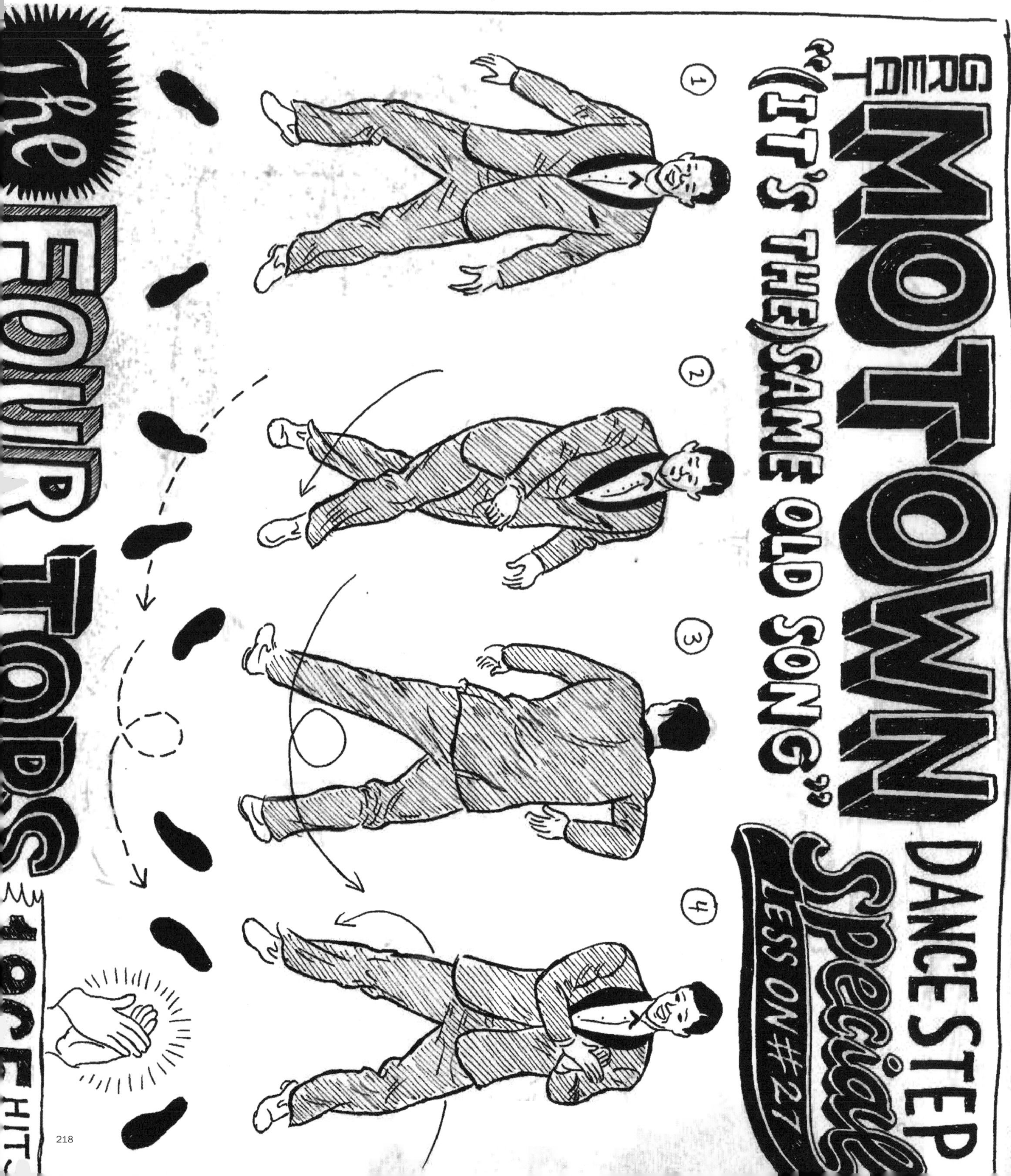

SONG CONTINUING — OR PLAYING — THROUGHOUT ENTIRE BOOK. THERE'S MUSIC FOR

14/09 – Extremely cold night. Around 2°. I went to St. Peter & Paul's Par[k] [t]o watch the lines of men getting their free dinners, but arrived too lat[e]. Then went downtown to the Shelter on (?) St to check things out. The place was packed. Outside, there was a black guy leaning backw[ards] over the bannister, in a very uncomfortable position. There was als[o] a young man leaning against the wall, smoking a cigarette, wa[tching] the guy leaning over the bannister. The young guy was an employee. The black guy wasn't quite asleep, but neither was he quite awake. His breathing was heavy and labored, and when h[e] inhaled, he nearly tipped over backwards; when he exhaled, he n[ear]ly slipped off the bannister frontwards. The employee watchi[ng]

shelter. He was too far gone, too incoherent – he might've been dead drunk or high on aerosol. Plumes of steam floated from his mouth – his breath – then quickly blew away. The employee – Danny, I think – seemed disgusted, but also concerned. Eventually, I asked the drunk guy if he was okay. He muttered something incomprehensible, finally sliding forward and collapsing. The security guards inside were very suspicious of me. I never got into the main room.

I had told them that I was a journalist working for the RFT which seemed to soften them a little, but open enough to all...

The place was really packed though.

...AT JUST MIGHT PARTIALLY FACILITATE ... Y INTEREST IN BRINGING MUSIC

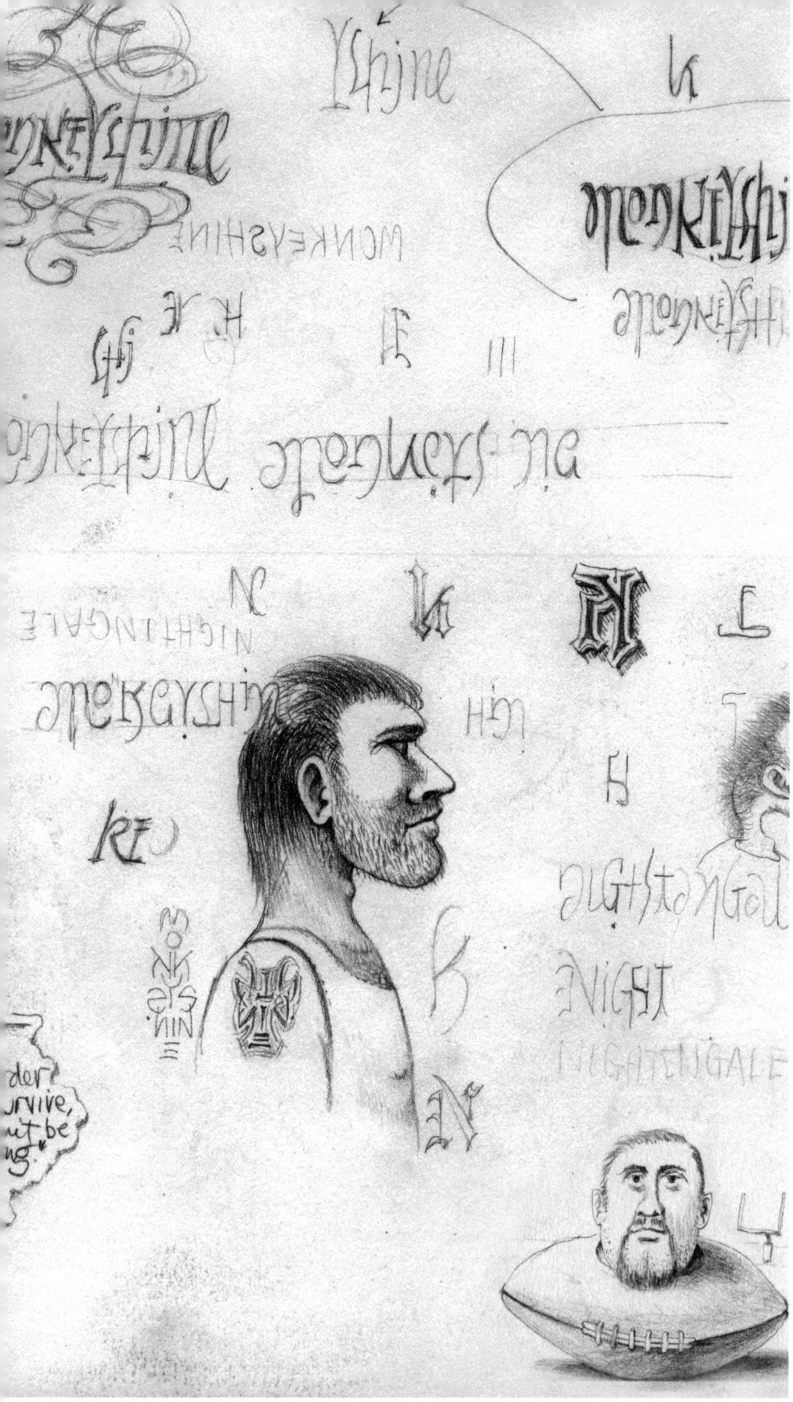

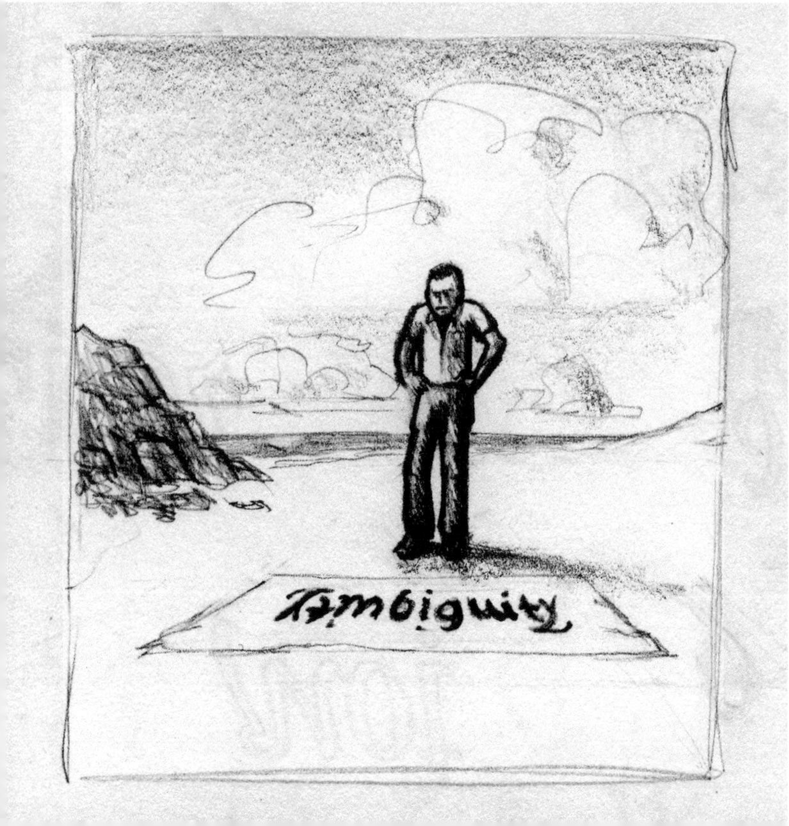

JOHN LANGDON

John Langdon, master of the art of ambigrams (typographic compositions that can be read up or down), and namesake of the protagonist in his friend Dan Brown's *The Da Vinci Code*, has kept a sketchbook for close to fifteen years. Early stages of logo work take place in a sketchbook, as does the development of an ambigram, whether a personal piece or a commission. Ideas for paintings are born there, too.

Langdon states that "the right-brained, open-minded, non-judgmental phases of my work happen in my sketchbook. It's the R&D department. Once ideas have reached a stage of refinement that I consider worthy of pursuit, they move to the next phase, either further exploration in Photoshop, or a left-brained, crafted-to-the-best-of-my-ability pencil drawing on tracing paper which, in turn, will be scanned for execution in Adobe Illustrator." The drawings of people are done for the pure enjoyment of drawing, and for these Langdon uses a pencil in a different way than when he is developing a concept or a design. "But with those drawings as an exception, the themes that run through all my work – wordplay, symmetry, ambiguity, and optical illusion – are present on every page of my sketchbooks." Langdon keeps four concurrent sketchbooks for no good reason other than to have one within reach when he wants it. The books here are from 2000–5.

전체교수회의자료
2006년 9월 6일(수) 오후 2
KMU
KOOKMIN UNIVERSITY SINCE 1946
국민대학교
아름다운 도전

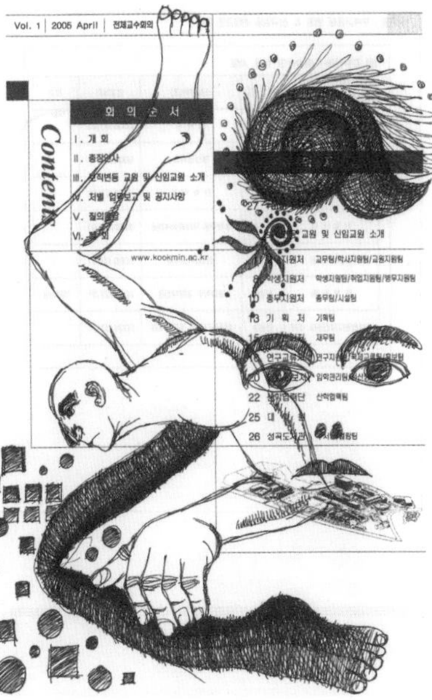

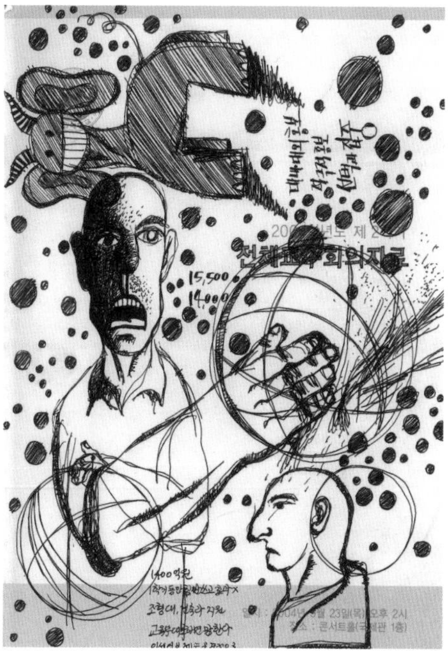

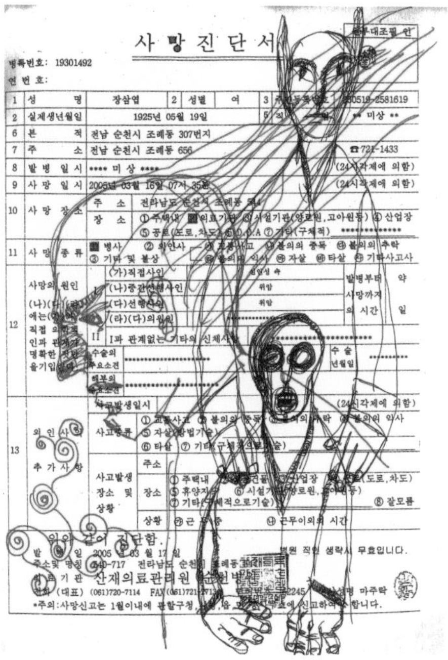

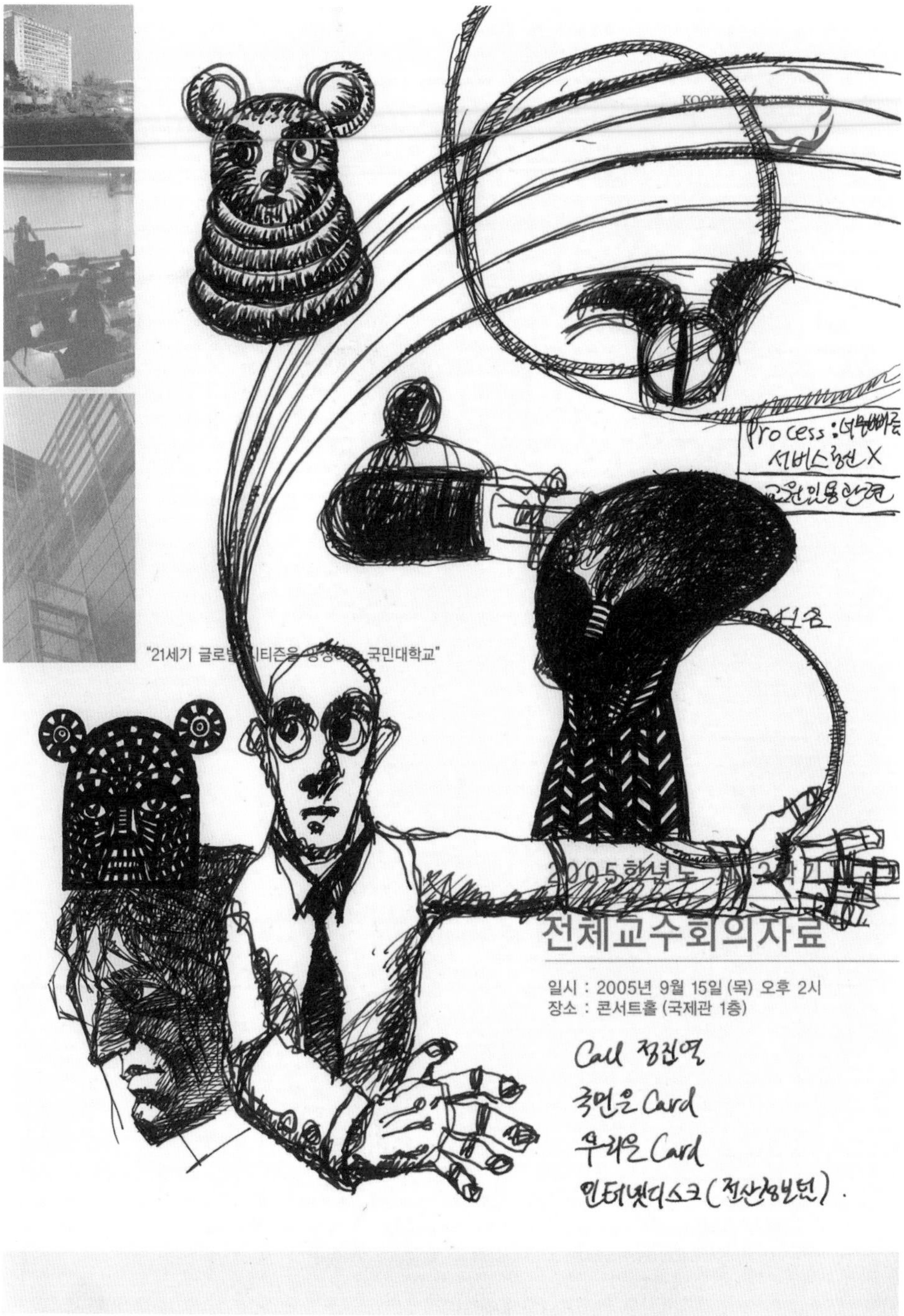

JACOB JOONHEE LEE

Jacob Joonhee Lee, a Korean designer and educator from Seoul, has over 100 sketches culled from client meetings, in addition to the more than twenty personal sketchbooks he has saved since 1986. Those, however, are his private domain. The ones shown here are "from long, official meetings where I doodle on the documents as both notes and daydreams."

The reason for these visual respites is that "first of all I sketch to make meetings not boring. Secondly, I try to get some inspiration from my inner thoughts through sketches." He also notes, "I don't sketch only for finished work, but I more likely sketch to make my brain fresh to get better ideas. My original sketches are usually more rough and harsh than finished work, which often becomes more clean and commercial to make clients and readers happy." Joonhee Lee likes to sketch "to express my feelings, always." His preference is to sketch an unusual figure or thing, or something that has personal resonance. "I like to draw all kinds of patterns from all kinds of cultures, Eastern or Western, old and new." And he will continue to draw at meetings – at least until he is caught.

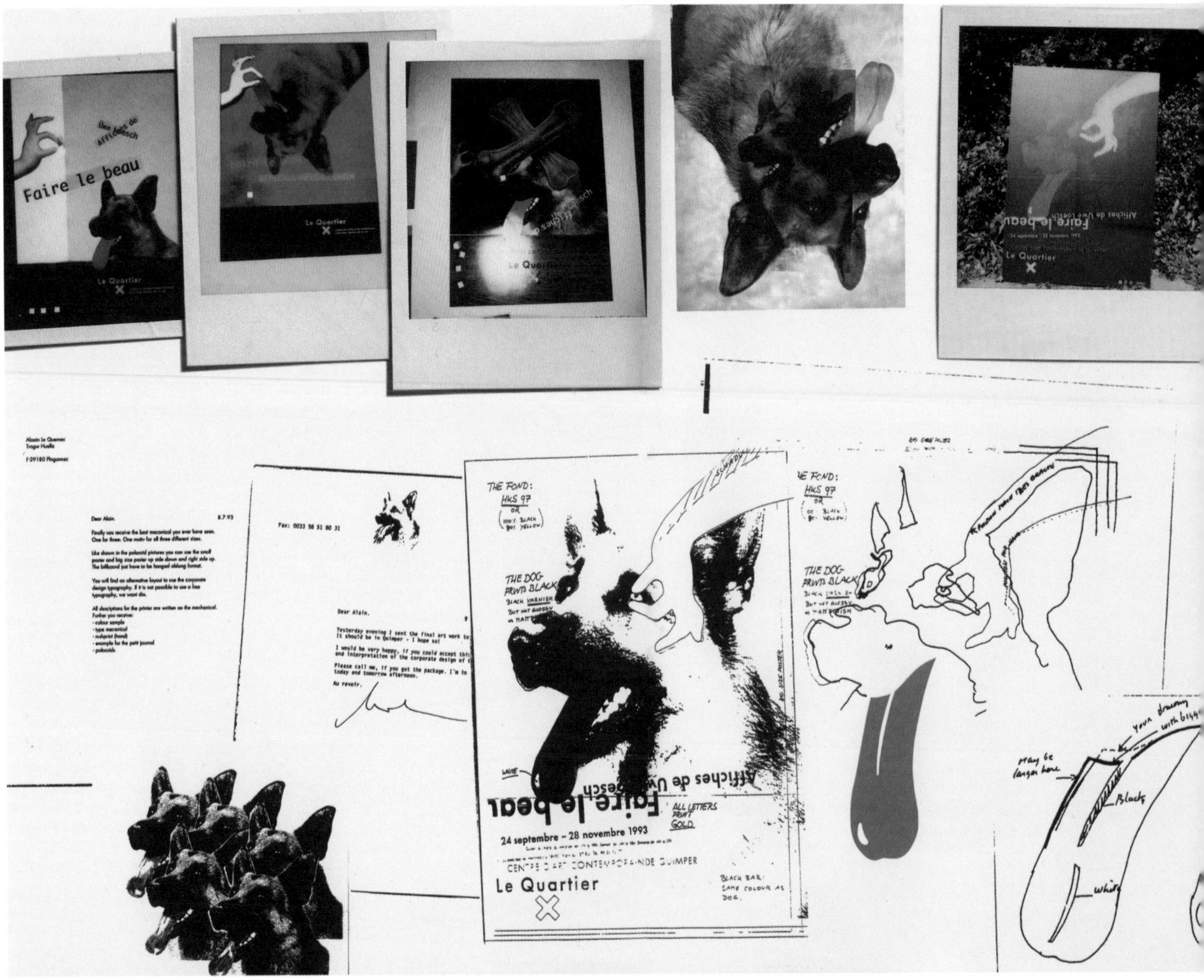
Faire le beau
Le Quartier
Alain Le Quernec
Trogor Huella
F-29180 Plogonnec
Dear Alain. 8.7.93
Finally you receive the best meconical you ever have seen.
One for three: One motiv for all three different sizes.
Like shown in the polaroid pictures you can use the small poster and big size poster up side down and right side up. The billboard just have to be hanged oblong format.
You will find an alternative layout to use the corporate design typography. If it is not possible to use a free typography, we wont die.
All desciptions for the printer are written on the mechanical.
Further you receive:
- colour sample
- type meconical
- rushprint (hand)
- example for the petit journal
- polaroids
Fax: 0033 98 51 80 31
Dear Alain,
Yesterday evening I sent the final art work to
It should be in Quimper - I hope so!
I would be very happy, if you could accept thi
and interpretation of the corporate design of
Please call me, if you got the package. I'm in
today and tomorrow afternoon.
Au revoir,
THE FOND:
HKS 97
OR
100% BLACK
80% YELLOW
THE DOG
PRINTS BLACK
BLACK VARNISH
BUT NOT GLOSSY
MATT
Affiches de Uwe Loesch
Faire le beau
ALL LETTERS
PRINT
GOLD
24 septembre – 28 novembre 1993
CENTRE D'ART CONTEMPORAIN DE QUIMPER
Le Quartier
BLACK BAR:
SAME COLOUR AS
DOG.
Your drawing
with bigger
May be
larger here
Black
White

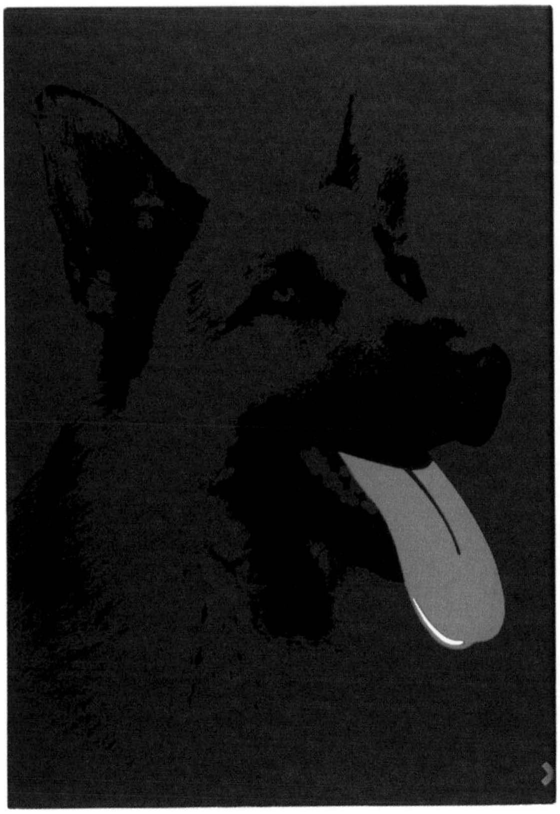

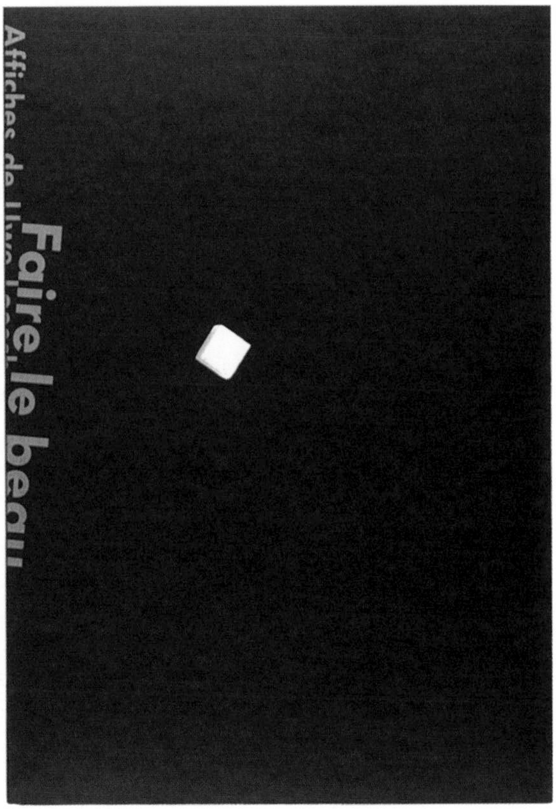
Faire le beau
Affiches de Uwe Loesch

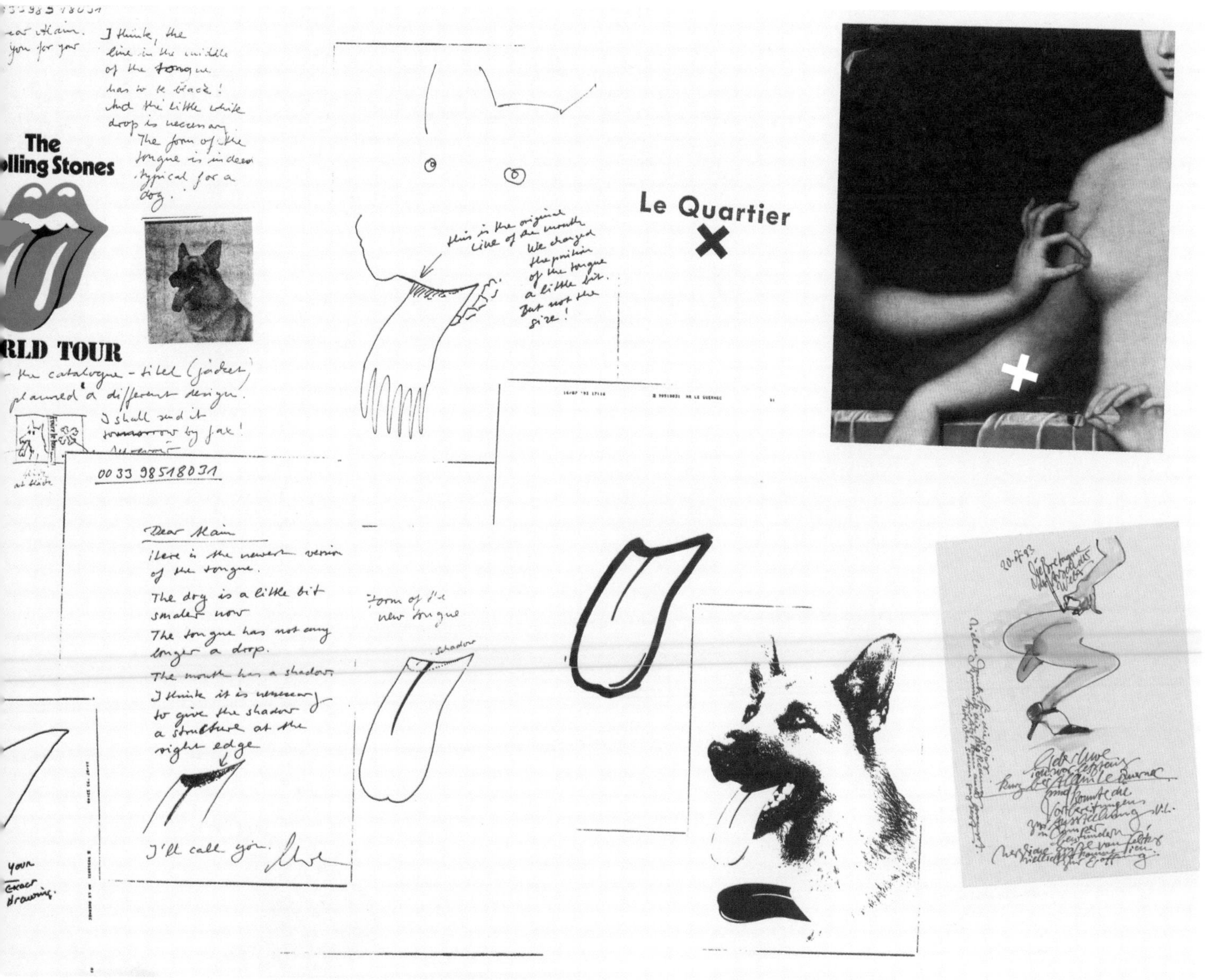

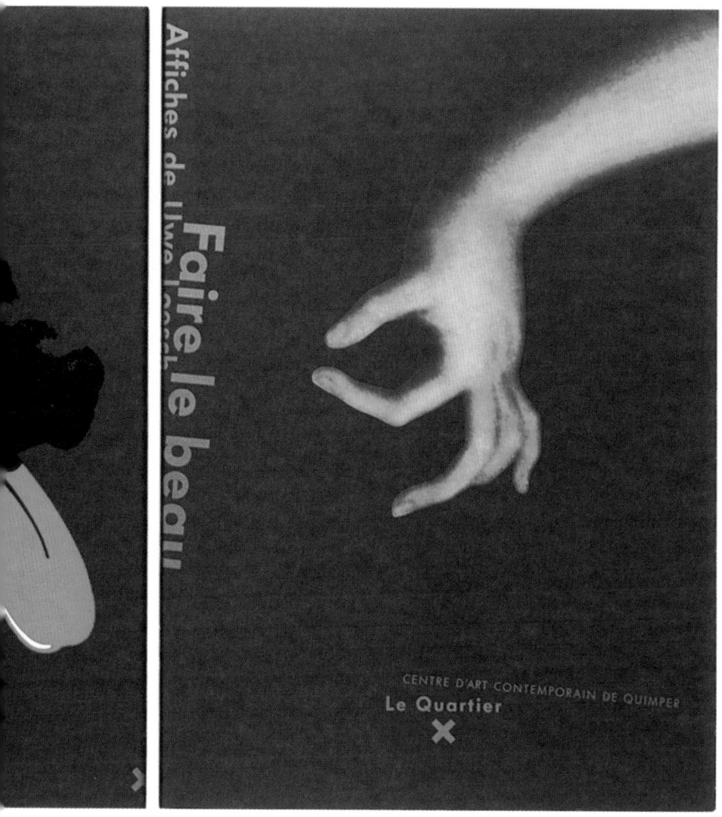

UWE LOESCH

Uwe Loesch, from Dresden, Germany, is an accomplished poster designer with work in the permanent collections of the Museum of Modern Art, New York; the Israel Museum, Jerusalem; Le Musée de la Publicité, Paris; the Library of Congress, Washington, D.C.; and the art library of the Staatliche Museen Preußischer Kulturbesitz, Berlin. Instead of sketchbooks, he keeps scraps of all kinds. The work represented here is the jacket for the catalog of his exhibition "Faire le beau. Affiches de Uwe Loesch" at the Centre d'Art Contemporain in Quimper, France, in 1993.

"The jacket documents the exchange of sketches between the curator of the exhibition, Alain Le Quernec, and me, discussing the form of the tongue of The Rolling Stones, which is more or less misquoted in the final artwork of the poster," Loesch explains. "The shepherd dog symbolizes Germany and the hand is a part of the famous painting of the School of Fontainebleau [the portrait of Gabrielle d'Estrées and the Duchess de Villars, 1594, Louvre, Paris]. It symbolizes France. The tongue symbolizes my generation. Not on the poster, but on the title of the catalog (under the jacket) is a piece of sugar. It symbolizes the communication process between sender and receiver (target group) in advertising."

ROSS MacDONALD

Ross MacDonald, illustrator and designer of props for motion pictures, has always been compelled to keep sketchbooks. "I used to cut school notebooks in half and use them," he slyly recalls. "In junior high, I had multiple binders filled with sketches for comics, Frank Frazetta-style book covers, even a couple with nothing but designs for weapons and armor."

MacDonald's books are "just to doodle ideas and preserve them for later perusal, inspiration, whatever." Moreover, "They are on any crappy paper I can find. As a result, they look better than my finished work," he says with a hint of self-deprecation. When asked what the most unusual aspect of the images might be, MacDonald quips, "They are unusually brilliant." The overwhelming theme is slapstick humor, "which seems to come up a lot," and "a general feeling of wise-assedness."

He keeps five "archiva" books – thick wads of sketches in bulldog clips that hang on the wall. Then there are a dozen or so from finished projects – kids' books, movies – and another dozen from projects in various states of suspended animation. "Some of those have been on hold for ten years, some I work on every few weeks or months," he says.

HEY, FELLERS!
DO YOUR BIT FOR THE
HOMELAND
YOU GET ALL THIS!
IT SEEMED LIKE A GOOD IDEA AT THE TIME...
5 YEARS AGO...
COMICS
INTERROGATION
HIT THE GROUND RUNNING
No. 31
GREEN GHOST
GAS GUN

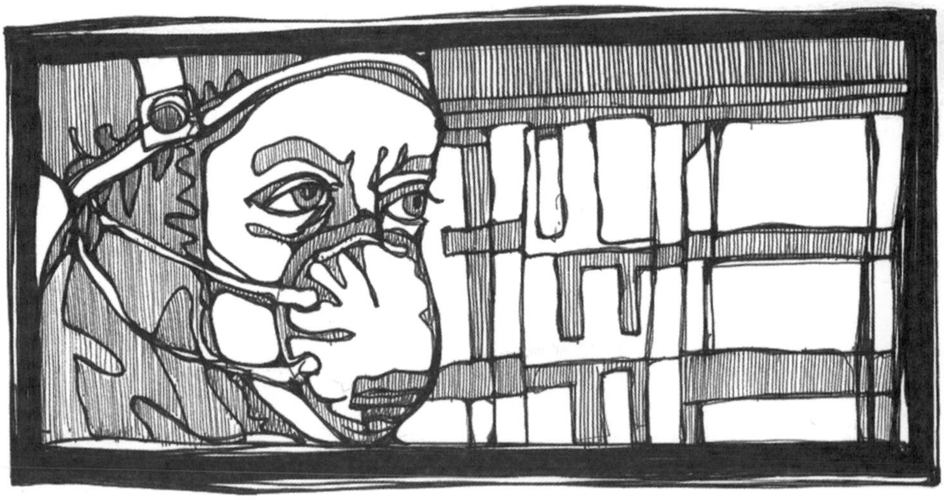

KERRY McELROY

Using a sketchbook as a travel diary is a venerable pastime. Australia-based designer Kerry McElroy says, "When I went overseas, instead of taking photos I drew anything that caught my eye. It then progressed to things that happened to me, and, looking back, I guess it became a dairy of events in my life."

To look at his sketches is to find various double or multiple meanings. "They may reflect a specific event, a relationship, even a quirky moment, sometimes a moment that I have drawn in code so that it won't embarrass anyone who looks at these pictures – or me, for that matter. So they are completely on show whilst also being quite private."

These images from 2000–8 show McElroy's daily life in black and white. "Sometimes I have drawn the same thing, but the pictures are not the same, as if my emotions and the experience are completely different. When I look back at these pages they make me smile. I think I am an optimist and that shows."

McElroy has "a lot of books, and of course one is always in my satchel wherever I go. That's why they get so worn: they are a part of my family, a part of me."

L. O. V. E.
*#@!≥
TITILATING

23.08.00
Green
Green brief - done in 10min
as not time left for creativity
So shot Items around the hoose
PROGRESS
WRITING TIFF
TIME REMAING.
Groovy
SPOT
SLUG

D
X
Q
SLUG
More
AARGH
FALLEN BRANCH
FRIDAY!
TUTANKHAMUN
Cancel
SATURDAY
DO NOT DISTURB

DAVID McLIMANS

David McLimans, an illustrator and designer specializing in collage, started his sketchbooks while in high school in 1965–67. Even though he skipped the next several years while he was in the US Navy, he returned to regular sketching again in the early 1970s and has "kept one kind or another ever since."

He maintains them for various purposes. "Little ones are for travel – quick notes and drawings." He also has collage books that, he says, "could be thought of as artist's books." McLimans adds, "I make them as objects. Sketchbooks give me the freedom I don't have when working on an assignment. They are sometimes roadmaps for future projects." He avers that his sketchbooks are "grittier, and show more accidents" than his finished work.

His books are thematic: "One book has a lot of war images. I did them at the outset of the Iraq invasion." Other dominant motifs are masks and letterforms. "The sketchbook I'm currently working in has a plant theme," he adds.

Even though McLimans has sketchbooks going back to the 1970s, and pages from the 1960s, he confesses that "I've either lost or purposely destroyed many of them. Around thirty now remain."

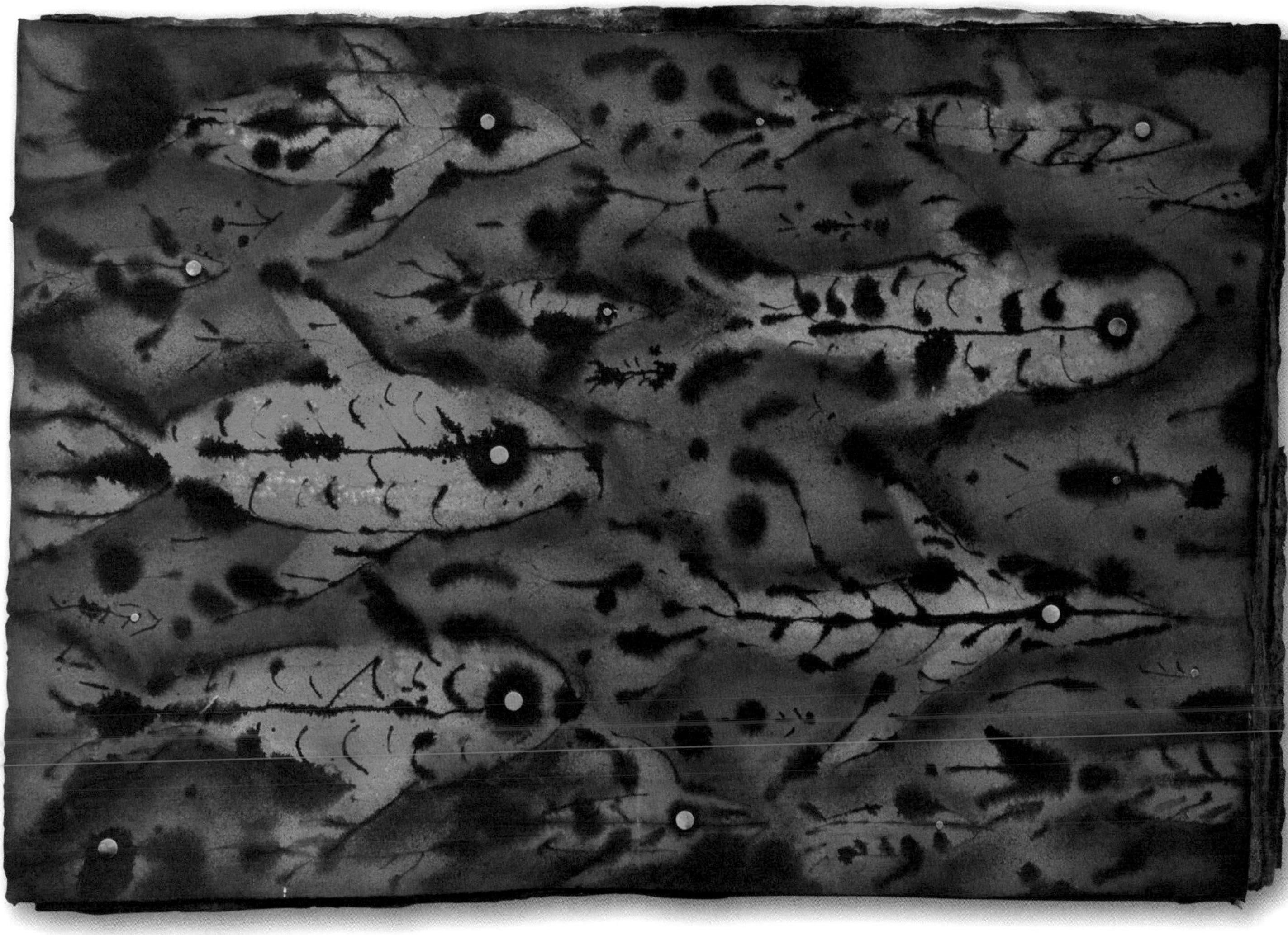

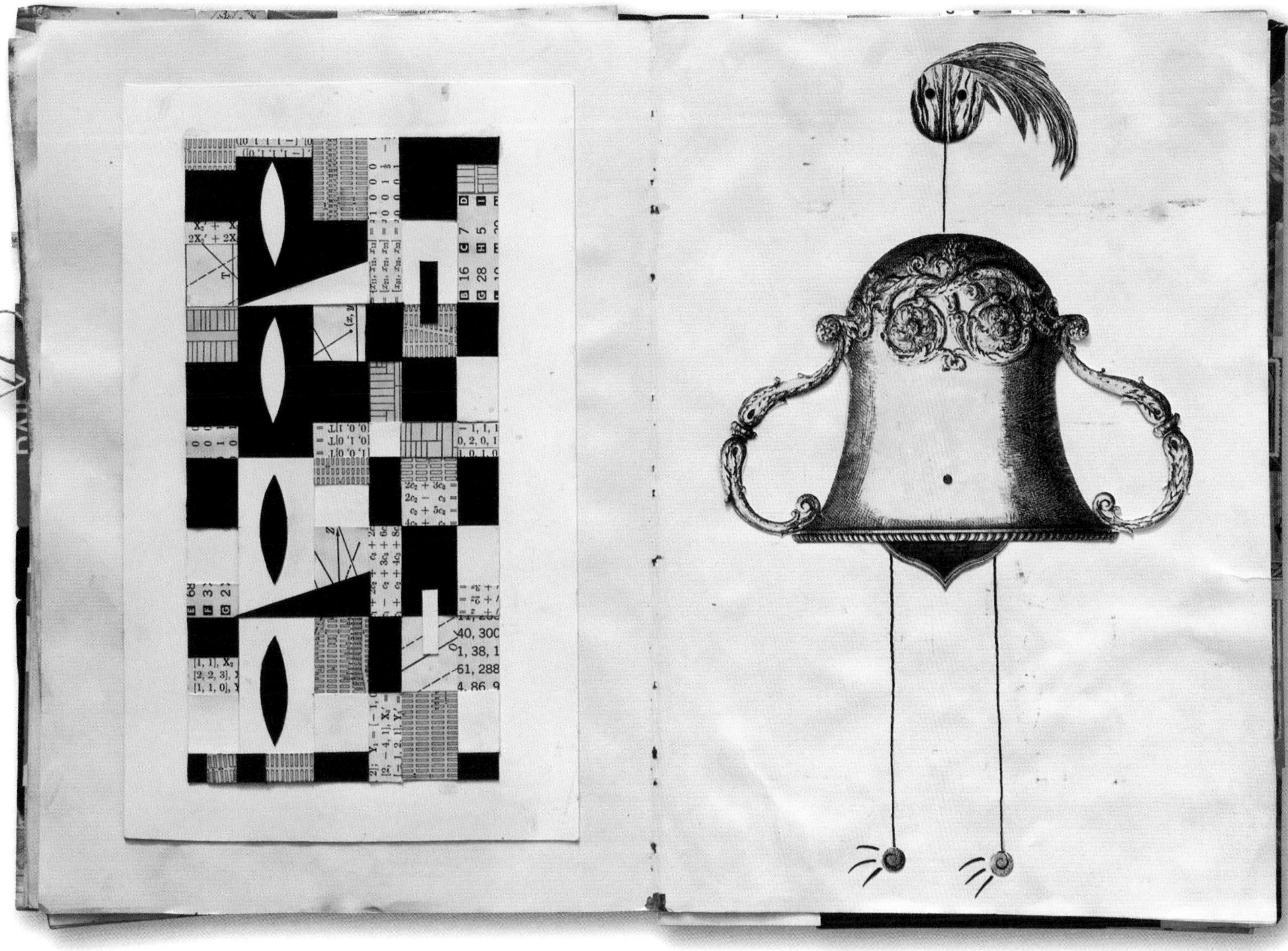

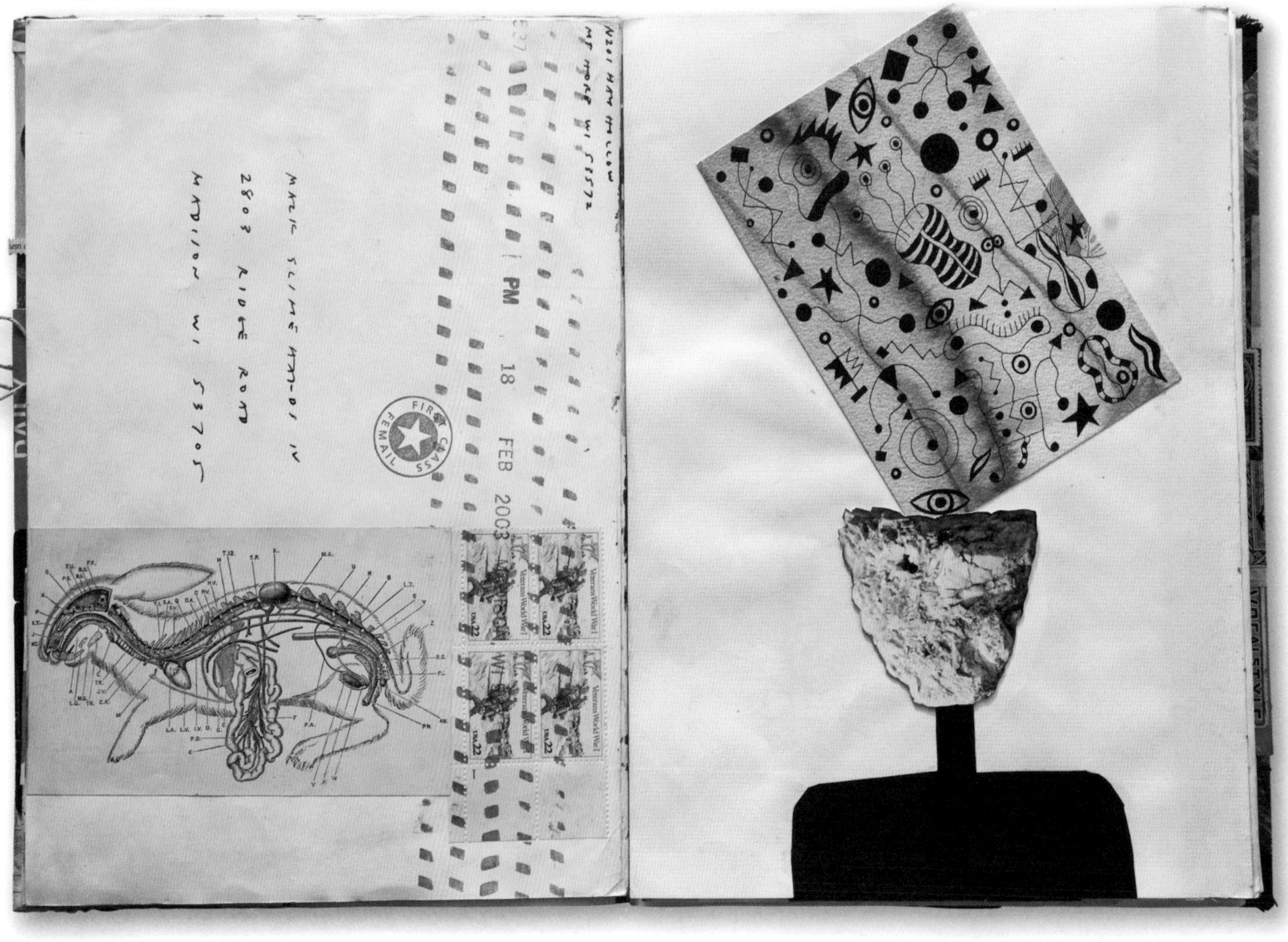
FIRST CLASS FEMAIL
PM
18
FEB
2003

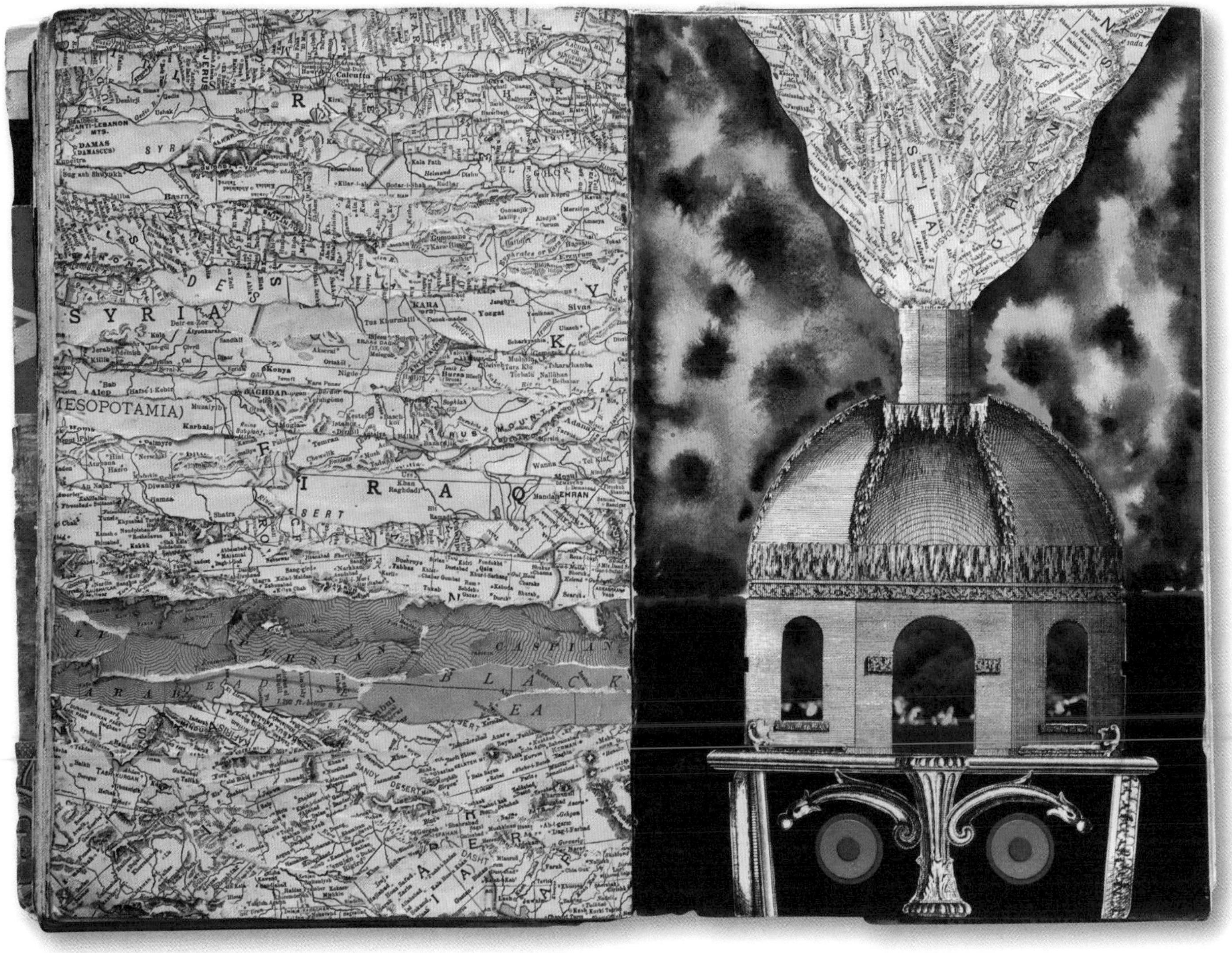
SYRIA
MESOPOTAMIA)

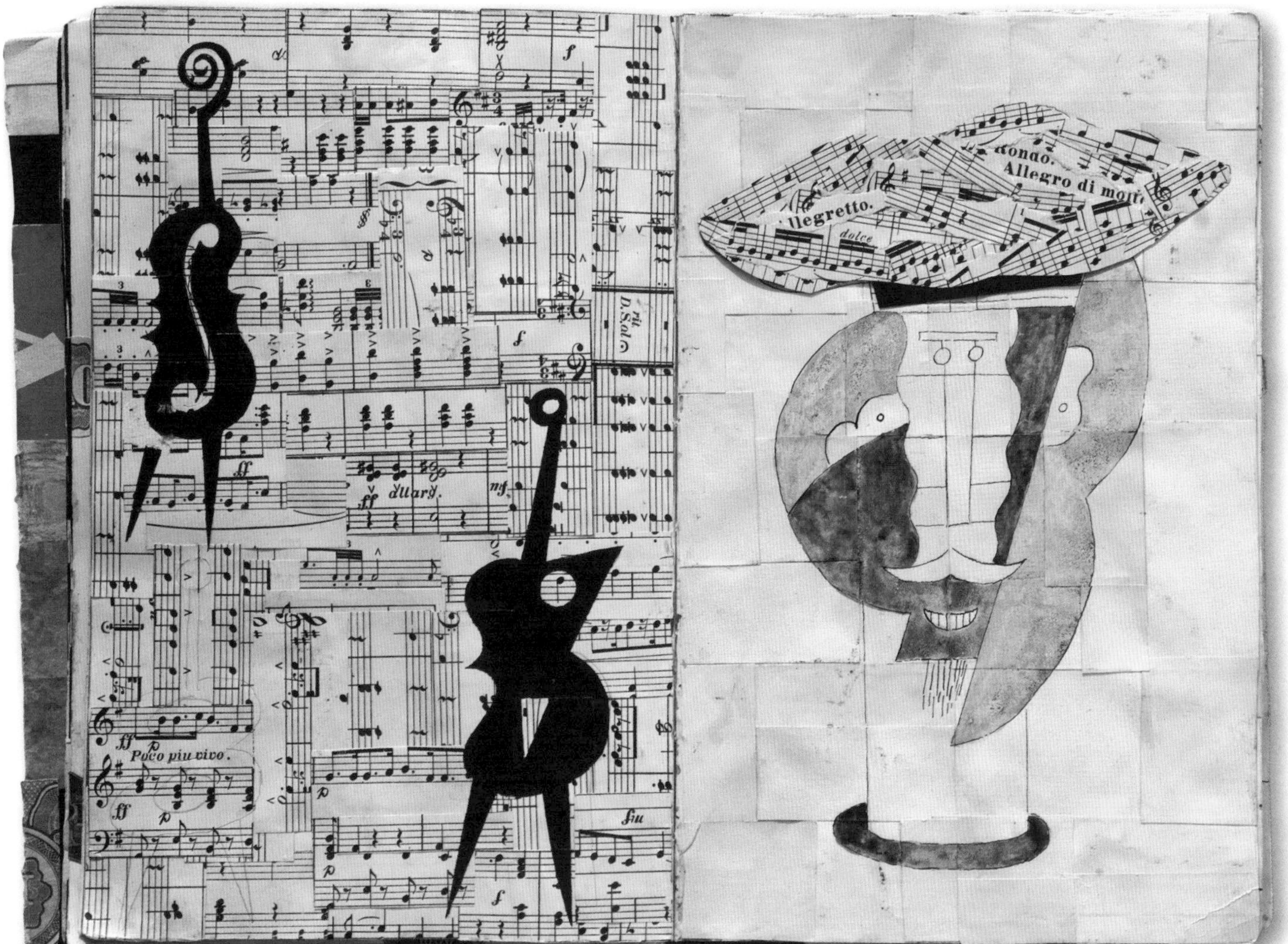
dolce
Poco piu vivo.

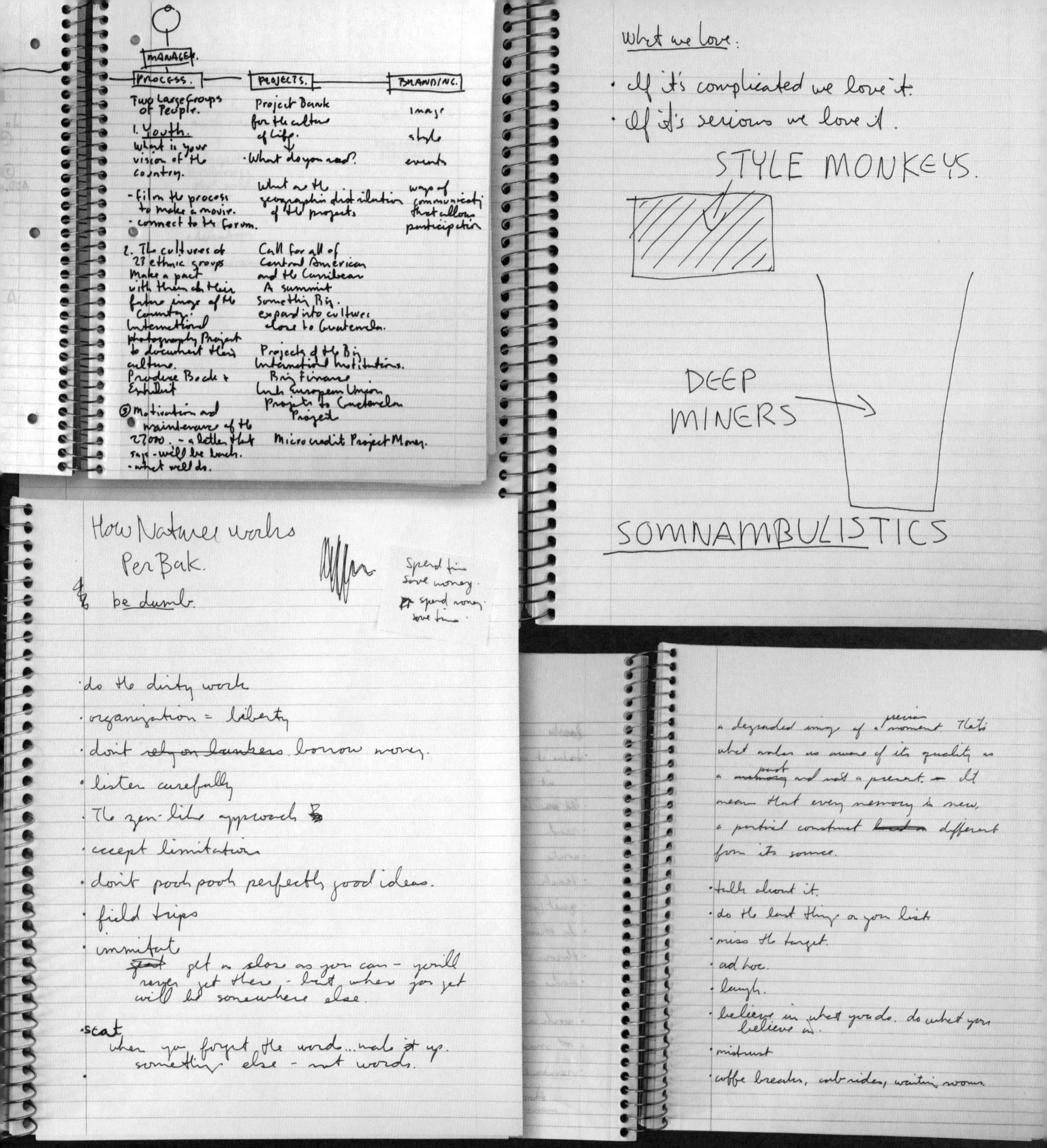

BRUCE MAU

Canadian designer Bruce Mau's sketchbooks are as economical and spare as his explanation for using them. He has kept a sketchbook "forever," he states: "They are as memory, since mine is failing."

The books are used for what he calls "first gestures," and he

What is the single most unusual aspect of these gestures and doodle images? The fact that "some of them are funny." And, "No," there is no theme to them.

Since he has been keeping them forever, he doesn't know how many

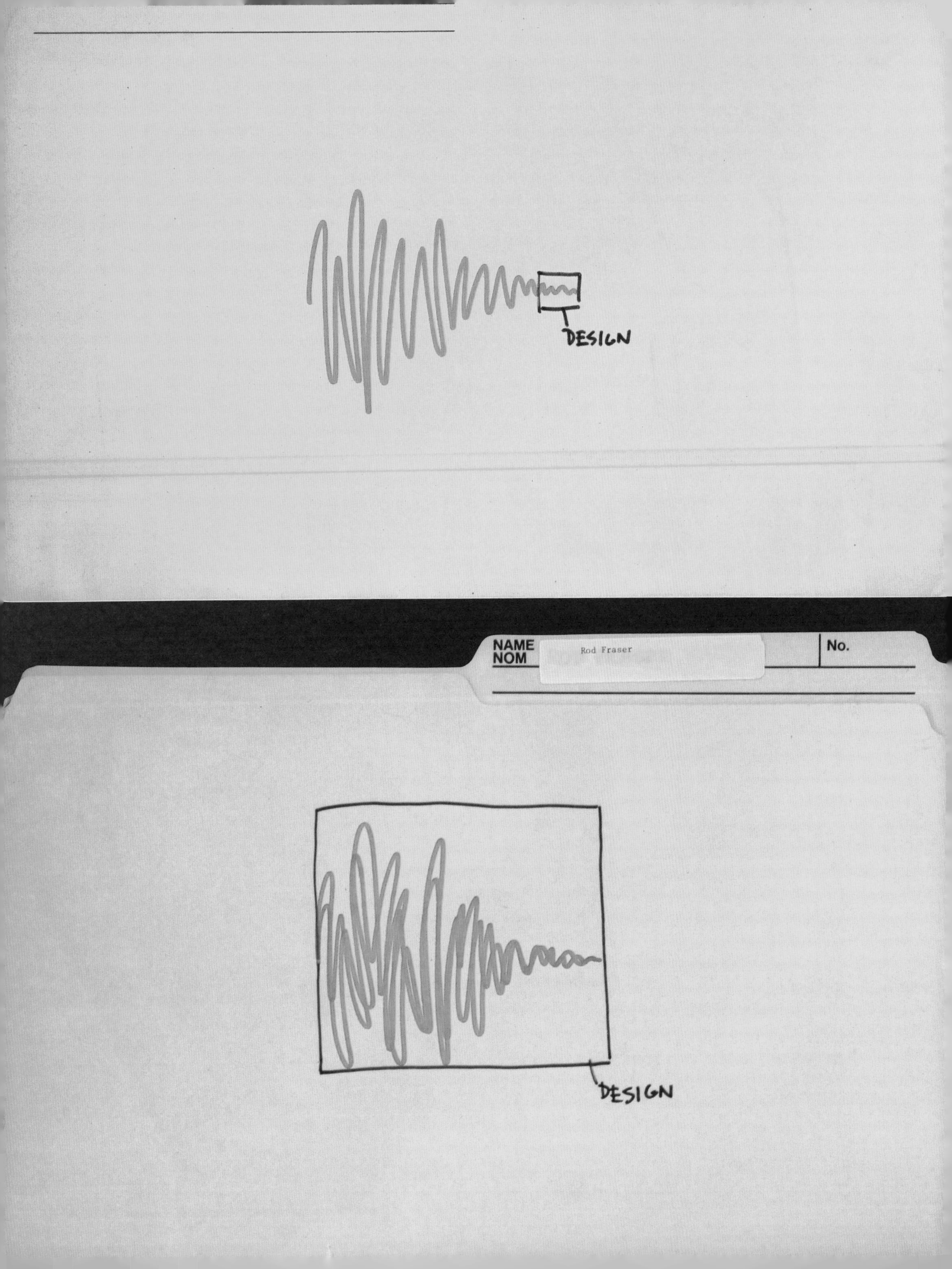
DESIGN
NAME
NOM
Rod Fraser
No.
DESIGN

CHAZ MAVIYANE-DAVIES

Zimbabwe-born, Boston-based political poster designer Chaz Maviyane-Davies has kept sketchbooks of sorts for the past thirty years. "In most cases I draw on the first scrap of paper in front of me and keep these loose sheets in various folders."

The purpose of these sketches is idea development: they "serve as early process scribbles to identify potential concepts to explore," he says. "They are predominantly commission/project-based. Though extremely rough, they allow me to contemplate the project research as a whole and envisage through matrixes, mapping, and linking thoughts, possibilities that I couldn't extrapolate in my mind. Drawing also allows me to unearth my visceral responses to the content."

The sketches in his folders are mainly thumbnails in pencil with rare elements of color. "My finished work still maintains the conceptual germ of the early sketch but would have evolved through many permutations to a more refined expression." He states that he is "looking for the human connection in many of my resolutions. As most of my work is social in nature, linking our humanity to our actions through the body is an important part of the creative personality I strive for in my communication."

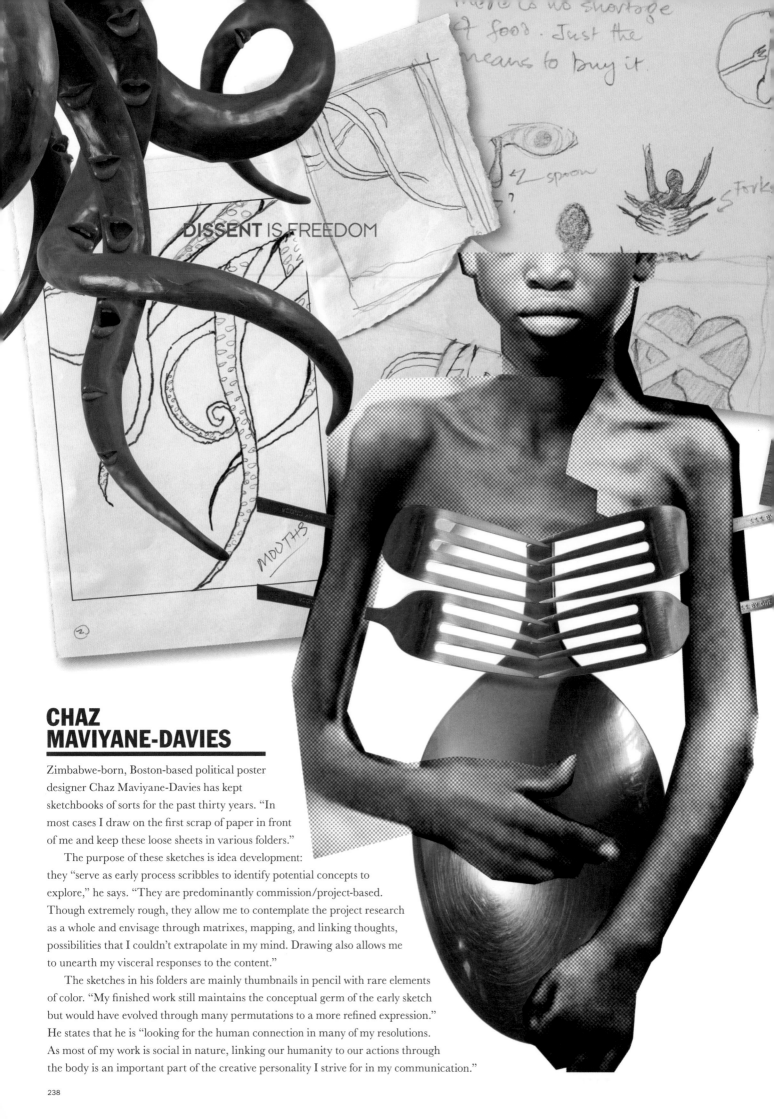

OWLEDGE WILL SET YOU FREE
THE BRITISH COUNCIL LIBRARIES
23 Jason Moyo Avenue, Harare
Tel: 790627 Fax: 737877
75 George Silundika Street, Bulawayo
Tel: 74815 Fax: 75816

The War Resisters League's
44th Annual Peace Award Dinner
honoring the work of Dennis Brutus,
Women of Zimbabwe Arise (WOZA)
and Gays and Lesbians of Zimbabwe (GALZ)
Friday, September 18, 2009, 6:30 pm
Judson Memorial Church
239 Thompson Street
New York City
STUBBORN HOPE:
Celebrating the Ongoing Struggles for
Justice and Peace in Southern Africa
For more info go to warresisters.org or call 212.228.0450

cut out Africa
Peace Awards

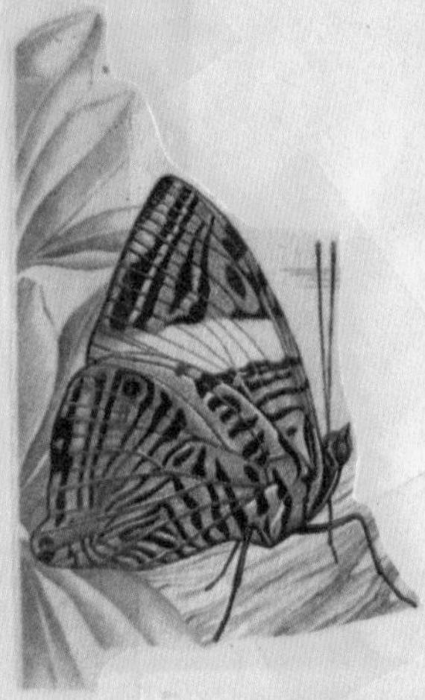

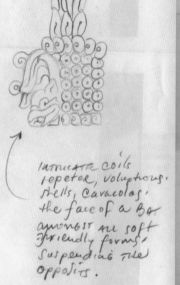

intricate coils
repeted, voluptous.
shells, caracolas.
the face of a BA
amongst all soft
friendly forms.
suspending the
opposits.

MAYA — PEOPLE OF THE CORN.

'MAYAN GLYPHS BEHAVE
'JUNGULAR' — INTRICATE,
VOLUPTUOUS, PREGNANT
COMPACT, ORGANIC
REPETITIVE YET IN
SEPARATE CLUSTERS
FLOW,

THE MAYA WORLD WAS
MADE UP OF THREE
LAYERED DOMAINS:
THE STARRY ARCH OF HEAVEN,
THE STONY MIDDLE WORLD
OF EARTH MADE TO FLOWER
AND BARE FRUIT BY THE
BLOOD OF KINGS, AND THE
DARK WATERS OF THE
UNDERWORLD BELOW.
ALL DIMENSIONS OF EXISTENCE
WERE INTERRELATED.

(WHITE)
N

(BLACK) W — BLUE GREEN — E (RED)

EAST SHOULD BE AT TOP OF MAPS.

S
(YELLOW)

THIS feels like corn —
ALL THIS TABLET
Feels like THE
VOLUPTUOUS, JUICY
corn.

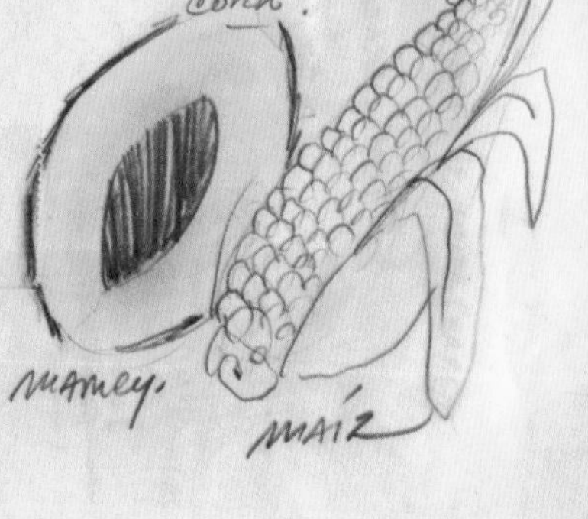

mamey.

MAÍZ

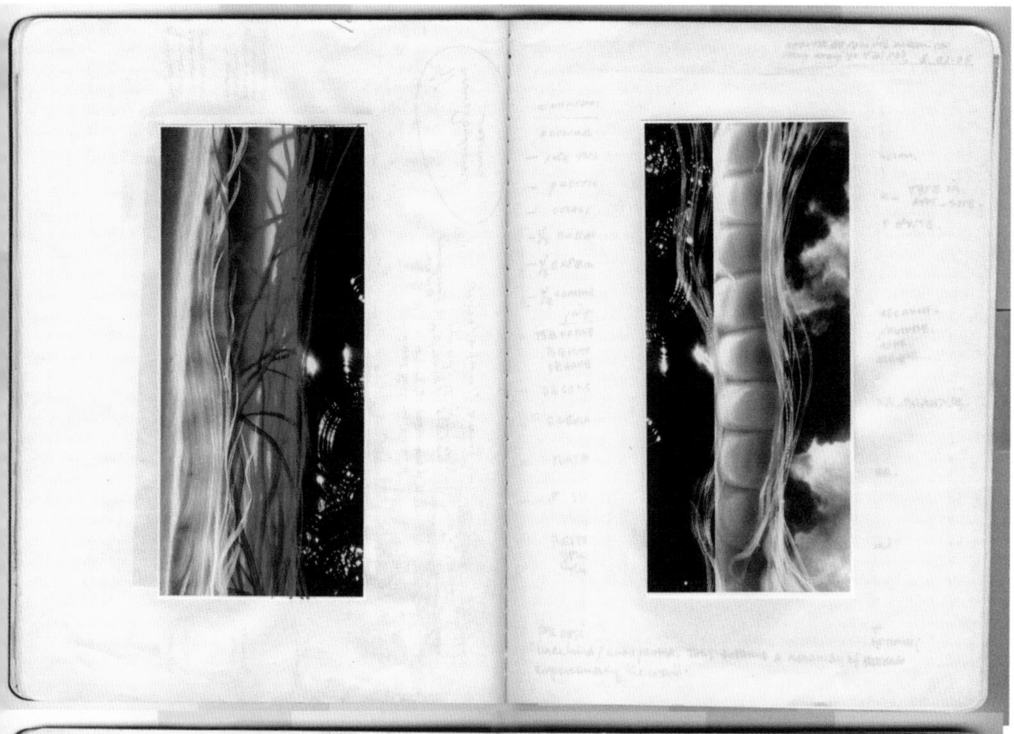

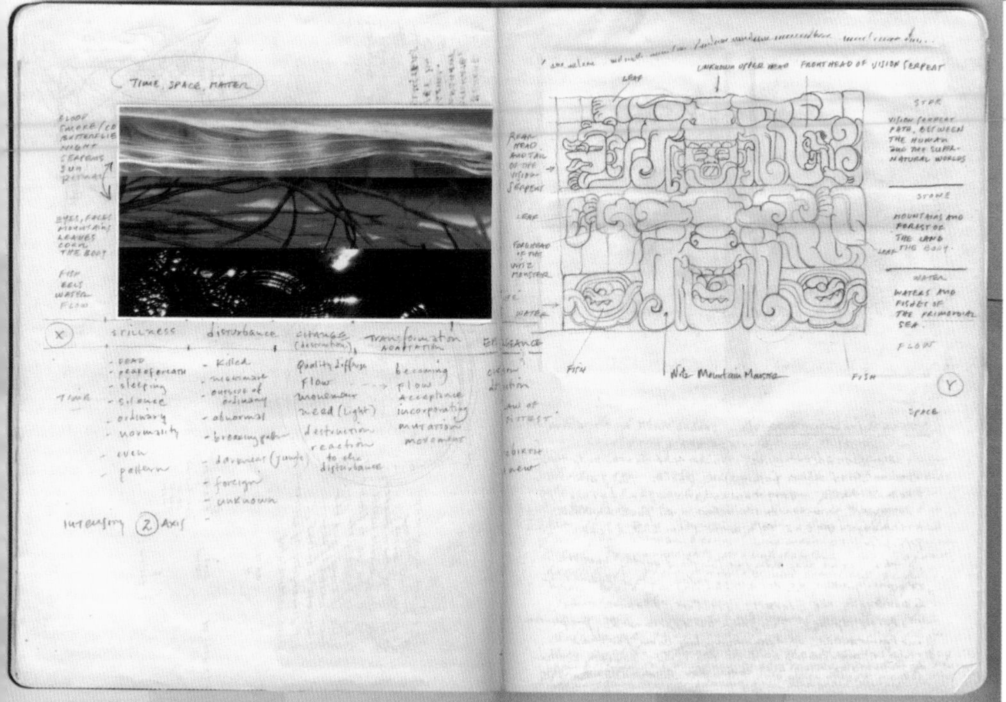

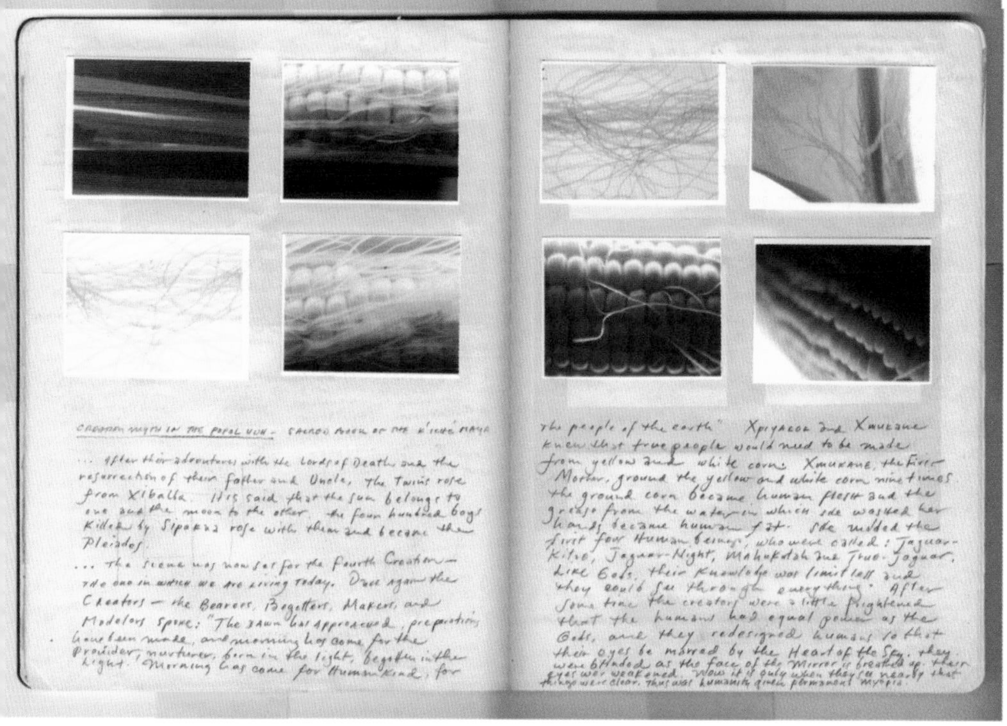

REBECA MÉNDEZ

Los Angeles designer and educator Rebeca Méndez keeps sketchbooks as records of projects, both for art and commerce. Those shown here are from June/July 2005 and refer to a project for Imaginary Forces, for which she was hired by Peter Frankfurt as an 'Ancient Maya culture specialist' and as creative director for the title sequence of *Apocalypto*, a film by Mel Gibson.

"I arrived at the creative direction for the title sequence by immersing myself in Maya history and specifically their cosmology as described in the Popol-Vuh, the 'council book' of the ancient Maya," Méndez explains. "Maya scholar Linda Schele in her book *The Blood of Kings* describes the ancient Maya world as 'made up of three layered domains: The starry arch of heaven, the stony middle world of earth made to flower and bear fruit by the blood of kings, and the dark water of the underworld below.' The design of the title sequence is based on these three layers. After analyzing the Mayan glyphs and carvings, it became apparent that the forms, geometry, and rhythm of the glyphs emerge from the formal qualities of maize – in the Popol-Vuh, it is described that the Maya people sprout from the maize plant and thus are known as 'The People of the Corn.'"

SUPERNATURAL WORLD.
1/3
REAL
MOUNTO
LAND.
2/3
YAXCHILAN. BIRDJAGUAR
3/3
XIBALBA/RIVERS.
CENOTES/RIVERS
CREATION/DESTRUCTION.
DATES
w/ HEADS.

BUTTERFLIES AT THE USUMACINTA RIVER.

→ YAX
JADE
GREEN
OF THE
JUNGLE.

← PIEDRAS
NEGRAS
MASK

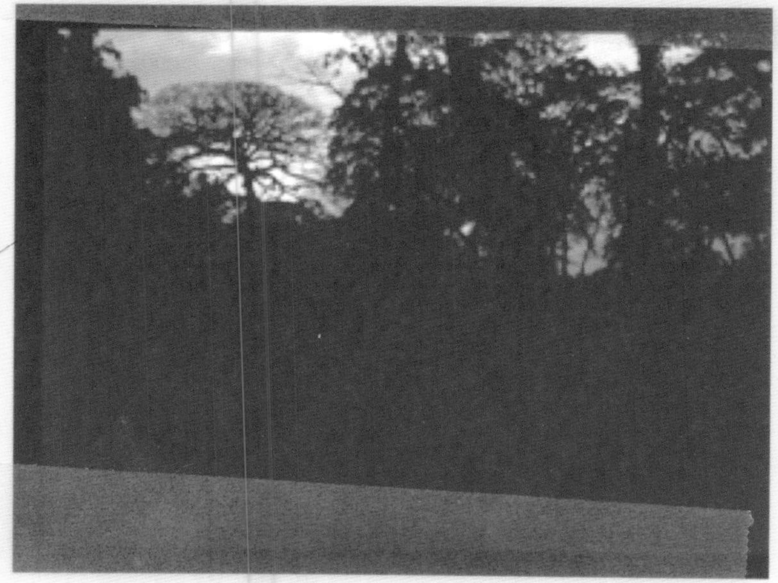

CEIBA

SACRED
TREE
OF THE
MAYA.

OROPENDOLA

RICK MEYEROWITZ

New York caricaturist and comic illustrator Rick Meyerowitz has had a sketchbook since he was a kid. The ersatz book was made of shirt cardboards "that my father nailed to a board for me," he happily recalls. "I would get splinters when I drew."

Since then he has used many different kinds. "They were different sizes, and I used them willy-nilly, several at a time. I like things orderly, so in 2000 I decided that from then on I'd use 4 × 6 in. [10 × 15 cm] books and that I'd finish one before I started another." Meyerowitz coins a unique term: "These books are idea kitchens for me. They're as likely to be filled with notes as drawings – about ideas, or literature, or even shopping lists." He always carries a 4 × 6 in. book, noting that "I can jam it into any pocket in anything I'm wearing. I can even carry it in my teeth if I'm swimming."

"Messiness is endemic to sketchbooks," Meyerowitz admits. "They can be incoherent and filled with mistakes, dumb ideas, bad drawings, half-thoughts, or useless information. The book is exactly the place to get everything wrong and not be embarrassed by it. It's for whatever comes to mind, whether idiotic or profound."

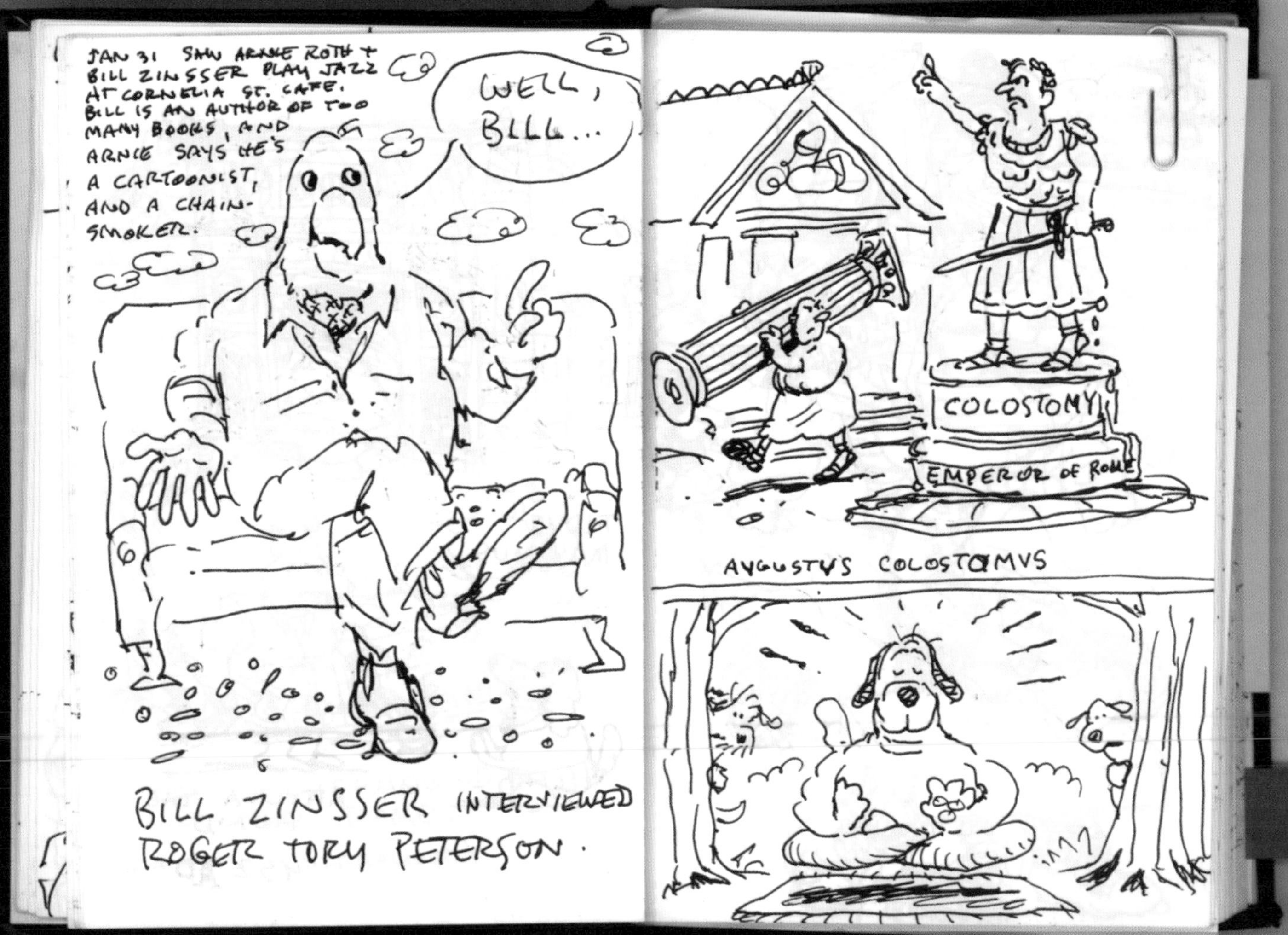
JAN 31 SAW ARNIE ROTH + BILL ZINSSER PLAY JAZZ AT CORNELIA ST. CAFE. BILL IS AN AUTHOR OF TOO MANY BOOKS, AND ARNIE SAYS HE'S A CARTOONIST, AND A CHAIN-SMOKER.
WELL, BILL...
BILL ZINSSER INTERVIEWED ROGER TORY PETERSON.
COLOSTOMY
EMPEROR OF ROME
AUGUSTUS COLOSTOMUS

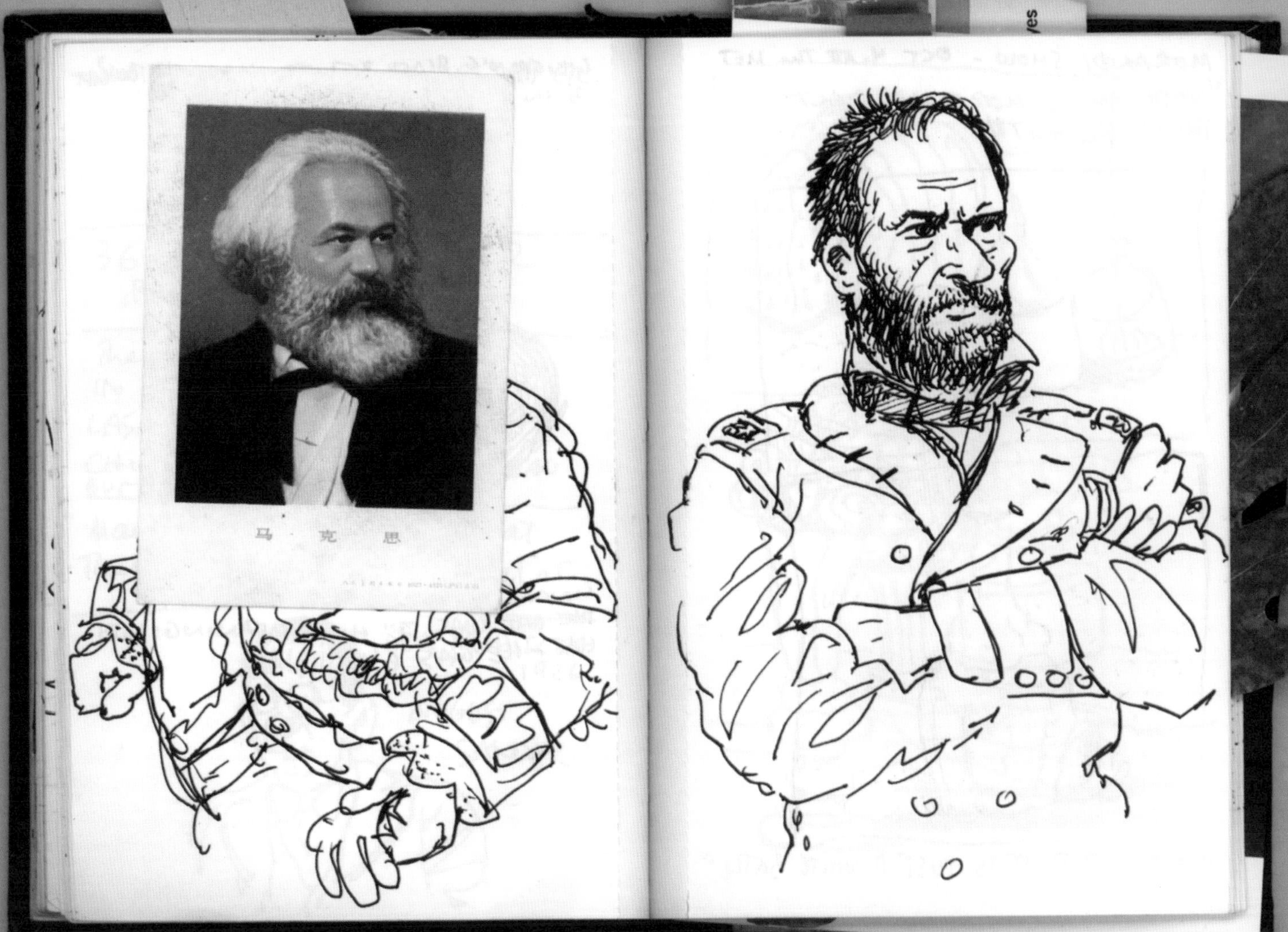
马克思

GIOVANNI FRANCESCO GRIMALDI

CHAMOMILE
FECHA
DUAL UNI-WHEELCHAIR

75 CENTS
Americans ignorant on religion
■ Half of teens think Sodom and Gomorrah were married. New book cites dangers of religious illiteracy, 1D
■ Pop quiz, 1D
Paramount Home Entertainment

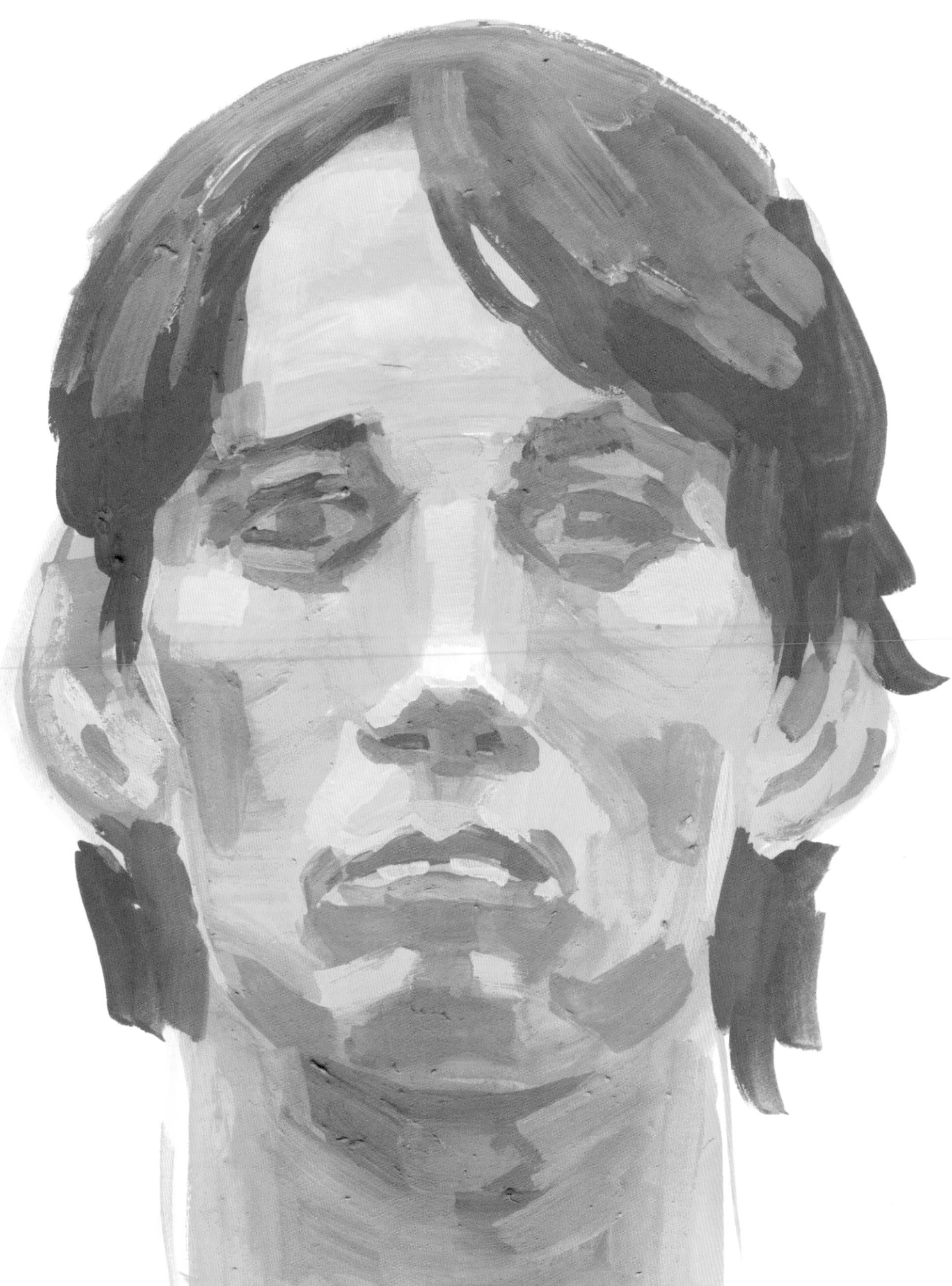

CHRISTOPH NIEMANN

Christoph Niemann, Berlin-based, internationally roving illustrator, has been using sketchbooks for the last twenty years, but never for real jobs. "The big danger with a sketchbook is that after doing a few nice drawings one becomes vain. You start drawing more carefully because you don't want to mess up the whole book with some half-baked doodles," he admits.

However, by way of explaining his process, he says, "Since scores of half-baked doodles are essential for coming up with ideas for me, I only do them on loose letter-size paper. My sketchbooks, about forty by now, are just very personal visual diaries. I almost exclusively draw in them when I travel."

The key separation for Niemann is that "when I work on a real job, all I care about is whether the reader gets (and likes) what I do. The sketchbooks are just for me. I find the process of drawing always difficult and exhausting, but I enjoy looking at old sketchbooks and finding a silly little watercolor that I made on some trip ten years ago."

The best is that "it feels like I am ten years old again: drawing just for the sake of drawing. No theme required."

JOHN CARLIN
NE FOR THE
DEAL
DATA GRID
3.14.05 TUESDAY
7PM
*PIG PARTY
S M L XL
ALL 3?
YEP
START SITE
B4 MOVIE
MOVIE RELEASED
JUNEISH/JULY
STILLS
100 SHIRTS
SEND SCOTT SEX HAUNT
HORNY
SCARED
UNCOMF
READ
RULES
MYSPACE
3★
WEBSITE
3 TIMES!
CHECK CAFEPRESS
NAW
3 · 18 · 06

NEIL NUMBERMAN

Neil Numberman, a nom de crayon for a New York-based cartoonist and illustrator who threatens rash reprisals if his real name is revealed, used to turn his lined paper notebooks into storyboards and what he calls "a character design hub." He would spend time doodling in these custom-made volumes: "Usually it is just something to keep me busy while I'm at lectures, on the train, or in any building that involves the government," he reports. "I sometimes like to amuse people in bars by drawing them. Note: Not everyone is amused. Even my most restrained sketches make fun in one way or another. Whether it's of person or a thing, I always capture some underlying goofiness." Still, the sketches are fairly precise. "I've had people say they are good enough to be finishes, and I'm slowly becoming convinced."

"I have maybe twenty-five organized books. But then I have seven or eight ratty cardboard boxes full of sketches on loose-leaf paper," he says. The sketches shown here are from Numberman's two years at the School of Visual Arts MFA Illustration program, from 2004–6.

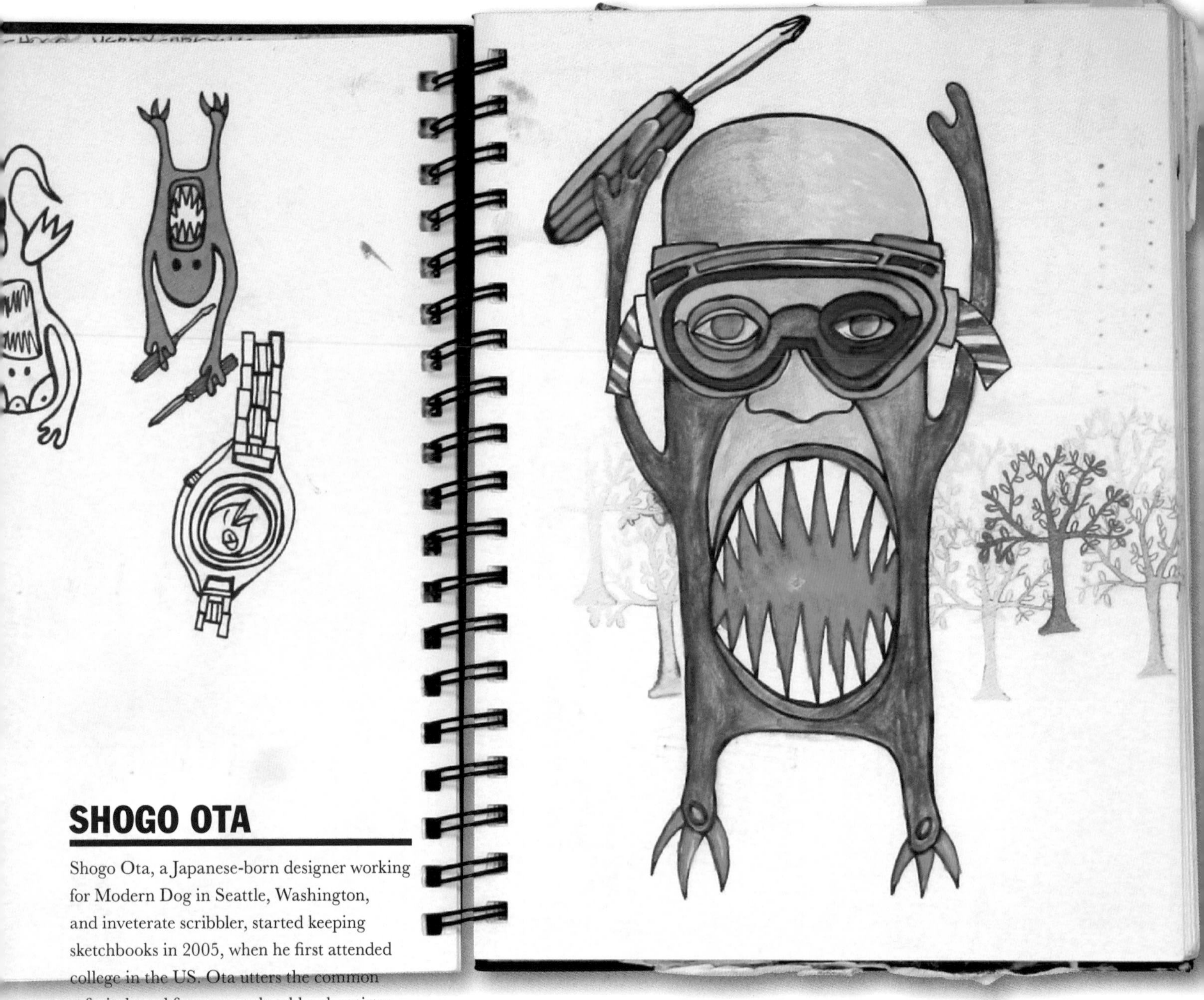

SHOGO OTA

Shogo Ota, a Japanese-born designer working for Modern Dog in Seattle, Washington, and inveterate scribbler, started keeping sketchbooks in 2005, when he first attended college in the US. Ota utters the common refrain heard from most sketchbook artists: "I keep them to keep track of ideas, and often those ideas are only half-baked." Whether quarter-, half-, or full-baked, they provide insight into the thought process of their maker, if only as jots or notes. But they can serve as the foundation for more fully realized work.

Ota is comfortable thinking in both English and Japanese and the books show his linguistic dexterity. "It's totally random," he explains. "In my sketchbooks you can see that I go back and forth. I also draw quite a bit with sumi-e. And sometimes not."

He has only four books (two small ones, two big ones) in his sketchbook oeuvre. And there are no recurring themes, although sometimes "you can tell what projects I'm working on at Modern Dog from what appears in the books." The book shown here is "relatively new," he reports. "My latest and most current one is from December 2008."

23
ROCKANDROLL
I'm Ready
Seattle's Color Printer™
LITHO CRAFT
866.789.7151

DESIGN VS ART
FRANKIE
MODERN DOG
DESIGN & ILLUSTRATION
USA
FAX 281 8293
MCM
TEL 282 8857
SEATTLE
太田翔伍
9/26/09
Bellingham Holly's House
Guaranteed 10 Years!
$1.98
RC-191
LUCKY STRIKE
"IT'S TOASTED"
Seattle's Color Printer™
LITHO CRAFT
866.789.7151

ABCDE
FGHIJ
KLNM
OPQR
STUV
3456789

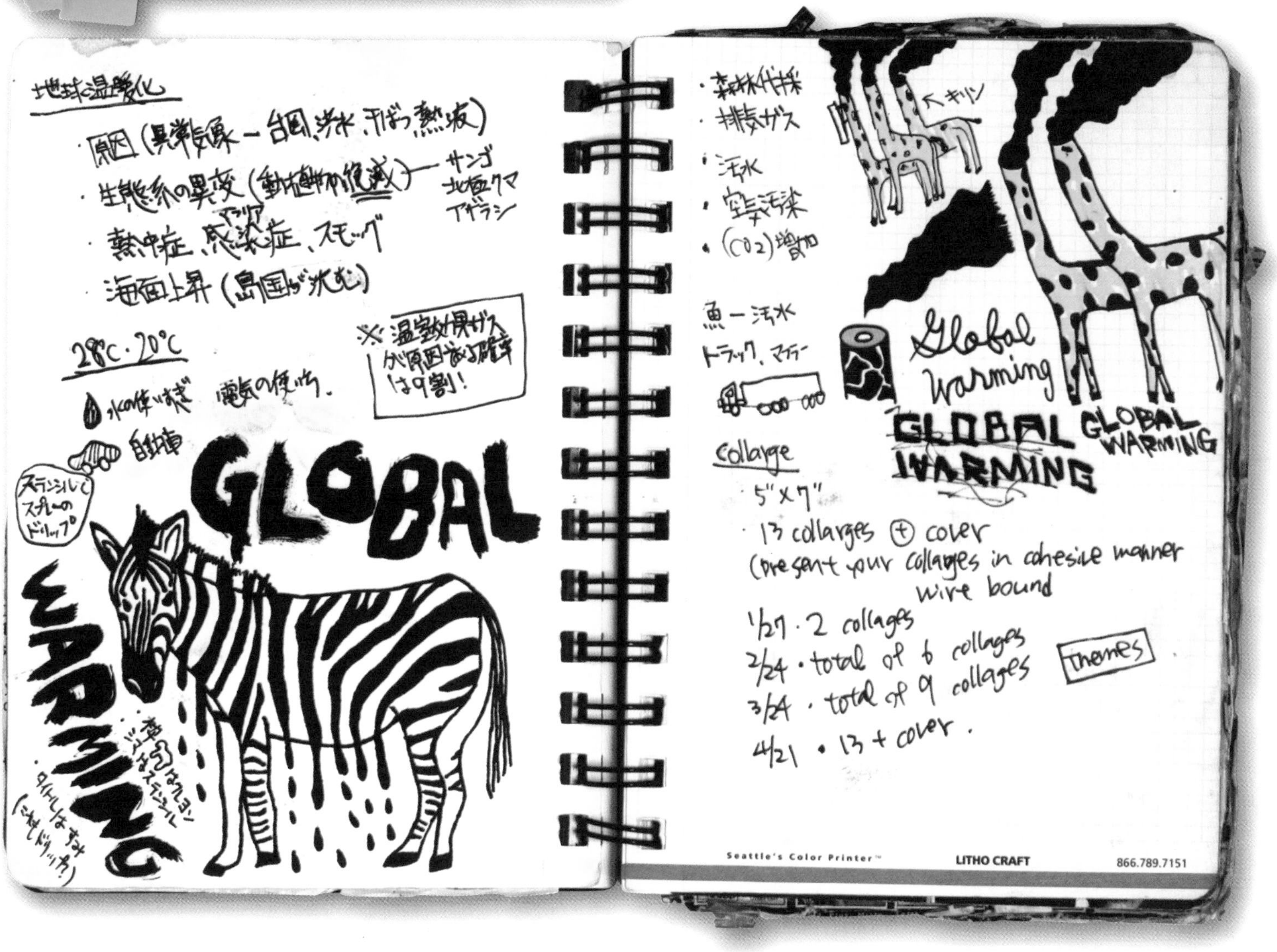
地球温暖化
原因（異常気象―台風、洪水、干ばつ、熱波）
生態系の異変（動植物の絶滅）―サンゴ 北極グマ アザラシ
熱中症、感染症、スモッグ
海面上昇（島国が沈む）
28°C・20°C
水の使いすぎ 電気の使い方。
自動車
ステンシルしてスプレーのドリップ
GLOBAL
WARMING
森林伐採
排気ガス
汚水
空気汚染
(CO2)増加
魚―汚水
トラック、マフラー
←キリン
Global Warming
GLOBAL WARMING
GLOBAL WARMING
collage
5"×7"
13 collages + color
(present your collages in cohesive manner
wire bound
1/27・2 collages
2/24・total of 6 collages
3/24・total of 9 collages
4/21・13 + color.
themes
Seattle's Color Printer™
LITHO CRAFT
866.789.7151

HEY! WHO PINCHED MY ASS?!!
the "LAST of the Red Hot WHATE CRIMES"
With
SCRIMSHAW JONES
YO BODIE
and
CRANK-ASS JOHNSON

EVERETT PECK

Cartoonist and illustrator Everett Peck, creator of the zany animated TV series *Duckman*, has maintained sketchbooks for thirty-five years. Looking at his effervescently wacky drawings, it makes sense – they are as sketchy as they are finished. Peck uses his book to "sometimes sketch things around me," he says, "but generally, for me, a sketchbook is a place to put down ideas." And he is consistent: there is not much difference between these images and his finished work. In fact, "sometimes I use the sketchbook image as finished art," he explains.

For Peck, in these sketchbooks (which cover the years 2002–9), each page is a fairly complete expression of a concept, "and if there is an underlying theme it is humor." Peck's every line is pregnant with wit. Add to that his hilarious characterizations and, well, humor is an understatement.

Although he is not certain exactly how many sketchbooks he has, Peck declares: "I know they take up a lot of shelf space in my studio and make a good TV stand."

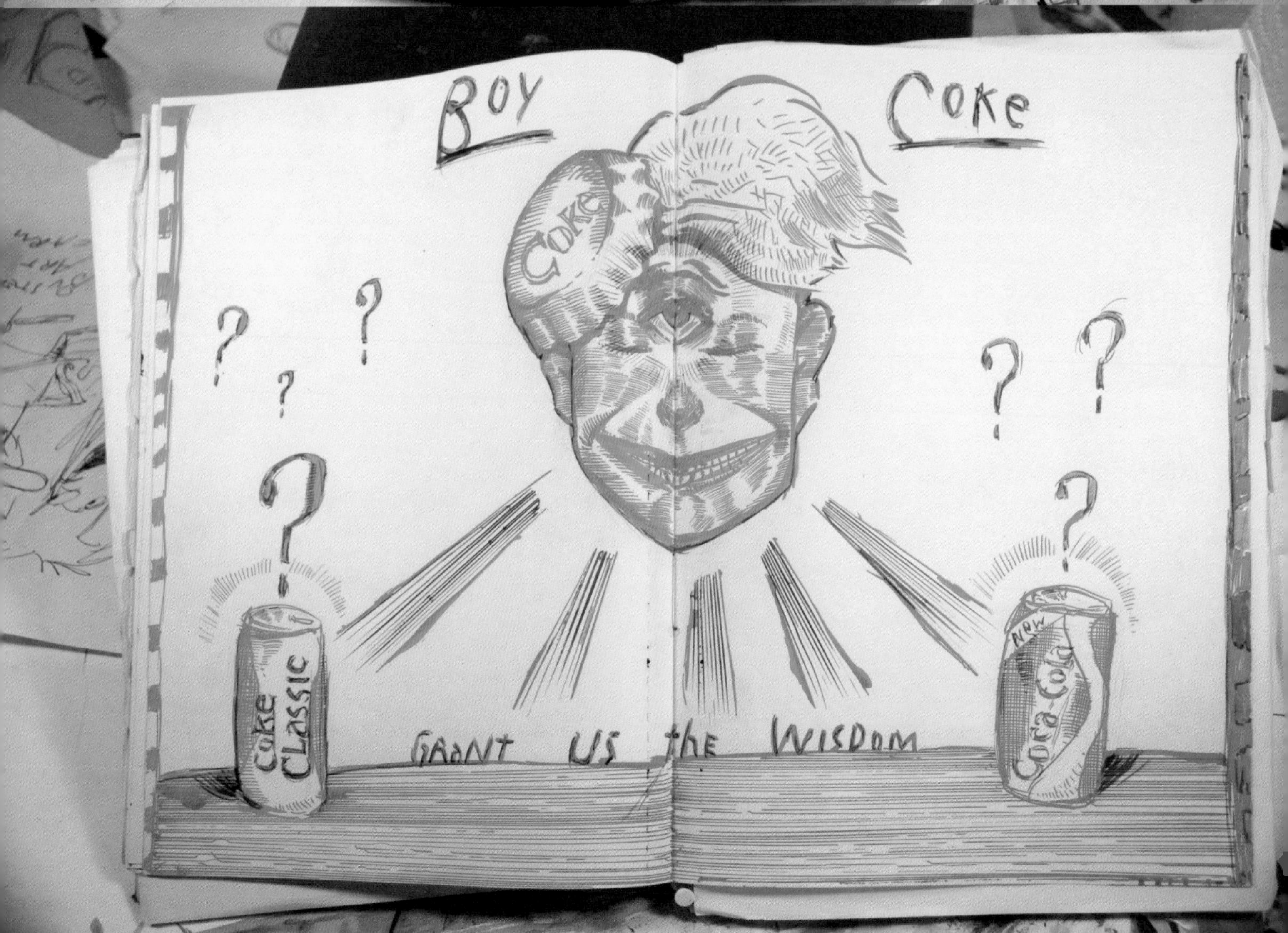
BOY
COKE
COKE
GRANT US THE WISDOM
Coke Classic
NEW
Coca-Cola

Hey KIDS!
Lets all Get together AND BRING BACK THAT GOOD OL'......
CRO-MAGNON
SENSE OF HUMOR!
THUD

Cape Baron Goose
Beautifully coloured head on King Vulture no feathers on head so that the sun can dry-up and kill parasites
SADDLE BROWN
SLATE BLUE
orange
Bright orange
Grey

DANIEL PELAVIN

New York illustrator, letterer, and type designer Daniel Pelavin's first "official" sketchbook was made in 1961 as a collection of individual loose-leaf pages bound into a folder. He still has it. But now he has graduated to bound books in which he spends considerable time generating and recording ideas; impromptu sketching from life. "They are a working tool," he firmly notes, "rather than a 'work of art' or presentation piece." He was even reluctant to let these be seen. "There are many 'bad' sketches, an inevitable part of the process of finally arriving at workable solutions," he adds.

The books are not, nor were they ever meant to be, thematic, but contain "lots of ambiguous mechanical, architectural constructions that range from fictitious 'Dr Frankenstein laboratory equipment' to electric fans, typewriters, power stations, jukeboxes, and robot faces." And though he will not admit it, they are actually quite beautiful in their roughness.

Pelavin has around forty books that have been used primarily for work, and ten or so others that contain imaginary constructions, figure studies, sketches from travel, and the occasional job sketches done during a vacation away from the studio.

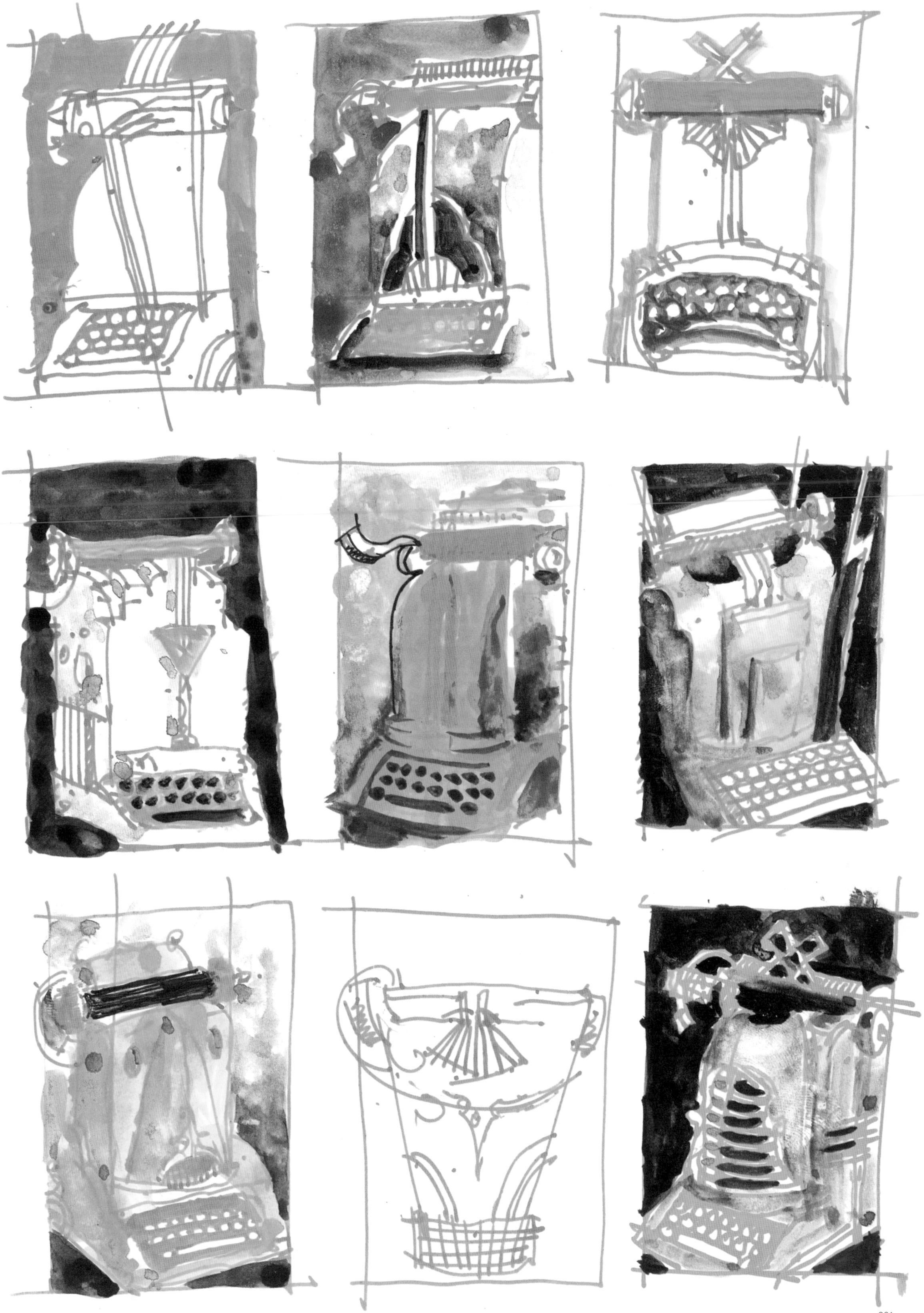

CARD GAMES

CARD GAMES

CARD GAMES

CARD GAMES

CARD GAMES

CARD GAMES

CARD GAMES

CARD GAMES

CARD GAMES
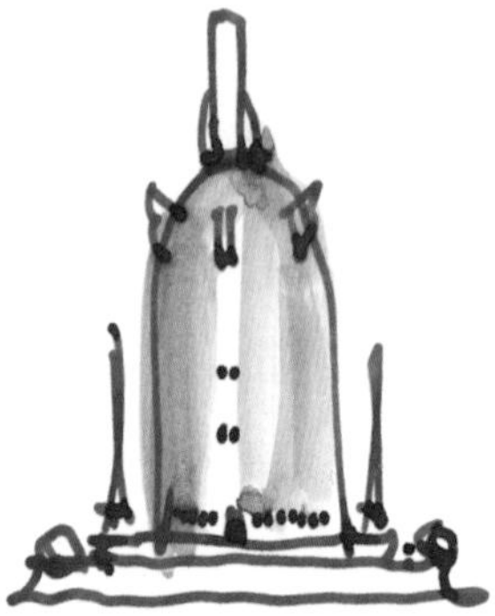

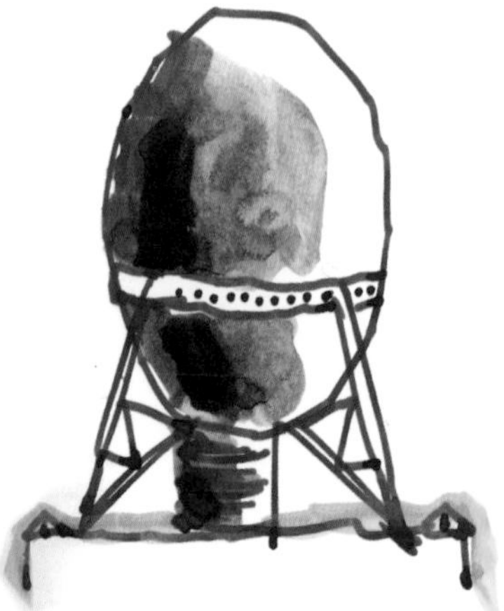

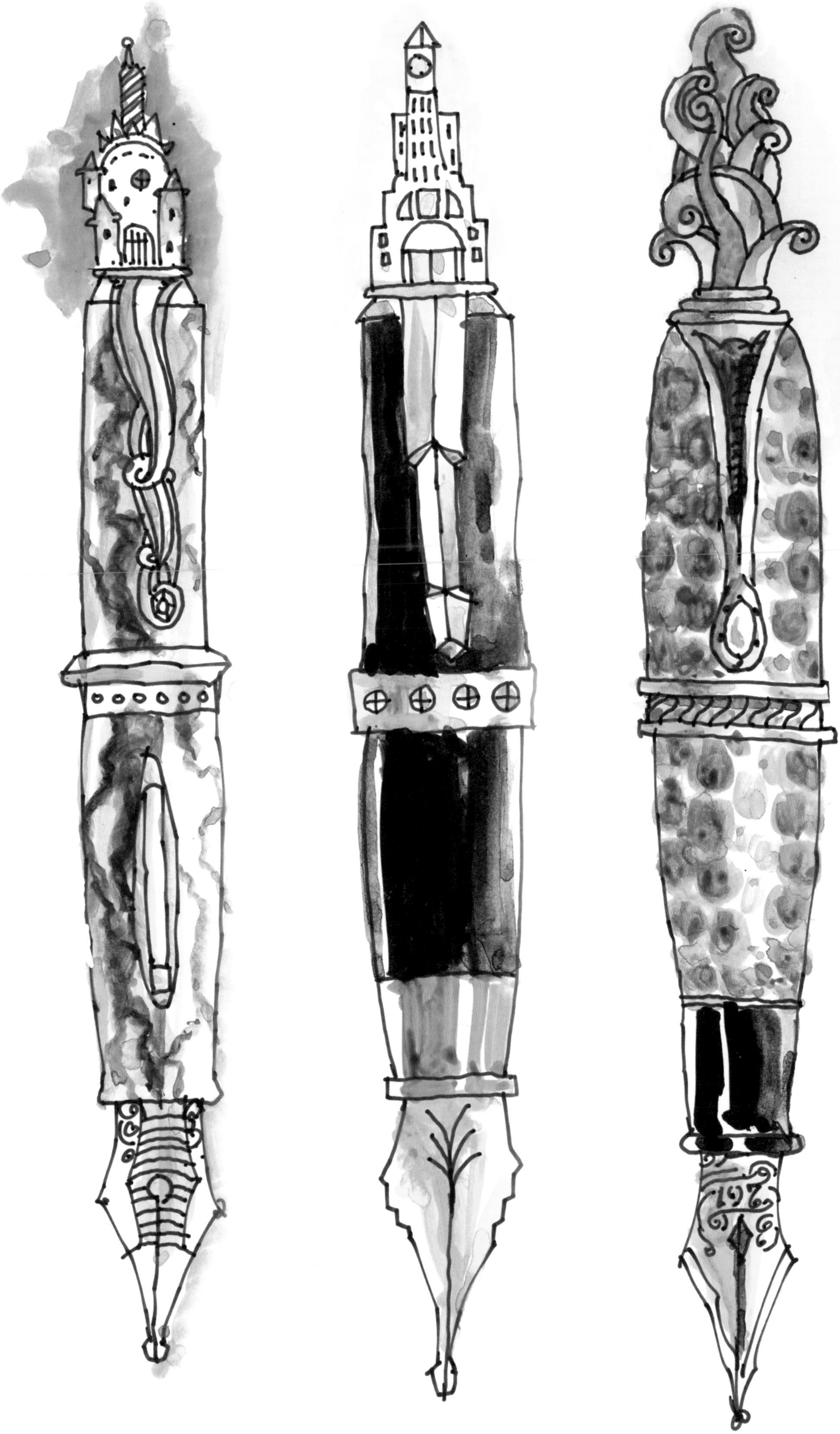

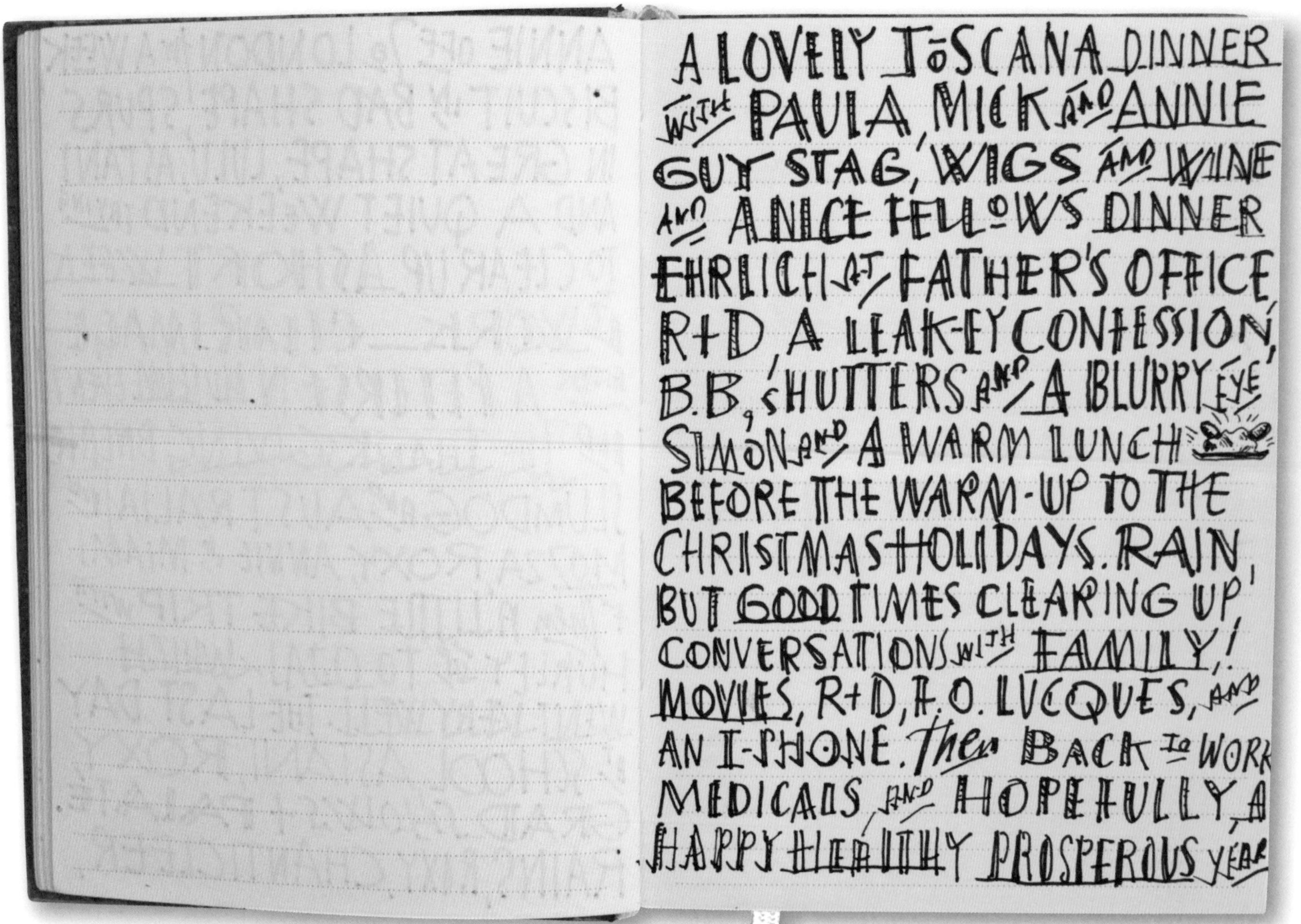
A LOVELY TOSCANA DINNER
WITH PAULA, MICK AND ANNIE
GUY STAG, WIGS AND WINE
AND A NICE FELLOWS DINNER
EHRLICH AT FATHER'S OFFICE
R+D A LEAK-EY CONFESSION,
B.B, SHUTTERS AND A BLURRY EYE
SIMON AND A WARM LUNCH
BEFORE THE WARM-UP TO THE
CHRISTMAS HOLIDAYS. RAIN,
BUT GOOD TIMES CLEARING UP,
CONVERSATIONS WITH FAMILY!
MOVIES, R+D, F.O. LUCQUES, AND
AN I-PHONE. Then BACK TO WORK
MEDICALS AND HOPEFULLY, A
HAPPY HEALTHY PROSPEROUS YEAR

SLOWLY BACK TO WORK
DOCTORS, JURY DUTY,
ASTANI AND A MOZZA PARTY,
FOLLOWED BY A CATARACT
OPERATION AND ALL OF THE
FOLLOW UP. The BRILLIANT
MAN ON WIRE + BACK ON
the BIKE WITH ROBIN. SPURS
STRUGGLING TO SURVIVE
MLK AND THE INAUGURATION
SHOWERS AND NO SHOWERS.
SPURS SCRAPING IN TO WEMBLEY
A BAD FEELING ABOUT QUIK
BAD NEWS FROM APTED, BUT
GOOD ASTANI PROGRESS.
THE DRIVEWAY AND A BAD COLD

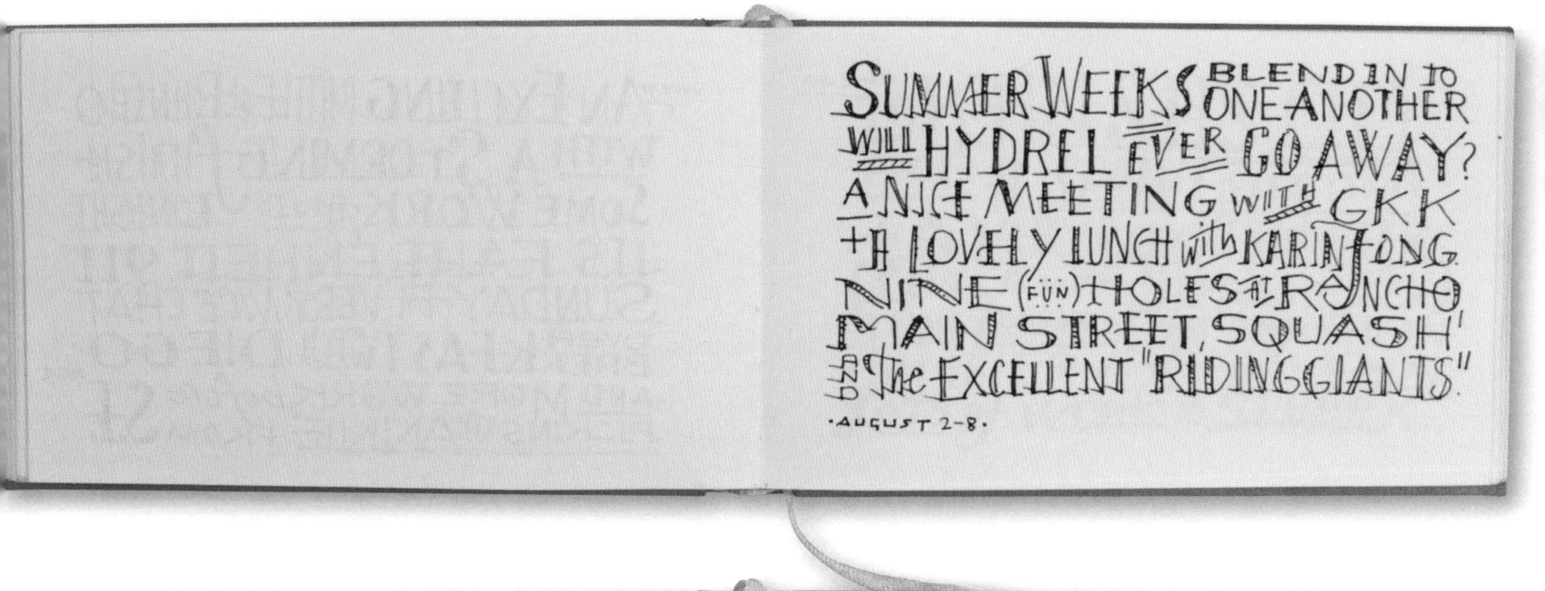
SUMMER WEEKS BLEND IN TO ONE ANOTHER
WILL HYDREL EVER GO AWAY?
A NICE MEETING WITH GKK
+ A LOVELY LUNCH WITH KARIN FONG
NINE (FUN) HOLES AT RANCHO
MAIN STREET, SQUASH
AND THE EXCELLENT "RIDING GIANTS"
AUGUST 2-8

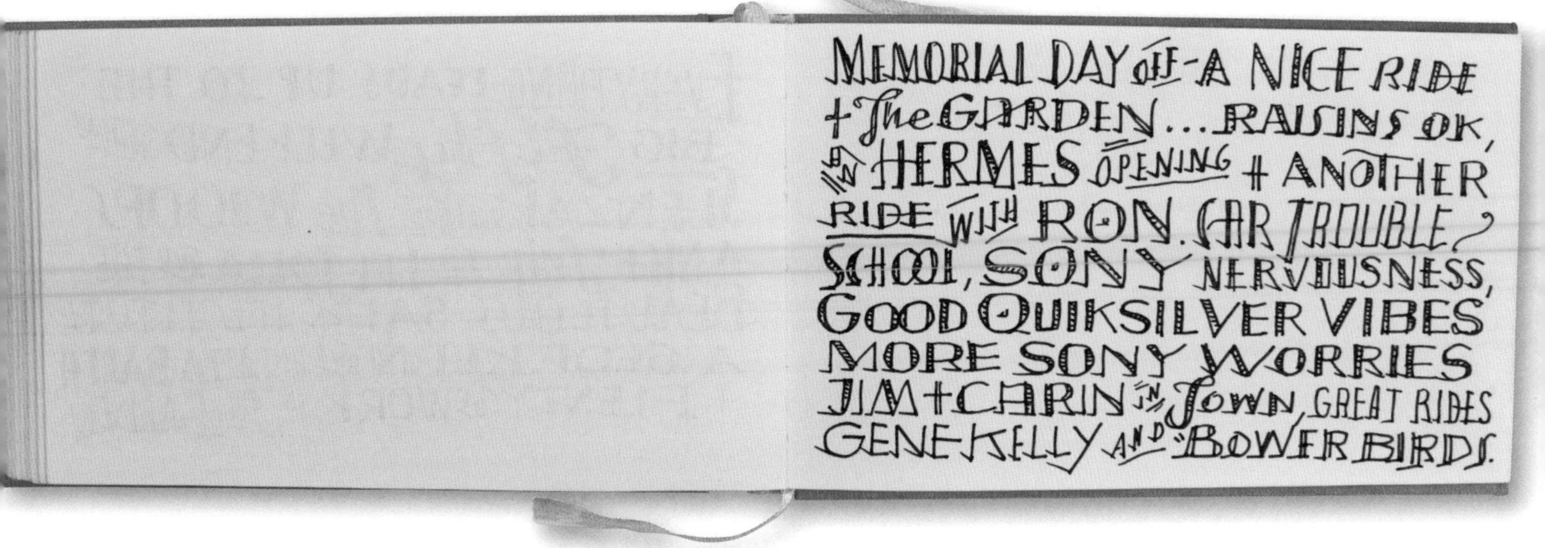
MEMORIAL DAY OFF - A NICE RIDE
+ THE GARDEN ... RAISINS OK,
AND HERMES OPENING + ANOTHER
RIDE WITH RON. CAR TROUBLE?
SCHOOL, SONY NERVOUSNESS,
GOOD QUIKSILVER VIBES
MORE SONY WORRIES
JIM + CARIN IN TOWN, GREAT RIDES
GENE KELLY AND BOWER BIRDS.

JANUARY 23RD 04
HOWARD HODGKIN
IN LITTLE SHOP
OF WHOLE FOODS

CLIVE PIERCY

Clive Piercy, English-born proprietor of the Santa Monica-based Air Conditioned design firm, has been keeping sketchbooks, as he says, "on and off for donkey's years." Of course, it is not clear how long donkeys survive in captivity, but Piercy has been actively practicing design for over twenty-five years. The sketchbooks are extremely detailed and beautifully rendered textual exercises, so we might assume he has been doing them for a long time. He considers them "a visual diary," and believes them to be "quite good," although he asked that this last statement be stricken from the record. Wit and humor are an essential component of Piercy's work, and he builds his graphic vocabulary on play and surprise. But he also says that he is "trying to make [the sketchbooks] a little poetic in style and language."

Although there is no theme, Piercy likes "wordplay, and these pages afford me the chance to stretch my associative wordsmithing limbs." These excerpts are taken from five books produced during 2004–9. And he is still going strong.

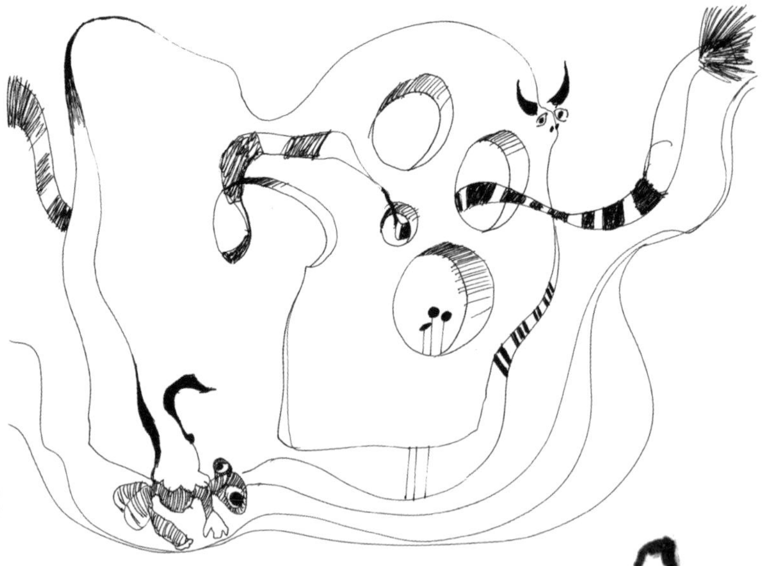

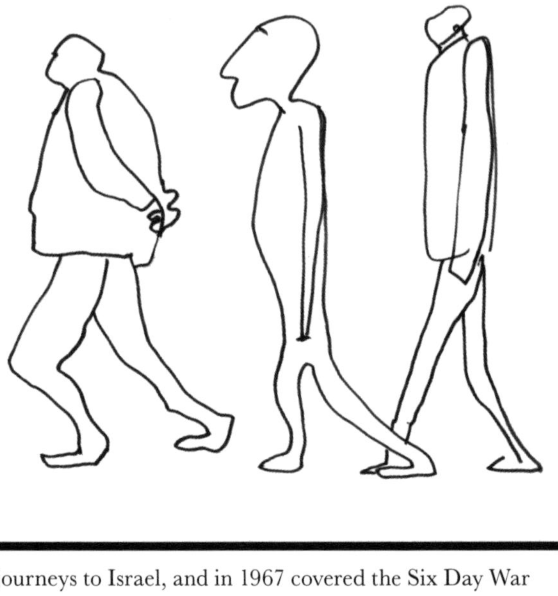

DAN REISINGER

Dan Reisinger is a Tel Aviv-based designer who in 1949 emigrated from Yugoslavia to Israel, where a year later, at age sixteen, he was accepted as a student – its youngest up to that time – at the Bezalel Academy of Art and Design in Jerusalem. He has been an avid sketchbooker ever since. It makes sense, too, since he has been a teacher for many decades and has encouraged their use.

The excerpts here span over fifty years of sketching, mostly from life. In the late 1950s he moved to London, where he studied three-dimensional design, and produced street and other scenes. He remained there until 1966, always sketching. That year he returned from his peripatetic journeys to Israel, and in 1967 covered the Six Day War between Israel and its Arab neighbors. The drawings show soldiers on both sides, prisoners, parades, and armaments. In addition there are records of bombed-out homes (in Gadot) and the insides of bomb shelters. Most of the images are style-less, but some, including those of tanks, are almost caricatures.

Many of Reisinger's sketches and finished works – posters and other graphic design, featured in numerous exhibitions – carry social, political, and cultural themes. The sketchbook is a respite from his more disciplined work and an exploration of art for its own sake.

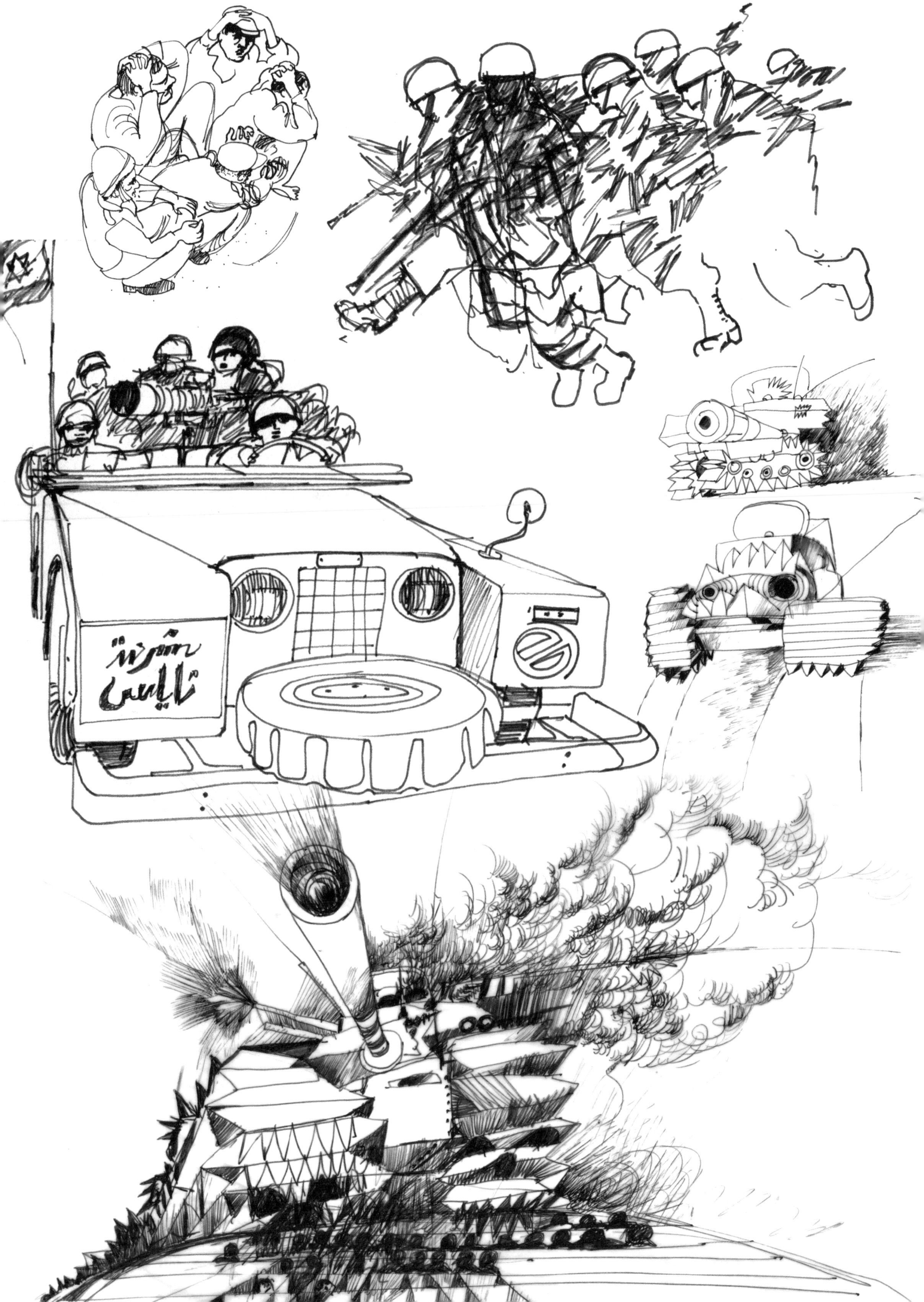
شرطة
نابلس

KNOKE 53

CARNABY STREET
DOMINO MALE FASHION
TOP TEN
LATEST FASHION FOR MAN
GAY
MALE FASH
THE ANIMALS
D. REISINGER

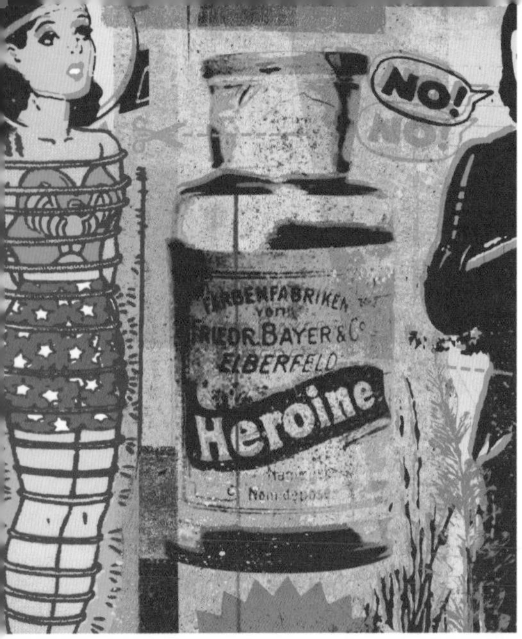
NO!
FARBENFABRIKEN
FRIEDR. BAYER & Co
ELBERFELD
Heroine
Nom déposé

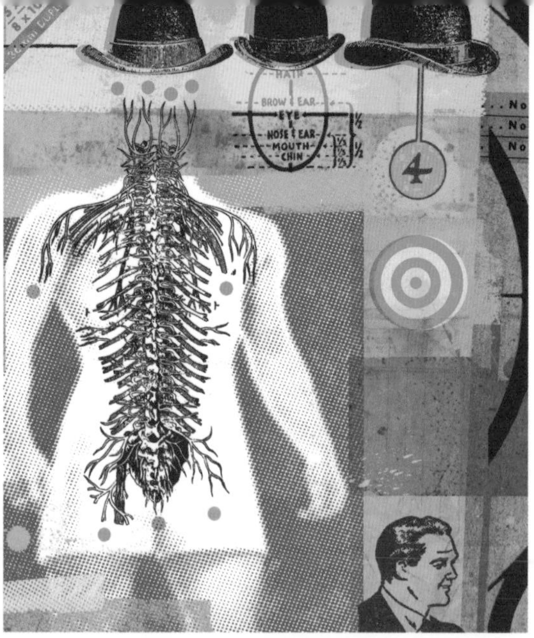
HAIR
BROW
EAR
EYE
NOSE
EAR
MOUTH
CHIN
4

4
8

us th
Drea
TAVLA I.
2
6
5
4
20
7
14
1
21
19
18
22
2
13

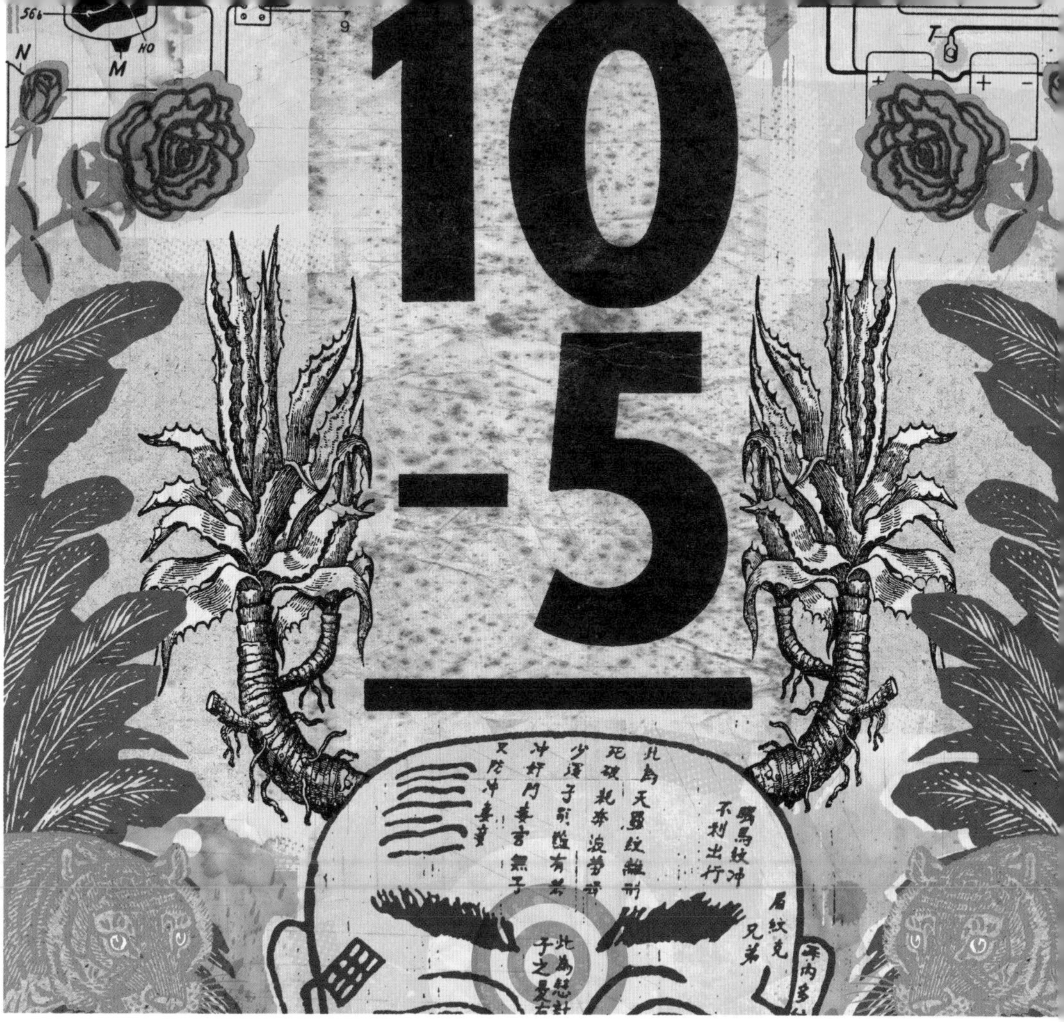

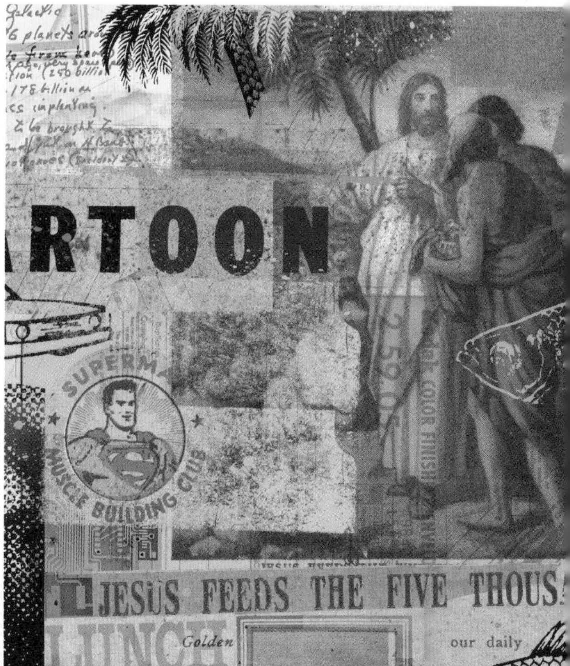

TIM ROBINSON

New York illustrator Tim Robinson started keeping sketchbooks when he lived in Brooklyn in the 1990s, and was an avid sketchbooker until around 2002. "Those books were actual collage made from bits of this and that, mostly street debris – things look best when they've been run over and stained repeatedly," he says. "Through the 1990s, I realized that I could find endless scraps for digital collage on the internet."

Collage was an early passion, with influences ranging from Robert Motherwell to Joseph Cornell. One virtue of Robinson's sketches was the inclusion of surprising words and phrases: "I started tearing up old dictionaries and comic books. There's also a family history element, because my dad [a graphic designer] gave me a pile of old ticket stubs and ephemera he had squirreled away. In my online searches I found that schematic representations of engines and wiring, even anatomy, were uploaded in high resolution. That is the strongest new theme: the combination of the technical and the organic; and always numbers."

Few of Robinson's physical sketchbooks survive. "I've saved probably three or four," he admits. "The rest have been broken up and sold off or framed in pieces for shows, recycled, and scavenged for newer work. They were not meant to be precious." The digital sketchbooks shown here "are easier to keep around," he says.

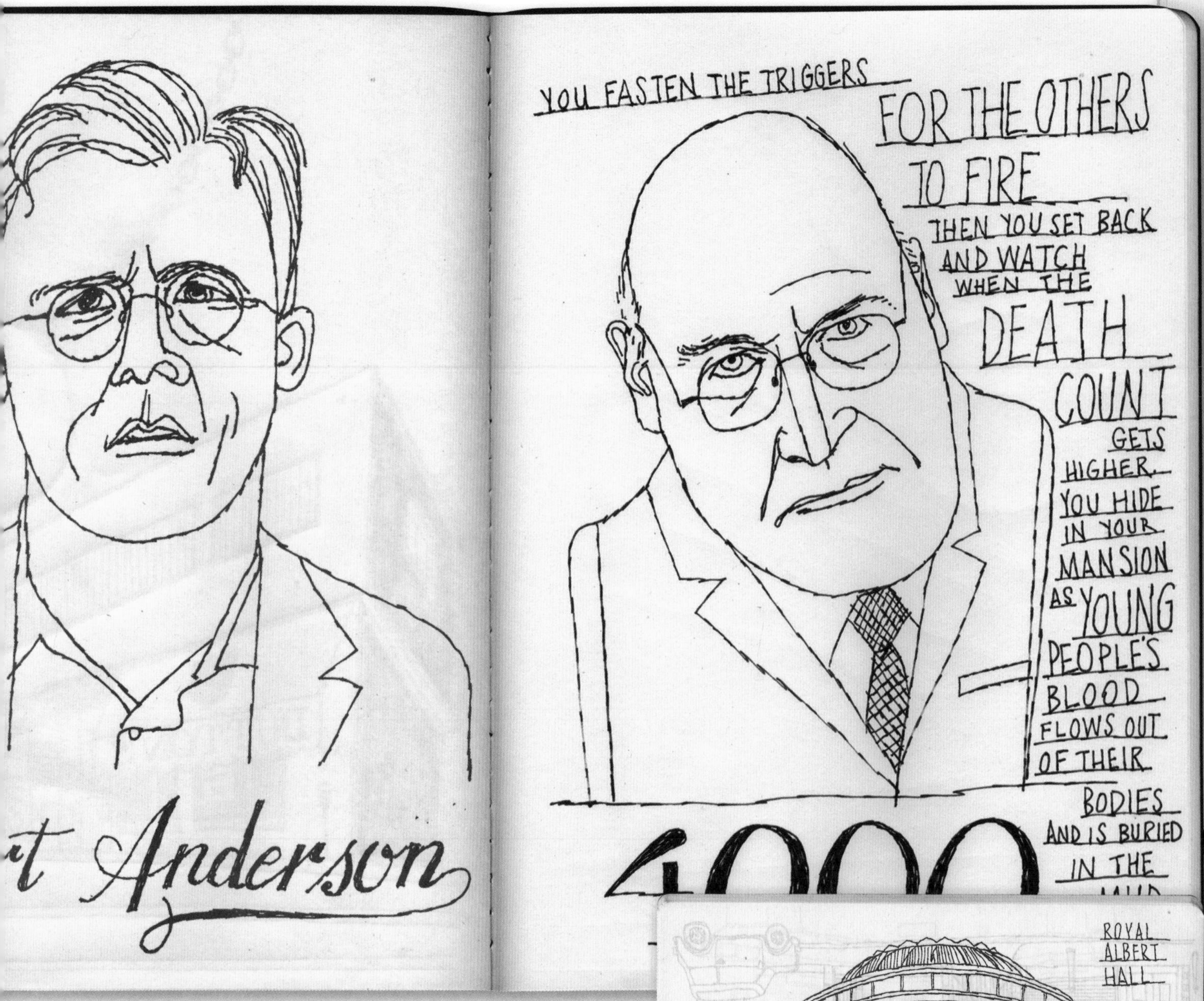

t Anderson
YOU FASTEN THE TRIGGERS
FOR THE OTHERS
TO FIRE
THEN YOU SET BACK
AND WATCH
WHEN THE
DEATH
COUNT
GETS
HIGHER
YOU HIDE
IN YOUR
MANSION
AS YOUNG
PEOPLE'S
BLOOD
FLOWS OUT
OF THEIR
BODIES
AND IS BURIED
IN THE

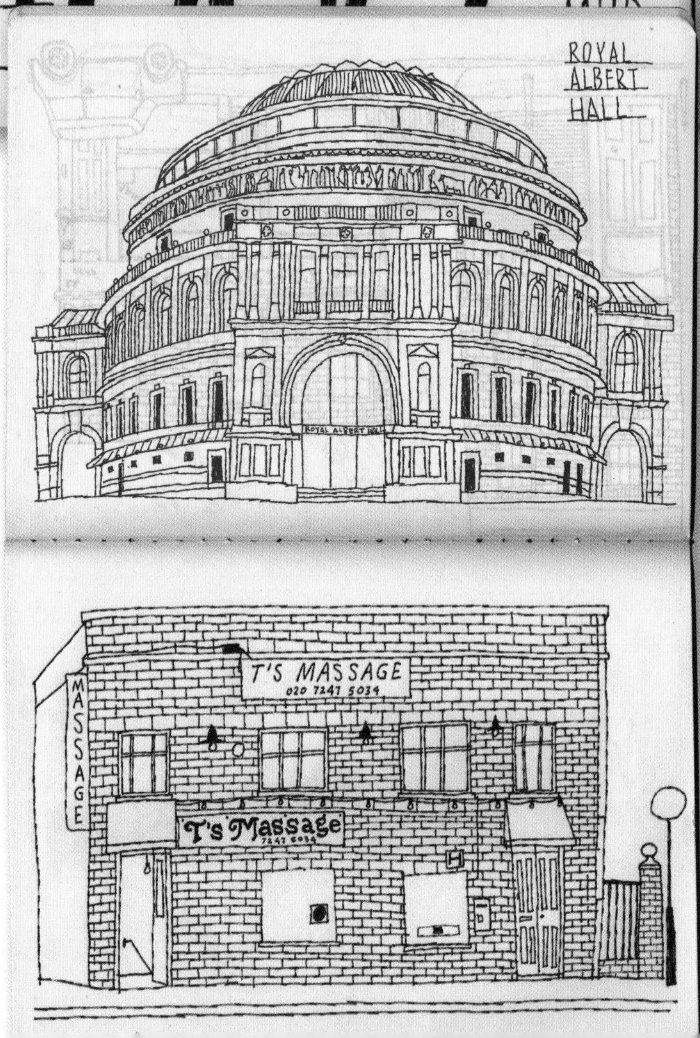

ROYAL
ALBERT
HALL
T'S MASSAGE
MASSAGE
T's Massage

PAUL ROGERS

Although children's book author and illustrator Paul Rogers has kept sketchbooks for most of his career, he began taking them more seriously in the last few years. "My students at Art Center [Pasadena] are great sketchbook keepers, and when I started teaching there I realized that I had lost a bit of the joy of simply filling a book with drawings."

Rogers says, "I was looking for a way to bring line into my work in a more active way, and I began looking at artists who used line as a major element in their work: Ben Shahn, David Stone Martin, Al Hirschfeld. I was thinking that I'd like to develop an approach to illustration that was more drawing-based than the design-focused assignments I typically get. Sketchbooks were a way to explore these ideas."

His books are almost entirely made up of line drawings that he will scan and then color on the computer, which allows him to be more flexible than he would be on a painting. "It's important to me that the finished piece stays fresh and doesn't look digital," he concludes. Most are done from photographs. "I not a big sit-on-the-street-and-make-a-drawing guy but I'll take a lot of photographs of a scene. I always try to make the drawings look spontaneous, even if they're made looking at a computer monitor in my studio or hotel room."

nt Had No
OVIN
NCE MY
BABY
EFT TOWN
I'M Going
WHERE THE
WEATHER
SUITS MY
CLOTHES

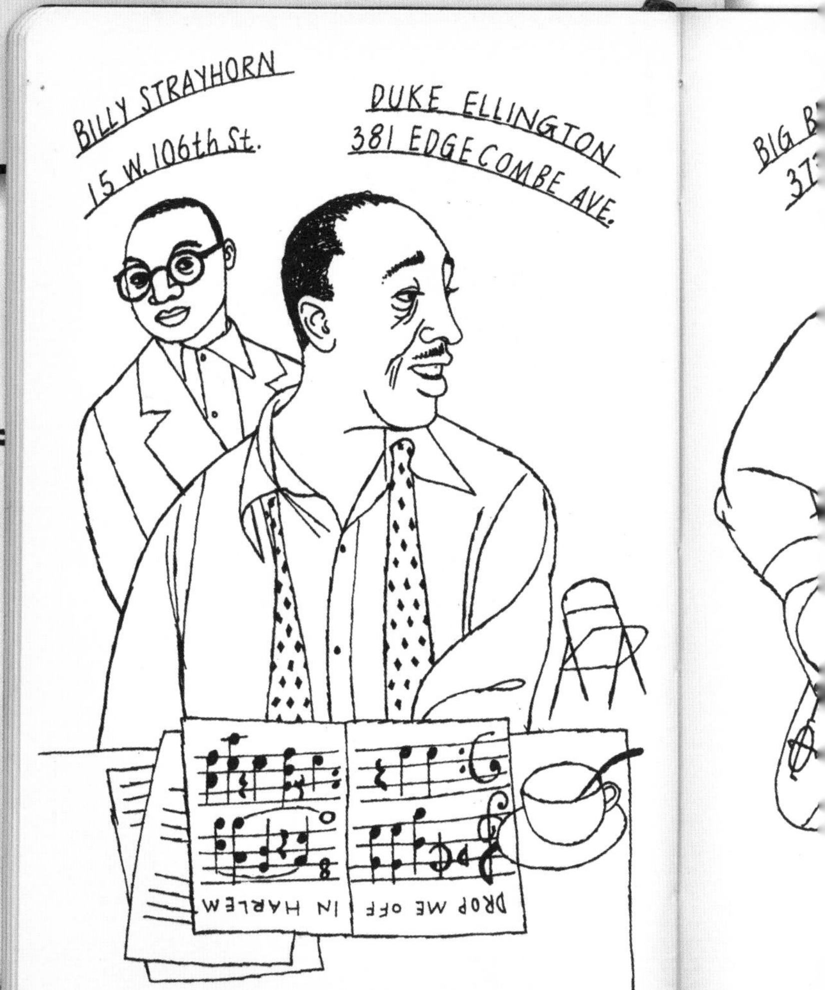
BILLY STRAYHORN
15 W. 106th St.
DUKE ELLINGTON
381 EDGECOMBE AVE.
DROP ME OFF IN HARLEM

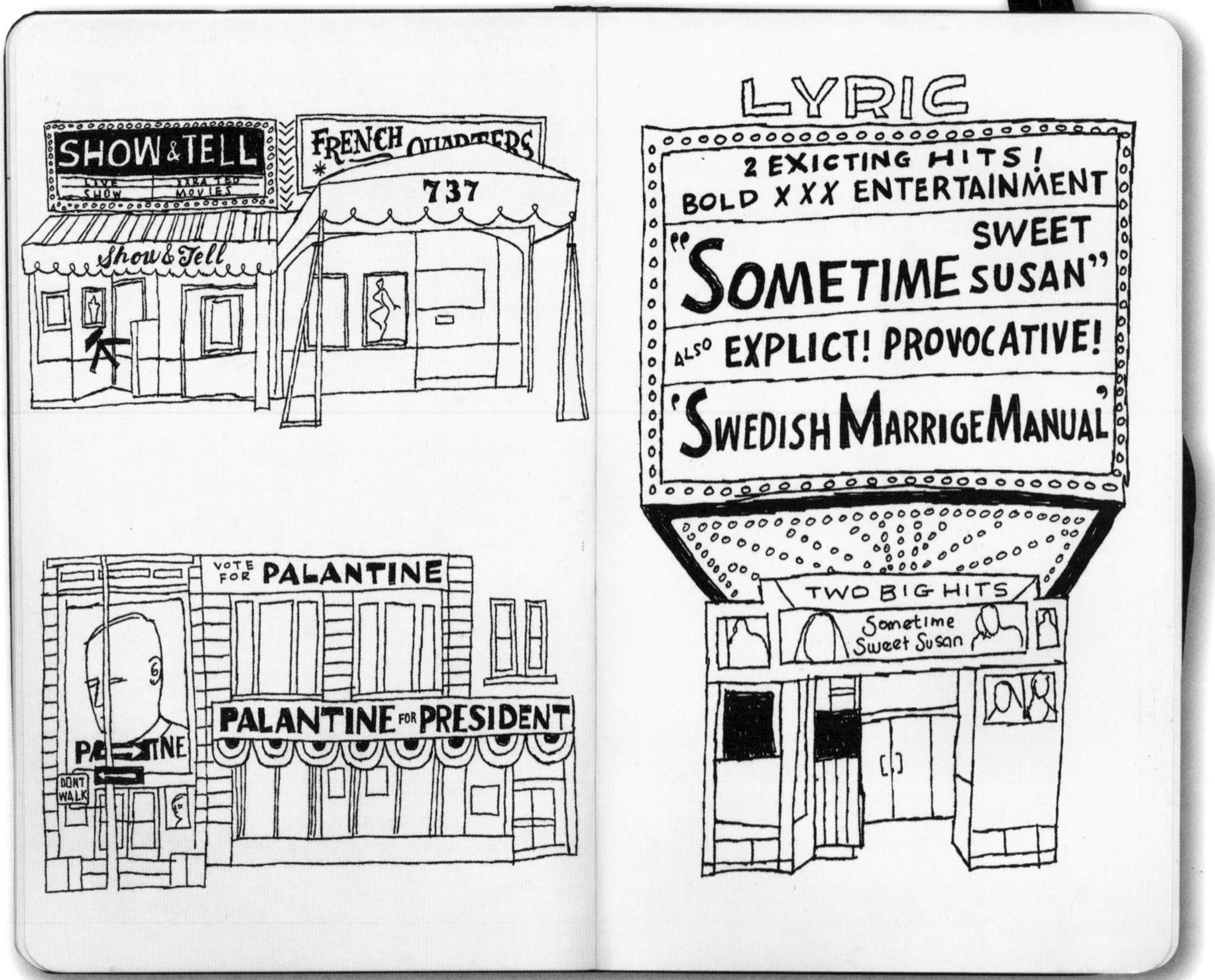
SHOW & TELL
LIVE SHOW
Show & Tell
FRENCH QUARTERS
737
VOTE FOR PALANTINE
PALANTINE FOR PRESIDENT
DON'T WALK
LYRIC
2 EXICTING HITS!
BOLD XXX ENTERTAINMENT
"SOMETIME SWEET SUSAN"
ALSO EXPLICT! PROVOCATIVE!
'SWEDISH MARRIGE MANUAL'
TWO BIG HITS
Sometime Sweet Susan

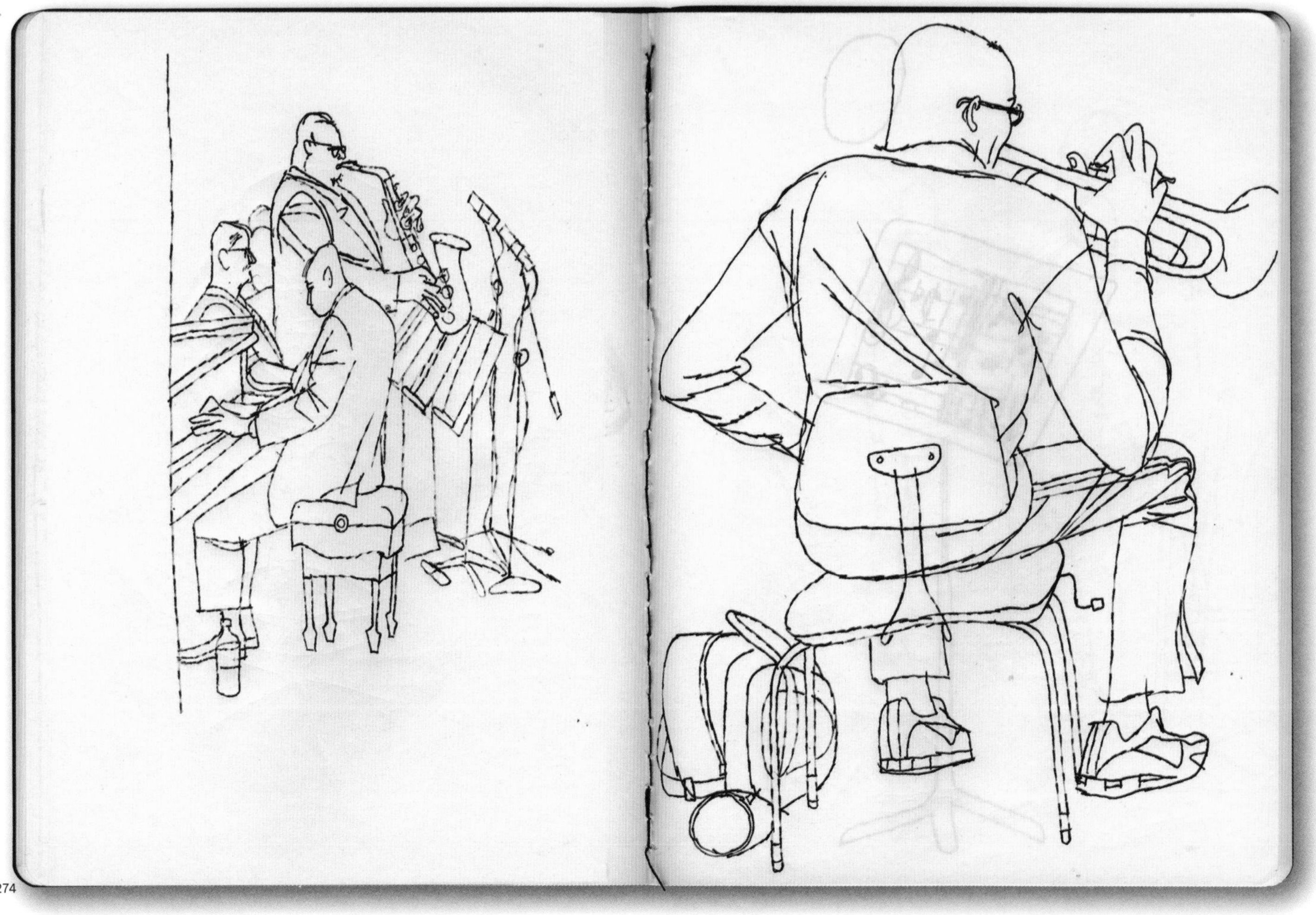

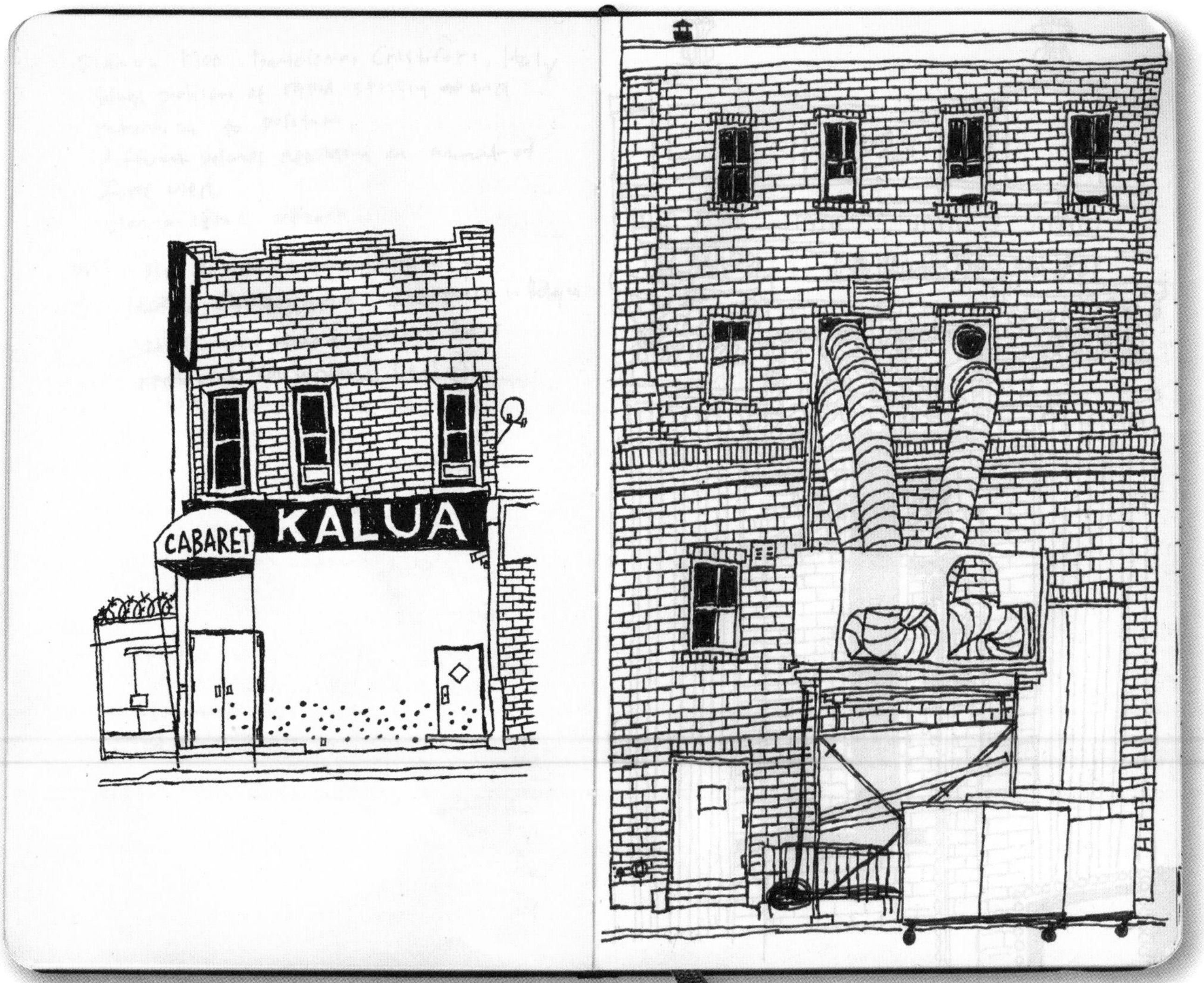
CABARET
KALUA

CRAYLEY PA
DRIFTERS
JACKIE WILSON
FRANK ZAPPA
HANK WILLIAMS
JOHNNY CASH
HOUSE OF OLDIES
Carmine St.

LAURIE ROSENWALD

Laurie Rosenwald does not keep a sketchbook in the strict sense. "Rather than sketches," she explains, "I have hundreds of random pieces of stuff, including photos, drawings from other jobs, details and bits of paper that I collect and use as starting points for other things." She never sketches in the strict sense, either. "I always say my roughs are a 'work in progress' and if a client doesn't like it, it's still a sketch. When they like it, of course, it's a finish. So everything I send is finished. It depends on how you look at it."

If she is taken at her word, Rosenwald's art is located in a netherworld between rough and finished. Which explains why the single most unusual aspect of these images is "their out-of-the-blue, leftfield, unrelated willy-nilliness." Oddly, Rosenwald says there are no inherent themes in her work, but "in my collections there are thousands of random things and they are all things I like."

When asked to date the images here, she comes up blank. They are "never, forever, I don't remember," she scrambles; "my work may be totally dated, timeless, or out of fashion," adding, "I have a couple of things on my site from 1979. Shhhh! Don't tell."

Tim
JELLY
PAST
PRESENT
FUTURE

STEFAN SAGMEISTER

Stefan Sagmeister, Austrian-born, New York-based designer and provocateur, has maintained his expansive sketchbooks for the past thirty years, since he was seventeen. He notes simply that the purpose is to "develop ideas." In fact, they contain the process of his work. "I find it easier to think about an idea once it's down on paper, which gives me the opportunity to squeeze it (until the juice runs down its legs)."

Perhaps the single most unusual aspect of these books is that "they are neat," he says with a smile. "I had kept very sloppy, all over the place sketchbooks for the first ten years and found them too cumbersome to be of any help in the future (when I go through and look for seeds of ideas)."

He has about a "dozen sloppy ones," and about "twenty-five large-format neat ones. I fill about one a year." The images here show the progression of the cover for his book *Things I Have Learned in My Life So Far* (2008).

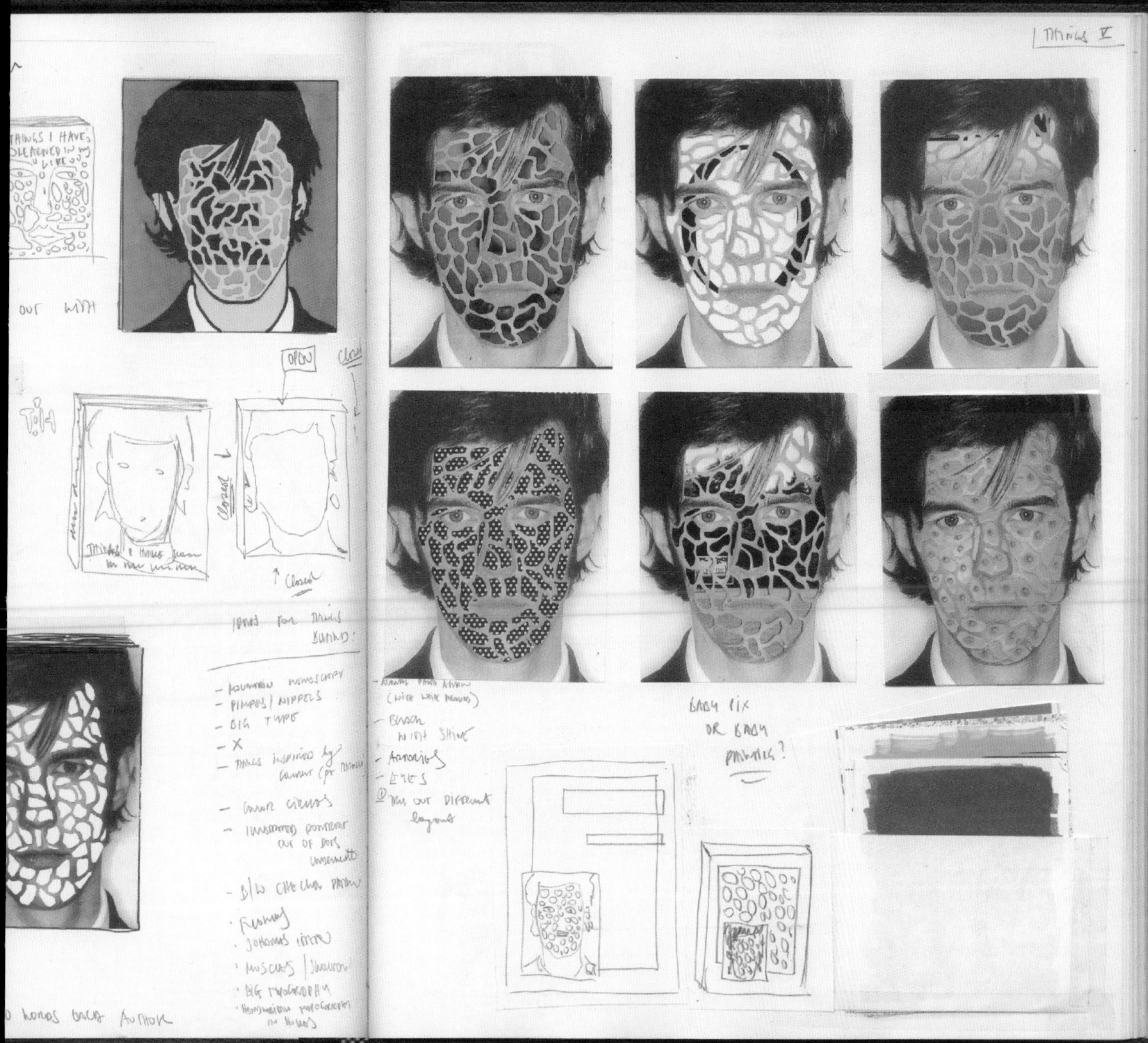
OPEN
Closed
IDEAS FOR THINGS BEHIND:
BABY PIX
OR BABY
PAINTINGS?

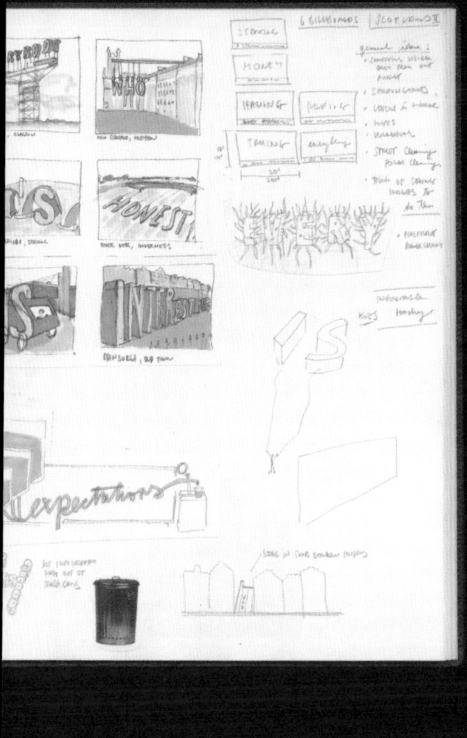

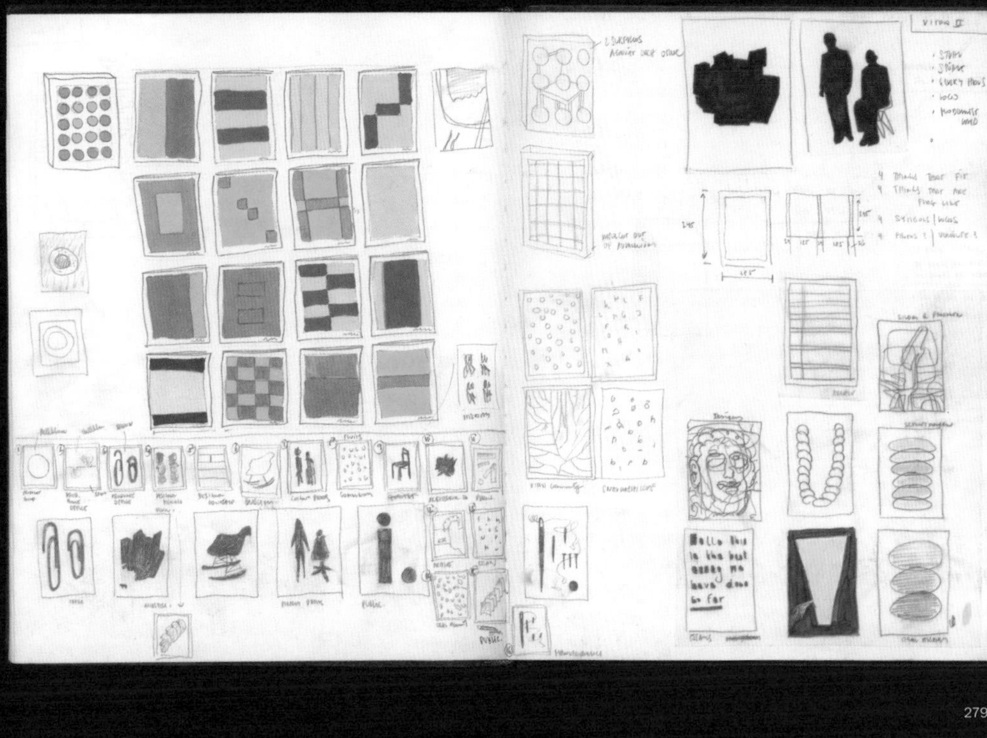

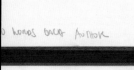

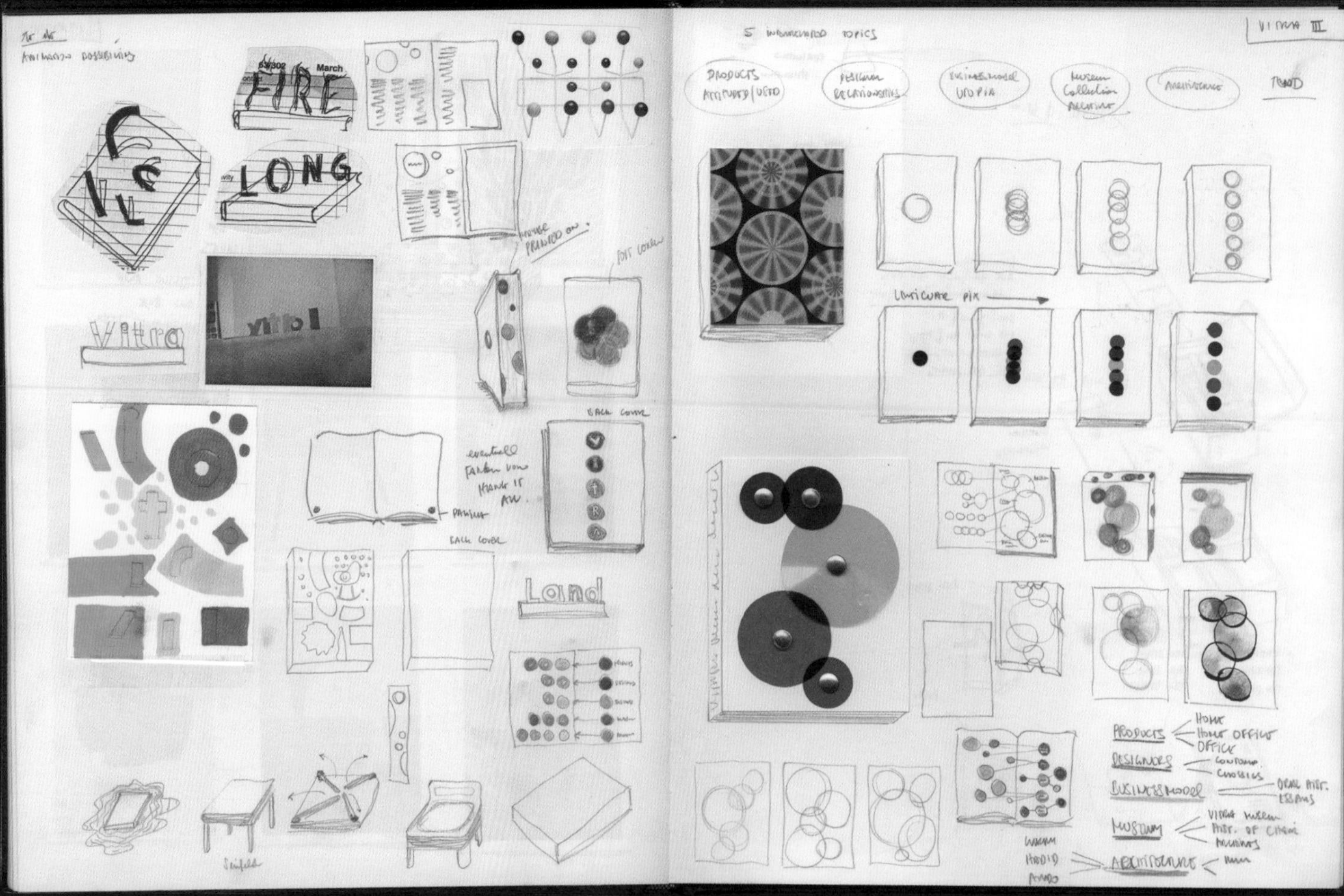

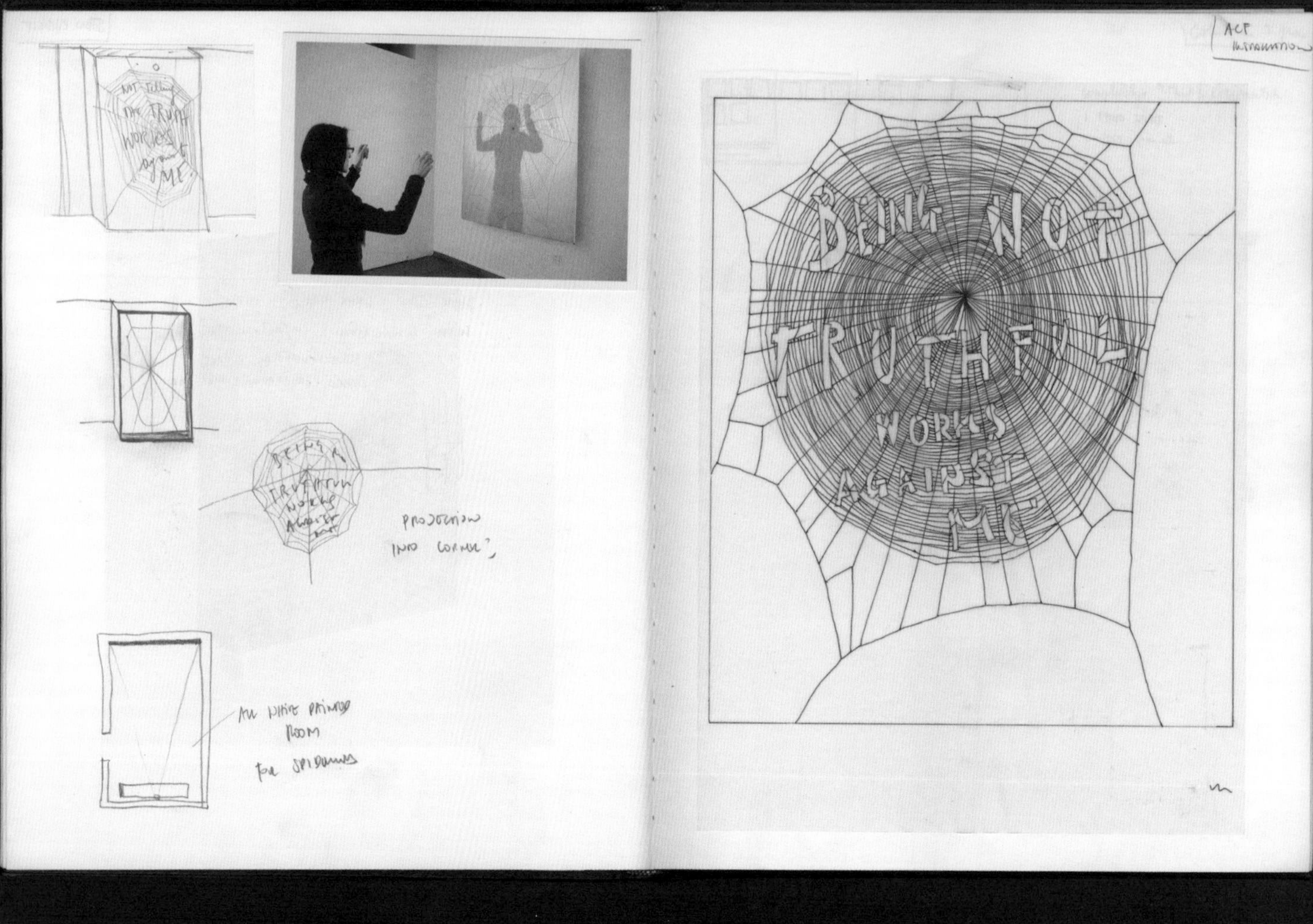

WINE
PAPER LASER CUT
PATTERN AS STORY DIAGRAMM
STORY PATTERN
To do:

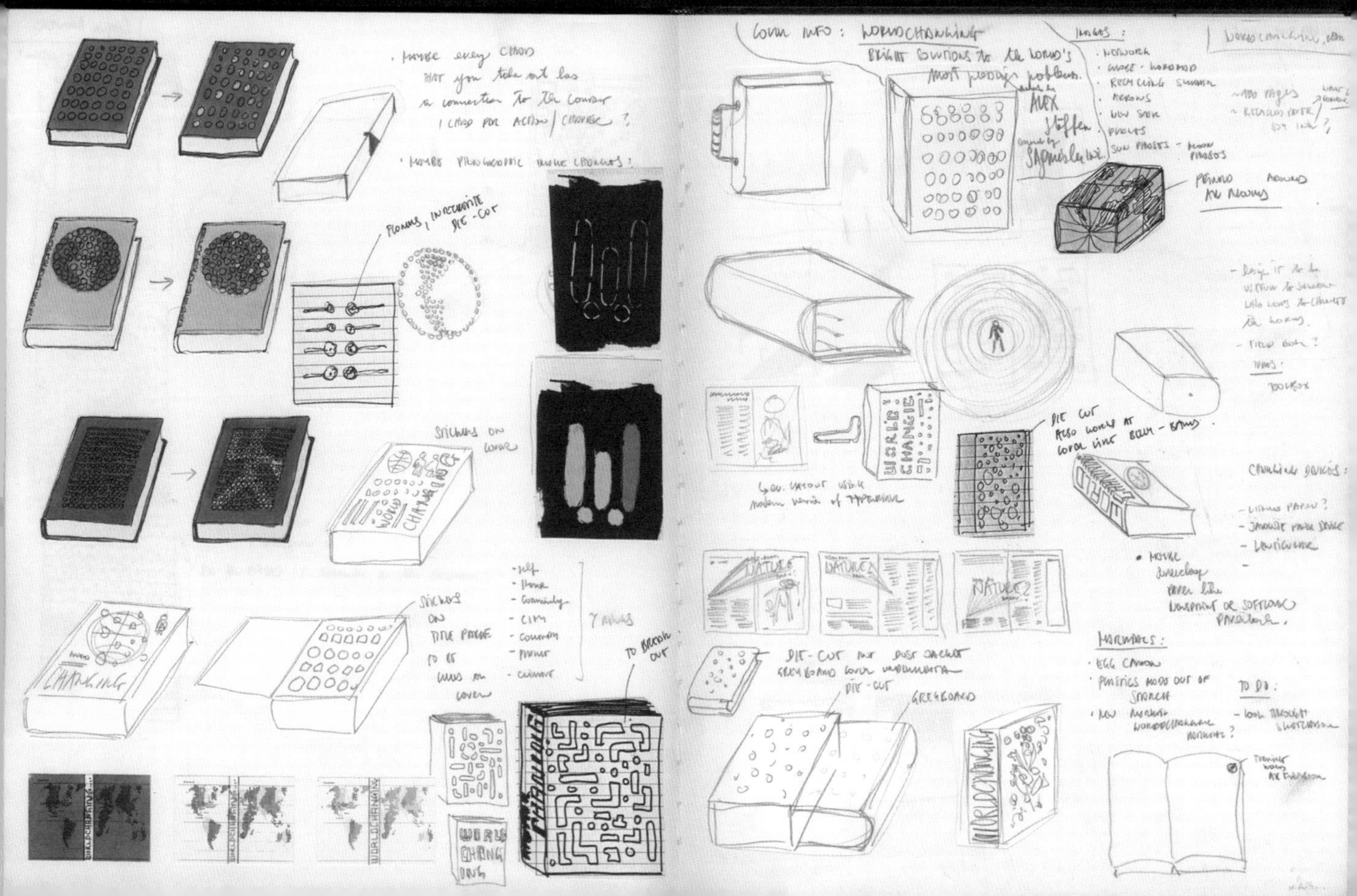
COVER INFO: WORLDCHANGING
BRIGHT SOLUTIONS TO THE WORLD'S MOST PRESSING PROBLEMS
ALEX STEFFEN
STICKERS ON COVER
TO BREAK OUT
DIE-CUT
GREYBOARD
MATERIALS:
EGG CARTON
TO DO:

(D) "CANNED" CANDIDATE

(A) BOUND FRIDGE

(B) GREEN STICKERS
A COLLECTION OF PRODUCT-TYPE BURSTS THAT CARRY "GREEN" PROMISES

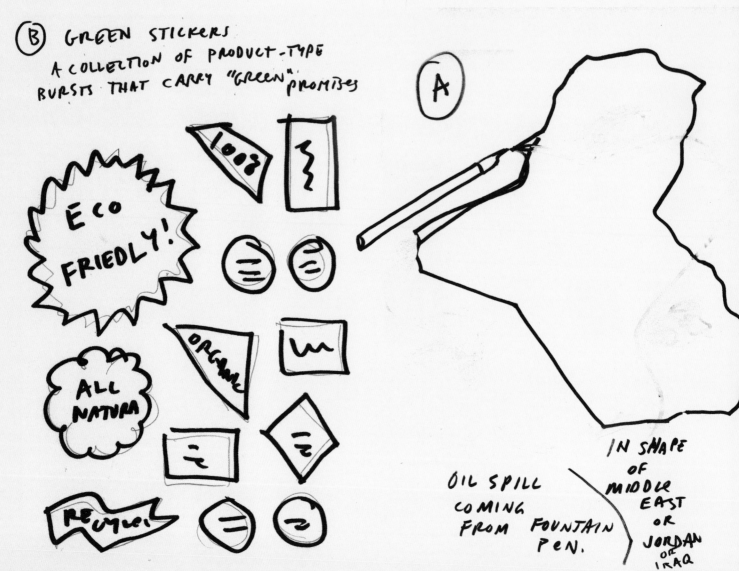

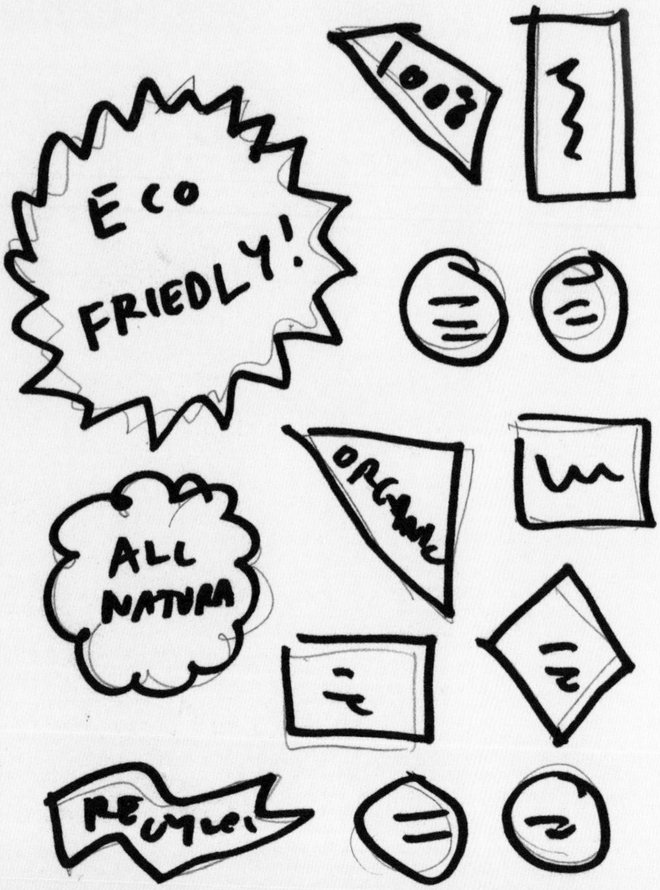

(A)

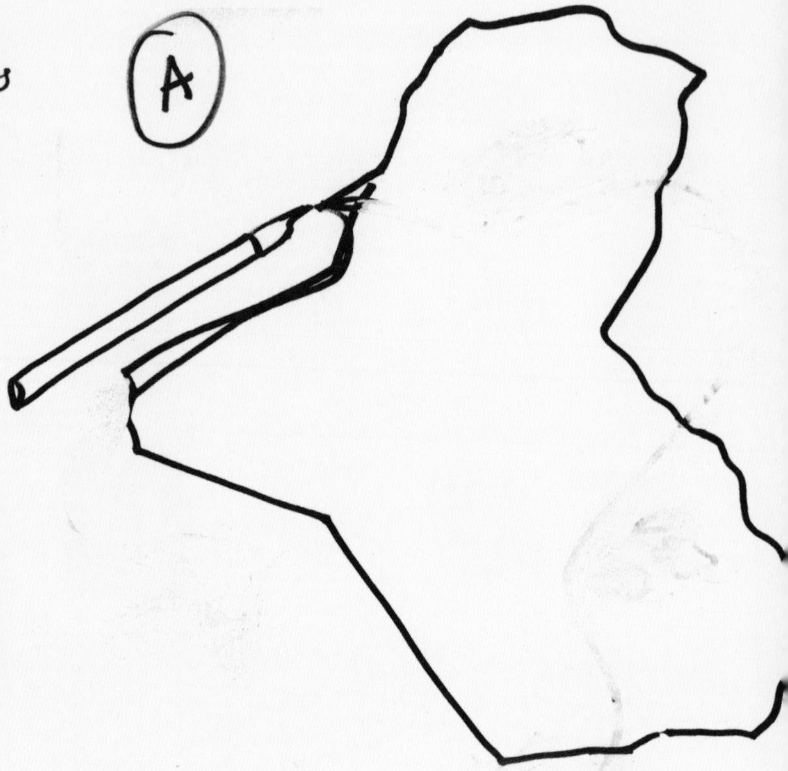

OIL SPILL COMING FROM FOUNTAIN PEN.

IN SHAPE OF MIDDLE EAST OR JORDAN OR IRAQ

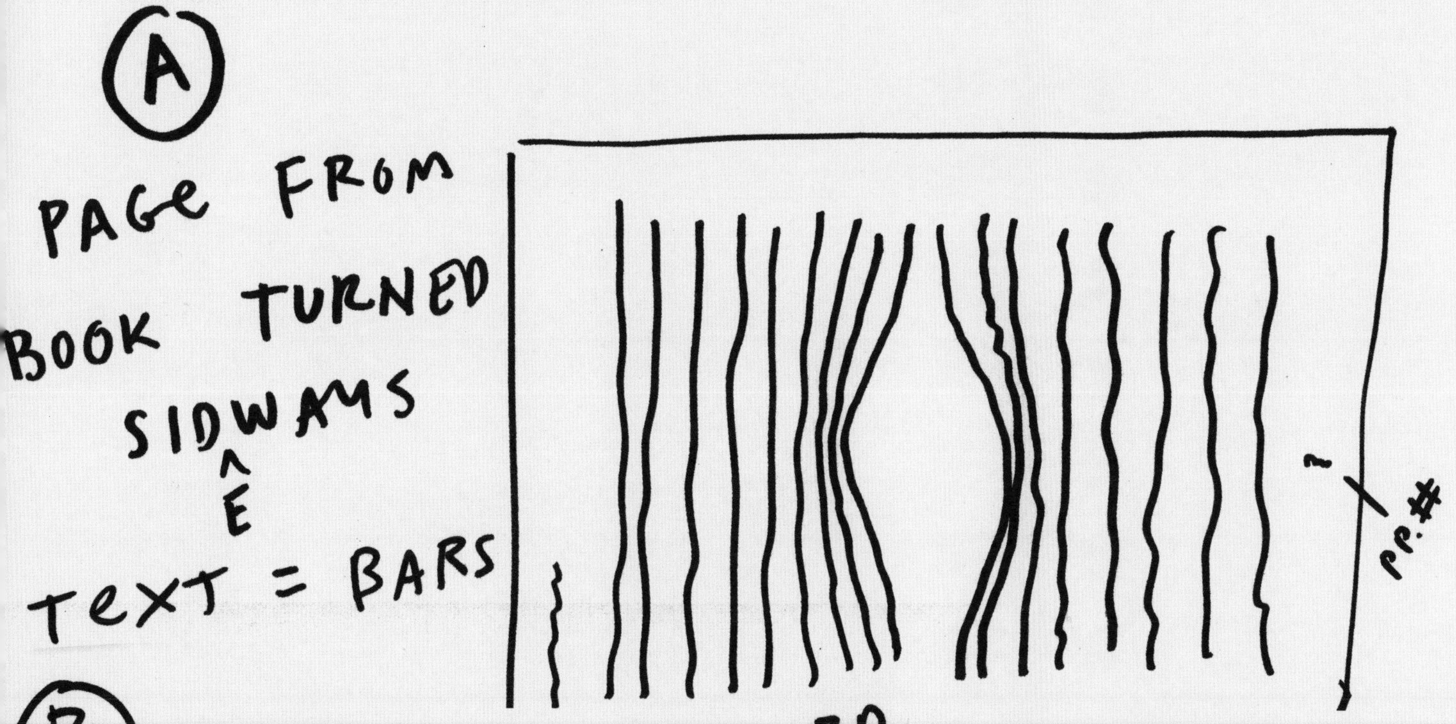

PAUL SAHRE

Paul Sahre, a New York designer and author, says, "I am not one for sketching in books: too much pressure." He admits that "any and all the sketches I have reproduced here were drawn quickly and were meant to articulate conceptual directions for a specific assignment, to be scanned or faxed to an art director somewhere."

"What's more," he adds, "these sketches always begin a discussion between myself and the art director and then between the art director and the editor. The sketches are a means of starting to figure something out and are rarely an end in themselves. The crappier and more formless (while still presenting an idea), the better."

Sahre is the first to note that, as sketches, "they are remarkably crappy, but I also hope they are 'ingenious'." These images are from 2000–9.

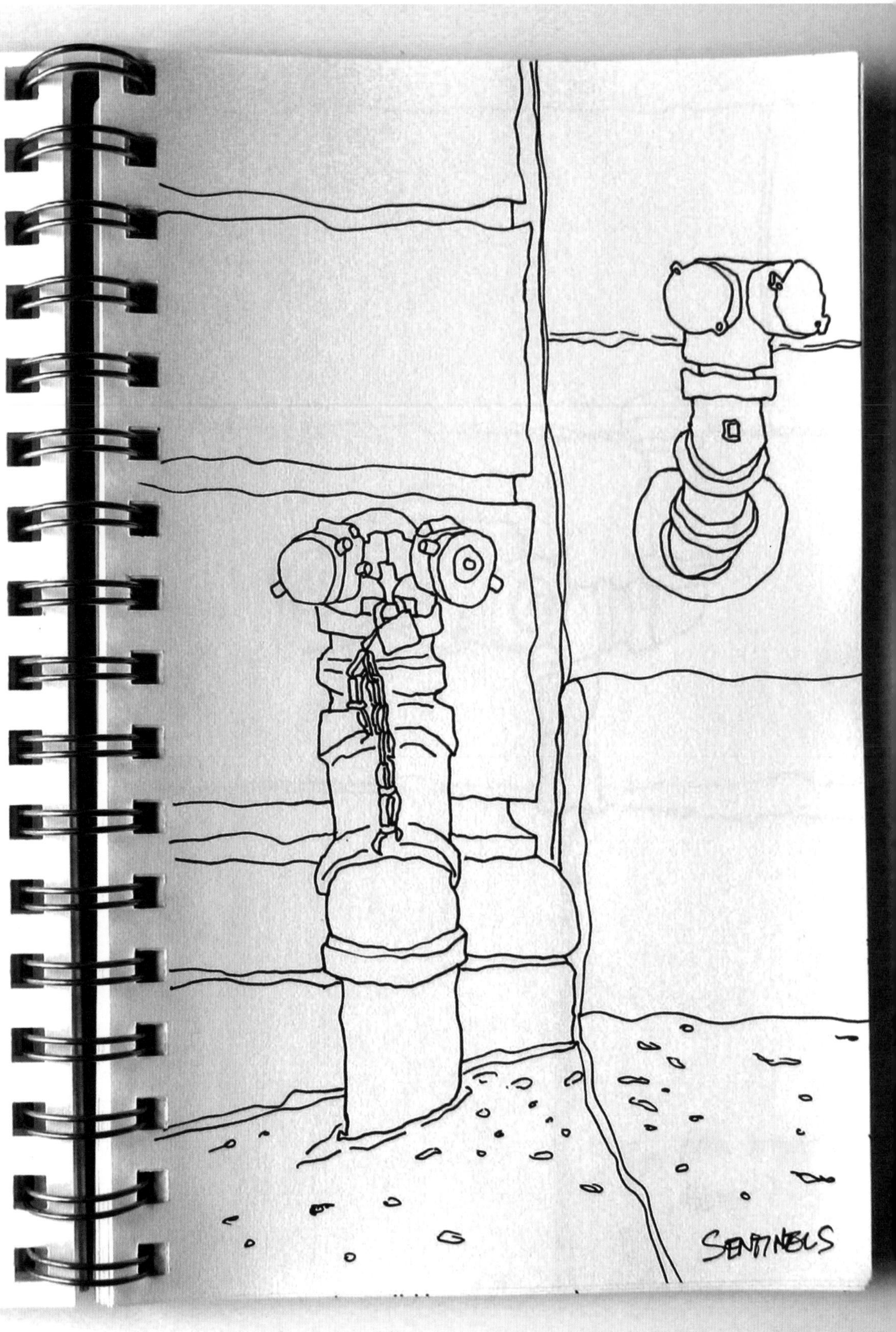

ZINA SAUNDERS

New York-based illustrator Zina Saunders has kept sketchbooks off and on for years, "though more off in the years since I've become a digital artist," she says. "I use them to play, to explore, to goof off. My sketchbooks are purely for my own amusement and I don't keep them for posterity." And yet based on what is shown here, the work has a certain timelessness that can be viewed over and over.

Saunders does note that "my sketchbook stuff is lonely line work, usually of objects; my finished work is paintings and digital woodcuts, usually of people." The ideas she preserves in them are objects of the everyday – of the street.

In 2009, her sketchbook was about the characters that "I see in hydrants and fireplugs scattered across the New York City landscape. Since my primary focus in my finished work is people, it seems that my sketchbooks wind up being pictures of mechanical objects, though I always imagine them having personalities. I can't seem to escape emotionality, no matter what I draw." What is vividly clear in these sketches and loose finishes is what she calls "the intimacy I have with inanimate objects."

When asked how many sketchbooks she maintains, her answer is as sharp and clear as the drawings she makes: "One at a time."

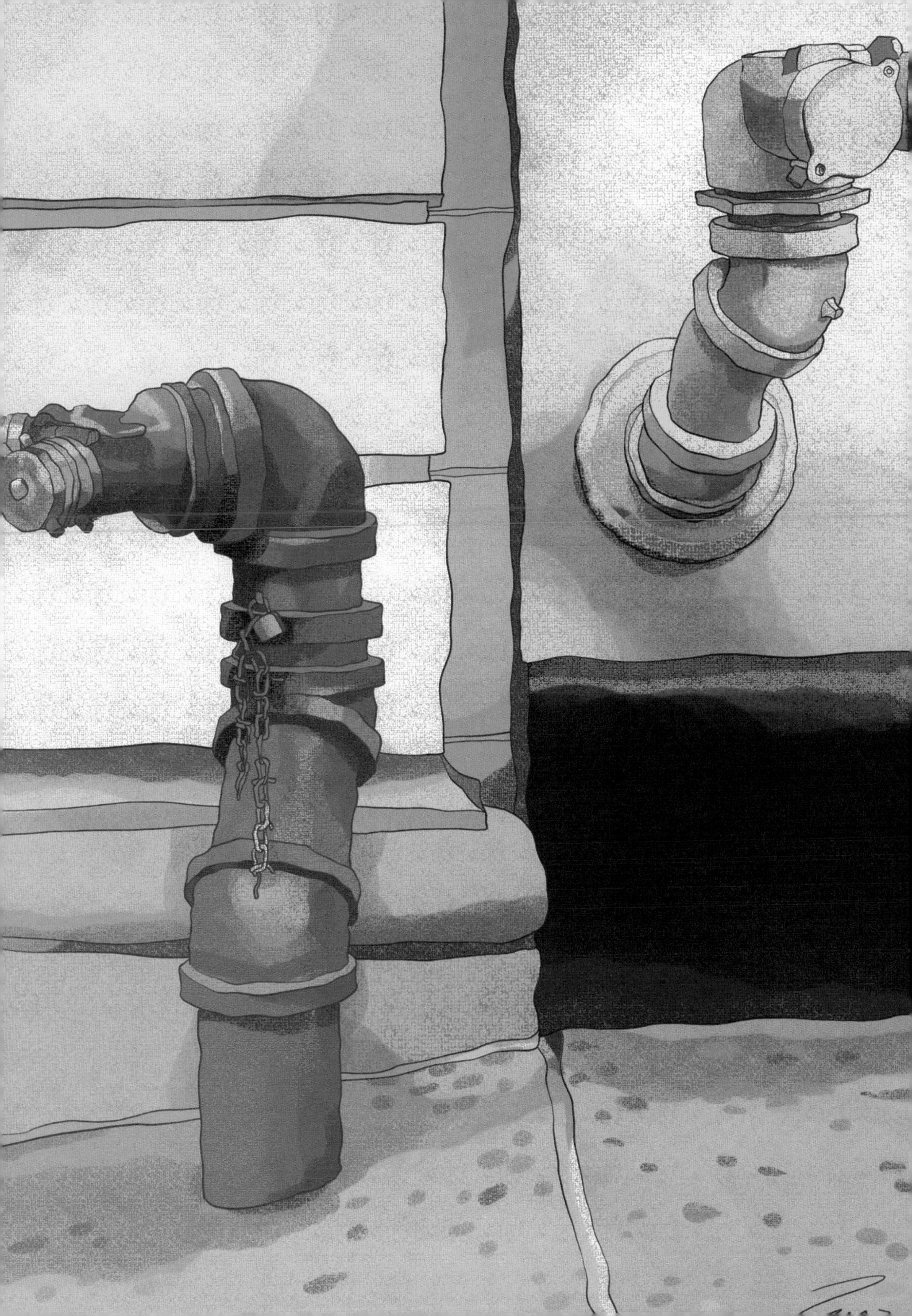

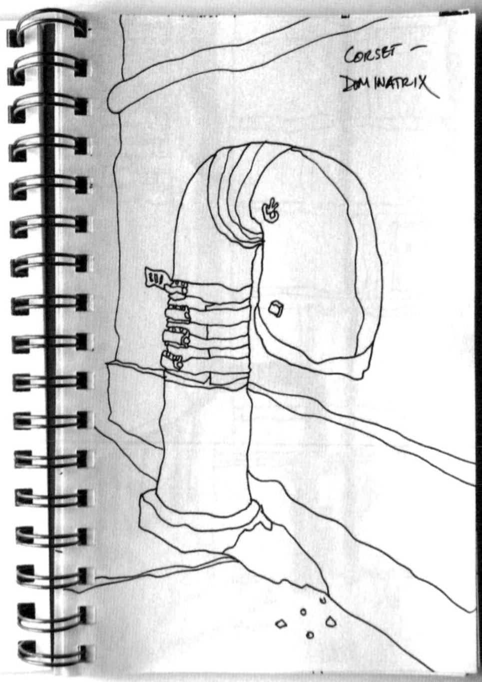
CORSET –
DOMINATRIX

BLACK SHEEP

HALF BLIND BEGGAR
GIVE

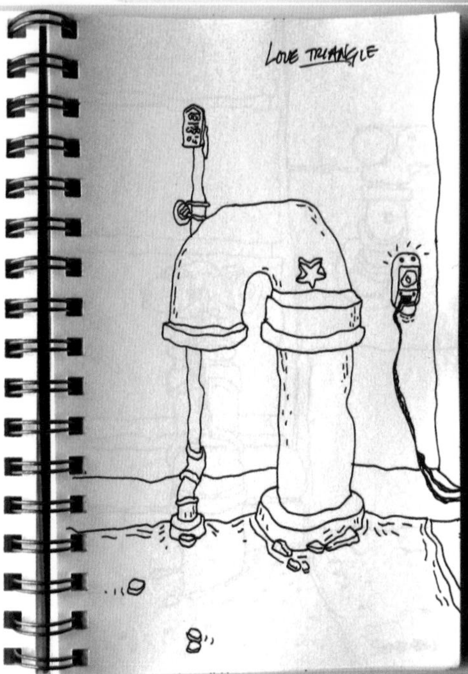
LOVE TRIANGLE

PALS

LITTLE
BIRD
DRINKING

STEPHEN SAVAGE

Stephen Savage, a New York editorial and children's book illustrator with a penchant for simple graphic lines, has always drawn pictures, but "it wasn't until my mid-twenties that I started working in a sketchbook," he notes. "Sketchbook work is practice time. I taught myself portraiture, for example, from drawing classmates and people on the subway. And my travel sketchbooks helped me develop a color palette for my children's books."

Savage is very precise, but the sketchbooks allow him to work spontaneously and chaotically. "Then when it comes time to do an illustration, I clean everything up. Truth is, I'm embarrassed by the sketchbooks. They're like my messy closet. I've never felt like one of those artists who could make something happen right there on the page. My work needs lots of additional designing."

About the content of his books, Savage says he has "lots of heads and lots of landscapes. I have two cardboard boxes filled with two kinds of sketchbooks: standard issue 8½ × 11 in. [21.5 × 28 cm] black hardbound books and small pocket sketchbooks." And each is stuffed to the gills with chaos.

JEFF SCHER

New York designer Jeff Scher, whose experimental and commercial animated short films are shown in major festivals, at the Museum of Modern Art, New York, and other museums, has long kept a sketchbook, "where stray thoughts take test drives." A nice, vivid metaphor; and there's more: "It's where my hands get to think out loud. It's where I discover what I'm thinking about by what comes out through the pen. It's where bad ideas get tinkered with and good ideas fester until a time comes when they are ready to drive."

Scher's notebooks are ongoing. "An idea might come and go and come back ten years later with new sneakers," he continues, metaphors streaming. "I work on them in the morning and late, late at night. They are stews of ideas; the finished work is always a distillation of one or two." His notebooks are of catalogs of "what ifs," "like maps to places I might go. They are often about ideas for other media, mostly film. There are notes for mechanical sculptures that I have no idea how to construct, and most likely won't get around to. If there is a theme it's thinking about motion, and different ways of seeing, recording, and creating it. Some pages have lots of layers. I like the stew of chaos from layers. Unexpected juxtapositions happen, and unlikely links sometimes emerge that lead to ideas for experiments."

washed
film by
SOME
Body
else
I'm sorry to say
that all my

despite the best of intentions
DURER
I AINT
PICTURE PERCUSSION IST.

POP TOP
a good title
go Oskar go
Fade Out, THE END
THE OPPOSITE OF FIRST CLASS
Blonde Alert
A Blinking Fight
Coalition of the Swilling
Blind Faith
ILEE Shnazzy Witless
Puppy Love
Garden of Audits
Smoker's heart
Last time Lucky
BIG DOG
PICTURES FROM AN EXECUTION
OOPS, WE'RE THE BARBARIANS
Blamme
Unrealistica
Knotical
JACK IN THE BOX
Cooler by the Shore

exPanding the Brand
Schabelhalten

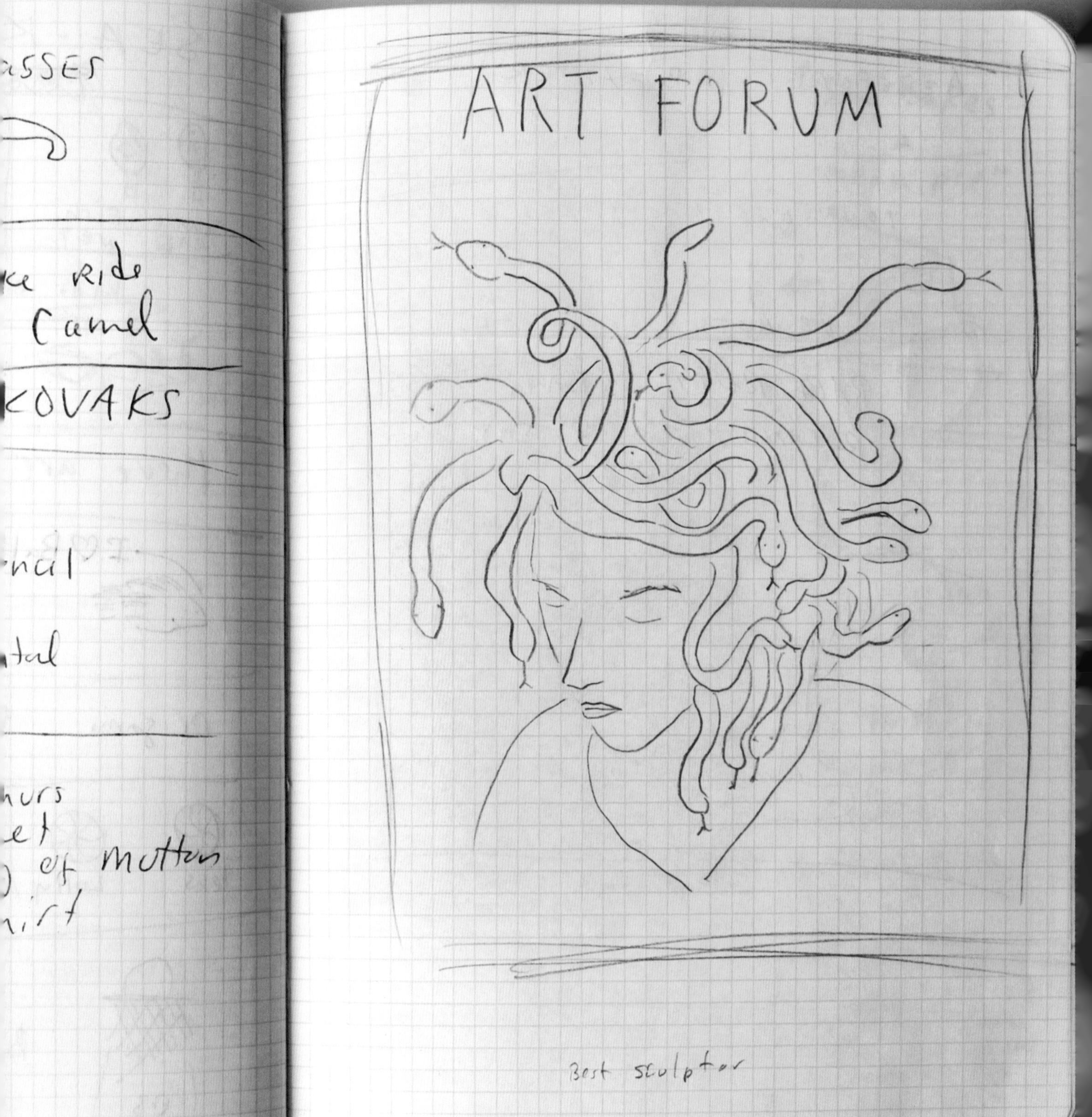

TAMARA SHOPSIN

Tamara Shopsin, a New York-based designer and illustrator known for her quirky humor and minimalist drawing, is something of a casual sketchbook-o-phile. She has kept a book on and off since high school and uses them to collect ideas that, she notes, "I don't have enough time for and don't like enough to do something with."

Does that mean the sketchbook is a storage bin or trash can? "Sometimes I have a bad idea over and over again," she explains. "And I won't stop having it until I write it down." So the sketchbook is a tool for occupational therapy.

"The drawings don't need to be visually attractive. The ideas are not thought all the way through. These sketches are hopefully the germ of something that will become better." As sketchbooks go, Shopsin says, "They are not that unusual, they are doodles and there are no themes that I can see, but I am pretty close to it."

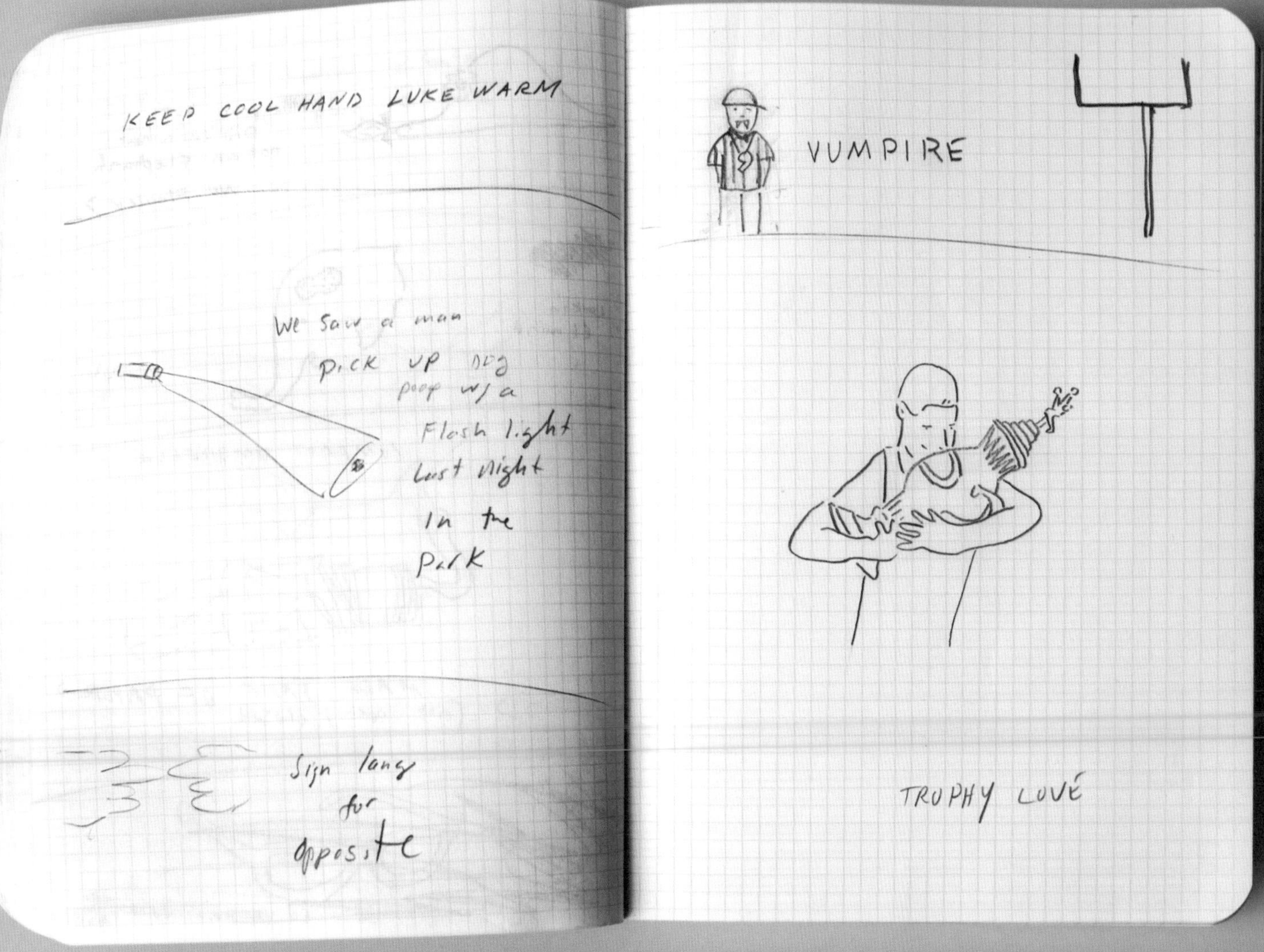
KEEP COOL HAND LUKE WARM
We saw a man pick up dog poop w/ a Flash light last night in the park
Sign lang for opposite
VUMPIRE
TROPHY LOVÉ

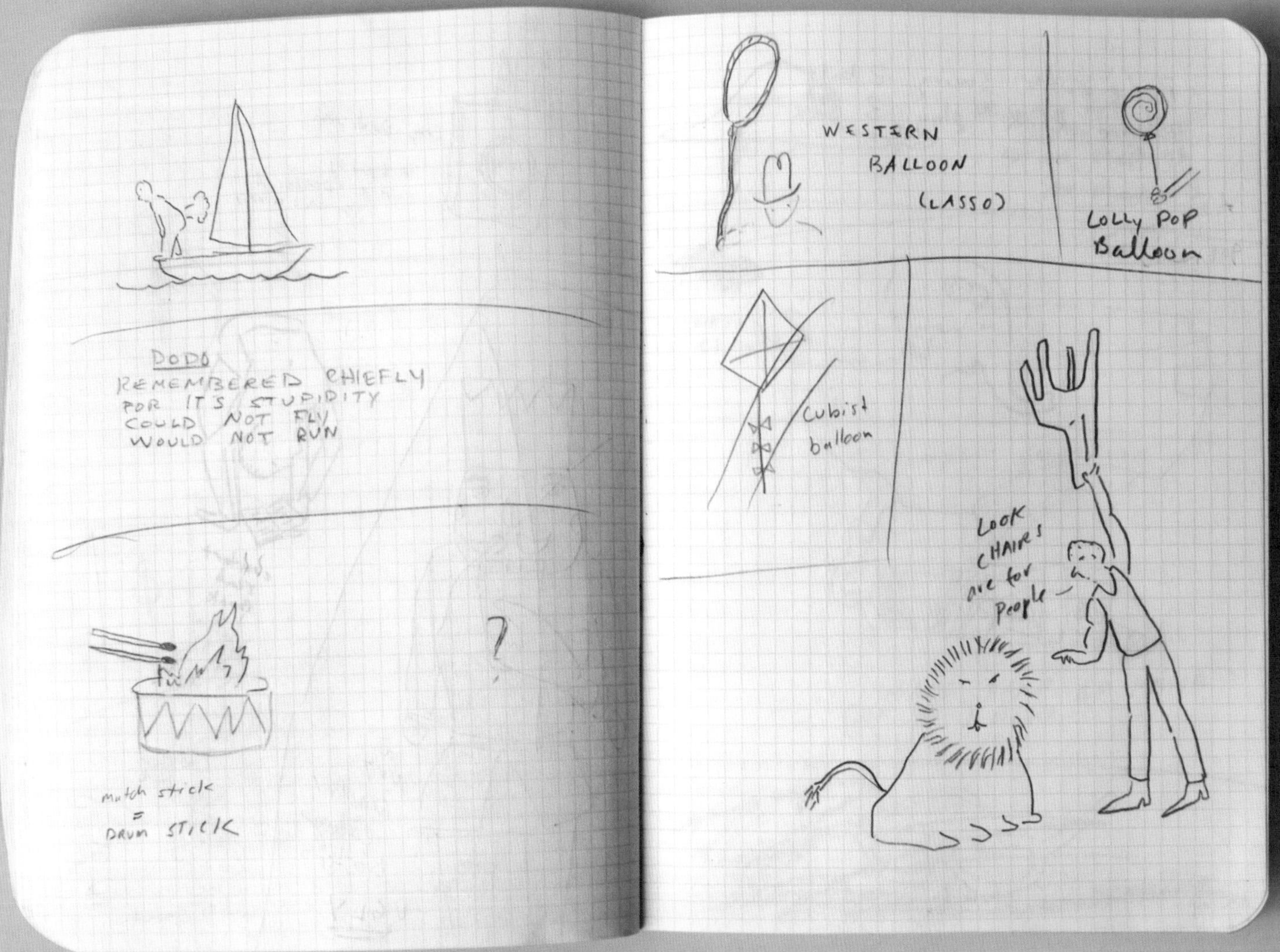
DODO
REMEMBERED CHIEFLY FOR IT'S STUPIDITY
COULD NOT FLY
WOULD NOT RUN
?
match stick = DRUM STICK
WESTERN BALLOON (LASSO)
LOLLY POP Balloon
Cubist balloon
LOOK CHAIRS are for People

BOSTON MA
2.1.01
Elwood Smith
41 Locust Grove Road
Rhinebeck NY 12572

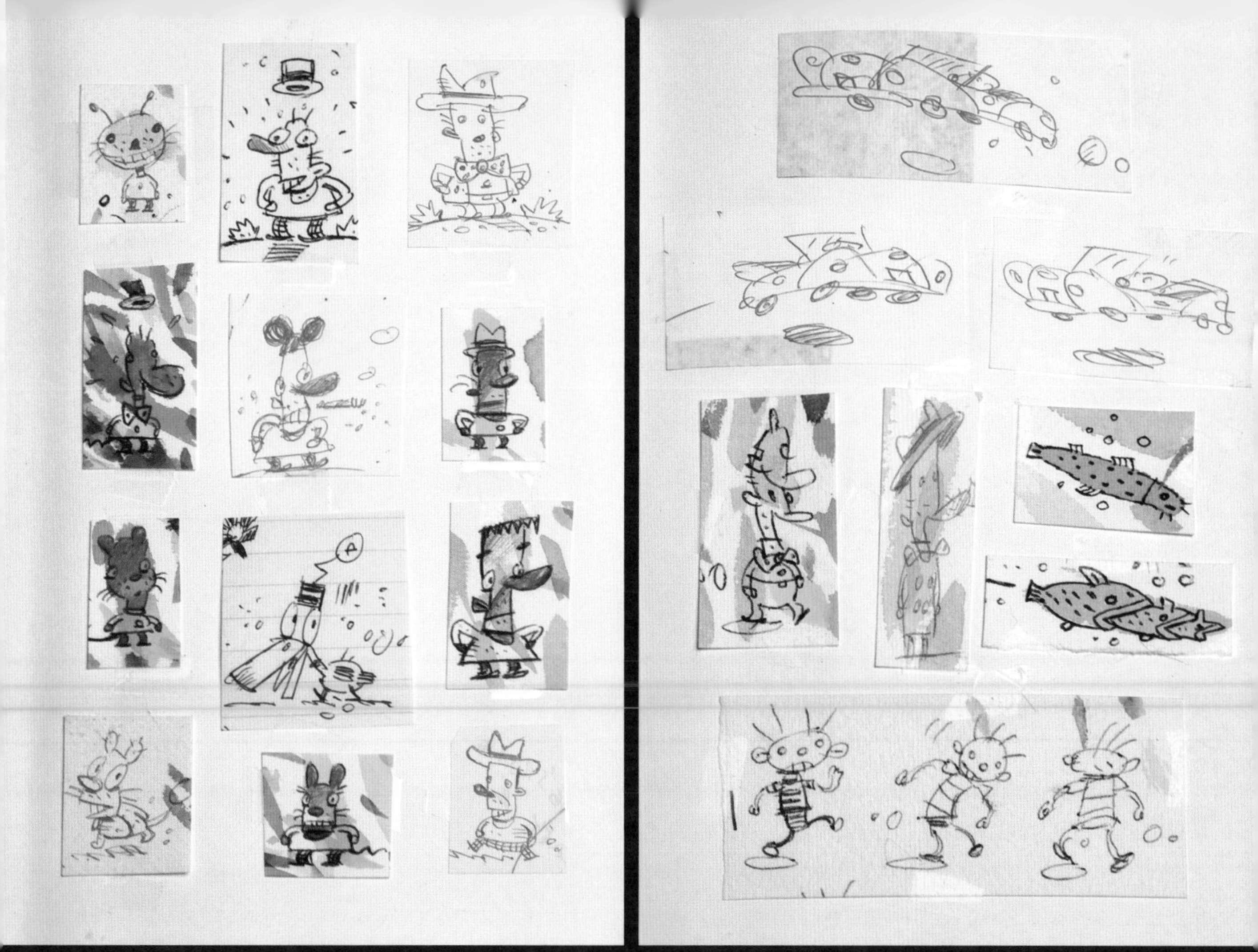

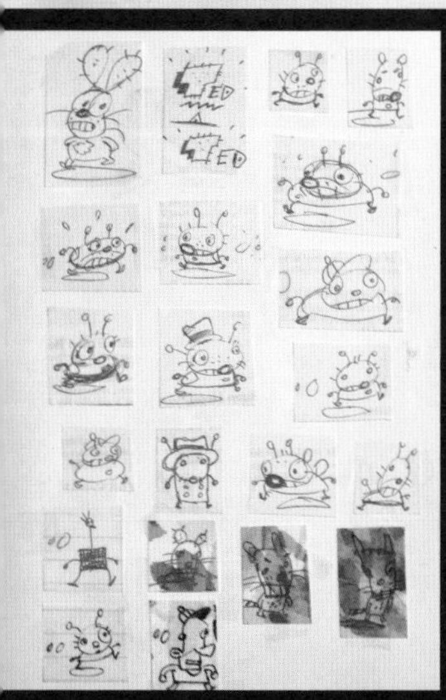

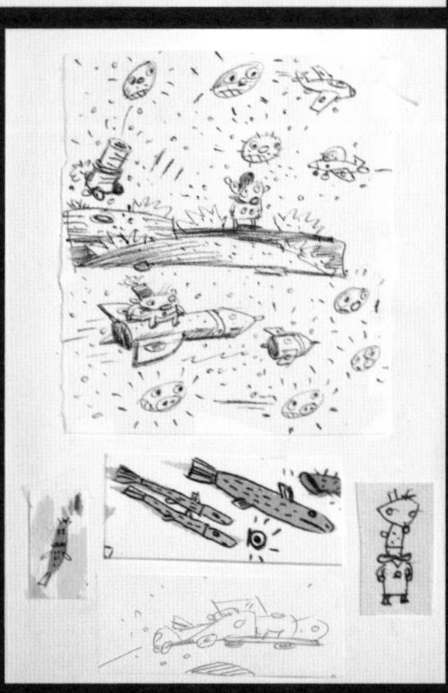

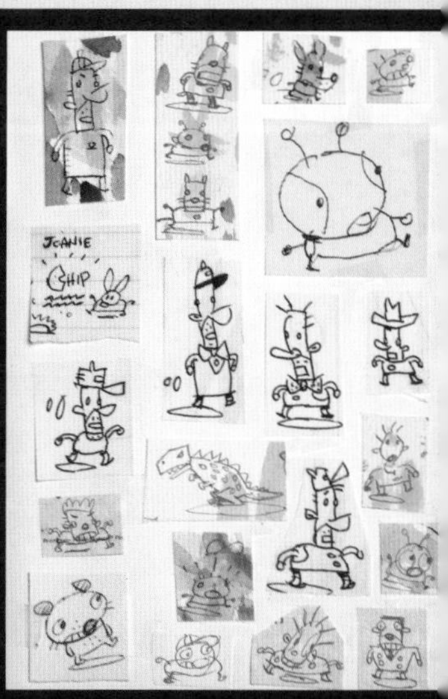

ELWOOD H. SMITH

llustrator and animator Elwood H. Smith says his sketchbooks are "just collections of doodles made while talking on the phone. I've been taping them into sketchbooks since about 1984."

After each conversation, he ends up with a page of some ten to hirty doodles. "I love drawing with a ballpoint pen, but I draw on vhatever is within reach; magazine subscription envelopes, lined yellow pads, and, if I'm in my studio, scraps covered with watercolor est splotches that I keep taped to my drawing table. Many of the saved mages appear in my commercial work and in my animation projects."

"I love to draw characters walking – hundreds of them just moseying along. Sometimes, they are running – fleeing something. They are mostly older men and usually are apprehensive. All of them are me, I guess." The human characters are often surrounded by bunnies peering over hills or accompanied by deranged cats or dogs. He also has a surfeit of nervous suns with faces; sawtooth bushes and land masses with prickly grass; small, worried animals peeking out from behind bushes; speeding cars, often filled with angry or stressed characters, make up this alternate universe. "I never tire of drawing these same images," he adds. "If I had

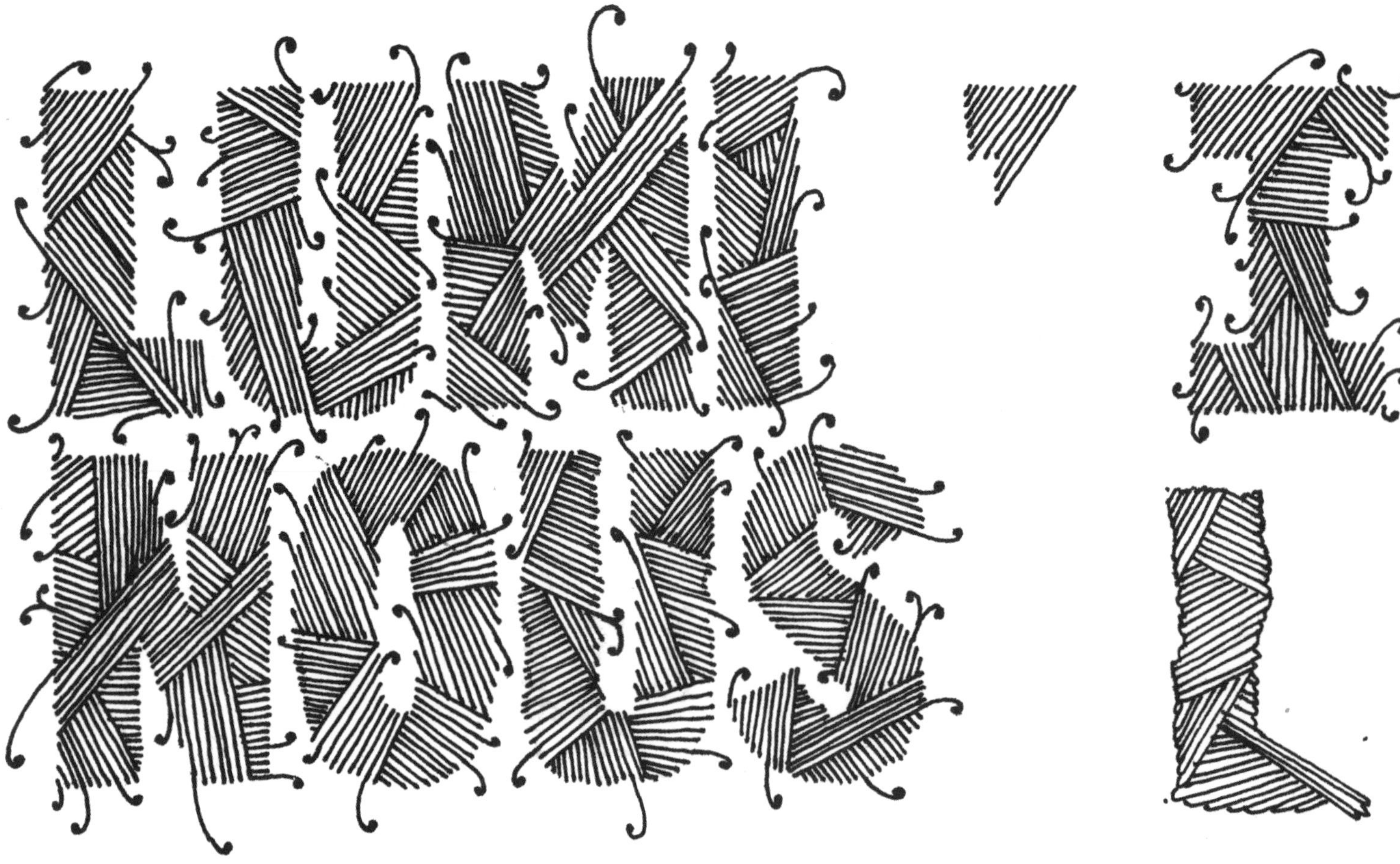

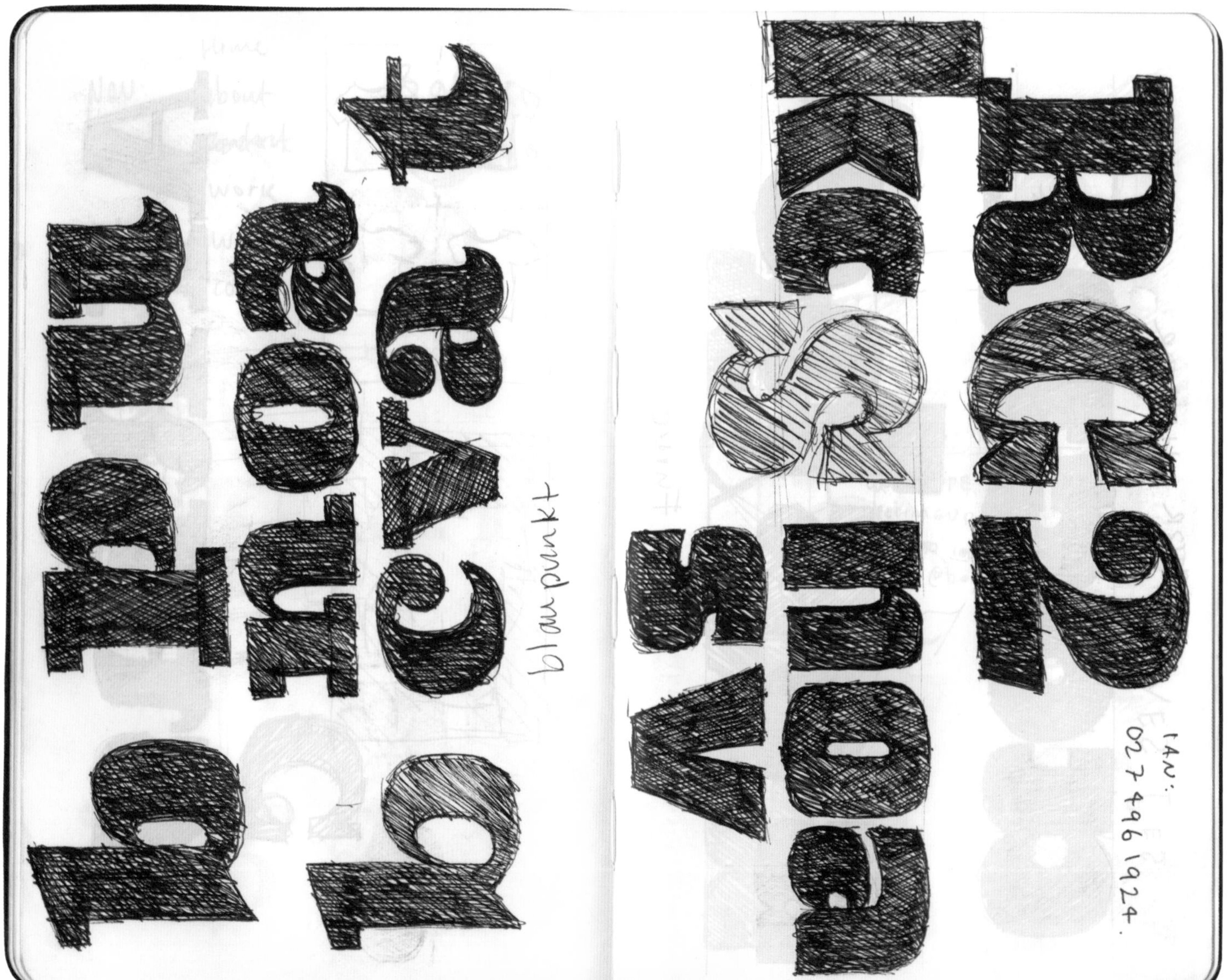
blaupunkt
IAN: 027 496 1924.

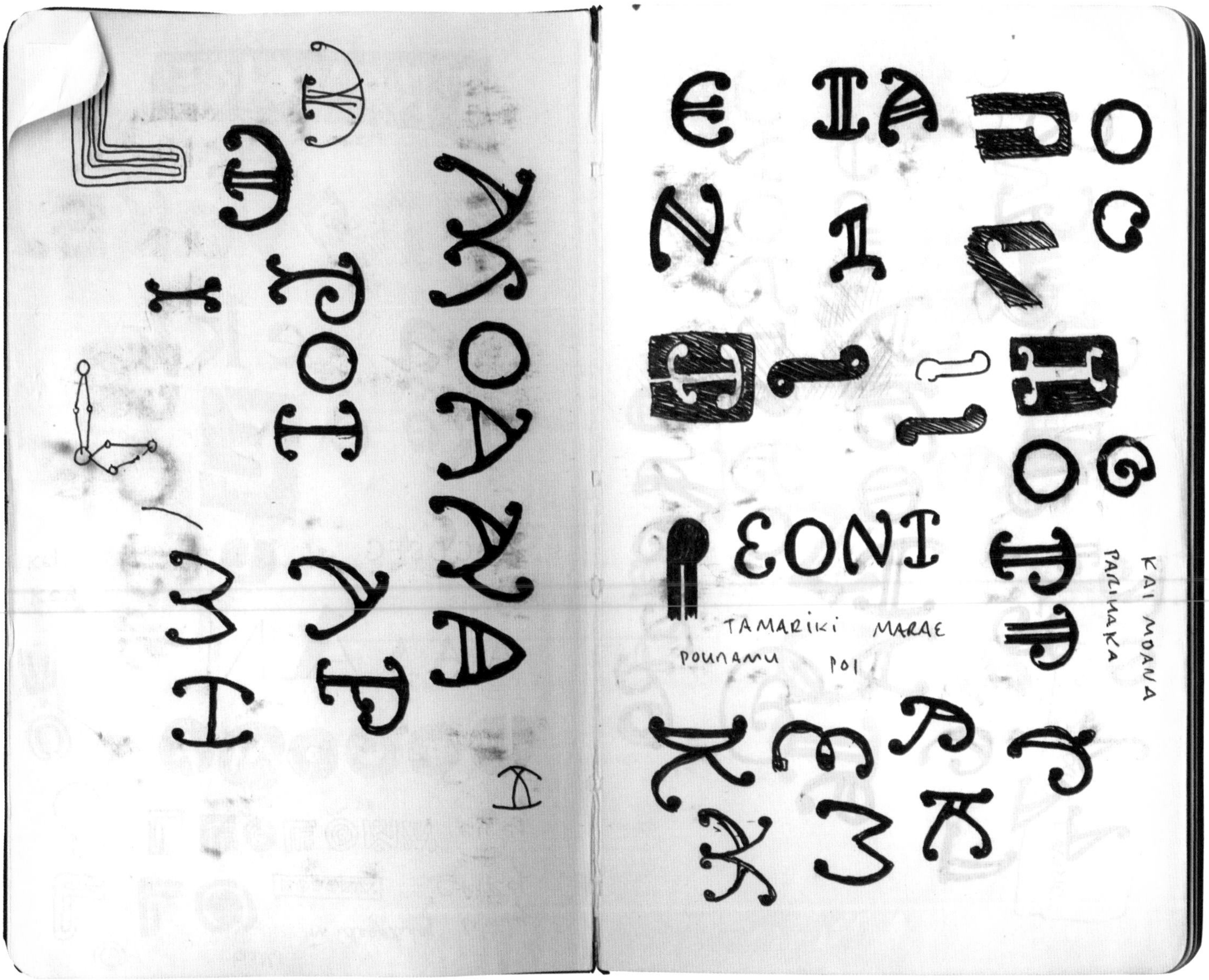

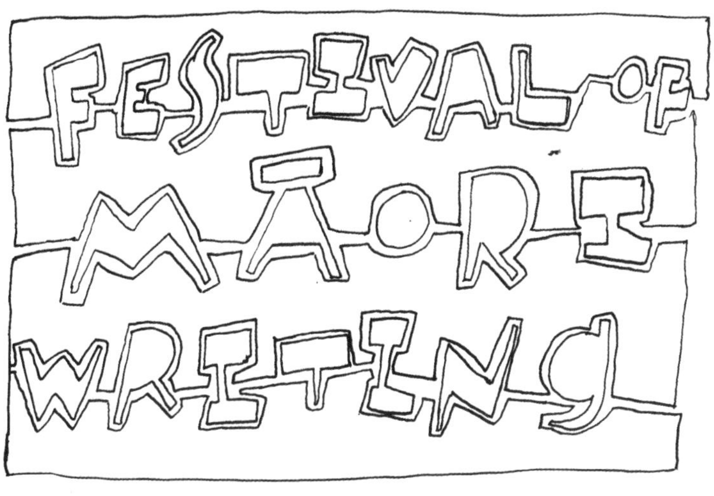

KRIS SOWERSBY

Ever since primary school, New Zealand designer Kris Sowersby has kept his sketchbook at the ready: "I have always felt compelled to draw and scribble notes to myself." It used to be for working out ideas: "At design school we had to hand them in as part of our assignments. When I started designing type, a sketchbook was for quickly drawing letters, to flesh out ideas or pin down a fleeting thought, like a butterfly collection. But these days it's mostly for phone numbers, lists, outlines – very mundane stuff."

His final typefaces bear little resemblance to his scribbles. "The sketches are quick roughs to see if a letterform will work or to nail a small detail," he notes. "I think that there is some sort of myth that by looking at someone's sketches you can see their 'thoughts' or 'processes,' that it reveals something essential to understanding their work." He challenges the viewer to see this insight, but Sowersby is understandably skeptical.

He currently keeps five books, primarily of type and typographical fragments. The ones excerpted here are from 2005–9.

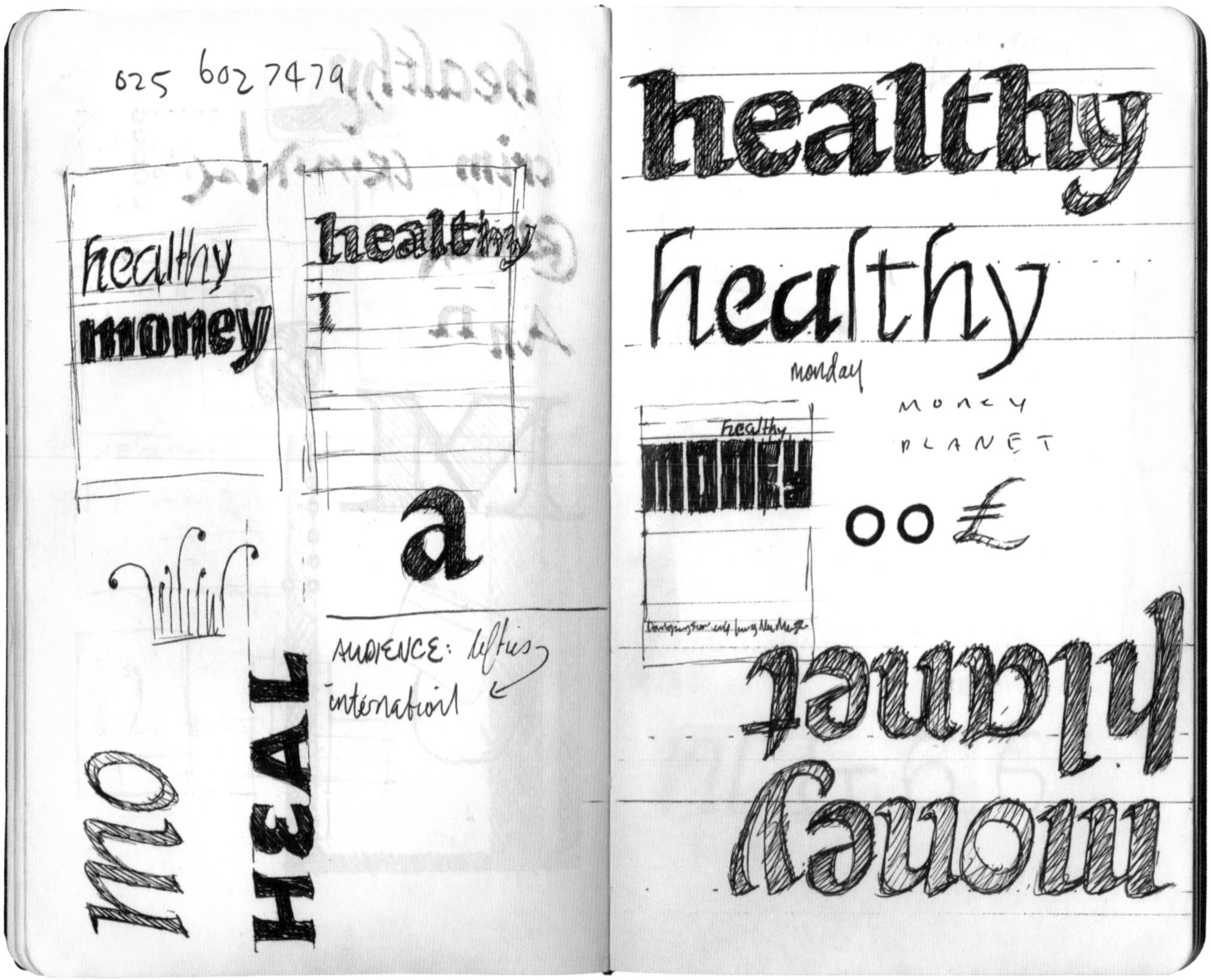
025 6027479
healthy
money
healthy
HEAL
AUDIENCE: lefties
international
healthy
healthy
monday
MONEY
PLANET
healthy
money

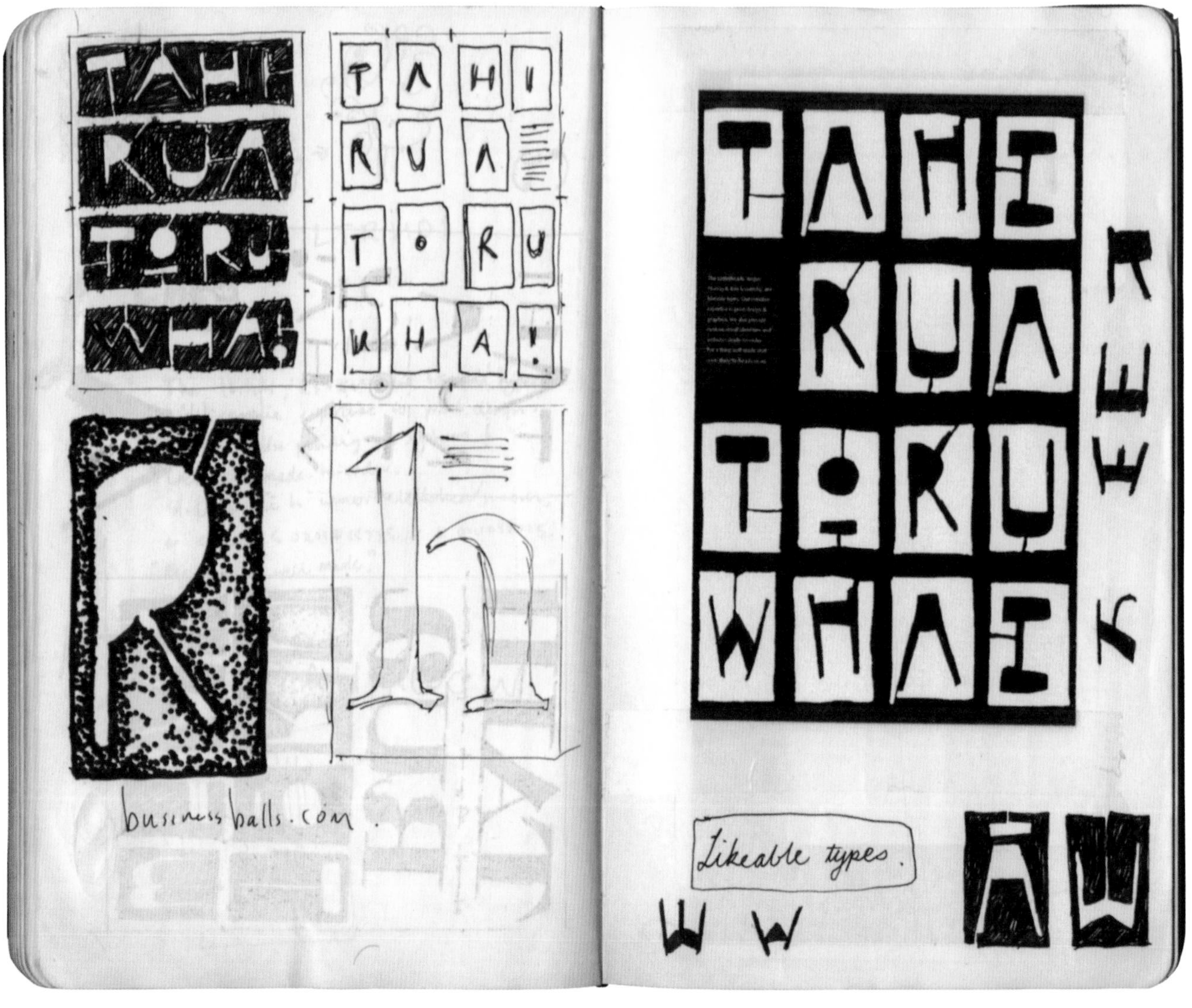
TAHI
RUA
TORU
WHA!
businessballs.com
TAHI
RUA
TORU
WHAI
Likeable types.

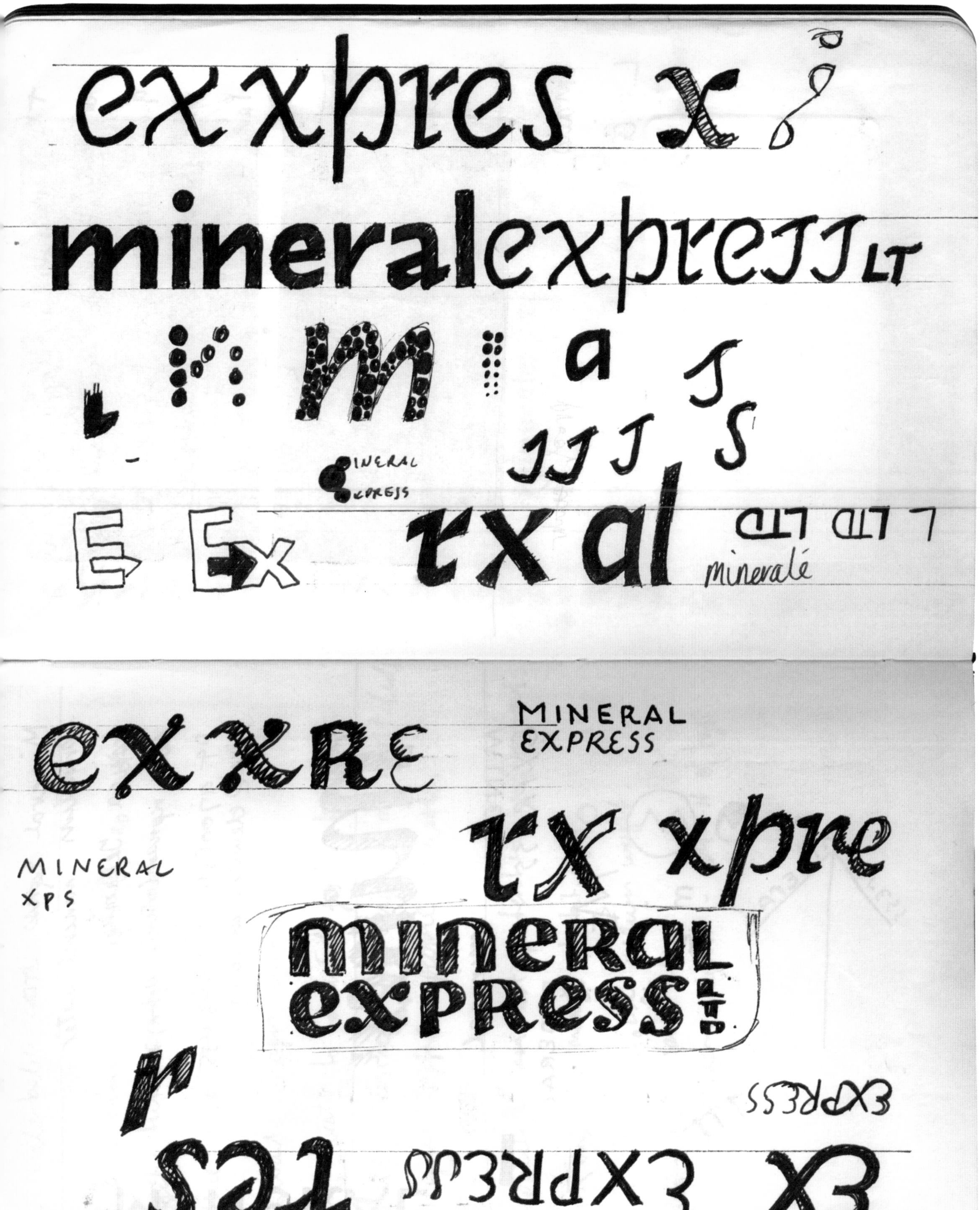
exxpres
mineralexpress LT
MINERAL
EXPRESS
minerale
MINERAL
EXPRESS
MINERAL
XPS
mineral
express
LTD

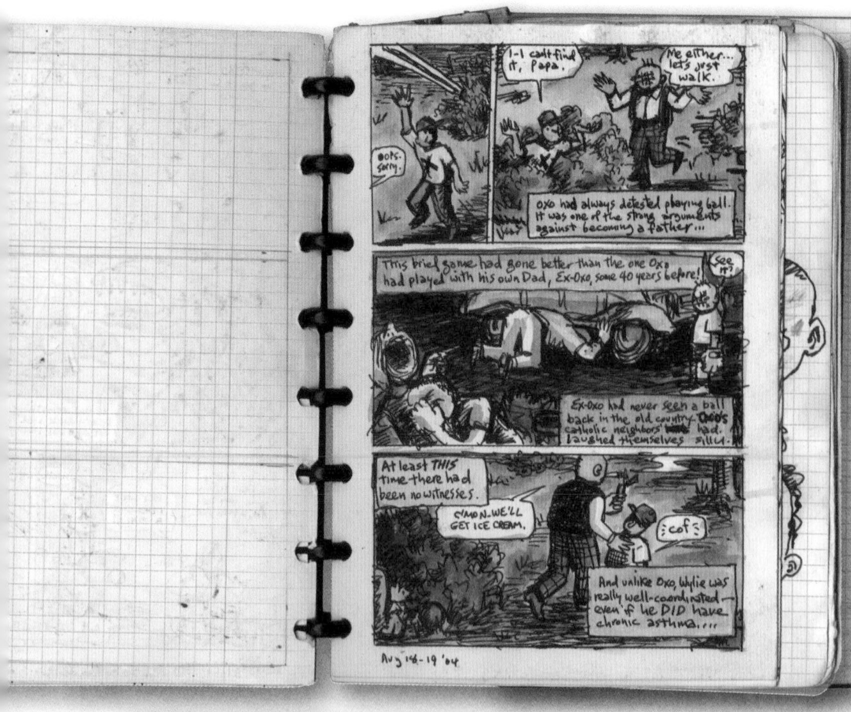

ART SPIEGELMAN

Art Spiegelman, the author of *Maus* and scholar of comics, has kept sketchbooks of one sort or another since the mid-1960s, "though often they are notebooks with as much or more prose and shopping lists as they are books of drawings." He admits he keeps them to "find out what I'm thinking," and "to complain without anyone interrupting."

They diverge from his comics because "in the finished work I redraw everything over and over, throttling it to within an inch of its life. These sketchbooks are mostly what Paul Klee referred to as 'taking a line for a walk,' with no planning or preliminary drafts. They have little to do with the final work, though they are often the seeds of what later become my comics."

The odd thing, admits Spiegelman, is that "I haven't torn them into shreds and discarded the images. There is an unseemly degree of self-absorption, alienation, and despair." He does not know how many books he has, but guesses "upwards of thirty over the years, though many, like the one here from 1992, can be only one or very few pages long before being abandoned. Lots is done on stray pieces of paper and kept in folders to avoid the inhibition I feel in front of any bound book."

Inventory of Fantasies, Fears, Dreams, Memories, Information, Notes, misinformation, Doodles and more. Taking Stock of what's in my head while preparing to file for Mental Bankruptcy and a great Depression~

6.11.
okay. At least PRETEND this is a piece of paper no one will ever see. You are being crushed by your own expectations and your projections of a Phantom Audience ready to disapprove or – worse, for someone of your neurotically insecure ilk – IGNORE you. The lurking fear that you're a washed-up has-been needs to be embraced. Maybe it can be a key to some sort of creative Liberation. FARGLE! FNAG! DIZOORAGGA! Yes. MIZZLEPIZZAWOKKA FUNNY PIGGAWOKKA. Penis. Penis. […] Random words random lines and how many typewriters have to be thrown at how many monkeys if one of them is ever to become Shakespeare. The sputtering […] brain […] addled by age and "cured" in tobacco, no longer capable of cohering. The Grand Themes are reduced to Fart jokes and self-absorbed depression. Of course self-loathing is just the pimple-infected, cellulite jiggling flip side of self-regard. From top to toe no stand-in for an actual heart. Keep the pen flowing til a revelation happens that that is valuable. (So did Charles Crumb reduce his writing to illegible scrawls as a way to avoid seeing his dark thoughts and unacceptable self fed back in a way that his […] could use as evidence condemning him to suicide???)
Down – Projected Audience eyeballs bombarding from one side; Projected Freudian censorious super-ego eyeballs bouncing in from the other til, finally one's own eyeballs roll up and show only the whites – unable to see or record anything.
Meanwhile – half-remembered: Hans Christian Andersen's The Ice Queen: Little Hans and little Greta in a […] childhood innocence love each other like Eden never stopped... but then the window Hans […] and a splinter of glass gets into Hans' eye. The glass splinter that keeps Hans from seeing Beauty or Goodness anymore, turns him toward the Ice Queen, a slave to the Death Mother.
(Woo. Got up to breathe a cigarette and look for myself on the internet and now back to our exercise: Keeping a pen moving to locate a self you can use. Where does the naive belief in Phoenix-like rising from one's own ashes into yet-another rebirth come from? Far older than the new testament Jesus resurrection stuff, the phoenix […] and probably as old as the religious impulse itself). Okay now move along, move along – there's nothing to see. Keep rolling this logorrhea off the pen tip... and for Christ's sake – Tell us a story. Once upon a time, little Tommy Hatchethead tried to pull the hatchet out of his head but the pain caused by jiggling the blade made him smart. He was bothered by the unsightly hatchet – made him look asymmetrical and repugnant to himself and others. Maybe a large cap could cover the axe enough to make him look more like everyone around him. And then, and then as he looked around he noticed – perhaps for the first time, or maybe it was something he noticed daily but forgot every day when he jiggled that ax-handle and renewed that innocence again... and he looked around at the crowds walking through the city around him and noticed they all wore large caps and they bulged in ways that made it seem probable that they all – every last one of 'em – had axe handles stickin out of their heads, bulging out of their caps. The End. No! Keep writing til you actually say something – or til you at least give up the illusion that you actually have anything to say!

"4.6 DWARVES (2.4 Dwarves laid off during economic downturn.)"
6.18.08
FIRE!
FOR GAS FIRES, PRESS ONE..
FOR ELECTRIC FIRES, PRESS TWO....
AND NOW FOR A SOOTHING MEDLEY OF VIVALDI HITS...
"Discussing a cable internet outage with TimeWarner."

4.7.07
HAT-MAN
ONCE A PLANET OF MEN IN HATS_CIGARETTE SMOKE SWIRLED AROUND THEM AND THEIR TRENCHCOATS HAD UP-TURNED COLLARS. WHA HOPPEN?
COKE
SURE, 'NEO-NOIR' IS FASHIONABLE BUT NOT THE LIDS WE ALL FLIPPED
AND TO TOP IT ALL OFF... FEDORAS HAVE BEEN REPLACED WITH CLOWN HATS!
OF COURSE, NOBODY MISSES THE HAT-GIRLS!
WHA HOPPEN? IT HAD SOMETHING TO DO WITH JFK!...
IT'S WHY THE HAT-MAKERS KILLED HIM

4.5.07 HORIZONTAL IN THE TRIBE OF THE VERTICALS DAYDREAMING ABOUT CURVY DIAGONALS...

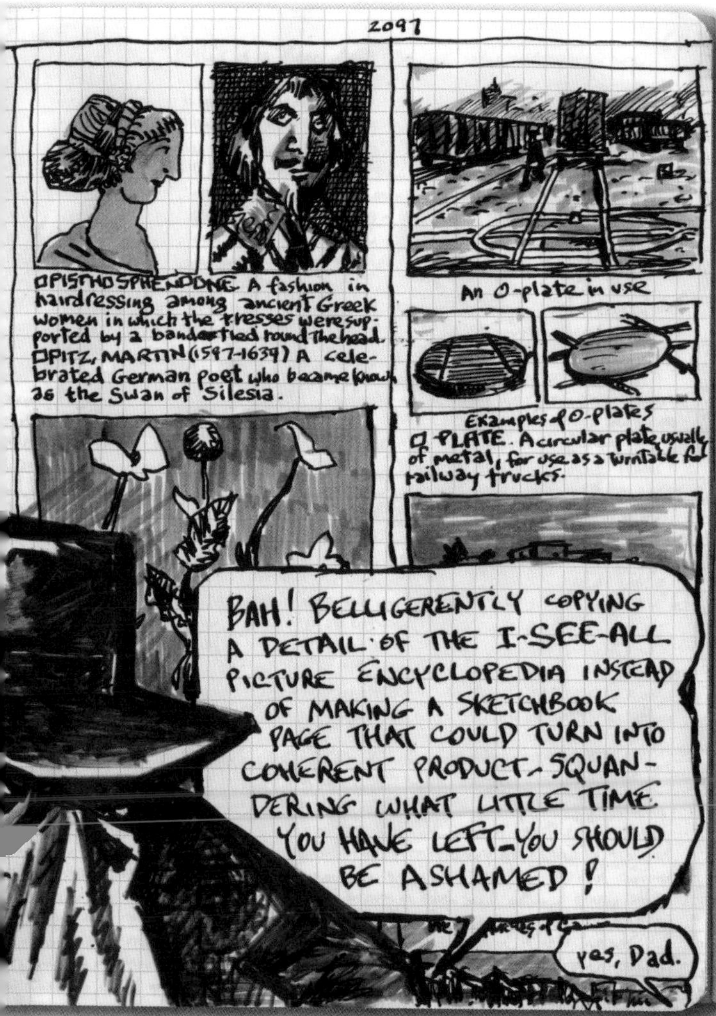
2097
OPISTHOSPHENDONE. A fashion in hairdressing among ancient Greek women in which the tresses were supported by a band or tied round the head.
OPITZ, MARTIN (1597-1639) A celebrated German poet who became known as the Swan of Silesia.
An O-plate in use
Examples of O-plates
O-PLATE. A circular plate usually of metal, for use as a turntable for railway trucks.
BAH! BELLIGERENTLY COPYING A DETAIL OF THE I-SEE-ALL PICTURE ENCYCLOPEDIA INSTEAD OF MAKING A SKETCHBOOK PAGE THAT COULD TURN INTO COHERENT PRODUCT- SQUANDERING WHAT LITTLE TIME YOU HAVE LEFT- YOU SHOULD BE ASHAMED!
yes, Dad.

DEATH THREATS
DAMN PREDATORS. THE @*!#% MAILBOX IS FULL AGAIN!
SO... LET'S FUCK!
6.15
6.16
AAH. BYOOTIFUL.. BYOOTIFUL...
WHATTH-?
DANG-I FORGOT!..
PAF!
IT SIMPLY AIN'T SAFE TO APPRECIATE SOMETHING, TO TAKE PLEASURE IN IT... SEEMS TO MAKE IT MORE LIKELY TO DISAPPEAR!
CANTCHA QUIT COMPLAINING ABOUT EVERY LITTLE THING?!!
HUH?
YOU KIDDING? I FIGGER IF I MAKE ENOUGH RUCKUS ABOUT THE LITTLE STUFF, THEY WOULDN'T DARE SEND ANY REALLY BAD STUFF MY WAY!

3-15-07

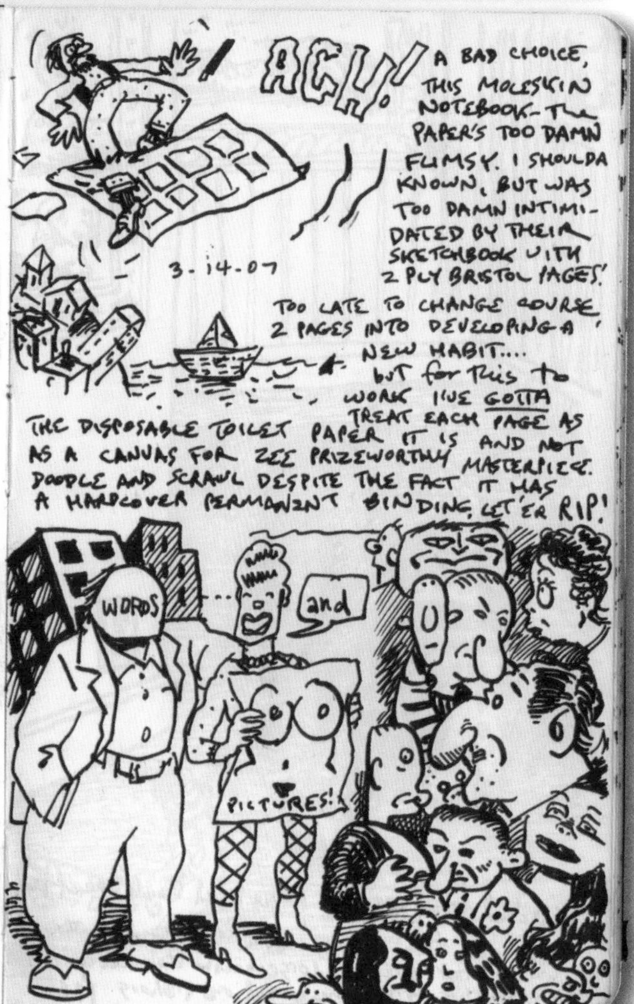
ACH!
A BAD CHOICE, THIS MOLESKIN NOTEBOOK- THE PAPER'S TOO DAMN FLIMSY. I SHOULDA KNOWN, BUT WAS TOO DAMN INTIMIDATED BY THEIR SKETCHBOOK WITH 2 PLY BRISTOL PAGES!
3-14-07
TOO LATE TO CHANGE COURSE, 2 PAGES INTO DEVELOPING A NEW HABIT.... but for this to work I'VE GOTTA TREAT EACH PAGE AS THE DISPOSABLE TOILET PAPER IT IS AND NOT AS A CANVAS FOR ZEE PRIZEWORTHY MASTERPIECE. DOODLE AND SCRAWL DESPITE THE FACT IT HAS A HARDCOVER PERMANENT BINDING. LET 'ER RIP!
WORDS
and
PICTURES!

RAW!
SALVAGED DOODLE 5-2-83
OFTEN

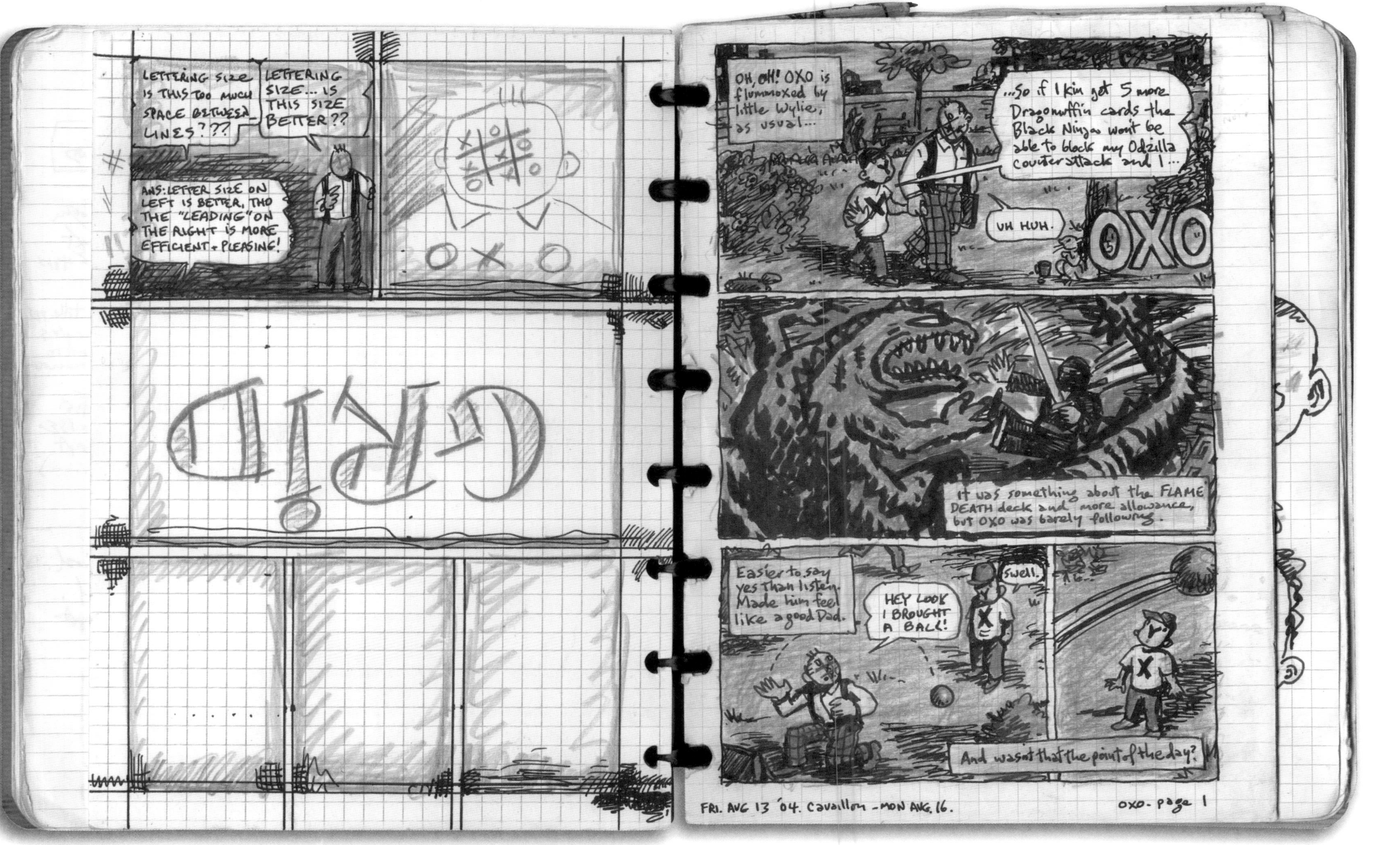
LETTERING SIZE IS THIS TOO MUCH SPACE BETWEEN LINES???
LETTERING SIZE... IS THIS SIZE BETTER??
ANS: LETTER SIZE ON LEFT IS BETTER, THO THE "LEADING" ON THE RIGHT IS MORE EFFICIENT + PLEASING!
GRID
OH, OH! OXO is flummoxed by little Wylie, as usual...
...So if I kin get 5 more Dragonmuffin cards the Black Ninja won't be able to block my Odzilla counterattack and I...
UH HUH.
OXO
It was something about the FLAME DEATH deck and more allowance, but OXO was barely following.
Easier to say yes than listen. Made him feel like a good Dad.
HEY LOOK I BROUGHT A BALL!
SWELL.
And wasn't that the point of the day?
FRI. AUG 13 '04. Cavaillon - MON AUG. 16.
OXO - page 1

BARRON STOREY

San Francisco-based comics artist and illustrator Barron Storey began his journals in 1976: "A high-water mark for my professional illustration career – and a disaster for my personal life. Inspired by the journals of my teacher, Robert Weaver, I turned to them to try to make sense out of what was happening." Storey uses his journals to "enhance observation, to get in touch with thought, to 'examine a life,' to develop skills suited to the capturing of experience – especially that which is subtle, multi-layered, ambivalent or paradoxical. (In a word, difficult to understand.) They have always been an attempt to find out what is true." He adds that he is "preoccupied with capturing experience. The books do not represent a conscious attempt to 'make art.' I love and revere all art and I study all art, but my interest is primarily in how it suggests the capturing of experience."

Some of his 160 journals are themed, "usually around a project that is prominent in my life at the time. For example, when I'm working on a play – my work on *Julius Caesar* led to 'Stories About Money.' Others are dedicated to long-running illustration assignments, such as the 'Rainforest Journal.' Most, however, are just records of my experience and thoughts. In fact, the themed ones often use external contexts as lenses to examine personal experience as well."

12
Here was a sees-you. Whence comes such another?
fin.
12

II.
HATE-FULL
A STORY of REVENGE
Over thy wounds, now, do I prophecy, which like dumb mouths, do ope their ruby lips to beg the the voice and utterance of my tongue:
A curse shall light upon the limbs of men. Domestic fury and fierce cival strife shall cover all the parts of Italy. Blood and destuction shall be so in use and dreadful objects so familiar that mothers shall but smile when they behold their infants quartered with the hands of war, all pity choked with custom of fell deed.
Had I as many eyes as thou has wounds, weeping as fast as they stream forth thy blood, it would become me better than to close in terms of friendship with thine enemies.
Spirit, come hot from Hell, cry Havoc!
13

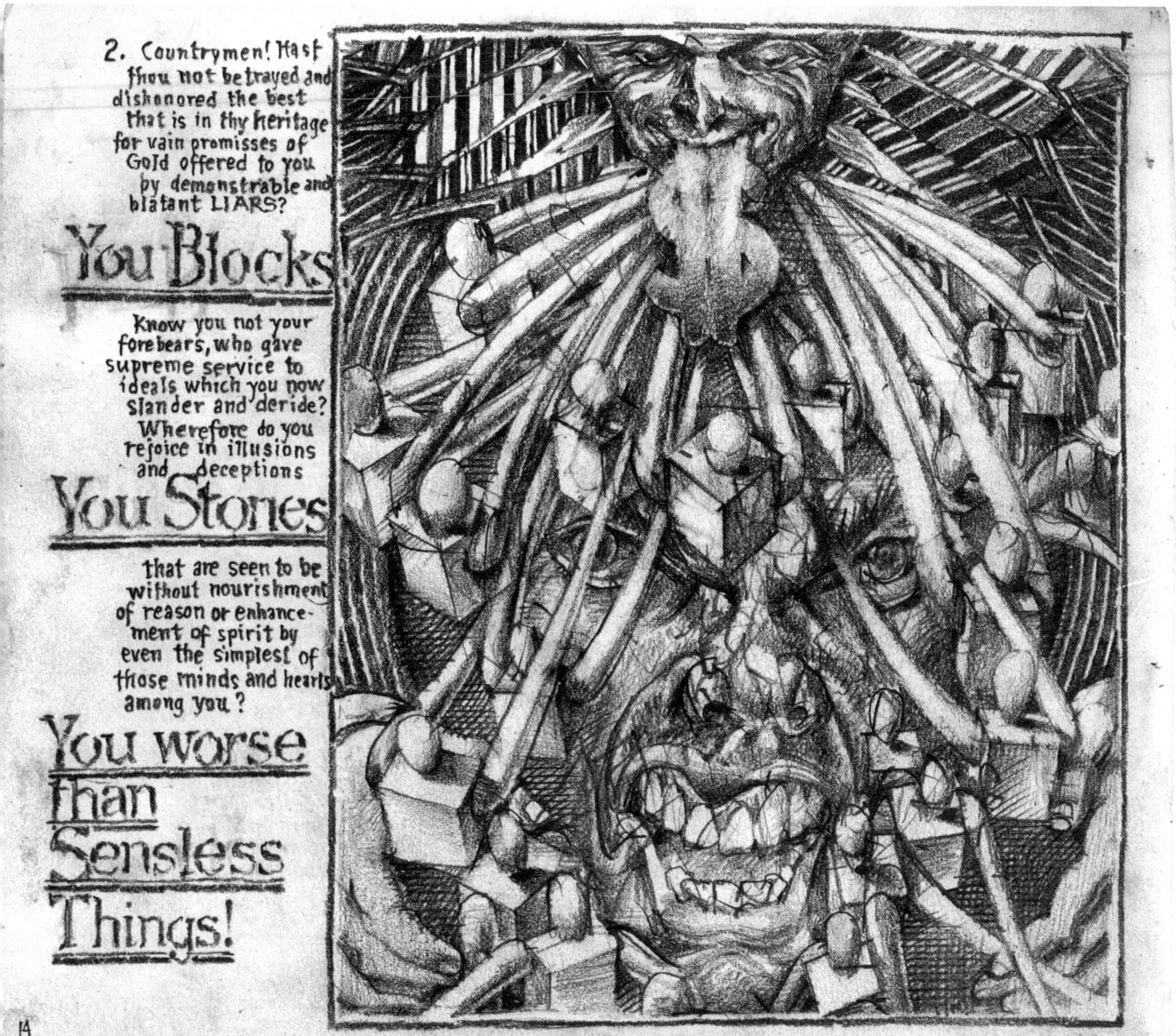
2. Countrymen! Hast thou not betrayed and dishonored the best that is in thy heritage for vain promisses of Gold offered to you by demonstrable and blatant LIARS?
You Blocks
Know you not your forebears, who gave supreme service to ideals which you now slander and deride? Wherefore do you rejoice in illusions and deceptions
You Stones
that are seen to be without nourishment of reason or enhancement of spirit by even the simplest of those minds and hearts among you?
You worse than Sensless Things!
14.

Thy worthless imaginings are all deceptions, such as thou would'st take as omens of good fortune to be are but the bait and lure to thy desperate soul– No path to salvation is indicated by them, fool!
YOU GON' BURN DUDE
THE LION STARTS TACKING STREET JIVE. IS THIS CALPURNIA'S PREMONITION OR IS IT MINE?
51.

Von Cassius... thinks too much.

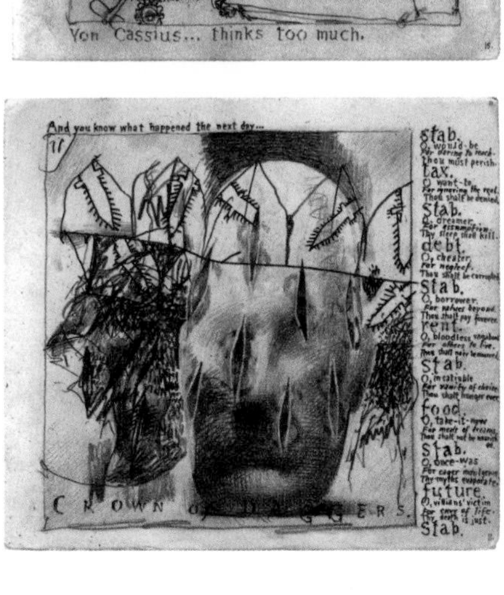
And you know what happened the next day...
CROWN OF DAGGERS.

A lioness hath whelped in the streets.
Graves have yawned and yeilded up their dead.
Fierce, fiery warriors fought upon the clouds.
Horses did neigh and dying men did groan
And ghosts did squeal and shriek about the streets
These things are beyond all use,
And I do fear them.
52

End of Part Four.

14. The paranoia that followed

36. The Dead Enjoying Music

People sleeping on the streets. Pimps and
prostitutes everywhere. Big slick cars
driving in to pick up the women. Angry,
hungry people
to whom begging
is shame and crime
is a given condition of life. It's
hell. My fear... is this the way
poor people feel all the time? It
can't have always
been this bad.
Isn't this shit the
result of... of.....
The end of Part Eight.

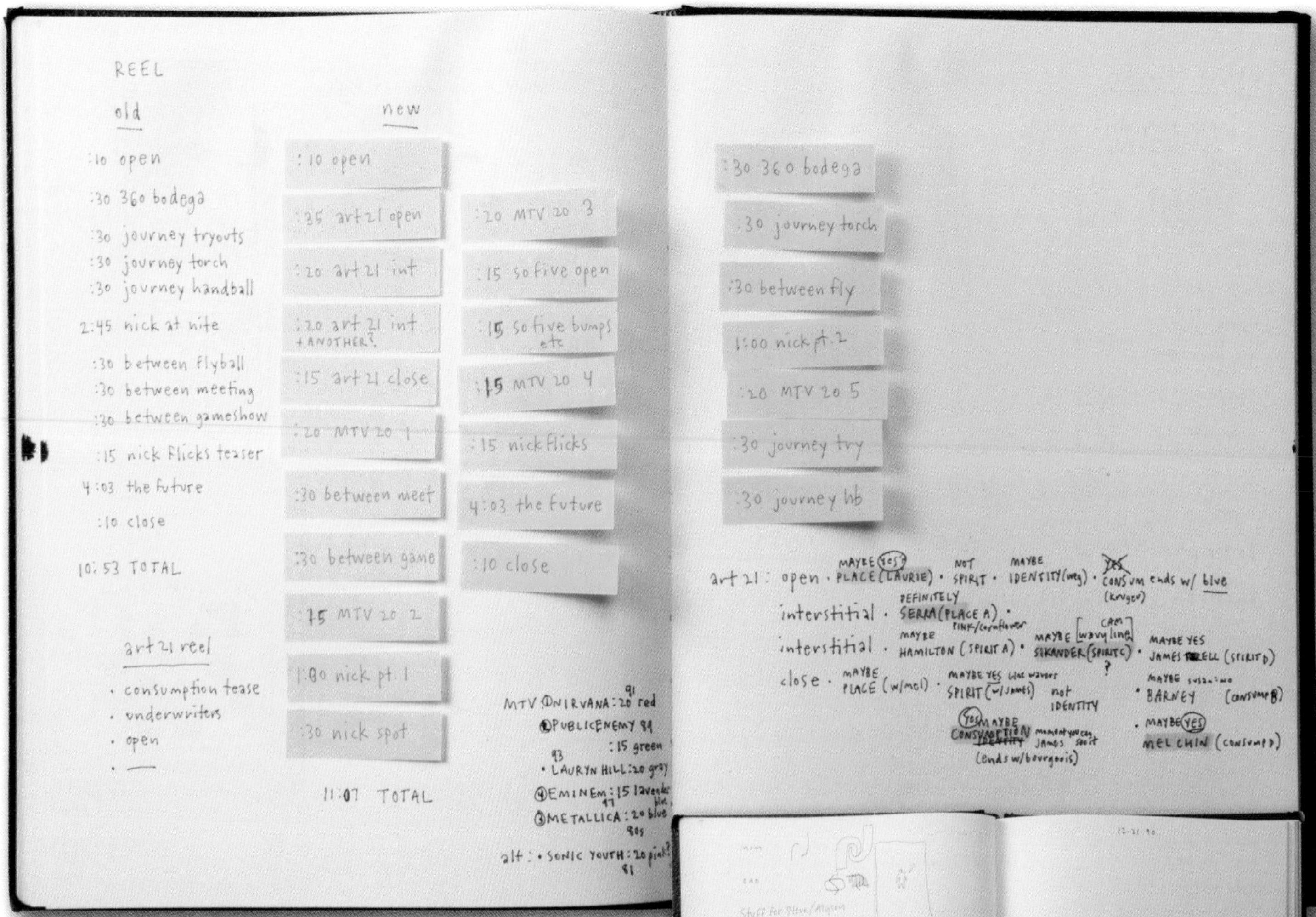

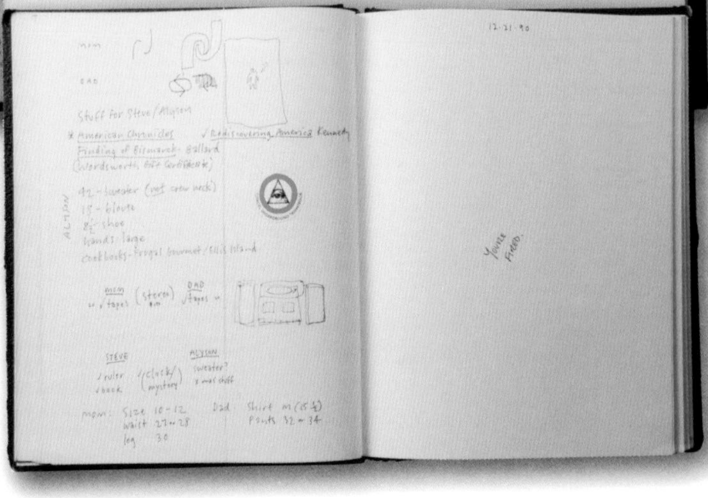

SCOTT STOWELL

Scott Stowell, whose New York firm Open is recognized for its expertise in accessible information design, got his first sketchbook twenty-three years ago, when a teacher at Rhode Island School of Design told him it would be key to everything he would subsequently do. "Since then," he confides, "my sketchbooks are for everything: ideas, notes, to-do lists, drawings, quotations, reminders, and occasional artifacts, like clippings, gum wrappers, etc."

Stowell, whose work is known for its modernist clarity cut with contemporary wit, admits, "I almost never use handmade elements in my work, but nearly everything in these books is handmade." He insists that "drawing makes a big difference – even if you can't see it in the final product."

These books are the quintessence of orderliness, and for Stowell there is nothing unusual about them. "They just look like what my life was about at a certain time. Today's pages look like today." He has approximately twenty books and "on average I go through one a year, but that varies. Good times fill more pages. The opposite is also true – sometimes one book lasts for a few years."

In one of his sketchbooks, Tibor Kalman, for whom he worked in the late 1990s, wrote during a client meeting: "You're fired." Needless to say, he kept that page.

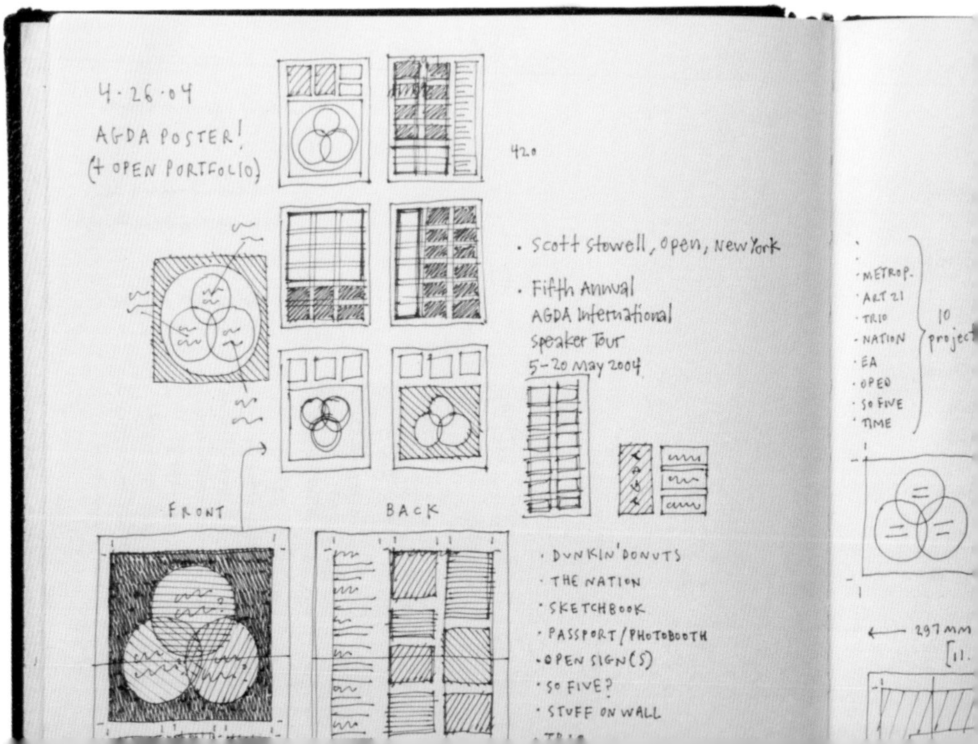

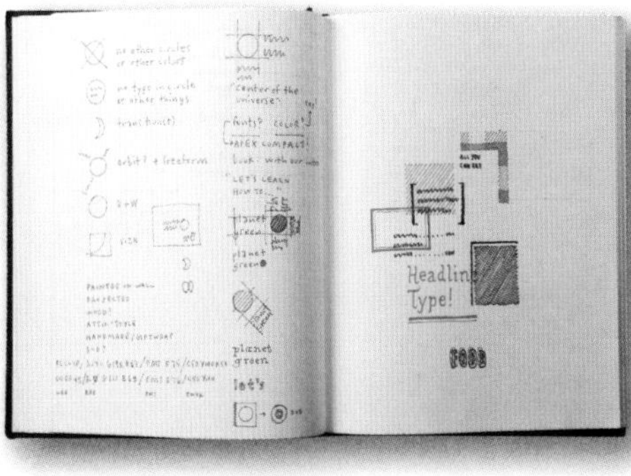

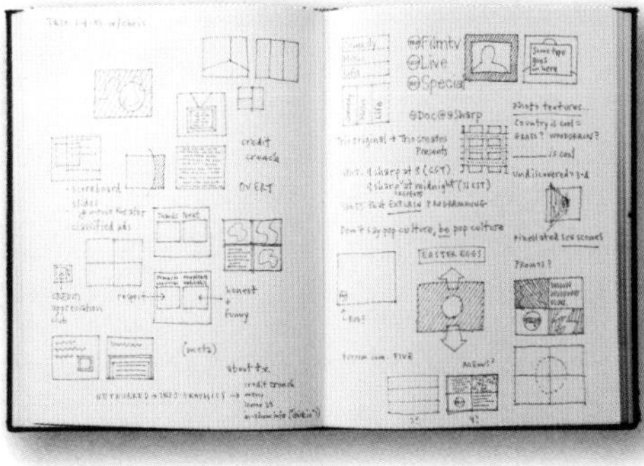

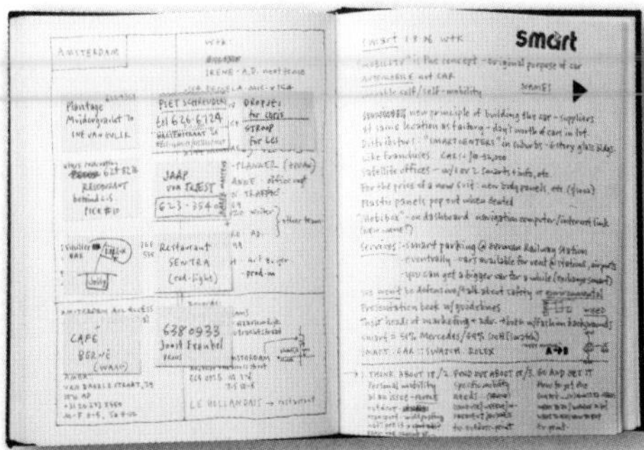

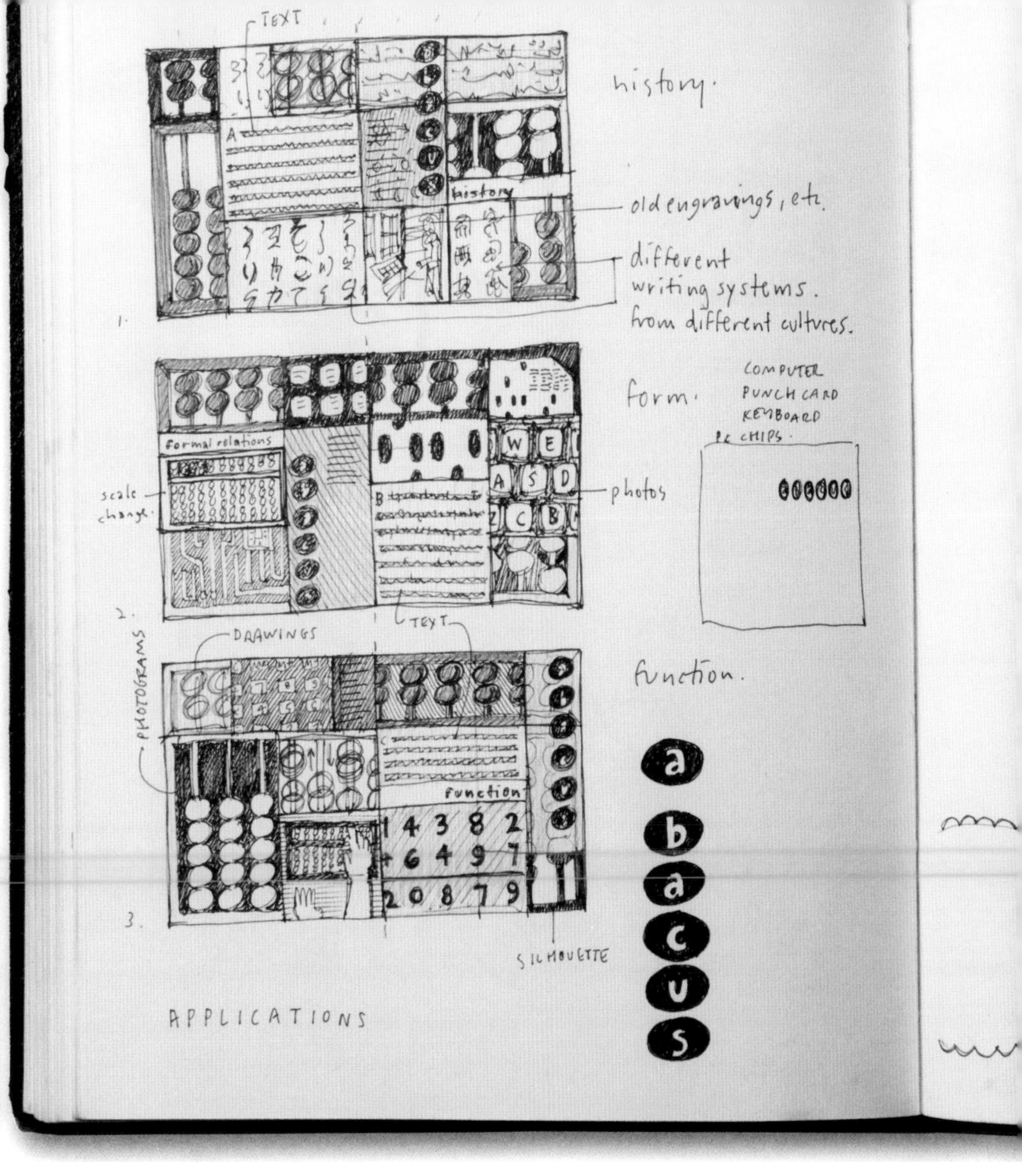
TEXT
history.
old engravings, etc.
different writing systems. from different cultures.
1.
form.
COMPUTER
PUNCH CARD
KEYBOARD
IC CHIPS.
formal relations
scale change
photos
TEXT
2.
DRAWINGS
PHOTOGRAMS
function.
function
3.
SILHOUETTE
a
b
a
c
u
s
APPLICATIONS

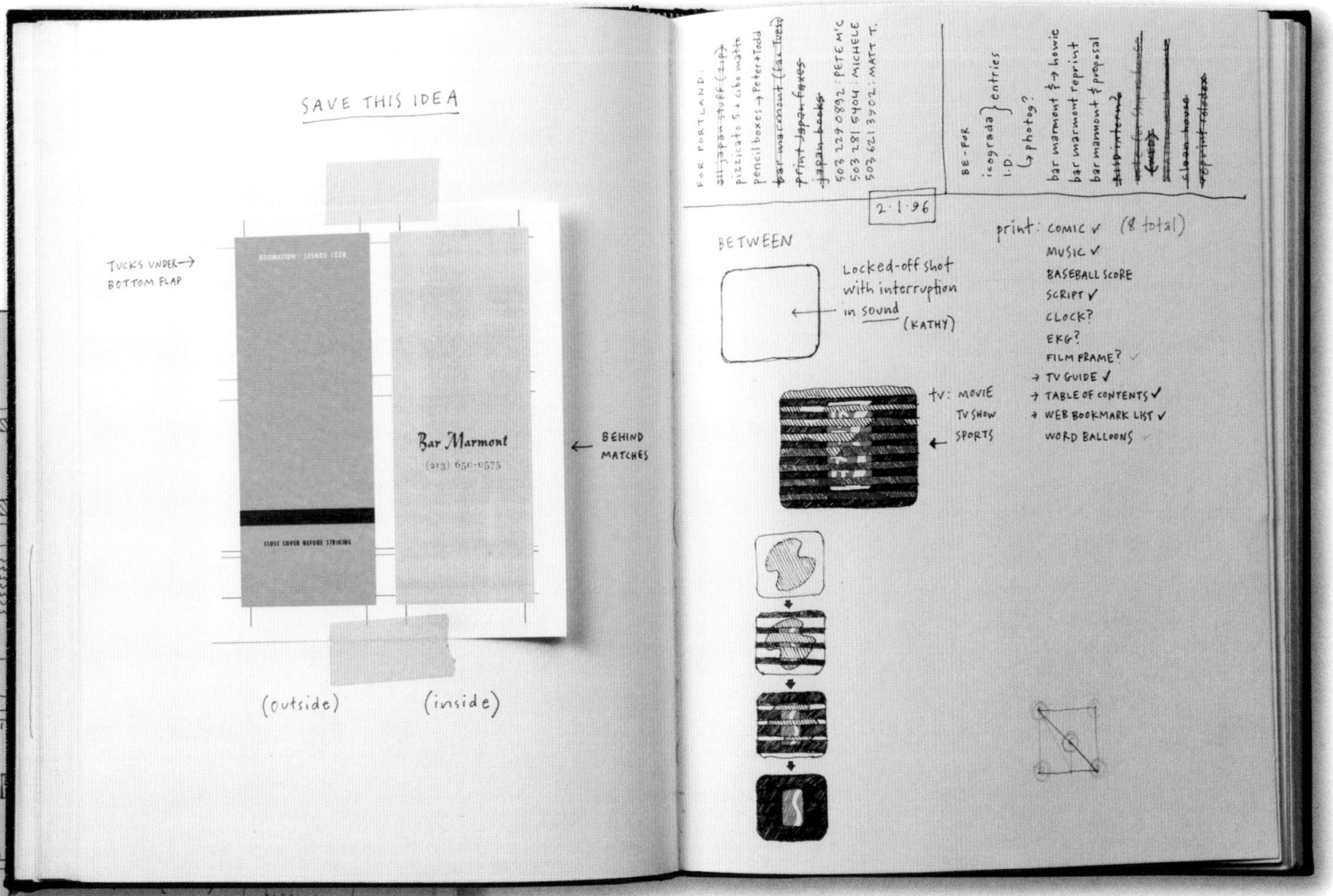
SAVE THIS IDEA
TUCKS UNDER→
BOTTOM FLAP
CLOSE COVER BEFORE STRIKING
Bar Marmont
(213) 650-0575
BEHIND MATCHES
(outside)
(inside)
2·1·96
BETWEEN
Locked-off shot with interruption in sound (KATHY)
tv: MOVIE
TV SHOW
SPORTS
print: COMIC ✓ (8 total)
MUSIC ✓
BASEBALL SCORE
SCRIPT ✓
CLOCK?
EKG?
FILM FRAME?
→ TV GUIDE ✓
→ TABLE OF CONTENTS ✓
→ WEB BOOKMARK LIST ✓
WORD BALLOONS

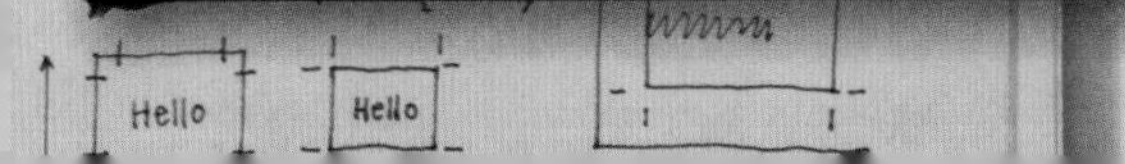
Hello
Hello

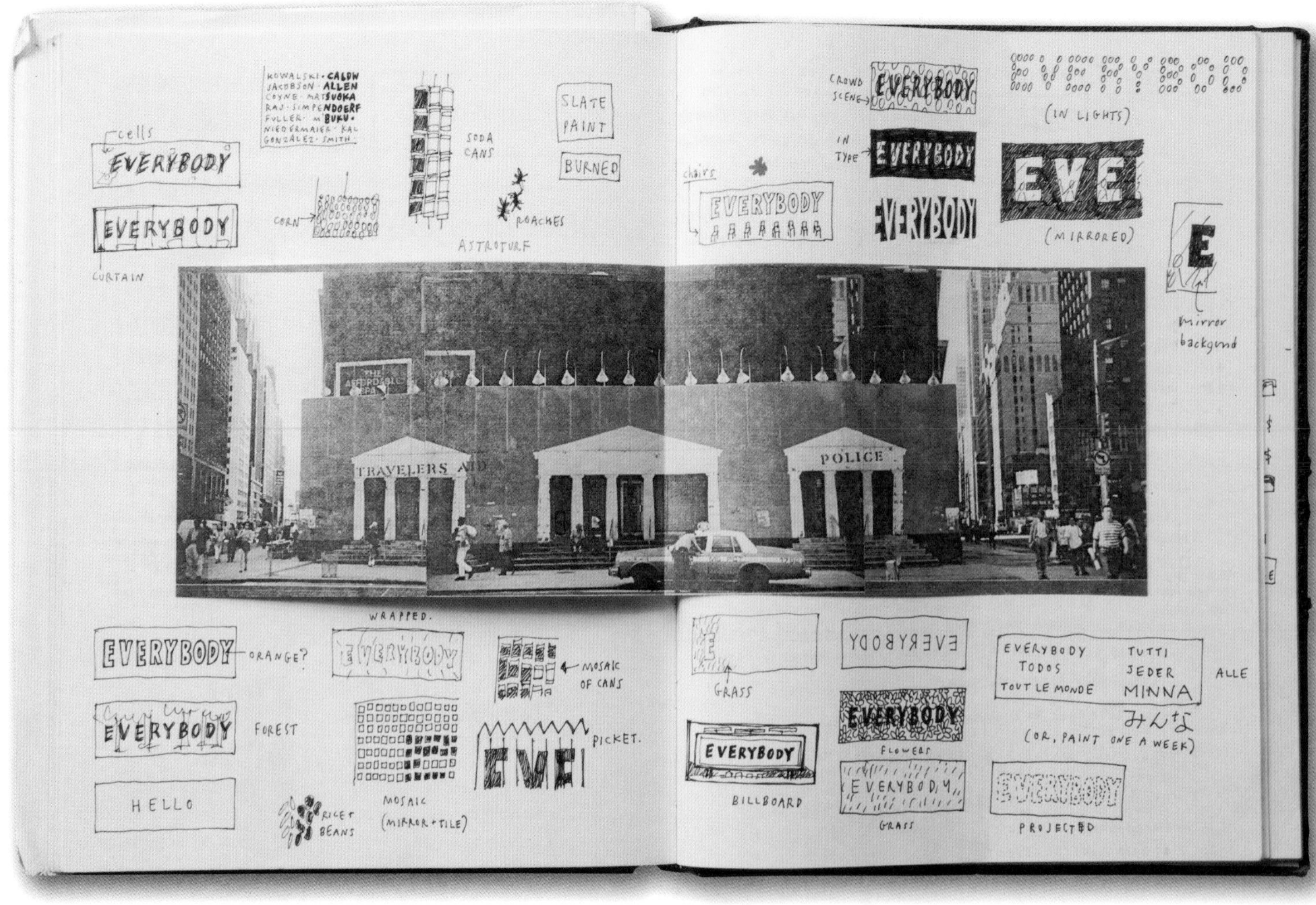
cells
EVERYBODY
EVERYBODY
CURTAIN
KOWALSKI · CALDW
JACOBSON · ALLEN
CORN
SODA CANS
ROACHES
ASTROTURF
SLATE PAINT
BURNED
CROWD SCENE
EVERYBODY
IN TYPE
EVERYBODY
(IN LIGHTS)
chairs
EVERYBODY
EVE
(MIRRORED)
E
Mirror backgrnd
TRAVELERS AID
POLICE
WRAPPED.
EVERYBODY
ORANGE?
MOSAIC OF CANS
FOREST
PICKET.
HELLO
RICE + BEANS
MOSAIC (MIRROR + TILE)
GRASS
EVERYBODY
BILLBOARD
FLOWERS
GRASS
EVERYBODY TODOS TOUT LE MONDE
TUTTI JEDER MINNA
ALLE
みんな
(OR, PAINT ONE A WEEK)
PROJECTED

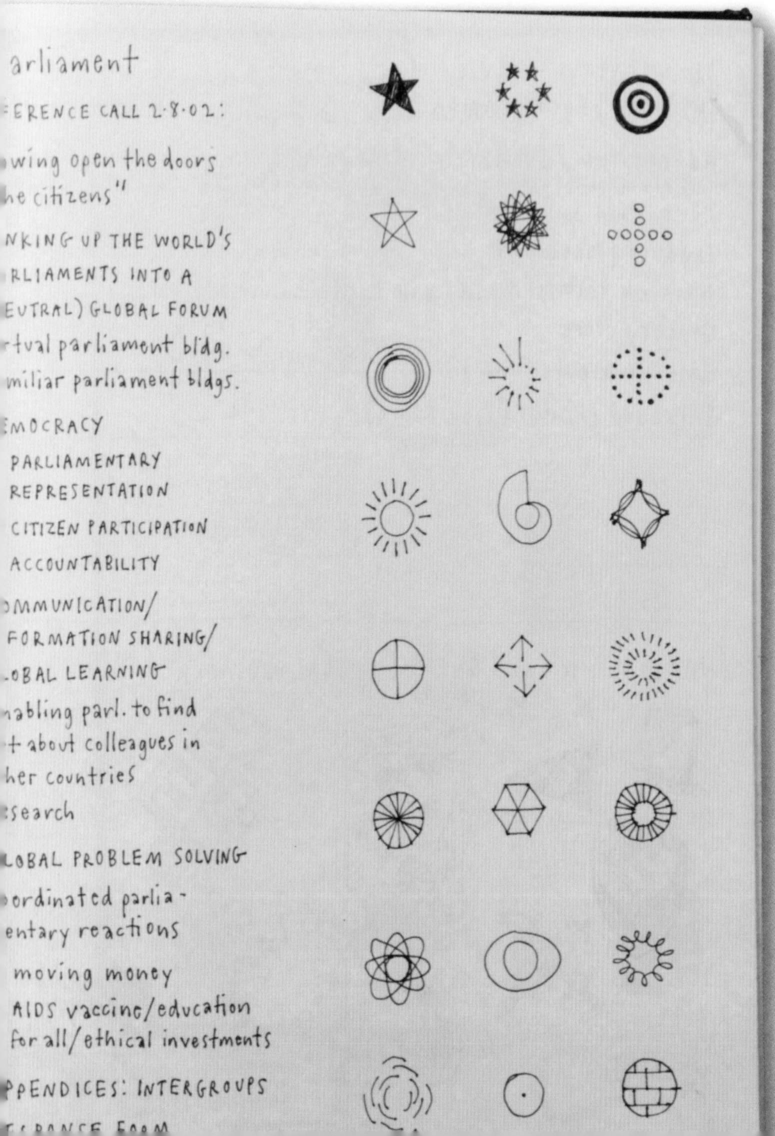
arliament
ERENCE CALL 2·8·02:
wing open the doors
he citizens"
NKING UP THE WORLD'S
RLIAMENTS INTO A
EUTRAL) GLOBAL FORUM
rtual parliament bldg.
miliar parliament bldgs.
EMOCRACY
PARLIAMENTARY REPRESENTATION
CITIZEN PARTICIPATION
ACCOUNTABILITY
OMMUNICATION/
FORMATION SHARING/
OBAL LEARNING
nabling parl. to find
t about colleagues in
her countries
esearch
OBAL PROBLEM SOLVING
oordinated parlia-
entary reactions
moving money
AIDS vaccine/education
for all/ethical investments
PPENDICES: INTERGROUPS

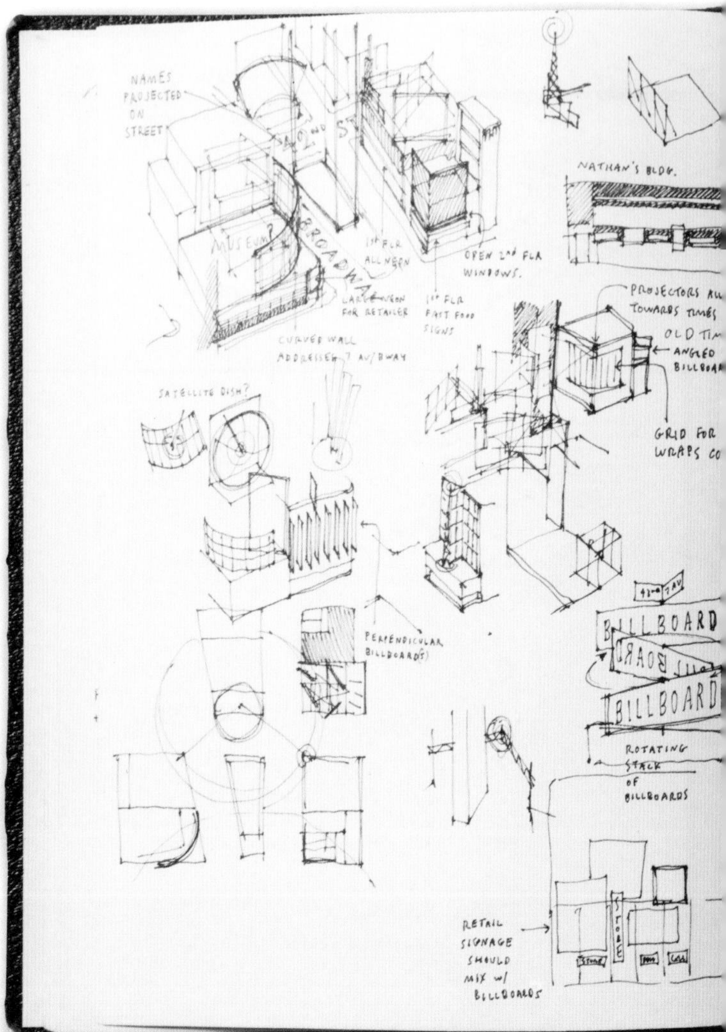
NAMES PROJECTED ON STREET
MUSEUM
BROADWAY
OPEN 2nd FLR WINDOWS.
NATHAN'S BLDG.
PROJECTORS A
CURVED WALL
SATELLITE DISH?
GRID FOR WRAPS
PERPENDICULAR BILLBOARDS
BILLBOARD
BILLBOARD
ROTATING STACK OF BILLBOARDS
RETAIL SIGNAGE SHOULD MIX W/ BILLBOARDS

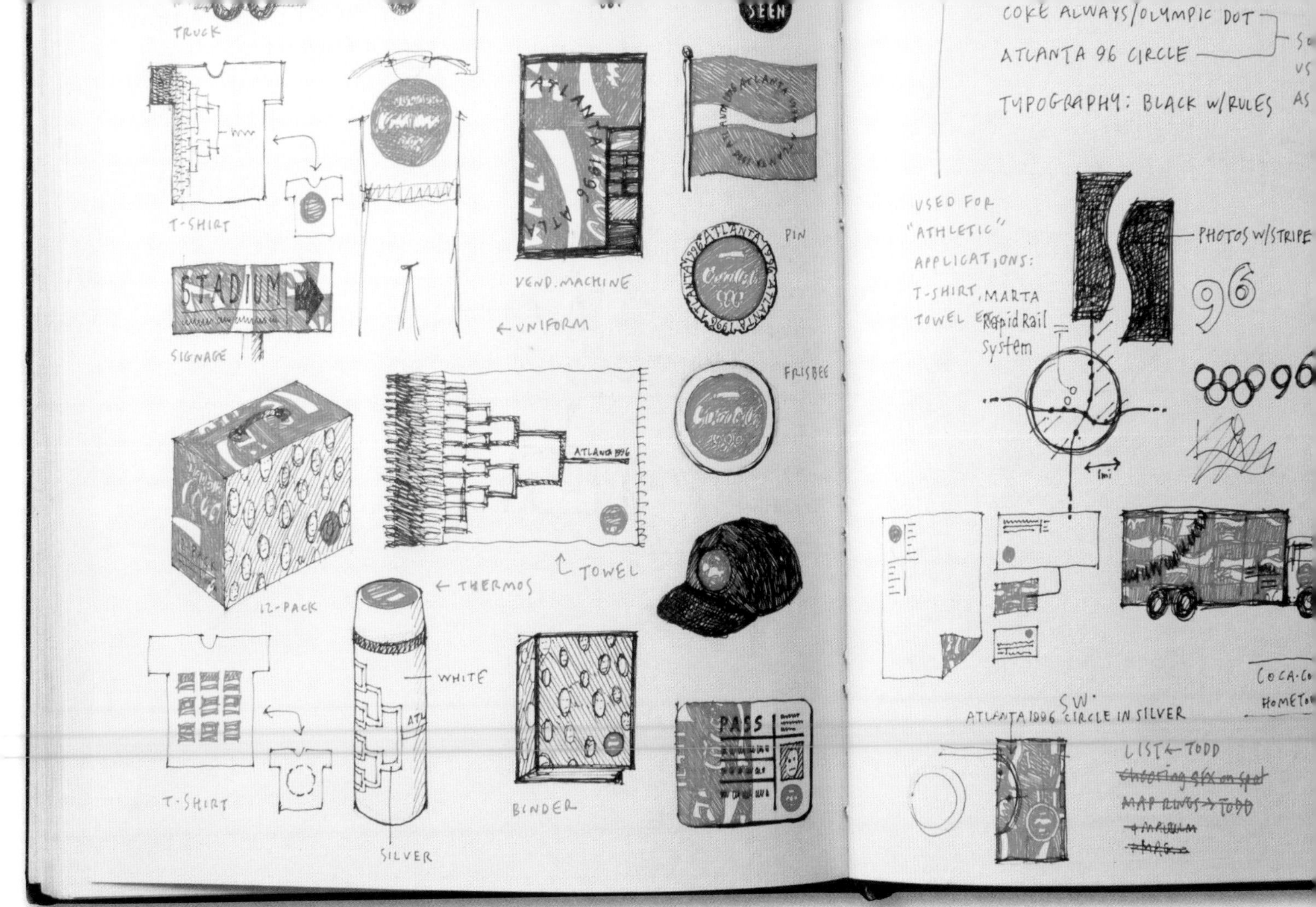
TRUCK
T-SHIRT
SIGNAGE
STADIUM
VEND. MACHINE
← UNIFORM
PIN
FRISBEE
ATLANTA 1996
TOWEL
← THERMOS
12-PACK
WHITE
SILVER
T-SHIRT
BINDER
PASS
COKE ALWAYS/OLYMPIC DOT
ATLANTA 96 CIRCLE
TYPOGRAPHY: BLACK W/RULES
USED FOR "ATHLETIC" APPLICATIONS:
T-SHIRT, TOWEL
MARTA Rapid Rail System
PHOTOS W/STRIPE
96
ATLANTA 1996 CIRCLE IN SILVER
LIST → TODD

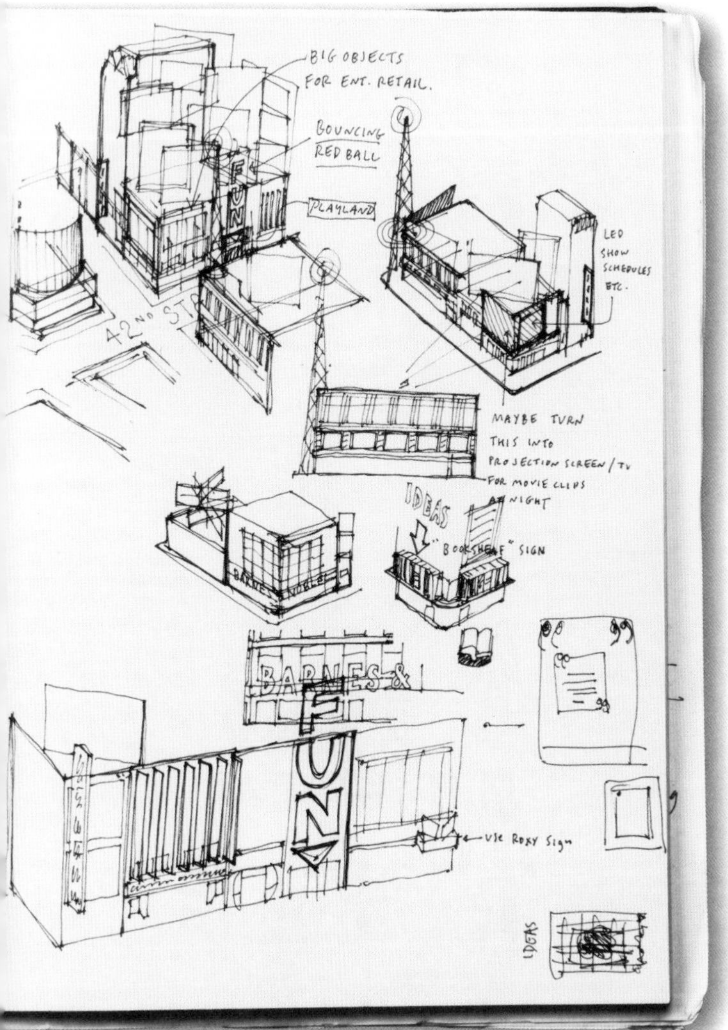
BIG OBJECTS FOR ENT. RETAIL.
BOUNCING RED BALL
PLAYLAND
LED SHOW SCHEDULES ETC.
42ND ST
MAYBE TURN THIS INTO PROJECTION SCREEN / TV FOR MOVIE CLIPS AT NIGHT
IDEAS
"BOOKSHELF" SIGN
BARNES &
FUN
USE ROXY SIGN

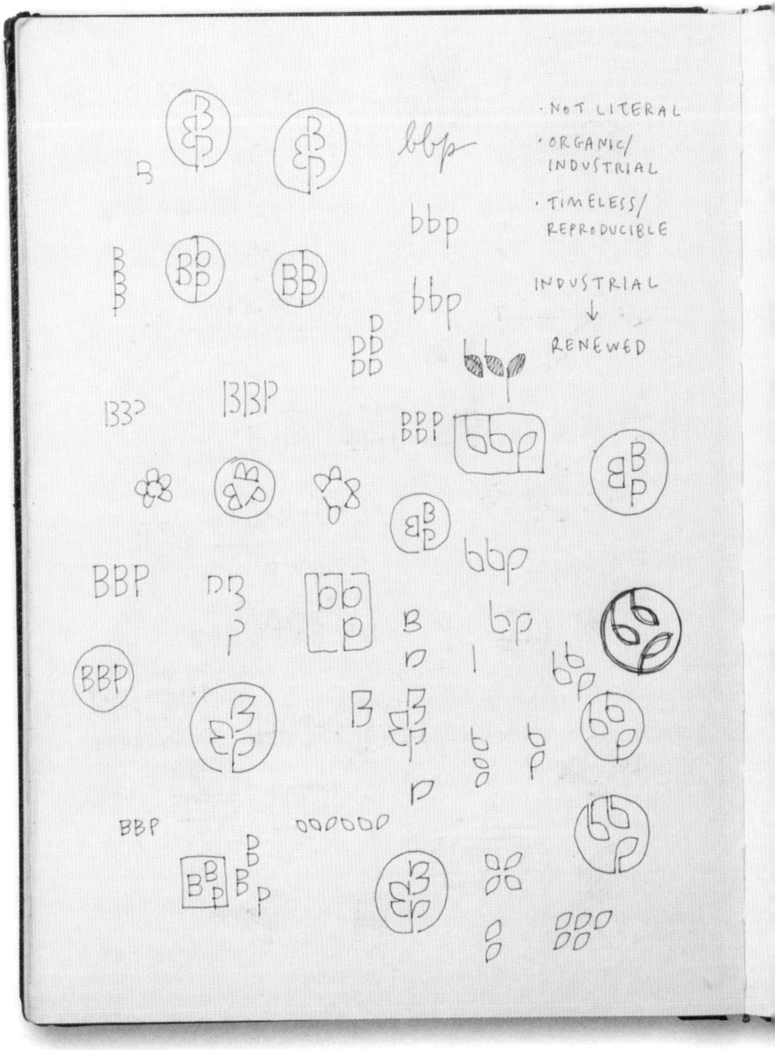
· NOT LITERAL
· ORGANIC/ INDUSTRIAL
· TIMELESS/ REPRODUCIBLE
INDUSTRIAL
↓
RENEWED
bbp
BBP

ISTVÁN SZUGYICZKY

István Szugyiczky, a designer from Budapest, Hungary, "always had sketchbooks, in fact several at the same time. They serve a very functional role, albeit a pleasurable one."

"The purpose of sketches for me, first of all, is not to forget an idea, and to have something to run after since the sketches often have better composition than the final image," he says with a kind of remorse, as if wondering why all work cannot be as fresh.

His sketches, of course, have an appearance of unfinished-ness and spontaneity. "There is a certain kind of rawness, and they have the ability to take me back to the very moment I drew them," he adds, and "there is no inherent theme as the sketches are mostly 'born' from sudden ideas."

Szugyiczky may work on multiple sketchbooks at the same time, but the books are not his only form of liberation. "I also draw on a lot of different papers from everywhere," he admits. The books shown here were made in 2008–9.

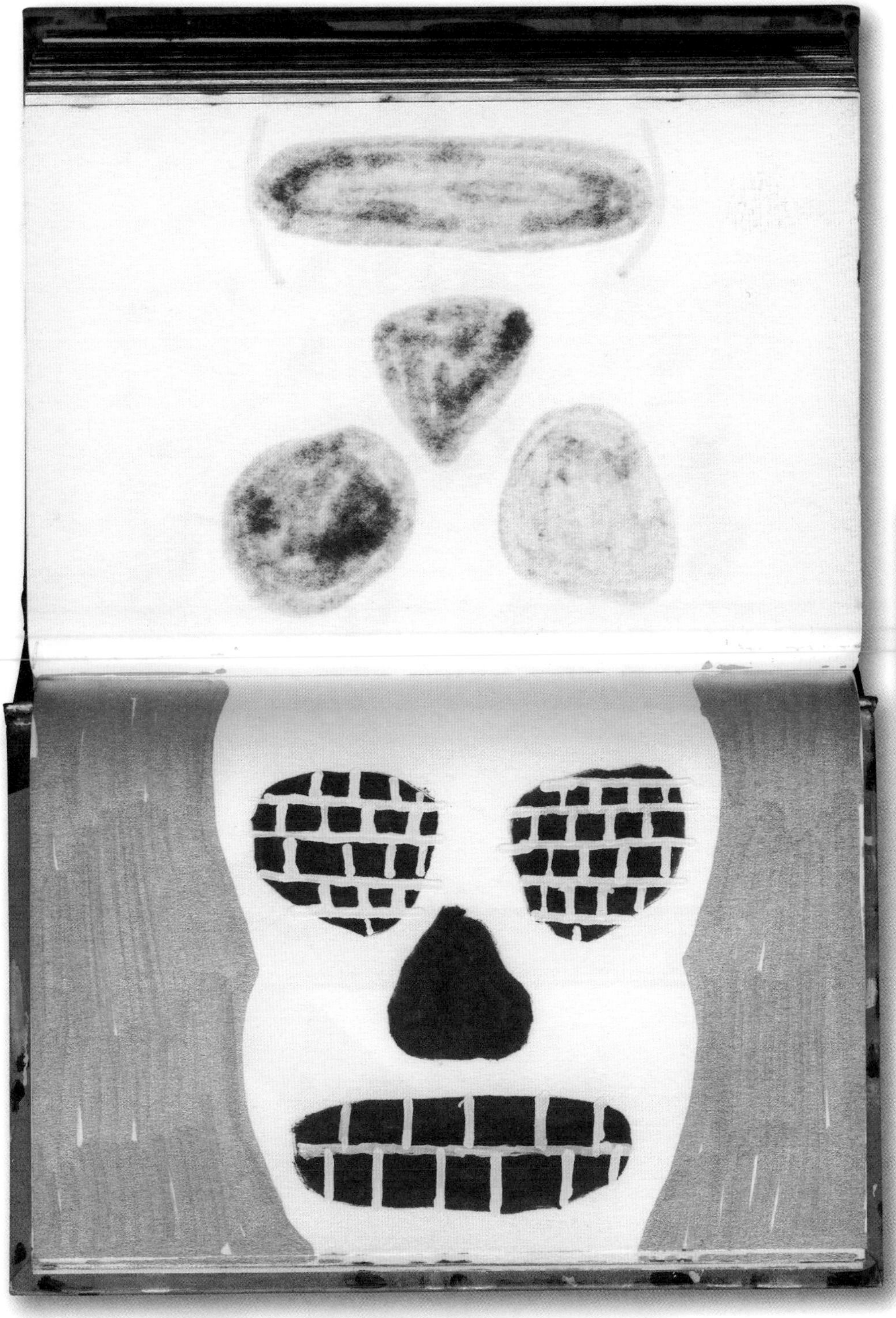

DAVID TARTAKOVER

Israeli designer and poster artist David Tartakover has given his sketchbooks a name: the "black books." He started in the mid-1970s, and confidently states: "I'll continue working on them as long as I'm able." Other than a few deviations, he has retained the same A4 format. Each is dated and arranged by the Hebrew order, progressing from right to left. "I keep them in chronological order in a bookcase," he proudly notes.

"The black books sit on the interface between a diary, an artist's book, a sketchbook and a scrapbook. They are a seismograph of my private and political everyday, canceling the distinction between them. As a totality the black books are a succession of responses and initiatives, plans and executions, and they contain the lexicon of images, forms, figures, and ideas that I'm engaged with, for almost four decades." These sketches were all done on the same day in May 2002, during the Israeli Defense Force operation in the West Bank, which started after a wave of suicide bombings in the heart of the big cities in Israel: Tel Aviv, Netanya, Jerusalem, and Haifa.

GARY TAXALI

Toronto-based illustrator Gary Taxali explains that his sketchbooks have a singular purpose: "To record my visual thoughts when I am away from my studio. I personally don't like drawing in books. I think that books are precious and it's hard to record uncensored thoughts and ideas. Scrap paper, the backs of phone bills, and old napkins are much better. I keep a filing cabinet where I store these drawings. I only use sketchbooks for convenience when I travel and don't have the means to draw randomly on paper, like when I'm on a plane," he says.

"As first recordings of ideas they go straight from the brain to the paper. The spontaneity makes them better. I try to emulate that as much as possible when doing finished work, but it is very hard."

The sketches are often the first realization of new concepts, characters, and compositions: "I don't know if that's unusual but it's wonderful to flip through the pages afterwards. I am reminded of where I was, physically and mentally, at that moment in time. They are true history books of any artist's life." These pictures date from 2005–8.

Paul's
SHOE
REPAIR

INCRED-
ULOUS...
28
+35
36
BUT INCREDIBLE

WOW
-flow

Crap
- BABY.
Cheryl
NO
CHOCO-
LATE
Never

What?
ROW
SKID
WASTIN
away
ALL MY
LIFE
Poor

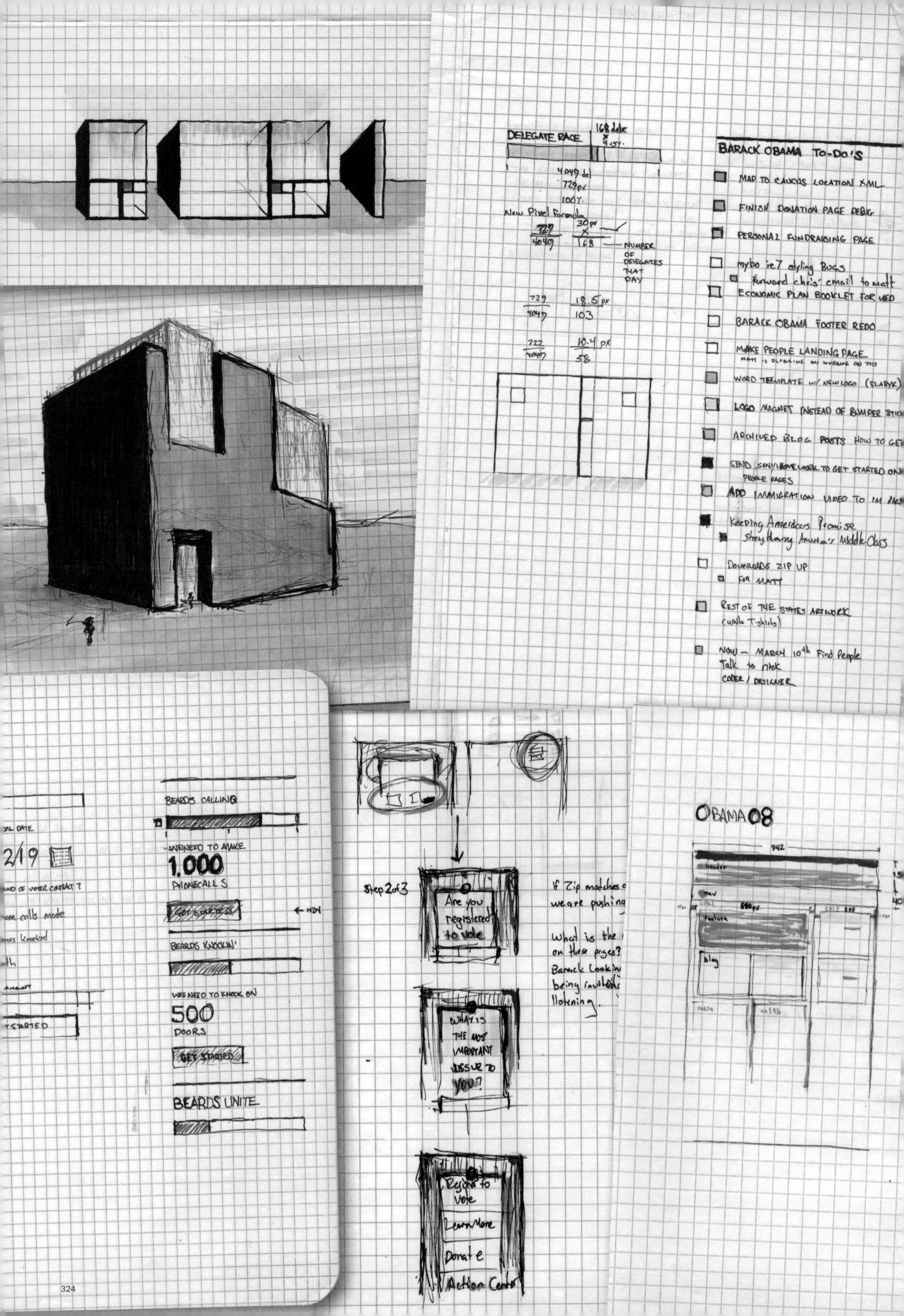
DELEGATE RACE
168 dele
4049 del
729 px
100%
New Pixel Formula
729 / 4049
30 px
168
NUMBER OF DELEGATES THAT DAY
18.5 px
103
10.4 px
58
BARACK OBAMA TO-DO'S
MAP TO CAUCUS LOCATION XML
FINISH DONATION PAGE DEBUG
PERSONAL FUNDRAISING PAGE
mybo ie7 styling Bugs
forward chris' email to matt
ECONOMIC PLAN BOOKLET FOR WEB
BARACK OBAMA FOOTER REDO
MAKE PEOPLE LANDING PAGE
WORD TEMPLATE w/ NEW LOGO
LOGO MAGNET INSTEAD OF BUMPER STICKER
ARCHIVED BLOG POSTS
ADD IMMIGRATION VIDEO
Keeping America's Promise
Strengthening America's Middle Class
DOWNLOADS ZIP UP
FOR MATT
REST OF THE STATES ARTWORK
(white T-shirts)
NOW – MARCH 10th Find People
Talk to nick
CODER / DESIGNER
BEARDS CALLING
WE NEED TO MAKE
1,000
PHONECALLS
GET STARTED
BEARDS KNOCKIN'
WE NEED TO KNOCK ON
500
DOORS
GET STARTED
BEARDS UNITE
2/19
Step 2 of 3
Are you registered to vote
WHAT IS THE MOST IMPORTANT ISSUE TO YOU?
Register to Vote
Learn More
Donate
Action Center
If Zip matches
we are pushing
What is the
on these pages?
OBAMA 08
942
header
nav
feature
blog

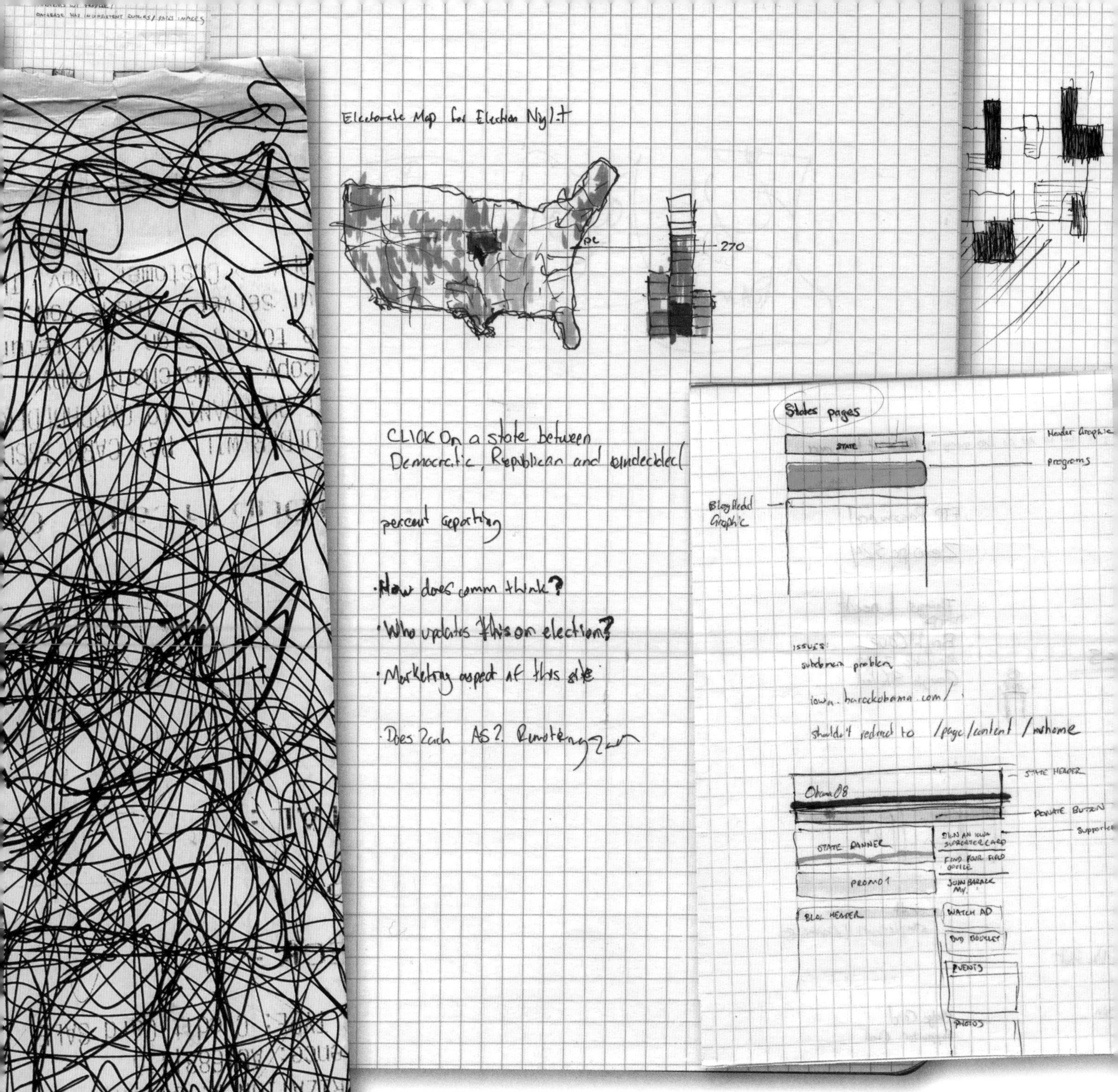

SCOTT THOMAS

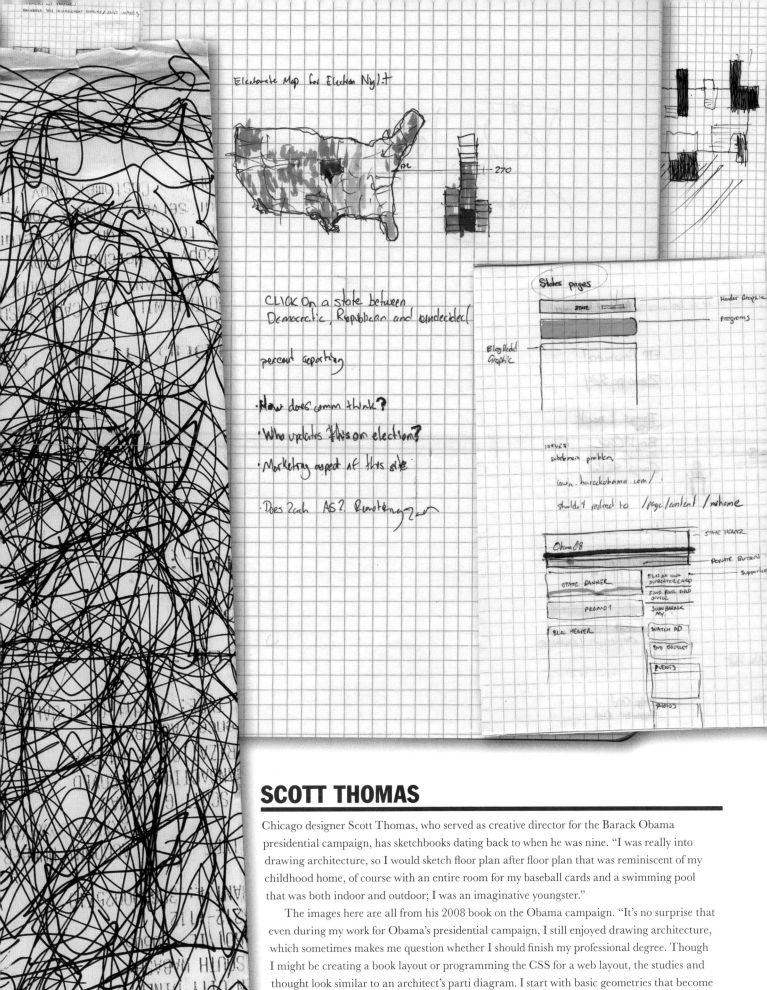

Chicago designer Scott Thomas, who served as creative director for the Barack Obama presidential campaign, has sketchbooks dating back to when he was nine. "I was really into drawing architecture, so I would sketch floor plan after floor plan that was reminiscent of my childhood home, of course with an entire room for my baseball cards and a swimming pool that was both indoor and outdoor; I was an imaginative youngster."

The images here are all from his 2008 book on the Obama campaign. "It's no surprise that even during my work for Obama's presidential campaign, I still enjoyed drawing architecture, which sometimes makes me question whether I should finish my professional degree. Though I might be creating a book layout or programming the CSS for a web layout, the studies and thought look similar to an architect's parti diagram. I start with basic geometries that become the container of information, the same way an illustrator starts with basic proportions and geometries before adding the information of detail to an image."

But, he says, "Sketching in today's environment seems to be accelerated, possibly due to the influence of technology. Much of my 'sketching' has to be done digitally in order to show process, otherwise people think you did the first thing that came to your head."

RICK VALICENTI

Rick Valicenti, Chicago-based designer and founder of Thirst, has been keeping sketchbooks for at least a decade. He claims there are two types of books for him: "Those in which I can do a series of expressions in a particular fashion, for instance, type studies, or overheard messages; and those I take to meetings to use as notebooks or ideation studies."

The books are spontaneous, and what's more, declares Valicenti, "interestingly, they are either beautifully composed or just simply messy as hell."

Although not necessarily thematic, "Some of the books are self-contained studies ... every page is an extension of the page before it." He has close to 100 books, "and because I have a home, a studio, and a storage facility, there are sketchbooks everywhere." The images here are from his expressionist books, in which he combines thoughts and letterforms into singular compositions. As he explains, "It is on these pages that the muse collaborated on this idea for the first time."

BUT
YOU
TOLD
ME YOU
LOVED
ME

MY
DO YOU
INFECTED
GROWN

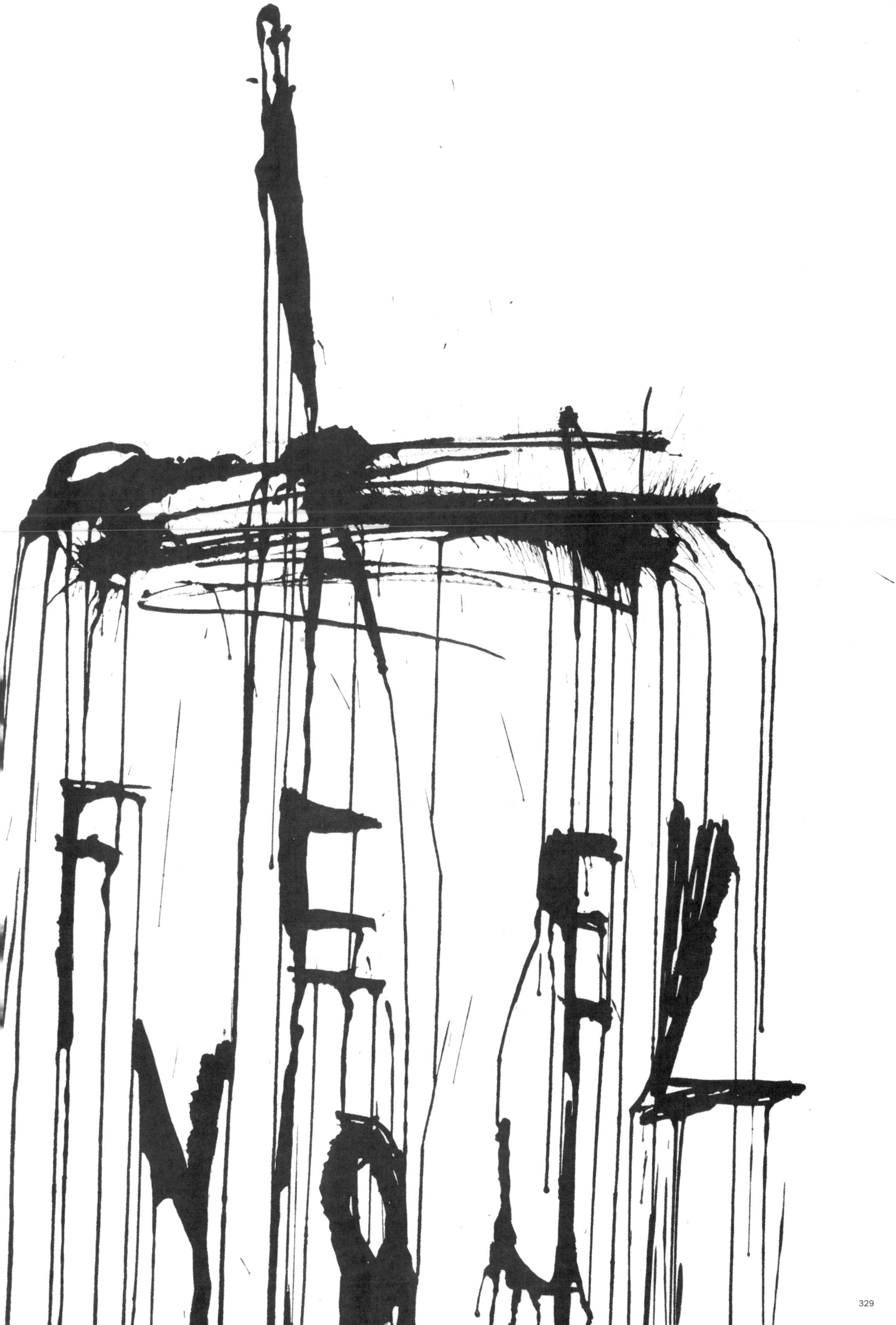

BOB VAN DIJK

Bob van Dijk, Dutch designer and proprietor of Lava Grafisch Ontwerpers, likes sketching, “but not in a book – for the process. If you turn a page in a book, you cannot look back at your work in one view – so I prefer to sketch on pages.”

Van Dijk makes sketches “every day, for fun, when I come home, to relax and keep me trained in characters and in situations. I like to have a ‘free’ way of working on the computer; I also use a Wacom Tablet. But I like to use just pencils – and I like the fact that you cannot copy a sketch. With the computer you can change everything,” he says.

“Sketching is just imagination, and combinations of things that happened to me that day,” he continues. “I start sketching and, while working, everything connects, like the characters start to communicate with each other – just like in normal life, when you add different people together in one space. I like storytelling and I make individual drawings for people I know. The knowledge I have about them forms the outcome later on.”

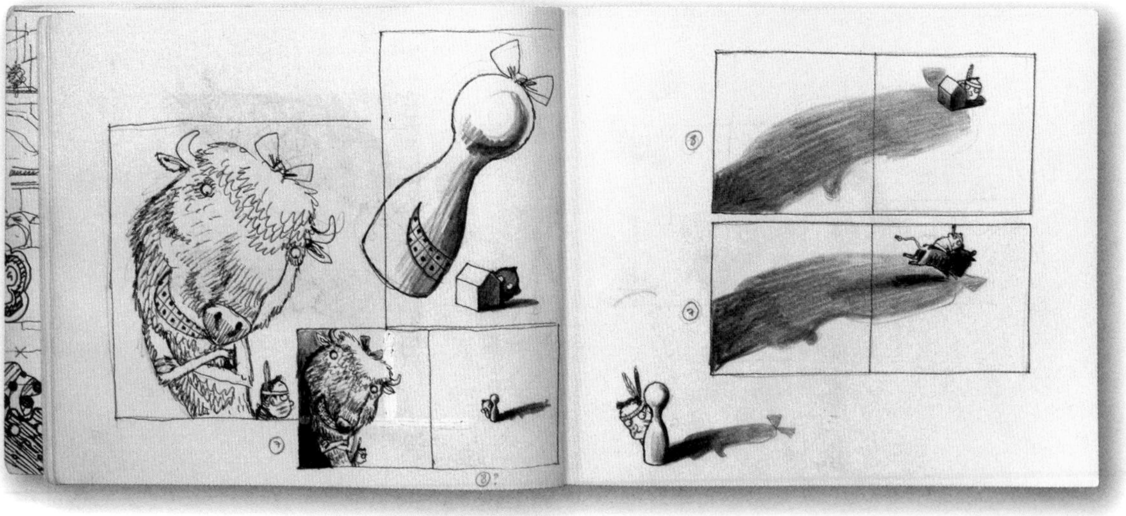

C O V E R.

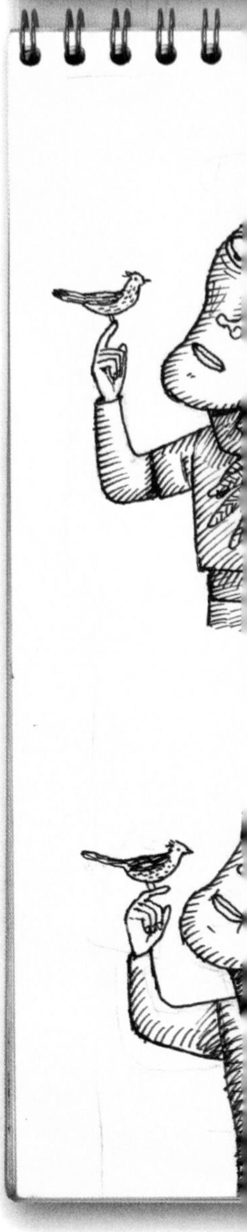

KLAAS VERPLANCKE

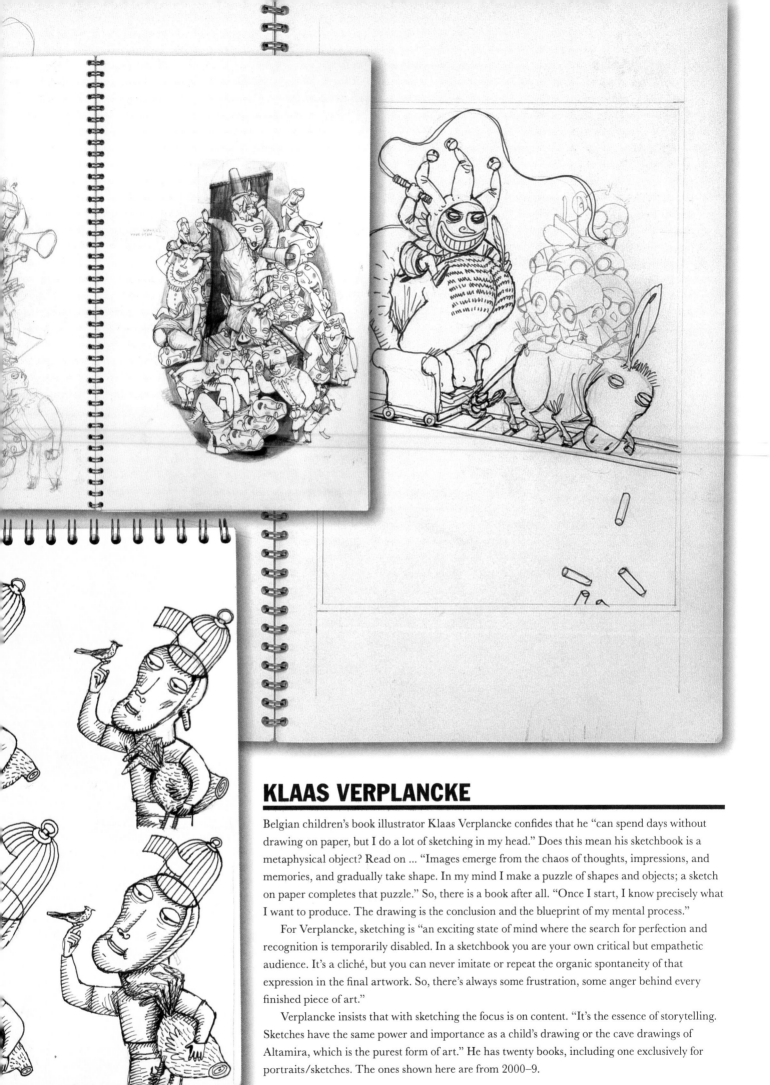

Belgian children's book illustrator Klaas Verplancke confides that he "can spend days without drawing on paper, but I do a lot of sketching in my head." Does this mean his sketchbook is a metaphysical object? Read on ... "Images emerge from the chaos of thoughts, impressions, and memories, and gradually take shape. In my mind I make a puzzle of shapes and objects; a sketch on paper completes that puzzle." So, there is a book after all. "Once I start, I know precisely what I want to produce. The drawing is the conclusion and the blueprint of my mental process."

For Verplancke, sketching is "an exciting state of mind where the search for perfection and recognition is temporarily disabled. In a sketchbook you are your own critical but empathetic audience. It's a cliché, but you can never imitate or repeat the organic spontaneity of that expression in the final artwork. So, there's always some frustration, some anger behind every finished piece of art."

Verplancke insists that with sketching the focus is on content. "It's the essence of storytelling. Sketches have the same power and importance as a child's drawing or the cave drawings of Altamira, which is the purest form of art." He has twenty books, including one exclusively for portraits/sketches. The ones shown here are from 2000–9.

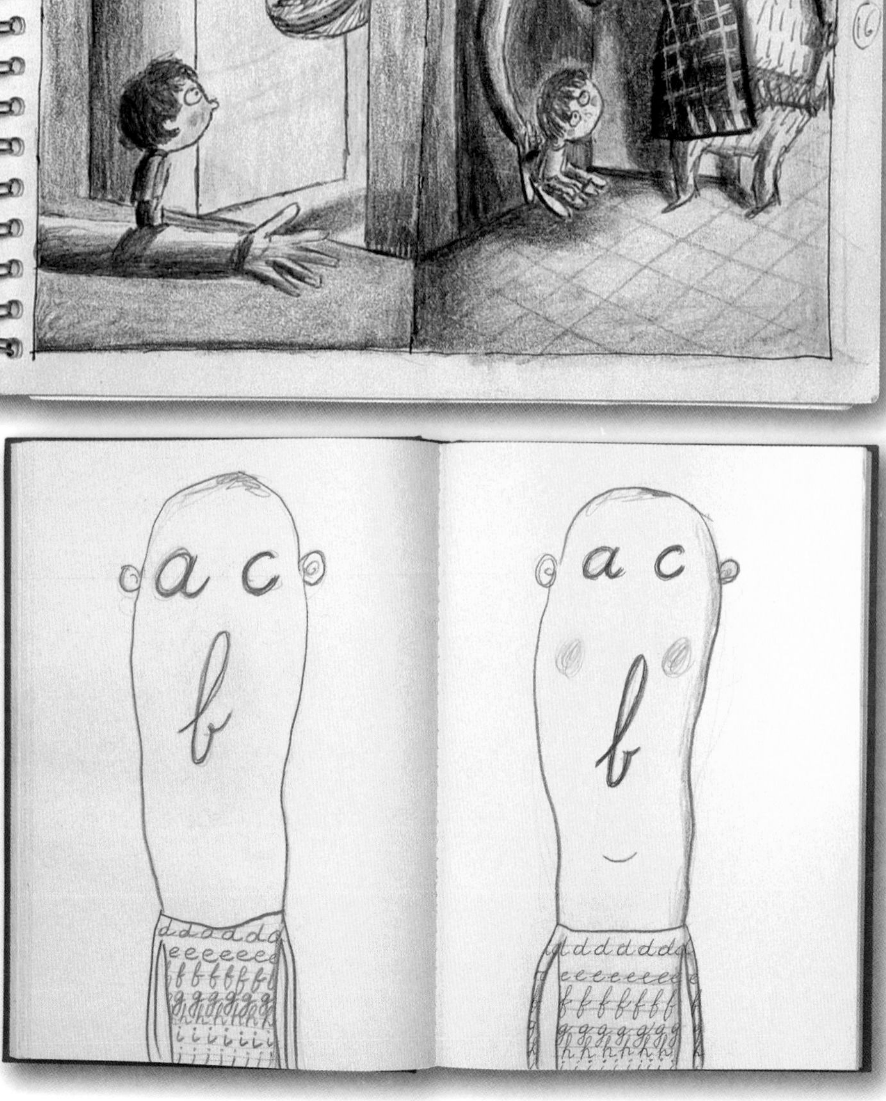
a c
b
a c
b

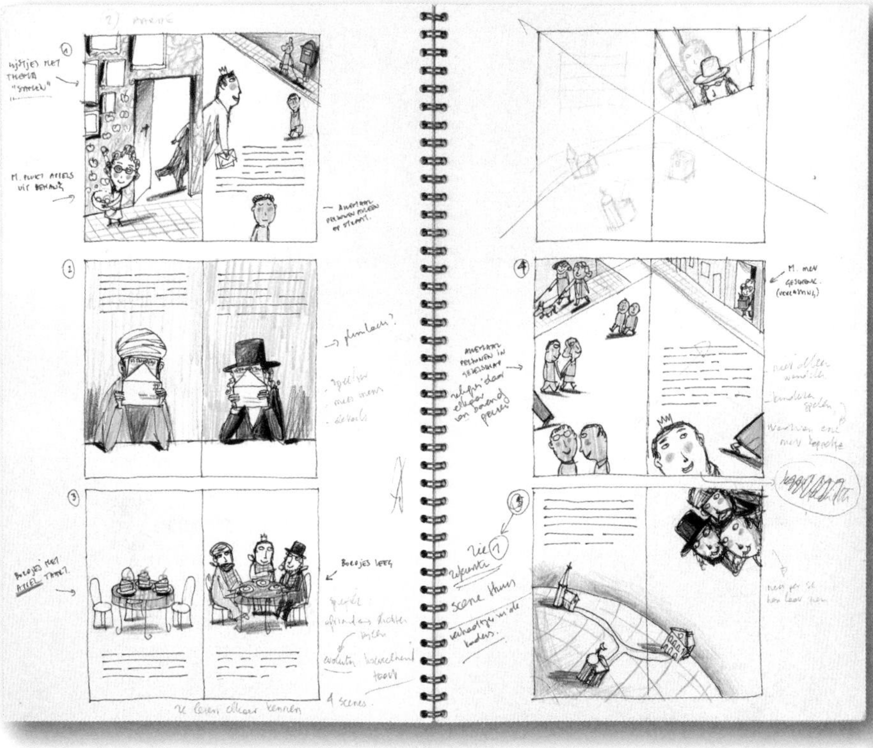

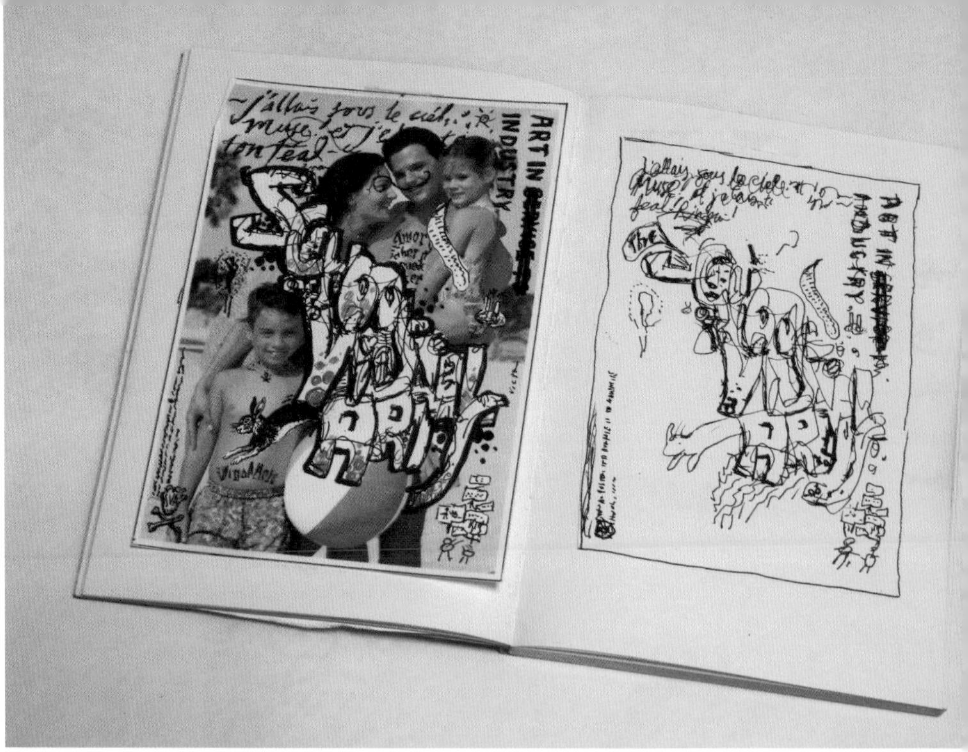

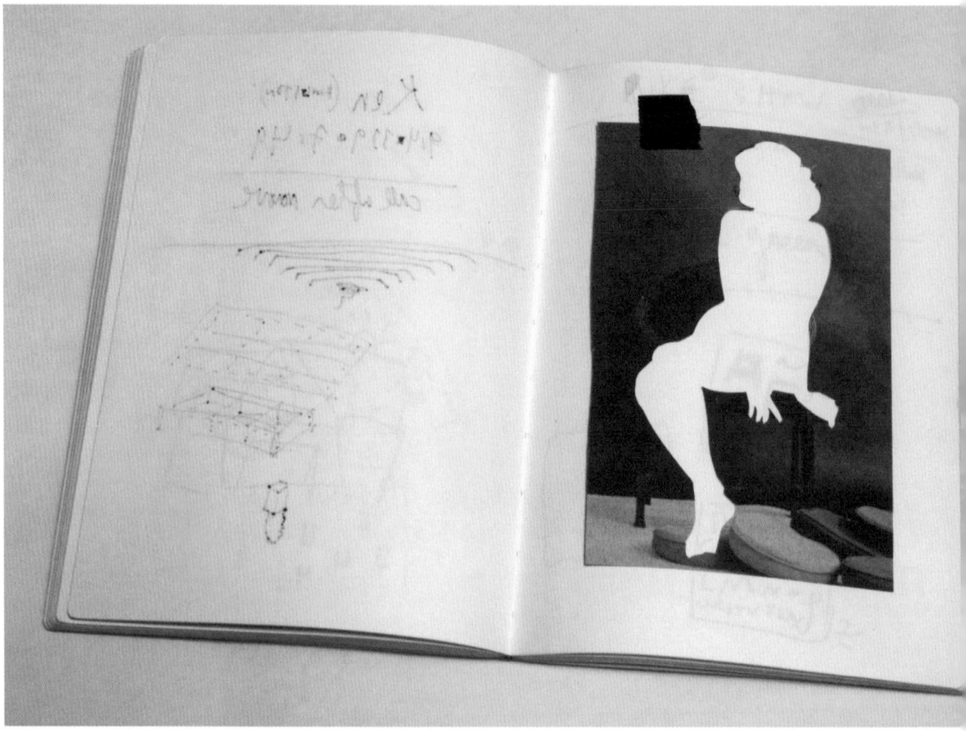

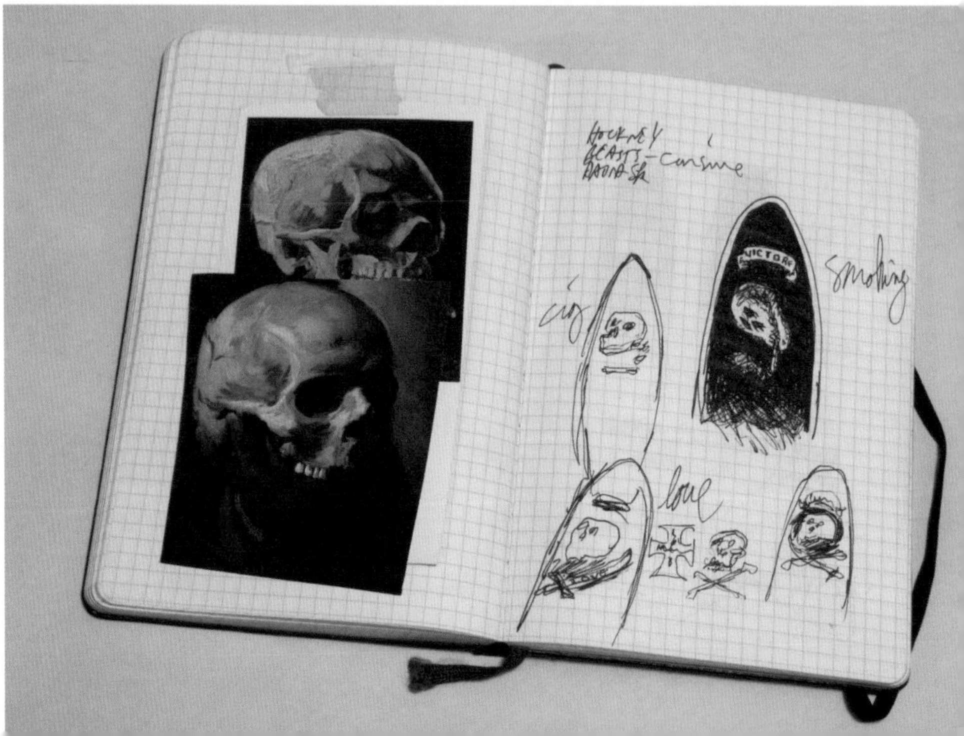

JAMES VICTORE

Known for his expressively sketchy, hand-wrought method, New York-based designer James Victore says he has always "used visual devices to keep track of things." The sketchbook is like a schedule: "I live by lists and reminders, so my sketchbook is a list of ideas to play out – eventually. Also, I use them to think through any design or project I am working on. When I do a good job with my sketches, all I have to do is follow them. They are my guide and shorthand."

He is not alone when he says, "I am always trying to match the damned immediacy of the sketch on any job." But the sketches also underscore a feeling he has about "the lousy nature of my drawing and handwriting skills. My sketchbooks are quite ugly." And that suits him just fine.

Victore has lots of books. "I go through maybe two or three a year. Sometimes more. I change sizes often. There are a few different kinds that I like. I try to have one with me all the time, so I prefer pocket-sized books. Early ones from when I was in school and when I was starting as a designer have pages ripped out. I must not have liked the work in them."

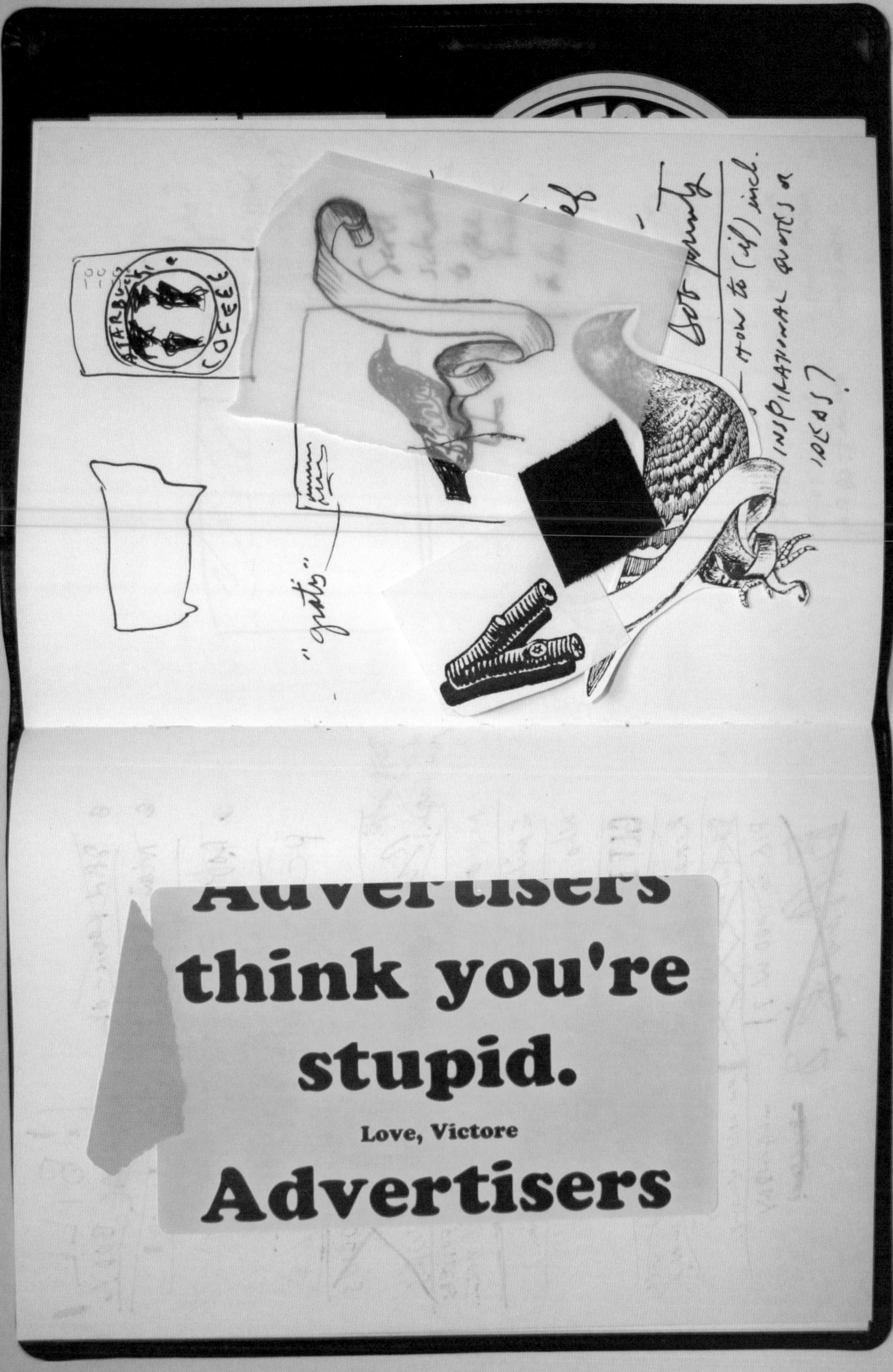
think you're
stupid.
Love, Victore
Advertisers

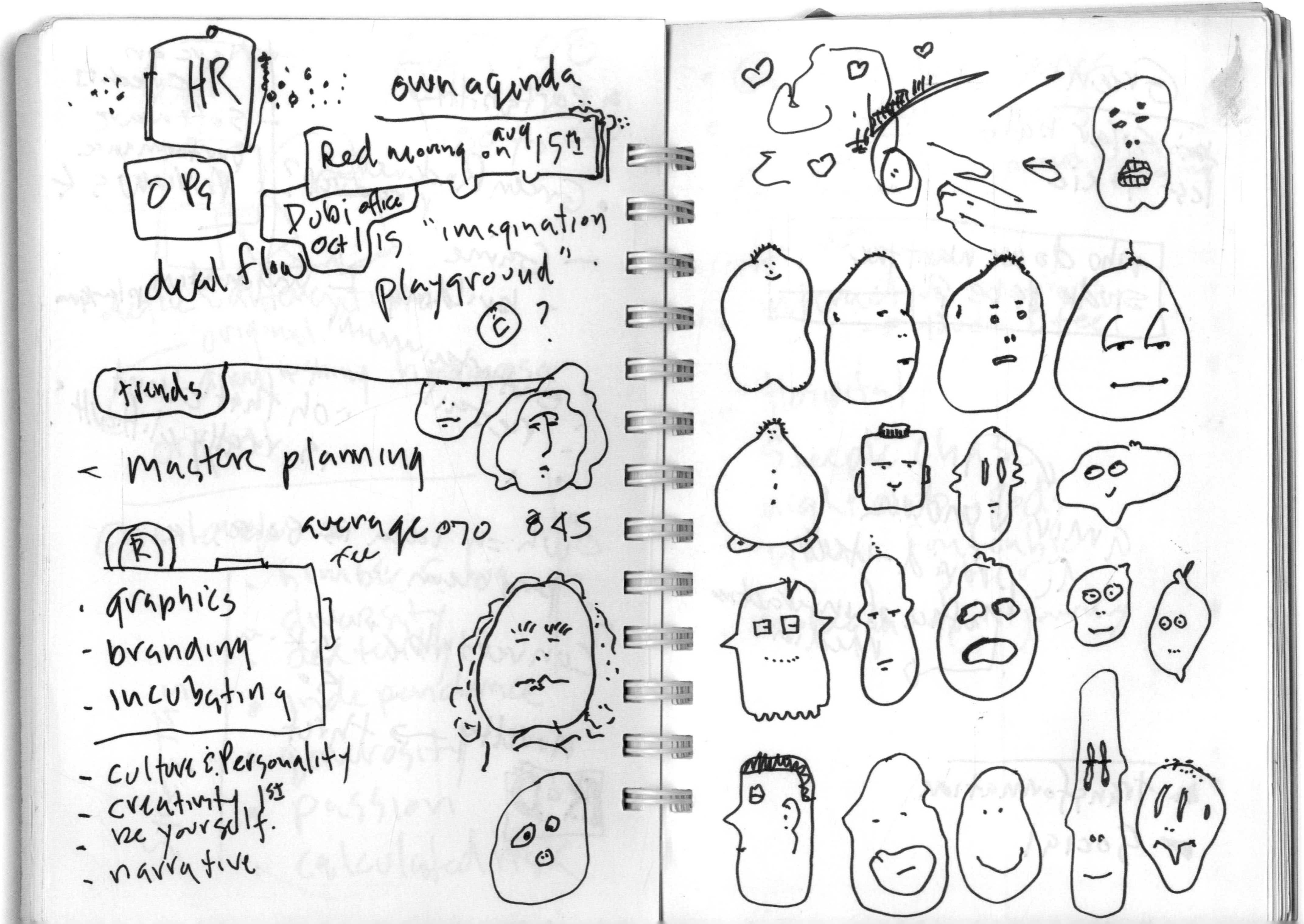
HR
OPS
own agenda
Red morning on Aug 15th
Dubi office
Oct 1 15 "imagination playground".
deal flow
©?
trends
master planning
average 070 845
fee
®
· graphics
- branding
- incubating
- culture & Personality
- creativity 1st
- be yourself.
- narrative

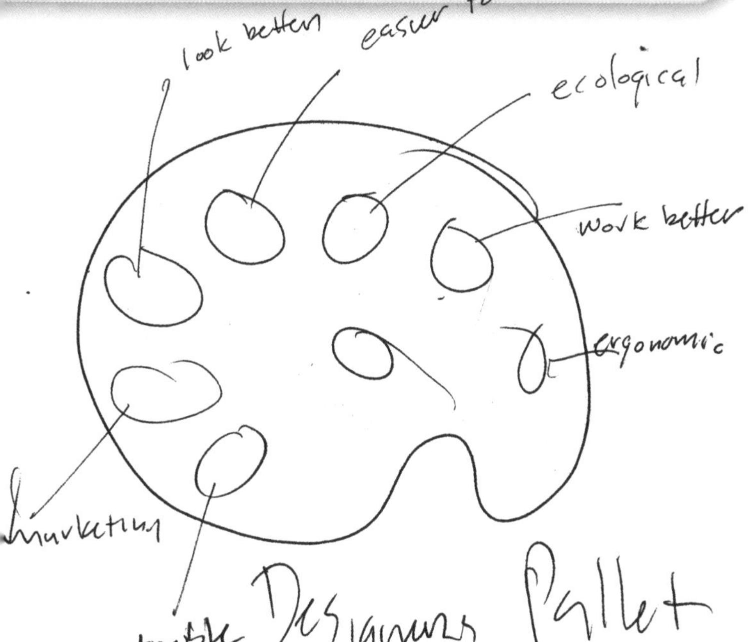

TUCKER VIEMEISTER

Veteran New York-based industrial designer Tucker Viemeister uses a sketchbook mostly to keep his notes and ideas in order – "It gives me a place to sketch out ideas that won't get lost. I use it every day," he says.

He is passionate about the form: "It has to be easy to carry, so I will carry it! And also to have nice paper – but not fancy." It is like canvas for him, except a canvas with doodles. "I don't edit (except when someone (like you) asks for pages – then I pick the best ones!)."

Viemeister says, "I learned about the cool black sketchbooks when I first went to Pratt and I was hooked. I used the big 8½ × 11 in. [21.5 × 28 cm] size. Years later, when I started working at Razorfish, Craig Kanarick give me a half-size Razorfish spiralbound notebook. The size is perfect – light cover, open flat, or fold inside-out. We copied them at Rockwell – so I have a complete set going back to 1997. In fact, we need to make more!"

KHOI VINH

Khoi Vinh, design director of *New York Times* Digital, has worked in sketchbooks for over twenty years. "I started in earnest in art school," he reports, "and have tried – with varying degrees of success – to keep working in them regularly ever since." Vinh settled on the format of sketchbook shown here because "I've always liked to paste items in my sketchbooks, and the loose-leaf format was much more accommodating." It was also a much cheaper format.

His sketchbooks are "a repository for all of my doodles, a work area where I can shift my brain into free-association mode just to see what comes out." Vinh suggests that pages in his sketchbooks are rife with Freudian hints at what is going on in his head, "but I'm loath to guess at what those themes might be." The act of working in these sketchbooks has been about "groping my way toward some kind of creative answer. With every doodle or piece of ephemera, I'm working out abstract or incomplete ideas about what my own 'voice' and 'visual vocabulary' are, how I communicate and what I like and what I don't. I'm not sure I'll ever really find all the answers, but that's what makes keeping these sketchbooks so enjoyable for me."

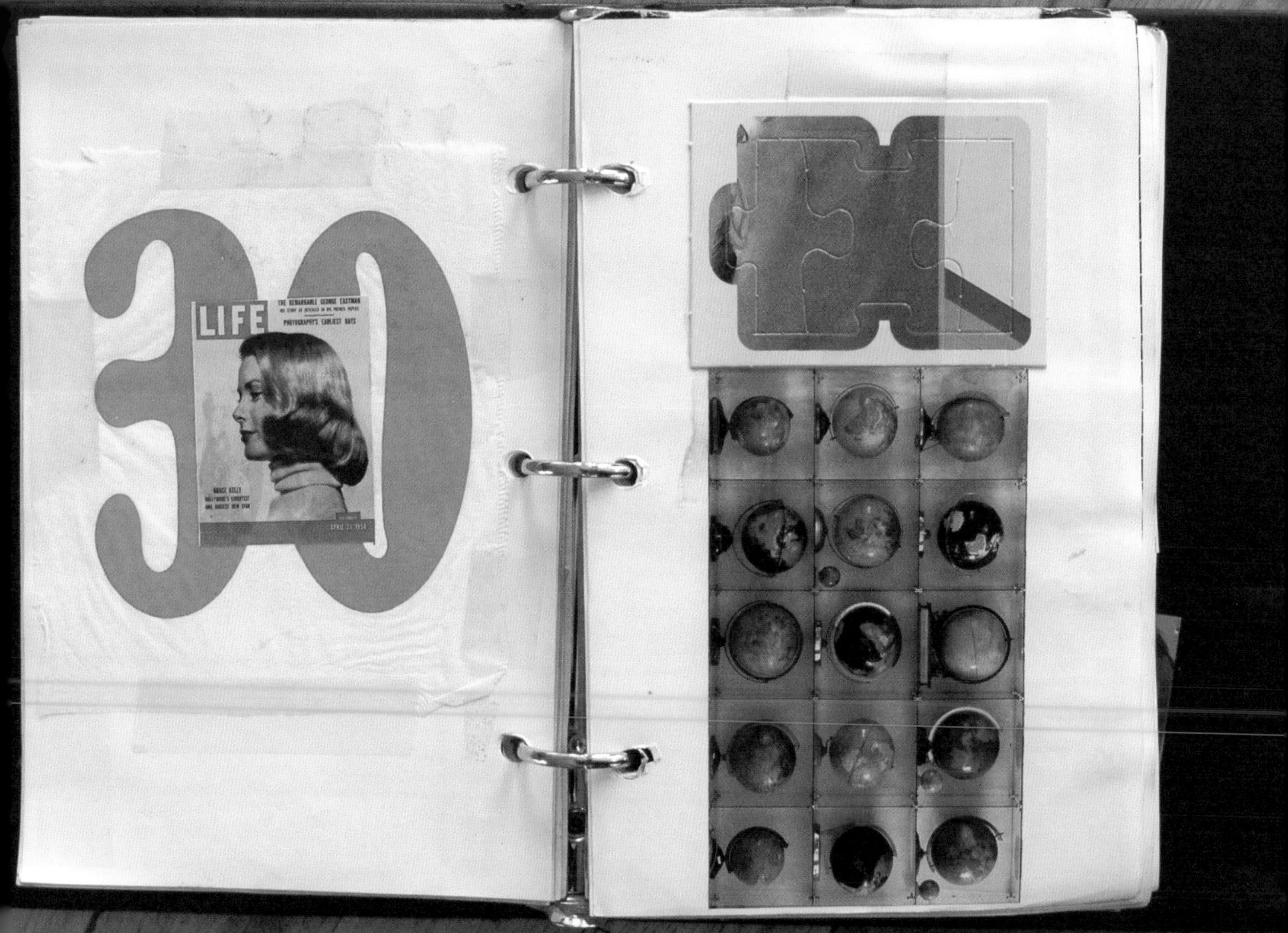

LIFE
THE REMARKABLE GEORGE EASTMAN
PHOTOGRAPHY'S EARLIEST DAYS
GRACE KELLY

Air Courier Travel
The Goods: If you long to see the world, have a sense of adventure and want to save a buck, then being an air courier on occasion might be the ticket. "With minor differences, it's exactly like traveling in coach class . . . only at half the cost," says Kelly Monaghan, author of *Air Courier Bargains.*
The Big Picture: An air courier is anyone who accompanies time-sensitive business cargo being shipped as passenger baggage on a regular commercial flight. Generally, he or she must travel alone, stay for a specified time and limit personal baggage to carry-on. In exchange, the courier is given a fare discount. Most of the tickets are for international round-trip travel. Available routes vary with global business cycles. This fall, Monaghan says, the Pacific Rim is hot. One courier company, Halbart Express (718-656-8189), is offering flights from New York to several Asian cities—Tokyo, Seoul, Singapore, Hong Kong—for $728 round trip. Halbart's New York-London quote from November 1 to December 11 is $200 round trip. There aren't any courier flights from Washington to Asia now, but Virgin Wholesale Express (718-244-7244) offers them daily from Dulles to London ($380). For more information, contact the International Association of Air Travel Couriers (561-582-8320; *www.courier.org*) or the Intrepid Traveler (212-569-1081; *www.intrepidtraveler.com*). The latter is a company owned by Monaghan, who is scheduled to speak Monday at 7:30 p.m. at Travel Books and Language Center in Bethesda (301-951-8533; free; reservations required).
The Last Word: Contrary to a common misperception, the courier usually doesn't carry anything through customs and often doesn't even see the shipment. On an established route, he or she runs no risk of being held legally responsible for the shipment's contents—that's the courier company's responsibility—according to several industry officials and U.S. Customs spokeswoman Patricia Coss. —*Bill O'Brien*
1
2
3
4
5
Remove this label, reinsert the battery, and plug in the power adapter before using your PowerBook.

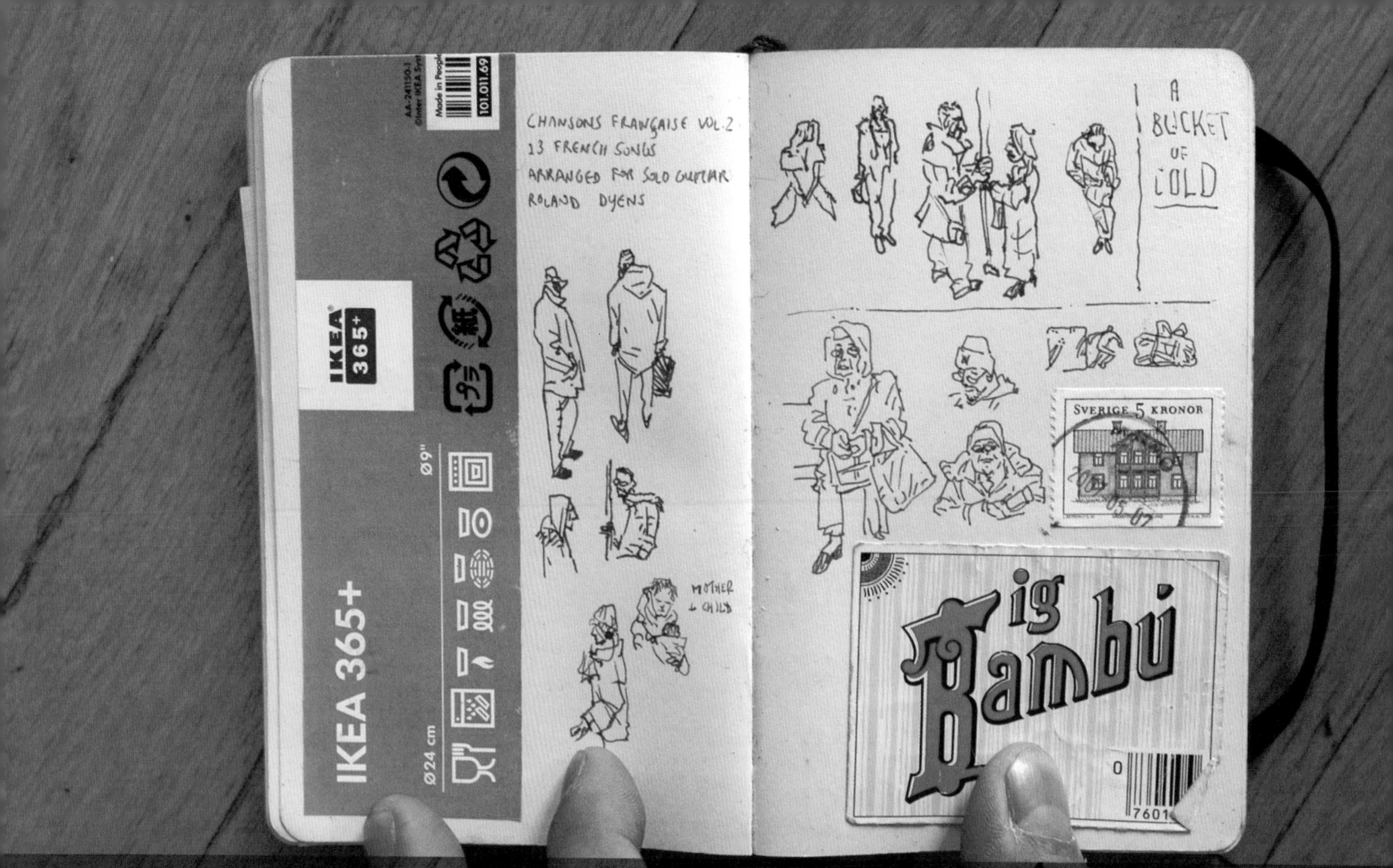
IKEA 365+
CHANSONS FRANÇAISE VOL.2
13 FRENCH SONGS
ARRANGED FOR SOLO GUITAR
ROLAND DYENS
MOTHER + CHILD
A BUCKET OF COLD
SVERIGE 5 KRONOR
ig Bambú

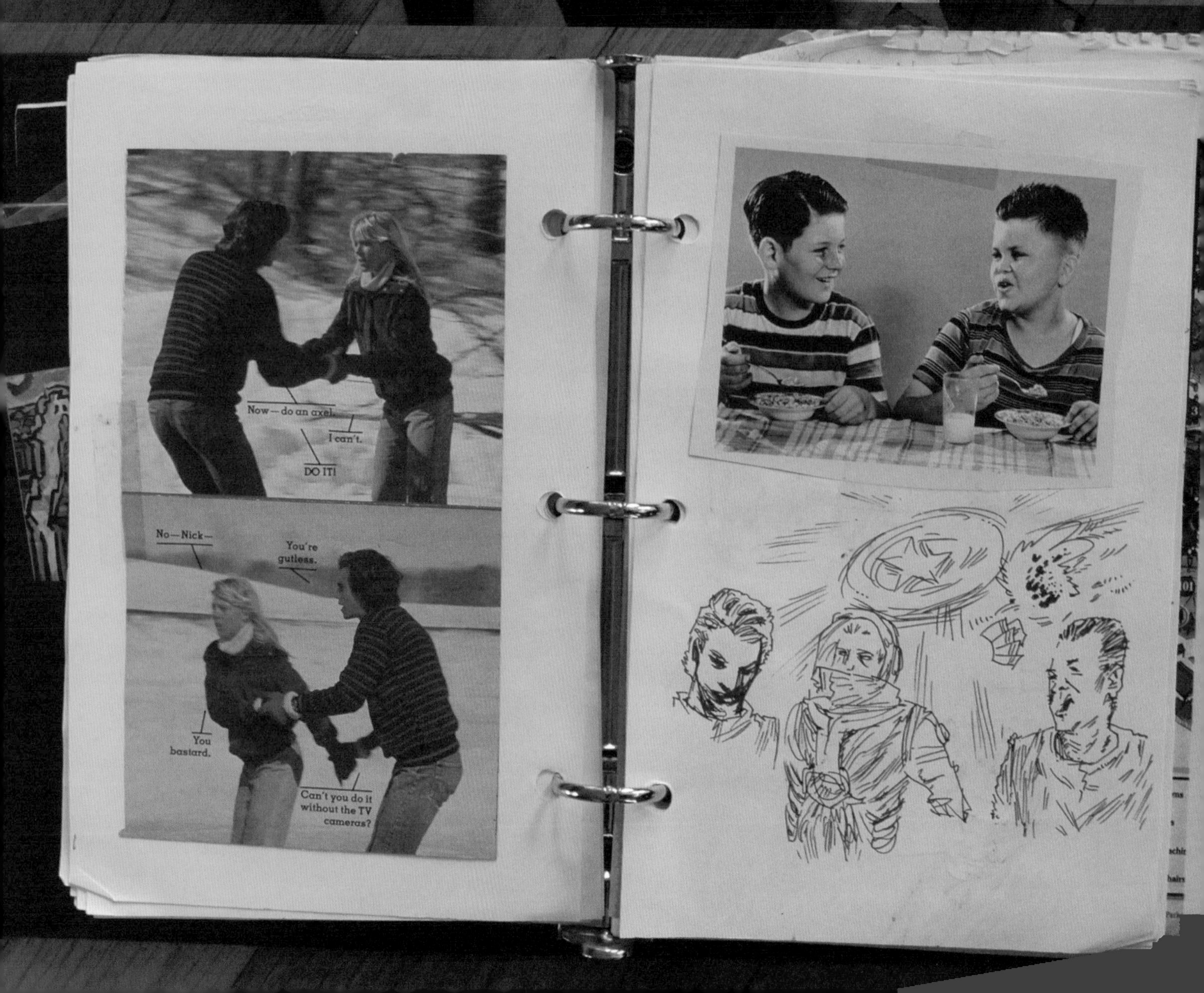
Now—do an axel.
I can't.
DO IT!
No—Nick—
You're gutless.
You bastard.
Can't you do it without the TV cameras?

10 Adhesive Layers
Total 4.6 ft x 4 in (1.4 m
AND CLAIRE FORLANI IN "BASQUIAT"

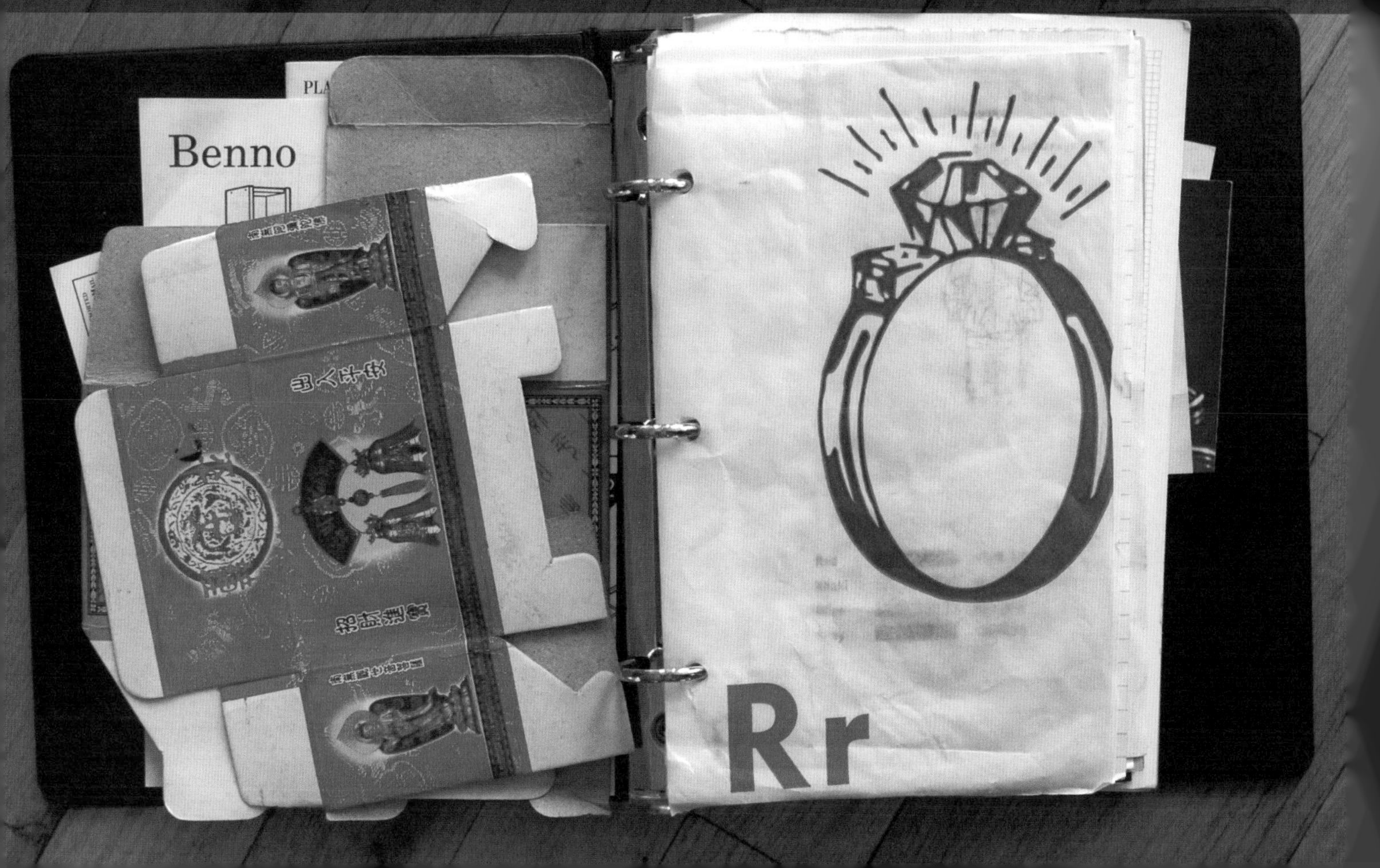
Benno
Rr

NATE VOSS

Nate Voss, a designer based in Omaha, Nebraska, has a backlog of sketchbooks ating back to when he was ten years old. Most of them are filled with comic drawings superheroes like Wolverine and video game haracters like Super Mario Bros," he reports.

Voss's sketchbooks allow him to work out erything from sizing and composition to stom lettering: "Almost every logo I've done ofessionally began life as a scan directly out my sketchbook." His sketches often have ore life to them than his final work, where oportions and mathematical correctness me into play: "This makes for solid, nsistent design, but I almost always find ere's a spark to the original that gets lost."

Voss usually scribbles a little Garfield Odie in the corners, who make off-color narks about how much they hate the work is plotting out. "I spent all of grade school mored with that comic strip. It's a very nfortable face to draw – a couple of ovals, f-circles, and some stripes – so I fall into ching them almost as a reflex against ative block. The comments are mine and ude language I'd not care to repeat here."

THIS IS IT! 2008 IS ALMOST OVER!
THAT'S... GOOD?
HELL YES THAT'S GOOD! I'VE BEEN BEAT UP AND KICKED AROUND BY THIS ROTTEN YEAR LONG ENOUGH!!
©2008 NATHAN VOSS www.3GPOINT.COM
NOW IT'S FINNALLY OVER! THERE'S NOTHING THAT STUPID SUNNOVA BITCH YEAR CAN EVEN DO ABOUT IT! HA HA!
SKZZZT!
KA-BOOM!
CONRAD?
I MIGHT HAVE SKIPPED THE NAME CALLING.

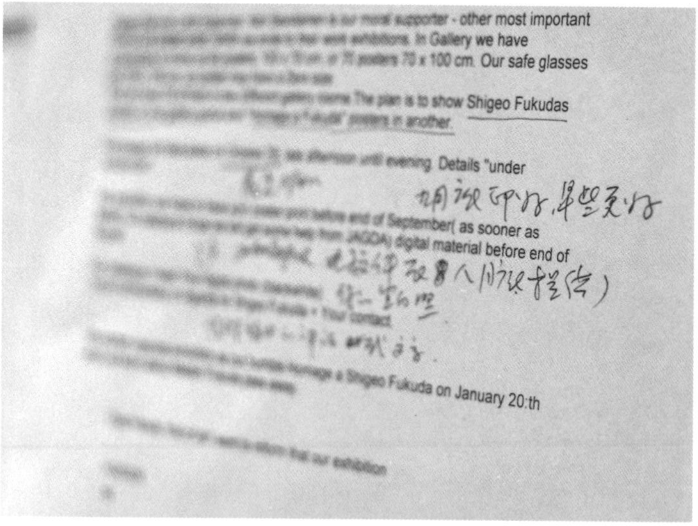

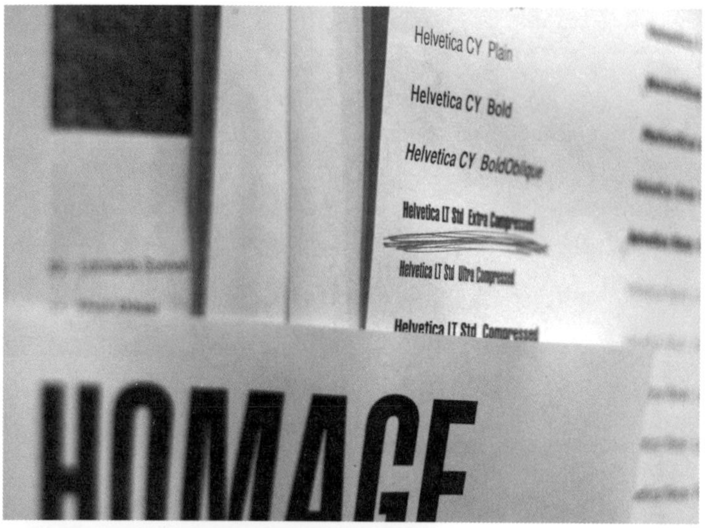

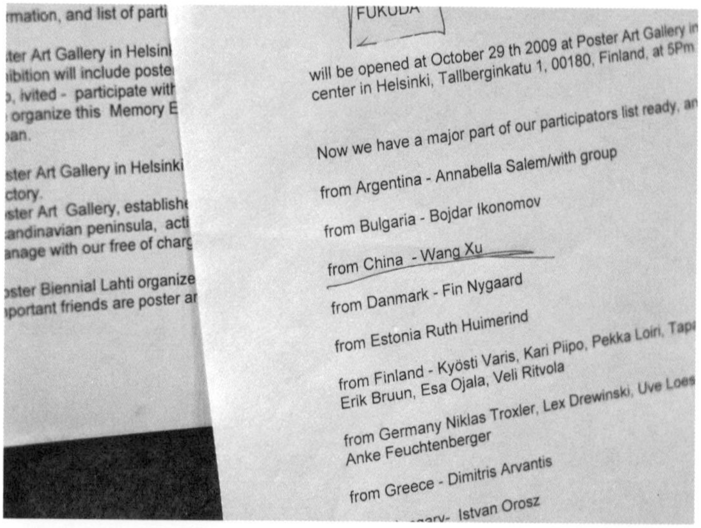

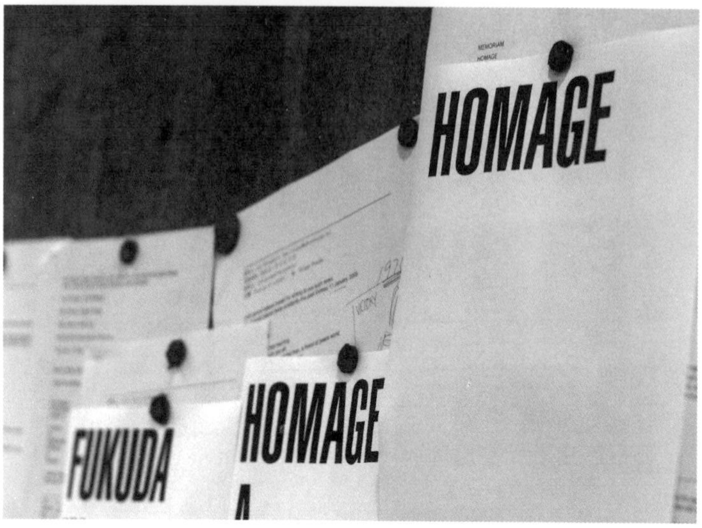

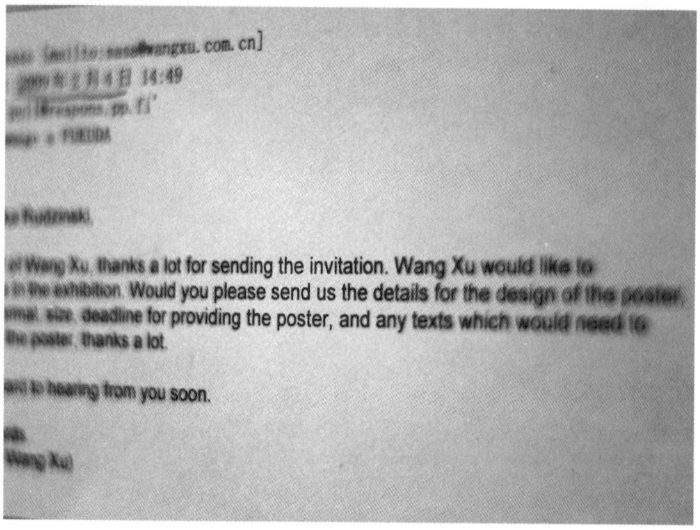

WANG XU

Wang Xu, from Beijing, uses every surface as an ersatz sketchbook. "Actually," he clarifies, "I don't have a sketchbook." Instead, he says sketching for him is, well, thinking. "I am thinking all the time, sometimes even thinking at midnight."

Rather than draw conventional sketches, he usually "would draw some simple schematic layout. This is for my communication or discussion with designers or computer operators." Most of these have not been kept, but fortunately he has preserved the images shown here.

Wang Xu has a philosophical view about what he calls the "sketchbook in the mind." He says it is a kind of "scientific and environmental protection." It can be changed or further developed all the time, or, for that matter, thrown away. Instead of writing things down, "I will keep necessary keywords in my cell phone as a memo or working instruction, and then start to put into practice the idea and the thinking in the computer." Such is the nature of the 21st-century sketchbook.

发送时间: 2009年1月17日 2:25
收件人: undisclosed-recipients:
主题: Passing of a giant... Mr. Shigeo Fukuda
VICTORY
HOMAGE
VICTORY
HOMAGE
VICTORY

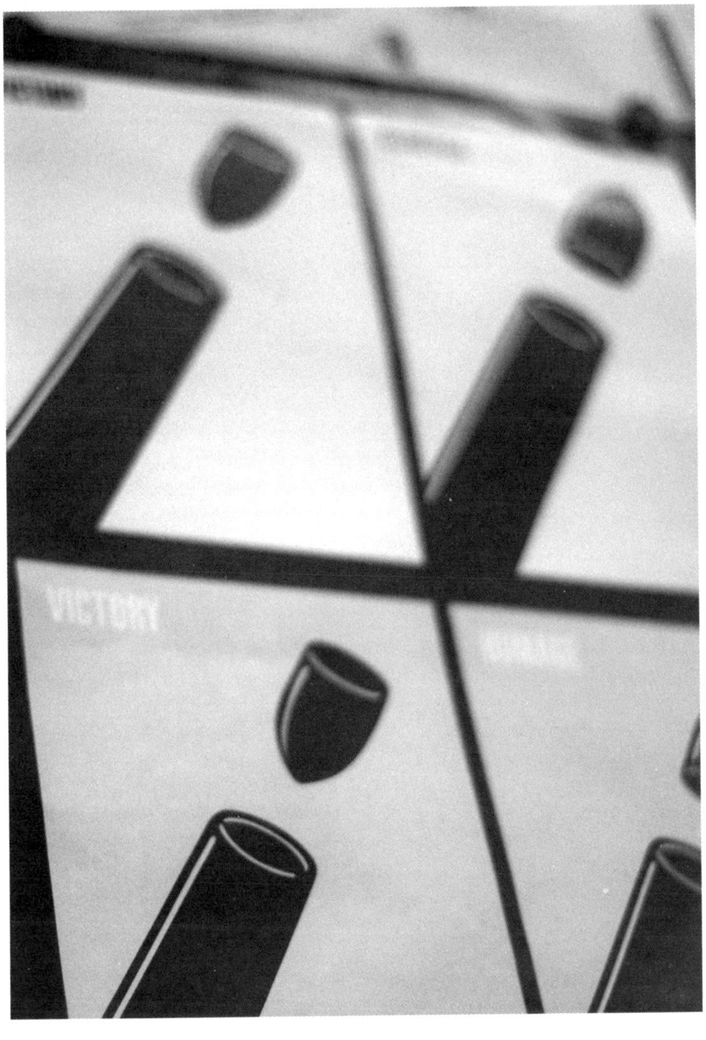
VICTORY

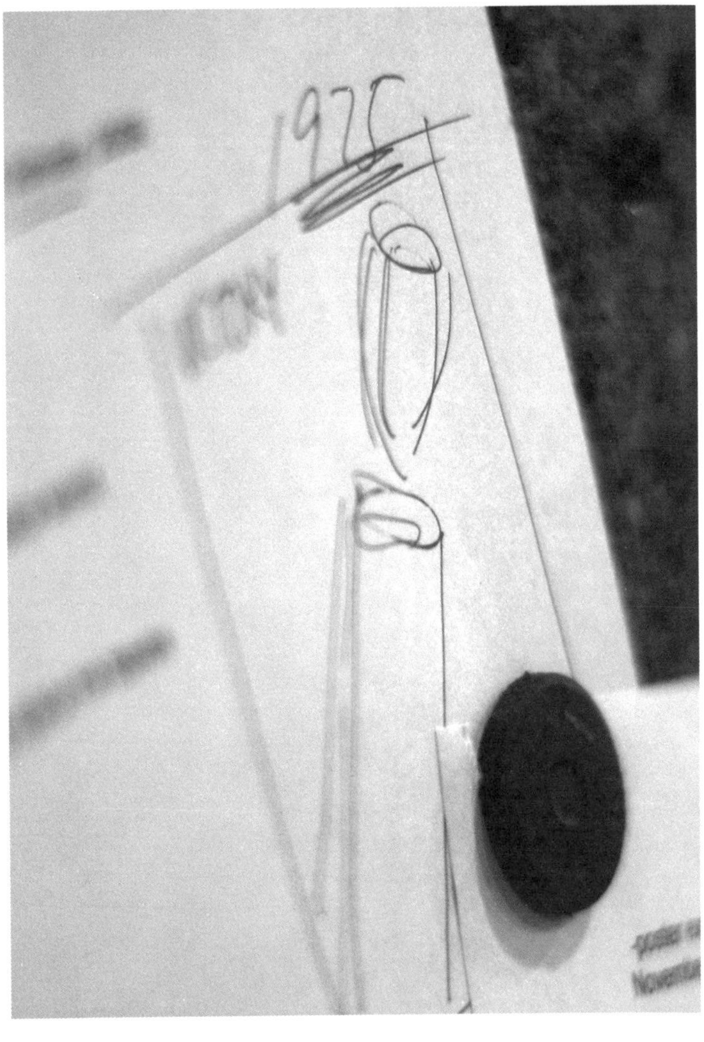

VCRETISATRI
CRETISATRI

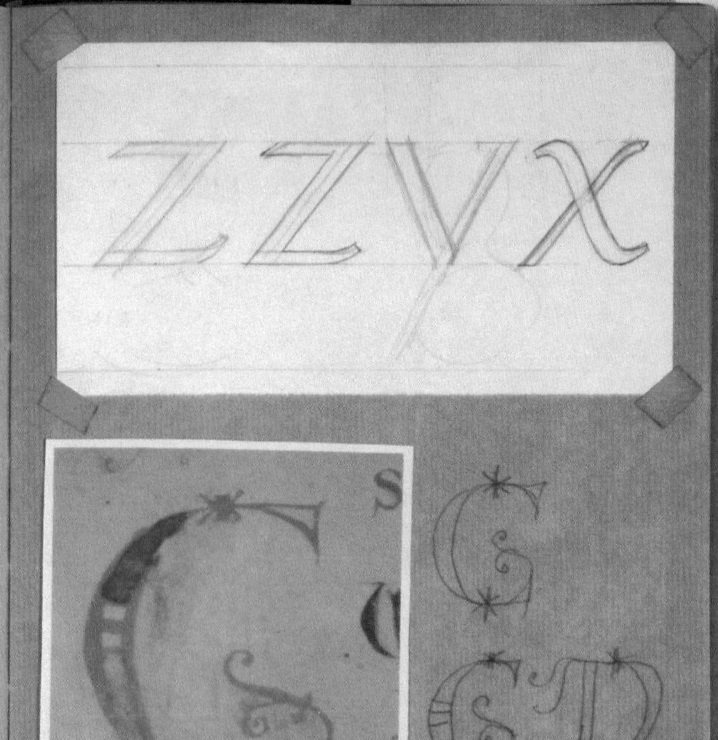
ZZYX

SPQR